CW00351118

Programming with Visual Basic® 6

Edward J. Coburn

Quantum Corporation

Brooks/Cole
Thomson Learning™

Australia • Canada • Denmark • Japan • Mexico • New Zealand • Philippines • Puerto Rico •
Singapore • Spain • United Kingdom • United States

BROOKS/COLE PUBLISHING COMPANY COPYRIGHT PAGE SKETCH

Sponsoring Editor: *Kallie Swanson*
Marketing Team: *Nathan Wilbur, Laura Hubrich*
Editorial Assistant: *Grace Fujimoto*
Production Editor: *Kelsey McGee*
Manuscript Editor: *Philip Jochnowitz*
Permissions Editor: *Mary Kay Hancharick*

Cover Design: *Laurie Albrecht*
Manufacturing Buyer: *Tracy Brown*
Interior Design/Typesetting: *Publishers' Design and Production Services, Inc.*
Cover Printing, Printing and Binding: *The Courier Co., Inc./Kendallville*

COPYRIGHT © 2000 by Brooks/Cole
A division of Thomson Learning
The Thomson Learning logo is a trademark used herein under license.

Visual Basic® and MSDN™ are either registered trademarks or trademarks of Microsoft Corporation in the United States and/or other countries.

For more information, contact:
BROOKS/COLE
511 Forest Lodge Road
Pacific Grove, CA 93950 USA
www.brookscole.com

All rights reserved. No part of this work may be reproduced, transcribed or used in any form or by any means—graphic, electronic, or mechanical, including photocopying, recording, taping, Web distribution, or information storage and/or retrieval systems—without the prior written permission of the publisher.

For permission to use material from this work, contact us by
Web: www.thomsonrights.com
fax: 1-800-730-2215
phone: 1-800-730-2214

Printed in the United States of America

10   9   8   7   6   5   4   3   2   1

Library of Congress Cataloging-in-Publication Data

Coburn, Edward J.
   Programming with visual basic 6 / Edward J. Coburn.
       p.   cm.
   Includes index.
   ISBN 0-534-36829-8
       1. Microsoft Visual Basic.   2. BASIC (Computer program language).
   I. Title.
QA76.73.B3C6314   199
005.26'8—dc21   99-14607

Contents

3 ▮ The Code Window and More Code   117

4 ▮ Using Loops and Arrays   195

5   More Labels, Buttons, and Text Boxes   261

6   Using Menus and Related Features   309

7   Using Dialog Boxes and Multiple Forms   361

8   Saving and Loading Files   415

9 Error Handling and Debugging 487

10 Accessing Databases 531

11   Additional Tools   591

12   Linking Applications   637

13   Browsing the Web   675

A   Appendix   Using ActiveX Controls   713

Preface

This book was designed for use in an introductory course in Visual Basic® 6.0. It can also be used for self-study—to help those with no prior programming experience in Visual Basic gain all the knowledge they need to use Visual Basic to create innovative and practical Windows programs. The hands-on lab exercises, with step-by-step instructions, enable the reader to become familiar quickly with the programming concepts and to gain proficiency in using all the tools. These exercises and the many sample screens make it easy for anyone to understand this book.

Objectives

After completing this book, the reader should be able to:

- Create and execute applications using a multitude of Visual Basic tools, statements, properties, and events.

- Understand the basic concepts of file access, and create and execute applications that can open, read from, save to, and close data files.

- Understand what relational databases are, how they are designed, and how to use Visual Basic to access them.

- Create applications that can pass data from one to the other using Dynamic Data Exchange (DDE) and Object Linking and Embedding (OLE) techniques.

- Create Web browser applications that can access World Wide Web Sites.

Organization

Most of the chapters in this book deal with the continuing construction of a Personal Information Manager (PIM) that includes notepad, alarm clock, address book, appointment calendar, To-Do list, and Web Browser. Work on this program begins in Chapter 5 and continues throughout the book. When it is finished, the reader will have a fully functional PIM that can be further modified to meet individual needs.

This book is organized around important pedagogical features. Performance objectives appear at the beginning of each chapter, step-by-step instructions explain each new Visual Basic concept, and a series of exercises is included so that readers can determine whether they have understood the material in the chapter. The **Performance Objectives** at the beginning of each chapter explain the basic level of performance that readers should expect to have attained when they finish the chapter. Each new term presented in this book is shown in **boldface**. These terms are also listed and defined in the **Glossary** at the end of the book. Virtually every Visual Basic concept is explained through the use of illustrative figures and step-by-step instructions that can be tried out in the lab.

In anticipation of some of the problems the reader may face, numerous **HINT** boxes help the new Visual Basic programmer successfully complete and understand each task. Information useful for avoiding potentially hazardous situations is given in **WARNING** boxes.

At the end of each chapter are four aids to reinforce what the reader has learned. The **COMMAND AND MENU SUMMARY** lists and defines each of the commands, tools, menu options, and properties that were discussed in the chapter, giving the reader a quick reference to keystrokes and options that may be difficult to remember. The **PERFOR-MANCE CHECK** provides a series of short-answer questions specially designed to help readers decide whether they fully understand the material introduced in the chapter. Then the **PROGRAMMING EXERCISES**, which give the students a chance to practice creating the same types of programs that were created in the chapter, help the reader identify any remaining trouble spots. In most chapters there is a **Debugging** exercise, marked with the icon 🛠, that guides the reader through the process of finding and correcting common programming errors. A reader who can successfully complete the **PERFORMANCE MAS-TERY** exercises truly understands the chapter. Here **Discovery** exercises, marked with the icon 🔍, introduce concepts and techniques that are new but are directly related to the chapter. The **For the Adventurous** exercises, marked with the icon 🏃, go beyond the chapter to challenge those readers eager to extend their reach.

Overview

There are 13 chapters and 5 appendices in this book. Here is a brief look at the contents of each chapter and appendix.

CHAPTER 1   INTRODUCTION TO VISUAL BASIC AND PROBLEM SOLVING

This chapter introduces the reader to programming in general and to Visual Basic in particular. It covers several important Visual Basic concepts and introduces the Visual Basic help system.

CHAPTER 2   YOUR FIRST APPLICATION

In this chapter the reader begins writing applications. Command buttons and text boxes are introduced, as are some actual Visual Basic commands. The Multimedia Control is included to show the reader that Visual Basic can be used to create fun programs as well as those that are more serious in nature.

CHAPTER 3   THE CODE WINDOW AND MORE CODE

Here the reader learns how to manipulate code in the code window. The mathematical use of numeric variables and the manipulation of string variables are dealt with in depth.

CHAPTER 4   USING LOOPS AND ARRAYS

Arrays are some of the most useful tools in any programming language. In this chapter the reader discovers how to use arrays within loops to save excess coding. The Do-While and For-Next loops are discussed in detail.

CHAPTER 5   MORE LABELS, BUTTONS, AND TEXT BOXES

The most often used elements in Visual Basic are labels, buttons, and text boxes. This chapter further expands on their use. Work on the PIM begins in this chapter with the creation of the notepad and the alarm clock. The reader is also shown how to compile programs.

CHAPTER 6   USING MENUS AND RELATED FEATURES

Virtually every Windows™ program uses menus. Visual Basic menus are easy to create. This chapter shows the reader how to create standard menus and also how to create custom menu buttons for giving programs a professional look.

CHAPTER 7   USING DIALOG BOXES AND MULTIPLE FORMS

Most Windows programs have more than one window. Additional windows are used for error messages, as dialog boxes, and simply as other parts of the program processes. This chapter shows how to use extra windows for these and other purposes.

CHAPTER 8   SAVING AND LOADING FILES

Few Windows programs can function without some type of data access. This chapter introduces sequential, random, and binary files and demonstrates how to open a file, save data, read data, and close the file. Both sequential and random files are illustrated. The appointment calendar is added to the PIM in this chapter.

CHAPTER 9   ERROR HANDLING AND DEBUGGING

Every programmer has problems while creating programs. In this chapter the reader learns about many Visual Basic tools that can help the programmer determine what errors are in a program and other tools that can help solve the problems.

CHAPTER 10   ACCESSING DATABASES

This chapter teaches the reader many techniques necessary in accessing relational databases. The reader will learn how to change records and how to add them to and delete them from a database. The address list is added to the PIM in this chapter.

CHAPTER 11   ADDITIONAL TOOLS

This chapter covers a number of important tools and techniques, including the use of graphics and drag-and-drop. The reader learns how to print reports by printing both the notepad and the To-Do list, which is added to the PIM in this chapter.

CHAPTER 12   LINKING APPLICATIONS

One of the most important innovations in Windows is that it enables us to have one application automatically send data to another application through the use of dynamic data exchange. This chapter illustrates several programs that send and receive data.

CHAPTER 13   BROWSING THE WEB

Access to the Internet and World Wide Web has become almost commonplace in the typical office. In this chapter you will discover some of the terminology necessary to understand how a Web browser works and will learn how to add a Web browser to the PIM.

APPENDIX A   USING ACTIVEX CONTROLS

ActiveX controls is a new buzzword in programming. In this appendix the reader learns how to create ActiveX tools to use in many different programs by simply adding them to the toolbar just like any other Visual Basic tools.

APPENDIX B   STANDARD PREFIXES

When programming in Visual Basic, we commonly use certain prefixes to define variables and controls. These prefixes are listed in this appendix.

APPENDIX C   VISUAL BASIC MENU SYSTEM

This appendix illustrates and explains all the options in the Visual Basic menu system.

APPENDIX D   TOOL BAR BUTTONS AND TOOLBOX TOOLS

This appendix illustrates the tool bar and briefly discusses of each of the buttons and tools.

APPENDIX E   GLOSSARY

This appendix briefly defines each of the Visual Basic terms introduced in the book.

Acknowledgments

Many people are involved in the production of a book like this. I want to take this opportunity to thank all the editors, managers, copyeditors, compositors, and designers who helped get it off the ground and contributed their skills through the long months of preparation.

One of the key ingredients in the success of any publication is the incisive comments made by the reviewers. The following people read and commented on the manuscript, offering invaluable advice and the benefit of their experience. Jim Forkner of Penn State University acted as technical consultant as well as reviewer. The other reviewers included Janice Burrell of Dillard University, William D. Haseman of the University of Wisconsin-Milwaukee, Beth McGrew of Connors State College, and Constantine Roussos of Lynchburg College.

Edward J. Coburn

Introduction to Visual Basic and Problem Solving

1.1   Chapter Objectives

After finishing this chapter you will be able to:

- Describe the steps you use in creating a program to solve a problem.
- Describe the major difference between programs written in Visual Basic and those created in other languages.
- Describe the four steps in creating a Visual Basic program.
- Describe what happens when Visual Basic recognizes an event.
- List the major Visual Basic elements that appear when you start the program.
- Explain the purpose of properties.
- Describe how you use the Visual Basic help system.

1.2   Introduction

This is a book about programming in Windows using the Windows programming language Visual Basic. It is not a book about hardware (the computer devices) or how to use Windows. Accordingly, we assume that you already know how to operate a computer and how to use the keyboard, mouse, monitor, disk drives, printer, and other standard devices. If you are not familiar with one or more of these devices, consult the lab assistant or your instructor. We also assume that you either have experience with Windows or have taken a Windows class. We discuss basic Windows elements only briefly and only when appropriate. Otherwise, we assume you are familiar with Windows concepts.

Depending on your point of view, your experience with the programming language you are using, and your approach to programming, writing programs can be either time-consuming and frustrating or pleasant, enjoyable, and even fun. To help you have an en-joyable experience in Visual Basic, we begin with a look at the programming process and how you can use that process to solve your business problems with Visual Basic. We com-pare the Visual Basic approach to the programming methods of other languages. After dis-cussing Visual Basic, we will take an in-depth look at the help system.

1.3   Problem Solving and the Programming Process

There is more than one approach to the solution of any problem, no matter how trivial. When a computer is part of the problem-solving equation, the number of possible ap-proaches can expand dramatically.

Suppose you are having trouble remembering the appointments you have made with clients or co-workers. You probably have already tried several different ways of solving this problem. Perhaps you have begun carrying around an appointment book. But you find that you often forget to check your book, or neglect to write down an appointment, or sim-ply let the meeting time come and go without realizing it. Next you turn to an electronic ap-pointment book—a small device, resembling a calculator, that enables you to store appointments. It may even have an alarm that sounds to remind you of each appointment. The alarm solves the problem of getting busy and forgetting that it's time for the meeting.

If you work at a desk, you may have a bulletin board where you post reminders of your meetings. A bulletin board presents the same problems as an appointment book, along with the additional problem that the notice may simply fall and vanish behind your desk.

The fourth approach—one that management often uses—is to have someone else, usu-ally a secretary, remind you of your meetings. With a bit of thought, you could probably come up with several more approaches to solving the same problem.

A computer gives you other problem-solving options. There are many Windows ap-plications that can be used to schedule your appointments. No matter how sophisticated they are, most programs of this type don't quite solve your problems. Or there may be no application available to help with your particular problem. That's where programming lan-guages like Visual Basic come in. With Visual Basic you can create an application—like an appointment book—that works precisely the way you want it to work.

How do you choose the best approach to solve your problem? If it's a common prob-lem, such as keeping track of appointments, alternatives present themselves quickly and easily. Programming problems, by contrast, require careful consideration and a systematic approach.

Programming to Solve a Problem

If you decide that the best approach for the problem you are trying to solve is to write a pro-gram, you will need to go through a series of steps in the programming process.

1. **Define the problem.** Your definition may range from a few sentences to hundreds of words. A detailed description of just what you are trying to accomplish generally re-sults in a better understanding of the problem. Your description may contain limiting conditions that you wish to impose on the solution—for example, that your program cannot have more than three windows and can use certain shortcut keys for your menu options.

2. **Design your program.** Use your definition to answer your design questions: How many windows will your program need? What will be in the windows? What data will be needed as input? What controls (command buttons and so forth) will be required?

Designing the code for those controls is the most important phase of the programming process. With a good design, carried out properly, you can save hours of program debugging and rewriting. Programmers who skimp on the design phase usually end up regretting it when they can't figure out why something isn't working the way it's supposed to.

3. **Create the program.** This step is generally the most fun. In most programming languages, this step is called program coding. In Visual Basic, programs contain so much more than code (as you will see shortly) that this step becomes more an act of creation than just coding. If you have spent enough time designing the program and are thoroughly familiar with the Visual Basic elements you need, this step should come easily.

4. **Test and debug the program.** While you are keying your Visual Basic code (commands), the system generally informs you if you have keyed a statement incorrectly. However, that doesn't mean you won't end up with errors in your code. For example, you may have a statement in your program to display some text in a particular box in the window, and your statement may use the name of the wrong box. The statement itself is "correct" in Visual Basic (because text could be placed in the named box), but it is incorrect for what you want the program to do (because the text will show up in the wrong box). Errors like this are generally called **logic errors.** To accomplish its objective, a program must be put together in a logical progression of steps. An error in this progression is an error in the "logic" of the program—a logic error. There are generally any number of logic errors in a completed program, and that's why the testing process is important. Visual Basic has many debugging tools and techniques that can help you find and repair logic errors. You will deal with them in great detail in later chapters, after you have learned enough Visual Basic to make the debugging experience worthwhile.

5. **Document the program.** If the program is for your own use, you may need minimal documentation. If it is to be used by others, they will probably need some type of written information about how to operate the program. The three categories of documentation are **program documentation,** the **user's guide** (or manual), and **on-line help.**

   ■ **Program documentation.** This includes the coding comments, generally created as the program is written and put directly into the program. Such comments are especially helpful during debugging and making future changes in the program—these are common occurrences. It is especially important to have comments on any code that is tricky or difficult to understand.

   ■ **User's guide.** This is a written document for the benefit of the user. It can be anything from a large or small manual to a page or two explaining how to operate the program. It may include such information as the format for entering dates, the range of values allowed for a certain entry, illustrations of the windows that will appear in the program, and explanations of the important options found in menus and dialog boxes.

   ■ **On-line help.** This may be extensive documentation, explaining everything the program is capable of doing, or brief, simple notes on the more complex program steps. Visual Basic has an extensive help system, which we will explore later in this chapter.

If you have followed the proper procedures in creating your program, it will probably function as it should for as long as it proves useful.

Programming Languages and Visual Basic

For a computer to solve a problem, the computer must be given precise instructions about how to do it. The computer must be guided, step-by-step, through the process necessary to solve the problem. As a group, these instructions make up a **program** or **application** (the two terms are interchangeable).

From the very first program ever written, programs have been linear in nature. That is, the computer begins with the first line of program code and executes the instructions one after another until it reaches the end of the program.

For example, suppose you want the computer to calculate the amount of your payment on a loan. To do this, the program needs you (the user) to input the amount of the loan, the period of the loan in years, and the interest rate. Next, the payment amount needs to be calculated. Finally, the program needs to display the calculated payment on the display screen. Using the popular programming language QBasic, such a program looks something like this:

SAMPLE QBASIC PROGRAM

```
INPUT "What is the loan amount"; Loan
INPUT "How many years is the loan for"; Years
INPUT "What is the interest rate"; Rate
NewRate = Rate / 100 / 12
Payment = Loan * ((NewRate * ((1 + NewRate) ^ (Years * 12))) /
↳(((1 + NewRate) ^ (Years * 12)) - 1))
Print "Your monthly payment is "; Using; "$#,###.##"; Payment
```

> **NOTE:** The ↳ symbol, used on the Payment statement above, indicates that the statement is continued on the next line because there is too much code to display on one line. This symbol is used throughout the book.

The first three lines of the program input the three pieces of data and store that input in the named fields (Loan, Years, and Rate). These fields are called **variables.** Variables are special storage locations within the computer where the program's data are stored. Following the three Input statements, the NewRate field (another variable) is calculated from the Rate field. This intermediary calculation is done to simplify the next calculation, which actually calculates the payment and stores that result in the variable called Payment. The last statement displays the payment on the screen.

This program executes step by step in the order of the statements. The particular program shown is only one way to determine a payment amount. The program can be written any number of ways, because there are many different ways to solve the problem. Regardless of the way the program is written, however, it is always linear in nature; that's how such programming languages work.

To get a feel for how this type of program works, you run a sample of the foregoing program.

1. Boot your computer into Windows.
2. Launch **Windows Explorer**. Copy the folders for Chapters 1 through 6 (Ch-1 through Ch-6) onto a blank disk. This disk is called your work disk. You will need to copy the folders from wherever they are stored on your system. To do this, you will need instructions from your instructor or lab assistant.
3. Put your work disk into drive A.
4. Launch **Windows Explorer** and change to the Ch-1 folder on drive A.
5. Launch the **Linear Monthly Payment** program to see the window as shown in Figure 1.1.

As you see, the first thing the program does is ask for the loan amount.

FIGURE 1.1
The sample Linear
program.

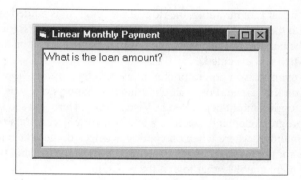

6. Key **1000** and press **Enter** and the program asks for the number of years of the loan.

7. Key **2** and press **Enter** and the program asks for the loan amount.

8. Key **8** and press **Enter** and the program displays the amount of the payment, which is $45.23.

Your display should look like the one in Figure 1.2.

Note that we have added an extra routine to the program that allows you to do additional calculations. This routine is not shown in the program listing given previously, but it makes the program easier to use.

9. Press **Enter** and the display clears, the first question being displayed again.

10. Key **1000**, **3**, and **9.5** for the three inputs (be sure to press **Enter** after each). The payment displayed is $32.03.

11. Try calculating a few more payments using different values for the three inputs.

12. Close the program. You are finished with it.

This is a nice program. As you discovered, however, one problem the program has is that you need to key all three inputs, whether or not they have changed since the last calculation. Also, if you key **100** instead of **1000** before you press **Enter**, there is no way to change the amount except to do the entire sequence again. In addition, there is no error checking in the program. If you enter invalid data for one of the Input statements, the program simply uses the invalid data and quite probably generates an error. You can add code to the program so that the amounts can be changed and error messages used if the data entered were incorrect. You can create a menu system to make data entry more flexible and easier. Regardless of the changes, the program will still be linear in nature.

Languages such as Visual Basic offer a completely different solution. Unlike standard linear programming languages, Visual Basic uses a new approach called **event-driven programming.**

FIGURE 1.2
The result of the
monthly payment
calculation.

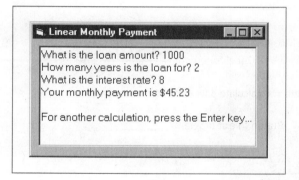

In linear programming, the flow of the program is guided on the basis of questions presented to the user. When the user enters one of the amounts, for example, the program goes on to the next input statement. The program begins at the top and goes directly through the code when it is executed.

In event-driven programming, however, the program flow is controlled by the objects drawn on the screen. For example, Figure 1.3 shows one way in which the Monthly Payment program might be created in Visual Basic. Here you see several of the standard Windows program elements, such as a text box for entering data (the Loan Amount); a set of option buttons, where when one option is selected, the others are automatically turned off (the Period); a list from which to select the Interest Rate; and two buttons, one to calculate the payment and the other to exit the program.

To use the program, enter the loan amount into the text box, select the period from the group of option buttons, and select the interest rate from the list. After these are keyed and selected, the **Calculate Payment** button is clicked and the monthly payment is displayed. In this program, the user controls the flow of the program by keying the data, selecting the elements, and clicking the **Calculate Payment** button. The user can select the interest rate and then key the loan amount or the other way around. There is actually no code in the program except behind the two buttons. The code for the **Calculate Payment** button is, essentially, the calculation statement for the payment amount, though there is also code to determine which item in the list is selected and which option button has been chosen. This is necessary to determine the numeric values for the interest rate and period.

To see how the execution of this program differs from that of the linear version, you can run this one.

13. Change to the **Explorer**, and run the program from the Ch-1 folder in drive A called **VB Monthly Payment**.

You see the display shown in Figure 1.3. The initial value of the period is 2 years, and the initial value in the interest rate list is 6.00. For the first sample, use the same calculation you used in the first program.

FIGURE 1.3
The Monthly Payment program created in Visual Basic.

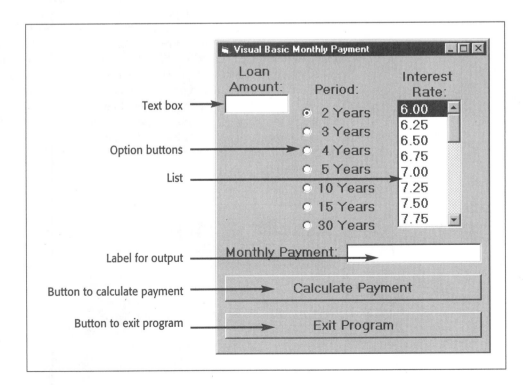

14. Key **1000** for the Loan Amount and select **8.00** for the Interest Rate by scrolling the list and clicking the **8.00** entry.

15. Click the **Calculate Payment** button, and you see $45.23 displayed as the Monthly Payment.

This is the same result you got with the other program. In this case, however, you could key just the Loan Amount and select the other elements rather than key them.

16. Pick **3** years and select **9.50** percent for the interest rate. Then click the **Calculate Payment** button.

The answer for this calculation is $32.03, just as it was before. This time you didn't need to rekey the Loan Amount.

17. Click **4** years and click the **Calculate Payment** button.

This time you simply clicked a couple of program elements to calculate a different result. In the other program, you would have had to rekey all three numbers. As you can see, this program is much more flexible than the previous one. For example, suppose you key the Loan Amount incorrectly. In the first program, you have to finish entering all the data and then start again. In the Visual Basic version, you simply rekey the Loan Amount.

The best thing about this Visual Basic program is that no code is required for any of the visual elements. That is, the programmer does not have to create any code for the list to enable the user to scroll the list or select the items from the list. The only code in the program resides behind the two buttons, and that code is executed only when the buttons are clicked. The code for one of the buttons is totally independent of the code for the other button. For example, the code for the **Exit Program** button has only three lines:

```
Private Sub cmdExit_Program_Click()
    End
End Sub
```

The first line tells the program that this section of code is a procedure (**Private Sub**) for the **cmdExit_Program** button that is to be executed when the user clicks (**_Click**) the button. The only code needed to exit the program is the End statement. The last statement, **End Sub**, simply tells Visual Basic that it has reached the end of the procedure. This code is completely independent of the code for the **Calculate Payment** button. That code is in a similar procedure for the clicking (**_Click**) of the **cmdCalculate_Payment** button.

1.4 About Visual Basic

As we have said, writing programs in Visual Basic is much like an act of artistic creation. Creating a Visual Basic application is almost like using a drawing program to create an illustration. In linear programming languages, page after page of coding is required to create the windows and controls, such as text boxes and lists, that Visual Basic gives you automatically. Rather than performing just the single step of coding a program's instructions, you go through four steps when creating a Visual Basic application.

1. First you draw the **form(s)** you want (see Figure 1.4). Forms are the windows that your application uses. If your application requires more than one form, you should probably finish most of the work on the first form before creating any other forms. Visual Basic creates the first form of every application for you. This gives you a starting point for your application, because every application must have at least one form.

FIGURE 1.4
Illustration of a form.

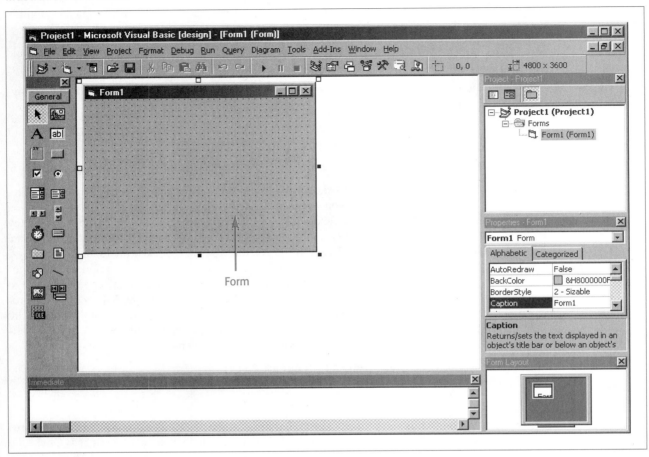

2. Next you place on the form any **controls** you might need (see Figure 1.3). Controls are the graphical objects in the window. They can include

   ■ Command buttons that the user can click on

   ■ Label boxes for displaying messages on the form

   ■ Text boxes that let the user enter text such as the Loan Amount

   ■ Lists from which the user can select one or more items

   ■ Option buttons where the user can select one of several items

   ■ Picture boxes, which can contain drawings, including icons, created in Paintbrush or some other graphics program

   ■ Timers that can be used to time events in the program for alarms and the like

   ■ File controls that enable the user to load files into a program and save them back to disk

3. Each of the controls has many **properties** that can be customized. For example, you can make the caption of a command button **Calculate Payment** or **Exit Program** (as shown in Figure 1.3), the command button can be resized so that it is larger or smaller than the one shown in Figure 1.3, and the font (letter style) used to display the caption on the button can be changed. Each of these changes is made by using the properties of the command button (see Figure 1.5).

4. Finally, you write the code for appropriate events, such as when a user clicks a button.

FIGURE 1.5
The connection between the command button caption and the caption property
in the Properties list.

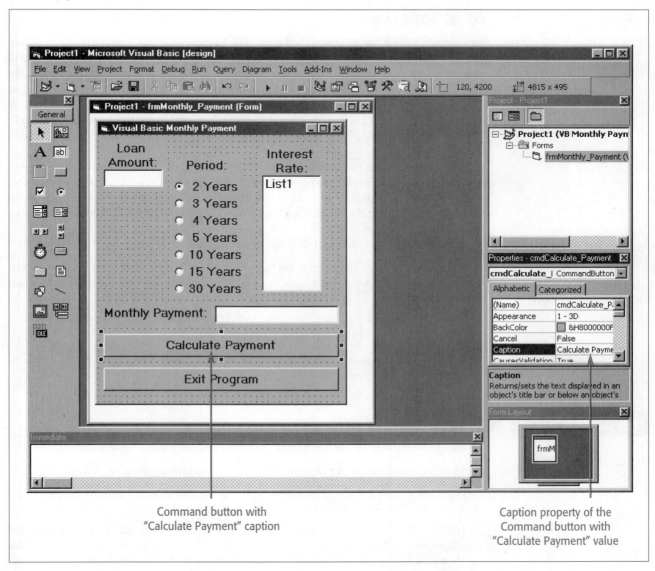

Command button with
"Calculate Payment" caption

Caption property of the
Command button with
"Calculate Payment" value

Visual Basic Controls

Setting up the forms with the appropriate controls is where the real power of Visual Basic lies and what makes Visual Basic so much fun to program. In languages without a preprogrammed visual interface (known as a Graphical User Interface, or GUI, pronounced "gooie"), it is a tedious process to create screen elements and code the program to interpret user actions such as keystrokes or mouse movements. In Visual Basic, all that is taken care of. All you do is select the object you want from a Toolbox display of the objects (shown on the left in Figure 1.4), move it to the position on the window where you want it, change any of the properties necessary (such as the size of the object), and you're done (with the control itself—you must still create the code needed for any user actions). The system already knows how to interpret keystrokes and mouse movements. The real beauty here is that you see every aspect of the form and its controls as they are created. There is never any question as to placement, captions, and so on, because you can see exactly what you are creating.

Visual Basic Events

For each object you create (forms and controls), Visual Basic has a predefined set of user actions, called **events,** that it recognizes. You write your program code to tell Visual Basic what you want the program to do in response to these events. In our sample program, for example, the form has a **Calculate Payment** button, and Visual Basic responds to your clicking the button by looking for the code for the **Click** procedure. If there is such code, it is executed; if not, the click of the button is ignored. Visual Basic looks for different code if the user double-clicks. Even simply moving the mouse cursor over the button generates an event for which you can create code.

The fact that Visual Basic intercepts all the user actions does not mean that you have to write code for each of the actions. You write code only for the events that have meaning to your program. If you want to recognize when the user double-clicks a button, you write code for that event, but if a single click has no meaning in your program, you write no code, and the event is ignored.

Briefly, here's how a Visual Basic program works:

1. An action is recognized as an event by some form or control. The action can be caused by the user (such as a mouse click or keystroke) or by the system itself (such as when a timer is used).

2. If there is code for the event, that code is executed; otherwise, the event is ignored.

3. The system then waits for the next event.

Now that you know in general terms how a Visual Basic program works, it's time to see what Visual Basic actually looks like.

1.5   Looking at Visual Basic

Launching Visual Basic is like launching any other Windows application. You double-click the icon if it is on the desktop or select it from one of the Start menu submenus.

1. Exit both of the sample Monthly Payment programs.

2. If the Visual Basic icon is on the desktop, click it. Otherwise, find it in the Start menu submenus, and then launch Visual Basic from that subgroup to see the dialog box shown in Figure 1.6. If you can't find Visual Basic in the Start menu subgroup, check with your instructor or lab supervisor.

As you can see, this dialog box enables you to start a new project, look for an existing project, or open a project that you recently opened. You are just getting ready to explore Visual Basic, so you start a new project. This is the default tab, and Standard EXE is the option you use.

3. Click the **Open** button to see the initial Visual Basic display shown in Figure 1.7.

Figure 1.7 shows that Visual Basic has all the normal Windows program elements, such as a Control menu icon; **Minimize, Maximize,** and **Close** buttons; and a menu bar. The other elements shown are unique to Visual Basic. These elements are shown **docked** together in the Visual Basic development window (the entire display window). Docking is Visual Basic's way of keeping the elements arranged so the windows that contain them don't overlap. If you wish, you can undock the elements so that they can be moved around within the development window. Shortly, we'll see how to do this.

FIGURE 1.6
The dialog box for starting a Visual Basic project.

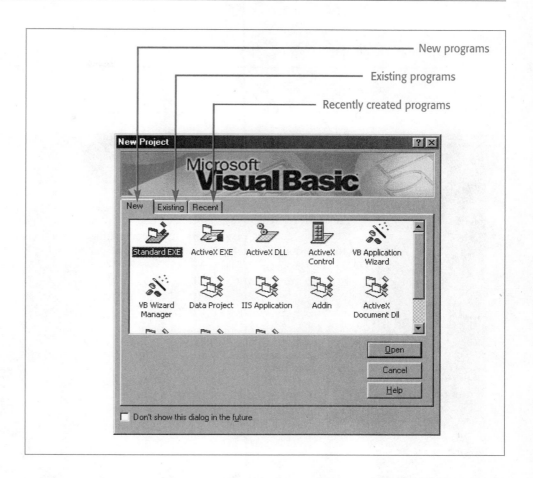

New programs

Existing programs

Recently created programs

The Tool Bar

Just under the menu bar is the **Tool bar.** Its icons represent some of the options found on the menus. For example, the icons with the small arrow (▶), double bars (❚❚), and small box (■) represent the **Start, Break,** and **End** options, respectively, on the **Run** menu.

1. Pull down the **Run** menu to see the three options as shown in Figure 1.8.

Note that the three icons from the Tool bar are shown on the menu, to the left of the menu options to which they are related. The **Start** option is available (to run the program), whereas the **Break** and **End** options are dimmed and not currently available. These options are used only when a program is executing, not when it is being created. Note also that the **Start** option can be executed with the **F5** function key (which is referred to as a **shortcut key**) and that you can stop the program's execution by using the **Ctrl** and **Break** keys together. We will discuss the use for each of the tools on the Tool bar when appropriate.

The Toolbox

Next, on the left side, is the **Toolbox** (see Figure 1.9). This is where you select the program controls to be placed on your form. For example, the Command Button control (▭) is used to add a button to your form. These controls will be discussed as they become useful.

The tools shown are only a small selection of the controls available, and your display may have more tools than the Toolbox in the figure. If so, don't worry about it. You will learn a bit later how you can add additional controls to your toolbox when you need them.

FIGURE 1.7
The initial Visual Basic display.

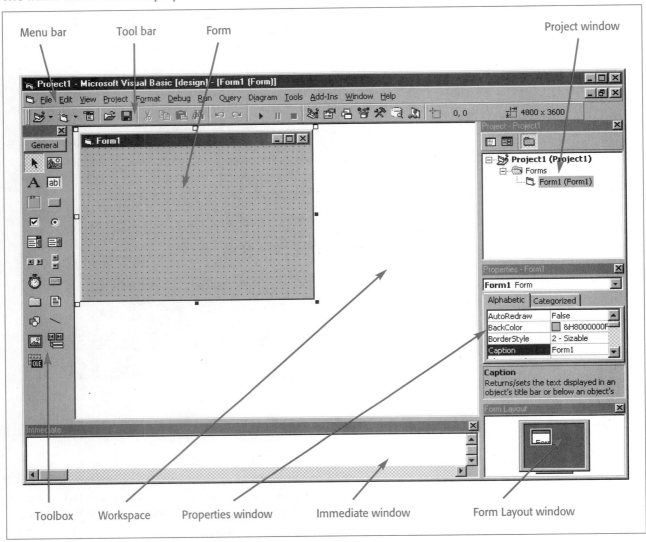

The Form

In the development window workspace, you can see a **Form** that has the default name of **Form1.** This is the beginning window for your program; it even looks like a normal window, with the **Control** menu icon, title bar, **Minimize, Maximize,** and **Close** buttons, border, and workspace.

The Form workspace is filled with a grid of dots spaced at regular intervals to help you align your controls. As the controls are placed on the form, they automatically align on the dots. If you decide that you don't want the controls to align to the grid, you can turn this alignment off.

The Project Window

To the right of the development window workspace are three windows: the Project window, the Properties window, and the Form Layout window. We will examine the **Project window** first (it should look like the one shown in Figure 1.10).

FIGURE 1.8
The **Run** menu, showing the **Start** option.

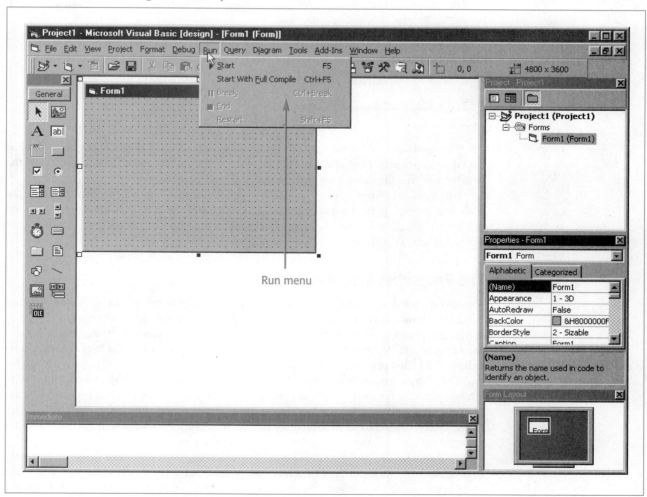

FIGURE 1.9
The Toolbox, showing the position of the Command Button control.

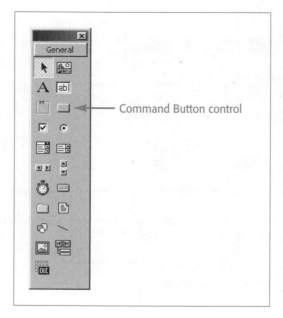

FIGURE 1.10
The Project window.

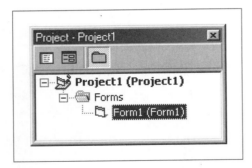

This is where Visual Basic keeps track of the various parts of your program, which is called your **project.** Note that the Project window shows the name of your project in the title bar and that the default name for all projects is **Project1.**

Just as many Windows programs have several different windows that can appear on the screen at various times, your programs can have multiple windows. If the current program did have multiple windows, they would all be listed in the Project window. As it is, only **Form1 (Form1)** is shown.

The Properties Window

The second window shown on the right is the **Properties window.** As we have said, each object in a Visual Basic program has many properties. Because different types of objects (a text box versus a control button, for example) vary in their purposes, Visual Basic has different properties defined for each type of object. These are shown in the Properties window (Figure 1.11) and can be changed there.

Each object in the project has its own set of properties. The **Object box** tells you to which object the currently displayed properties belong. Each property has a name and a default or initial setting, which is the value of the property. Some of the property settings, such as the size and placement of a control, can be changed with mouse actions, but most are changed either by using the property window while you are creating the program or dynamically while the program is running. For example, the Caption property is currently highlighted, and its setting is **Form1.** As we pointed out earlier, **Form1** is the name of the form as shown on the title bar. It is unlikely that you want your window to be called **Form1**

FIGURE 1.11
The Properties window.

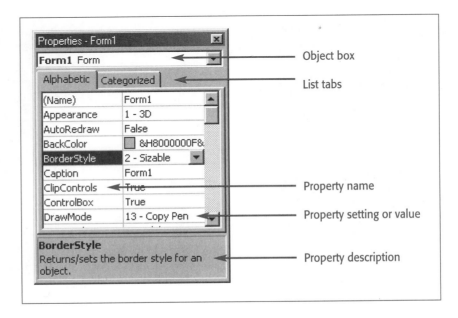

when you are creating a program, because the name in the title bar is usually related to the name of the program. You probably want to change the caption to something more appropriate as the program is being created. This is done by using the Property window. Then, as the application is being executed, you may want to change the window title again to reflect the application name along with the name of the file that is being used in the application. So you might want to change the form caption to **Notepad** now and to **Notepad - Filein** after the Notepad application has loaded the Filein file.

Let's see just how easy it is to change the setting of the Caption property. If the Caption property is already highlighted, all you have to do is key the new caption. If not, you merely click the property and then key the new caption.

1. Click the Caption property if necessary.

2. Key **Clicking Practice** and you see the text appear in two places—in the Properties window on the Caption line and on the title bar of the form.

The Caption is only one of the many properties available for a form. To see others, you can scroll or enlarge the Properties window, but to do that you must undock the window.

3. Double-click the Properties window title bar, and you see that it becomes an independent window.

4. Enlarge the Properties window so that it appears as shown in Figure 1.12 (or make it as large as you can).

As you can see, even with the expanded window, other properties are still not shown. A few of the more important properties (some showing in the list, some that you can't see unless you scroll the window) are as follows:

- **Name,** which is the name of the control that you use in your code to refer to the control. The default name of each control begins with the type of control (**Text** for a text box, **Command** for a command button, **Form** for a form, and so on), followed by the number of the control. For example, if a text box is the third text box you have placed in the window and you have not changed the name of the other two, its name will be **Text3**. If you have changed the names of the first two text boxes, the new one will be **Text1** again. You can leave the Name with its default, but if the object is to be used in your code, it is easier to remember which object is which if the name is related to the object's purpose. For example, if you have a command button with a caption of **OK,** a better control name than **Command1** might be **OK_Button**. In addition, it is a good idea (and a Microsoft standard) to begin each control name with an abbreviation indicating the type of control. Thus, the name of the command button becomes **cmdOK_Button.** A list of the standard control name prefixes is shown in Appendix B. We use these standard prefixes throughout this book.

- **Text** or **Caption** is the text that shows up in the object. The form caption shows up on the title bar of the window (as you have seen). A command button caption is displayed on the button, and the text of a text box is displayed in the text box.

- **Enabled** is used to activate or deactivate a control when the application runs. A text box may be disabled—for example, when the text is purely for display purposes and you do not want it to be changed. If it is disabled, it still appears in the window but does not respond to events (mouse movements and keystrokes).

- If you want the control not to appear at some point in your application, you can turn it off visually by using the **Visible** property. So you may have a command button that will appear in the window sometimes and will not appear at other times.

- **ControlBox**, **MinButton**, and **MaxButton** are controls that appear only on forms, and these properties are used to turn them on or off. Normally, you want your form to have all three of these controls, but there may be occasions when, for example, you do not want the user to maximize or minimize the form.

FIGURE 1.12

The enlarged Properties window, showing more properties and their settings.

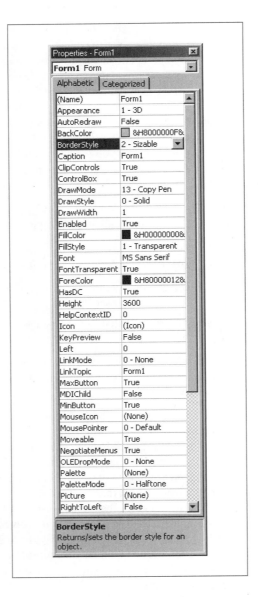

■ **BackColor** and **ForeColor** are used to change the background and foreground colors of the control. The background color is the color of the control itself (the form, for example), and the foreground color is generally the color of the text that appears in or on the control.

We will explore these and many other properties more fully as we have need for them in our programs. Changing the properties and watching the control automatically change is one of the joys of using Visual Basic. As you use more of the properties throughout the book, you will come to appreciate this special type of Visual Basic magic.

5. Scroll through the Properties list to see the rest.

If any of the properties shown in the Properties window is not familiar to you, you can read through the brief description of the property in the Properties description at the bottom of the Properties window. If that explanation is not sufficient, you can look the property up in the Help system, which we will discuss shortly.

Note that the Properties window has two tabs near the top, labeled **Alphabetic** and **Categorized.** The Alphabetic listing is the default form and is what you are currently reading. Sometimes, however, it is useful to have the properties listed by category.

6. Click the **Categorized** tab to see the display in the Properties window change to one similar to that shown in Figure 1.13.

Now several categories are shown in the list, beginning with Appearance. Each of the properties listed under the category heading is related to that topic. Note that the Appearance category has the properties of Appearance, BackColor, Caption, and ForeColor, along with others that are related to the appearance of the control.

The categories can be collapsed to make the Properties window a bit easier to read by clicking the box with the minus sign in it (⊟).

7. Click the collapse box for the Appearance category, and all the properties under the category title vanish.

Now the collapse box has changed to an expand box, with a plus sign in it (⊞), that lets you redisplay the properties.

8. Click the expand box to redisplay the properties.

FIGURE 1.13
The Property categories.

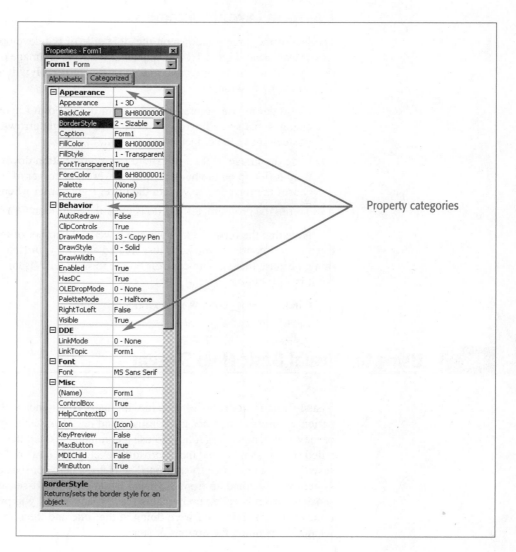

Property categories

FIGURE 1.14
The Form Layout
window, showing your
form.

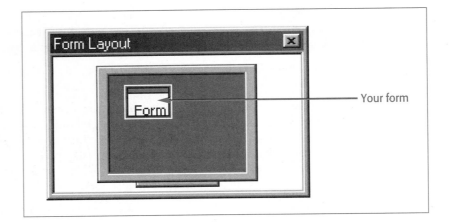

9. Explore the properties a bit more, then double-click the title bar of the Properties window to have Visual Basic redock the window.

The Form Layout Window

The last of the three windows on the right side of the development window is the **Form Layout window** (Figure 1.14). This window shows an image of the desktop with the positioning of the various forms that make up your project. It will also let you move the forms around on the desktop.

1. Move the mouse pointer over the form in the Form Layout window, and the pointer changes to a symbol with up, down, left, and right arrows. This pointer indicates that you can move the object by dragging it.

2. Drag the image of the form (hold the mouse button down and move the mouse), and drop it (let up on the button) in the lower right corner of the desktop illustration. This causes the form to show up in the lower right corner when the program is executed.

3. To run the program, all you do is click the Start icon (▶) on the Tool bar.

Note that the form shows up in the lower right corner of the desktop just as predicted. Even more important, you have just created and run your first program. It doesn't do anything, because there are no controls on the form to tell Visual Basic to perform some task, but it is a program.

4. Click the Stop icon (■) to exit the program.

1.6   Using the Visual Basic Help System

Visual Basic is an extensive system with many commands and options. Even the most experienced users sometimes get confused and need assistance with some of the techniques, or they may simply forget how to use a command. To aid the user, Visual Basic has a detailed Help system, called the Microsoft Developers Network™ (MSDN™) Library, that can save time and minimize frustration. The Help system consists of two parts: the Help menu system that is called up from the menu bar and a context-sensitive Help system. **Context-sensitive Help** is called up by using the **F1** key. When you press **F1**, Visual Basic determines which activity you were doing at the time and then brings up an appropriate Help window explaining the options or steps.

> **HINT:** In order to follow the steps in this section, you must have access to the MSDN Library CDs or have the MSDN Library installed on your network. Most of the Help topics are located in the MSDN Library. If you don't have access to the MSDN Library, you should still read through this section and then experiment with the Help topics at your first opportunity.

The Help Menu

The **Help** menu is called up with the Help command, on the right end of the menu bar.

1. Click **Help** on the menu bar; the **Help** menu drops down as shown in Figure 1.15.

This menu has several different categories of information available. Briefly, here is what each of them is for:

- **Contents...** brings up the MSDN Library window with the Contents tab selected. Contents is a list of Help topics that you can choose from for more information. You select the appropriate topic from the list to jump to a Help window that will tell you how to use Visual Basic or get quick access to key reference topics.

FIGURE 1.15
The **Help** menu.

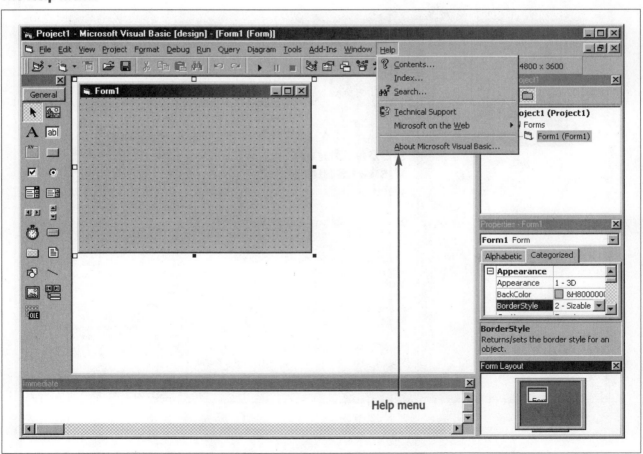

Help menu

- **Index...** brings up the MSDN Library window with the Index tab selected. The Index is a list of the topics in the Library that you can use to look up a particular topic.

- **Search...** brings up the MSDN Library window with the Search tab selected. Search allows you to look for a Library topic by the keywords found within the topic.

- **Technical Support...** gives you information about the various ways you can get help from Microsoft if you are having difficulty with Visual Basic.

- **Microsoft on the Web** gives you a list of Microsoft Web sites where you can get additional information about Visual Basic and other topics.

- **About Microsoft Visual Basic** provides important information about this version of Visual Basic and includes the copyright, version, serial number, and the name of the registered user. It also has a button to allow you to obtain system information, such as how much free memory there is on your computer.

You can explore most of these options on your own. For now, let's take a few moments to look at the Library window, because it will lead us to other Help topics.

The Library Window

1. Click **Contents...** on the Help menu to see the window shown in Figure 1.16.

FIGURE 1.16
The initial MSDN Library display.

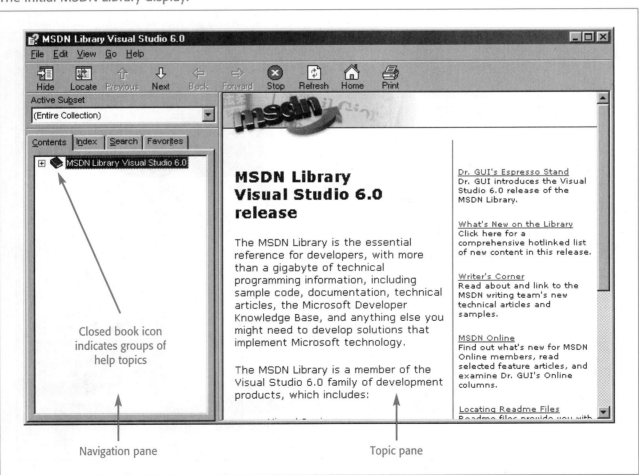

In this window you see two different display sections. The one on the left is called the **Navigation pane** because this is where you will navigate among the topic headings to find the particular topic in which you are interested, and the one on the right is called the **Topic pane** because this is where the topic information will actually be displayed. Notice the three tabs we mentioned in the Navigation pane as well as a fourth tab, **Favorites,** that can be used to bookmark favorite topics or ones that you look at frequently so they are quickly available. As in all Windows programs with tabs, to switch to one of the other tab sheets, you simply click on that tab. The tab displays are called sheets because they represent sheets of paper within the tabbed display. In this case, you are looking at the Contents sheet.

In the **Navigation pane,** the items in the workspace marked with a book icon (📖) are groups of topics that expand when the icon (or the words following it) is double-clicked. You can also expand the group when you click the plus box (⊞) to the left of the topic in the same way you expand folders in Windows Explorer. The group of topics indicated by the icon will also expand if you double-click it. The Navigation pane has a horizontal scroll bar, so as you move into the various groups and topics within those groups, you can scroll the pane to better see the group and topic titles. Also, the Library window can be resized and the data within will automatically reposition itself to fit within the workspace; you can maximize the window if you wish.

2. Click the plus box beside the one topic group shown to see it expand as shown in Figure 1.17.

The open group item now shows an open-book icon (📖) to indicate that the group is open. The new group items shown underneath are all references to topics in the Library. Notice that many of them are not about Visual Basic. This Library is a reference to many products that make up Visual Studio 6.0, which is a group of many programming tools, one of which is Visual Basic. You will see many topics that are not related to what we are going to be doing in this book. As a matter of fact, the information you would normally be looking for is found in one of the groups, labeled **Visual Basic Documentation.**

3. Click the **Visual Basic Documentation** topic to see it expand as shown in Figure 1.18.

Now you see additional groups as well as an actual Help topic called Visual Basic Start Page. The topics are always marked with the page icon (📄) shown on the topic in Figure 1.18. Let's navigate a few more groups to see what an actual Help topic looks like.

4. Double-click the **Reference** group to open it as shown in Figure 1.19.

In this group you will see the Language Reference group. Notice in Figure 1.19 that the navigation pane has been scrolled a bit horizontally to show a better view of the groups and topics. Feel free to scroll your displays any time to get a better view of what we are discussing.

5. Double-click the **Language Reference** group to open it and see the group of topic groups shown in Figure 1.20.

Now you need to open the Objects group.

6. Double-click the **Objects** group to open it as shown in Figure 1.21.

Notice that you now have an alphabetical list of topic groups.

7. Double-click the **C** group to see the list of Help topics shown in Figure 1.22.

Now you can see a series of Help topics rather than just new groups.

8. Click the **CommandButton Control Help** topic.

If you don't have the MSDN CD in the CD drive or stored on the network somewhere, you will see a message similar to the one shown in Figure 1.23. This tells you to insert the CD so the system can access the needed information.

FIGURE 1.17

The Library window with the group expanded.

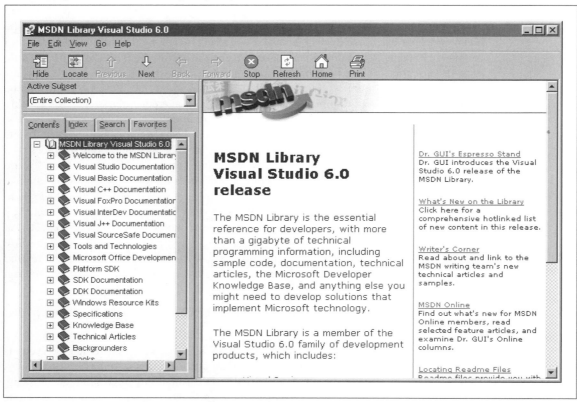

FIGURE 1.18

The Visual Basic Documentation group expanded.

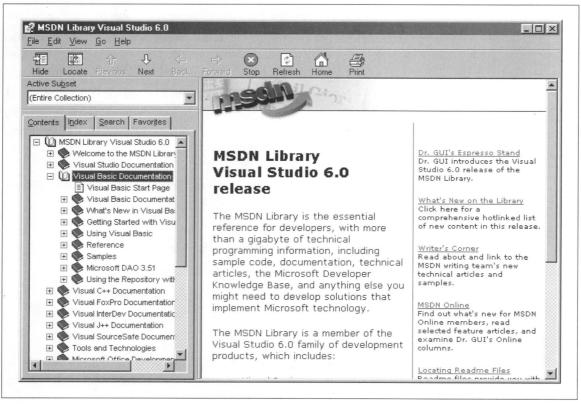

FIGURE 1.19
The open Reference group.

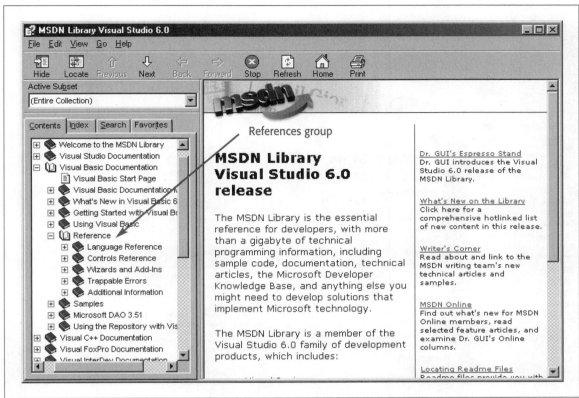

FIGURE 1.20
The Language Reference group

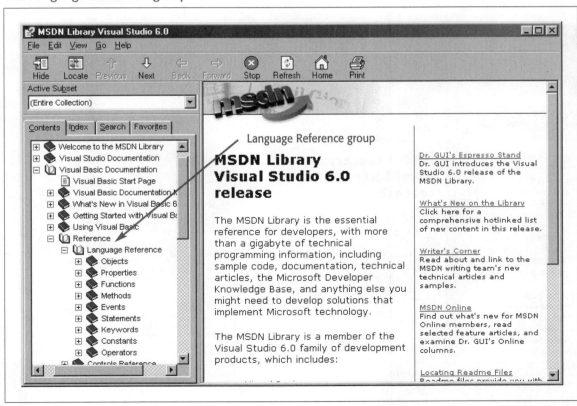

FIGURE 1.21
The Objects group.

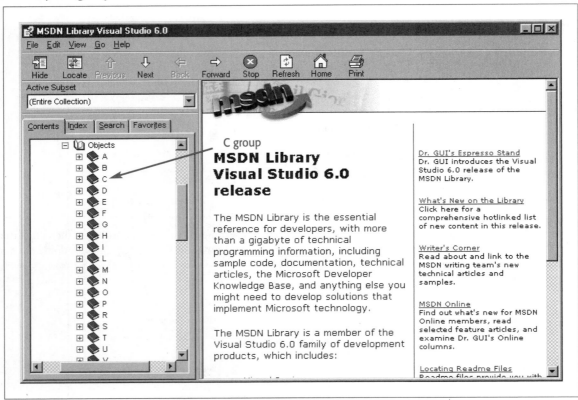

FIGURE 1.22
The list of Help topics within the C group of Properties.

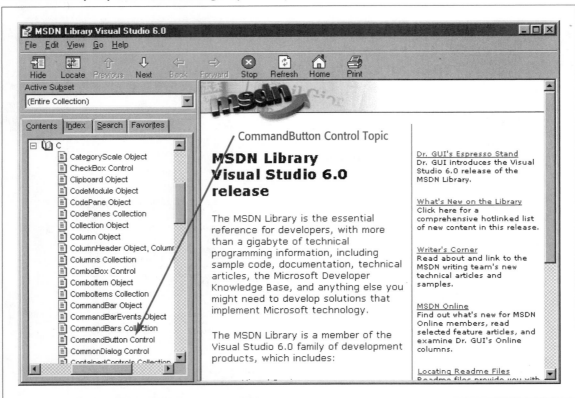

FIGURE 1.23
The window telling you
to insert the MSDN CD.

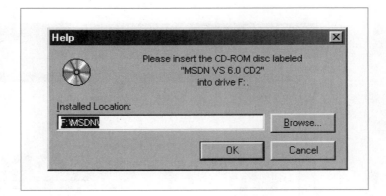

9. If you saw the message in Figure 1.23, insert the CD in the CD drive and then click the **OK** button to see the topic information as shown in Figure 1.24. If you don't have a CD, you cannot do the subsequent steps but you should still read through them. In such a case, click the **Cancel** button.

In many Help windows, additional information is available beyond what is contained in the window itself. This additional information is given in the form of **Glossary items** and **Additional Topic items**. These items in a Help window are printed in blue and underlined.

FIGURE 1.24
The CommandButton Control Help topic.

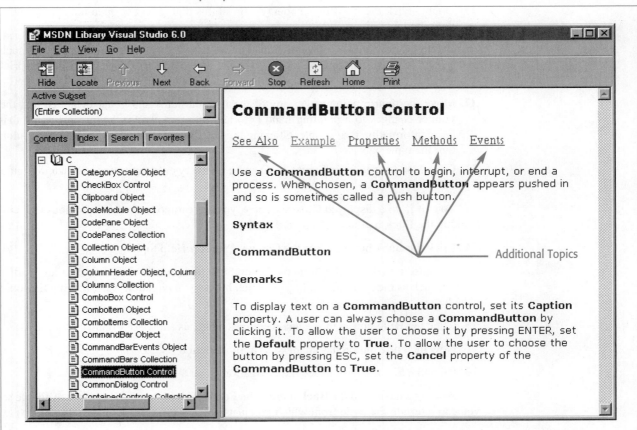

FIGURE 1.25
The list of See Also topics.

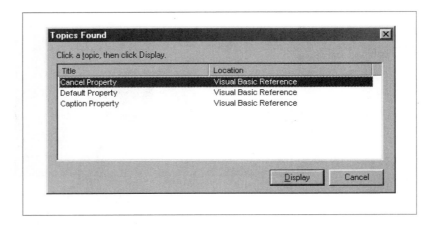

They will either take you to a different Help topic window that may or may not have links to additional help topics or, as in the case of the items shown in this window, may present you with a list of additional topics from which to choose. The term **See Also** is an Additional Topic item in this window, as are several others on the same line. This window does not have any Glossary items, but you will see some in the next window.

10. Click **See Also** to call up the dialog box of the additional topics available shown in Figure 1.25.

    As you can see, there are three topics that are related to the CommandButton Control.

11. Double-click the **Caption Property** item in this dialog box to open the Library window shown in Figure 1.26.

    In this window, you see several items that we have indicated are Glossary items, such as the terms **icon** and **run time.** Clicking on one of these Glossary items will bring up a brief explanation of the term.

12. Move the mouse pointer over any of the marked items and you will notice that the pointer changes to a pointing hand ( ) and the item changes color, indicating that more information is available. Clicking the item pointed to will bring that information into the topic pane.

13. Click **icon** (as shown in Figure 1.26) and a Glossary entry appears as shown in Figure 1.27.

    To exit from a displayed Glossary entry, you have to go back to the previous topic by clicking the **Back** button ( ) on the toolbar.

14. Click the **Back** button to see the Caption Property Help topic.

    You just used the **Back** button on the toolbar. Other buttons on the toolbar are worthy of note, such as the **Hide** button ( ), which hides the navigation pane, making the topic pane larger.

15. Click the **Hide** button to see just the topics panel, as shown in Figure 1.28.

    Now the **Hide** button has changed to a **Show** button ( ).

16. Click the **Show** button to see the navigation panel appear again.

    After you have used the **Back** button, the **Forward** button ( ) becomes available so you can return to the topic from which you just came.

17. Click the **Forward** button to return to the **icon** Glossary item.

FIGURE 1.26

The Caption Property Help window showing several glossary items.

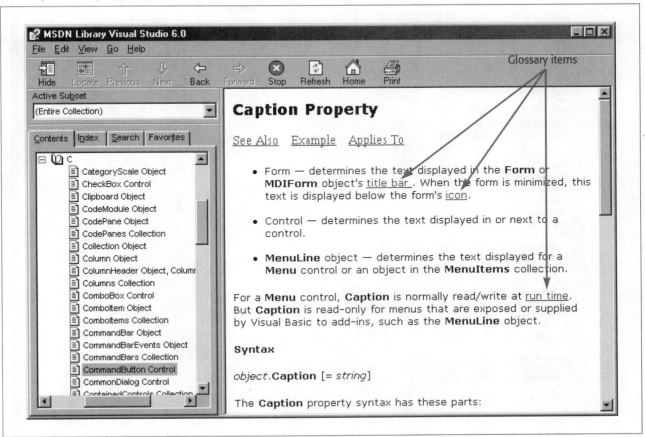

Now the **Previous** ( ) and **Next** ( ) buttons, which were previously dimmed and unavailable, become available. These buttons let you move between Glossary entries.

18. Click the **Previous** button to see the **host application** Glossary entry. This is the entry that appears in the Glossary list right before the **icon** Glossary entry alphabetically.

19. Click the **Next** button to see the **icon** Glossary entry again. Click the **Next** button a second time to see the Glossary entry for **identifier,** which is the next one in the Glossary list.

Now the Glossary entries become part of the history list and if you click the **Back** button, you return to the Glossary entry you just viewed.

20. Click the **Back** button once to see the **icon** Glossary entry. Click the **Back** button several more times until you reach the Caption Property Help topic again.

At the end of the toolbar buttons is the **Print** button ( ), which allows you to print the currently displayed Help topic or that one and all the topics subordinate to it. Before you print any topic, you need to be sure there is a printer connected to your computer and that the printer is turned on and ready to receive the output from the computer. If not, Windows gives you an error message when you try to print.

21. Click the **Print** button and you see the dialog box shown in Figure 1.29.

FIGURE 1.27
The **icon** Glossary entry.

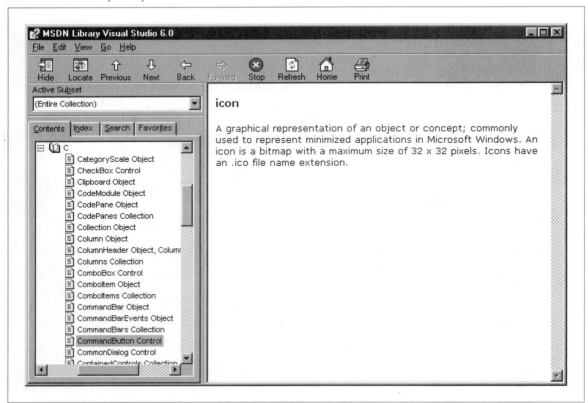

FIGURE 1.28
The topic pane with the
navigation pane hidden.

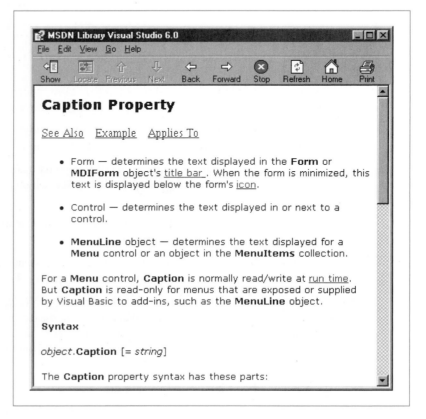

FIGURE 1.29
The Print Topics dialog box.

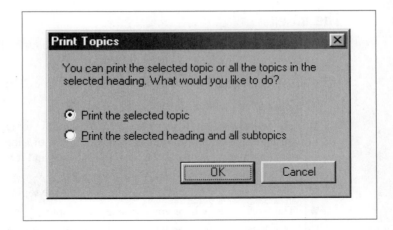

As you can see, this dialog box asks whether you want to print just the currently selected topic or that topic and those to which it is linked. We will print just the selected topic.

22. Click the **OK** button and the Print dialog box shown in Figure 1.30 will appear.

23. You don't need to change anything here, so you can simply click the **OK** button and the topic in the topic pane will print, though any Additional Topic items will not be printed, since they are links rather than normal text.

FIGURE 1.30
The Print dialog box.

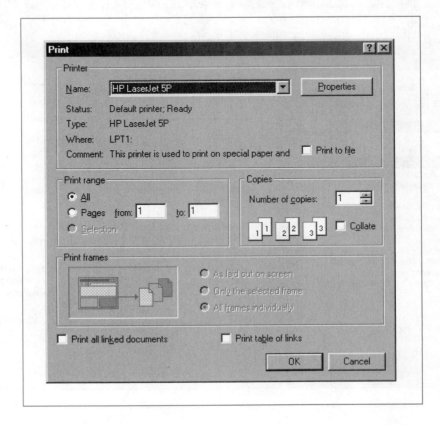

The Index

The Contents sheet is fine if you just want to peruse the topic. But if you want to look up something specific, the Index saves you time.

1. Click the **Index** tab to see the Index sheet as shown in Figure 1.31.

There are three elements in this window:

■ The pull-down list, where you select the specific topic subset you want to look through. By default, the subset is the entire set of Library topics. Visual Basic Documentation is one of the available subsets and if you select it, you see only topics related to Visual Basic.

■ The entry box, where you enter the name of the topic for which you are looking.

■ The workspace, where you can select the topic.

Let's begin by selecting the Visual Basic Documentation subgroup.

2. Pull down the Active Subset list and scroll it to select the Visual Basic Documentation.

Now any of the topics that are not related to Visual Basic are dimmed and unavailable for selection.

Let's look for a topic and see how the system helps zero in on the topic. Suppose that you are looking for information on the Caption property. You simply enter as much of the word "Caption" into the entry box as necessary for the related topics to show up in the

FIGURE 1.31
The Index display.

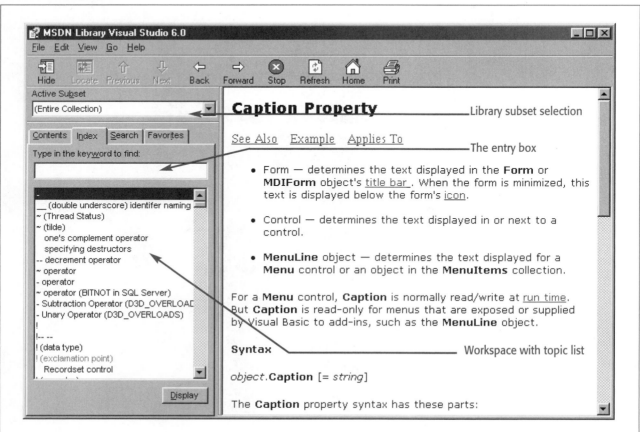

FIGURE 1.32
The dialog box that appears when you try to select a Help topic not in the selected topic subset.

workspace. As you enter the letters, Windows comes successively closer to the topic you are seeking.

3. Key **C** into the entry window and the topics in the workspace change with the first "C" topics shown.

4. Key **A** (following the **C** already entered) and the highlighted topic becomes **CA.** This topic is dimmed, so if you try to select it you get an error.

5. Double-click the **CA** topic to see the error dialog box shown in Figure 1.32.

We are getting closer to the topic we actually want.

6. Key **PT** and you see the **Caption Property** topic in the list.

7. Double-click the **Caption Property** topic and a Topics Found dialog box appears. There are, as you can see, a series of topics on the Caption Property.

8. Click the **Cancel** button to exit from the Topics Found dialog box.

It is important to realize that the topics in any Help system are organized as the author of the Help system thought best. Sometimes you have to try several alternative wordings before you find the Help topic in which you are interested. Suppose that you had tried to find the Help topic we just found by looking up Properties instead of Caption Property. You would find a lot of topics, but not the one you were looking for (at least not directly).

Searching for a Topic

If you have tried several different approaches to find the topic you need and are still unable to find it, you can use the Search sheet to help. Let's see how you would look up information on how to minimize a window form.

1. Click the **Search** tab and you see a window like the one shown in Figure 1.33.

To use this window, type the name of the topic you are looking for and then click the **List Topics** button.

2. Key **Minimize** and click the **List Topics** button.

A small dialog box appears, informing you that the search can be canceled if it seems to be taking too long, or if you decide you are not searching for the right topic, or if for any other reason you want to cancel the search. After a minute or so, the list of topics will appear as shown in Figure 1.34.

3. Double-click the first topic found, which begins with "A form can't be ..." as shown in Figure 1.34. The topic will change to the one shown in Figure 1.35.

Notice that the new topic has the word *minimize,* or forms of the word, highlighted. Since this is the word you searched for, it wants to show you where that word is in the new topic. If you examine the navigation panel, you notice that the topics are ranked. The ranking

FIGURE 1.33

The Search sheet display.

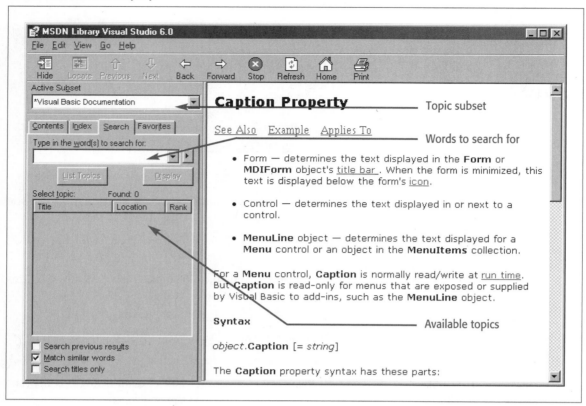

FIGURE 1.34

The list of topics found during the search.

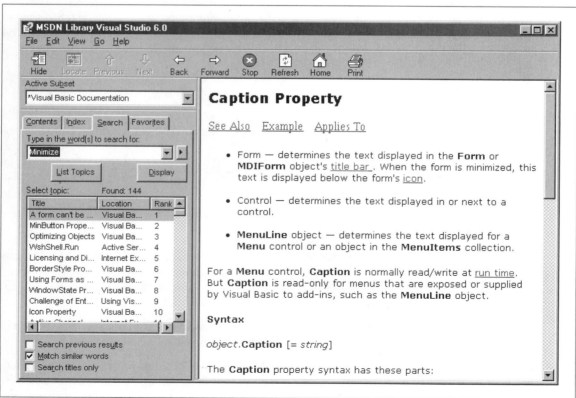

FIGURE 1.35

The new topic that contains the word *minimize*.

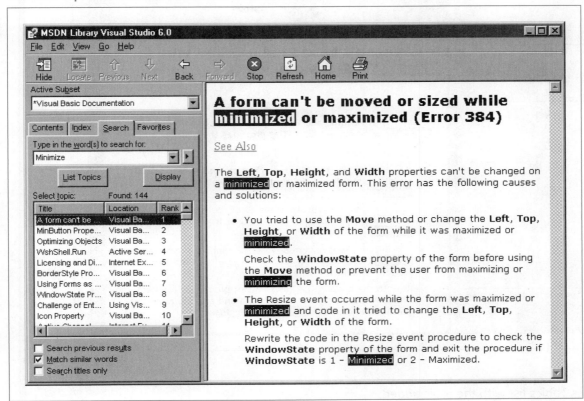

is based on the number of times the word searched for is found in the topic. Thus, the topic ranked 1 has the most instances of the search word, the topic ranked 2 has the second most, and so on.

4. Perform a few more searches until you are comfortable with the process.

Favorites

If you have searched for Help topics and discovered a few that you think might be helpful in the future, you can save them, so you don't have to look them up again, by storing them in the **Favorites** list.

1. Click the **Favorites** tab to see the display shown in Figure 1.36.

   Here you see the current topic shown in the entry box at the bottom and the **Add** button is available so you can add the current topic to your Favorites list.

2. Click the **Add** button to add the topic to the list as shown in Figure 1.37.

   Now, if you ever need to return to this topic, it is available for immediate selection.

3. Click the **Back** button to return to the previous topic and then double-click the topic in the list to return to it.

   As you might expect, the **Favorites** list is saved even after you exit from the Help system. The next time you go into the Help system and change to the **Favorites** sheet, whatever topics you have added to the list will be there.

FIGURE 1.36
The Favorites sheet.

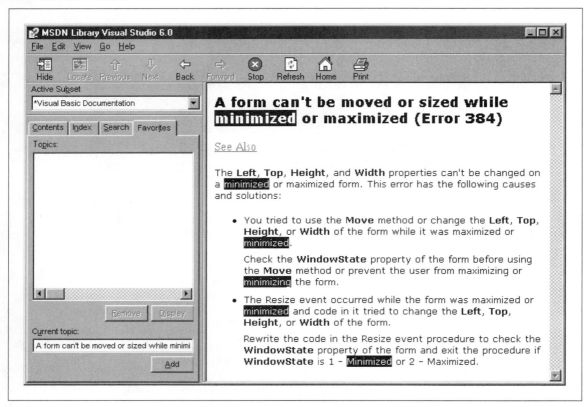

FIGURE 1.37
The Favorites Topics list with the topic added.

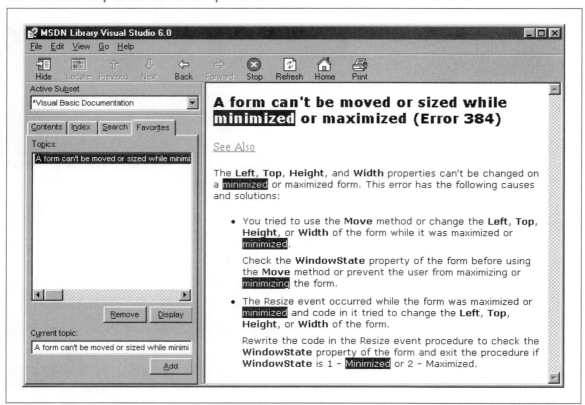

FIGURE 1.38
The PictureBox control.

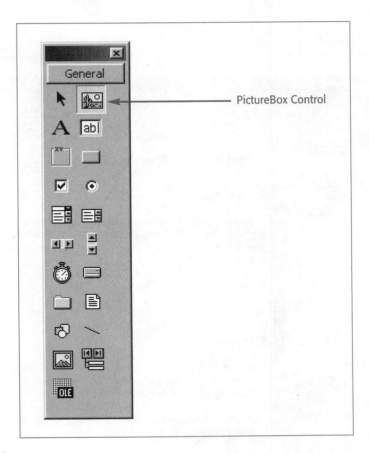

PictureBox Control

Sometimes, however, you add a topic to the list that you later decide you will not need to view any longer and you wish to remove it. Or you may simply have too many topics in the list to comfortably find the ones you need and you decide to remove a few of them to make finding the most important ones easier. Notice that since you have a topic in the list, the **Remove** button is now available.

4. Click the **Remove** button and the topic is removed from the list. The selected topic is always the one removed, but, since you only have one topic, it is automatically the one selected and, thus, the one removed.

5. Close the **Library** windows before moving to the next section.

CONTEXT-SENSITIVE HELP   Using the Index or Search sheet brings up your requested information, but, in some cases, an even quicker way is to let Visual Basic determine what information you need by using **context-sensitive Help**. Context-sensitive Help is called up by pressing the **F1** key. When it is pressed, Visual Basic determines what you were working with when you pressed **F1** and brings up a Help window on that topic.

1. Click the **Caption** property in the Properties window to select it. You may need to scroll the list a bit to find the **Caption** property.

2. Press **F1** and the Help window for the **Caption** property appears, just as you have seen previously. Close the Library window.

Context-sensitive Help windows are available for virtually anything you might be doing in Visual Basic. As you have just seen, there are topics for the properties, but there are also topics for the menus, most Visual Basic commands, and most of the tools.

FIGURE 1.39
The PictureBox Control Help topic.

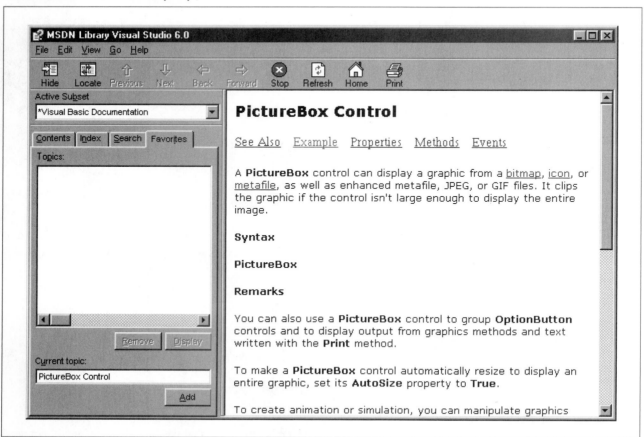

3. Click the **PictureBox** control in the toolbar, as indicated in Figure 1.38, and then press the **F1** key to see the PictureBox Control topic as shown in Figure 1.39.

HELP SYSTEM EXAMPLES   One final way that the Visual Basic Help system can assist you is with example code. You probably noticed the term Example on some of the Help topics. These are examples of code using the event or property that is referred to in the Help window. We will try a sample just to see how you might use one of these examples to learn more about the topic at hand.

1. Switch to the Index sheet, key **FillColor,** and double-click the **FillColor** property topic. When the list of topics found appears, click the one specifying that it is the Visual Basic Reference (the last one of the four shown) to see the topic shown in Figure 1.40. Notice the Example topic.

2. Select **Example** and a new topic appears (Figure 1.41).

   This topic has the sample code and a short explanation of what the code is, what it does, and how to install the code so you can execute it. To use the code, you need to select just the lines of code without the comment lines at the top of the display, copy the code to the Windows clipboard, and then paste it into a form as explained in the topic.

3. Highlight the necessary lines by positioning the cursor at the beginning of the first line and dragging the mouse to the end of the section of code as shown in Figure 1.42.

4. Press **Ctrl-C** (hold down the **Ctrl** key and press **C**) to copy the code.

FIGURE 1.40
The FillColor topic.

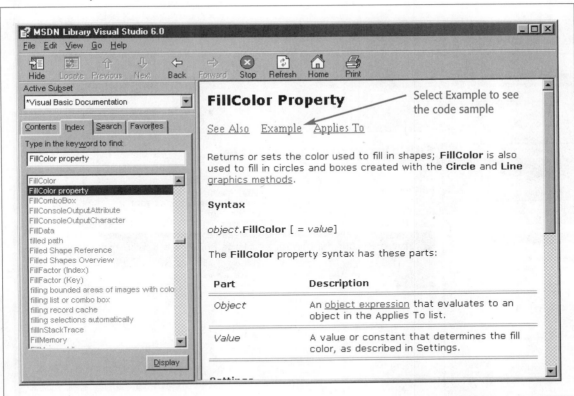

FIGURE 1.41
The Example for the FillColor property.

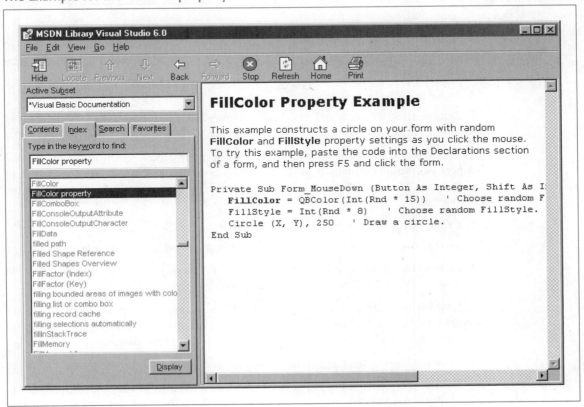

FIGURE 1.42

The Example topic, showing the selected code.

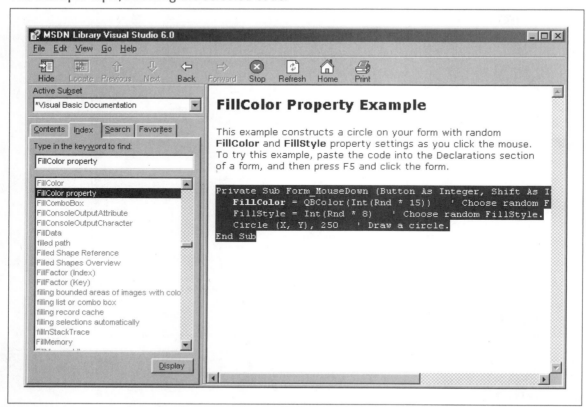

Now the code is on the Windows clipboard and can be pasted into the code window of the object for which the code is designed. In this case, the code is meant for the code window of a form.

5. Close the **Library** window.

6. Double-click the form and the code window shown in Figure 1.43 appears. This is where you insert your code.

Notice that your cursor is currently positioned in the code at the insertion point. This is where you would normally begin to enter your code. In this instance, we want to create a new section of code with the code we copied. Thus, we need to move the cursor below the existing code.

7. Use the arrow keys to move the cursor below the End Sub statement.

Now you are ready to paste the code from the clipboard into the code window.

8. Press **Ctrl-V** (or select the Paste option on the Edit menu) to paste the code into the window. Your window now looks like the one in Figure 1.44.

Now we are ready for the fun part. We have a program ready to run. Unlike the one we ran earlier in the chapter, however, this program will actually do something. Of course, running a program in Visual Basic is easy, as you saw earlier in the chapter.

9. Click the **Run** button (▶) on the button bar and your blank form appears.

Though you can't tell yet, the program is actually running. To see what the program is doing, all you need to do is position the mouse pointer on the form and click the button.

FIGURE 1.43
The form code window.

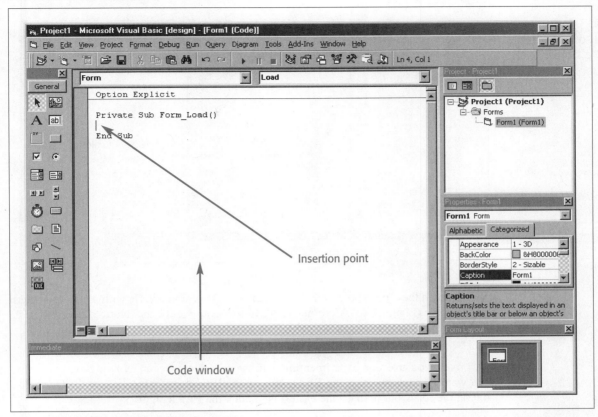

FIGURE 1.44
The code window with the code pasted in.

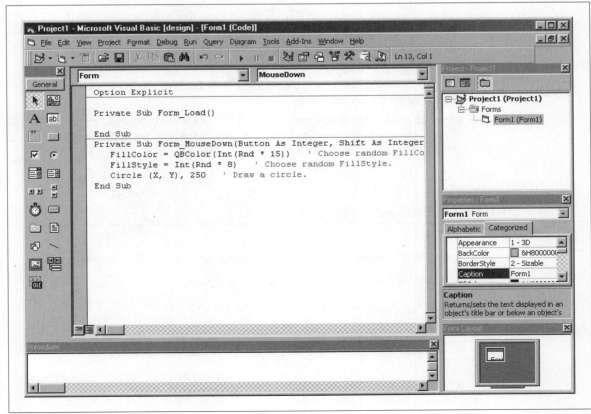

FIGURE 1.45
The result of pressing
the mouse button.

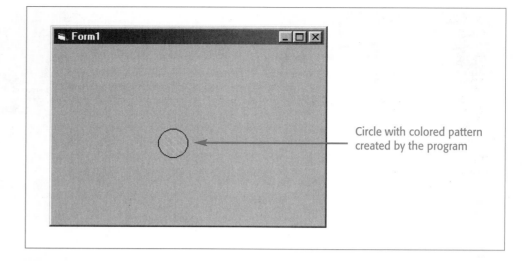

Circle with colored pattern
created by the program

10. Position the mouse pointer in the form and click. A small circle with a colored pattern appears (Figure 1.45). Continue to move the mouse and click. Notice that each circle has a different pattern and/or color. The patterns and colors are chosen randomly by the program.

When you are done experimenting with the program, you can exit the program in several ways, such as by using the **End** option on the **Run** menu or by clicking the **Close** button on the form, but perhaps the easiest is to click the **End** icon (■).

11. Click the **End** icon (■) and the program will terminate.

LEAVING THE LAB   If you are working in a lab, when you are finished with your session, you should always follow these steps (including this time):

1. Exit from Visual Basic, saving your program if necessary. This time you don't need to save the program. Most of the time you would, but you were only experimenting.

2. Exit from Windows (unless you are instructed to leave Windows active).

3. Turn off the computer (unless the policy in your lab is different). Check with your lab person for the proper procedure.

4. Clean up your area, being careful not to leave any disks or papers behind, and if you did any printing in the session, be sure to reset the printer the proper way (and turn it off if so instructed) and clean up any excess paper you may have accumulated.

1.7   Command and Menu Summary

In this chapter you learned to use the following keystrokes:

F1 is used to call up a context-sensitive help screen.

In this chapter you learned to use the following menu options:

■   **Help:**

   ■   **Contents...** brings up the MSDN Library window with the Contents tab selected.

   ■   **Index...** brings up the MSDN Library window with the Index tab selected.

- **Search...** brings up the MSDN Library window with the Search tab selected.
- **Technical Support...** gives you information about the various ways you can get help from Microsoft if you are having difficulty with Visual Basic.
- **Microsoft on the Web** gives you a list of Microsoft Web sites where you can get additional information about Visual Basic and other topics.
- **About Microsoft Visual Basic** provides important information about Visual Basic.

In this chapter you learned to use the following buttons (or icons):

- The **End** icon allows you to terminate the execution of your program.
- The **Start** icon allows you to execute your program.

1.8 Performance Check

1. Which of the five steps of the programming process do you consider the most important, and why?

2. Which type of documentation is generally the easiest for the user to find while using the program?

3. In simple terms, what is a program?

4. What type of programs do most programming languages create?

5. What type of programming does Visual Basic use?

6. In a Visual Basic program, how is the program flow controlled?

7. What is the first step in creating a Visual Basic program (during the coding step of the programming process)?

8. In general terms, what is a command button called?

9. What is an event?

10. What is the grid in the form workspace for?

11. What is the default control name of the initial form?

12. What is the default caption of the initial form?

13. If you added three command buttons and did not change their control names, what would the control name of the third button be?

14. What property would you use if you did not want your program window to have a minimize button?

15. What is context-sensitive help?

16. What key do you use to call up context-sensitive help?

17. What is the purpose of underlined entries in a help window?

18. What is a Glossary entry?

19. What option in the help system will give you direct system information about your computer?

_____

20. What is the Annotate option on the Options button menu for in the Help system?

_____

1.9   At the Computer

1. This exercise will give you practice launching Visual Basic and exploring the Help system. At the computer, do each of the following:

   a. Boot the computer and launch Windows.

   b. Launch Visual Basic (from the appropriate program subgroup on the Start menu).

   c. Click **Help** and click **Contents...**

   d. Double-click the **MSDN Library Visual Studio 6.0** group. Then click the plus box beside the **Visual Basic Documentation** topic, click the plus box beside **Reference,** and click the plus box beside **Language Reference** to call up a list of programming language topics.

   e. How many groups are listed under Language Reference?

_____

   f. Double-click **Events** to view the alphabetical groups and then double-click **C**. What is the first topic in the C events list of topics?

_____

   g. Click the first **Topic** in the list.

   h. Click **See Also.** What is the new topic?

_____

   i. Click the **Index** tab and key **H**. What is the first available topic in the list?

_____

   j. Scroll the list and find **Handle Property.** Double-click the topic. What is the word in the first paragraph that is shown in boldface?

_____

   k. Scroll to the bottom of this topic. There is a Glossary item called **Windows API.** Click it. What does API mean?

_____

   l. Click the **Back** button and then scroll back to the top and click the **See Also** link. What is the name of the next topic?

_____

   m. Click the **Example** link. What is the first line of the code example?

_____

   n. Click the **Back** button. Click the **See Also** link. What is the first topic in the dialog box?

_____

   o. Click the **Cancel** button and then close the **Library** window and end your session properly.

2. This exercise will give you practice working with the Help system. At the computer, do each of the following:

   a. Boot the computer, launch Windows, and launch Visual Basic.

   b. Pull down the **Help** menu and click **Contents...** Change the Active subset to Visual Basic Documentation if necessary.

   c. What is the first topic group?

_____

   d. Open the **MSDN Library Visual Studio 6.0** group. Then open the **Visual Basic Documentation** topic, open **Reference,** and open **Language Reference.**

   e. Open the **Events** group and open the **A** group of topics.

   f. What is the first topic in the group?

_____

   g. Click this topic.

   h. What is the first Glossary entry in the topic?

_____

i. Scroll the topic and click the **focus** Glossary entry. What is the last word in the glossary?

_____

j. Click the **Back** button. Click **Applies To.** What is the last topic in the dialog box?

_____

k. Cancel out of the dialog box and switch to the Index tab.

l. Key **L**. What is the first available index entry?

_____

m. Key **O** (after the L). What is the first available index entry?

_____

n. Switch to the Search tab.

o. Key **COM**. What is the first item in the list?

_____

p. Key **P** (after COM). What is the only item in the list?

_____

q. Close all the Help windows and end your session properly.

3. This exercise will give you practice working with the help system by creating an **Example** program. Go into the lab and do each of the following:

a. Boot the computer, launch Windows, and launch Visual Basic.

b. Open the Help window.

c. Find the Line Method topic.

d. Click the **Example** link.

e. Copy the example and open the code for the **Form_Click** procedure by double-clicking the form and then moving the cursor out of any existing code.

f. Paste the copied code there.

g. Run the program and click the form.

h. Exit from the program.

i. Close all the Help windows and end your session properly.

1.10   Performance Mastery

1. You tutor several people in using Visual Basic. Create a step-by-step tutorial on how to use the Help system. Use the previous exercises and the chapter text as samples, but create your own steps. You can use either the Notepad or the WordPad program to write your tutorial or you can write it out by hand.

2. You decide you want to know something about the Circle method. Call up the Help window for the Circle method and run a program using the **Example** code.

Your First Application

2.1   Chapter Objectives

After finishing this chapter you will be able to:

- Add a command button and a text box to a form.

- Change the size and position of a button and a text box.

- Use assignment statements and If Tests in programs.

- Run programs.

- Save a program to disk and load a program from disk.

2.2   Introduction

With the preliminaries out of the way, it is time to see just how easy and enjoyable it really is to create a Visual Basic application. In this chapter you will create your first application. You will "start small" by learning how to construct applications using buttons, text boxes, and the multimedia control that allows a program to play music and sounds as well as display animations and videos.

This chapter begins with a brief look at the first application you will create.

2.3   Creating Your First Application

Because we are just beginning to explore Visual Basic, we will create a program with three buttons to provide functionality and a text box in which to display messages. The code we will write will tell the application what to do when the buttons are clicked.

FIGURE 2.1
The Clicking Practice program.

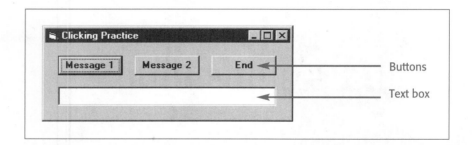

FIGURE 2.2
The form after clicking the **Message 1** button.

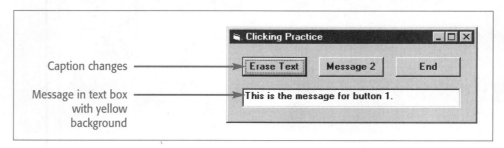

A Brief Look

To get a feel for the project, you will begin by executing a finished version of the program.

1. Boot your computer into Windows and launch Explorer.

2. Put your practice disk in drive A, and launch the **Clicking Practice.exe** program in your Ch-2 folder to see the display shown in Figure 2.1.

We have three buttons and a text box in this program. When the user clicks the first button, a message appears in the text box, and the text box changes to yellow. When the user clicks the second button, a different message appears in the text box, erasing the first message, and the text box changes to red with the text in yellow. The third button is used to exit from the program.

3. Click the **Message 1** button; a message appears in the text box, and the background of the text box becomes yellow as shown in Figure 2.2. Also, the caption of the **Message 1** button becomes **Erase Text.**

4. Click the **Message 2** button and a different message appears. This time, the background color of the text box is red, and the text itself is yellow. The caption of the **Message 2** button becomes **Erase Text**, and the caption of the first button becomes **Message 1** again.

5. Click the **Erase Text** button; the text disappears and the color of the text box changes back to white.

6. Click the **End** button and the program ends.

As you can see, each of the buttons performs a different function. That is, the code behind each of the buttons functions independently of the code behind any of the other buttons. Let's see how this works.

Getting Started

As you saw in the previous chapter, Visual Basic automatically creates your first application form. It does this because every Windows application must have at least one form (window) to be an application.

1. Launch Visual Basic.

2. Change to the Properties window, click **Caption**, key **Clicking Practice**, and click the form.

You should give every object used in a project a name rather than simply allowing the program to use the default names assigned to it. This project is going to be for Clicking Practice, so it makes sense to call the form something similar. Thus, we will name our form **Clicking_Practice**. But remember that we are going to use the Microsoft standard prefixes, and the standard prefix for a form is **frm**. So the name of our form will be **frmClicking_Practice**. The name of the control name property is actually **(Name)**. The parentheses allow the property name to be placed at the top of the alphabetical property list because the parentheses will be sorted before the alphabetic property names.

3. Click **(Name)** and **frmClicking_Practice**, and press **Enter**.

You have already created an application. The form itself will actually operate as a program. It won't really do anything, because it has no controls (except the Control menu box and the **Minimize, Maximize**, and **Close** buttons), but it is an application. To create an application that actually does something, you need to add a few controls to the form. First, however, you have to decide what type of program you want to create and design that program. Remember that each program should be designed first, though our designs in this chapter will be minimal because the applications will not be very sophisticated.

To begin, you might want to sketch the form so you will know approximately where you want to put the buttons and text box. At this point, however, we have not said enough about buttons and text boxes for you to create a sketch. Besides, as you will shortly see, it's so easy to add objects to the form and readjust them that you may as well forgo designing a form and simply create it. You do need to know, however, what elements you want on your form and how many there will be. We have already made the decision to use three buttons and one text box.

Adding the Command Buttons

There are two ways to add controls to a form. If you double-click the control on the Toolbox, the control automatically appears in the middle of the form. You can also click the control (just once) and then "draw" the control on the form. We will explore both of these methods.

Let's start by putting a command button on the form by double-clicking.

1. Move the mouse cursor to the Toolbox, and double-click the **CommandButton** control (as shown in Figure 2.3).

Now a command button appears on your form as shown in Figure 2.4. This is not the proper location for the button, but as you will see, it takes very little effort to adjust the button so that its placement is correct.

Note that the button has a three-dimensional look. It appears to be sitting on the form just as if it had actually been placed there. Visual Basic 6 has many objects that can appear three-dimensional. Using these objects gives your forms a professional look.

2. Drag the button to the upper left corner, leaving one row of the grid dots above the button (not counting the row of dots that just peeks out under the title bar) and one column to the left (as shown in Figure 2.5).

Command1 is not what we want as a caption on the button. Let's change it.

3. Change to the Caption property in the Properties window, and key **Message 1**. This indicates that the first message will appear when the button is clicked. Now your button should look like the one shown in Figure 2.6.

FIGURE 2.3
The Toolbox with the
CommandButton
control indicated.

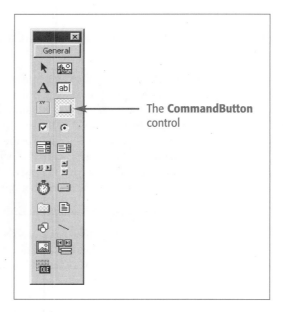

The **CommandButton**
control

HINT: You can always change to the Properties window and call up the first property beginning with the keyed letter when you use **Ctrl-Shift** and the first letter of the property you want. For example, to call up the Caption property, you would press **Ctrl-Shift-C**, and the Cancel property would be selected. Then you would press **Ctrl-Shift-C** again to select the Caption property.

FIGURE 2.4
The form with the command button in the middle.

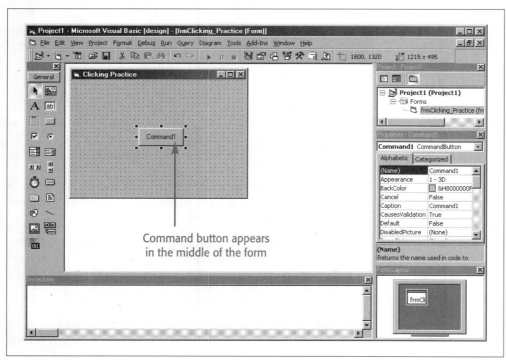

Command button appears
in the middle of the form

FIGURE 2.5
The new position of the command button.

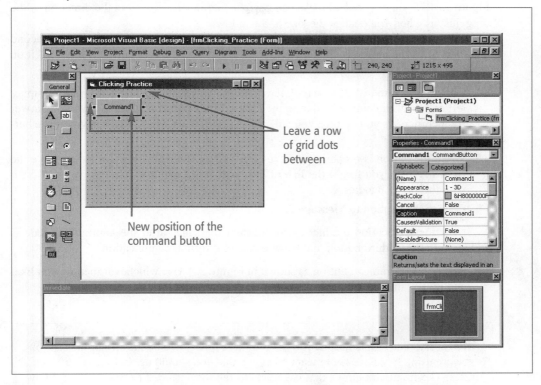

FIGURE 2.6
The sizing handles that can be used to change the size of the button.

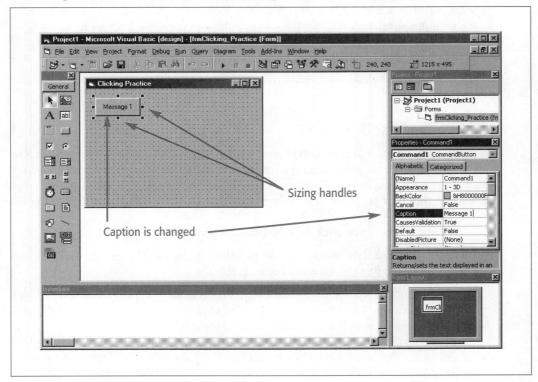

If this button were not quite long enough for the caption, the size of the button could be changed. Around the edge of the button are small boxes called the **sizing handles** (see Figure 2.6). If you drag one of these handles, the button will expand in the direction of the drag, just as when you change the size of a window.

Now we want another command button beside the first so that we can see a second message when the button is clicked. This time you will add the button by "drawing" it on the form. Examine Figure 2.7. This is where we want the next button to be.

4. Click the **Command Button** tool, move the mouse pointer to where we want the upper left corner of the button, and drag the mouse to the position where we want the lower right corner. As you do this, you will see an outline box that shows you where the button will be.

5. When the button is properly sized, just release the mouse button. If it is not quite the right size or if you forgot the line of dots between the buttons, just move or resize it with the sizing handles.

6. Change the caption to **Message 2**.

Now the application produces two different messages after the appropriate code is added. Let's add a third button that lets the user exit from the application.

7. Add a third command button as shown in Figure 2.8. Use whichever method you like, and review the steps if necessary.

> **HINT:** The size of the buttons you use is generally dictated by the size of the caption you are using. That does not mean, however, that you should use buttons of different sizes. The first two buttons that we added to the form needed to be as wide as they are to accommodate the caption we used. The third button could be quite a bit smaller, but if you made it smaller, the visual balance of the form would be disturbed. Forms generally look better when the buttons are all the same size. Sometimes, however, a button in a different part of a form may actually fill the spacing of the form better if it is a different size from the other buttons on the form. There is no one correct size for a button. How you size and place controls on a form depends on style, design, and, perhaps, artistic taste.

Adding the Text Box

Now we are ready to add the text box in which the messages will appear. Just to see how the properties work, we will use them to change the size and position of the text box, rather than doing it with the mouse. That way, you will be familiar with a few more of the properties and with how properties are changed (not all of them can be adjusted by using the mouse).

To add a text box, you click the **TextBox** control in the Toolbox.

1. Double-click the **TextBox** control as indicated in Figure 2.9, and the text box will show up on the form as shown in Figure 2.10.

Note that the text box seems to be recessed. This is more of the three-dimensional look we mentioned earlier. The TextBox property **Appearance** allows you to change the look from three-dimensional to flat. However, you will leave this text box just the way it is.

Just as with the command buttons, the text box will automatically be placed in the center of the form when you double-click the tool and will always be the default size you see now. The position can be changed the same way you changed the position of the button, and

FIGURE 2.7
The second command button.

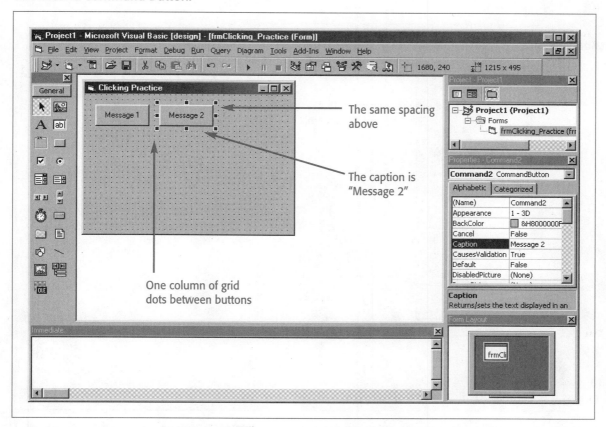

FIGURE 2.8
Adding the **End** button.

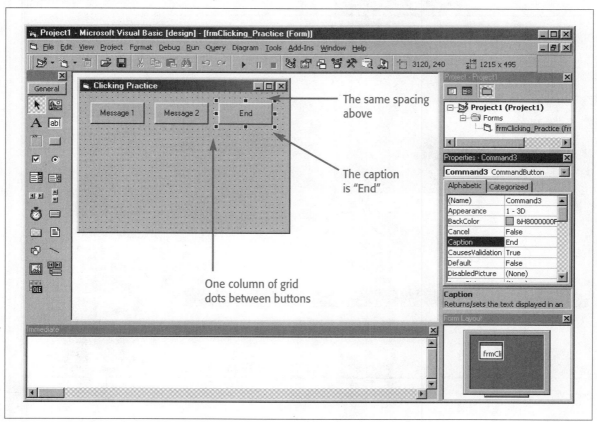

FIGURE 2.9
The **TextBox** control.

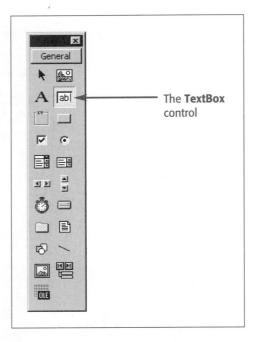

The **TextBox**
control

FIGURE 2.10
The text box in the default position and default size.

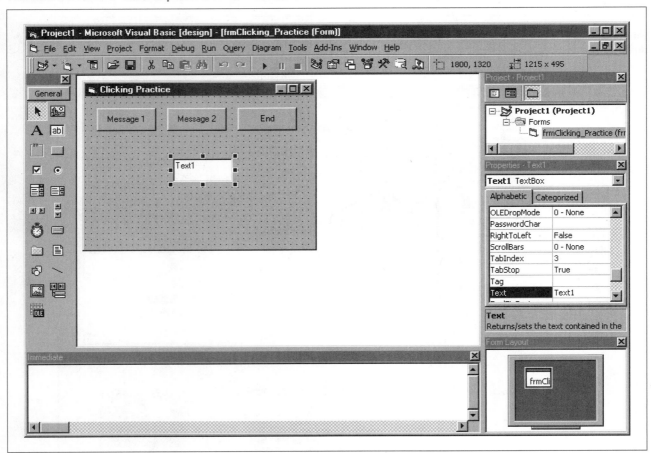

it can be resized with the sizing handles. As we have said, this time we will use the properties. You will end up with the text box positioned as shown in Figure 2.11.

The first property we want is the one that will align the text box with the left end of the buttons. This is the **Left** property.

2. Switch to the Properties window, and click the **Left** property.

The setting is currently 1800 (yours may be slightly different, depending on the size of the form), but 1800 what? What unit of measurement is being used? A video display is made up of an array of dots called **pixels,** and you might suspect that the 1800 represents the current position of the text box in pixels. You can use pixels as the measurement if you wish (you will see how in a later chapter), but the default measurement that Visual Basic uses is one that is more suitable to all the devices on which you might want the display to be shown, including printers. Many printers use a smaller scale than pixels. Thus Visual Basic defaults with its own unit of measurement, **twips** (Type WIdth Properties). A twip is very small—there are 1440 twips in an inch.

All measurements of controls on a form are related to the form, not to the desktop. That is, if the **Left** property is set to 1800, the left edge of the text box is 1800 twips from the left border of the form, rather than from the left edge of the desktop or the Visual Basic workspace. We actually want the left edge to be 240 twips from the left border.

3. Key **240**, and press **Enter**.

FIGURE 2.11
The position of the text box.

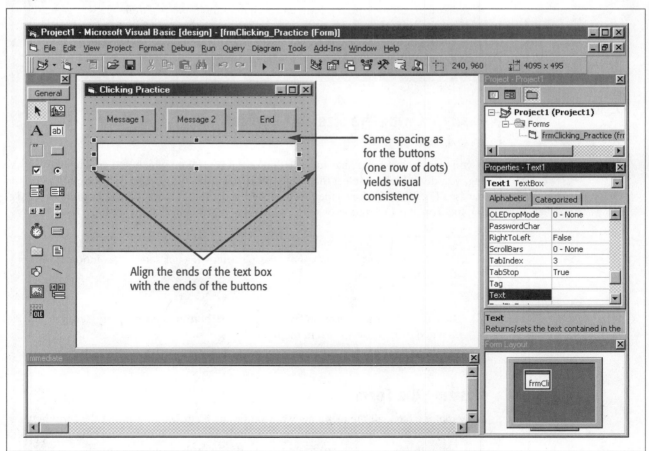

This will cause the text box to move to the left, aligned with the buttons. Now you need to move the box up so that it is underneath the buttons.

4. Click the **Top** property, key **960**, and press **Enter**.

Now the text box is under the buttons with a row of grid dots exposed between. Because the buttons are separated from the top of the form by a row of grid dots, it helps to balance the form by leaving the same amount of spacing between the buttons and the text box.

The text box needs to be widened to accommodate the message to be printed there. This is done with the **Width** property.

5. Switch to the **Width** property, key **4095**, and press **Enter**.

This will make the right edge of the text box align with the right edge of the **End** button.

There is only one more change to make to the text box. If you look back to Figure 2.11, you will see that there is nothing in the box, whereas your box has **Text1** in it. Sometimes you will want to have text in your text box when your application is initially executed. For this application, however, we would like the box to be empty.

6. Switch to the **Text** property, and erase the current setting by using the **Del** key for each character or by highlighting the entire entry and then pressing **Del**.

7. Click the text box. Now the text box will be empty and your form should match the one shown in Figure 2.11.

> **HINT:** It is usually easier simply to draw a control in the position where you want it rather than adding it to the form and then moving it into position. We will generally give you a reference by showing you the form with the control in the proper location. We will often give you the Top and Left placements as well, so you can be sure that your controls are where they should be to follow the example.

Easily Viewing the Size and Position of a Control

If you want to know the size and position of the control on which you are currently working, you don't have to select the properties to see the settings. The right side of the button bar (see Figure 2.12) shows the position of the upper left corner, which it indicates by giving the **Top** and **Left** property settings, and the **Width** and **Height** settings.

> **HINT:** Your display may not show these settings if your screen resolution is set to 640 by 480.

1. Switch back to the form and select the first button. The property settings will be changed from those shown in the figure.

2. Select the next button and observe the new settings.

Resizing the Form

Now that we have all the elements we want on the form, we notice that the form is wider (slightly) and taller than it needs to be. We could leave it this width and height, but it will look better if it is a more appropriate size for the controls contained within.

FIGURE 2.12
The **Width** and **Height** settings.

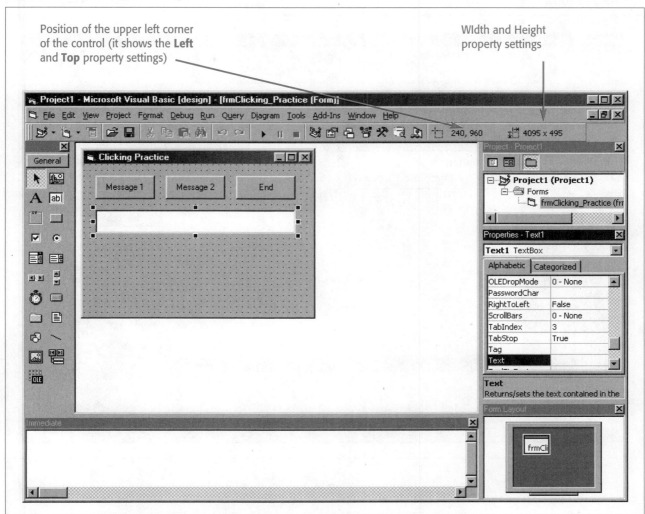

1. Shrink the form horizontally and vertically (click the form to make it the active control and use the sizing handles) until it appears as shown in Figure 2.13.

    Note that we balanced the spacing between the controls and the border so that it is consistent (again, this makes it look better).

The Code Window

Every object (controls and forms) you use in a Visual Basic program has a number of events that Visual Basic will recognize and for which you can write code. In our application, we want to write code for the three buttons.

To view the code, you call up the **code window** for the object by double-clicking the object, by pressing **F7** after highlighting the object (though this shortcut key is not indicated on the **View** menu), or by using the **Code** option on the **View** menu.

1. Double-click the **Message 1** button, and the Code window shown in Figure 2.14 appears.

FIGURE 2.13
The resized form.

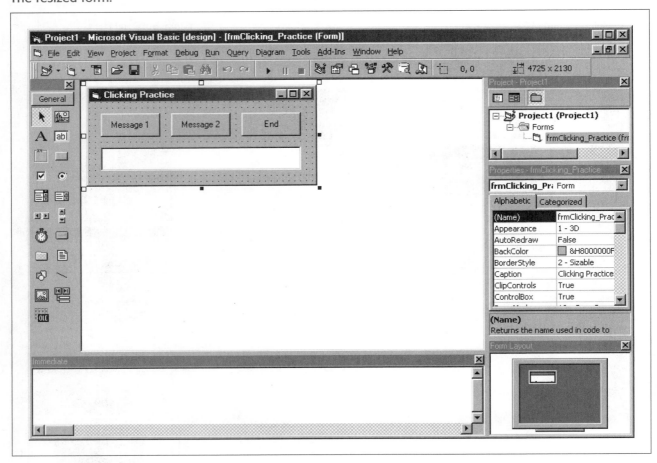

HINT: Don't be concerned if your Code window displays more code than is shown in the figure. All this means is that you opened the Code window previously by double-clicking one of the other objects.

The first thing to observe is that this is the code window for **Form1** in general. Although we opened the code window for the Command1 command button, there is a set of code for each form, and that code is displayed in the code window for that form. You can tell what code set you are working with by checking the name of the form shown in the title bar. It is still called **Form1**. This is because, even though we changed the name of the form, we have yet to save the program to disk with the new name. The name shown in the title bar of the code window is the name of the form as it is stored on disk. As we mentioned, if you use multiple forms in your application, there will be a separate code window for each form. The name of the current form is shown in the title bar. If you restore the code window by using the **Restore** button as shown in the figure, the form and the code window will both show up, and the code window title bar will show the name of the form.

2. Click the **Restore** button to see the separate displays as shown in Figure 2.15.

FIGURE 2.14

The code window.

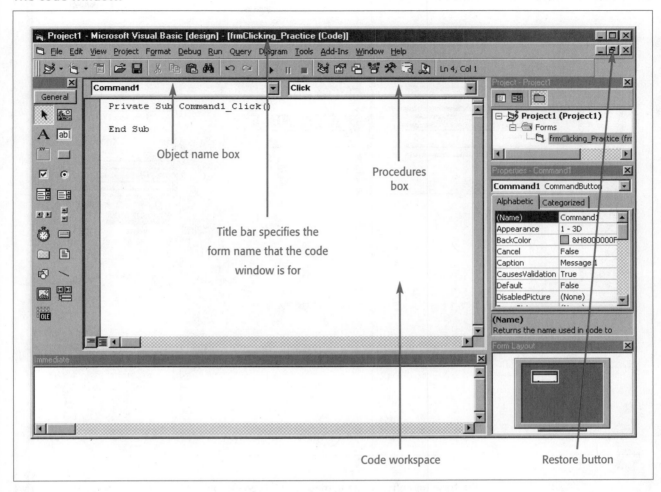

Look again at Figure 2.14. The first thing to notice is the **Object name box,** which holds the names of all the objects that are related to this form, including the form itself. The **Procedures box** holds the list of all the events, such as click and keystroke, that Visual Basic recognizes. You can write separate code for every event, though generally you need only code for one or two of the possible events for any particular object. The default object is the one that was selected when the code window was called up, in this case Command1, which is the control name (Name) of the first button. The default event is Click (a single click).

The **code workspace** takes up most of the window. Note that Visual Basic has already put part of the code in the workspace for you. All the code for events is set up as **procedures.** The first line of procedure code begins with the keyword **Private,** followed by the keyword **Sub,** followed by the object name, Command1, and the event for which the code is being written, which in this case is Click. **Private** is a classification of the procedure and will be discussed in Chapter 3. The last line of code is simply **End Sub**. The parentheses at the end of the first line of code are used to bring data (called **parameters**) from the rest of the program into the procedure. This will be explored later.

Note that the name of the current object (the first button) is Command1. Though this is usable, it is not very indicative of the purpose of the particular button. This name can be changed to something a bit more meaningful, so before we begin writing code, let's go back

FIGURE 2.15
The separate form and code window.

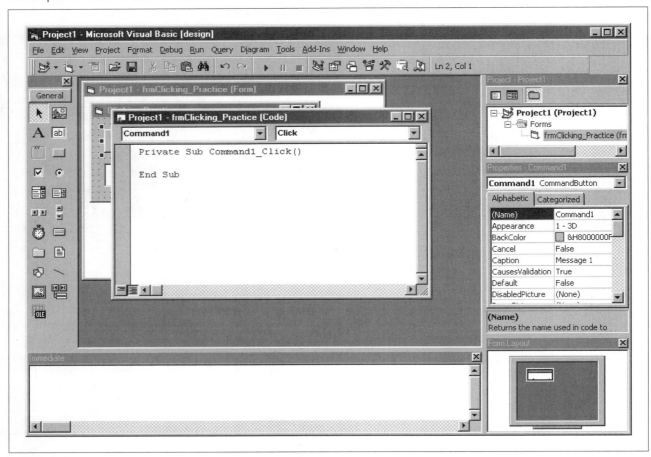

to the form and change the names of the three buttons. (If we're going to change one, we might as well change them all.) Remember that we will use the Microsoft standard prefixes on all our control names, and the standard prefix for command buttons is **cmd**.

Using the standard prefixes on the control names allows Visual Basic to sort the controls into groups in the lists of control names. Then, when we are looking for a particular object, we can look in that group in the list and find it more easily. If all the command buttons have the prefix cmd and we don't use that prefix for any other object, then all the command buttons will be sorted together because they all begin with cmd.

3. Click the form and then click the first button on the form. Switch to the Properties window, select the (Name) property, key **cmdMessage_1**, and press **Enter**.

HINT: Note that as you change to the next button, the property selected doesn't change. This is a handy feature of Visual Basic. It assumes that as you switch from control to control, you will want to modify the same property in each. It will generally save time to place all your controls of the same kind (all buttons, for example) on the form and then change the settings of a particular property on all those controls at the same time. This way, you don't have to continually select new properties from the Properties window.

4. Switch back to the form, select the next button (by either clicking it or pressing the **Tab** key), and change the control name to **cmdMessage_2**.

You don't actually have to change back and forth continually between the windows. You can change objects by using the pull-down list in the Object box of the Properties window.

5. Click the down arrow to the right of the Object box, select Command3 from the list, and change the control name to **cmdEnd**.

The prefix we will use for a text box is **txt**. Thus, we will use txtOutput for the name of the text box in this program.

6. Change the name of the text box to **txtOutput**.

These names are a lot more meaningful and easier to associate with the appropriate object than are the automatically assigned default names. Visual Basic will keep track of how many controls there are and of their names, but you still need to find and use the controls based on their names. Control names like **Command1** are just not very helpful.

Because spaces are not allowed in control names, an underline character between words is used to make them easier to read. This is a common practice among programmers. The easier it is to read a control name, the easier it is to find the control name in a list or in the code window.

7. Double-click the first button to call up the code window again.

Now look at the name of the procedure. Before it was **Command1_Click,** but now it is **cmdMessage_1_Click**. Visual Basic will automatically update procedures for such changes where it can. It cannot, however, make all the adjustments in your code that changing a control name might necessitate. It is much better to change your control names before you begin to write your code to avoid the problems that making changes later might cause.

Note that your code window also has the code for the **Command1** button. Once the code window for an object event is opened, Visual Basic registers that event and retains the code even if the object name is changed. There really is no harm in leaving them in the program, but having a lot of extraneous procedures that the program is not actually using can make your real procedures harder to find. So let's get rid of the Command1 code.

8. In the code window, highlight the code for the Command1 procedure, and press the **Del** key.

9. Click the scroll arrow on the right end of the Object box to display the list of objects on the form (Figure 2.16).

As you can see, there is an entry for each of the objects you have created thus far in this application. In addition, there is one for the Form itself. To see the code for any of the objects, you select the object you are interested in from the list, and the code for the Click procedure will generally appear first. This is true when it is the first in the event list. If there is already code for an event for the object, however, the existing code will appear for all such events.

Note that the list of object names is in alphabetical order, and the buttons are sorted together because they all begin with the cmd prefix. Again, using the prefixes gives you grouping of like objects in any control lists you use.

10. Press **Esc** or click the mouse in the code window to drop out of the list.

The only code we need to use when the user clicks the button is to print a message in the text box. We will make the message simple but meaningful.

11. Press **Tab** (to indent the code—a good practice that we will use often) and key **txtOutput.Text = "This is the message for button 1."**. The code will appear as shown in Figure 2.17.

FIGURE 2.16
The list of objects.

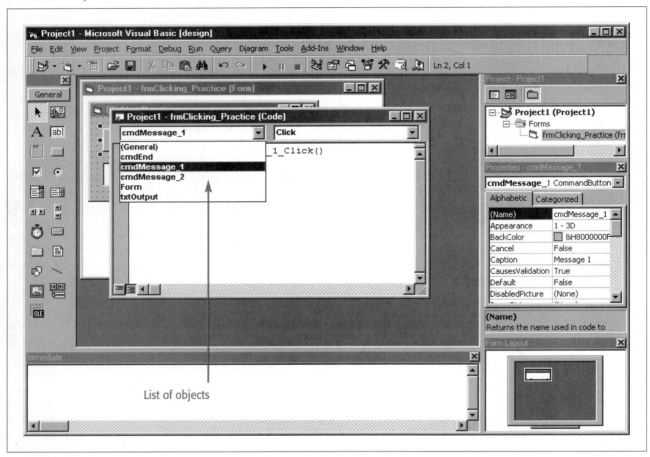

FIGURE 2.17
The Code window, showing the added line of code.

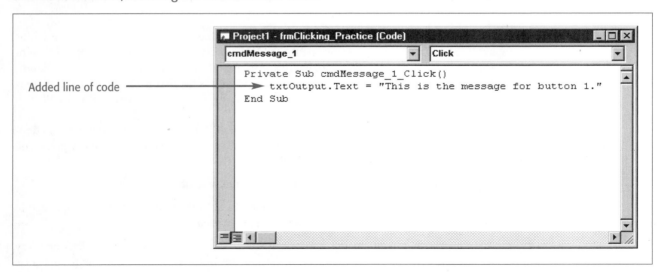

The statement we entered is called an **assignment statement.** The formal format of the statement is

```
[Let] varname = expression
```

Because this is the first time we have used the format for a statement, we will cover all four pieces of the format. First, any portion of a format that is in italics is to be used as specified. Thus, the word *Let* is to be used exactly as stated (though in this case, the word *Let* is optional). Then any element that is shown in normal, boldfaced print is a variable portion of the format that can be expressed any way the programmer deems necessary. Whenever an element of the format is surrounded by brackets, [], it means that this part of the statement is optional. In this case, the *Let* portion of the statement is optional, and most programmers don't use it. Next we have the **varname,** which is where the variable or property is shown. It is the name to which the value of the variable or property is assigned. It is the programmer's responsibility to decide what the variable name is supposed to be. Then comes the equals sign, which acts as the assignment operator. Finally, the **expression** is what is being assigned to the **varname.** It is called an expression because many assignment statements use an expression such as a mathematical calculation on the right side of the assignment statement. Again, the programmer is responsible for the form of the **expression.**

We are assigning (or storing) the **expression** on the right side into the **varname** on the left side of the equals sign. Sometimes an assignment statement will assign a value to a variable, which is a storage location for the value. At other times, an assignment statement will store the data into an object property, as we are doing in the example.

Any text that appears in the expression portion of an assignment statement must be surrounded by quotation marks. This is necessary so that Visual Basic will know precisely where the text begins and where it ends. Otherwise, it is too easy for Visual Basic to misinterpret some of the text. For example, the keyword **Sub** is used at the beginning of each procedure. If you used the word *Sub* in text that was not in quotes, Visual Basic would interpret *Sub* as the beginning of a procedure. But when you enclose the text in quotes, as soon as Visual Basic sees the quotes, it ignores what is in them (except for making the appropriate assignment). Such groups of text in quotes are called **text strings** or **literals.**

When referring to objects on your forms (generally in assignment statements), you first refer to them by the object name and then by the property you are changing. In the assignment statement in Step 11, the name of the text box is **txtOutput**. Then the second part of the assignment name, **Text**, is the property we are changing. Thus, we are changing the value of the Text property in the **txtOutput** text box to the text given on the right side of the assignment statement. You will use many such statements in your Visual Basic programs.

Each object has a default property, and the default property of a text box is Text. Thus, we could have made the assignment as follows:

```
txtOutput = "This is the message for button 1."
```

Note that the property is not shown with the object name. Doing an assignment this way, although technically correct, is generally not a good idea. It is always much better to mention the property directly. Then there is never any question about which property is being used.

Believe it or not, that's all the code that is needed for the first button. Now let's put a similar message in the code for the second button.

12. Pull down the list of objects and select **cmdMessage_2.**

The beginnings of the code (Private Sub and End Sub) will appear just as they did for the first button (Figure 2.18), and you will still see the code for the first button.

13. Press **Tab** and key **txtOutput.Text = "Visual Basic is so much fun! (message 2).".**

FIGURE 2.18
The predefined code for the second button and the code for the first button.

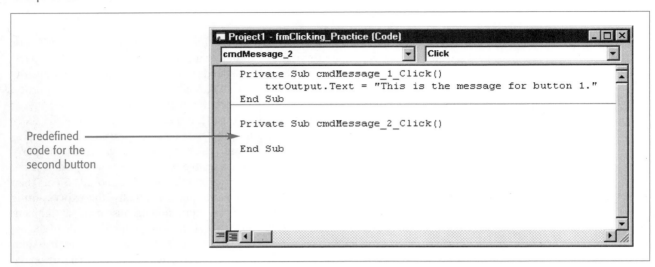

Predefined
code for the
second button

This statement assigns the second message to the same text box the first assignment statement did. That makes sense; there is only one text box on the form.

Well, we're just about finished. The only thing left is to create the code for the **End** button.

14. Pull down the list of objects and select **cmdEnd**.

15. Press **Tab** and key **End**.

The **End** command tells Visual Basic to exit from the program.

This gives you code for all three of the buttons, and your code window should look like the one shown in Figure 2.19 (with the code window maximized). Note that the sections of code are alphabetized just like the list in the Object name box and that the only sections of code that show up are the ones where you have actually put in some code. If you have code for multiple events for an object, all that code will appear alphabetized by event within the object's listings. So you can change to the code segments for the various objects and the events used within by simply moving the cursor from one procedure to the next. If you want to enter code for any event that doesn't already have code, however, you will have to pull down the Event list to change to that code segment, because it will not show up in the code window until there is code in it.

Now we are ready to find out how well our program works.

2.4 Running Your Application

Running an application, as we saw in the last chapter, is done through the use of the **Run** menu, the shortcut key, or the **Start** button. In the last chapter we used the **Start** button, so this time we will use the **Run** menu to execute our program.

1. Pull down the **Run** menu and select the **Start** option. After a short time, your application will appear as shown in Figure 2.20.

This window looks just the same as it did during construction, except that the grid dots are gone. They show up to help you align your controls only while you are creating the program. Because the program looks virtually the same when you are creating it as when you

FIGURE 2.19
The code window with the keyed code.

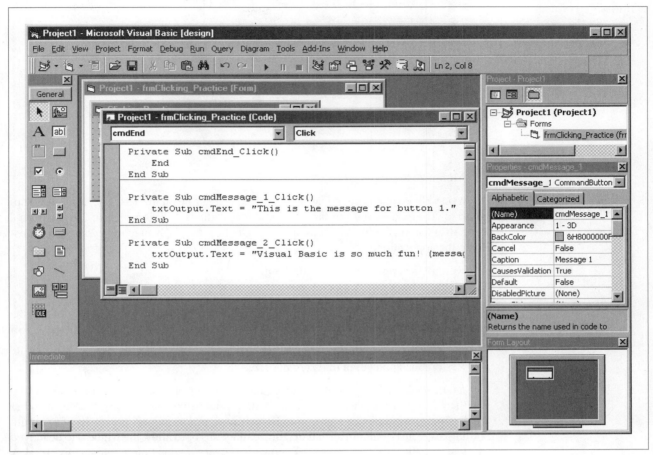

are finished, there is never any doubt about what the finished product will look like. Note that the window has a Control menu icon and **Minimize**, **Maximize**, and **Close** buttons. As mentioned earlier, these will automatically be part of every application unless they are turned off.

Let's see how the application works.

2. Click the **Message 1** button.

Immediately, the message we created for the first button appears in the text box.

3. Click the **Message 2** button.

Now the second message appears in the text box.

4. Click the first button again, and the first message reappears.

This program is not too fancy, but it also wasn't very difficult to create. As you learn more about Visual Basic, your applications will get ever more sophisticated—but not much more difficult to create. You will discover that you can create some very nice, useful, and fun programs in Visual Basic with minimal effort.

As we have said, your program automatically includes the **Minimize**, **Maximize**, and **Close** buttons and the Control menu icon. Let's be sure they work as they are supposed to work.

FIGURE 2.20
Your application
window.

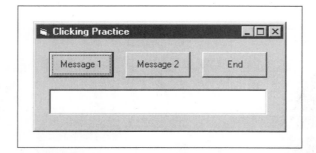

5. Minimize the application.

You will see that the application is reduced to a button on the Taskbar, just as it is supposed to. The icon used is the same as that on the form itself. It is a generic one that Visual Basic uses automatically. You will discover later how to assign an icon of your own choosing to the application.

6. Restore the application to the desktop.

7. Maximize the application.

The maximized application takes up the entire desktop but utilizes none of it except the space required for the buttons and text box. This is a case where you might want to turn off the **Maximize** button; it is of no value to maximize this application.

8. Restore the application to its regular size.

You can also use the Control menu icon to close the application and to move and resize the window, or you can move and resize the window with the mouse just as in any other application. Once again, the power of Visual Basic and Windows proves itself. You did nothing to create the minimize and maximize functions or to allow the window to be moved and resized. Visual Basic gives these powers to every application automatically. It takes someone who has programmed in another language to appreciate all the coding that Visual Basic saves by furnishing these techniques to every application automatically.

The only button in our program that we haven't tried is the **End** button.

9. Click the **End** button, and Visual Basic exits from the application.

You can also use the **End** option on the **Run** menu, the **End** icon (■) on the Tool bar, the **Close** button, or the **Close** option on the Control menu icon menu, or you can simply double-click the control menu icon to terminate the program execution.

2.5 Saving Your Application

After you spend any length of time creating an application, you should save it to disk. The memory of the computer is only temporary—the disk is the only safe place for your application. Unless it is a short process, like our first sample application, don't wait until you have finished the application. It can be very disheartening to have worked for a long time getting an application just so, only to have the power go down or the computer lock up on you and cause you to lose all your work. You should save your application to disk every ten minutes or so. Then, if something does happen, you can go back to the last saved copy and reconstruct just the few minutes of work that was lost. Saving your application takes only a few seconds; it is very cheap insurance.

Saving the Application Yourself

Saving your application is done through the use of the **File** menu, or you can simply click the Save icon ( ) on the Toolbar. We will use the **File** menu this time so you can become familiar with it.

1. Pull down the **File** menu as shown in Figure 2.21.

As you can see, there are four save options (two Save and two Save As): two to save the project, which can consist of multiple forms and modules, and two to save the currently selected form (frmClicking_Practice). Saving forms will come later. For now, we will simply save the entire project (which will also cause the form to be saved).

Initially, when you save a project, the **Save Project** and **Save Project As...** options function similarly. That is, until a project has been saved, it doesn't have a name, so Visual Basic will ask you for a name for each of the forms and the project if you use the **Save Project** option. If you use the **Save Project As...** option, Visual Basic will ask for the new name of the project but will save the forms with their previous names. If you want your forms to have new names as well, you use the Save frmClicking_Practice As... option. After a project has been saved once, Visual Basic will know the name of the project and the related files, and the **Save Project** option will simply store the project and associated forms to disk without prompting.

FIGURE 2.21
The **File** menu.

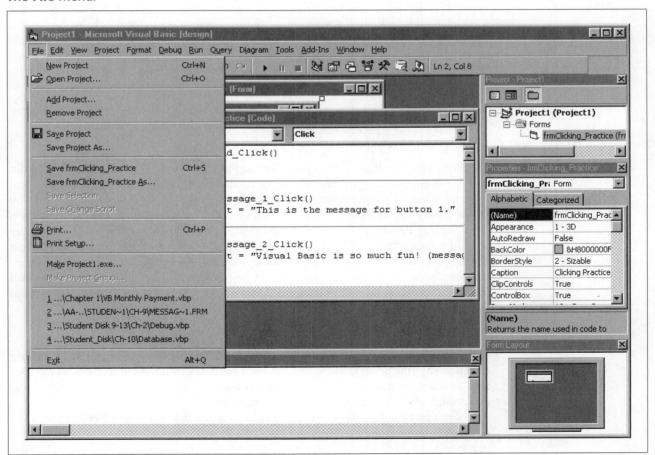

FIGURE 2.22

The first dialog box for saving a project.

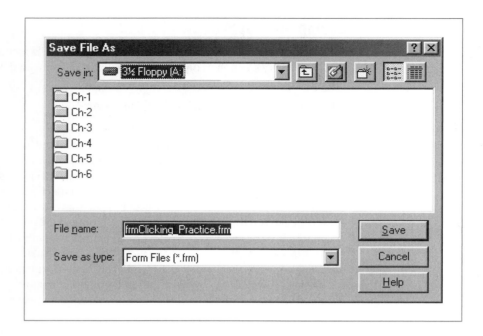

2. Select the **Save Project** option, and you see a dialog box similar to the one shown in Figure 2.22 (though yours will not be displaying the folders on drive A yet).

This is the first of two dialog boxes you will see. This one requests the filename for the form in your application. If you had multiple forms in your application, a dialog box would appear for each form. Note that the default filename is **frmClicking_Practice.frm**. This is the default Name of the form file, because it is the name you gave the form. This name will be fine for the name of the file stored on disk, so you won't need to change it. But you do need to tell Visual Basic where to save the file. You will save the file on your practice disk.

3. Insert your practice disk in drive A, select drive A in the list of drives, and change to the Ch-2 folder (the root directory of the practice disk is shown in the figure).

4. Click the **Save** button.

Now a similar dialog box appears for the project name (defaulted to the Ch-2 folder on drive A automatically). Generally, it is a good idea to give the project and the first form the same name. If you have multiple forms, they cannot all have the same name, but you might want them to have similar names. For example, say you called your first form **frmClicking_Practice**. Form 2 might be called **frmClicking_Practice_Alarm** (if it were an alarm clock), form 3 **frmClicking_Practice_Input** (if it were an input form of some type), and so on. That way, when you look at your disk directory, you will instantly recognize which files are related to a particular project. Another way to differentiate one project from another is to store each project in a separate folder. This approach is especially useful for large projects.

5. Key **Clicking Practice** and press **Enter**.

Now you have saved two files, **frmClicking_Practice.frm** (the form) and **Clicking Practice.vbp** (the project). Basically, the form file contains information about all the controls and code necessary to construct the form, and the project file contains a list of the forms (and other files) that the application requires.

Now that these files have been saved once, you can choose the **Save Project** option the next time you want to save them, and Visual Basic will immediately save the files with no prompting.

FIGURE 2.23
The Options dialog box.

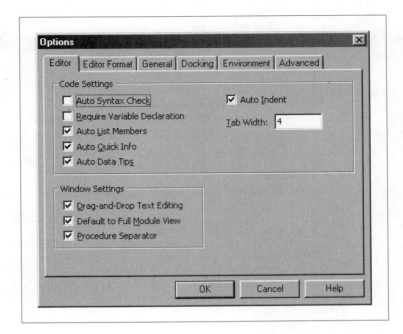

Saving the Application Automatically

Although it's important to save your program every ten minutes or so as you are creating it, there is another way to safeguard your work. You can make Visual Basic automatically save your program when you run it. This is done by specifying an option on the **Options...** item of the **Tools** menu.

1. Pull down the **Tools** menu and select **Options...** to see the dialog box shown in Figure 2.23.

   You need to change one of the options on the **Environment** sheet.

2. Click the **Environment** tab to see the display shown in Figure 2.24.

   As you can see, there are three different options for saving your program when you run it:

- Save Changes
- Prompt to Save Changes
- Don't Save Changes

If you select **Save Changes**, your program will automatically be saved for you. **Prompt to Save Changes** is used when you want to be given a choice of whether or not the program is to be saved. This is handy when you are making changes that you want to try out before you save them. The third option will cause your changes not to be saved at all. In this case, you will have to be sure to save your program frequently, because Visual Basic will not do it for you. Most of the time, you will want Visual Basic to save the program automatically whenever you run it.

3. Click the **Save Changes** option to turn it on (if necessary).

4. Exit from the dialog box by clicking the **OK** button.

Now your program will be saved automatically every time you run it. And we will assume that's what is happening. We will not remind you to save your program before it is run.

FIGURE 2.24
The **Environment** sheet
of the Options dialog
box.

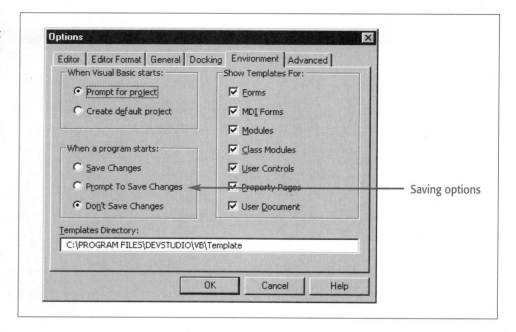

This change was saved. Now Visual Basic will use this option and save your programs automatically whenever they are run. If this is inappropriate at any time, you can change to one of the other two options.

> **HINT:** If you are using a lab computer, it is a good idea to check this option each time you begin a session. Another user may have reset this option, and you will not be saving your programs even though you think you are. Visual Basic will always ask for the file names to be saved when you execute the program for the first time, but it will not ask again after the forms and project have been initially saved.

2.6   Program Design

We mentioned in Chapter 1 the importance of designing a program before you begin creating it so that you have some idea of the direction in which you are heading, but we didn't really tell you how to do this. Now that you have created your first application, it is time to look at how a program is designed.

In the past, programmers have used many approaches to program design. Two of the most popular have been **flowcharts** and **pseudocode.** A flowchart is a pictorial representation of the flow of the program from one step to the next, whereas pseudocode is a written design created with a language that approaches the language code itself without actually being the code of the language. Neither of these approaches, nor any of the other myriad program design approaches, is exactly appropriate for Visual Basic, because Visual Basic is such a departure from the linear type of programming done in the past. We need some type of design system that lends itself to event-driven programming. Thus, we will use an outline system plus pseudocode that will enable us to designate the various program elements clearly and add the code to the elements where it is appropriate. We will begin by designing the program we just completed.

The main element of every program is the overall project. We will designate that with the project name. The name of our project is Clicking, so that will be the first thing in our design.

```
Project Clicking
```

Because every program will have one form to which everything else is subordinate, we will append the name of that form to the project so that it highlights the rest of the design.

```
Project Clicking - frmClicking_Practice
```

We will follow that with an outline of the main program elements that spring from the main form. Thus far, these elements are limited to buttons and text boxes.

```
Project Clicking - frmClicking_Practice
   A.  cmdMessage_1
   B.  cmdMessage_2
   C.  cmdEnd
   D.  txtOutput
```

There is currently very little pseudocode for each of these objects. Essentially, cmdMessage_1 and cmdMessage_2 display a message in the text box txtOutput, and cmdEnd exits the program. Each of these buttons carries out its code for the Click event as shown:

```
Project Clicking - frmClicking_Practice
   A.  cmdMessage_1
       1.  Click
           Display a message in txtOutput text box
   B.  cmdMessage_2
       1.  Click
           Display a message in txtOutput text box
   C.  cmdEnd
       1.  Click
           Exit the program
   D.  txtOutput
       Used to display messages from cmdMessage_1 and
cmdMessage_2
```

Note that under each of the objects in the outline, we listed the event and then the code under the event. The exception to this is the txtOutput text box, which has no event code defined for it. Later on we will create text boxes where we will add code, but in this sample program, there is no code for the text box. Note also that the pseudocode for the click procedures does not specify the messages that will be displayed. Remember that this is merely a design, not program code. The idea of a design is to give us a path to follow when creating the program; it need not give us all the specifics. We decide those specifics when we actually code the program.

2.7 Modifying Your Application

Generally, any application worth creating takes more than the few minutes it took to create this first application. It no doubt took you much longer than a few minutes for this project, but most of that time was spent reading the instructions. You probably spent only 10 or 15 minutes actually working on the project. It will often take you several sessions to complete a larger Windows application. So you need to be able to retrieve a project from disk. You just saved your first project to disk, so you should be able to retrieve it. But first, we will erase the project that is still in Visual Basic. Otherwise, you won't see anything happen when you load the project from disk, because the new project will simply overwrite the current project, and they are the same one.

Starting a New Project

To erase a project, you merely tell Visual Basic to start a new project.

1. Pull down the **File** menu and select New Project.

   Visual Basic erases the current project and presents you with the New Project dialog box. If you had made any changes to the current project since the last time it was saved, Visual Basic would prompt you to determine whether you want to save the changes. But you made no changes, so there is no need for prompting.

2. Click the **OK** button to use the default **Standard EXE** type of application. This gives you a new program with the starting form.

Loading a Project

Now you are ready to reload your project. This is done with the **Open Project...** option.

1. Pull down the **File** menu and select **Open Project...** to see the dialog box shown in Figure 2.25.

   This dialog box gives you a list of all the projects, which are all the files on the disk with an extension of **vbp** (for Visual Basic Project). Then you can either key the filename you want or select it from the list of existing files. If the project you want to load is one you stored recently (as it is in this case), you can change to the **Recent** tab, and those files will appear in a list from which you can choose the appropriate one. Your file is in this **Existing** list, so you don't need to use the **Recent** list.

2. Double-click **Clicking Practice.vbp** to load the project.

   Now you will see the form you created earlier. The first change we are going to make is to the buttons or, more precisely, to the code for the buttons. When the user clicks one of the buttons, a message is displayed in the text box. If the user clicks that same button a second time, the same message is displayed, so it's hard to tell that anything has happened.

FIGURE 2.25
The Open Project...
dialog box.

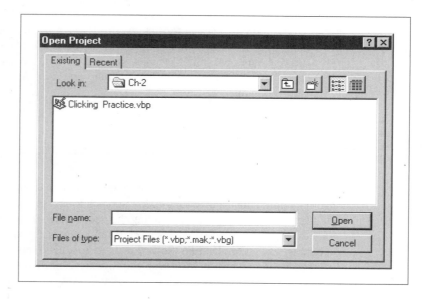

Instead, we want the text box to be cleared when the user clicks either of the buttons the second time (without clicking the other button). In other words, if the user clicks button **1**, the message will appear. Then, if the user clicks button **1** again without first clicking button **2**, the text in the box will be erased. Because the function of the button will be changed, we will want the caption of the button to reflect the new purpose. We also want to make the same changes for the second button.

3. Call up the code window for the first button.

The only code here is the one line (not including the given procedure code) to put the message in the text box. The first thing we need to do is change the caption on the button. After the user clicks the button, the message is written in the text box. Then the button should reflect its new purpose. We mentioned earlier that most of the property settings can be changed while the program is running, which is called **runtime,** and this is a case where that capability will come in handy. Let's change the caption of the button to **Erase Text**.

4. Press the **End** key to move the cursor to the end of the line of code (**Home** will jump the cursor to the beginning of the line) and press **Enter**.

This will create a new line for you to enter the next line of code. Note that this line is automatically indented to where the previous line was. Indenting code in coding groups (there are several different types of coding groups, as you will discover) makes the groups easier to see and interpret.

5. Key **cmdMessage_1.Caption = "Erase Text"** (see Figure 2.26).

This assignment statement begins with the name of the button, followed by the name of the property to be changed. This is the way we defined the left side of an assignment statement earlier. Then the right side of the assignment has a literal (text in quotes) like the other assignment statement.

FIGURE 2.26
The new statement.

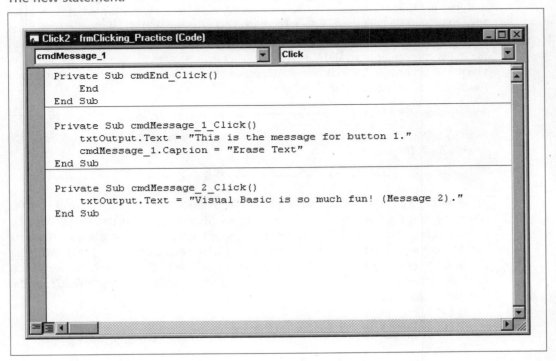

```
Click2 - frmClicking_Practice (Code)

cmdMessage_1                              Click

    Private Sub cmdEnd_Click()
         End
    End Sub


    Private Sub cmdMessage_1_Click()
        txtOutput.Text = "This is the message for button 1."
        cmdMessage_1.Caption = "Erase Text"
    End Sub


    Private Sub cmdMessage_2_Click()
        txtOutput.Text = "Visual Basic is so much fun! (Message 2)."
    End Sub
```

Now we run into a problem. This code will display the message in the text box and change the caption. But we also want the button to blank the text box if this button is the one that has most recently displayed the message in the text box. The way the code is written, it will always display the message in the box; there is no provision for erasing the text. What we need is a way to determine what is currently in the text box so that we can decide whether the message needs to be displayed or the box needs to be blanked. We need an If Test.

The If . . . Then . . . Else Statement

One of the more important statements in any programming language is the **If Test.** It allows the given statements to be executed only when a certain condition is true. One format of the command is

```
If condition Then
    Thenpart
Else
    Elsepart
End If
```

As you can see, there are various parts to this command. We will begin by discussing the **condition.** A condition is a test that is generally specified with **relational** (or **Boolean**) **operators** that define a relationship between two elements. (Other things can be used for the condition, and we will cover them as they become necessary.) Essentially, there are six relational operators: equal (=), not equal (< > or > <), less than (<), greater than (>), less than or equal to (< = or = <), and greater than or equal to (> = or = >). As an example, suppose we have two variables, A and B (remember that a variable is simply a storage location for a value) with A=5 and B=6. If we used the conditional **IF A=B**, the test would be false (or the test would fail), because A is 5 and B is 6 and they are not the same (equal). If we used **IF A<B** as the conditional, the test would be true because 5 is less than 6.

The conditional guides Visual Basic to the next part of the statement that is to be executed. If the test is true, the **Thenpart** of the If Test is executed and the application continues after the **End If** statement. If the test is false, the Elsepart is performed. If there is no **Else** (it is optional), then when the test is false, the program will simply jump beyond the **End If** statement and continue. Either of these "parts" can be one or many statements, and the statements can be any valid Visual Basic statements, such as assignment statements. As you progress through this book, you will learn many other Visual Basic statements that can function as a statement in one of the If Test "parts."

> **HINT:** Don't key any of the code until you are instructed to do so. The code to be keyed will be given again.

Now that you know, in general terms, how the If Test works, let's see if we can put together the code for blanking the text box. What we need is a test to determine whether the button has just been clicked. We are going to change the button caption when the button is clicked, so we can test that caption to see whether it has been changed. If it says "*Message 1*", the button has not been clicked (otherwise it would say "*Erase Text*", and we would know the button had been clicked). We want to see if the button says "Erase Text", and the first part of the If Test looks like this:

```
If cmdMessage_1.Caption = "Erase Text" Then
    txtOutput.Text = ""
Else
```

When you use the quotation marks with nothing between, they indicate an empty literal or a **null string.** Thus, txtOutput.Text = "" assigns to the text box an empty literal (""), which blanks it out.

We aren't finished with the Thenpart, however. Once the text has been blanked, the user should be able to put the text back into the box, and the caption on the button should indicate that. To do this, we need to change the caption of the button back so that it reflects the original purpose. So we need to add another line to the If Test. It will then be

```
If cmdMessage_1_Button.Caption = "Erase Text" Then
    txtOutput.Text = ""
    cmdMessage_1.Caption = "Message 1"
Else
```

This new statement gives the button its original caption. This takes care of the part of the If Test where the text had just been displayed in the text box. We haven't yet dealt with the original purpose of the button. That code will go in the Elsepart, because if the caption of the button is not "*Erase Text*", then it must be "*Message 1*", and we need to display the message when the button is clicked. The Elsepart will be

```
Else
    txtOutput.Text = "This is the message for button 1."
    cmdMessage_1.Caption = "Erase Text"
End If
```

But we still need one more statement. We know that if we have just written message 1 in the box, message 2 cannot be in the box. Suppose for a moment that we had just clicked button 2. If we set up button 2 to do the same thing as we are setting up button 1 to do, then button 2 would say "*Erase Text*" right after the message had been put in the box. But after we click button 1 and put message 1 in the box, message 2 is no longer there, and it would be valid to put message 2 there again. Therefore, we want to change the caption of button 2 so that it says "*Message 2*" again. Now, if button 2 had never been clicked, the caption would already be "*Message 2*", but there is no harm in changing a caption to the same caption that is already there. We could check (with an additional If Test) to see if the caption has been changed before we change it, but this is a waste of effort. It doesn't matter what the caption currently is, because we know what we want it to be. Therefore, we will add one more statement to the Elsepart.

```
Else
    txtOutput.Text = "This is the message for button 1."
    cmdMessage_1.Caption = "Erase Text"
    cmdMessage_2.Caption = "Message 2"
End If
```

This makes the entire If Test:

```
If cmdMessage_1.Caption = "Erase Text" Then
    txtOutput.Text = ""
    cmdMessage_1.Caption = "Message 1"
Else
    txtOutput.Text = "This is the message for button 1."
    cmdMessage_1.Caption = "Erase Text"
    cmdMessage_2.Caption = "Message 2"
End If
```

Let's add this code now.

1. Move the insertion point to the beginning of the first line of code (not the Sub statement).

2. Press **Enter**. This will add a blank line at the insertion point. Press the **Up Arrow** key to move the insertion point up to the previous line.

3. Key **If cmdMessage_1.Caption = "Erase Text" Then** and press **Enter**.

4. Press **Tab** (to indent), key **txtOutput.Text = ""** and press **Enter**.

5. Key **cmdMessage_1.Caption = "Message 1"** and press **Enter**.

6. Press **Backspace** (the cursor will drop back to the previous indent point), key **Else**, and press **Enter**.

7. Press **Tab** and **Del** to pull the next line up, already indented.

8. Press **Down Arrow, Home,** and **Tab** to align the next line under the previous line.

9. Press **End** and **Enter**.

10. Key **cmdMessage_2.Caption = "Message 2"** and press Enter.

11. Press **Backspace** and key **End If**.

That completes this section of code, and your code window should have the code shown in Figure 2.27.

Now we need to put virtually identical code in the cmdMessage_2 code. Because it will be so similar, let's copy this code rather than rekeying all of it.

Copying Text

To copy text, you must first select it. You could select the entire procedure (including the **Sub** and **End Sub** statements), but all you really need is the If Test code.

1. Move the cursor to the beginning of the first line of the If Test code, and highlight all the lines of code except the very last line (**End Sub**), as shown in Figure 2.28.

The selected text will be highlighted as the cursor is moved if you hold down the left mouse botton. After the text is selected, it is ready to be copied. When Visual Basic copies

FIGURE 2.27
The code window, showing the code in the program so far with the If Test indicated.

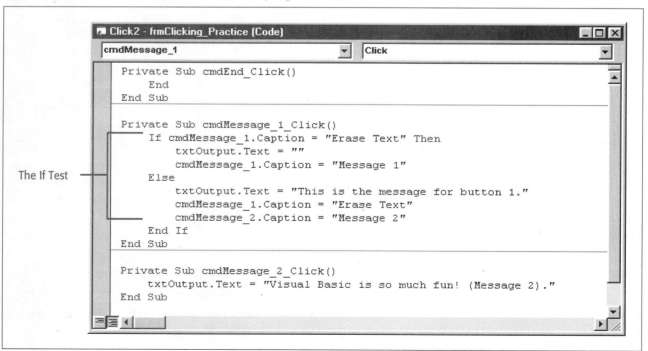

FIGURE 2.28
The highlighted code.

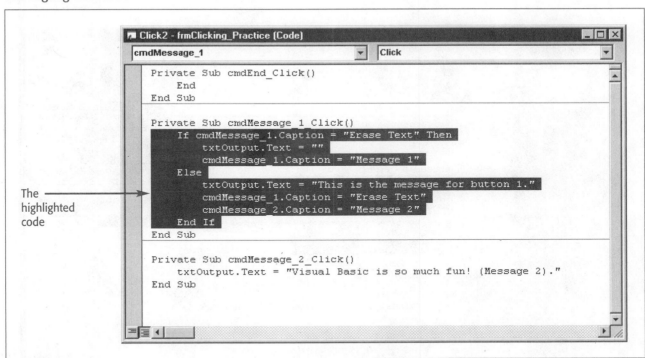

The highlighted code

text (or moves it), it places the text to be copied on the **clipboard,** a temporary storage area that all Windows applications can access. Then that clipboard text can be **pasted** elsewhere in the code. The copying is done using the **Edit** menu, which has several options that let us manipulate the code.

2. Pull down the **Edit** menu as shown in Figure 2.29.

The four options of interest right now are **Cut** (shortcut key **Ctrl-X**), which will delete the text from the current location and place it on the clipboard; **Copy** (shortcut key **Ctrl-C**), which will leave the text where it is but place a copy of it on the clipboard; **Paste** (shortcut key **Ctrl-V**), which will take the text from the clipboard and copy it into the code at the current cursor location; and **Delete** (shortcut key **Del**), which will remove the text without putting it on the clipboard. Because we don't want to remove the highlighted text, but merely wish to place it on the clipboard, we will use the **Copy** option.

3. Select **Copy** from the menu.

Though nothing seems to happen to the highlighted text, Visual Basic has actually placed a copy of it on the clipboard. Now we need to switch to the code for the message 2 button and paste the copied text there.

4. Move the cursor down in the code to the cmdMessage_2 code.

5. Place the cursor at the beginning of the first line of the code (again, not the Sub statement) and press **Ctrl-V**, the shortcut key for the **Paste** option.

HINT: You can also use the object menu that is called up when you right-click the selected text. It contains only the *Cut, Copy, Paste, Delete,* and *Select All* options as shown in Figure 2.30.

FIGURE 2.29
The Edit menu.

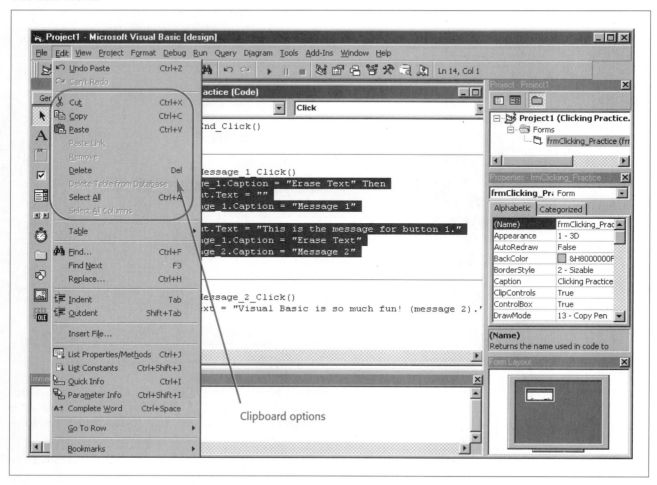

The code from the other window will instantly appear with the two lines of previous code on the end, as shown in Figure 2.31. Now we need to edit this code so that it is correct for the second button rather than the first.

On the first line of the If Test, we only need to change cmdMessage_1 to cmdMessage_2 so that it will test the second button caption rather than the first.

6. Move the cursor to the left of the 1 in cmdMessage_1, press **Del**, and press **2**.

The second line is okay as it is because we still want to erase the text. Then the third line just needs the two 1s changed to 2s.

7. On the third line, change the 1 in cmdMessage_1 to 2 and the 1 in "Message 1" to 2.

That takes care of the If part of the If Test. On the first line of the Elsepart, the text itself is incorrect. The correct text is in the line that was already in the code and is now at the end of the If Test. Let's get a little more practice by moving it to the correct location.

8. Move the cursor to the line that contains "Visual Basic is so much fun!…," select it, and press **Ctrl-X** to cut the text (we didn't need it where it was).

9. Move the cursor to the beginning of the related line in the Elsepart (the line containing "This is the message for button 1").

FIGURE 2.30
The object menu for the selected text.

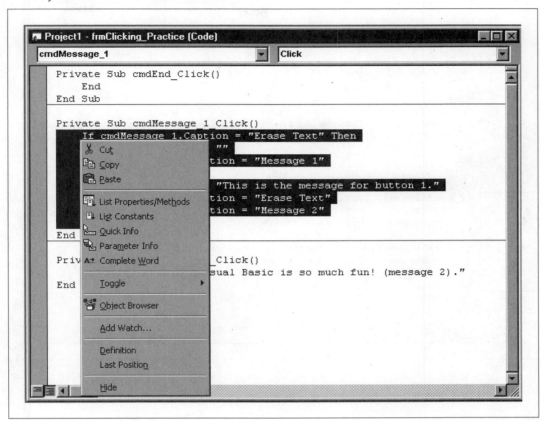

10. Press **Ctrl-V** (for paste) and the line will appear.

11. Indent the new line as it should be.

Now you have a second txtOutput.Text line that should be removed.

12. Move the cursor anywhere on the second txtOutput.Text line, and press **Ctrl-Y** to delete the line.

Now the final two lines need to have their button numbers reversed. The cmdMessage_1_Caption should be "Message 1", and the cmdMessage_2_Caption should be "Erase Text".

13. Change the 1 in cmdMessage_1_Caption to 2 and the 2 in cmdMessage_2_Caption to 1. Also change "Message 2" to "Message 1".

This concludes the necessary changes. Your code should be as shown in Figure 2.32.

Changing the Colors of the Text Box

There are two colors of interest for most objects: the **BackColor,** which is the color of the background, and the **ForeColor**, which is the color of whatever text is displayed in or on the object.

FIGURE 2.31

The code after pasting the copied code.

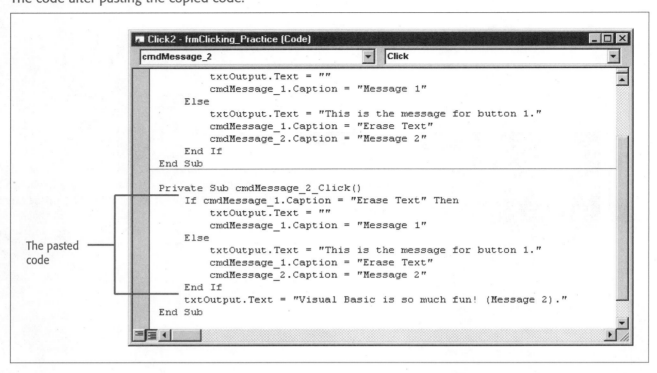

The pasted code

```
Click2 - frmClicking_Practice (Code)

cmdMessage_2                          Click

            txtOutput.Text = ""
            cmdMessage_1.Caption = "Message 1"
        Else
            txtOutput.Text = "This is the message for button 1."
            cmdMessage_1.Caption = "Erase Text"
            cmdMessage_2.Caption = "Message 2"
        End If
    End Sub

    Private Sub cmdMessage_2_Click()
        If cmdMessage_1.Caption = "Erase Text" Then
            txtOutput.Text = ""
            cmdMessage_1.Caption = "Message 1"
        Else
            txtOutput.Text = "This is the message for button 1."
            cmdMessage_1.Caption = "Erase Text"
            cmdMessage_2.Caption = "Message 2"
        End If
        txtOutput.Text = "Visual Basic is so much fun! (Message 2)."
    End Sub
```

FIGURE 2.32

The changed code.

```
Click2 - frmClicking_Practice (Code)

cmdMessage_1                          Click

            If cmdMessage_1.Caption = "Erase Text" Then
                txtOutput.Text = ""
                cmdMessage_1.Caption = "Message 1"
            Else
                txtOutput.Text = "This is the message for button 1."
                cmdMessage_1.Caption = "Erase Text"
                cmdMessage_2.Caption = "Message 2"
            End If
        End Sub

        Private Sub cmdMessage_2_Click()
            If cmdMessage_2.Caption = "Erase Text" Then
                txtOutput.Text = ""
                cmdMessage_2.Caption = "Message 2"
            Else
                txtOutput.Text = "Visual Basic is so much fun! (Message 2)."
                cmdMessage_2.Caption = "Erase Text"
                cmdMessage_1.Caption = "Message 1"
            End If
        End Sub
```

When we display the text for the first button, we want the background color to be yellow. This requires only a single statement:

```
txtOutput.BackColor = vbYellow
```

Note that this statement follows the standard assignment format. **vbYellow** is a special predefined Visual Basic (thus the vb prefix) variable that translates to the special code Visual Basic needs to change the background color to yellow. There are other predefined variables for the seven other standard colors. There are also many other predefined variables that we will discuss as we have need for them.

1. Change to the code for the **Message 1** button, and key the previous BackColor statement just above the End If statement as shown in Figure 2.33.

Though we are not going to change the foreground color (the text) from black in this routine, we are going to do it in the **Message 2** button click event. We are going to change the background color to red and the text to yellow. Because we are going to change the text color to yellow in the other button click event, we will have to change the color back to black here. (Otherwise, we would be displaying yellow text on a yellow background and wouldn't see any text.) This requires the statement

```
txtOutput.ForeColor = vbBlack
```

2. Key this statement following the BackColor statement.

Now, we want the background color of the text box to change back to white when the user clicks the **Erase** button, so in the code that precedes the Else statement, we need a statement to do that. We could also change the foreground color, but because we aren't displaying any text in that portion of the procedure, there really is no need to do so.

3. Key the appropriate ForeColor statement above the Else statement to give the code shown in Figure 2.34.

FIGURE 2.33

The added BackColor statement.

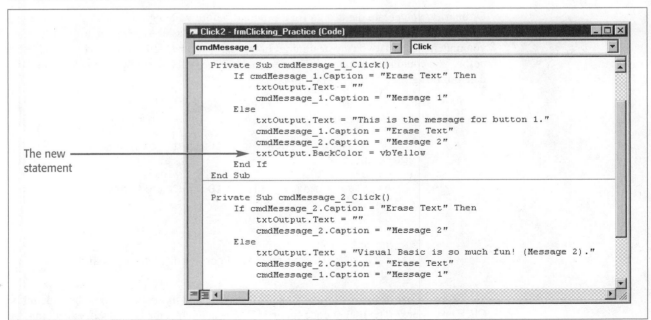

The new statement →

```
Click2 - frmClicking_Practice (Code)

cmdMessage_1                          Click

Private Sub cmdMessage_1_Click()
    If cmdMessage_1.Caption = "Erase Text" Then
        txtOutput.Text = ""
        cmdMessage_1.Caption = "Message 1"
    Else
        txtOutput.Text = "This is the message for button 1."
        cmdMessage_1.Caption = "Erase Text"
        cmdMessage_2.Caption = "Message 2"
        txtOutput.BackColor = vbYellow
    End If
End Sub

Private Sub cmdMessage_2_Click()
    If cmdMessage_2.Caption = "Erase Text" Then
        txtOutput.Text = ""
        cmdMessage_2.Caption = "Message 2"
    Else
        txtOutput.Text = "Visual Basic is so much fun! (Message 2)."
        cmdMessage_2.Caption = "Erase Text"
        cmdMessage_1.Caption = "Message 1"
```

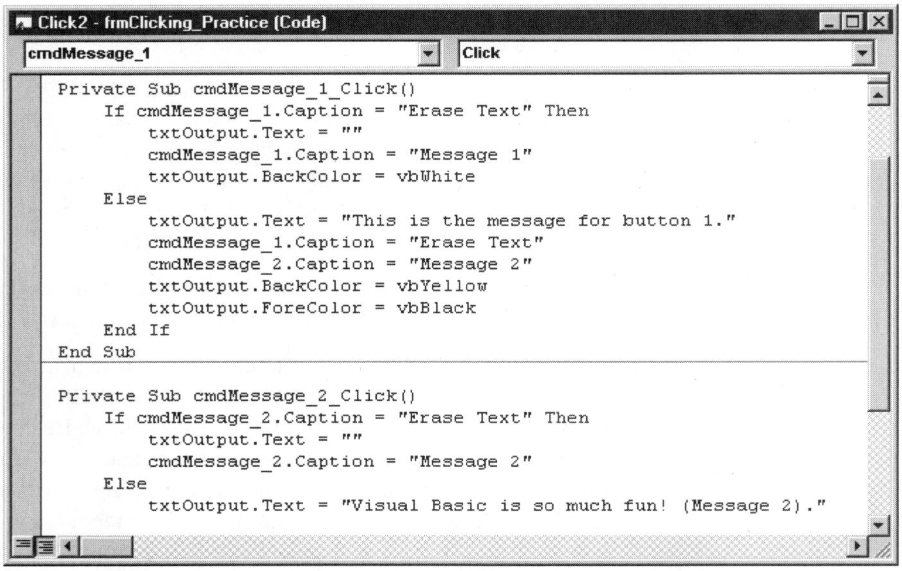

FIGURE 2.34

The complete code for the **Message 1** button.

```
Click2 - frmClicking_Practice (Code)                    _ □ X
cmdMessage_1                        ▼   Click                        ▼
Private Sub cmdMessage_1_Click()
    If cmdMessage_1.Caption = "Erase Text" Then
        txtOutput.Text = ""
        cmdMessage_1.Caption = "Message 1"
        txtOutput.BackColor = vbWhite
    Else
        txtOutput.Text = "This is the message for button 1."
        cmdMessage_1.Caption = "Erase Text"
        cmdMessage_2.Caption = "Message 2"
        txtOutput.BackColor = vbYellow
        txtOutput.ForeColor = vbBlack
    End If
End Sub

Private Sub cmdMessage_2_Click()
    If cmdMessage_2.Caption = "Erase Text" Then
        txtOutput.Text = ""
        cmdMessage_2.Caption = "Message 2"
    Else
        txtOutput.Text = "Visual Basic is so much fun! (Message 2)."
```

That concludes the changes for the **Message 1** button. Now we need to add to the code for the **Message 2** button.

4. Switch to the code for the cmdMessage_2_Click procedure. Key the appropriate statements to change the background color of the text box to red and the foreground color to yellow. Be sure to change the background color to white in the Else part of the If statement.

Be patient. We will test the program after we explore a few more items.

Updating the Design

Ordinarily, you create the design for a program before you begin to code it. We are doing the process a bit backwards, but that's only because it's easier to design a program if, first, you understand what you are designing. In this case, you needed to know what an If Test is before you could incorporate it into a design. Now we will use our new knowledge and update our design. Thus far, our design is

```
Project Clicking - frmClicking_Practice
    A. cmdMessage_1
        1. Click
            Display a message in txtOutput text box
    B. cmdMessage_2
        1. Click
            Display a message in txtOutput text box
    C. cmdEnd
        1. Click
            Exit the program
    D. txtOutput.Text
        Used to display messages from cmdMessage_1 and
        ↳ cmdMessage_2
```

Much of our design will not change. All we changed in the program is the code in the Click procedures. The pseudocode for an If Test is much like the code itself, except that we don't need to be specific about messages. The pseudocode for our changed Click procedure for cmdMessage_1 is

```
1. Click
     If button caption is "Erase Text" Then
         Erase the text in the text box
         Change the caption on the button back to its
         ↳original and the change background color to white
     Else
         Display a message in txtOutput text box changing
         ↳the display colors
         Change the caption on the button to reflect new purpose
         Change the caption on the message 2 button back to its
         ↳original
     End If
```

You will note that actually more writing is needed for the pseudocode here than for the actual code. This is often the case. We use pseudocode to tell us what is supposed to be happening, and sometimes it actually takes less code to get the computer to execute our design than it takes for us to understand what we are trying to get the computer to do. The nice thing about pseudocode, however, is that it is not formal. It doesn't matter how we write the design as long as it makes sense when we translate it into code. When writing the code, however, we need to follow the precise rules of Visual Basic, or we will get errors.

The design for the If Test for the other button would be similar.

Some Additional Samples

One If Test sample will probably not give you much of a feel for the use of the structure (an If Test is called a structure because it generally consists of many statements). Thus, we will take the time to explore a few more If Test samples (the conditional parts of them, at least) before moving on to discover how well our new application works.

Testing the Text   When we set up the test in our code, we tested the caption. We could just as well have tested the text to see whether it had been changed. Thus, instead of

```
If cmdMessage_1.Caption = "Erase Text" Then
```

the test could just as easily have been

```
If txtOutput.Text = "This is the message for button 1." Then
```

This tests the text in the text box to see whether it matches the text that was just shown there. The rest of the If Test could be exactly the same as it was, because if the text is correct, we know the text is there and ready to be erased, which is the same thing that the original conditional was determining.

An important thing to remember about testing text is that upper- and lowercase are important. If you are testing "This", you will not get a match if the text you are testing happens to be "this". The easiest way around this problem is to change all the text to upper- or lowercase; Visual Basic has a function for each of those conversions. **UCase** will return a version of the text all in uppercase, whereas **LCase** will return a version of it all in lowercase. The format of the UCase function is

```
UCase(stringexpression)
```

The **stringexpression** is called the **parameter** of the function and, in this example, is the string or variable that you want to change to uppercase. The format of the LCase statement is similar. Here is a sample If test using the UCase function:

```
If UCase(txtOutput.Text) = "THIS IS A SAMPLE"
```

When you are using UCase or LCase, it is imperative that you use the proper case on what you are comparing against. Note that

```
If UCase(txtOutput.Text) = "This is a sample"
```

would always be false because the UCase function would return a version of txtOutput.Text in all uppercase, and the literal is mixed case.

Testing Properties   Other property settings can be tested (the text that we checked for is, after all, the property setting for the Text property, and a caption is another property setting). We could, for example, test to see whether an object is visible or not. Visible is a property that is either true (setting value of True) or false (setting value of False). Thus, if we wanted to determine if a button was visible, we could use an If Test similar to the following:

```
If cmdEnd.Visible = True Then
```

This just compares the Visible property setting of the cmdEnd to see if it is True.

> **HINT:** When you are testing a value to see if it is True, your If Test can actually be shortened, because you don't need the = True part of the conditional. That is, the above test could actually be written
>
> ```
> If cmdEnd.Visible Then
> ```
>
> This can be done because an If Test is supposed to be determining whether a test is true, and if you test a variable that can be True or False, you get a True/False result. Thus, asking if cmdEnd.Visible = True is the same thing as just asking if cmdEnd.Visible, because each of these expressions will be either True or False.

Another example of an If Test would be a test to determine whether the background color of a form had been changed to a certain color. The test might be

```
If frmClicking_Practice.BackColor = vbRed Then
```

Here the **BackColor** property is compared to the variable vbRed. (Recall that vbRed is a predefined constant.)

Testing Variables   There are many types of variables, other than the properties, that can be used in Visual Basic. The most commonly employed are **numeric variables,** which are used to store numbers that can be used in calculations; **string variables,** which are used to hold text information; **date variables,** which are used to hold dates and times; and **variants,** which are a special type of variable that Visual Basic uses to hold whatever type of data is being assigned to it. The default variable type is variant because it is the most flexible. Any of these variables can be used in an If Test.

Variable names can be up to 255 characters long and can include numbers, letters, and the underscore (_). No special characters (such as parentheses, colons, commas, or periods) or spaces are allowed. The only other restrictions are that the first character of the name must be a letter and that the variable name cannot be a word that has special meaning to Visual Basic (such as **Sub**).

> **HINT:** The same rules hold for naming controls.

There are several types of numeric variables that determine the way the data are stored and how large the numbers can be. The variable names for such variables use special characters following the variable name (such as AMT%, where % indicates that the variable is an integer) to indicate the type of numeric variable. String variables are indicated by using a dollar sign ($) on the end. Name$ would automatically be a string variable. Variables can also be declared as a particular variable type, which eliminates the need for the type indicator. All of this will be covered in much more detail in the next chapter.

It is always a good idea to declare your variables, and it is generally not a good idea to use variants. In the next few pages, you will see some examples wherein variants can cause problems.

Just as we use special designations on control names to classify them (such as cmd for Command Button or txt for Textbox), it is standard practice also to use three characters to classify the type of declared variables. A string variable named Input_Name might instead be called strInput_Name, where str means the variable is a string, and an integer variable, which is used to store numbers, might be called intAmount rather than just Amount.

Using variables in an If Test is not much different from what you have already seen. For example, suppose your application is asking for an amount that cannot exceed 5000 or be less than 1000 and the integer variable that the data are stored in is called intInput_Amount. You will need an If Test to be sure that the amount falls within the specified range. You could start with the conditional as follows:

```
If intInput_Amount > 5000 Then
```

The Thenpart would be some type of error message (because the amount is supposed to be less than or equal to 5000). Unfortunately, this gives us a test only for the top of the range. We still need a test for the bottom of the range. Somehow we need to combine two tests. For this purpose, Visual Basic offers two **connectives** that can be used: **And** and **Or.** The **And** connective tells Visual Basic that the entire test is true only if both parts of the test are true. For example, assume that intAmount_A is 5, intAmount_B is 6, and intAmount_C is 8. The If Test

```
If intAmount_A > 4 Then
```

would be true because intAmount_A is indeed greater than 4. The test

```
If intAmount_B < 7 Then
```

would also be true, whereas

```
If intAmount_C < 7 Then
```

would evaluate to false. If we combined the first two conditionals as

```
If intAmount_A > 4 And intAmount_B < 7 Then
```

then because intAmount_A > 4 is true and intAmount_B < 7 is true, the entire test would evaluate to true. On the other hand,

```
If intAmount_A > 4 And intAmount_C < 7 Then
```

would be false, because intAmount_C < 7 is false even though intAmount_A > 4 is true. Remember, for an And compound conditional to be true, both parts of the conditional must be true.

The Or conditional, on the other hand, is true if either part is true.

```
If intAmount_A > 4 Or intAmount_C < 7 Then
```

would be true, because intAmount_A > 4 is true. This test would be false only if both parts of the test were false.

Knowing how the connectives work, we decide we need to use the Or connective for our range check. We can change our If Test conditional to

```
If intInput_Amount > 5000 Or intInput_Amount < 1000 Then
```

This compound conditional tells Visual Basic to check the first conditional and, if the amount is not larger than 5000, to check the second conditional. If it is also false, the Then-part (the error message) is not executed.

> **HINT:** Because variants change types on the basis of the data being stored in the variable, it is a good idea to have specifically declared variables when using If Tests. Otherwise, the results of your If Tests can sometimes be difficult to predict.

We used an integer rather than a string for this test purposely. Using text fields for numeric comparisons is risky. What if the user entered "10000"? 10,000 is greater than 5000 numerically, but text fields are evaluated by Visual Basic character by character, beginning on the left side, until something doesn't match. Visual Basic finds that the first characters of this comparison (5 and 1) don't match and that 1 is less than 5. Thus, the entry will pass the range test when it actually shouldn't. What we need is a numeric comparison on the entry. Visual Basic compares numbers the same way we do, and 10,000 is indeed larger than 5000.

Sometimes, however, the entry you need to check or work with will be text, not numeric. Input from a text box, for example, is text (or stringdata) rather than numeric. Visual Basic has a function to convert a string value into a numeric value. The function is **Val**. It will start on the left end of a text string, remove all the leading blanks, and begin picking up numeric digits until it runs into a character it does not recognize as numeric. For example, the following will store the value 1400 in the variable intAmount:

```
intAmount = Val(" 1400 S. Street")
```

> **HINT:** The Val command is only one of many Visual Basic functions that you can use to manipulate numeric and string variables. We will explore several more in the next chapter.

Using this command and a string variable, we make the assignment

```
intAmount = Val(strInput_Amount)
```

Then we immediately follow with the If Test.

```
If intAmount > 5000 Or intAmount < 1000 Then
```

A numeric field assignment would be

```
intAmount = 5000
```

whereas a string field assignment would be

```
strAmount_Text = "5000"
```

Note that quotation marks are used. Remember that quotation marks are necessary for strings but are not used for numbers.

A conditional cannot be used to compare numeric data and string data, because they are evaluated differently. For example,

```
If intAmount = strAmount_Text Then
```

would cause Visual Basic to give you an error if the variables intAmount and strAmount_Text had been specifically declared as integer and string fields, respectively.

A Final Word on If Tests

If Tests can be used in series. That is, you can use a second test (using the command **ElseIf**) as the Elsepart of the first test. Suppose, for example, you are trying to execute a series of statements that depend on the value of a variable as shown:

```
If txtBox.Text = "1" Then
    Thenpart 1 (since we don't really care what is being done)
ElseIf txtBox.Text = "2" Then
    Elsepart 2
ElseIf txtBox.Text = "3" Then
    Elsepart 3
Else
    Elsepart 4
End If
```

In this statement, if any test is true, the statements in that section of the code are executed and the rest of the statements are skipped. For example, if the value of txtBox.Text is "2," that Elsepart would be executed, and then control would drop completely out of the rest of the If Test.

You can also use one If Test inside another. This is called **nesting** the If Tests. A sample follows.

```
If txtBox.Text = "1" Then
    If txtBox_2.Text = "1" Then
        Thenpart 1
    Else
        Elsepart 1
    End IF
Else
    Elsepart 2
End If
```

In this case, if the first test is true, control passes to the Then part of the first test to find the second test. If that test is true, the Then part of it is executed (Thenpart 1). If the second test is false, its Else part (Elsepart 1) is executed. If the first test is false, the Else part of it (Elsepart 2) is executed.

If you have a series of compound conditionals that you need to use, you don't have to put them all on one line. Any Visual Basic statement can be continued by using the underline symbol at the end of the line. This can be especially useful for the If Test. For example, suppose you need to test five variables. You could always write the statement as one line, as

```
If strField_1 = "Sample" And strField_2 = "Sample" And
↳strField_3 = "Sample" And strField_4 = "Sample" And
↳strField_5 = "Sample" Then
```

But if you placed each of the conditionals on a separate line, the If Test might be easier to read.

```
If strField_1 = "Sample" And _
    strField_2 = "Sample" And _
    strField_3 = "Sample" And _
    strField_4 = "Sample" And _
    strField_5 = "Sample" Then
```

This is the same statement as before. The underline character tells Visual Basic to continue the statement with the code found on the next line. This technique can be used on any statement to enhance readability; it is just more commonly used on If Tests.

Trying Your New Application

Now that we have learned a bit more about the If Test, let's try out your new application. Normally you would want to save your program, but remember that now Visual Basic will save your program automatically. Thus, you only need to run the program.

1. Run the program.

    Your window will look exactly the same as it did before.

2. Select the first button.

    The text will appear in the text box just as before, but this time the caption on the button will change (see Figure 2.35) and the background color of the text box will be yellow. It will say **Erase Text**. Now, if the application works properly, when you click button 2, the second message should appear, the caption of the second button should change to **Erase Text**, and the caption of the first button should change back to **Message 1**.

3. Select button 2 (see Figure 2.36).

    Did everything change as it was supposed to? Good.

4. Select button 1, and the text, captions, and colors will change again.

5. Select button 1 again. This time the text in the box will be erased, and the caption of button 1 will again say **Message 1**. The background color of the text box will become white.

6. Select both buttons a few more times to satisfy yourself that the application is working properly.

FIGURE 2.35
Running the new version of the program.

Caption on the button is now changed

Background is now yellow

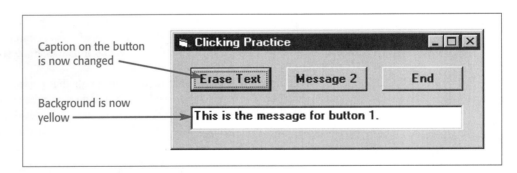

FIGURE 2.36
The results after clicking button 2.

Button 1 caption is now what it was originally

Message is changed, as are the colors

Button 2 caption is now changed

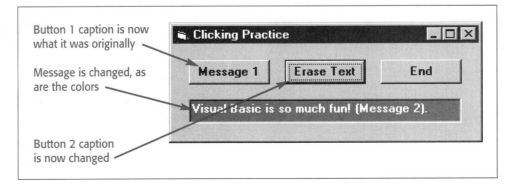

FIGURE 2.37
The text with the
Enabled property set to
False.

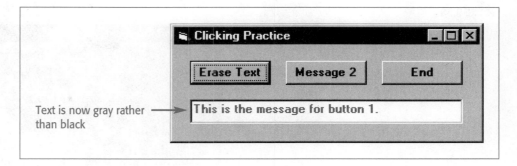

Text is now gray rather → This is the message for button 1.
than black

One Final Change

There is still one change to the application that we should make. It is a minor change but will serve to illustrate property changes.

1. Select all the text in the text box.
2. Key **This is changed**.

Note that you can change the text in the box. Because this program is supposed to display messages, it does not need to allow you to change the text (nothing would be done with the changed text anyway). Therefore, we should fix the application so the text cannot be changed. This is done by **disabling** the text box.

3. Select the **End** button to exit the application.
4. Select the text box.
5. Change to the Enabled property in the Properties window.

Note that the setting for Enabled is True. We need it to be False.

6. Press **F**. The setting will become False.
7. Execute the program again.
8. Try to select the text box. Notice that nothing happens.
9. Select the two buttons to be sure that nothing else happened to the program.

Something else did happen. Now the text is gray rather than black (see Figure 2.37). Even selecting the **Message 2** button does not change the foreground color to yellow as it is supposed to do. Gray is the color that Windows uses when something is disabled. Menu options, for example, are gray when they are not available (disabled). This standard Windows technique cannot be changed. Any time an object is disabled, the text will be gray rather than the color to which the background color is set.

There is an alternative way to set up a box so that text cannot be entered. You can use a **label** rather than a text box. You will learn how to do that in the next chapter.

10. Exit the program when you are satisfied.

2.8   Printing Your Code

ALERT: To do this next section, be sure that you have a printer attached to your computer and that the printer is turned on and ready to receive data.

FIGURE 2.38
The Print... dialog box.

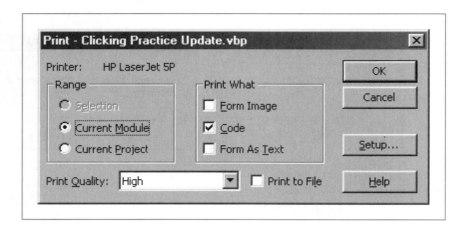

One final thing needs to be discussed about this program: printing your code. As your programs get longer, you may find it more convenient at times to be able to view more of the program at once than you can see in the code window. To do this, you will need to print the program using the **Print...** option from the **File** menu.

1. Pull down the **File** menu and select **Print...** (shortcut key **Ctrl-P**) to see the dialog box shown in Figure 2.38.

This dialog box has two separate parts: *Range* specifies how much of the program you want to print (the selected elements, the elements of the current form, or the elements of the entire program) and *Print What* allows you to specify which elements of the program you want to print (the form as an image, the form as text that will give you the properties, or the code). You must select one or more of the elements on the right. If you try to print without selecting an element, you will get an error message.

Because there is only one form, you can use either the **Current Module** or the **Current Project** option.

2. Select all three of the element options so you will see what the printout of each looks like.

3. Select **OK** to print. If you are not sure your printer will print the graphics of the form, check with your instructor or lab assistant before you begin printing.

The code will print on one page, the form as text (showing the properties) will print on another, and the form image will print on a third. Note that only procedures that have code in them are printed. The other object procedures are ignored. If the code of the program exceeds one page in length, additional pages print automatically, and each page is numbered at the top.

2.9   The Multimedia Control

Now that we have finished the serious portion of this chapter, we will play a little, although what we are going to discover can be useful too. The **Multimedia Control** allows you to play music passages, sound effects, animations, and videos. Incorporating these features can enliven an otherwise basically boring program.

Before we attempt to write such a program, we will load the finished product to see how this kind of program works.

Viewing the Program

> **NOTE:** If your computer doesn't have a sound board and speakers, it will probably not produce any sounds. You can still experiment with the program, however, because the animations will still be displayed.

1. Launch the Music And Animation program from your Ch-2 folder to see the form shown in Figure 2.39. Note that as the program loads, it plays a sound file.

   As you can see, this application plays two different music pieces and two animations. It performs different tasks, depending on what button is selected. It also has two additional buttons to stop the music and animations.

   This program assumes that the sound files are in the Media folder in the Windows folder on the C drive. If your system doesn't have that folder or there are no sound files in it, your program will not play any sounds even if your system has a sound card and speakers. In this case you will need to check with your instructor or lab assistant to determine where sound files might be located on your computer.

2. If your computer has speakers and the introductory sound played when you ran the program, click the **Play Bach** button.

3. Click the other music button, and then click the **Stop the Music** button. The music will stop playing.

4. Click the **View Window Switch** button to start one of the animations, which begins with the display shown in Figure 2.40.

FIGURE 2.39
The **Music And Animation** program.

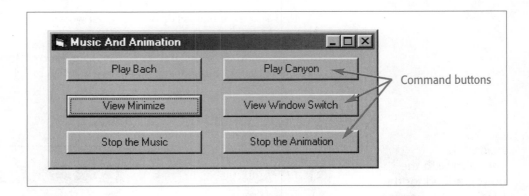

FIGURE 2.40
The initial display of the **View Window Switch** animation.

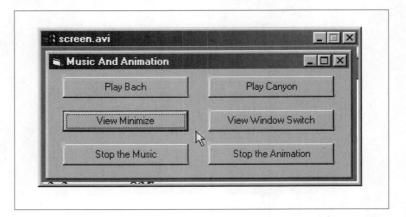

Notice that this animation is an illustration of switching between two program windows.

5. Click the **Minimize** button, and a different animation starts. Before this animation is finished, click the **View Window Switch** button. This animation begins again and the other is canceled.

6. Start one of the animations, and click the **Stop the Animation** button before the animation is finished. Note that this button stops the animation.

7. Start one of the animations, and click the **Stop the Music** button before the animation is finished. Nothing happens.

You can see how the buttons work with this program. The process that begins with the **Play** or **View** button can be interrupted with the appropriate **Stop** button. If you start an animation and click the **Stop the Music** button, the animation will continue to play. Remember that each section of code used in an event, such as clicking a button, is independent of the code for a different event, such as clicking a different button.

8. Play with the Music And Animation program for a bit until you are familiar with the functions, and then exit from the program.

Writing the Multimedia Program

With this preliminary demonstration out of the way, it is time to start digging into Visual Basic for real.

The first thing you need to do is begin a new project.

1. Start a new project.

2. Change the name of the form to **frmMusic_And_Animation**.

We need a series of buttons on our form, but we will begin with just one so that we can introduce the **Multimedia Control**.

3. Add a button to the form, and change the name to **cmdBach** and the caption to **Play Bach**. Size and position the button as shown in Figure 2.41.

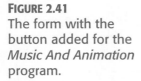

FIGURE 2.41
The form with the button added for the *Music And Animation* program.

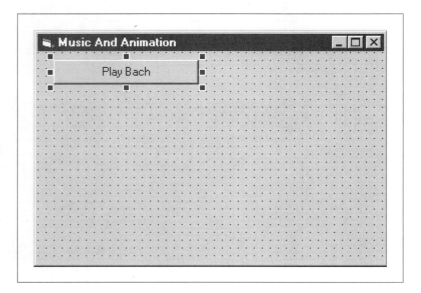

Now we need to add the Multimedia Control to the form. The problem is that it isn't one of the standard Visual Basic tools. To use it, we have to add it. This is done with the **Components...** option of the **Project** menu.

4. Pull down the **Project** menu, and select the **Components...** option (shortcut key **Ctrl-T**) to see the dialog box shown in Figure 2.42.

There are three tabs on this dialog box, but we are on the one we need.

5. Scroll the list until you find the entry for **Microsoft Multimedia Control 6.0**.

6. Click in the box on the left side of the **Microsoft Multimedia Control 6.0** entry, and then click the **OK** button.

Now your Toolbox will show a new control.

7. Double-click the **Multimedia Control** as shown in Figure 2.43. This will add the control to your form. Move the control to the position shown in Figure 2.44. Then change the name of the control to **mmcMusic**. The prefix is for MultiMedia Control.

Note that the Multimedia Control has the same nine buttons that are generally found on a CD (compact disc) player. Some or all of these buttons become active when the control is used. The number of active buttons depends on what the control is being used for.

When you use this control in your applications, you can choose whether the user will be able to use the buttons or the program will handle the control functions. In this application, we want the buttons to control the use, and we will actually hide the multimedia controls from the users (we will add another control for the animations).

In using this control, two properties are important: **DeviceType** and **Filename**. We will begin by setting the **DeviceType** property. This property is used to tell the control what type of multimedia file it is to play. Here are the types that are typically used:

■ **WaveAudio** is used to play WAV files, which are generally sound-effect files.

■ **Sequencer** is used to play MID and RMI files, which are generally Midi music files.

■ **AviVideo** is used to play AVI files, which are animations.

FIGURE 2.42
The **Components** dialog box.

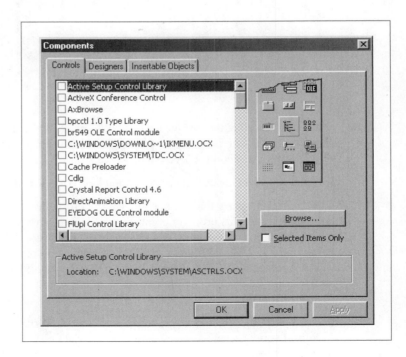

FIGURE 2.43
The Multimedia Control.

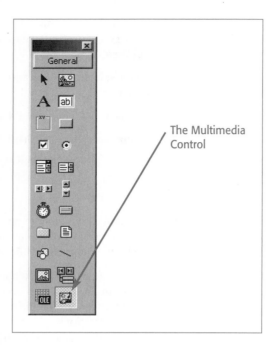

The Multimedia
Control

FIGURE 2.44
The Multimedia Control
added to the form.

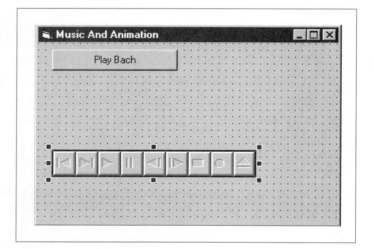

We will use all of these values in this program. As in the sample program we examined earlier, we want our program to play a WAV file when the program begins. So the DeviceType for this control needs to be WaveAudio.

8. Change to the DeviceType property and key **WaveAudio**.

The other property that we need to set up before the control will actually play audio files is **Filename**. This property points to the file we want the control to play. The file we want to hear when the program begins is called **The Microsoft Sound.wav**. It can generally be found in the **C:\Windows\Media** folder on your computer if you are running Windows 95 or in the **C:\WinNT\Media** folder if you are running Windows NT. If there are no files in either place on your computer, ask your instructor or lab assistant where your WAV files can be found.

9. Switch to the Filename property, and key **C:\Windows\Media\The Microsoft Sound.wav** or whatever pathname is appropriate.

Setting these two properties is only part of what is necessary for the control to play the WAV file. Now you must tell the control what to do by giving it a command with the **Command Method**. We have already discussed properties. A **method** is a property for the object that is available only when the program is running. Thus, a method is used only in code. The format of the Command Method is

```
[Form.]MMControl.Command = Cmdstring
```

The [Form.] portion of the command is necessary only when the command is referencing a control on a form other than the one that the command is on. We mentioned previously that a Visual Basic program can, and generally does, use multiple forms. When it does, and a control on one form needs to be referenced on another form, the name of the command is appended to the name of the form with a period between. For example, if you want to assign a literal to a text box on the form frmExtra from code located on the form frmFirst, you would use a command similar to

```
frmExtra.txtDisplay.Text = "This is to be displayed in the
↳ text box."
```

The second element in the format is **MMControl**. This is the name of the control that is the subject of the method being used. Following that comes the method **Command**, separated from the method by a period. The last portion of the format is for what is being assigned to the method **(= cmdstring)**. For this method, cmdstring can have a variety of values, but we are currently interested only in three:

- **Open** is used to tell the control to open the file that has been specified in the Filename property.
- **Play** is used to tell the control to play the file that was just opened.
- **Close** is used to tell the control to stop playing the file and close it.

Because we want to play the WAV file when the program begins, we need to have some place to put the statements to play the file that will be executed before the user does anything in the program. The first thing that every program does is load the first form, and the first event that is triggered when a form is loaded is the **Form_Load** procedure. If we put statements in the Form_Load procedure, they will run as the form is displayed on the desktop.

10. Double-click the form to open the code window in the Form_Load procedure.

You might think that the first statement we need is for the Open method. Normally that would be correct. In this case, because the computer can play only one sound file at a time, we need to use the Close method first. We need to be certain that no other music piece or sound file is being played. The Close method is how we do that. The required statement is

```
mmcMusic.Command = "Close"
```

11. Add this statement to the procedure.

Now we do need the Open method statement.

```
mmcMusic.Command = "Open"
```

12. Key this statement into the procedure.

Then we need the Play method.

```
mmcMusic.Command = "Play"
```

13. Key the Play statement into the procedure following the Open statement.

This is all that we need to play the WAV file. You should have three statements as shown in Figure 2.45.

FIGURE 2.45

The statements in the Form_Load procedure.

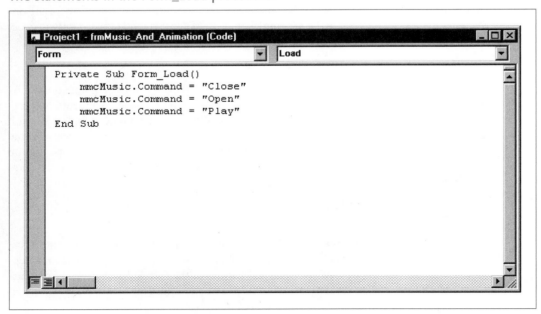

14. Run the program. The WAV file should sound the same as the sample program you practiced with at the beginning of the chapter.

15. Exit from the program.

16. Open the code window for the ***Play Back*** button, and key a Close method statement.

We mentioned that WAV files use a DeviceType of WaveAudio, whereas MID and RMI use a DeviceType of Sequencer. This means that to play the music with the buttons, you will have to change the DeviceType. This is done with an assignment statement of the format

```
[Form.]MMControl.DeviceType = device
```

Following this format, the statement we need is

```
mmcMusic.DeviceType = "Sequencer"
```

17. Key this statement following the Close statement.

This changes the DeviceType, but the other property we set, Filename, needs to be changed also. The format for this statement is similar:

```
[Form.]MMControl.Filename = stringexpression
```

In this statement, the stringexpression is the pathname and filename of the Filename you are assigning. Thus, the statement we need for the **Bach** button is

```
mmcMusic.Filename = "C:\Windows\Media\Bach's Brandenburg
  ⮑Concerto No.3.RMI"
```

18. Key this statement, substituting an appropriate pathname if the one shown is not where your files are located.

Now that we have the proper DeviceType and the Filename of the file that we want to play, the next step is to open and then play that file just as we did before.

19. Key the Open and Play statements we used in the Form_Load procedure, or copy them from that procedure and paste them here.

That's all that's needed. Your code should now look like that in Figure 2.46.

20. Run the program. After the startup sound plays, click the **Play Bach** button. The Brandenburg Concerto should begin playing.

21. Let the entire music piece play out, or exit from the program and the playing will stop. You can also experiment with the buttons on the Multimedia Control if you wish.

Now we can add the button that we will need to play the other music piece.

22. Add another button to your form so that it looks like the one in Figure 2.47.

23. Change the caption of the new button to **Play Canyon** and the control name to **cmd-Canyon**.

FIGURE 2.46
The code for the Form_Load and the cmdBack_Click procedures.

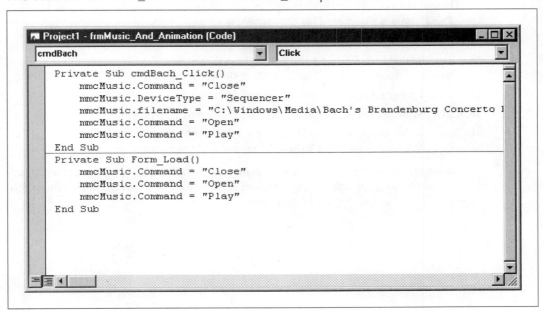

FIGURE 2.47
The **Music And Animation** form after the next button is added.

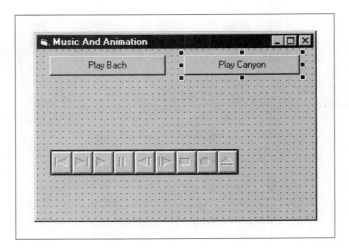

24. Copy the code from the **cmdBach_Click** procedure, and paste it in the _Click procedure of the new button.

This code is perfect for the other button except for one thing: the Filename property is
set to the same file as for the other button. We need to change the filename so that it points
to the file that is appropriate for the caption of the button. That filename is **Canyon.MID**.

25. Change the Filename statement to reflect the new filename.

```
mmcMusic.Filename = "C:\Windows\Media\Canyon.MID"
```

26. Run the program. Click either of the buttons and then click the other. The first music
piece will be interrupted, and the second piece will begin playing.

The last thing we will do in this section is to add the **Stop the Music** button. Adding
the buttons and the second Multimedia Control for the animations is left as an exercise at
the end of the chapter.

27. Add the **Stop the Music** button, change the control name to **cmdStop_Music**, and
change the caption to **Stop the Music,** as shown in Figure 2.48.

There is only one statement needed for the code in the **cmdStop_Music_Click** procedure. Think about it a minute. That's right. We need a Close method statement to close the
music file.

28. Open the code for the **Stop the Music** button, and key the Close method statement.
The completed code should look like that shown in Figure 2.49.

29. Run the program and click one of the music buttons.

30. Click the **Stop the Music** button, and the music will stop playing.

31. Practice with the program until you are sure you know just how it is functioning. Then
exit from the program, exit Visual Basic, and end your session properly.

The program you experimented with at the beginning of the Multimedia Control section also had buttons for animations. You will add the animations to your program in Programming Exercise 4 at the end of the chapter.

FIGURE 2.48
The **Music And
Animation** form after
adding the **Stop the
Music** button.

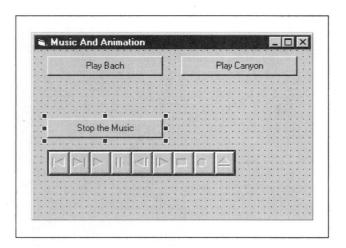

FIGURE 2.49
The completed code.

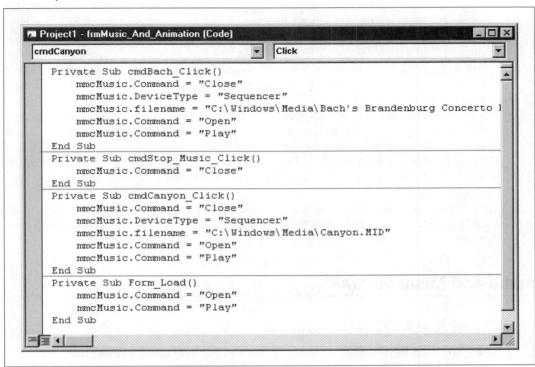

2.10 Debugging Your Programs

One of the most difficult things about programming is finding the errors that inevitably creep into programs. The process of finding the errors in a program is called **debugging,** because an error is generally referred to as a **bug.** At the ends of most of our chapters, you will find a section called "Debugging Your Programs." It contains hints about what errors you might make in programs that deal with the topics covered in the chapter and what you might do to correct those errors.

Generally, if you enter the name of a method or event incorrectly, Visual Basic will warn you when you press **Enter** to go to the next line, or it will tell you when you run the program. Such errors are known as **syntax errors,** which are errors in the syntax, or words and methods, of the language. Visual Basic won't know what to do if you specify a command incorrectly, so you will get an error. That's not to say you can't make errors in your programs, however.

One of the most common errors that programmers make in Visual Basic programs is to set a property to the wrong value. The color of the text box is set incorrectly, or an object is disabled when it is not supposed to be. When such things happen, one of the easiest things to do is print the application's properties and code. Look for the places in the code where properties are changed or where a change is supposed to be made but the statement to make that change is missing. Also, check the initial settings of the properties to be sure they are what you think they are.

You might have a problem if you are using the Multimedia Control. If you have set one of the properties incorrectly, it will not tell you. If you misspell the name of the file that the control is to play, nothing will happen, but you will get no error. Also, if you specify the wrong DeviceType, the file will not play but Visual Basic will not tell you that you have done something wrong. For example, if you mean to set the DeviceType property to "Sequencer" but spell it "Sequencr" (there should be an "e" before the "r"), nothing will happen when you run the program. You will not get an error, but neither will the sound file play. So it is important to check all property settings if your program is not performing properly.

Another common error is to put code in the wrong procedure. For example, you want the program to end when you click on a button you have called **Exit,** but when you selected the procedure in which to put the code, you picked the wrong one and just didn't notice. Thus, even though you have an End statement associated with the **Exit** button, the program will not end when the button is clicked. Here you need to check carefully to be sure the code is where you think it is.

If you are careful with the object properties and their values and with where you put the code for the events, you should be able to get your programs to run with minimal extra effort.

2.11   Command and Menu Summary

In this chapter you learned to use the following keystrokes:

- **Ctrl-A** is the shortcut key for the **Save File As...** option on the **File** menu.
- **Ctrl-C** is the shortcut key for the **Copy** option on the **Edit** menu.
- **Ctrl-P** is the shortcut key for the **Print...** option on the **File** menu.
- **Ctrl-S** is the shortcut key for the **Save File** option on the **File** menu.
- **Ctrl-V** is the shortcut key for the **Paste** option on the **Edit** menu.
- **Ctrl-X** is the shortcut key for the **Cut** option on the **Edit** menu.
- **Ctrl-Y** deletes a single line of code in the code window.
- **End** moves the cursor to the end of a line of code in the code window (also in a text box).
- **F5** is the shortcut key for the **Start** option on the **Run** menu.
- **F7** is the shortcut key for the **Code** option on the **View** menu.
- **Home** moves the cursor to the beginning of a line of code in the code window (also in a text box).

In this chapter you learned about the following properties:

- **BackColor** changes the background color of the object.
- **Caption** changes the caption of a command button or the title (in the title bar) of a form.
- **DeviceType** allows you to specify the type of file you want the Multimedia Control to play.
- **Enabled** turns on or off access to the object by the user during runtime.
- **Filename** allows you to specify the name of the file you want to play with the Multimedia Control.
- **ForeColor** changes the foreground color of the object.
- **Height** determines the height of the object.

■ **Left** determines the position of the left side of the object within the form.

■ **Name** allows you to change the control name of an object to something more suitable than the default name given it by Visual Basic.

■ **Text** contains the text that is displayed in the text box.

■ **Top** determines the position of the top of the object within the form.

■ **Visible** allows an object to appear (if the value is True) or not appear (if the value is False) on a form.

■ **Width** determines the width of the object.

In this chapter you learned about the following methods:

■ **Command** allows you to specify the function that you want the Multimedia Control to perform. The functions discussed are **Open**, **Close**, and **Play**.

In this chapter you learned about the following functions:

■ **LCase** is used to change text to all lowercase.

■ **UCase** is used to change text to all uppercase.

■ **Val** is used to convert string data into numeric data.

In this chapter you learned the following object and variable prefixes:

■ **cmd** is for command buttons.

■ **frm** is for forms.

■ **int** is for integer variables.

■ **mmc** is for Multimedia Controls.

■ **str** is for string variables.

■ **txt** is for text boxes.

In this chapter you learned about the following menu options:

■ **Edit:**

   ■ **Copy** (shortcut key **Ctrl-C**) copies the selected code to the clipboard without removing it from its current location.

   ■ **Cut** (shortcut key **Ctrl-X**) copies the selected code to the clipboard while removing it from its current location.

   ■ **Delete** (shortcut key **Del**) erases the selected code.

   ■ **Paste** (shortcut key **Ctrl-V**) copies the code found on the clipboard into the current location in the code window.

■ **File:**

   ■ **New Project** lets you start a new project with an empty form.

   ■ **Open Project...** lets you load a previously saved project.

   ■ **Print...** (shortcut key **Ctrl-P**) lets you print just selected parts of your program or all of it.

   ■ **Save (form name)** (shortcut key **Ctrl-S**) is used to save an individual form file to disk.

   ■ **Save (form name) As...** (shortcut key **Ctrl-A**) is used to save an individual form file to disk with a name different from the one it currently has.

   ■ **Save Project** lets you save a project to disk.

   ■ **Save Project As...** lets you create a duplicate project by saving an existing project with a different name.

■ **Run:**
- ■ **End** is used to terminate the execution of a program.
- ■ **Start** (shortcut key **F5**) is used to start execution of a program.

■ **View:**
- ■ **Code** (shortcut key **F7**) calls up the code window for the selected object.

In this chapter you learned about the following Toolbox tools:

This tool is used to add command buttons to the form.

This tool is used to add a Multimedia Control to the form.

This tool is used to add text boxes to the form.

In this chapter you learned about the following Toolbar icon:

This tool is used to save the project to disk.

2.12   Performance Check

1. What has to be added to the original form that Visual Basic gives every new project to make an application executable?

2. Where do objects that are added to a form always initially appear?

3. What are the small boxes that appear on the border of an object called and what are they for?

4. Why should all the buttons on a form generally be the same size?

5. What is the property to set the position of an object from the left side of the form?

6. What is a twip and how big is it?

7. What is the Width property for?

8. At a glance, where can you see the positioning on the form of the currently selected object?

9. How do you call up the code window for a particular object?

10. When you are making changes in the code window, how do you change from the code of one object to the code of another object without leaving the code window?

11. Why would you change the control name of an object?

12. What is **F5** for?

13. What is incorrect about the following assignment statement?

    ```
    txtOutput.Text = This is a sample
    ```

14. What is incorrect about the following assignment statement (assuming that cmdEnd is an object)?

```
cmdEnd = True
```

15. On what menu do you find the New Project option?

16. What is the purpose of the Val command?

17. Assuming that intEntry is an integer, what is wrong with this statement?

```
intAmount = Val(intEntry)
```

18. Given intAmount = 5, intInterest = 7, intDividend = 5, strInput = "Yes", and strResponse = "Test", specify whether each of the following evaluates to True or False.

a. `If intAmount > intInterest Then`

b. `If intAmount < intInterest Then`

c. `If intAmount <> intDividend And`
`  ⤷intInterest > 6 Then`

d. `If intAmount > 4 Or strInput <>`
`  ⤷"Yes" Then`

e. `If strResponse = "No" Then`

f. `If strResponse = "Test" Then`

g. `If intAmount = strResponse Then`

h. `If intAmount <> 6 And`
`  ⤷intDividend <> 6 And`
`  ⤷intInterest <> 8 Then`

i. `If intInterest <= 8 Or`
`  ⤷intDividend >= 1 Then`

19. What is the shortcut key **Ctrl-V** for?

20. What is the difference between code cut from the code window and code copied from the code window?

21. What is the DeviceType property used for?

22. What function must be used in the Multimedia Control Command method prior to the Play statement?

23. What property specifies the background color of the object?

24. What is a bug?

25. What is the UCase function used for?

2.13 Programming Exercises

NOTE: In these exercises, we will give you some of the forms you need to create your programs. We will show you only the form without the rest of the Visual Basic system in the background. This way, you will be able to concentrate on just the form itself.

FIGURE 2.50
The completed form for
Programming
Exercise 1.

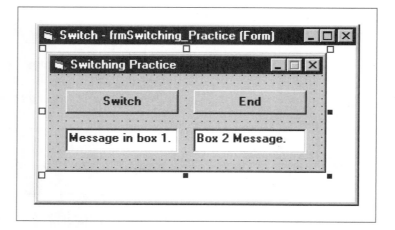

1. For this exercise you will create a window with two buttons and two text boxes. One button will end the program, and the other will allow you to exchange the messages in the two windows. The form design is shown in Figure 2.50. The design for the program is

```
Project Switch - frmSwitching_Practice
    A.  cmdSwitch_Button
        1.  Click
            Switch the messages in txtBox_1 and txtBox_2
    B.  cmdEnd
        1.  Click
            Exit the program
    C.  txtBox_1
        Used to display messages to be switched
    D.  txtBox_2
        Used to display messages to be switched
```

This exercise will give you practice adding buttons and text boxes to a form and adding code to the application. Study the design and then, at the computer, do each of the following:

a. Get into Visual Basic.

b. Put your work disk in drive A (to save your project).

c. Switch to the Properties window, select the Caption property, key **Switching Practice**, and press **Enter**. Then change to the (Name) property, key **frm-Switching_Practice**, and press **Enter**.

d. Double-click the Command Button tool.

e. Drag the button to the upper left corner, leaving one row of the grid dots above the button (not counting the row of dots that just peeks out under the title bar) and one column to the left.

f. Move the mouse button to the sizing handle in the middle of the right side, and drag the right side until the width is 1695 (check the right side of the button bar or the Properties window for the width).

g. Switch to the Caption property in the Properties window, key **Switch**, and press **Enter** (see Figure 2.50 for the completed form, showing the button).

h. Switch to the (Name) property in the Properties window, key **cmdSwitch**, and press **Enter**.

i. Select the Command Button tool, and draw the **End** button on the form as shown in Figure 2.50. Change the (Name) property to **cmdEnd** and the Caption property to End.

j. Select the Text Box tool.

k. Draw the text box on the form as shown in Figure 2.50.

l. Change to the Text property, key **Message in box 1**, and press **Enter** (see Figure 2.50 for the completed text box).

m. Add the second text box with the text **Message box 2** (so the text will be different from the text in the first text box and you will be able to tell the difference when they are switched).

n. Change the control names of the two text boxes to **txtBox_1** and **txtBox_2**.

o. Adjust the size of the form until your completed form looks like the one in Figure 2.50.

p. Double-click the **Switch** button to call up the code window.

Now you need code to switch the text in the two text boxes as given in the design. You might think that you could do it as

```
txtBox_1.Text = txtBox_2.Text
txtBox_2.Text = txtBox_1.Text
```

The problem with this is that after the text from box 2 is moved into text box 1, the original text in text box 1 is not there any more, so when the second statement is executed, the text that is now in text box 1 (the text from text box 2) is moved into text box 2. This moves the text from text box 2 back into text box 2, accomplishing nothing. What you need is a way to temporarily save the text from text box 1 before moving the text from text box 2 in there. This is done with a temporary string variable (remember that a text box contains string data):

```
strTemporary = txtBox_1.Text
```

Now the text from text box 2 can be moved in as

```
txtBox_1.Text = txtBox_2.Text
```

And then the text from the temporary variable is moved into text box 2:

```
txtBox_2.Text = strTemporary
```

q. Press **Tab**, key **strTemporary = txtBox_1.Text**, and press **Enter**.

r. Key **txtBox_1.Text = txtBox_2.Text** and press **Enter**.

s. Key **txtBox_2.Text = strTemporary** and press **Enter**.

t. Close the code window, click the form (on the form, not on any object), change to the Maxbutton property, and press **F** (for False, which will turn off the maximize button).

u. Open the code window for the **End** button, press **Tab**, and key **End**. Close the window.

v. Pull down the **File** menu, select Save Project, key **Switching Practice**, press **Enter**, key **frmSwitching_Practice**, and press **Enter** (once for the form and once for the project).

w. Run your program and select the **Switch** button a few times to satisfy yourself that the application is doing what it is supposed to do (note that the maximize button is disabled). Select the **End** button.

ALERT: For this next step you must have, either networked or attached to your computer, a printer that is turned on and ready to receive data.

x. Pull down the **File** menu, select the **Print** option, turn on all the print elements, and select **OK**.

y. After everything has printed, exit Visual Basic and shut down the system properly.

2. For this exercise you will create a window with five buttons and six text boxes as shown in Figure 2.51. You will be able to key information into one of the text boxes and then use the buttons to store those keyed data into one of the other five storage text boxes. Then, after the keyed data are stored in one of the boxes, the caption will change to show that you can copy the text from that box back to the entry box so it can be moved to a different storage box. The design for the program is

```
Project Storage - frmText_Entry_Storage
    A. cmdStore_In_1
       1. Click
           If button caption says move Then
              Move the data in txtStorage_1 to the text entry box
           Else
              Move text from the entry box to txtStorage_1
           End If
    B through E - These are the same as for cmdStore_In_1 button
    F. txtStorage_1
       Used to store the text taken from the text entry box
    G through J - These are the same as for txtStorage_1
    K. txtEntry
       Used to enter the text to be stored in txtStorage_1
         ↳through txtStorage_5
```

The exercise will give you practice adding buttons and text boxes to a form and adding code to the application. Study the program design and then, at the computer, do each of the following:

a. Get into Visual Basic.

b. Put your work disk in drive A (to save your project).

FIGURE 2.51
The form for
Programming
Exercise 2.

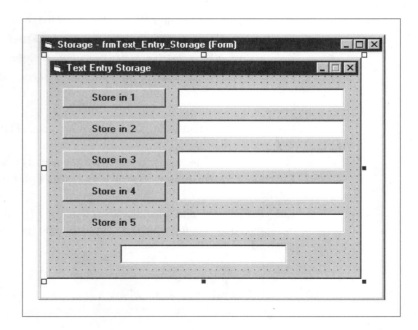

c. Change the caption of the form to **Text Entry Storage** and the name of the form to **frmText_Entry_Storage**.

d. Add a button to the form and position it as shown in Figure 2.51. The caption should be **Store in 1** and the name should be **cmdStore_In_1**. The button is at position 240, 240, and its width is 1935.

e. Add the other four buttons as shown in the figure. The left position, height, and width are all the same as those of the other buttons, whereas the tops are at 840, 1440, 2040, and 2640, respectively. The captions of the buttons should be changed to the ones shown in Figure 2.39.

f. Add the first text box (to the right of the first button at position 2400, 240 with width 3135), erase the text, and change the control name to **txtStorage_1**.

g. Add four more text boxes, position them so that they are aligned with the first text box and the buttons, erase the text, and change the control name settings to **txtStorage_2** through **txtStorage_5**.

h. Add the last text box to the form, position it as shown in the figure (1320, 3240 with width 3135), erase the text, and change the control name setting to **txtEntry**.

i. Call up the code window for the first command button.

You want the code to be able to move the text that the user keyed into the entry box to the storage box beside the button and then erase the text in the entry box. Then, after it has been moved, you want to change the caption of the button so that it will reflect the new purpose of moving the text from the storage box back to the entry box. You can use If Test logic similar to that used in the chapter for testing the status of the button. The code you need is

```
Sub cmdStore_In_1_Click ()
    If cmdStore_In_1.Caption = "Move To Entry Box" Then
        txtEntry.Text = txtStorage_1.Text
        cmdStore_In_1.Caption = "Store in 1"
        txtStorage_1.Text = ""
    Else
        txtStorage_1.Text = txtEntry.Text
        txtEntry.Text = ""
        cmdStore_In_1.Caption = "Move To Entry Box"
    End If
End Sub
```

The If Test conditional is testing the caption to see whether it has been changed from the original "Store in 1". If the caption has been changed, the code should move the text from the storage box back to the entry box (**txtEntry.Text = txtStorage_1.Text**), change the button caption back to what it was before (**cmdStore_In_1.Caption = "Store in 1"**), and then blank out the text in the storage box (**txtStorage_1.Text = ""**). If the caption is the original, the code needs to move the text from the entry box to the storage box (**txtStorage_1.Text = txtEntry.Text**), erase the entry box text (**txtEntry.Text = ""**), and then change the caption to reflect the new purpose (**cmdStore_In_1.Caption = "Move To Entry Box"**).

j. Key the code as shown.

k. Select all the If Test code and copy it to the clipboard.

l. Change to the code for the next command button, paste the code in, and change all the references to storage box 1 to 2 and the reference to cmdStore_In_1.Caption to cmdStore_In_2.Caption.

m. Paste the code into the three other command buttons and modify it in each.

> **HINT:** You could have changed the control names of the command buttons, but because they all serve essentially the same purpose and the number already on each one tells you its position and purpose, it was not necessary (this time) to change the control names. Actually, you didn't need to change the control names for the text boxes either (you did that simply for the practice).

n. Change the setting of the Maxbutton property (on the form) to false so there will not be a **Maximize** button.

o. Select the entry box and the TabIndex property. Change the setting to 0. This property tells Visual Basic which object is the first one to have the cursor on when the program is started. You want the user to begin with the entry box, so you set the TabIndex to 0 (which is the first number).

p. Save the form and project in the Ch-2 folder on drive A as **Storage**.

q. Run your program and key something in the entry box. Click one of the buttons; the text should appear in the text box beside that button, the button caption should change, and the text in the entry box should be erased. Click that button again; the text in the box beside the button should be erased to reappear in the entry box, and the button caption should change back to the original caption.

r. Experiment with the program a bit more until you are satisfied that it operates correctly. Then exit from the program.

> **ALERT:** For this next step you must have, either networked or attached to your computer, a printer that is turned on and ready to receive data.

s. Pull down the **File** menu, select the **Print** option, turn on all the print elements, and select **OK**.

t. After the printing is finished, exit Visual Basic and shut down the system properly.

3. For this exercise you will create a window with five buttons and five text boxes as shown in Figure 2.52. The first text box will begin with text in it, and then the buttons will move that text to another text box (erasing the text from the previous one). Where the text is moved will be guided by the buttons (look at the captions on the buttons in the figure). Note that the buttons and text boxes are not related by position. The design for this program is

```
Project Skipping - frmPassing_Practice
    A. cmdNext_Box
        1. Click
            If txtBox_1 has text Then
                Move text to txtBox_2
                Erase text in txtBox_1
            Else If txtBox_2 has text Then
                Move text to txtBox_3
                Erase text in txtBox_2
            Else If txtBox_3 has text Then
                Move text to txtBox_4
                Erase text in txtBox_3
            Else If txtBox_4 has text Then
                Move text to txtBox_5
                Erase text in txtBox_4
```

FIGURE 2.52
The form for Programming Exercise 3.

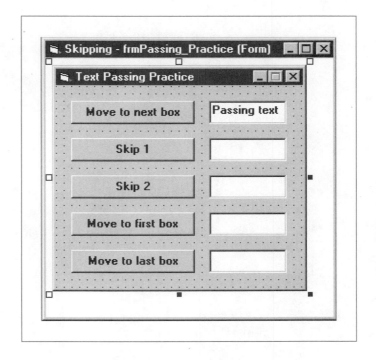

```
                   Else
                       Move text to txtBox_1
                       Erase text in txtBox_5
                   End If
        B. cmdSkip_1
            1. Click
                   If txtBox_1 has text Then
                       Move text to txtBox_3
                       Erase text in txtBox_1
                   Else If txtBox_2 has text Then
                       Move text to txtBox_4
                       Erase text in txtBox_2
                   Else If txtBox_3 has text Then
                       Move text to txtBox_5
                       Erase text in txtBox_3
                   Else If txtBox_4 has text Then
                       Move text to txtBox_1
                       Erase text in txtBox_4
                   Else
                       Move text to txtBox_2
                       Erase text in txtBox_5
                   End If
        C. cmdSkip_2
            1. Click
                   If txtBox_1 has text Then
                       Move text to txtBox_4
                       Erase text in txtBox_1
                   Else If txtBox_2 has text Then
                       Move text to txtBox_5
                       Erase text in txtBox_2
                   Else If txtBox_3 has text Then
                       Move text to txtBox_1
                       Erase text in txtBox_3
```

```
                    Else If txtBox_4 has text Then
                        Move text to txtBox_2
                        Erase text in txtBox_4
                    Else
                        Move text to txtBox_3
                        Erase text in txtBox_5
                    End If
            D.  cmdFirst_Box
                1.  Click
                    If txtBox_2 has text Then
                        Move text to txtBox_1
                        Erase text in txtBox_2
                    Else If txtBox_3 has text Then
                        Move text to txtBox_1
                        Erase text in txtBox_3
                    Else If txtBox_4 has text Then
                        Move text to txtBox_1
                        Erase text in txtBox_4
                    Else
                        Move text to txtBox_1
                        Erase text in txtBox_5
                    End If
            E.  cmdLast_Box
                1.  Click
                    If txtBox_1 has text Then
                        Move text to txtBox_5
                        Erase text in txtBox_1
                    Else If txtBox_2 has text Then
                        Move text to txtBox_5
                        Erase text in txtBox_2
                    Else If txtBox_3 has text Then
                        Move text to txtBox_5
                        Erase text in txtBox_3
                    Else
                        Move text to txtBox_5
                        Erase text in txtBox_4
                    End If
            F.  txtBox_1
                Used to store the text as it is passed from box to box
            G through K - These are the same as for txtBox_1
```

This exercise will give you practice adding buttons and text boxes to a form and adding code to the application. Study the design and then, at the computer, do each of the following:

a. Get into Visual Basic.

b. Put your work disk in drive A (to save your project).

c. Change the caption of the form to **Text Passing Practice** and the name of the form to **frmPassing_Practice**.

d. Add a button to the form and position it as shown in the figure. The caption should be **Move to next box** and the control name should be **cmdNext_Box**. The button is at position 240, 240, and its width is 1935.

e. Add the other four buttons with captions as shown in the figure. The left position, height, and width are all the same as those of the other buttons, whereas the tops are at 840, 1440, 2040, and 2640, respectively, with control names of **cmdSkip_1**, **cmdSkip_2**, **cmdFirst_Box**, and **cmdLast_Box**, respectively.

f. Add the first text box (to the right of the first button at position 2400, 240 with width 1215), change the text to **Passing Text**, and change the control name to **txtBox_1**.

g. Add the other four text boxes, position them so that they are aligned with the first text box and the buttons, erase the text, and change the control name settings to **txtBox_2** through **txtBox_5**.

h. Call up the code box for the first command button.

In order to move the text from one box to any other, you first need to know what box the text is in. If you look back at the design, you will see that all we have to do to determine which text box the text is in is to look in that box. An appropriate If Test is

```
If txtBox_1.Text <> "" Then
```

This checks the first text box, and if it is not blank, we are ready to move the text to the next text box down:

```
txtBox_2.Text = txtBox_1.Text
```

and erase the text in the first text box:

```
txtBox_1.Text = ""
```

Using similar logic for the other text boxes, the rest of the If Test is as follows:

```
ElseIf txtBox_2.Text <> "" Then
    txtBox_3.Text = txtBox_2.Text
    txtBox_2.Text = ""
ElseIf txtBox_3.Text <> "" Then
    txtBox_4.Text = txtBox_3.Text
    txtBox_3.Text = ""
ElseIf txtBox_4.Text <> "" Then
    txtBox_5.Text = txtBox_4.Text
    txtBox_4.Text = ""
Else
    txtBox_1.Text = txtBox_5.Text
    txtBox_5.Text = ""
End If
```

i. Key the code as shown.

j. Select all the If Test code and copy it to the clipboard.

k. Switch to the code for each of the command buttons, paste the code in, and make the necessary changes so that the code fits the purpose of the new button, following the program design given earlier.

l. Change the setting of the Maxbutton property (on the form) to false so that there will not be a maximize button.

m. Save the form as **frmPassing_Practice** and the project as **Skipping** in the Ch-2 folder on drive A.

n. Run your program and try out each of the buttons until you are satisfied that the program operates correctly. Then exit from the program.

ALERT: For this next step you must have, either networked or attached to your computer, a printer that is turned on and ready to receive data.

o. Select the **Print** option from the **File** menu, turn on all the print elements, and select **OK**.

p. Exit Visual Basic and shut down the system properly after everything has printed.

4. In this exercise you will finish the work on the Music And Animation program, which will give you practice working with buttons and the Multimedia Control. At the computer, do each of the following:

   a. Get into Visual Basic.

   b. Load the Music And Animation program you created in this chapter.

   c. Add a second Multimedia Control and three more buttons until your form looks like the one in Figure 2.53.

   d. Change the captions of the buttons to the ones shown in the figure, and give the new objects appropriate control names.

   e. Open the code window for the **View Minimize** button. Key an appropriate Close statement for the new Multimedia Control.

   f. In this chapter, you learned how to specify the DeviceType property. To play an AviVideo animation, you must set the DeviceType to AviVideo. Key an appropriate DeviceType statement.

   g. The Filename property needs to be set to the Screen.AVI file as in this chapter. Key the appropriate Filename statement. The Screen.AVI file is in the **"A:\ch-2"** folder.

   h. Key appropriate Open and Play statements.

   i. Copy all the code to the **View Window Switch** button, and change the name of the file in the Filename statement to **Switch.avi**.

   j. Open the code window for the **Stop the Animation** button, and key the appropriate statement.

   k. Shrink the form so that the Multimedia Controls can no longer be seen. When using this program, you don't need to see the controls.

   l. Run the program and click one of the **View** buttons. That animation should begin playing.

   m. Click the other **View** button; the first animation should stop, and the other should begin playing.

   n. While the animation is playing, click the **Stop the Animation** button to stop playing the animation.

   o. Experiment with the program until you are satisfied that it operates correctly. Then exit from the program.

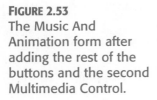

FIGURE 2.53
The Music And Animation form after adding the rest of the buttons and the second Multimedia Control.

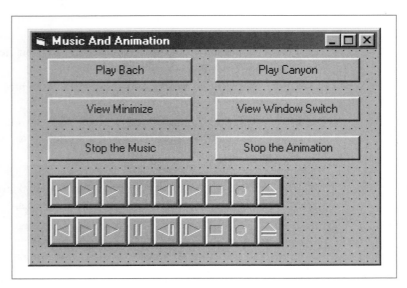

ALERT: For this next step you must have, either networked or attached to your computer, a printer that is turned on and ready to receive data.

    p. Select the **Print** option from the **File** menu, turn on all the print elements, and select **OK**.

    q. Exit Visual Basic and shut down the system properly after everything has printed.

5. Most programs have an About dialog box that appears when you select an About option on the Help menu. You decide you want to experiment with an About dialog box to prepare for future programs. This application will give you practice with the Multimedia Control and buttons. At the computer, do each of the following:

    a. Get into Visual Basic.

    b. Put your work disk in drive A (to save your project).

    c. Add a text box to the form. A text box can use more than one line, which is controlled by the **Multiline** property. Change the Multiline property to True.

    d. Key the following in the Text property of the text box:

The About Dialog Box Program

Copyright (Put current year here.)

by (Your name goes here.)

    e. Add a Multimedia Control to the form, and set the properties so that it will play one of the sound files, either music or sound effects.

    f. Add an **Exit** button that will exit from the program. If this were added to another program, the About form would simply be removed and the program would continue with the main form of the project. We'll see how to do this later in the text.

    g. Test the program and then exit from it.

ALERT: For this next step you must have, either networked or attached to your computer, a printer that is turned on and ready to receive data.

    h. Select the **Print** option from the **File** menu, turn on all the print elements, and select **OK**.

    i. Exit Visual Basic and shut down the system properly after everything has printed.

6. You decided you wanted to experiment with colors, so you wrote a program in which you could press a button to use the color entered into a text box to determine the color of the form background. The problem is that the program doesn't work. This exercise will teach you a few methods of looking for errors in your programs. At the computer, do each of the following:

    a. Get into Visual Basic.

    b. Put your work disk in drive A, and load the Debug project from the Ch-2 folder.

    c. Run the program to see the form shown in Figure 2.54.

    d. The first thing you should notice it that there is no caption in the title bar. The program should be called **Color Changes**. Exit from the program using the **Exit** button. Oops, an error. What's wrong? That's right. The Exit command is incorrect. Fix it, and press **F5** to continue to exit the program.

    e. Put the caption on the title bar and then run the program.

FIGURE 2.54
The Debug form.

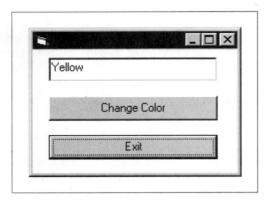

Because you were just experimenting with colors, you set your program up for only three colors, Red, Blue, and Yellow. As you can see, the background of the form is currently Yellow. You want to change it to Blue.

f. Key **Blue** in the text box and click the **Change Color** button. The background color changes to Blue. Very good.

g. Now change the color back to Yellow by keying **Yellow** into the text box and clicking the button. That doesn't work.

h. Exit from the program and open the code window for the button. Find the code for the change to Yellow. Examine the If Test. What do you see? "Yellow" is spelled as "yelow" (one l), and it also isn't capitalized. As you learned in this chapter, case is important in an If Test. Correct the errors so the test will work.

i. Run the program and change the background to Blue and then back to Yellow. Change the color to Red. The color becomes Black. Now what?

j. Exit from the program and examine the If Test for the change to Red. Note that the variable in the BackColor statement is "Red" rather than "vbRed" as it should be. Visual Basic doesn't know what "Red" is and changes the color to its default of Black.

k. Fix this statement, and then thoroughly test the program to be sure it is now working properly. Exit from the program.

> **ALERT:** For this next step you must have, either networked or attached to your computer, a printer that is turned on and ready to receive data.

l. Select the **Print** option from the **File** menu, turn on all the print elements, and select **OK**.

m. Exit Visual Basic and shut down the system properly after everything has printed.

2.14   Performance Mastery

1. You have just learned about text boxes and buttons, so you decide to write a program to practice what you have learned. Write a program that has two buttons and two text boxes. When you click the first button, its associated text box will have a message in it and the other text box will be erased. When you click the second button, the same thing happens in reverse. Design the program carefully, and then create it using the given form design and your program design. Be sure to use appropriate names for all your objects. After you have created the program, save it as **Buttons and Boxes** with the form saved as **frmButtons_And_Boxes**, test it, and then print all the elements.

2. You like working with the colors that you used in the text boxes in this chapter. You decide to write a program with a button for each of eight colors, which are vbBlack, vbRed, vbGreen, vbYellow, vbBlue, vbMagenta, vbCyan, and vbWhite. When the button is pressed, the background color of the form is to be changed to the color represented by the button. Because the form will already be that color, you should disable the button so it cannot be pressed again. When the next button is pressed, the previous button needs to be enabled again. The easiest way to do this is to test the color of the form before changing it and turn on the button that is associated with the color of the form at that time. Design the program carefully, and then create it using the given form design and your program design. Be sure to use appropriate names for all your objects. After you have created the program, save it as **Button Colors** with the form saved as **frmButton_Colors**, test it, and then print all the elements.

3. As a prelude to a more complex program, you decide to practice translating a product code into its product name. Your program needs to have two text boxes: one for your entry of the code and the other for outputting the expanded product name. Add a button to do the translation. You will need an If Test to determine the proper product code and its related product name. Use product codes and names like Org for Orange, Pea for Peach, and so on. The program should be able to translate at least ten different codes. Design the program carefully, and then create it using the given form design and your program design. Be sure to use appropriate names for all your objects. After you have created the program, save it as **Translation** with the form saved as **frmTranslation**, test it, and then print all the elements.

4. In preparation for the next chapter, in which you will learn a lot about calculations, you decide to practice with a simple calculation. You design a form like the one shown in Figure 2.55. The text box in the upper left is used for input of the number to be added to one of the totals in the three text boxes at the bottom. The text box in the upper right is where the user will enter Left, Middle, or Right to indicate to which of the three text boxes at the bottom the number is to be added. To add a value for the text box to one of the others, you will need a statement like the following:

```
txtLeft_Out.Text = Str(Val(txtLeft_Out.Text) +
 ↳ Val(txtData_In))
```

The Str function is used to translate a numeric value to a string value so that it can be displayed in a text box.

FIGURE 2.55
The form for Performance Mastery Exercise 4.

Design the program carefully and then create it, using the given form design and your program design. Be sure to use appropriate names for all your objects. After you have created the program, save it as **Text Box Addition** with the form saved as **frmText_Addition**, test it, and then print all the elements.

5. You have decided that just for practice, you will create a program that will manipulate markers in text boxes. You design a form like the one shown in Figure 2.56. When you click the **Horizontal** button, the first and third rows should have X's put in them, the background color of the text boxes should be changed to yellow, and the second row should be erased. When you click the **Vertical** button, the first and third columns should have X's put in them, the background color should be changed to green, and the second column should be erased. The **End** button should end the program. Design the program carefully and then create it, using the given form design and your program design. Be sure to use appropriate names for all your objects. After you have created the program, save it as **Design** with the form saved as **frmDesign_Practice**, and then print all the elements.

6. You want to create a simple calculator with buttons 1 through 9 that will add the number of the button (1 through 9) to a running total that will be displayed in a text box. Design and create the calculator form, giving all the elements appropriate names, and then write the necessary code to make the calculator function properly. Save the application as **Calculator** when you are finished, and print all the elements.

To do this application, you will need a little extra information (which will be covered in detail in the next chapter). To add a value to a number, you use an assignment statement such as

```
intTotal = intTotal + 1
```

This would retrieve the current value of a variable called intTotal and add 1 to it, storing it back in intTotal. You already know you can convert a text string to a value using the Val function. Well, there is another function to change a numeric variable to a string value. That function is **Str** and would be used as

```
txtOutput.Text = Str(intTotal)
```

This takes the value in Total, changes it to a string, and stores that string in txtOutput.Text.

FIGURE 2.56
The form for
Performance Mastery
Exercise 5.

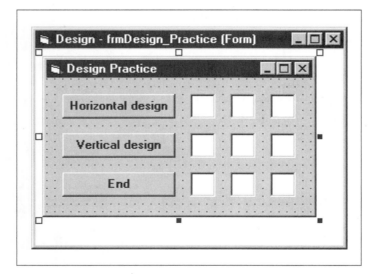

7. You decide to experiment with the sound files on your computer. You want to write a program that will play ten different sound files, one after the other. Create a new program with a Multimedia Control and a single button. Change the Filename property of the Multimedia Control to reflect the filename of the first sound file you want to play. The Multimedia Control has a **Done** event. In the code for this event, add a large If Test that will test the value of the Filename property. If the filename is the first filename, change it to the second; if it is the second, change it to the third; and so on. Add a text box and display the filename of the file being played. Save the application as **Sound Player**. Test the program to be sure it is working properly. When finished, print all the elements.

8. In preparation for the next chapter, in which you will learn a lot about calculations, you decide to practice with a simple calculation. Design a form with three text boxes and one button. The first text box is for the input of a number. The second text box will be used to input either A for addition or S for subtraction. The third text box will be used for the output of the result of the calculation. The button will be used to test whether the calculation is to be addition or subtraction and then to perform the calculation. To add a value for the text box to one of the others, you will need a statement such as the following:

```
txtAmount_Out.Text = Str(Val(txtAmount_Out.Text) +
↳ Val(txtData_In))
```

The Str function is used to translate a numeric value to a string value so that it can be displayed in a text box. To subtract, you simply change the plus symbol to a minus sign, which is the symbol for subtraction.

Design the program carefully and then create it, using the given form design and your program design. Be sure to use appropriate names for all your objects. After you have created the program, save it as **Text Box Addition** with the form saved as **frmText_Addition**, test it, and then print all the elements.

9. You decide to add a sound file to a program you are writing but are not sure of the sound file you want to use. You decide to write a program that will allow you to play each sound in the folder, pausing between them. The program should display the name of the file in a text box so that you will know which file was played. Then it should allow you to click a button to go to the next file to be played. This program will require you to read the directory of the folder to get each of the filenames to be displayed and played. This will require you to use a new statement.

To read the directory of a folder, you need to use the **Dir** function, which has the format

```
Dir[(pathname[,attributes])]
```

The **pathname** refers to the pathname where the file is to be found, along with the type of file for which you are looking. For example, the WAV files you want to play are probably found in the **"C:\Windows\Media"** folder, so this would be the first part of the pathname. But you also need to specify the type of file. This is done with a specification like **"*.WAV"**. Put together, the pathname would be **"C:\Windows\Media*.WAV"**.

The attributes in the function indicate what type of element you are looking for. In this case you want the directory of a folder, which is a value of 16. This can also be specified using a predefined Visual Basic variable called **vbDirectory**. When you do this, the entire function looks like

```
Dir "C:\Windows\Media\*.WAV", vbDirectory
```

That this is a function means that Visual Basic executes the command and then returns something to the program. In this case, it returns the name of the file that is found.

This format of the command is the one to use for reading the first file in the folder. To read subsequent ones, you use only the Dir function by itself. Thus, the entire command should be used in the Form_Load procedure, whereas the Dir function by itself should be used in the button procedure that tells the program to play the next file.

Because this function is returning a filename, the function should become a part of the Filename property assignment used. The statement to read the first filename in the folder and assign it to the Filename property is

```
mmcPlay.Filename = "C:\Windows\Media\" &
    Dir("C:\Windows\Media\*.wav", vbDirectory)
```

The ampersand (**&** symbol) in the statement appends (**concatenates**) the filename result of the Dir command to the pathname. This is necessary because the Filename property needs to have the entire pathname of the file in order for the file to be found.

In addition to this statement in the Form_Load procedure, you need to use the rest of the statements required to play a WAV file.

In order to play a new file with the button, you have to be able to determine when the first file is finished. The Multimedia Control has an event called **Done** that is executed when the file being played finishes. You want the next file to be played when the button is pressed, so all you do in the Done event is signal the user that the program is ready to play the next file. The easiest way to do this is to enable and disable the button. Disable it when the file is playing, and enable it when the program is ready to play the next file. This is done with the **Enable** property of the button. The format of the Enable property statement is

```
object.Enabled [= boolean]
```

where **object** is the object that is being enabled or disabled and the **boolean** referred to is either **True** to enable the object or **False** to disable the object. Thus, the statement in the Done event should be

```
mmcPlay.Enabled = True
```

to turn the button on.

Then, in the button routine, you need to turn the button off and you need to find the name of the next file to be played. To do this, you don't need the entire form of the Dir function; you need only the function name itself. The statement you need is

```
mmcPlay.filename = "C:\Windows\Media\" & Dir
```

Add to this all the rest of the statements needed to play a file, and your program should be ready. Save the program as **Folder Sounds** and thoroughly test it. When satisfied, print all the elements.

The Code Window and More Code

3.1   Chapter Objectives

After finishing this chapter you will be able to:

- Show how to split the code window.
- Explain how to use the search and replace feature of the code window.
- Demonstrate how to use the Immediate window.
- Describe scope and how it affects the programs.
- Demonstrate how to use the various string-handling functions in your programs.
- Demonstrate how to use the Label control in your programs.

3.2   Introduction

In the last chapter, you learned how to enter code for an object into the code window. You also saw how you can copy code from the window to the clipboard so that it can be pasted back using the same or a different procedure. Additional manipulation techniques are available in the code window to help you, and after a brief look at how a Visual Basic program is structured, we will examine them.

When you can handle the code window better, we will look at a variety of Visual Basic commands that will prove useful for your future applications. You will also learn how to use the Label control on your form and how to use the Immediate window to help you debug your programs.

FIGURE 3.1
Illustration of the elements of a Visual Basic program.

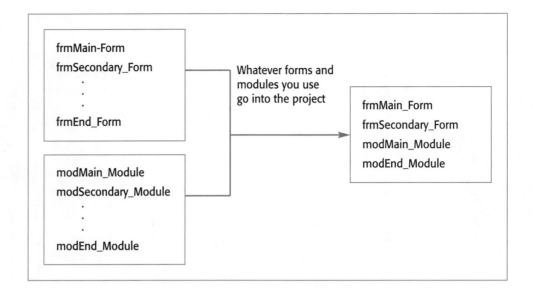

3.3   Understanding Projects

Before we delve more deeply into the coding of a Visual Basic program, it is important that you understand the actual structure of a Visual Basic program. A program is made up of two different types of elements: forms and modules. We have already discussed and used forms. A **module** is a special window where you can only place declarations and code. A module, unlike a form, includes no visual elements, only code.

A project can be composed of any number of forms and modules, but because one module can contain all the global procedures and variables that are necessary for a project, it is generally not necessary to use more than one module. Suppose, however, that you are part of a group of programmers creating a complicated program. You may use a module for your part of the program, and some of the other programmers may use different modules for their parts. When the program segments are combined into one program, it will have several modules. Also, there may be instances where you want to use several modules in your programs to keep various program elements separate. Suppose, for example, you have a program that displays bar charts and you put your bar chart routines into a module. Now you decide to add to your program routines to display pie charts. It might be less confusing to put the pie chart procedures into another module rather than incorporating them into the module that contains the bar chart procedures.

Given all this, the structure of a Visual Basic program may be pictured as shown in Figure 3.1.

3.4   More About the Code Window

You learned how to call up the code window in the last chapter. To learn more about how to use the code window, we need an application that has code we can use. Let's use the code in the Clicking Practice application that we created in Chapter 2. Before we do this, let's create a new project called Clicking Practice Update in the Ch-3 folder so that we don't inadvertently erase the original Clicking Practice project by saving our changes.

1. Get into Visual Basic, put your work disk in drive A, and open the Clicking Practice application found in the Ch-2 folder.

2. Using the **Save File As...** option on the **File** menu, save the form as **frmClicking_Practice** (the original name) in the Ch-3 folder, and then save the project (using the **Save Project As...** option on the **File** menu) as **Clicking Practice Update** in the Ch-3 folder. Again, this is simply a safety precaution.

3. Put the form on the workspace and open the code window for the **Message 1** button.

As you practice changing the code in the next few sections, be careful not to save the program. If you do, whatever changes you have made to the code will be saved, and you may end up with a program that will no longer function. If you do happen to save it inadvertently, you can always go back to the version saved in the Ch-2 folder.

Splitting the Window

The code window can be divided into two separate windows with the same or a different procedure in each window.

HINT: In this chapter and the rest of the book, we will seldom show all the elements of the Visual Basic system in our illustrations, but rather will show only the part of the screen we are currently discussing. This is done to conserve space and to help you see exactly what part of the screen is our current focus.

1. Move the cursor to the split bar as shown in Figure 3.2, and the mouse pointer will change shape to (↕) to indicate that the bar can be moved.

FIGURE 3.2
The code window showing the split bar.

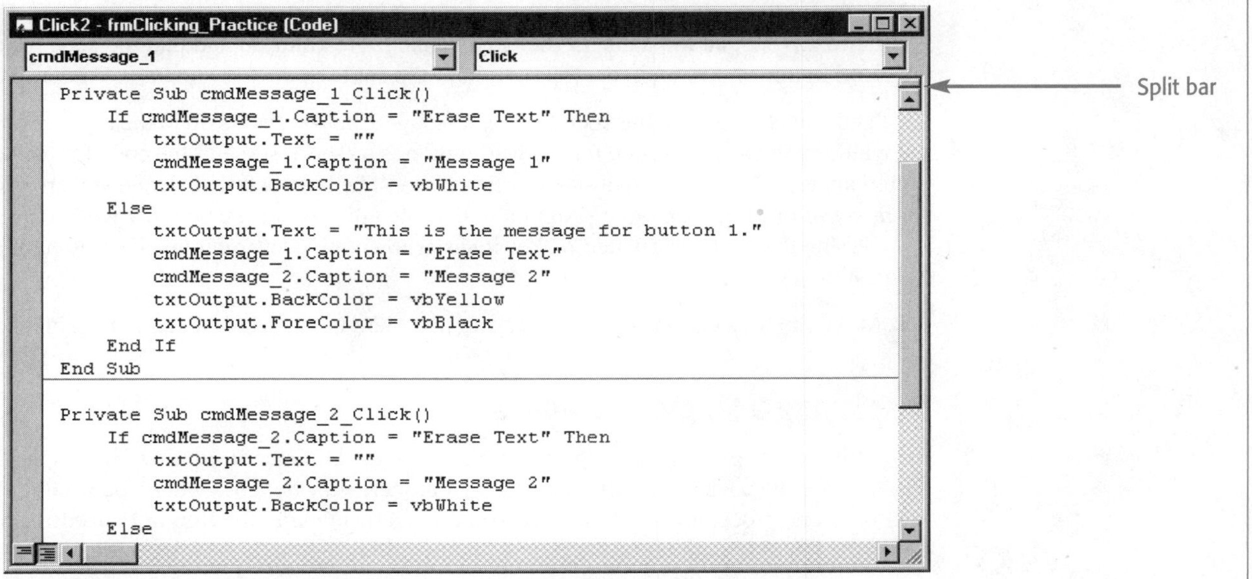

```
Click2 - frmClicking_Practice (Code)                          _ □ ×

cmdMessage_1              ▼      Click                    ▼

Private Sub cmdMessage_1_Click()                              ▲   ◄────  Split bar
    If cmdMessage_1.Caption = "Erase Text" Then
        txtOutput.Text = ""
        cmdMessage_1.Caption = "Message 1"
        txtOutput.BackColor = vbWhite
    Else
        txtOutput.Text = "This is the message for button 1."
        cmdMessage_1.Caption = "Erase Text"
        cmdMessage_2.Caption = "Message 2"
        txtOutput.BackColor = vbYellow
        txtOutput.ForeColor = vbBlack
    End If
End Sub

Private Sub cmdMessage_2_Click()
    If cmdMessage_2.Caption = "Erase Text" Then
        txtOutput.Text = ""
        cmdMessage_2.Caption = "Message 2"
        txtOutput.BackColor = vbWhite
    Else                                                     ▼
```

FIGURE 3.3
The divided window, showing different code sections in each window section.

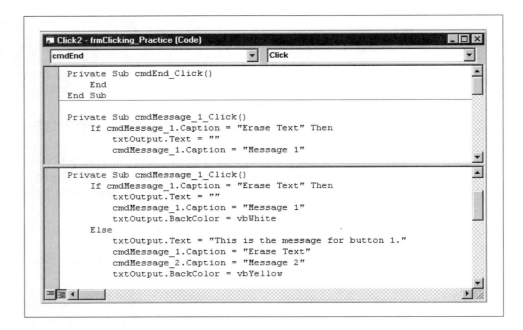

```
Click2 - frmClicking_Practice (Code)

cmdEnd                              Click

        Private Sub cmdEnd_Click()
            End
        End Sub

        Private Sub cmdMessage_1_Click()
            If cmdMessage_1.Caption = "Erase Text" Then
                txtOutput.Text = ""
                cmdMessage_1.Caption = "Message 1"

        Private Sub cmdMessage_1_Click()
            If cmdMessage_1.Caption = "Erase Text" Then
                txtOutput.Text = ""
                cmdMessage_1.Caption = "Message 1"
                txtOutput.BackColor = vbWhite
            Else
                txtOutput.Text = "This is the message for button 1."
                cmdMessage_1.Caption = "Erase Text"
                cmdMessage_2.Caption = "Message 2"
                txtOutput.BackColor = vbYellow
```

2. Drag the bar down, and a gray bar will indicate how far down you have moved the bar.

3. Release the mouse button when you have moved the bar down approximately to the middle of the window.

Now there are two separate sections of the window. Each section can contain a different part of one procedure, or each section can contain a different procedure.

You may be wondering why you would need to split the window when most, if not all, of your code from the various procedures can already be seen in the code window. As you learn more, your program will get larger. Soon the code for one procedure may fill the entire code window. And so, to see the code for two procedures at the same time, you will need to split the window.

4. In the code window, click in the top section. Then, on the form, double-click the **End** button. Note that the name of the object changes to cmdEnd and that the code for the **End** button shows up in the top portion of the split window as shown in Figure 3.3.

You can also see that the code for the **Message 1** button shows up in the top section of the window. Because the code for the **End** button is so short, some of the code for the next button appears. But as we mentioned earlier, it won't be long before the code you are using for many of the objects in your program will exceed the size of the window workspace.

Having the window divided makes it easier to copy code from one object to another. You can practice this on your own.

5. Move the split bar back up to the top so that there is one window section again.

Displaying a Single Procedure

Currently, the display is showing multiple procedures in the code window. It is generally easier to use the code window in this format, but there may be times when you want to display only one procedure at a time. You can do this by clicking the **Single Procedure** button in the lower left corner of the code window as indicated in Figure 3.4.

1. Click the **Single Procedure** button to see one procedure in the workspace as shown in Figure 3.4.

FIGURE 3.4

The code window, showing one procedure in the workspace.

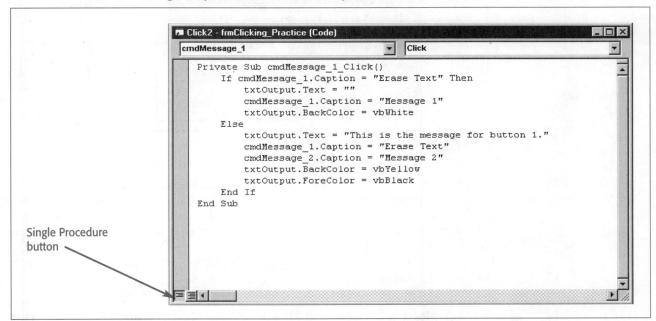

Single Procedure
button

2. Click the **Multiple Procedure** button just to the right of the other button to see the multiple procedure display again.

3. Switch back and forth a few times. Try it with a split window, too. When you are thoroughly familiar with the way it works, switch the window back to the multiple procedure display mode and one workspace (not split).

Searching

As your programs get longer, there may be occasions when you want to examine certain entries but are not sure where all those entries are in the code. For example, suppose you are using an object and then decide to change the name of that object. You will need to be sure you change all instances of the object name, or your code will have errors. In such a case, using the search techniques of the code window can be of value.

There are two ways to conduct a search. You can just let Visual Basic find all instances for which you are searching, or you can have Visual Basic find the instances and then replace all or only some of the entries with something else. We will explore each of these techniques.

We will begin by looking at the **Find...** option on the **Edit** menu.

1. Move the insertion point to the top of the code.

2. Pull down the **Edit** menu and select **Find...** (shortcut key **Ctrl-F**) to see the dialog box shown in Figure 3.5.

The first thing you should notice in this dialog box is the entry box, where you define your Visual Basic search. Then you can decide how much of the available code you want to look through to find your entry. You can search through just the text you have selected. This is the last option of the four and is disabled because you have not selected any text. You can search in just the Current Procedure, and Visual Basic will find your entry only in the current object code. You can search in the Current Module, which means Visual Basic will search in the code of all the objects on the current form or in the current module.

FIGURE 3.5

The **Find...** dialog box.

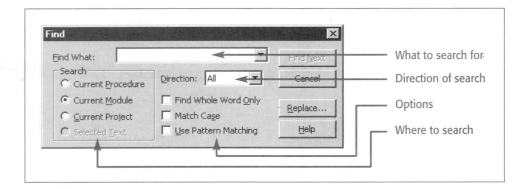

Current Project allows Visual Basic to search through the entire program. Remember that you can have multiple forms in one program (we will explore how to do this in a later chapter). You can also have more than one project loaded into Visual Basic at the same time. That's why the window specifies Current Project instead of something like Entire Project or All Modules.

The **Replace...** button allows you to switch directly to the **Replace...** dialog box (discussed in the next section).

Because we have so little code, let's search in the entire module.

3. Key **Message**, click **Current Module**, and press **Enter**, which will select the **Find Next** button.

Instantly Visual Basic will shift focus to the code window, and the first instance of "Message" will be highlighted as shown in Figure 3.6. If this is not the instance you were looking for, you can have the program go on to the next (or the previous) one.

4. Click **Find Next** again and Visual Basic will highlight the next instance of "Message."

5. Click **Find Next** several more times to see how this works.

The **Find...** dialog box has a list of directions that can be searched. If you pull down the list, you can choose among All, Up, and Down.

6. Pull down the Direction list and select Up. Then click the **Find Next** button to highlight the previous instance of "Message."

7. Press the **Find Next** button several times until the search loops back around to the top of the procedure.

Note that there are three options available for you to refine the way you want your search carried out. First, there is the **Find Whole Words Only** option. When this is on, it tells Visual Basic to find only whole words. This avoids finding the search word in other words. For example, in your search for "Message," you noticed that "Message" was found within object names such as "cmdMessage_1." If you had used the **Find Whole Words Only** option, the "cmdMessage_1" entry would have been skipped. To see how this works, let's tell the program to search for "is" with the **Find Whole Words Only** option on.

8. Click **Find Whole Words Only**, key **is** for the search word, and select **Find Next**.

The first instance of "is" that the program found followed immediately after "This," which has "is" as part of "This." "This," however, was skipped because we used the **Find Whole Words Only** option and the character string "is" is only a portion of the character string "This" (see Figure 3.7).

9. Click the **Find Next** button a few times until you are satisfied.

The second option is **Match Case**. Normally you will want to ignore the case of the characters so that you can find "MESSAGE," "MeSSage," and "Message" when searching

FIGURE 3.6
The searched-for word is found in the code.

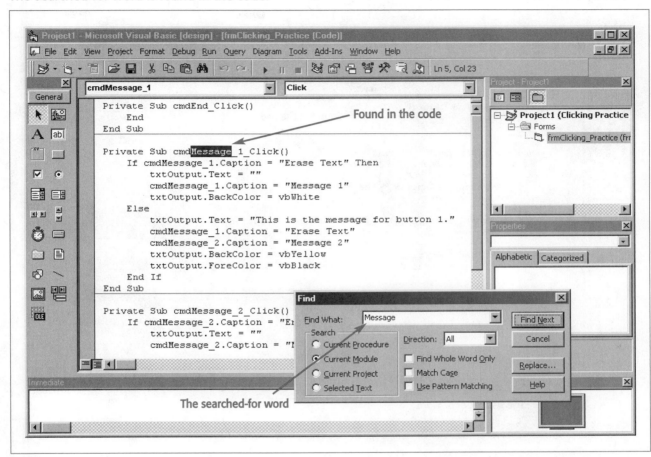

for "message." There may be times, however, when you want to search for something that is case-specific. When you do, you can turn on **Match Case** option.

The third option is **Use Pattern Matching**, which allows you to search for a wide variety of different pattern types rather than looking for a particular entry. To match a pattern, you use what are called **metacharacters.** These metacharacters are used as follows:

* * is a **multiple-character wildcard** that matches zero or more characters. For example, the pattern a*a matches aa, A3a, aBa, and aBbBA.

* ? is a **single-character wildcard** that matches any one character. For example, the pattern a?a matches aaa, a3a, and aBA, but not aBBBa.

* # is a **numeric wildcard** that matches any one character 0 through 9. For example, the pattern a#a matches a0a, a1a, and a2a, but not aaa nor a10a.

* [class] is a **character class** that matches any one character in the given class. Classes are generally specified with ranges, which can be specified by separating starting and ending characters with a hyphen. The class must be surrounded by square brackets. For example, [n-z] matches any alphabetic characters from n through z, but not those from a through m. Because the pattern matching is not case-sensitive, n-z works for both lowercase and uppercase letters.

A class can contain multiple clauses, each separated by a comma. Each clause can consist of a single character or a range of characters. For example,

FIGURE 3.7
The results of the first search for "is".

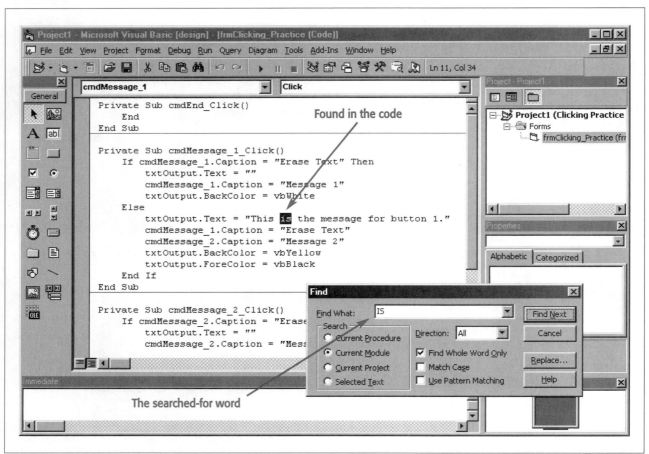

[*,T-Z,0-9] matches asterisks, any letters from t through z (case of the characters is ignored), and all numbers. As the example shows, to search for the metacharacters, *, ?, or #, you must search for them as a case by enclosing them in square brackets.

If you use a tilde (~) in front of the class, which is the only place where it's allowed, it reverses the class test. For example, [~a-z] matches anything but letters; [~0-9] matches anything but numbers.

Let's try a couple of samples.

10. Move the cursor to the top of the code window (you can use **Ctrl-Home** or use the mouse) and then key **U*O** into the Find What entry box.

11. Click the **Find Whole Words Only** option to turn it off. If you leave it on while searching for a pattern, most of the time you won't find what you want because it is unlikely that your pattern stands alone.

12. Click the **Use Pattern Matching** option and then the **Find Next** button.

The first pattern that is found is "utput.BackCo" in "txtOutput.BackColor = vbWhite" (see Figure 3.8). Note that this selection begins with "u" and ends with "o."

13. Click the **Find Next** button twice more.

The program found "utto" within "button."
Let's try a different pattern.

FIGURE 3.8

The results of the pattern-matching search.

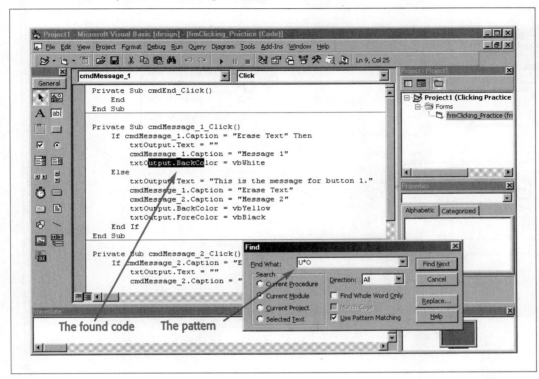

14. Move the cursor to the top of the code listings and then highlight the current pattern, key **[F–H,=]**, and press **Enter**.

This pattern will search for all letters F through H inclusive and equals signs. Note that it stopped on the "g" in cmdMessage_1_Click (Figure 3.9).

15. Click the **Find Next** button, and the program will stop on the "f" in "If".

16. Click the **Find Next** button twice, and the search will find the equals sign.

17. Continue to click the **Find Next** button until you are satisfied that you understand exactly how the [F–H,=] case works.

18. Practice the search techniques a few more times, using search patterns of your own design, until you are thoroughly comfortable with the procedure. Be sure to use each of the metacharacter and case techniques at least once. Turn off the **Pattern Matching** option before you exit the dialog box.

Replacing

If you ever need to change the name of an object in a program on which you have been working for a while, you will quickly understand the importance of the **Replace...** option, which allows you to replace one entry with another.

1. Move the insertion point to the top of the code in the code window, and then pull down the **Edit** menu and select **Replace...** (shortcut key **Ctrl-H**) to see the dialog box shown in Figure 3.10.

In this dialog box, you will see an extra text entry box for entering the text you want to Replace With. As we mentioned previously, on the Find dialog box there is a **Replace**

FIGURE 3.9
The results of the [F-H,=] pattern search.

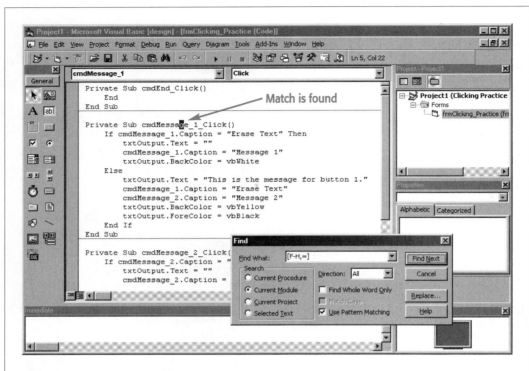

FIGURE 3.10
The **Replace**... dialog box.

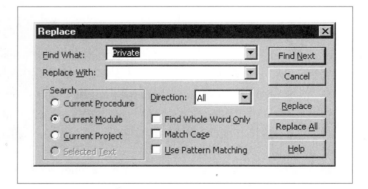

button, but it simply takes you from the Find dialog box to this dialog box. On this dialog box, the **Replace** button actually replaces data. The text you key into the Find What text box is searched for when you select the **Find Next** button. If it is found and you select the **Replace** button, the text in the Replace With text box replaces the found text. Then the searching begins again automatically without the need to select the **Find Next** button again. Now, if you want to search for and replace all instances, you can use the **Replace All** button. This will search and replace throughout the selected area without prompting you for each replacement.

2. Key **Caption** in the Find What entry box and press **Tab**.

3. Key **XXX** in the Replace With entry box and press **Enter**.

Instantly the program will locate "Caption," and the program will wait for you to tell it what to do (Figure 3.11). If you want to replace the entry, you select the **Replace** but-

FIGURE 3.11
The code found using Replace.

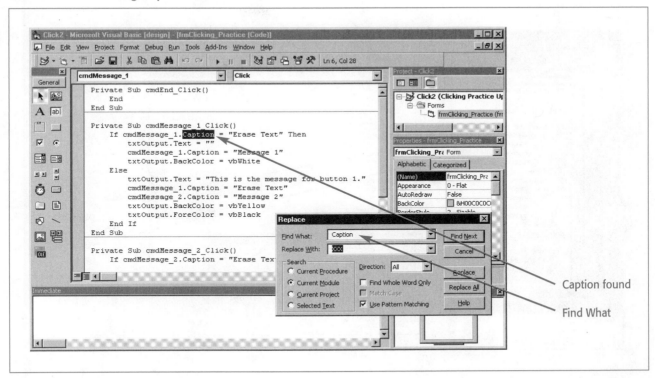

ton. If not, you select the **Find Next** button to let the program look for the next instance of "Caption."

4. Click the **Replace** button, and Visual Basic will move on to the next instance of "Caption," leaving "XXX" where the first instance was found, as shown in Figure 3.12.

Note that Visual Basic did not tell you that there was anything wrong with the statement, even though there is no XXX property. The Replace function doesn't do any syntax checking as it does its replacements.

5. Click the **Find Next** button, and this instance of "Caption" will be left as is.

As we have said, if you want to replace all instances of the search word without being prompted, you can use the **Replace All** button.

6. Click the **Replace All** button, and a confirmation dialog box (Figure 3.13) will appear after all the replacements are finished.

Note that all "Caption" properties are now "XXX."

7. Click the **OK** button to exit from the confirmation dialog box, and then click the **Cancel** button on the Replace dialog box.

8. Execute the program and select the **Message 1** button. The error dialog box shown in Figure 3.14 appears.

Note that Visual Basic also highlights the property with which it has a problem. It will always stop on the line with the error and highlight it so that you will know exactly which statement is in error.

9. Exit your program and then, before you continue, try a few more replacements using a variety of entries and patterns. Be sure not to save the program, or the manipulations you make to the code will be stored and the program will no longer function properly.

FIGURE 3.12
The replacement of "Caption" with "XXX."

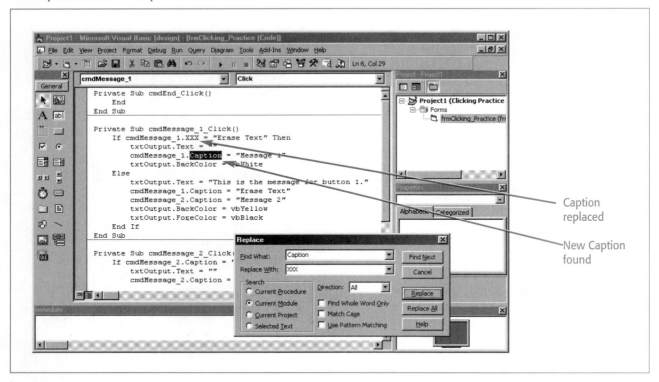

Caption replaced

New Caption found

FIGURE 3.13
The confirmation box that appears after the replacing is finished.

FIGURE 3.14
The error that appears because there is no XXX property.

3.5 Using the Immediate Window

Now that we have explored how to use the code window, it is time to examine another window that can prove useful. At the bottom of the Visual Basic environment window is the **Immediate window** (see Figure 3.15). It is called that because whatever code you key into the Immediate window is executed immediately. In order to see how you can use this window, you will reload the program you were just editing.

1. Reload the Clicking Practice Update program by exiting Visual Basic without saving the current version.

2. Run the program and select the **Message 1** button.

To use the Immediate window to explore values in the program, you don't have to exit the program. All you need to do is pause it. You can do this in several ways. Probably the easiest is to click the Break icon (▮▮) on the tool bar.

FIGURE 3.15
The Immediate window.

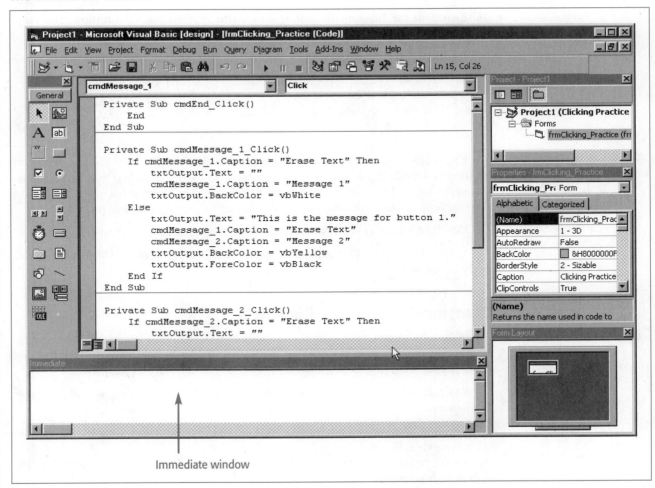

Immediate window

FIGURE 3.16
The Immediate window, showing the result of the Print command.

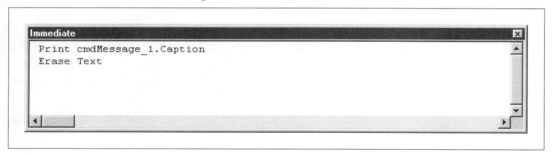

3. Click the Break icon (▮▮) on the tool bar.

Nothing much seems to happen, except that the break icon is now disabled and the run icon is enabled. More important, however, you can now use the Immediate window. If you had tried to print the caption for the **Message 1** button before you ran the program, you would have received an error message. Visual Basic wouldn't have known what the button was. Also, if you had tried to enter a command in the Immediate window before pausing the program, Visual Basic would have simply beeped at you, letting you know the window was not available.

4. Switch to the Immediate window, key **Print cmdMessage_1.Caption**, and press **Enter**. This is a command to Visual Basic to display the button caption.

> **HINT:** If the Immediate window is not showing, press **Ctrl-G** and it will appear. The question mark is a shortcut for the Print command, so the previous command could have been entered as **?cmdMessage_1.Caption**.

You will see that the caption is "Erase Text" as shown in Figure 3.16. The caption of the form is indeed "Erase Text" (but you probably knew that already). You have just displayed the value of the caption of the button. You can display the value of any element of a Visual Basic program that has an actual value, including variables and properties.

5. Key **?txtOutput.Text** and press **Enter** (remember that ? means Print).

This will give you "This is the message for button 1." as a result. This is what is currently stored in the text box.

Changing Values During Runtime

One of the most important functions you can perform using the Immediate window is changing values while the program is running. This can be invaluable when you are trying to find errors in your programs. To see how this works, we will try a small example.

1. Key **txtOutput.Text = "This is a sample."** in the Immediate window, and then press **Enter**.

Now look at the program form. Note that the text box has "This is a sample." displayed in it as shown in Figure 3.17.

This same technique can be used to change the value of any variable or property being used in your program.

FIGURE 3.17
The results of the
assignment statement
executed in the
Immediate window.

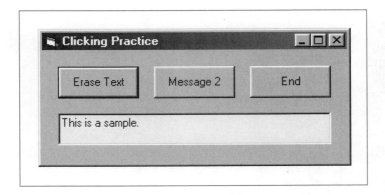

2. Key **cmdMessage_1.Caption = "Sample Caption."** and press **Enter** to see the caption of the button change (Figure 3.18).

Note that the caption appears on the button on two lines. This is because the caption is too long to fit across the button. This is easily fixed by increasing the width of the button, which can also be done using the Immediate window. Before we change the width, however, let's see what the width is currently.

3. Key **?cmdMessage_1.Width** and press **Enter**.

This will give you 1215, the current width of the button. Because we don't know how wide we will need to make the window to accommodate the new size of the caption, let's try adding just 100 twips.

4. Key **cmdMessage_1.Width = 1315** and press **Enter**.

The caption is still on two lines, and though the button is actually wider than it was, you probably cannot tell; 100 twips is only a small amount. Of course, you could continually try new, slightly greater width values, but let's just pick a size that will work.

5. Key **cmdMessage_1.Width = 1615** and press **Enter** to see the results as shown in Figure 3.19.

Now the caption shows up on one line, but the button is too wide because it overlaps the **Message 2** button. If we needed the caption to be able to display "Sample Caption," we would have to reposition the buttons on the form and change the size of the form (which can also be changed by using the Immediate window, because its Width property is the same type of property as the width property of the button). But we are just practicing, so rearranging our objects is not necessary.

FIGURE 3.18
The result of the new
assignment statement.

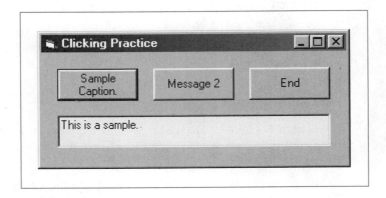

FIGURE 3.19
The button is now
wider because of the
assignment statement.

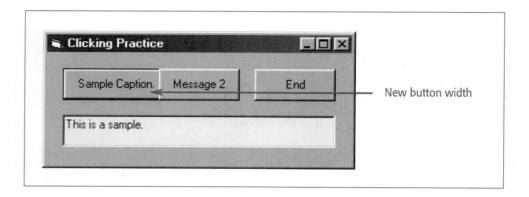

FIGURE 3.20
The digit to change
from 6 to 2.

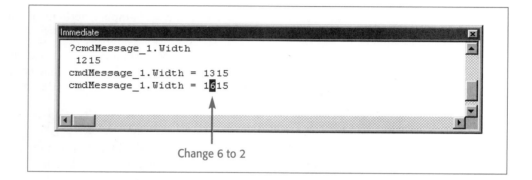

Remember that you can reuse any of the code in the Immediate window by simply clicking the line in the window and pressing **Enter.** This can be handy when you need to redo an Immediate window command that you have used previously. You can also change any keyed information currently in the window. For example, rather than keying the command **cmdMessage_1.Width = 1215** to change the width of the button back to what it was, you can position the insertion point on the 6 in the command **cmdMessage_1.Width = 1615** and change the 6 to a 2.

6. Position the insertion point on the 6 in the command **cmdMessage_1.Width = 1615,** press **Del**, key **2**, and press **Enter** (Figure 3.20).

This changes the width of the button back to what it was.

It is important to realize that any changes you make to variable or property values using the Immediate window are not permanent changes. If the program has a statement in it that changes the value you just changed in the Immediate window, the value will indeed change.

7. Press **F5** to restart the program and click the **Message 2** button.

Note that the caption of the **Message 1** button is now Message 1 again. Thus, the program still functions as it is supposed to, and whatever value changes it is supposed to make will continue to be done.

Using the Debug.Print Statement

If you need to observe value changes while the program is running, you can make the program display values in the Immediate window automatically. This is done with the **Debug.Print** statement.

1. Pause the program, highlight all the text in the Immediate window, and delete it. This will allow you to see just what your Debug.Print statement will be displaying for you.

2. Position the insertion point at the end of the End If statement in the **cmdMessage_1_Click** procedure, press **Enter** to create a new line, and key **Debug.Print cmdMessage_1.Caption**.

3. Run the program and click the **Message 1** button.

Note that the button caption "Erase Text" shows up in the Immediate window as shown in Figure 3.21.

You can use multiple Debug.Print statements in your program. Anywhere it might be useful to display the value of a program object, you can use a Debug.Print statement. Unfortunately, if you use a lot of them and you are displaying similar values with some of them, the output in the Immediate window can quickly become confusing. This defeats the purpose of the Debug.Print statements. They are supposed to help you determine why your program is not functioning properly. They are not supposed to make the job more difficult by displaying too much similar information in the window. For example, suppose you are displaying the values of the captions of both of your message buttons in the Immediate window. When the value is Message 1 or Message 2, you can tell which of the procedures is displaying in the window, but when the value is Erase Text, the value could have come from either button procedure.

A good technique to help you determine which value is being displayed in the Immediate window is to print the name of the element for which you are displaying the value.

4. Pause the program, position the insertion point at the end of the End If statement in the cmdMessage_2_Click procedure, and press **Enter** to create a new line.

5. Key **Debug.Print "cmdMessage_2.Caption = "; cmdMessage_2.Caption**.

Note that you use the name of the property twice: once in quotes, which makes it a literal so it will display exactly that way when the Debug.Print statement executes, and once to get the actual value of the caption.

6. Run the program, and click the **Message 2** button to see the output shown in Figure 3.22.

FIGURE 3.21
The Immediate window, showing the result of the Debug.Print statement.

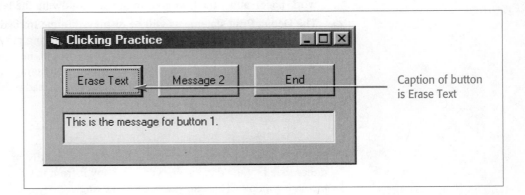

Caption of button is Erase Text

FIGURE 3.22
The output from the second Debug.Print statement.

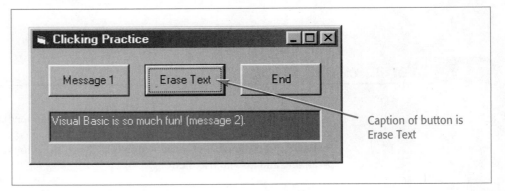

Caption of button is Erase Text

Now the Immediate window will have the name of the property followed by the value. When you use this technique, there is never any confusion about what value is being displayed. There is, however, the possibility that you may want to print the value of a property or variable in several places in a procedure so that you can follow how the value changes as the procedure is executed. If you do this, which statement is being shown at any one time can again become confusing. There are various ways to prevent this. One is simply to number the statements in some manner, such as

```
Debug.Print "1. cmdMessage_2.Caption = "; cmdMessage_2.Caption
```

and

```
Debug.Print "2. cmdMessage_2.Caption = "; cmdMessage_2.Caption
```

This is only one technique. You may find some other method of identifying your statements that better suits your needs.

Additional Tips for Use of the Immediate Window

You have seen how the Immediate window can be useful. There are a few more helpful things to know about this window.

- You should use the cursor control keys or the mouse to move around in the Immediate window, reserving the use of the **Enter** key for executing the statements.

- The Immediate window can be scrolled like any other window to retrieve previously used statements or simply to look at results that have been scrolled off the workspace.

- The cursor controls work in the Immediate window the same way they work in the code window. For example, **Home** goes to the beginning of the line, **End** goes to the end of the line, **Ctrl-Home** goes to the first line in the window (not in the workspace), and **Ctrl-End** goes to the line following the last displayed line.

- The Debug.Print statements will be displayed in the Immediate window wherever the insertion point currently is. If you have been exploring previous statements or results in the window, you will probably want to reposition the cursor at the end of the displayed information in the window before re-executing your program. That way, any new results will be displayed at the bottom instead of being interspersed in the previous information.

> **HINT:** If you need to display something that is lengthy in the Immediate window, rather than key the data again, you can copy it from the code and paste it in the Immediate window. This can save a lot of keying.

3.6 Variables and Scope

Now that you know the ins and outs of the code and Immediate windows, it's time to explore some important Visual Basic coding techniques. Because much of programming revolves around the use of variables, we will begin by looking at the types of variables available and how to use them.

Types of Variables

We briefly discussed variables in the previous chapter. It is now time to add to that discussion.

We mentioned that there are various types of variables and that type can be specified by using a special character placed on the end of the variable name or by declaring the variable to be a certain type. When you declare the variable type, you do not have to use a type-indicator character.

Before we discuss how to declare variables, let's look at the types of variables available. Table 3.1 gives the type name; the standard prefix used (such as int for integer and str for string); a description of the variable, including how many bytes the variable requires to be stored; the type-indicator character (if any); and the range of values that can be stored in the variable. The Object variable type contains an object reference rather than an actual value. *Objects,* in this case, does not refer to objects such as buttons and text boxes. Declared objects are very different and are beyond the scope of this discussion.

TABLE 3.1
The types of Visual Basic variables.

Type	Type Abbreviation	Description	Type Indicator	Range
Integer	int	Two-byte integer	%	–32,768 to 32,767
Long	lng	Four-byte integer	&	–2,147,483,648 to 2,147,483,647
Single	sng	Four-byte floating-point	! (or none)	–3.37E+38 to 3.37E+38
Double	dbl	Eight-byte floating-point	#	–1.67E+308 to 1.67E+308
Currency	cur	Eight-byte fixed decimal of four digits	@	–9.22E+14 to 9.22E+14
String	str	Fixed length: 1 byte per character; variable length: 10 bytes plus 1 byte per character	$	Fixed length: 0 to 65,500 characters; variable length: 0 to 2 billion characters
Variant	vnt	Any variable type	(none)	Date values from Jan 1, 0000 to Dec. 31, 9999; numeric values are same range as for Double variables; string values are same range as for String variables
Boolean	bln	Two-byte	(none)	True or False
Byte	byt	One-byte	(none)	0-255
Date	dtm	Eight-byte floating-point	(none)	Date values from Jan 1, 0000 to Dec. 31, 9999; times from 0:00:00 to 23:59:59

The table specifies the range of values that can be stored in each variable type and the amount of memory required for that storage. For example, an **Integer** variable and a **Long** (integer) variable both store **integer** values, or those without decimals, but the Long variable can store a larger value than an Integer variable and requires more memory for that storage. In order to write efficient programs that conserve the valuable resources of the computer, you need to use the proper variable for the purpose. If you need to store a person's age, a value that will never exceed three digits, there is no needed to use a Long variable when an Integer variable will hold the value just fine. But if you need to store the population of a large city, the 32,767 limit of an Integer variable would fall far short of the maximum value you would need, so a Long variable would be your only option.

The **Single** and **Double** variables are used to store **floating-point numbers,** or numbers that have a decimal point with an unspecified number of decimal positions. Floating-point numbers are used to store extremely large or extremely small numbers that are generally represented in **exponential notation,** which is similar to the **scientific notation** with which you may be more familiar. Exponential notation indicates the number and how many decimal positions it requires. Thus, 156,000, would be represented as 1.56E5, which would be 1.56×10^5 in scientific notation. The E5 (10^5) represents the five positions that would be generated if you multiplied 1.56 by 10^5, or 10,000. You many also view this as moving the decimal point the specified number of positions to the right. Starting with 1.56 and moving the decimal point five positions to the right gives you the number 156,000.

Floating-point numbers can also have a negative number between the E and the following number, as in 1.56E–5. This time, instead of moving the decimal to the right, you need to move the decimal five places to the left, or divide 1.56 by 10^5. This yields the number .0000156.

Either Single or Double variables can be used to store floating-point values. The difference is in the range of the number that can be stored in each. Double variables have twice the amount of storage for the number, so they can store values much larger and much smaller than can Single variables. Again, you should determine the type of data you need to store and choose the type of variable that is appropriate.

The **Currency** data type stores numbers with a fixed decimal point of four positions. Currency is generally used in calculations involving money. Floating-point numbers can sometimes be subject to small rounding errors, and when you are doing financial calculations, it is important that everything be totally accurate. When doing such calculations, use the Currency data type.

A **String** variable is used to store textual data. It can store from 0 to approximately 2 billion characters. The amount of storage used is not fixed. It is automatically adjusted as the data are placed there.

A **Boolean** variable is used to store the Boolean values True and False. If you need a variable in your program that should be either true or false, you can use a Boolean variable so that you can test for True or False. This can make your programs easier to interpret.

The **Date** variable is used to store dates and times. There are several date functions in Visual Basic that can help you determine, among other things, the number of days between two dates.

The **Byte** variable can be used to store a one-character value. This can save a tremendous amount of storage under certain conditions. If you have numbers that cannot be any larger than 255, they can be stored as Bytes. A Byte variable requires only one byte of storage, whereas an Integer variable requires two bytes. Thus, if the integer values you need in your program will never be larger than 255, you can halve your storage requirements by using Byte variables rather than Integers.

We mentioned **Variant** variables in the previous chapter and would like to reiterate that your use of Variants should be limited. Visual Basic automatically determines the type of storage a Variant requires, but that determination is not always the most efficient. Also, the program takes extra execution time (albeit a small amount) to make that determination every time the variant is referenced. Unless there is some overriding reason why you need to use a Variant variable, you should always use a defined type.

Naming Variables

In addition to using standard prefixes, there are a few other rules about the names of your variables. We briefly covered these rules in the previous chapter, but they are important enough to discuss in more depth. Keep in mind that we are discussing naming variables, but the same rules apply to naming controls.

- They must begin with a letter. If you are using the standard prefixes, this is not a problem because the prefixes are letters. A variable name such as 19Amount is not allowed.
- The name can contain only letters, numbers, and the underscore. No punctuation characters or spaces are allowed. "intAmount Input" is not a valid variable name because of the space. It should be changed to "intAmount_Input" using the underscore. Likewise, "intAmount-Input" is not allowed because of the dash.
- The name cannot be more than 255 characters long.
- The name cannot be a reserved Visual Basic word such as Sub, because these words have special meaning to Visual Basic.

> **HINT:** Visual Basic does not require that you use the standard prefixes. It is just a very good idea and is highly recommended.

Your variable names should be related to the variables' purposes. If you are using a variable as a counter, call it something like intCounter instead of intA. If the variable is used to calculate a total, a good choice might be intTotal, intSub_Total, or intGrand_Total.

Types of Declarations

A variable can be declared in two different ways: implicitly and explicitly.

Implicit Declarations   *Implicit declaration* simply means that the variable is defined when it is used. For example, you can use a statement such as

```
strTemp_Text = txtOutput_Text.Text
```

If strTemp_Text had not been previously declared, Visual Basic would automatically create a variable called strTemp_Text. It would default to Variant type (which means it would have the wrong prefix—str instead of vnt) and would contain a copy of the text found in the txtOutput_Text text box. Although it is convenient to allow Visual Basic to declare variables for you, this practice can lead to problems. Suppose, for example, your procedure using the above statement needed to have code such as the following:

```
Sub cmdButton_1_Click ()
    strTemp_Text = txtOutput_Text.Text
    txtOutput_Text.Text = ""
    txtText_Out.Text = strTem_Text
End Sub
```

On the surface, it looks as if this code takes the text out of the txtOutput_Text text box, saves it in strTemp_Text, erases the text out of txtOutput_Text.Text, and then assigns the saved text into the txtText_Out text box. But look closely. On the txtText_Out.Text line, strTemp_Text is misspelled (strTem_Text). This code, then, would always assign an empty string to txtText_Out.Text because strTem_Text has no value assigned to it.

The Option Explicit Statement   To avoid this type of problem, Visual Basic gives you a special **Option Explicit** statement. When this statement is used in a module, every variable must be explicitly declared or an error will occur when the program is executed. The Option Explicit statement affects only the specific module or form in which it is located. Because this is the case, and because you will probably want to use the statement in every module and form, Visual Basic has a way to add the statement automatically to every form and module. Let's see how to set this up and how the Option Explicit statement can help us.

1. Pull down the **Tools** menu and select the **Options...** option to see the dialog box shown in Figure 3.23. Your dialog box will probably open with the Editor tab selected, as shown in Figure 3.23, but if it doesn't, click the Editor tab.

2. Click the **Require Variable Declaration** option to turn it on (if it is already on, be sure not to turn it off) and select **OK**.

   This option will stay set until you turn it off.

3. Pull down the **File** menu and select **New Project**. When Visual Basic asks whether you want to save the changes to the Clicking Practice Update project, select **No** and then select **OK** on the New Project dialog box.

   There is only one form in this program, but Visual Basic has already added the Option Explicit statement to it.

4. Call up the code window for the form, and you see the Option Explicit statement that was automatically added to the declarations in the procedure just above the Form_Load procedure.

   Now let's see what happens if we implicitly declare a variable.

5. In the Form_Load procedure, key **intAmount = 5** as the only code in the procedure.

   Because you have not explicitly declared intAmount, it is being implicitly declared, and Visual Basic should give you an error.

FIGURE 3.23
The Options dialog box,
showing the Editor tab.

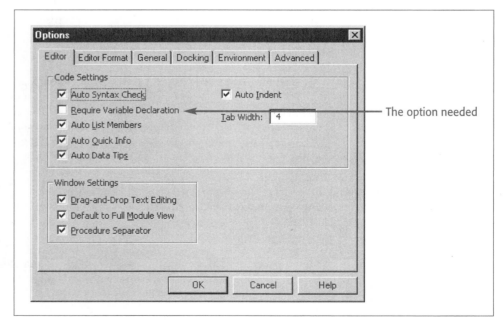

6. Run the program, and the error shown in Figure 3.24 will appear.

Every variable you now use in your program must be explicitly declared, or you will continue to get this error.

7. Click the **OK** button to respond to the error.

Explicit Declarations Now that we have set our program up so that we will have to explicitly declare our variables, it is time to see just how to do that.

There are five different ways in which a variable can be declared: **Dim**, **Static**, **Public**, **Private**, and **Global**.

The simplified version of the format for a Dim declaration statement is

```
Dim varname As type
```

Here, *varname* refers to the name of the variable you are declaring, and *type* is the type of variable you are declaring it to be.

The formats of the Static, Public, Private, and Global statements are the same except for the declaration command itself.

If you declare a variable in a procedure, it must be declared with either Dim or Static, and both types are **local** to the procedure. This is referred to as the **scope** of the variable. Local scope means that the variable is available for use only in the procedure where it is declared. Local variables declared with Dim remain in existence only as long as the procedure is executing. That is, once the procedure has finished, any variables that were local to the procedure no longer exist, and their values are erased. If you want a variable to retain its value after the procedure has finished, you declare the variable as Static instead of Dim. Static variables retain their values as program control moves in and out of a procedure.

Let's see how this works.

1. Start a new project without saving the previous one.

2. Add a button to the form and call it **cmdInput_Amount** with a caption of **Click Here**.

3. Add a text box called **txtOutput_Counter**.

4. Open the code for the Click event procedure for the button and key the following statements:

```
Dim intCounter As Integer
intCounter = intCounter + 1
txtOutput_Counter.Text = Str(intCounter)
```

The statement **intCounter = intCounter + 1** is a counter statement. It adds 1 to the value that is stored in intCounter and stores the new value back into intCounter. In other words, it increases the value of intCounter by 1. The idea is that intCounter will count the number of times the user clicks this button.

The **txtOutput_Counter.Text = Str(intCounter)** statement takes the value of intCounter and stores it in the text box. Because intCounter is a number, it must be translated to a string

FIGURE 3.24
The error generated by the implicit declaration of intAmount.

before it can be displayed. The **Str** function does this. You will learn about such functions later in this chapter.

> **HINT:** If you use the Str function to translate intCounter, and intCounter has 1 (one) in it, you might think that txtOutput_Counter.Text would be one byte long. That's not the case. Because part of every number is a sign, Visual Basic reserves an extra byte before every number for the sign. Thus, the length of txtOutput_Counter.Text would be two bytes, not one.

5. Run the program without saving it and click the **Click Here** button; 1 shows up in the text box, just as it should (Figure 3.25).

6. Click the button again; 1 is still in the text box.

7. Click the button several more times. The value displayed in the text box doesn't change.

Because intCounter is declared with the Dim statement, intCounter is redefined and initialized each time the procedure is run. Thus, each time you click the **Click Here** button, intCounter will become 0 again, and adding 1 to that gives 1 each time.

For intCounter to be used as designed, it needs to be declared as Static.

8. Exit from the program.

9. Change the Dim statement to Static.

10. Run the program without saving it and click the **Click Here** button; 1 shows up in the text box. That's okay.

11. Click the button again. This time, 2 is in the text box (Figure 3.26).

The first time you clicked the **Click Here** button, intCounter was declared and initialized (to 0). At the end of the procedure, intCounter was 1 because it had been increased by 1. The next time you clicked the button, because intCounter is declared as Static, it was not reinitialized and retained the value of 1. And so, at the end of the procedure, intCounter was incremented and became 2.

12. Click the **Click Here** button again. This time, 3 is displayed.

13. Click the button a few more times to see that the value displayed continues to increase.

14. Exit from the program.

You can also use Dim and Static to declare a variable in the (General) procedure, and it becomes local to the form, or a **form-level** variable. That is, the value of a variable declared in the (General) procedure will be available to the procedures for all the objects on the form. It will not, however, be available to other modules or forms. If a variable is declared with the Dim declaration, then as the program exits from the form and reloads the form, that variable is redeclared and reinitialized. A static variable will retain its value when the form is exited and reloaded.

There will be occasions when you want to be able to have access to a variable in all the procedures in the program. Such variables are called **global.** They are declared as Global or Public in the (General) procedure of a module. Global variables are available to all procedures in the program and always retain their values as long as the program is still executing. If you have a variable you want to declare in a module and you want it to be form-level rather than global, you can declare it in the (General) procedure using Private or Dim. Such variables are, essentially, always static because variables declared in a module are always retained in the computer's memory. Accordingly, the Static declaration is not allowed in the (General) procedure in a module. You can use the Dim and Static declarations in your user-defined procedures set up in a module. You will learn how to do this in a later chapter.

FIGURE 3.25
The program code and the form, showing the output.

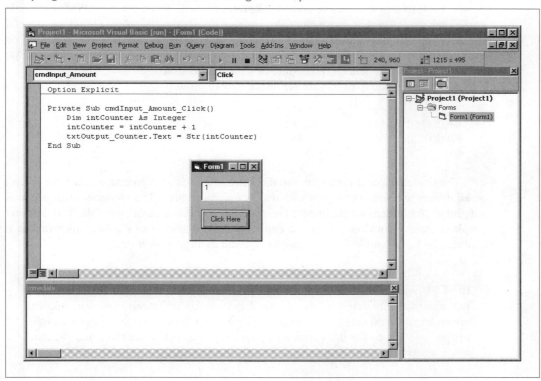

FIGURE 3.26
The output after the Dim statement is changed to Static.

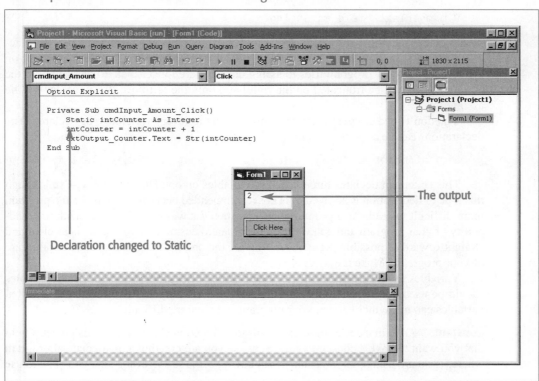

We have been using standard prefixes for our variable declarations. There is another prefix portion that can be useful in instantly recognizing the scope of a variable. If a variable is local to a procedure, no additional prefix is used. Thus, we would use a variable name such as intAmount, as we have already been doing. If a variable is global, you should use a "g" prefix; gintAmount would represent a global integer. The "m" prefix is used on those variables that are form-level in scope; mintAmount would represent a variable that was declared in the (General) procedure of a form or module.

A few more examples of variable declarations follow.

```
Static intAmount As Integer
Global glngInput_Amount As Long
Public gcurMoney_Input As Currency
Dim mstrText_Field As String
```

The first example declares the variable intAmount within a procedure (no extra prefix) as an integer and specifies that it will always retain its value. The second sample declares glngInput_Amount as a long integer and specifies that it is a global variable. The third example declares gcurMoney_Input as currency and specifies it as Public, which makes it global. The last example declares mstrText_Field as a form-level string.

> **HINT:** If you forget to specify the data type when declaring a variable, Visual Basic will automatically assign variant as the data type. Unfortunately, you probably will not realize this and may have unexpected results in your program. Always remember to specify the type for the variable in your declaration statement to avoid the automatic assigning.

When declaring strings, you can specify them with a length that is changeable, or you can specify the precise length you want. To do this, you would change the last statement in the foregoing list to

```
Dim mstrText_Field as String * 20
```

This specifies that the mstrText_Field variable will always be 20 characters long. If the actual data in the field do not fill the field, it will be padded on the right with blanks. If, on the other hand, your program tries to assign data that are longer than 20 characters to the field, the data will be truncated on the right, and only the leftmost 20 characters will be assigned.

You don't need a separate declaration statement for every variable to be declared. The declarations can be combined, as in

```
Dim intAmount As Integer, lngResult As Long, strSample_Text As String
```

This statement declares three different variables on one Dim statement. Even though this type of declaration is allowed, it is not recommended because it can make the program more difficult to read. As a programmer, you should always be concerned with the readability of your program and do everything you can to ensure that your code is as clear and straightforward as possible. Remember, you are the one who is going to have to take care of your programs. Make it easy on yourself.

Variables should always be declared with the smallest scope possible. Global variables should be used only when absolutely necessary for the purpose. Extensive use of global variables can make maintaining your programs much more difficult.

Constants   One final declaration that needs to be mentioned is **Const**. It designates a field that you want to have a constant value. Suppose you are creating a mathematical program wherein you are using pi a lot. Rather than keying 3.14159265 every time you need to use pi in your program, you could create a constant called PI and use that in the calculations instead. The form of the statement to do that is

```
Const sngPI = 3.14159265
```

This would be a local declaration. If you wanted the constant to be available throughout the many forms and modules of your program, you could declare the constant as global by placing the statement in the (General) procedure of a module and changing it to

```
Global Const gsngPI = 3.14159265
```

Using this constant, a statement such as

```
sngResult_Amount = sngInput_Amount + 3.14159265
```

could be simplified to

```
sngResult_Amount = sngInput_Amount + gsngPI
```

> **HINT:** This statement is adding gsngPI to the variable sngInput_Amount and placing the result in sngResult_Amount. We will discuss mathematical statements shortly.

Scoping Practice

There are many different rules for declaring variables and the scope of those variables, so it will be instructive to create an application using several of the different variable types.

1. Start a new project without saving the previous one. It was just for practice.
2. Add two buttons to the form; call them **cmdButton_1** and **cmdButton_2**, and use similar captions.
3. Add a text box to the form under the buttons, calling it **txtOutput**, and erase the text in the box.
4. Open the code window for **cmdButton_1** and key the following lines within the procedure:

```
Dim strText_Sample As String
strText_Sample = "Sample text from Button 1."
txtOutput.Text = strText_Sample
```

This declares the variable strText_Sample as a string, assigns the literal "Sample text from Button 1." to the variable, and then stores the contents of strText_Sample (Sample) in the text box. Now let's add code for the second button.

5. Change to the Button *2* code and key the following two statements:

```
strText_Sample = "Text for Button 2"
txtOutput.Text = strText_Sample
```

6. Run the program, saving it as **Scope Practice**.

Note that you get the "Variable not defined" error. This happens because strText_Sample is defined in the **cmdButton_1** procedure, which makes it local to just that procedure, but it is not declared in the **cmdButton_2** procedure. To fix this, we will create a form-level declaration.

7. Select **OK**, exit the program, and change to the **cmdButton_1_Click** procedure.

FIGURE 3.27

How to cut and paste the Dim statement.

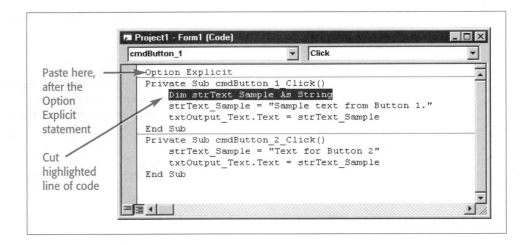

Paste here, after the Option Explicit statement

Cut highlighted line of code

8. Highlight the Dim statement and cut it from the code.

   Because we want to create a form-level declaration, we don't want a duplicate declaration in the procedure. Declaring a variable twice in your program, in two different locations, with two different scopes can be extremely confusing and should be avoided.

9. Change to the (General) procedure and paste the Dim statement after the Option Explicit statement (Figure 3.27).

10. Run the program again and select **Button 1**. The text will appear.

11. Select **Button 2**, and the new text will appear.

12. Click **Button 1**, and the text for that button will appear again.

   Now the variable is defined for both of the existing procedures and for any other procedure that may be created on this form.

13. Exit from your program.

   Now we have seen how scoping works on a procedure and form level. What would happen if we added a second form to the program and tried to access strText_Sample in a procedure on that form? That's right. We would get an error again. Declaring strText_Sample in the (General) procedure of form1 makes it local to that form. No other form would have access to it. If, however, we declared strText_Sample as global in a module, it would then be available to every form and module we added to the program.

   You will see some of this usage in later chapters. Right now, we need to break away from writing code to discuss an important topic: adding *comments* (remarks) to our code.

3.7   Adding Comments to Your Code

As your programs get longer and more complex, it becomes more important to add comments to your code so that when you go back to make modifications to the programs at some future time, you will be able to figure out what is going on in them. Figuring out what is happening in your sections of code may seem simple now, but we have only scratched the surface of the programming commands available in Visual Basic. As you learn how to use more statements, procedures, and events, it will become ever more difficult to determine what is going on in each procedure.

Putting comments into a program is a simple process. You merely put an apostrophe (') anywhere in the line of code, and what follows becomes a comment, ignored by Visual Basic.

> **HINT:** The command REM can be used instead of the apostrophe, but only at the beginning of a line. Most programmers prefer to use the apostrophe because it is less intrusive and more convenient.

1. Call up the code window for **Button 1**, position the insertion point at the beginning of the Sub line, key **' The procedure for Button 1**, and press **Enter**.

   Note that the comment changes color to green (if you have a color monitor). Though we haven't mentioned it before, keywords such as Sub, Dim, and String are shown in the code window in blue. This is done so that it is easier to tell one type of code from another. The comments always stand out in the code window because they are green.
2. Key **'** (a single apostrophe) and press **Enter**.

   This will give you a blank line between the comment line and the program code (Figure 3.28). It just makes the coding easier to read.

> **HINT:** You don't actually need the apostrophe to get the blank line. You can simply leave a blank line in the code. You can set your comments off whichever way you like.

We mentioned that Visual Basic ignores comments. This is easy to demonstrate.

3. After the strText_Sample assignment statement, add another line (Figure 3.29):

   ```
   ' strText_Sample = "Comment"
   ```

Now, if the comment is not ignored, then when the button is selected, the text box should have "Comment" in it instead of "Sample text from Button 1."

FIGURE 3.28
The two comment lines.

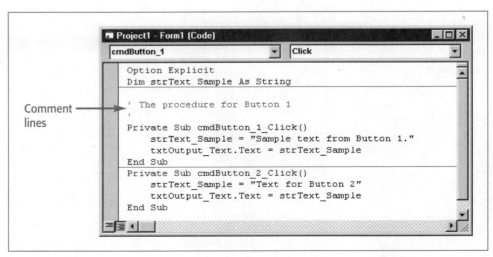

FIGURE 3.29
The inserted comment
line.

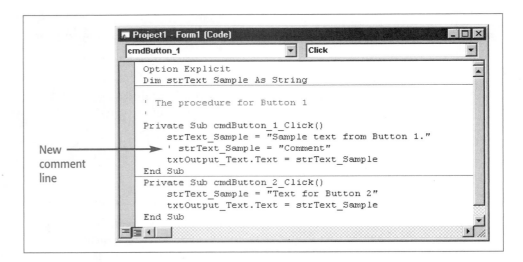

FIGURE 3.29
The inserted comment
line.

4. Run the program and select **Button 1**.

As you see, Sample text from **Button 1** shows up in the text box. That means the assignment on the comment statement was ignored. To prove this, we will remove the apostrophe from the statement.

5. Exit from the program, remove the apostrophe from the assignment, run the program again, and select **Button 1**.

This time Comment did appear in the text box.

Comments do not have to be on separate lines. You can add comments to the end of a statement if you wish.

6. Exit from the program, remove the added assignment statement because we don't need it, go to the end of the Dim statement, and key ' **This will make strText_Sample local to this form**.

7. Change to another line and note that the new code is changed to green. This indicates that the text following the apostrophe is a comment (Figure 3.30).

Adding comments to the ends of statements can make a program much easier to figure out long after the code is written. We will use many such comments in our programs.

8. Add comments to the rest of the program and then save it again.

FIGURE 3.30
The comment added to
the end of the
statement.

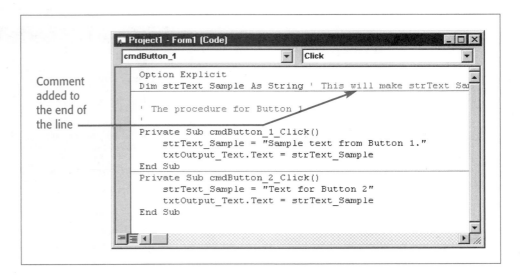

3.8 Mathematics

Computers were originally invented to do mathematical processing that took humans too long to accomplish. Though computers have progressed light years beyond their crude precursors, number crunching is still one of their primary uses. Even in a visual language such as Visual Basic, processing numbers is important. In the course of this book, we will be creating programs to calculate results, total columns of figures, and do many similar calculations.

Creating Calculations

Calculations are generally done in Visual Basic through assignment statements. That is, the expression is the right side of the assignment statement, and the left side is where the result of the calculation is stored. Take, for example, the following addition calculation:

```
intResult_Amount = intNumber_1 + intNumber_2
```

Visual Basic will add the value of the variable intNumber_1 field to the value of the variable intNumber_2 field and put the result in the intResult_Amount variable. Other calculations are done in a similar fashion with the symbols – for subtraction, * for multiplication, / for division, ^ for exponentiation, and parentheses to dictate the order in which the calculations are performed. Table 3.2 lists the various operations available for calculations in Visual Basic and the precedence number of each. The precedence numbers reflect the **order of operations.** Note that parentheses have the highest precedence. Operations within parentheses are always evaluated before operations outside the parentheses. If there are operations with parentheses within parentheses, the operations within the innermost parentheses are always evaluated first.

When Visual Basic performs mathematical operations, it does them in the same order in which you have been taught to do them. Operations with lower precedence numbers are done before those with higher precedence numbers. If two operations have the same precedence, the calculations are performed from left to right. In the equation 4 + 5 * 6 / 3, the multiplication is performed first as 5 * 6 = 30. Then the division is done as 30 / 3 = 10. Finally, the addition is done as 4 + 10 = 14, and the result of the calculation is 14.

As we have said, parentheses can be used to change the order of operations. If the foregoing problem were specified as (4 + 5) * 6 / 3, the result would be different. Operations within parentheses are performed first, so the first calculation would be 4 + 5 = 9, followed by 9 * 6 = 54 and then 54 / 3 = 18.

TABLE 3.2
Mathematical operators and their precedence.

Operator	Operation	Order of Precedence
()	Parentheses	1
^	Exponentiation (raises a number to a power)	2
–	Negation	3
*, /	Multiplication and division	4
\	Integer division	5
Mod	Modulo arithmetic	6
+, –	Addition and subtraction	7

You are no doubt familiar with this already, but you are probably less familiar with **integer division** (\) and **modulo arithmetic** (Mod). The integer division operator is used to divide two numbers, as is the regular division operator. The difference is that the result of the regular division operator can be a decimal number, whereas the result of the integer division operator is a truncated integer. By truncated we mean that the decimal portion of the result is dropped, not rounded. If you calculate 11 / 4, the result is 2.75. If you calculate 11 \ 4, the result is 2.

The modulo arithmetic operator is used for division also, but the result is only the remainder of the division. If you calculate 11 Mod 4, the result is 3, the remainder of the division of 11 by 4. Modulo arithmetic can be useful for a variety of calculations. A simple example is leap year. Every fourth year is a leap year, in which an extra day is added to the calendar. If you are doing any calculations in which you are using the number of days between two dates, it might be necessary to know whether the year is a leap year. To find out, all you need do is take the year Mod 4 and determine whether there is a remainder. That is, if the year is 1998 Mod 4, the result is 2, the remainder. That means that 1998 is not a leap year. If the year is 2000 Mod 4, the result is 0, which indicates that the year 2000 is a leap year, as is the year 2004.

When entering mathematical calculations in Visual Basic, you do not enter the dollar sign ($) or the percent symbol (%). If you want to use percentages, you must convert them to their decimal equivalents by dividing them by 100. For example, 15% translates to .15.

For a little hands-on practice with calculations, we will create a simple program with a button and a text box.

> **HINT:** Have you remembered to set the auto save function? If not, you may want to now. You should save your programs periodically as you are creating them to keep from losing any important changes, and using the auto save function is the easiest way to make sure this is being done.

1. Create a new project and add a button and text box. Change the caption of the button to **Calculate** and the control name to **cmdCalc**. Erase the contents of the text box and change its control name to **txtOutput**.

2. Open the code window for the button, and key the following two lines of comments above the Sub statement.

```
' A program for practicing calculations
'
```

3. Add the following lines of code to the procedure.

```
Dim intResult As Integer
Const intAmount = 10
txtOutput.Text = Str(intAmount + 5)
```

If you recall, we mentioned that the Str function is used to change numeric data to string. We use that function again here. Now, if the program runs correctly, the text box should display 15 when the button is selected.

4. Run and save the program as **Calculation Practice**. Select the **Calculate** button.

Note that 15 does show up in the text box (Figure 3.31).

> **HINT:** Because intAmount is a constant, a statement such as intAmount = intAmount + 5 would result in an error. A constant is just that, constant. It cannot be changed.

FIGURE 3.31
The code and the program output.

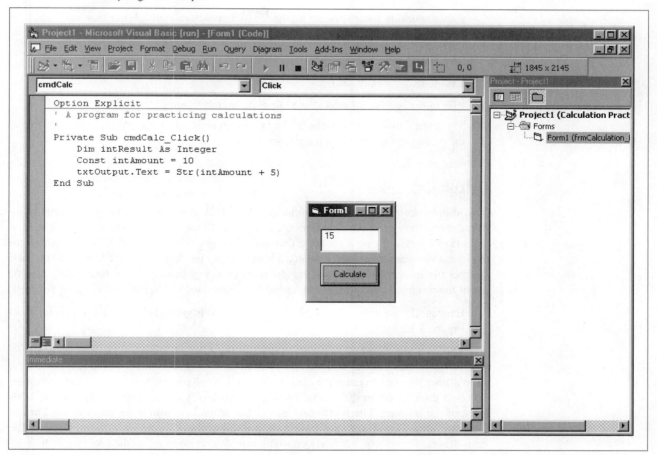

Let's try some other calculations.

5. Exit the program and change the addition symbol to the subtraction symbol. Run the program and select the **Calculate** button to see 5 (the difference between 10 and 5).

6. Exit the program and change the addition symbol to the multiplication symbol. Run the program and select the **Calculate** button to see 50 (the product of 10 and 5).

7. Exit the program and change the multiplication symbol to the division symbol. Run the program and select the **Calculate** button to see 2 (the result of 10 divided by 5).

Let's try a few examples to be sure our understanding of the order of operations is clear.

8. Exit the program and change the assignment to the following:

```
txtOutput.Text = Str(intAmount + 5 * 3)
```

9. Run the program and select the **Calculate** button to see 25. The multiplication is done first (5 * 3 = 15), and then the addition (10 + 15 = 25).

Now try it with parentheses.

10. Exit the program and change the statement to

```
txtOutput.Text = Str((intAmount + 5) * 3)
```

11. Run the program and select the button to see 45. This time the addition is done first (10 + 5 = 15), and then the multiplication (15 * 3 = 45).

    Exponentiation means taking a number to a power, or multiplying that number by itself the given number of times. 5 ^ 3 is the same as 5 * 5 * 5, or 125. Let's investigate this.

12. Exit the program and change the statement to

    ```
    txtOutput.Text = Str(5 ^ 3)
    ```

13. Run the program and select the **Calculate** button to see 125.

14. Try several other calculations in your program until you are sure you know how to use the math symbols and parentheses properly.

Calculating Sales

Now that we know how to use calculations, let's look at a practical example of how those calculations may be used. A common calculation is that of sales amounts and the related sales tax. We will create a program that does this type of calculation. It is a program created for a company that sells Widgets. This company needed a program that could be used to enter the sales of Widgets of three different colors and calculate the total sales. A sample of the program has already been created for you to look at before you create it yourself.

1. Execute the program in the Ch-3 folder called **Widget Sales** to see the form shown in Figure 3.32.

    This is a program that is used to calculate the sales of three products, Blue Widgets, Red Widgets, and Yellow Widgets. As you can see, the first column of each text box on the form allows the user to enter the quantity of each of the products ordered by the customer. The first three boxes in the second column of text boxes are for entry of the current sales price of the product. The fourth text box in the second column is for entry of the current sales tax rate. These text boxes have a default value already entered in them. Because the sales prices of products stay fairly constant, it makes sense to set up the program so that the user doesn't have to re-enter the same sales price each time. The same is true of the sales tax rate. Text boxes are used so that if they do change, the new prices or tax rate can be entered by the user and no change to the program is required.

    The third column is made up of **labels** rather than text boxes, and is used to show the extended price (quantity * sales price). The fourth column, which also consists of labels, is

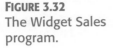

FIGURE 3.32
The Widget Sales program.

Widget Sales, Inc.				
	Quantity Ordered	Current Sales Price	Extended Price	Subtotal
Blue Widgets		1		
Red Widgets		2		
Yellow Widgets		3		
Current Sales Tax Rate		6	Sales Tax	
			Sales Total	
Calculate Sale	Clear Screen	Exit	Print Receipt	

used to display the subtotals, calculated sales tax, and grand total. Since the contents of a label cannot be changed, it is better to use labels than to use text boxes. This prevents the user from accidentally changing the results of the calculated fields.

2. Move the mouse pointer over one of the text boxes, and you will see the cursor change shape. Now move the pointer over one of the labels. The mouse pointer doesn't change. Try to click in one of the labels and nothing will happen. This is because you cannot enter data into a label. A label is only for display purposes.

You already know how to print the form from the Visual Basic print window. You can also print the form from within a program. You will learn how to do that in this chapter.

3. Key **100** in each of the three quantity text boxes, and click the **Calculate Sale** button to see the results shown in Figure 3.33.

The third column on the form shows the extended prices of $100.00, $200.00, and $300.00. The fourth column shows the subtotals of $100.00, $300.00 ($100.00 + $200.00), and $600.00 ($300.00 + $300.00). Under that is the sales tax amount of $36.00 ($600.00 * .06) and the grand total of $636.00 ($600.00 + $36.00).

4. Click the **Clear Screen** button.

All the labels are erased, as are the quantity text boxes. The prices and sales tax rate are left alone, however. We wanted these data to be supplied by default, so it would make no sense to clear them out.

5. Key **100**, **200**, and **300** in the quantity text boxes, and click the **Calculate Sale** button. This time, the total sales will be $1,484.00.

6. Click the **Print Receipt** button, and the form you see on the screen will be printed on the printer.

7. Change the Current Sales Price of the Blue Widgets to **3.56** and click the **Calculate Sale** button. Now the total sales will be $1,755.36. This shows that the calculations will produce decimal values.

8. Play with the program a bit more, trying various quantities and sales prices. Print a few of them out for reference as you work on creating the program. When you are comfortable with the way the program works, minimize it so you can refer to it if you feel the need.

FIGURE 3.33
The Widget Sales program, showing the calculation results.

Creating the Widget Sales Program

Now that you understand what the program is to accomplish, it is time to create the program yourself.

Setting up the Form

1. Start a new program.

2. Change the caption of the form to **Widget Sales, Inc.** and the control name to **frmWidget_Sales**.

   We will start out by adding a label to the form; we will need many of them.

3. Add a label to the program using the tool shown in Figure 3.34. Change the Caption property to **Blue Widget** and position it as shown in Figure 3.35.

   A label has a property called **AutoSize** that allows Visual Basic to determine the maximal size that the label needs to be to accommodate the contents. It is a Boolean (True or False) property with a default value of False.

FIGURE 3.34
The Label tool.

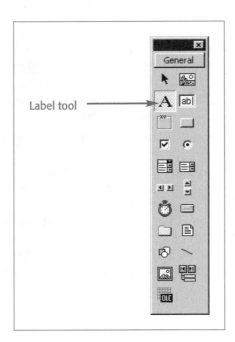

FIGURE 3.35
The form with the first label added.

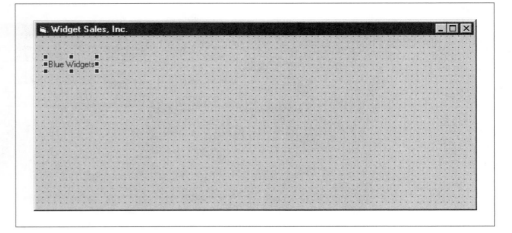

4. Change the AutoSize property to True.

Because we are going to need a number of labels that are to be used simply for column headings, row labels, and similar uses, it is easier to give the first one a standard name and then create several more with the same name. You will see how this is done in a moment.

5. Change the control name of the label to **lblMiscellaneous,** because it is a miscellaneous label (note the **lbl** prefix).

6. Select the label and copy it (**Ctrl-C**). Paste the copy back onto the form (**Ctrl-V**). The query shown in Figure 3.36 appears immediately.

This query is asking whether you want to create a control array. A **control array** is basically a group of objects of the same kind that have a common name. By creating a control array, you can have a series of labels that will show up in object lists as one item. You will learn much more about control arrays in the next chapter. For now, just click the **Yes** button; you do want to create an array of labels.

7. Click the **Yes** button.

This places the new label in the upper left corner.

8. Change the caption of the label to **Red Widgets** and move it to the position shown in Figure 3.37.

9. Paste the label onto the form nine more times, change the captions, and position the labels as shown in Figure 3.37. You will not be prompted to create a control array a second time.

10. Add seven text boxes to the form, and position them as shown in Figure 3.38. Be sure to key the values shown into the Text property of the appropriate text boxes.

FIGURE 3.36
The query window that appears when you are pasting a second label.

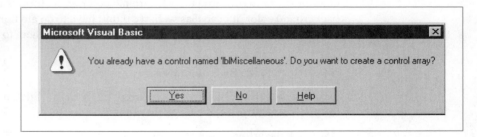

FIGURE 3.37
The form with the new labels.

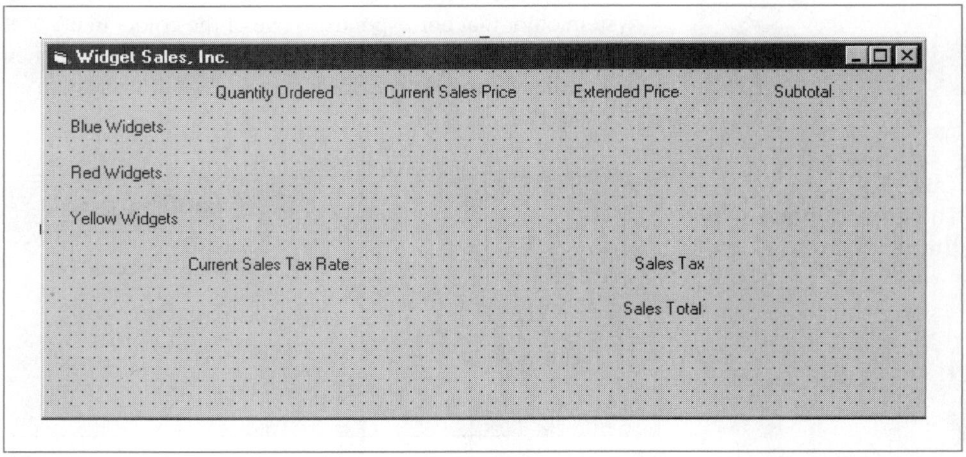

FIGURE 3.38
The form with the text boxes and buttons added.

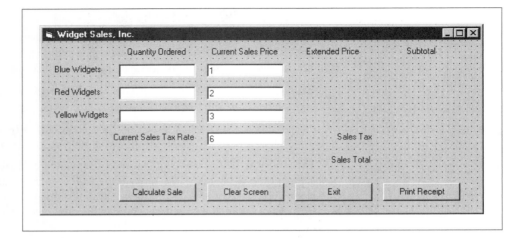

11. Change the control names of the text boxes to those shown in Table 3.3.

12. Add the buttons, position them, and change the captions so that your form looks like the one in Figure 3.38. Use appropriate control names for the buttons.

Now you need to create some more labels. This time, however, we want each of the labels to be separate so that we can write the appropriate data into them. We also want them to look like the text boxes. This requires changes to a couple of properties.

13. Add a new label to the form and, for now, don't worry about where to position it. You'll see where to put it later in this section. Change the control name to **lblBlue_Extended,** delete the text automatically, and put in the caption.

Labels are generally used to give names to other objects on the form, such as the labels we previously used, so their background color is usually made the same as the background color of the form. Because the background color of the form is gray, and that is the default background color of a label as well, we didn't have to do anything to make our previous labels blend into the form. Now, however, we don't want them to blend in. We want them to be white.

14. Change to the BackColor property of the label.

Note that there is a small down arrow on the right. Clicking it will cause a dialog box to appear so that you can change the color.

15. Click the arrow to see the dialog box shown in Figure 3.39.

There are two tabs on this dialog box. With the current color settings, you can pick a system color that corresponds to one of the colors that Windows uses for other purposes. If you chose the color of the Active Border from the list, then if you ever changed the Windows color for the Active Borders in the Windows system colors, the next time this program

TABLE 3.3
The control names for the text boxes.

	Quantity Ordered	**Current Sales Price**
Blue Widgets	txtBlue_Ordered	txtBlue_Price
Red Widgets	txtRed_Ordered	txtRed_Price
Yellow Widgets	txtYellow_Ordered	txtYellow_Price
Current Sales Tax Rate		txtSales_Tax_Rate

FIGURE 3.39
The pull-down color
selection dialog box.

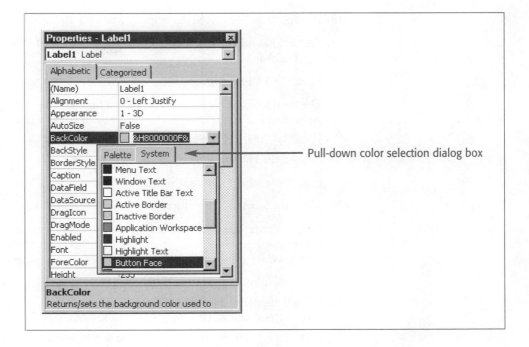

Pull-down color selection dialog box

was run, the color of the label would correspond to the new color. We don't want that to happen. We want the BackColor always to be white. Thus, you should use the **Palette** tab.

16. Click the **Palette** tab to see the colors available for the label background as shown in Figure 3.40.

17. Click the white color box as shown in Figure 3.40.

Now the background color is white, but the label doesn't look like the text boxes. We have to put a border around the label with the **BorderStyle** property.

FIGURE 3.40
The colors available for
the label.

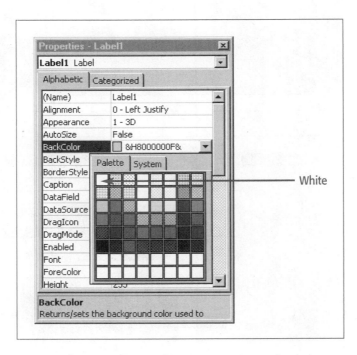

White

18. Change to the **BorderStyle** property and click the arrow.

This list has only two choices, **0 - None** and **1 - Fixed Single**. It is currently **0 - None**. You need to change it.

19. Click the **1 - Fixed Single** item.

The label looks like the text boxes except for one thing. It is thinner top-to-bottom. The **Height** property needs to be set to the same height as the text boxes, and that setting is 285. The **Height** property defines the height of an object.

20. Change the **Height** property of the label to **285**.

Finally the label looks as it should.

21. Move the label to the position illustrated in Figure 3.41.

Next, you need six more labels that look just like this one. You could create them as you did the last one—by adding it and changing all the properties—but it is easier just to copy them. When you do this, all the properties are already set.

22. Select the label (if it isn't still selected) and copy it to the clipboard.

23. Paste the label to the form. When asked whether you want to create a control array, click the **No** button. This time you want separate elements.

24. Paste the label five more times. All the labels appear in the upper left corner.

25. Move the labels into the appropriate positions as shown in Figure 3.42.

FIGURE 3.41
The form with the label added.

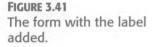

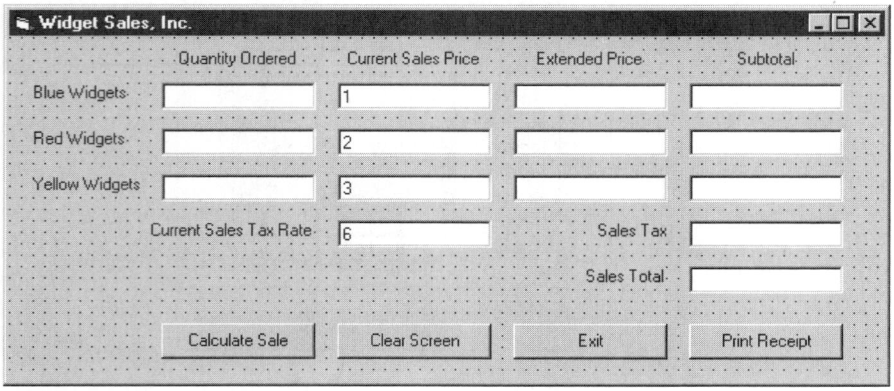

FIGURE 3.42
The form with the new labels added.

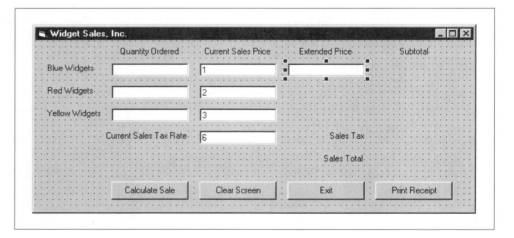

26. Change the control names of the new labels to correspond to those given in Table 3.4.

27. Save the program as **Widget Sales**.

Designing the Program We are finally ready for the design of the code. The first thing to do is calculate the extended price. This is done by multiplying the quantity by the price.

```
Project Widget Sales - frmWidget_Sales
    A.  Calculate button
        Multiply Blue Ordered by Blue Price to give Blue Extended
        Multiply Red Ordered by Red Price to give Red Extended
        Multiply Yellow Ordered by Yellow Price to give Yellow Extended
```

Then these extended prices are totaled into the subtotal column (though the first one is just a copy of the extended price).

```
        Copy Blue Extended to Blue Subtotal
        Add Blue Subtotal to Red Extended to give Red Subtotal
        Add Red Subtotal to Yellow Extended to give Yellow Subtotal
```

Yellow Subtotal is the total of all the extended prices, so it is used to calculate the Sales Tax, which is added to the Yellow Subtotal to yield the Total. Because the Sales Tax Rate is entered as an integer, it must be divided by 100 to yield a percentage.

```
Multiply Yellow Subtotal by Sales Tax Rate divided by 100 to give
 ↳ Sales Tax
Add Sales Tax to Yellow Subtotal to give Total
```

The rest of the design follows.

```
    B.  Clear button
        Erase all the fields except the Current Sales Prices and
         ↳ Current Sales Tax Rate
    C.  Exit button
        Exit the program
    D.  Print Receipt button
        Print the receipt on the printer
    E-G. Quantity Ordered text boxes
        Used to input the Quantity Ordered for each product
    H-J. Current Sales Price text boxes
        Used to input the Current Sales Price amount (generally used
         ↳ with default amount)
    K.  Current Sales Tax Rate text box
        Used to input the Current Sales Tax Rate (generally used with
         ↳ default amount)
```

TABLE 3.4
The control names of the labels.

	Extended Price	**Subtotal**
Blue Widgets	lblBlue_Extended	lblBlue_Subtotal
Red Widgets	lblRed_Extended	lblRed_Subtotal
Yellow Widgets	lblYellow_Extended	lblYellow_Subtotal
Sales Tax		lblSales_Tax
Sales Total		lblTotal

```
L-M. Extended Price labels
     Used to display the calculated extended prices
N-P. Subtotal labels
     Used to display the extended price subtotals
Q.  Sales Tax label
    Used to display the calculated sales tax amount
R.  Sales Total label
    Used to display the calculated total sales amount
There are additional miscellaneous labels for labeling program elements
```

Now we are ready to write the code.

The First Calculations   Most of the code for this program will be behind the **Calculate Sale** button.

1. Open the code window for the **Calculate Sale** button.

Because we are going to be using the calculated extended prices in most of the rest of the calculations, we will begin by setting up three integer variables to store these extended prices.

2. Key the following three Dim statements in the procedure.

```
Dim sngBlue_Extended As Single
Dim sngRed_Extended As Single
Dim sngYellow_Extended As Single
```

Next, we need to calculate the extended prices with a statement similar to the following:

```
sngBlue_Extended = Val(txtBlue_Ordered.Text) *
↳ Val(txtBlue_Price.Text)
```

We have to use the Val function to translate the ordered and price fields to numeric values so that they can be used in calculations.

3. Key an appropriate comment and then the foregoing statement, along with the other two statements you need—one for Red_Extended and one for Yellow_Extended.

Now the extended prices must be put into the labels. Given what we have learned so far, the following statement would probably be used.

```
lblBlue_Extended.Caption = Str(sngBlue_Extended)
```

The problem is that all that will be displayed is a number. We would really like to display the data in currency format. Remember that the test program displayed all the rest of the fields with dollar signs and two decimal positions as you saw in the sample program. To do this, we need a new function.

Formatting Numbers

Thus far, we have used the Str function to convert our numbers so that they can be displayed. With the Str function, however, all we get is plain numbers. What if we want commas or dollar signs, as shown in the sample program? For that, we will need a function that has more capabilities than Str. We need to be able to specify the particular formatting we want. This is done with the **Format** function. With Format, we can indicate the number of decimal places that a number must have, the number of leading or trailing zeroes, and even whether we want to use a dollar sign.

You use the Format function like the Str function except that after the value, you supply the format string that specifies the formatting you want to use. The format characters, which must be enclosed in quotation marks, are shown in Table 3.5.

TABLE 3.5
The format characters.

Symbol	Brief Description
0	Digit placeholder.
#	Print a digit or blank.
.	Indicates the position of the decimal point.
,	Separates for thousands and millions.
\	Displays the next character as is.
%	Percentage placeholder.
E- E+ e- e+	Scientific format.
−, +, $, (,), or space	Literal characters display exactly as given.
"ABC"	Strings in quotes display exactly as given.

The first format symbol is 0 (zero). It will cause a digit to be displayed if the expression has a digit in the position where the 0 appears in the format string. If there is no digit in that position, a zero is displayed. If the expression has more digits than there are zeros to the right of the decimal separator in the format string, the expression is rounded to as many decimal places as there are zeros. If there are more digits to the left of the decimal separator than there are zeros in the format string, those digits are displayed as is.

The number symbol (#) will also display a digit if the expression has a digit in the position where the # appears in the format string. This symbol works like the 0 digit placeholder, except that leading and trailing zeros aren't displayed if the number has the same number of digits or fewer digits than there are # symbols on either side of the decimal separator in the format string.

A period (.) is used as the decimal placeholder. In some locales, a comma is used as the decimal separator. The decimal placeholder determines how many digits are displayed to the left and right of the decimal separator. If the format expression contains only number signs to the left of this symbol, numbers smaller than 1 begin with a decimal separator. To display a leading zero with fractional numbers, such as 0.15, use 0 as the first digit placeholder to the left of the decimal separator, as in "##0.##". The actual character used as a decimal placeholder in the formatted output depends on the Number Format that has been set up previously in Windows.

When you use the percentage placeholder (%), the expression is multiplied by 100 and the percent character (%) is inserted in the position where it appears in the format string.

A comma (,) is used to denote the thousand and million separators. In some locales, a period is used as a thousand separator. The thousand separator separates thousands from hundreds within a number that has four or more places to the left of the decimal separator. Standard use of the thousand separator is specified if the format contains a thousand separator surrounded by digit placeholders (0 or #). If you need to scale your numbers, you can use two adjacent thousand separators or a thousand separator immediately to the left of the decimal separator. This works whether or not a decimal is specified. It will cause the number to be divided by 1000 and rounded as needed. You can use a format string of "###,." to display 100,000 as 100. Any number smaller than 1000 is displayed as 0. A format string of "###,," can be used to display 100 million because 100. means "scale the number by dividing it by 1000, rounding as needed." For example, you can use the format string "##0,," to represent 100 million as 100. Numbers smaller than 1 million are displayed as 0. The actual character used as the thousand separator in the formatted output depends on the Number Format that has been previously set up in Windows.

You use an E with a plus or minus symbol (E–, E+, e–, e+) to display your expression in scientific notation. The number of digit placeholders to the right of the E determines the number of digits in the exponent. If you use a minus sign to the left of the E, a minus sign will be used for negative exponents but a plus sign will not be used. For example, a format string of "#E–##" will display the number 156,000 as 1E5 and the number .0156 as 1E–2. If you use a plus sign in the format, then a plus or minus will appear in the displayed output. A format string of "#E+##" will display 156,000 as 1E+5.

The characters –, +, and $ are floating characters that are displayed where the digit display dictates. That is, they are displayed to the left of the last digit that the format causes to be printed. A format string of "$###,000" would display 15,125 as $15,125 and 12 would be displayed as $012.

To display a character that has special meaning as a literal character, precede it with a backslash (\). The backslash itself isn't displayed. Using a backslash is the same as enclosing the next character in double quotation marks. To display a backslash, use two backslashes (\\).

To display any characters that have no special format meaning, simply include the characters inside the format string. For example, if you display 12.5 using the format string "Bal = $###.00" you will see Bal = $12.50. The characters "Bal =" are displayed, and then the actual format string is used.

The following are a few more examples to help you understand just how to use the formatting characters:

Format(1234.50, "######.##") = 1234.5 (zero not shown as decimal position)

Format(1234.56, "###,###.000") = 1,234.500 (trailing zeros with comma added)

Format(1234.56, "$#,###,###") = $1,234 (decimals lost with dollar sign added)

Format(1234.56, "+##,###.##") = +1,234.56 (plus sign replaced dollar sign)

Format(–1234.56, "+##,###.##") = –+1,234.56 (plus sign shows along with minus sign)

If you need a number displayed with standard formatting, there are four predefined formats. They are shown in Table 3.6.

Some examples of the use of the predefined formats follow.

Format(–1240.127,"Fixed") = –1240.13 (no comma, rounded to two decimal positions, minus sign for negative)

Format(–1240.127,"Standard") = –1,240.13 (comma, rounded to two decimal positions, minus sign for negative)

TABLE 3.6
The predefined formats.

Format name	Description
Currency	Displays a number with a dollar sign and two decimal points. If there are enough digits to the left, a thousand separator is used. If the number is negative, it is displayed in parentheses. Rounding is done automatically.
Fixed	Displays a number with at least one digit to the left and two to the right of the decimal point. If there are no digits to the left, a zero is displayed. Negative numbers are displayed with a minus sign. Rounding is done automatically.
Standard	The same as fixed, except that a thousand separator is used and negative numbers are displayed in parentheses.
Percent	Multiplies the number by 100 and displays two decimal digits followed by a percent symbol (%). Rounding is done automatically.

Format(–1240.127,"Currency") = ($1,240.13) (dollar sign, comma, rounded to two decimal positions, parentheses for negative)

Format(–1240.12789,"Percent") = –124012.79% (no comma, percent symbol on the end, rounded to two decimal positions, parentheses for negative)

Back to the Code   Thus far in the Widget Sales program, we have calculated the extended sales amounts, and now we are ready to display them in the labels. We know how the Format function works and can use it to display the data in our program. For this program, the predefined currency format will work well. The statements needed should be similar to this one for sngBlue_Extended:

```
lblBlue_Extended.Caption = Format(sngBlue_Extended, "Currency")
```

1. Add to the program the foregoing statement and the other two that are needed (Figure 3.43).

According to the design and the form, the next logical things to calculate and display are the subtotals. The first subtotal is the same as sngBlue_Extended, so you can use almost the same statement as before.

2. Key the needed statement to display lblBlue_Subtotal.

Then you need to calculate lblRed_Subtotal. This is the total of sngBlue_Extended and sngRed_Extended.

3. Key the statement to display lblRed_Subtotal. Use a similar statement for lblYellow_Subtotal.

Now comes the sales tax. For this, you need to take the yellow subtotal field and multiply that by the current sales tax field, which is divided by 100 to make it a percentage. This is done as follows:

```
lblSales_Tax.Caption = Format((sngBlue_Extended + sngRed_Extended +
 ↳ sngYellow_Extended) * Val(txtSales_Tax_Rate.Text) / 100,
 ↳ "Currency")
```

FIGURE 3.43
The new statements added after the existing ones.

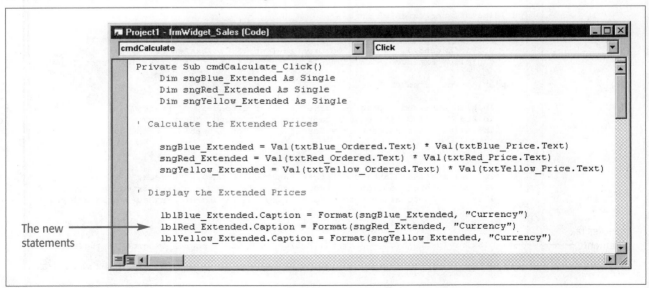

4. Key this statement into the procedure as shown in Figure 3.44.

You might wonder why, given that the three extended fields have already been totaled into the lblYellow_Subtotal label, it isn't used in the equation. The problem is that the label is formatted, and formatted fields don't work in calculations or in Format functions. The Val function would need to be used, and because the first character of the formatted field is a dollar sign, the Val function would return zero. Remember that the Val function begins at the left side of the string and stops at the first non-numeric character.

The final statement that is required is one to calculate the total. All that's needed is to add the subtotal and the tax amount, but there is actually an easier way. Because you are multiplying the subtotal by the sales tax percentage, you can actually do that same multiplication calculation by adding 1 to the percentage so that you are multiplying by 100 plus percent. For example, if the subtotal is $100 and the tax rate is 6%, you multiply 100 by .06 to get $6. Then if you add 1 to the .06 tax rate and multiply by that total, you are multiplying by 1.06, so you get $106, which is the same as the result of adding $100 and the $6 tax. Thus, the statement we need for the total is

```
lblTotal.Caption = Format((sngBlue_Extended + sngRed_Extended +
↳ sngYellow_Extended) * (Val(txtSales_Tax_Rate.Text) / 100 + 1),
↳ "Currency")
```

5. Key this statement into the program.

This gives you the entire procedure as shown in Figure 3.45.

6. Run the program, and key **100** into each of the Ordered text boxes. Click the **Calculate Sale** button. The result should be $636.00, just as it was when you experimented with the sample program (Figure 3.46).

FIGURE 3.44
Where to add the sales tax assignment statement.

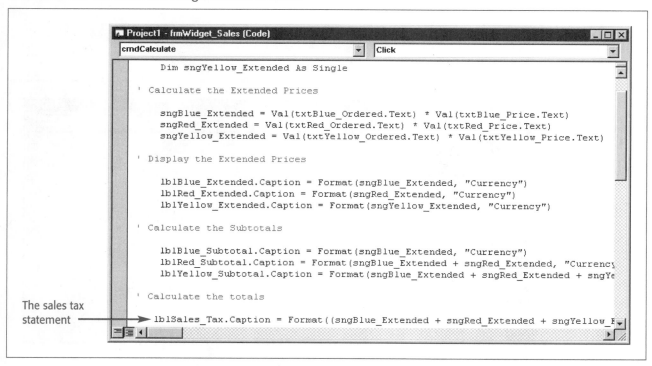

FIGURE 3.45
The entire procedure.

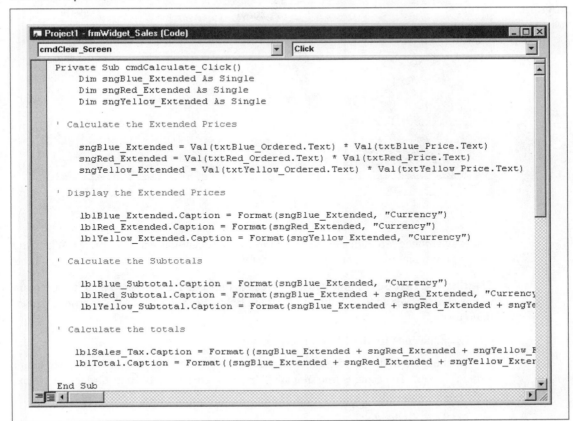

```
Project1 - frmWidget_Sales (Code)                                    _ □ ×
cmdClear_Screen              ▼    Click                               ▼
    Private Sub cmdCalculate_Click()
        Dim sngBlue_Extended As Single
        Dim sngRed_Extended As Single
        Dim sngYellow_Extended As Single

    ' Calculate the Extended Prices

        sngBlue_Extended = Val(txtBlue_Ordered.Text) * Val(txtBlue_Price.Text)
        sngRed_Extended = Val(txtRed_Ordered.Text) * Val(txtRed_Price.Text)
        sngYellow_Extended = Val(txtYellow_Ordered.Text) * Val(txtYellow_Price.Text)

    ' Display the Extended Prices

        lblBlue_Extended.Caption = Format(sngBlue_Extended, "Currency")
        lblRed_Extended.Caption = Format(sngRed_Extended, "Currency")
        lblYellow_Extended.Caption = Format(sngYellow_Extended, "Currency")

    ' Calculate the Subtotals

        lblBlue_Subtotal.Caption = Format(sngBlue_Extended, "Currency")
        lblRed_Subtotal.Caption = Format(sngBlue_Extended + sngRed_Extended, "Currency
        lblYellow_Subtotal.Caption = Format(sngBlue_Extended + sngRed_Extended + sngYe

    ' Calculate the totals

        lblSales_Tax.Caption = Format((sngBlue_Extended + sngRed_Extended + sngYellow_E
        lblTotal.Caption = Format((sngBlue_Extended + sngRed_Extended + sngYellow_Exter

    End Sub
```

FIGURE 3.46
The results of the
Widget Sales program.

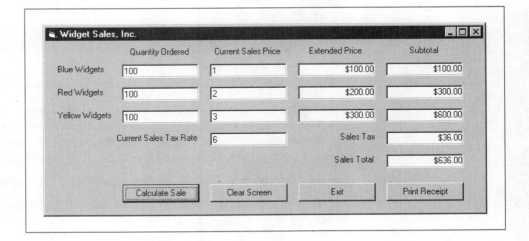

7. Key **100**, **200**, and **300** into the quantity text boxes, and click the **Calculate Sale** button. This time, the total sales will be $1,484.00.

8. Change the Current Sales Price of the Blue Widgets to **3.56** and click the **Calculate Sale** button. Now the total sales will be $1,755.36. This shows that the calculations will produce decimal values and that the Format function will display them properly (Figure 3.47).

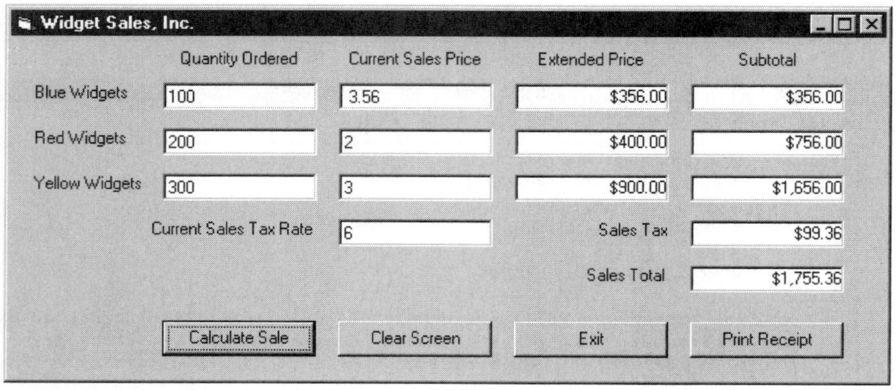

FIGURE 3.47
The results of the
Widget Sales program,
showing decimal
values.

FIGURE 3.47
The results of the Widget Sales program, showing decimal values.

9. Play with the program a bit more, trying various quantities and sales prices. When you are confident that the program works the way it is supposed to, exit it.

Clearing the Text Boxes and Labels   There is only one more thing to do to the program in this chapter. We added a button to clear the fields. We need to add the appropriate code to do this.

1. Open the code for the **Clear Screen** button.

You learned in the previous chapter that you can empty a text box by assigning a null string (" ") to it. The same is true of a label. Thus, to empty the txtBlue_Ordered text box, you need a statement like

```
txtBlue_Ordered.Text = ""
```

2. Add this statement to the program, along with the rest of the statements needed to clear all the labels and text boxes, except the ones for the current sales prices and the current sales tax rate.

3. Test the program by calculating a sale, and then click the **Clear Screen** button. Be sure all the fields are emptied properly.

4. Continue to test the program until you are satisfied that everything is working properly.

Printing the Receipt   Data can be printed in two ways from a Visual Basic program. You can print the data in some type of report format, which you will learn to do in a later chapter, or you can print the data as displayed on the form. The latter is a much easier way to print the data, and it is the way we are going to print the receipt for Widget sales.

1. Exit from the program and open the code window for the **Print Receipt** button.

To print the form requires only one statement: **PrintForm,** which has the format

```
[Formname.]PrintForm
```

As you can see, the name of the form is optional. If used, it tells Visual Basic to print that specific form. Otherwise, the current form is printed. Your program has only one form, so all you need is the PrintForm statement by itself.

2. Add the PrintForm statement to the code.

3. Run the program, and key **100** in each of the order text boxes. Click the **Calculate Sale** button, and then click the **Print Receipt** button to print the form. The form should be printed on the printer.

4. Exit the program.

5. Open the code window for the **Exit** button and key the appropriate statement.

6. Retest the program until you are satisfied that everything is working properly.

3.9   String Handling

In Visual Basic, virtually all input is done with text boxes. This input text is handled as string variables, and most programs you create will require this text to be processed in some manner. Fortunately, Visual Basic gives us a number of functions we can use to handle the string-type manipulations that are often necessary. We can determine the length of a string, combine several strings into one, divide a string into smaller strings, and search a string to locate specific characters. We will now discuss each of these functions and create a program to help us see how they work. As usual, we will begin with a brief look at the program you are going to create.

The String Practice Program

1. Run the **String Practice.exe** program found in the Ch-3 folder on your work disk to see the form shown in Figure 3.48.

What you see here is a program to test the various string manipulation functions you are going to learn how to use. You will key the data the program needs to work with, and then we will discuss what the program is doing.

2. Key **This is a test** into the left text box on the top row.

3. Key **for string manipulations** into the right text box.

4. Switch to the Left text box and key **3**.

5. Switch to the Right text box and key **7**.

6. Key **3** into the top text box beside Mid. Key **6** into the bottom text box.

7. Click the **Combine** button, and all the labels will be filled with results as shown in Figure 3.49.

FIGURE 3.48
The String Practice program form.

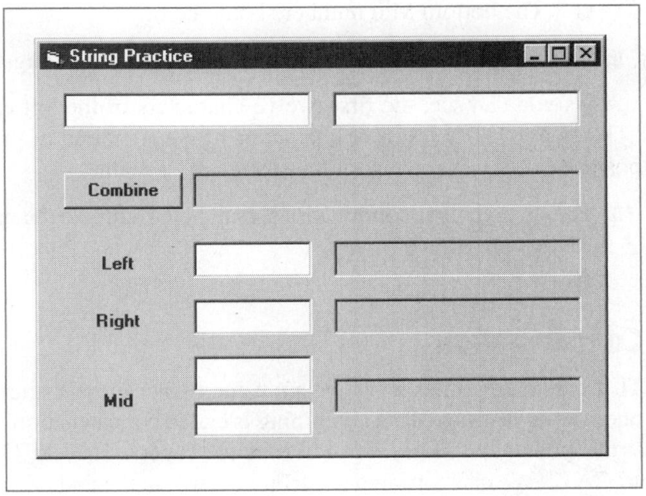

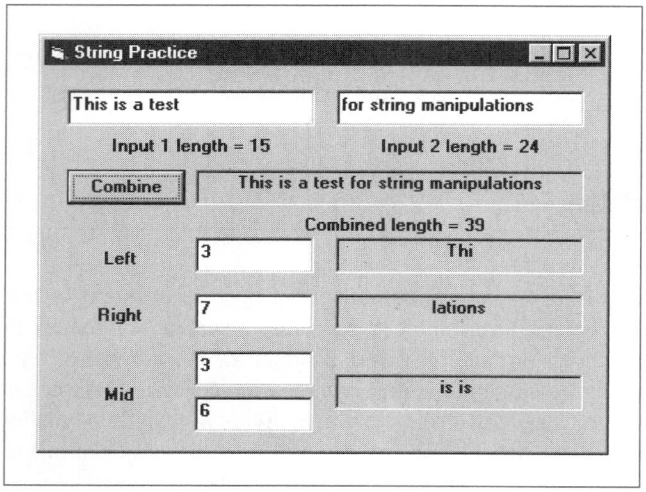

FIGURE 3.49

The results of using the **Combine** button in the String Practice program.

The first string manipulation we are going to discuss is the process of combining two strings, which is called **concatenation.** The text box beside the **Combine** button has the combined string of the two text boxes above it, and the combined length of the two strings is shown as 39, which is the total of 15 and 24.

The **Left** function will yield a **substring,** which is a portion of a larger string, of the specified number of characters on the left end of the subject string. The subject string here is the combined string, and the first three characters on the left are "Thi," just as shown.

The **Right** function yields a substring of the specified number of characters from the right of the subject string. As you can see, the seven rightmost characters of the string are "lations," which are the rightmost characters of manipu**lations.**

The last function, **Mid**, is used to get a substring from the middle of the subject string. The substring begins at a specified number and yields another specified number of characters. In this case, the Mid function begins at the third character and yields six characters. Thus, you get "is is " (with a space at the end).

8. Think about each of these manipulations a bit before continuing. Then change the numbers as follows:

   ■ The Left number should be 12.

   ■ The Right number should be 4.

   ■ The top Mid number should be 25.

   ■ The bottom Mid number should be 6.

9. Click the **Combine** button for the results shown in Figure 3.50.

As you can see, the first twelve characters of the left end of the combined string are "This is a te". The last four characters of the right end of the string are "ions". Starting at position 25, six characters of the string are "g mani".

10. Try several other combinations, and then minimize the program before going on to create this program yourself.

Concatenation

There are many times when we are using two or more strings that we want to combine into one, as you just saw. This combining is called concatenation, and we use the ampersand (&) as the symbol for this function. For example, suppose strField_One = "TOM" and strField_Two = "CAT". We can concatenate strField_Two on the end of strField_One with the statement

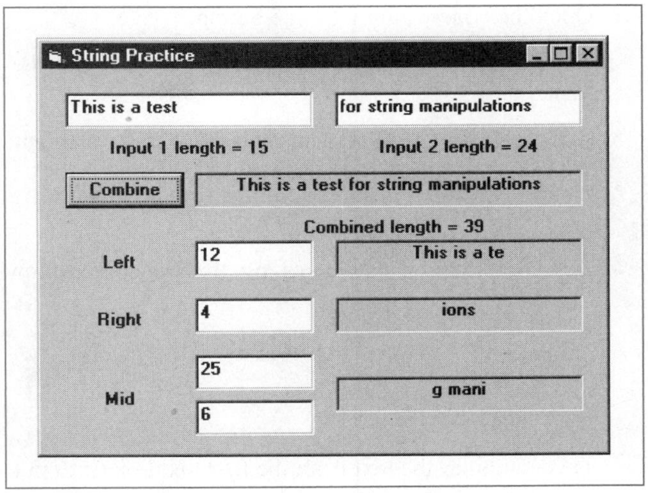

FIGURE 3.50
The String Practice program with the second set of results.

strConcatenated = strField_One & strField_Two, and then strConcatenated will contain "TOMCAT".

> **HINT:** The plus symbol (+) can sometimes be used for concatenation as well. In some situations, however, it can cause problems (especially if you are using variants), so you should always use the ampersand when doing concatenation.

Let's create the program you just experimented with to see just how this works.

1. Start a new project, and set up the form as shown in Figure 3.51. Name the form **frmString_Manipulations** and give it the caption **String Practice**. Be sure to leave the space between the boxes just as shown, because we need the room for the rest of the objects that we will add as we go.

   The top two text boxes will be used to key the two strings to be combined, and the bottom box will be used to display the concatenated string. Make the control names of the text boxes **txtInput_1** (the top one on the left), **txtInput_2**, and **txtConcatenated**, and name the button **cmdCombine**.

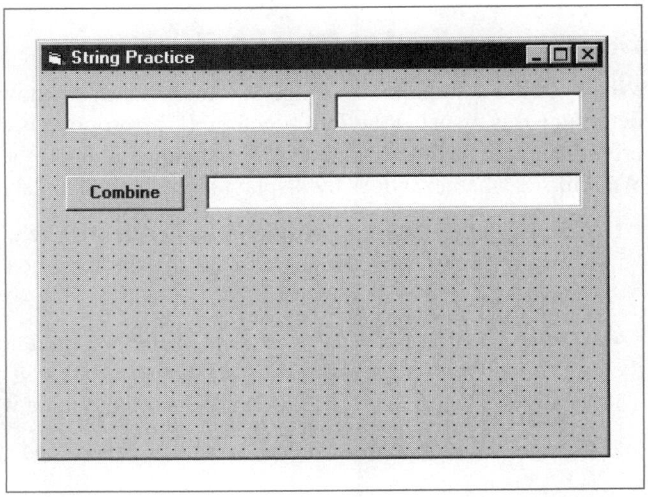

FIGURE 3.51
The initial form for practicing string manipulation.

2. Open the code window for the button.

To combine the strings and display that result in the output box requires only one statement.

3. Add the following statements above the Sub statement:

```
' Combine button procedure to practice manipulating string variables
'
```

4. Key the following statements into the procedure following the Sub statement:

```
'
' Concatenate the strings
'
txtConcatenated.Text = txtInput_1.Text & txtInput_2.Text
```

This combines the text from the first text box (txtInput_1.Text) with the text from the second text box (txtInput_2.Text) and copies the resultant combination into the output box (txtConcatenated.Text). The comments will serve to designate the operation, and the comments we will add to the rest of the statements will separate the different operations of the procedure from each other.

5. Run the program, saving the project as **String Manipulations**.

6. Key **This is in box 1** in the first text box, key **This is in box 2** in the second text box, and select the **Combine** button.

You will see the entry "This is in box 1This is in box 2" in the Concatenated text box. The T will be against the 1 unless you keyed a space following the 1.

7. Key a few more text samples and combine them. Do this until you are certain you understand precisely what is happening.

8. Exit the program.

> **HINT:** When keying your code, always be sure to leave a space between the variable name and the &. If you don't, Visual Basic will interpret the & symbol as the variable type indicator for a long integer.

Determining the Length of a String

When you are manipulating strings, it is often handy to know how long a string is. You can determine this by using the **Len** function. If the program is concatenating the strings properly, the length of the two input strings should add up to the length of the resultant string. We will see whether it does by displaying the lengths in labels.

1. Add a label to the form, position it under the first text box, and erase the caption as shown in Figure 3.52. Make sure you size the label box so that it is the same width as the text box.

Though you don't have any text in the label box right now, you need to change one of the properties so that the text that does end up in the box will be centered under the text box. That's why it is important for the label box to be the same width as the text box.

2. Change to the Properties window, select Alignment, and change the setting to **2 - Center**.

FIGURE 3.52
The form with the label added.

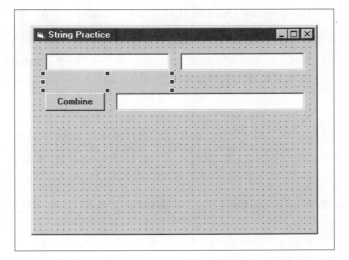

> **HINT:** When you are changing the alignment and a few other properties that have numbered options, you can select the option by number. That is, to select Center, you could have just entered 2.

3. Change the control name of the label box to **lblLength_1**.

4. Put a label box under each of the other two text boxes, making sure they are the same width as the text boxes. Then erase the captions and change the Alignment settings to Center. Use control names of **lblLength_2** and **lblCombined_Length**.

5. Open the code window for the **Combine** button.

As we mentioned, we want to use the Len function to determine the lengths of the various strings. The form of the function is simple:

```
Len(stringexpression)
```

The **stringexpression** can be either a variable or a literal. For example, you can use the function this way:

```
intLength = Len("Sample")
```

In this case, intLength will contain 6, because "Sample" is six characters long. You can also use the function this way:

```
intLength = Len(strSample)
```

Now, if strSample contains the word "Sample", intLength will contain 6 again. If strSample were to contain "encyclopedia", the intLength would contain 12 because there are twelve characters in "encyclopedia".

Using the Len function, we want to display the lengths of the contents of the two input text boxes under them and the length of the contents of the combination box under it. Your first instinct might be to use a statement something like

```
lblLength_1.Caption = Len(txtInput_1.Text)
```

The problem with this is that the Len function returns a number, and that is not appropriate to assign to the Caption property because it is a text field. You need to convert the numeric data to string data with the Str function.

Using the Str function, the Caption statement becomes

```
lblLength_1.Caption = Str(Len(txtInput_1.Text))
```

6. Now you can add the following statements to the button code under the current statements (see Figure 3.53):

```
'
' Display the lengths of the output fields
'
lblLength_1.Caption = Str(Len(txtInput_1.Text))
lblLength_2.Caption = Str(Len(txtInput_2.Text))
lblCombined_Length.Caption = Str(Len(txtConcatenated.Text))
```

7. Run the program, key **This is in box 1** in text box 1 (be sure there is a space at the end) and **This is in box 2** in text box 2, and select the **Combine** button.

Now the length of the text in the box is centered under each of the boxes. You will note that the length of the text in the first box is 17, the length of the text in the second box is 16, and the total length is 33. This is just what it should have been.

The only problem with this display is that the length displays are not very descriptive. It would be better if they said something like

```
Input 1 length = 17
```

It's not difficult to change them so they read this way, and doing so will illustrate another common use of concatenation and give you a bit more practice. What you need to do is concatenate a literal in front of the length value.

This time, rather than end your program, you will only temporarily suspend it (this often called a "break"). Then, after you have made your changes, you can continue the program where you left off, and you won't have to rekey the text in the text boxes.

8. Click the **Break** icon (⏸) on the tool bar (you could also use **Ctrl-Break**).

FIGURE 3.53
The new statements.

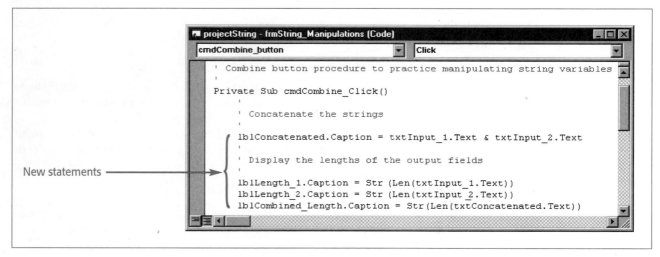

9. Switch to the code window and change your three statements to

```
lblLength_1.Caption = "Input 1 length =" & Str(Len(txtInput_1.Text))
lblLength_2.Caption = "Input 2 length =" & Str(Len(txtInput_2.Text))
lblCombined_Length.Caption = "Combined Length =" &
↳ Str(Len(txtConcatenated.Text))
```

Note that we put a space between the word "length" and the equals sign contained in the character string but not after the equals sign. There will automatically be a space between the equals sign and the converted number because the Str function will leave a space in front of the value it returns.

10. Pull down the **Run** menu and note that where the menu used to have **Run**, it now has **Continue**. This allows you to continue a program from the point where it was interrupted. Select **Continue**.

The text is still in the text box and the length displays haven't changed. They haven't changed because you haven't executed the code yet.

> **HINT:** You cannot always pause the code for the changes you want to make. Some changes affect the logic of the program too greatly for Visual Basic to continue the program where it left off. In such cases, however, Visual Basic warns you that the change you are about to make will mean you cannot continue your program.

11. Select the **Combine** button. Now your display should have the full messages underneath the text boxes, as shown in Figure 3.54.

12. Enter a few more strings, combine them until you are thoroughly familiar with what is happening, and then exit the program.

FIGURE 3.54
The completed length messages.

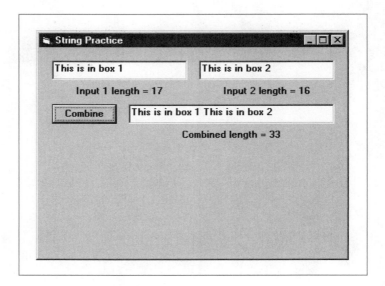

Copying a Substring

Now that you know how to combine strings, you are ready to learn how to copy part of a string, which is called a **substring.** There are three functions that you can use to create a substring from just the part of the string you want: **Left**, **Right**, and **Mid**.

> **HINT:** These string manipulation functions can also be named with a dollar sign on the end: Mid$, Left$, and Right$. The results of the functions are the same whether you use the dollar sign or not.

Left   The **Left** function allows you to create a substring from the specified number of characters from the left side of a string. The format of this function is

```
Left(stringexpression, length)
```

Here again, **stringexpression** can be a variable or a literal. **Length** is the number of characters you want in the substring. A sample statement using the Left function is

```
strOnly_Five = Left(strTo_extract, 5)
```

This statement uses the Left function to extract the first five characters from the string strTo_Extract. If strTo_extract contained "encyclopedia", then strOnly_Five would contain "encyc", the left-most five characters.

Let's add the Left function to our program.

1. Terminate your program execution.

2. Switch to the form and do the following (as in Figure 3.55):

   a. Add a label with the caption **Left**, make it the same size as the button, align it under the button, and center the caption. This label will not be used in any procedure, so you don't need to worry about the control name.

   b. Add a text box to the right of label, align its left edge with the left edge of the combined text box above it, align the right edge with the right edge of the txtInput_1

FIGURE 3.55
The form after adding the labels and text box for the Left function.

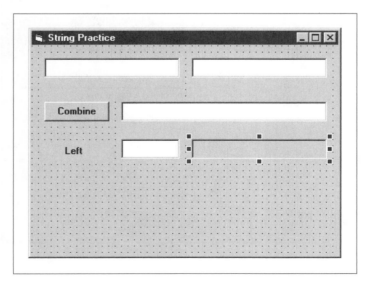

text box, erase the text, and use a control name of **txtLeft_In,** because it will be used to input the size of the substring you want to copy.

c. Add a label to the right of this new text box, align its edges with the edges of the Input_2 text box, delete the caption, and change the control name to **lblLeft_Out,** because this will be where you output the substring. To make this box look more like the other boxes, pull down the properties list, select BorderStyle, and change the value to 1 - Fixed Single. This puts a box around the label. The background color defaults to gray rather than white like the text boxes, but that's okay because it differentiates it from the text boxes.

We will still use the **Combine** button to tell the program when to do its string manipulations. Thus, you need to add the appropriate code to the button. But just what is the appropriate code? We want to copy the substring from the text contained in the combined text box, so the Left function should begin with

```
Left(txtConcatenated.Text
```

What about the length? It will be keyed in the text box we called txtLeft_In, so it's easy to assume that the rest of the function should be

```
Left(txtConcatenated.Text, txtLeft_In.Text)
```

Can you see the problem with this? txtLeft_In.Text is a string, and the function needs a number. You learned in Chapter 2 that the function Val is used to convert a string into a numeric value. Thus, we need to use the Val function to change txtLeft_In.Text to a number. This means that the Left function should become

```
Left(txtConcatenated.Text, Val(txtLeft_In.Text))
```

All that remains is to assign this function to the label that we called lblLeft_Out.

3. Open the code window again, and add the following statements to the end of the existing code (see Figure 3.56).

FIGURE 3.56
The new statements.

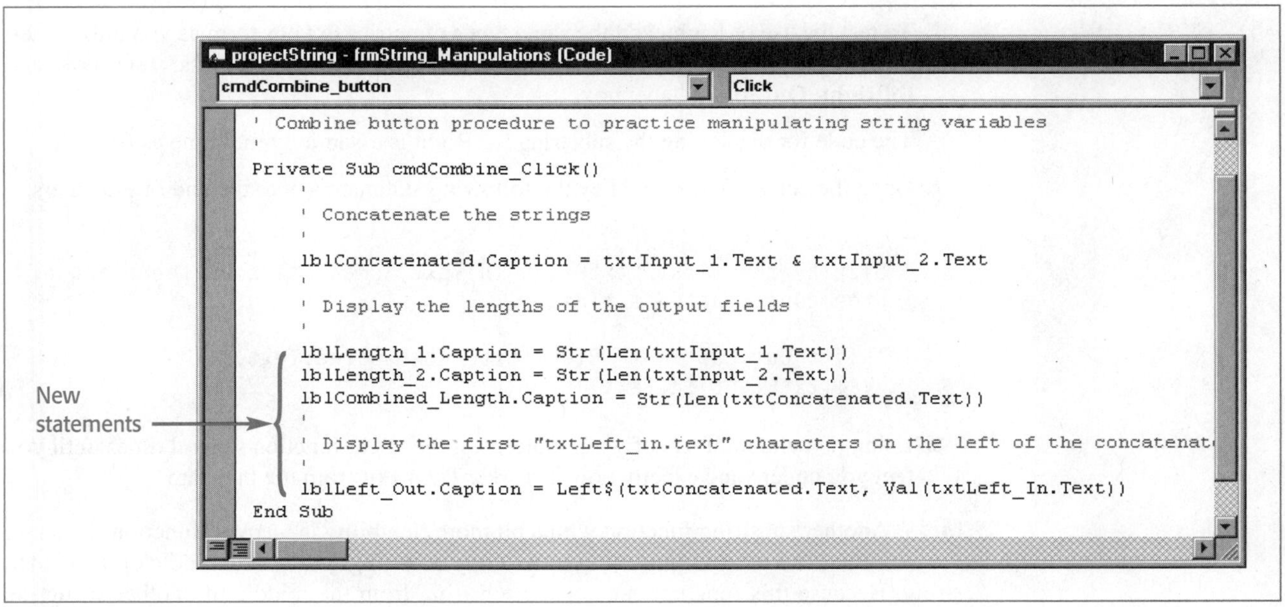

```
projectString - frmString_Manipulations (Code)

cmdCombine_button          ▼    Click                              ▼

    ' Combine button procedure to practice manipulating string variables
    '
    Private Sub cmdCombine_Click()
        '
        ' Concatenate the strings
        '
        lblConcatenated.Caption = txtInput_1.Text & txtInput_2.Text
        '
        ' Display the lengths of the output fields
        '
        lblLength_1.Caption = Str(Len(txtInput_1.Text))
        lblLength_2.Caption = Str(Len(txtInput_2.Text))
        lblCombined_Length.Caption = Str(Len(txtConcatenated.Text))
        '
        ' Display the first "txtLeft_in.text" characters on the left of the concatenat
        '
        lblLeft_Out.Caption = Left$(txtConcatenated.Text, Val(txtLeft_In.Text))
    End Sub
```

New statements →

```
'
' Display the first "txtLeft_In.Text" characters on the left of
⮡ the concatenated string
'
lblLeft_Out.Caption = Left(txtConcatenated.Text,
⮡ Val(txtLeft_In.Text))
```

4. Run the program; key **This is in box 1** in the first text box, **This is in box 2** in the second text box, and **6** in the Left input text box; and select the **Combine** button.

Now the program will run as before, except that the Left output box will have "This i" in it, the first six characters of the combined string.

5. Enter a few other numbers in the input box for the Left function, clicking the **Combine** button each time (until you are fully conversant with what the function is doing), and then exit from the program.

> **HINT:** If you use a length for the substring you want to copy that is longer than the length of the original string, the Left function will return the entire original string. The same is true of the Right and Mid functions.

Right   Just as the Left function copies the specified number of characters from the left end of a string, the **Right** function copies the specified number of characters from the right end of a string. The format of the function is virtually identical to that of the Left function:

```
Right(stringexpression, length)
```

As you can see, this function is formed the same way the Left function is formed, and it works in the same manner. Using the example we used before, the code for the Right function would look like

```
strOnly_Five = Right(strTo_extract, 5)
```

If strTo_extract contained "encyclopedia", strOnly_Five would contain "pedia", the five characters from the right end.

1. To test the use of Right, add the same types of entries to your form as you did for Left (see Figure 3.57). Use the control names **txtRight_In** for the text box and **lblRight_Out** for the label box.

The code for displaying the substring for Right is essentially the same as for Left.

2. Open the code window and key the following statements onto the end of the others:

```
'
' Display the first "txtRight_In.Text" characters on the right of
⮡ the concatenated string
'
lblRight_Out.Caption = Right(txtConcatenated.Text,
⮡ Val(txtRight_In.Text))
```

3. Using text and numbers of your choice, test the Right function several times until you feel you understand exactly how it works. Then exit from the program.

Mid   Another substring function with a bit more flexibility is the **Mid** function. It can do the job of either Left or Right and can also copy substrings out of the middle of the named string. Because this function can copy a substring from the middle of another string, its

FIGURE 3.57
The form with the addition of the Right function objects.

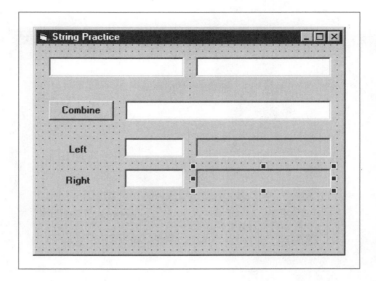

form is a little more complex than those of the other two functions. It requires the use of not only the length of the substring you want to copy, but also the starting position of that substring within the string expression. The format of the function is

```
Mid(stringexpression, start[, length])
```

Within the parentheses of the function, the string comes first, followed by the starting position in the string and then the length of the substring. Note that the **length** is actually optional. We will discuss this feature at the end of this section.

Using the same example again, we will copy five characters out of the middle of the string expression, starting at position 3. The Mid statement is

```
strOnly_Five = Mid(strTo_extract, 3, 5)
```

If strTo_extract contained "encyclopedia", then strOnly_Five would contain "cyclo", the five characters beginning at the third character. A second example is

```
strOnly_Three = Mid(strTo_extract, 8, 3)
```

If strTo_extract contained "encyclopedia", then strOnly_Three would contain "ped", the three characters beginning at the eighth character.

To add a Mid function to our program is only a little more complicated because we need to input two numbers.

1. Add two more text boxes and a label as shown in Figure 3.58. Center the Mid label between the two input text boxes, and center the output label box also. Use the control names **txtMid_Start_In** for the top text box, **txtMid_Length_In** for the bottom text box, and **lblMid_Out** for the label box.

The code for Mid is essentially the same as before, except for inclusion of the second number that is needed.

2. Open the code window, and key the following statements onto the end of the others:

```
'
' Display the "txtMid_Length_In.Text" characters from the
⮑ concatenated string starting at "txtMid_Start_In.Text"
'
lblMid_Out.Caption = Mid(txtConcatenated.Text,
⮑ Val(txtMid_Start_In.Text), Val(txtMid_Length_In.Text))
```

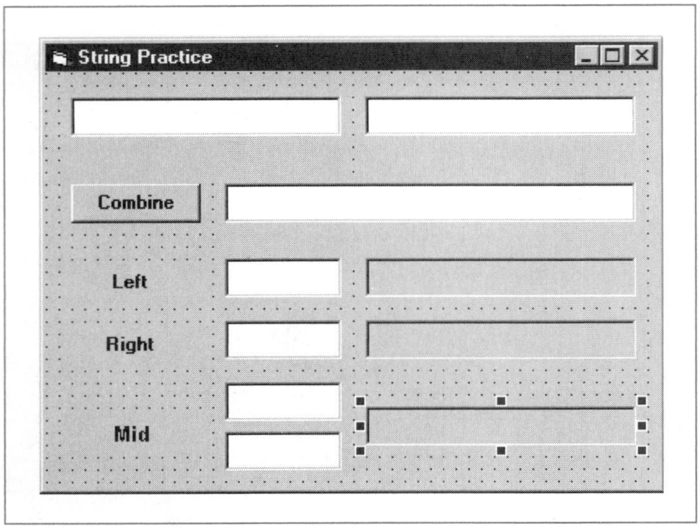

FIGURE 3.58
The form with the addition of the Mid function objects.

3. Using text and numbers of your choice, test the Mid function several times until you feel you understand exactly how it works. Then exit the program.

We mentioned that the length parameter of the Mid function is optional. This is because you will sometimes want to copy all the characters from the right side of a string but won't know how many characters that is. In such cases, you can use the Mid function without the length specification, and the Mid function will copy all the characters from the starting position to the end of the string. An example is

```
strTo_The_End = Mid(strTo_extract, 3)
```

If strTo_extract contained "encyclopedia", then strTo_The_End would contain "cyclopedia", all the characters from the third character to the end of the string.

There is a potential problem with this program. You can select the **Combine** button with no numbers entered into the Left and Right entry boxes. If the subject of the Val function is empty, the function will return zero. Thus, if there is no entry in the Left text box, the function **Val(txtLeft_In.Text)** will yield zero. Given this, the Left function will simply copy a substring of length zero. This is a valid substring.

If the starting number text box for the Mid function is empty, however, the program will result in an error. Though a string can have a length of zero, it does not have a zero position. So if the Val of the starting position for the Mid function is zero, the function will give you an error.

Because we already know how to test for the value of a string, we can solve this potential problem. All we need to do is test the value of the starting position text box to see if it is zero. As we just mentioned, if either textual data or nothing is in a text box, the Val function on that text box will return zero. Thus, we can test for an empty text box or one that has textual data (which are invalid for this program) with the following If Test:

```
If Val(txtMid_Start_In.Text) = 0 Then
```

4. Key this statement in front of the Mid statement.

Now, if this If Test is true, it means the user has not keyed anything into the starting position text box and we cannot allow the Mid function to be executed. But if the user is doing something wrong, we need to inform the user somehow. Later on, you will learn how to display dialog boxes on the screen for use in such situations. For now, we will just use the Mid output text box to give the user a message. We can do this with the statement

```
lblMid_Out.Caption = "Starting Position Missing"
```

More of an explanation would probably make it easier for the user to understand the omission, but the label is not very large, and this message is all that will fit. However, we can do one more thing to draw attention to the message. We can make it appear in red with the statement

```
lblMid_Out.ForeColor = vbRed
```

5. Key these two statements, followed by the **Else** statement.

If the text box actually has something in it, the caption can be displayed properly. So the Mid statement needs to follow the Else statement, as it does. It should, however, be indented.

6. Indent the Mid statement properly.

Because we have changed the ForeColor property to red to display the error message, we should be sure the Mid output will be displayed in black just as the rest of the output is displayed. Thus, we need to change the ForeColor to black.

7. Key the appropriate ForeColor statement and the **End If** statement.
8. Run the program, and click the **Combine** button before keying anything into the text boxes. The error message should appear in the Mid output label.
9. Key something into the text boxes, and click the **Combine** button again. The result of the Mid function should be displayed in black.
10. Practice with the program a bit more until you are sure it is working properly, and then exit it.

Trimming Extra Spaces

Sometimes when you are processing strings, there will be spaces on one end or the other. For example, suppose you have created a database application in which the first name is stored in one field and the last name is stored in another field. When you use the whole name to address an envelope, you will want to print the name with the first name followed by the last name. But suppose that all the first names are stored in a field that allows for a first-name size of 15 characters, and because most first names are not that long, they will all have extra spaces on the end. If the first name is Fred, there will be 11 spaces on the end, so if you concatenate "Fred" with the last name, you have an output that looks like

```
Fred           Smith
```

This is not what you want. You need to remove the spaces at the end of the first name. Visual Basic has three functions that can be used to trim excess spaces: one for the right, **RTrim**, one for the left, **LTrim**, and one for both, **Trim**.

"Fred" has spaces on the right, so you can use the following statement to remove the spaces and concatenate the last name onto the first name.

```
strWhole_Name = RTrim(strFirst_Name) & strLast_Name
```

The result will be the name

```
FredSmith
```

But this isn't what you want either. What happened? Because the RTrim function removed all the spaces on the right, there were none left to separate the first and last names. You will have to add one yourself:

```
strWhole_Name = RTrim(strFirst_Name) & " " & strLast_Name
```

Now the output will be as you want it:

```
Fred Smith
```

To test using RTrim and LTrim, we won't have to change the form, just some of the code. But before we change it, let's look at the current result of putting blanks on the ends of the inputs.

1. Run the program and key **Fred** followed by three spaces in the first input box, key five spaces followed by **Smith** in the second input box, and key a number in the start input box for the Mid (the program will give you an error if you don't). Then select the **Combine** button.

Your combined field will have the name with eight spaces between the first and last names.

2. Pause the program (press **Ctrl-Break** or use the **Break** icon) and open the code window.

Find the statement to concatenate the two inputs,

```
txtConcatenated.Text = txtInput_1.Text & txtInput_2.Text
```

We need to change this statement to

```
txtConcatenated.Text = RTrim(txtInput_1.Text) & " "
 ↳ & LTrim(txtInput_2.Text)
```

3. Change the statement as specified, press **F5** to continue the program, and select **Combine** because the entries are still in the text boxes.

Now your output will be what you wanted. Note that the combined length of the inputs no longer matches the total of the lengths of the two input fields. This is only to be expected; you have removed a lot of spaces.

When you want to be sure of removing all spaces around a string, Trim is probably the preferred function. To employ it instead of LTrim and RTrim in the previous statement, you would use

```
txtConcatenated.Text = Trim(txtInput_1.Text) &" " &
 ↳ Trim(txtInput_2.Text)
```

You may be wondering why you would ever want to use LTrim or RTrim when the Trim function does both. The answer is that sometimes you don't want to remove the spaces from both ends of a string. When this is the case, you must use either the LTrim or the RTrim function, whichever is appropriate.

4. Test the program using some other inputs, and change the code using RTrim, LTrim, and Trim in a variety of ways until you are thoroughly familiar with the functions. Then exit and print the program.

With this final change, your program code should look like the one in Figure 3.59.

Searching a String

When you are using long strings, it is sometimes necessary to locate a particular substring embedded in the whole string. Let's suppose, for example, that we have a database application in which we have stored the entire name in one field with the last name followed by the first name, as in "Smith, Fred". This is fine in the database program because it allows the data to be sorted by last name, but it is not convenient for printing on an envelope. We want to turn the name around and remove the comma so that the name is printed properly. Unfortunately, the string functions we have learned so far are of no help in locating the first

FIGURE 3.59
The completed code.

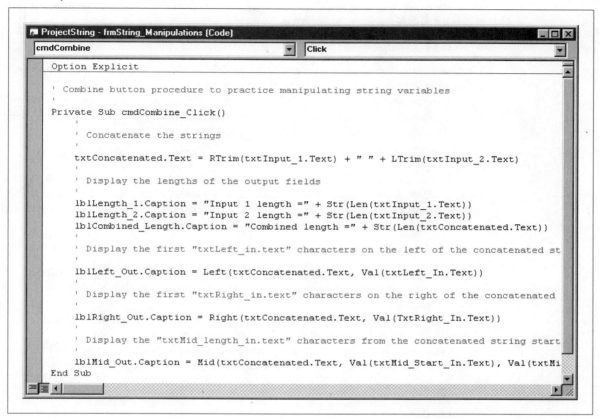

```
ProjectString - frmString_Manipulations (Code)

  cmdCombine                              ▼   Click                                ▼

  Option Explicit

  ' Combine button procedure to practice manipulating string variables
  '
  Private Sub cmdCombine_Click()
      '
      ' Concatenate the strings
      '
      txtConcatenated.Text = RTrim(txtInput_1.Text) + " " + LTrim(txtInput_2.Text)
      '
      ' Display the lengths of the output fields
      '
      lblLength_1.Caption = "Input 1 length =" + Str(Len(txtInput_1.Text))
      lblLength_2.Caption = "Input 2 length =" + Str(Len(txtInput_2.Text))
      lblCombined_Length.Caption = "Combined length =" + Str(Len(txtConcatenated.Text))
      '
      ' Display the first "txtLeft_in.text" characters on the left of the concatenated st
      '
      lblLeft_Out.Caption = Left(txtConcatenated.Text, Val(txtLeft_In.Text))
      '
      ' Display the first "txtRight_in.text" characters on the right of the concatenated
      '
      lblRight_Out.Caption = Right(txtConcatenated.Text, Val(TxtRight_In.Text))
      '
      ' Display the "txtMid_length_in.text" characters from the concatenated string start
      '
      lblMid_Out.Caption = Mid(txtConcatenated.Text, Val(txtMid_Start_In.Text), Val(txtMi
  End Sub
```

and last names in the string. We cannot, for example, assume that the last name is always five characters in length, as it is in this particular instance. That would not work with the next name in the file, which happens to be "Thompson, Alice". If we copied only the first five characters as the last name, we would end up with the last name of "Thomp". What we need is some way to search through the string to locate the comma separating the last and first names.

> **HINT:** Finding and copying substrings is known as **parsing** the string.

The **Instr** function was designed to fill this need. The format of the Instr function is

InStr([start,]string1, string2)

As you see from this format, to use Instr, you give the function the beginning position in the search string, which is optional, the name of the string you are searching, and then the substring you want to find. The function returns the position in the searched string where the substring starts. The following is an example of how the Instr function is used:

intSubstring_Position = Instr(1, strSearch_String, ",")

Now, if strSearch_String contains "Thompson, Alice", the search begins at the first character, continues until a comma is found, and then stores the position where it is found in intSubstring_Position. In this case, intSubstring_Position would contain 9.

Okay, you know how to find the comma. Now, how do you extract the two substrings so that they can be printed on the envelope? Because the comma position is in intSubstring_Position, you need to use the Left function to copy the last name up to that point (one less than intSubstring_Position). That would be

```
strLast_Name = Left(strSearch_String, intSubstring_Position-1)
```

If intSubstring_Position is 9, then one less than that would be 8, and strLast_Name would receive the leftmost eight characters of strSearch_String, or "Thompson".

Now what about the first name? You can apply a similar technique, using the Mid function. Because the Mid function lets you specify where the extraction will begin, all you need to do is begin one character past where the comma was found. That gives the statement

```
strFirst_Name = Mid(strSearch_String, intSubstring_position+1)
```

This works, but what if the strSearch_String has a space between the comma and the first name? We cannot assume there is a space, so we need to start just after the comma, but if there is a space, we end up with a space before the first name. To solve this problem, we simply use the Trim function, which changes the Mid statement to

```
strFirst_Name = Trim(Mid(strSearch_String, intSubstring_position+1))
```

This also solves the problem of spaces on the right end of the first name. If spaces remained on the right end, there would be extra spaces between the first and last names after we combined them.

We will not add anything to our program to experiment with the Instr function. Programming Exercise 2, at the end of this chapter, offers practice with Instr.

If you want to use Instr to search a string beginning at position 1, you don't actually need to use the 1 in the function, because the starting position is optional. That is,

```
Instr(1, strSearch_String, "ABC")
```

functions the same as

```
Instr(strSearch_String, "ABC").
```

Also, if the Instr function does not find the substring you asked it to find, the result is zero. That is, if you use the statement

```
intSubstring_Position = Instr(1, strSearch_String, ",")
```

and there is no comma in strSearch_String, then intSubstring_Position will have a value of zero.

1. Exit from Visual Basic and exit from the system properly.

About Program Design

When you are adding string manipulation statements to your program design, a simple statement of the required process is all that is necessary. Remember, a program design is just that, a design. It should not have the actual programming statements, but rather just enough information to enable you to create the programming statements from the design. For example, the statement to copy the first name, middle initial, and last name out of a string could be specified in the design with the simple statement

```
Separate name string into first, middle, and last
```

This records enough information so that, as you create the program, you will be able to tell what you intended to do at that point in the program. Thus, the design for the practice program we created in this chapter would be something similar to the following:

```
Project String Manipulation - frmString_Manipulations
```

```
A   and B. txtInput_1 and txtInput _2
    Used to input text to be manipulated
C.  cmdCombine
    a) Click
       Concatenate text from txtInput _1 and txtInput _2 and
       ↳ store in txtConcatenated text box
       Use number from txtLeft_In to extract Left substring
       ↳ from concatenated text and store in lblLeft_Out
       Use number from txtRight_In to extract Right substring
       ↳ from concatenated text and store in lblRight_Out
       If txtMid_Start_In invalid
          Display error message
       Else
          Use numbers from txtMid_Start_In and
          ↳ txtMid_Length_In to extract Mid after substring
          ↳ from concatenated text and store in lblMid_Out
       End IF
D.  txtConcatenated text box
    Used to output concatenated text
E   Through G are simply labels for Left, Right, and Mid
H.  txtLeft_In text box
    Used to input number for Left function
I.  txtRight_In text box
    Used to input number for Right function
J.  txtMid_Start_In text box
    Used to input starting position for Mid function
K.  txtMid_Length_In text box
    Used to input length of substring to extract for the Mid
    ↳ function
L.  lblLeft_Out label
    Used to output result of Left function
M.  lblRight_Out label
    Used to output result of Right function
N.  lblMid_Out label
    Used to output result of Mid function
```

We should point out that the labeling of the elements in a design (N for lblMid_Out label, for example) and the order in which those elements are listed is arbitrary. Generally, it is a good idea to group items of the same kind, such as all the input boxes, as we did for this design. Alternatively, you can group topic elements, such as all the Left elements followed by all the Right elements, and so on.

3.10 Debugging Your Programs

One of the errors most commonly made in writing code is keying the name of a variable incorrectly. If you are not consistent with the spelling of your variables' names, you can easily create a bug in your program. The easiest way to solve this problem is always to use the Option Explicit statement. Then if you key a variable name incorrectly, as soon as the program tries to execute the statement with the undeclared variable, an error occurs.

As our example program demonstrated, a user can enter invalid data into a text box or simply not enter the data at all. If your program is dependent on the data's being entered and entered correctly, it is important that you test that input to be sure it is valid for what you need. You will see other examples of testing for valid input as this book progresses.

You have now been introduced to a number of conversion functions. A common mistake when using such functions is to have the wrong type of data in the parameters of the functions. The parameter of the Val function, for example, must be a string value, either as a variable or as an object property. Functions like the Mid function can have some parameters that are numeric and others that are string. If you put the parameters into the function in the wrong order, Visual Basic will think the parameter is of the wrong type, when, in fact, the parameters are correct but are just in the wrong sequence. Thus, when using functions, you need to take extra care that the parameters are of the proper type and that they are in the proper sequence if there is more than one.

As you might imagine, when you are creating calculation equations, it is important that you follow the order of operations precisely. If you put parentheses in the wrong place, for example, the result of your calculation will be incorrect.

Variable scope can also cause problems for those programmers who are not careful. We mentioned that you should use the smallest (local) scope possible for all variables and should use global variables only when you have an overriding reason to do so. There are many examples in which global variables cause problems. If you declare a global variable and use that variable in procedure A, and then, within that procedure, call procedure B and use the same variable there, you will have changed the value of the variable in procedure A. This may or may not cause problems in procedure A, but you should be careful to avoid such possibilities. Simply declare the necessary variables in each of the procedures and avoid using global variables.

One thing you can do to help eliminate some of the problems you may have debugging your programs is to document them thoroughly. Then, if you are having problems with one of your procedures, you can look through the procedure and your comments will tell you what you had in mind when you wrote it.

3.11   Command and Menu Summary

In this chapter you learned to use the following keystrokes:

- **Ctrl-Break** is the shortcut key for the **Break** icon.
- **Ctrl-F** is the shortcut key for the **Find** function on the **Edit** menu.
- **Ctrl-H** is the shortcut key for the **Replace** function on the **Edit** menu.
- **F3** is the shortcut key for the **Find Next** option on the **Edit** menu.
- **F5** is the shortcut key for the **Start** option on the **Run** menu and also for the **Continue** option after you have used the **Break** icon.

In this chapter you learned about the following commands and functions:

- **Const** is used to declare a field that is not a variable because its value cannot be changed.
- **Dim** is used to declare a variable that is local to the procedure unless it is used in the (General) procedure where the variable becomes local to the form. The value of the variable is lost when the procedure or form is exited.
- **Format** allows you to create a format string to specify how your output is to be displayed.
- **Global** is used to declare variables whose values are available to the entire program.
- **Instr** is used to search a string for a specified substring.
- **Left** is used to copy a substring of the specified length from the left side of a string.

- **Len** is used to determine the length of a string.
- **LTrim** is used to trim off the blanks from the left side of a string.
- **Mid** is used to extract a substring of the specified length, beginning at a specified location within a string.
- **Option Explicit** will cause Visual Basic to verify that the variables you have used in your program have all been properly declared.
- **PrintForm** is used to print the form on the printer.
- **Private** is used to declare a form-level variable in the (General) procedure of a form but cannot be used in a module.
- **Public** is used to declare a global variable in the (General) procedure of a module.
- **Rem** is used to add comments to your program, but most programmers use the apostrophe (') instead of Rem.
- **Right** is used to copy a substring of the specified length from the right side of a string.
- **RTrim** is used to trim off the blanks from the right side of a string.
- **Static** is used to declare a local variable in a procedure so that the value is retained after the procedure is exited.
- **Str** is used to convert numeric data to string data.
- **Trim** is used to trim off the blanks from both ends of a string.

In this chapter you learned about the following properties:

- **AutoSize** lets you set up a label so that it automatically adjusts its size to the size of the text put in it.
- **BorderStyle** lets you put a box around a label and change the way the border looks on a text box.
- **Height** defines the height of an object.

In this chapter you learned the following object and variable prefixes:

- **lbl** is for labels.
- **lng** is for Long.
- **sng** is for Single.
- **dbl** is for Double.
- **cur** is for Currency.
- **vnt** is for Variant.
- **bln** is for Boolean.
- **byt** is for Byte.
- **dtm** is for Date.

In this chapter you learned about the following menu options:

- **Edit:**
  - **Find...** (shortcut key of **Ctrl-F**) lets you search for a specified entry through all the code or just a section of it.
  - **Replace...** (shortcut key of **Ctrl-H**) lets you search for a specified entry and change that entry to something else. You ask for verification of each change or change all instances without prompting.

■ **File:**

■ **New Project** erases the current project and begins a new one. If you have made changes to the current project since the last time it was saved, Visual Basic asks if you want to save the changes to the current project before it is erased.

■ **Run:**

■ **Continue** (shortcut key of **F5**) lets you continue the execution of a program from where it left off when you used the **Pause** button.

In this chapter you learned about the following Toolbox tool:

■ **A** The tool to add label boxes to the form.

In this chapter you learned about the following tool bar icon:

■ **II** The icon to pause the execution of the program.

3.12 Performance Check

1. What is the scope of declarations placed in (General)?

2. What is the purpose of the **Find...** option when you are using the code window?

3. What does the **Match Whole Word Only** option on the Find... dialog box do when it is turned on?

4. What is the shortcut key for the **Replace** option?

5. What is a metacharacter?

6. What are the four metacharacters? _____ , _____ , _____ , and _____ .

7. Why do you have to turn off the **Match Whole Word Only** option when using metacharacters?

8. What is a module?

9. What type of variable is declared as Public in the (General) procedure of a module?

10. What keyword is used to declare a constant?

11. What type of variable is Variable&?

12. Show the statement required to concatenate the variables strFirst and strLast and place the result in strWhole.

13. What is the Len function used for?

14. If strEmpty = " " (it is empty), what would be the value in intEmpty after the statement **intEmpty = Len(strEmpty)**?

15. If strInput = "ABCDEFGHIJKLMNOPQ", what would the function Right(strInput, 4) yield?

16. If strInput = "ABCDEFGHIJKLMNOPQ", what would the function Left(strInput, 8) yield?

_____

17. If strInput = "ABCDEFGHIJKLMNOPQ", what Mid function would you use to extract a substring of "GHIJK"?

_____

18. If strInput = "ABCDEFGHIJKLMNOPQ", what would the function Instr(4, strInput, "C") yield?

_____

19. If intAmount = 157, precisely what would be in strAmount after the statement **strAmount = Str(intAmount)** was executed?

_____

20. What is the purpose of the Format statement?

_____

21. What would be the output for Format(13234.545, "######.##")?

_____

22. What would be the output for Format(13234.56, "###,###.000")?

_____

23. What Format pattern should you use to output $1,289 if the input number is 1289.56?

_____

24. What would be the output for Format(13234.567, "Currency")?

_____

25. What predefined format is used to display the Format output with dollar signs?

_____

26. Assume the following:

    intAmount_1 = 6

    intAmount_2 = 15

    intAmount_3 = 3

What is intResult in each case?

a. intResult = intAmount_1 + intAmount_2 * intAmount_3

b. intResult = (intAmount_1 + intAmount_2) * intAmount_3

c. intResult = (intAmount_1 + intAmount_2) ^ intAmount_3

d. intResult = (intAmount_2 + intAmount_1) * intAmount_3

e. intResult = intAmount_1 ^ intAmount_3 / intAmount_3

f. intResult = intAmount_1 ^ (intAmount_2 / intAmount_3)

g. intResult = intAmount_1 − intAmount_2 / intAmount_3

h. intResult = (intAmount_1 − intAmount_2) / intAmount_3

3.13 Programming Exercises

1. For this exercise you will change the text box used for the concatenated inputs in the String Manipulation program to a label. The exercise will give you practice in deleting a text box, adding a label, and changing your code. We will not show any design, because the only change to the design is the conversion of a text box into a label. At the computer, do each of the following:

  a. Get into Visual Basic.

  b. Put your work disk in drive A.

  c. Open the String Manipulation project.

  d. Select the text box where the output for the concatenation is put.

    e. Press **Del** to delete the text box.

    f. Add a label in place of the text box and do the following:

        1) Expand and align it just as the text box was.

        2) Erase the caption.

        3) Change the control name to **lblConcatenated**.

        4) Put a border around it.

    g. Open the code window for the **Combine** button.

    h. Pull down the **Code** menu, select **Replace...**, key **txtConcatenated.Text** as **Find What,** press **Tab,** key **lblConcatenated.Caption** as **Replace With,** and select the **Replace All** button.

    i. Save the new project as **String Manipulation Update.**

    j. Run the program to make sure it works after the changes.

    k. Print all the elements.

    l. Exit Visual Basic and exit the system properly.

2. This exercise will give you practice in using the Instr function. The design for the program is

```
Project Instr Practice - frmInstr_Practice
    A.  cmdSplit
        1.  Click
            Use the Instr function to divide the text given in the
            ↳txtWhole_Name text box into first and last name and
            ↳put the first name in the txtFirst_Name text box and
            ↳the last name in the txtLast_Name text box
    B.  cmdPrint
        1.  Click
            Print the form
    C   through E are labels for the text boxes
    F.  txtWhole_Name text box
        Used to input the whole name for splitting
    G.  txtFirst_Name text box
        Used to output first name
    H.  txtLast_Name text box
        Used to output last name
```

Study the design carefully and then, at the computer, do each of the following:

    a. Get into Visual Basic.

    b. Put your work disk in drive A.

    c. Create a form as shown in Figure 3.60. You will need to do each of the following:

        1) Begin a new project, and name the form **frmInstr_Practice** with a caption of **Instr Practice**.

        2) Add the text box for the whole name, erase the text, and change its control name to **txtWhole_Name**.

        3) Add the label under the text box as shown, change the caption to **Whole Name**, and center it.

        4) Position two label boxes for outputting the first and last names as shown, put a box around them, erase the captions, and use the control names **lblFirst_Name** and **lblLast_Name**.

        5) Add labels under the output boxes, and change and center the captions as shown.

FIGURE 3.60
The form for
Programming
Exercise 2.

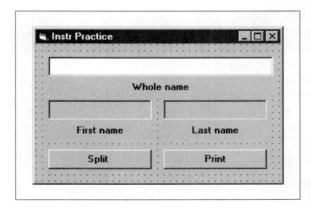

6) Add a button under the First name label, size it as shown in the figure, change the caption to **Split**, and change the control name to **cmdSplit**.

7) Add the **Print** button with the control name **cmdPrint**.

d. Open the code window for the **Split** button. The code will be similar to that illustrated in this chapter. Key each of the following statements as they are explained. Begin by keying appropriate comment statements before the Sub statement. The Instr statement and comments will be

```
'
' The Instr function finds the comma after the last name
'
intPosition = InStr(txtWhole_Name.Text, ",")
```

To find the last name requires the statement

```
'
' The Left function copies just the last name
'
lblLast_Name.Caption = Left(txtWhole_Name.Text, intPosition - 1)
```

And you will use the Right function to find the first name (the RTrim function is not needed because the name is being placed into a label, not positioned in front of the last name).

```
'
' The Right function finds the first name
'
lblFirst_Name.Caption = Right(txtWhole_Name.Text,
↳ Len(txtWhole_Name.Text) - intPosition - 1)
```

This works by copying the entire length of the name minus the position of the comma and one more (the space following the comma).

e. Open the code window for the **Print** button and add the appropriate statement.

f. Save the project as **Instr Practice**.

g. Try executing the program using various names such as **Smith, Fred** until you are satisfied that it works as expected (be sure to leave a space following the comma, because the statements expect it to be there). Print several of the samples as you progress.

h. Print all the elements, and then exit Visual Basic and shut down the system properly.

3. XYZ Corporation uses a list of inventory part numbers. The designation following the first dash is for the color of the item, and the number following the slash is the quantity on hand. For example, the part number 123-RE-BG45/15 has a color designation of RE and a quantity on hand of 15. Using the color designations of RE for red, GR for green, YE for yellow, and BL for blue, write a program that allows the user to input a part number and then, upon the user's selecting the button, displays the color and the quantity. This exercise gives you practice in using the various string functions. Given this information, design the program. Then, at the computer, do each of the following:

a. Get into Visual Basic.

b. Put your work disk in drive A.

c. Start a new project.

d. Change the caption of the form to **Inventory Determinations** and the name to **frmInventory_Determinations**.

e. Add a text box for entering the inventory part numbers, erase the text, use the control name **txtPart_Number**, and add the label **Part Number** centered under it.

f. Add a button beside the text box with a caption of **Determine**. Add a **Print** button that can be used to print the form.

g. Add two labels with borders, one for the color and one for the quantity, and erase the captions. Then add the labels **Color** and **Quantity,** centered under the boxes.

h. Open the code window for the button and add the appropriate code and comments. You will need an If Test to determine what the color designation translates to.

i. Save the project as **Inventory Determinations**, and then test the program using the part numbers 123-RE-BG45/15, 133-BL-GD67/95, 147-YE-HQ668/46, and, 1-BL-4/67. Print the form for each of these samples.

j. Print all the elements, and then exit Visual Basic and shut down the system properly.

4. When software manufacturers copy disks for distribution to their customers, it is vital that the disks be copied precisely. Even the slightest error might render the programs stored on a disk unusable. One of the techniques software manufacturers use to ensure that they produce accurate copies is called a **check digit** (or **check sum**). After a disk is copied, each byte on the disk is translated to its equivalent numeric storage code and added to an accumulated total. This accumulated total is called the check digit. After every byte of the disk is totaled, this check digit is compared to the check digit calculated for the original disk, and if the two numbers match, it is assumed that the disk was copied correctly. If they don't match, there must have been an error on the copied disk. The mere fact that they match, however, doesn't actually prove that the copy is correct; there are a number of errors that might occur that would not cause the check sum result to be incorrect. This is merely one test that is used for copy verification.

You are to write a check digit program. Rather than reading the bytes on a disk, however, your check digit will be calculated from a series of bytes input from a text box. To calculate the check digit, you will need a new function to change the byte to its numeric storage code. The **Asc** function is used for this purpose, and a sample statement is

```
intStorage_Code = Asc(strInput_Byte)
```

where intStorage_Code would contain the number code for the character in strInput_Byte.

Given this information, design a program to calculate the check digit using a text box for entering the digit, a button to cause the determination, and two labels to output the storage code and the check digit (the sum of the storage codes). Then, at the computer, do each of the following:

a. Get into Visual Basic.

b. Put your work disk in drive A.

c. Start a new project.

d. Change the caption of the form to **Check Digit** and name the form **frmCheck_Digit**.

e. Add a text box for entering the character to be used, erase the text, and use the control name **txtInput_Character**.

f. Add a button beside the text box with the caption **Total** and the name **cmd_Total**.

g. Add two label boxes with borders, one to display the storage number of the current character and one for the check digit, and erase the captions. Then add the labels **Storage Code** and **Check Digit,** centered under the boxes.

h. Open the code window for the button and add the appropriate code. You will need a calculation statement to accumulate the total. A statement such as

```
intTotal = intTotal + intNew_Number
```

is necessary.

i. Save the project as **Check Digits**.

j. Test the program by continually entering various keyboard characters. Use letters, numbers, and special characters. Make a list of ten such characters and run the program twice, comparing the check digit each time. It should be the same. What are the check digits of the five characters A, a, 7, (, and $? _____

k. Print all the elements and then exit Visual Basic and shut down the system properly.

5. You are a volunteer at a local school, and the math teacher has asked for a favor. She is teaching her students how to do squares and square roots and has asked you to create a program that will determine the answers. This exercise will give you practice inputting from a text box, converting the string to a number, and doing calculations. To do this exercise, you will need to use the square root function, which has the format **Sqr(number)**. Design the program and then, at the computer, do each of the following:

a. Get into Visual Basic with your work disk in drive A.

b. Start a new project.

c. Add the text box for inputting the number and a label describing the input.

d. Add four labels: two to label the output and two others for that output, one for the square and the other for the square root.

e. Add a button to do the calculation, and add a **Print** button to print the form.

f. Write the code and then save the project as **Square Root**.

g. Test the program to be sure it works properly, printing several of the results as you go. Print all the program elements to turn in with your form printouts.

h. Exit Visual Basic and shut down the system properly.

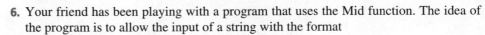

6. Your friend has been playing with a program that uses the Mid function. The idea of the program is to allow the input of a string with the format

```
name_1 - amount - name_2
```

and copy the amount out of the middle. Your friend wants to be able to display the two names and the amount in separate labels.

The problem is that your friend cannot get the program to work and has asked your help in debugging it. At the computer, do each of the following:

a. Get into Visual Basic and load the **Parsing Practice** program from the Ch-3 folder on your work disk.

b. Run the program, key **One - 15 - Three** in the text box, and click the **Do It** button. Immediately you will get an error. The error is "Invalid procedure call or argument". This means that one of the parameters in the function is somehow wrong. Click the **Debug** button to see, highlighted, the statement that has the error. It is the statement

```
intResult_2 = InStr(intResult, txtInput.Text, "-")
```

c. Move the mouse pointer over the intResult variable, and you will see a small window showing the value of the variable.

Note that it is 0 (zero). That's the problem; the function cannot begin at zero. Thus, the problem is not in this statement but in the one that gave intResult as a result. That statement is

```
intResult = InStr(txtInut.Text, "-")
```

Look carefully at the statement and you will see that txtInut.Text is spelled incorrectly. It should be txtInput.Text. This error occurred because the user didn't use the Option Explicit statement.

d. Change txtInut.Text to txtInput.Text. Exit and run the program again. Key **One - 15 - Three** into the text box, and click the **Do It** button.

Now the program works, but the output is not correct. In the output box for Name_1, you can see the dash. This is because the Mid statement copies from 1 to intResult. But intResult is where the dash is. The statement needs to copy to intResult_2.

e. Pause the program, change the statement, restart the program, and click the button again.

That works, but the number is missing from its output label. The statement that generates that output is

```
lblNumber.Caption = Mid(txtInput.Text, intResult, intResult_2)
```

It doesn't have a syntax error, so about the only thing that could be wrong is the intResult and intResult_2 values. You can see the values by using a Debug.Print statement.

f. Pause the program, put a Debug.Print statement on a new line above the Mid statement, restart the program, and click the button.

You will see that the value of each of the variables is 5. Why? Look at the second InStr statement. It begins its search where the other search left off. That means it is beginning to look for the dash at the dash, which, of course, it will find immediately. It needs to begin after the dash.

g. Pause the program, change the statement so that it will begin after the dash, restart the program, and click the button.

Now you see the output, but it is not correct. First the dash shows before the number.

h. Correct this and then retry the program.

Too much is being displayed in the number field. The problem is that the third parameter of the Mid function is wrong. It needs to be the difference between the dashes.

i. Correct this and then retry the program.

The final problem is that Name_2 shows the dash first just as the other search did.

j. Correct this and then retry the program.

The program should now display the output correctly.

k. Test the program with other combinations and then document the program properly. Print all the elements, and then exit Visual Basic and shut down the system properly.

3.14 Performance Mastery

1. You work at a business that faxes pages for customers. The first five pages that need to be faxed cost $1.35 each, and any others are 97 cents each. Design and create a program that will allow you to input the number of pages and will then display the cost of those pages. Add a print button so that you can print the result for the customer. Save the program as **Fax Calculations**, and then test the program using several numbers, printing the results. Print the program elements.

2. Date verification is an important job in a lot of programs. You have been assigned the job of creating a program that will allow the entry of a date and then will verify that each part of the date is correct. The date can be entered with either slashes or dashes. A few of the possible entries are **1/2/2000**, **01/11/2000**, **1-02-2000**, and **01-02-2000**.

    Design and create a program that will allow the date to be entered into a text box and then will verify each part of the date as follows:

    a. The month cannot be more than 12 or less than 1.

    b. The days cannot be less than 1, nor can they exceed the number of days allowed for that month (you don't need to worry about leap year; pretend that February cannot have more than 28 days).

    c. The year must be more than 1990 but less than 2001.

    Display an error message if any part of the date is incorrect, including mixing symbols, as in 1-02/2000. If the date is correct, display each part of the date in its own box with an appropriate label. Be sure to add a **Print** button so that the results can be printed. Save the program as **Date Verification**. Test the program by entering several dates in the possible formats, and print the results. Print the program elements when you are satisfied that the program is working properly.

3. You are going to be given a project soon in which the users will be asked to input a variety of numbers that are required to be within a certain range. You have decided to write a program to test out the technique. Your program should allow the input of three numbers. The first number is to be used as the bottom of the range, the second as the top of the range, and the third as the actual input. Add a label in which you can display a message indicating whether the number is within the range or not and a **Print** button to print the results. Design and then write the program, saving it as **Input Verification**. Test the program and then print all the elements.

4. You work for a retail store. You have been given the task of writing a program that will determine the markup on the products that the store sells. Write a program that will allow the input of the wholesale cost of a product and will then display the retail price, which includes the markup. The markups should be calculated as 15% when the wholesale price is less than $50, as 17% when the wholesale price is at least $50 but less than $75, as 19% when the price is at least $75 but less than $100, and 21% when the price is $100 or greater. Design and then write the program, saving it as **Price Markups**. Test the program and then print all the elements.

5. The retail store you work for gives its customers charge cards. Each month, a finance charge is added to the customer's balance. If the balance is $10 or less, the finance charge is 50¢. If the balance is more than $10, the finance charge is 1.5% of the outstanding

balance. It is your job to write a program to do the necessary calculations. Design and then write the program, saving it as **Finance Charges**. Test the program and then print all the elements.

6. The retail store you work for pays its sales clerks a straight salary of $150 per week plus 20% commission on what they sell up to and including $500 worth of merchandise and 25% commission on everything they sell over $500. Thus, if they sell $750 worth of merchandise, they earn 20% commission on $500 and 25% commission on $250. It is your job to write a program to do the necessary calculations. Design and then write the program, saving it as **Commissions**. Test the program and then print all the elements.

7. Fred, in the payroll department, has asked you to write a program that he can use to prepare the weekly payroll. Your program will need to input whether the employee is hourly (and if so, the rate of pay) or salaried (and if so, the salary received). Then the pay should be calculated, taking into account a 20% federal tax rate, a 2% state tax rate, and a 6.75% FICA rate (or use the current FICA rate if your instructor supplies it). The percentage for retirement that is deducted from the pay before taxes should also be entered. People who are paid on an hourly basis have to belong to the union, and the union gets 1% of the pay after taxes. Hourly personnel receive time and a half for all hours over 40. The output of the program should show the gross pay, each of the deductions, and the net pay. Design and then write the program, saving it as **Payroll Calculations**. Test the program and then print all the elements.

8. You have a friend who is a teacher. She has asked you to write a program that she can use to calculate the end-of-term grades for her students. Your program will need to input six grades, total them, display the average, and then assign a letter grade. Each of the first five exams is worth 50 points and the final is worth 100, so there is a possible total of 350 points. The letter grades are to be assigned as follows: 90 and above, an A; 80 or more but less than 90, a B; 70 or more but less than 80, a C; 60 or more but less than 70, a D; and less than 60, an F. Design and then write the program, saving it as **Grade Calculations**. Test the program and then print all the elements.

9. Your young niece is just learning how to read a calendar. You decide to write a program that will allow her to enter the number of the month (January is 1, February is 2, and so on) and display the number of days in the month. Ignore the fact that February has 29 days in a leap year. Design and then write the program, saving it as **Days in the Month**. Test the program and then print all the elements.

10. A local high school teacher is teaching his students about Fahrenheit and Celsius temperatures and has asked you to write a program in which one of the temperatures can be entered and the program will calculate the other. The formula is **Fahrenheit = (9/5)Celsius + 32**. The user should be able to enter a temperature and a code indicating whether the temperature is entered in degrees Celsius or Fahrenheit, and then see the translated temperature in an output text label. Design and then write the program, saving it as **Temperature Changes**. Test the program and then print all the elements.

11. You have been asked by your boss at the electric company to write a program to calculate customer charges. The user will need to input the name of the customer and the kilowatt-hours (kWh) used and then the program will display the charges. There should be a **Print** button to print the form that could then be sent to the customer. The charges are to be calculated according to the following schedule: $1.37 for the first 17 kWh, the next 55 kWh at $0.0389/kWh, the next 125 at $.0355/kWh, the next 200 at $0.0325/kWh, the next 200 at $0.0315/kWh, and any more at $0.0296/kWh. Design and then write the program, saving it as **Electric Charges**. Test the program and then print all the elements.

12. You work for a manufacturing facility that uses a number of parts in the manufacturing process. You have been given the task of writing a program that can be used to determine when a part needs to be reordered and how many parts are to be reordered.

Write a program that will allow the input of a product name and quantity on hand and will output the reorder quantity. If the reorder quantity is less than the quantity on hand, put zero in the reorder quantity to signify that the product does not need to be reordered. Use the product names, quantities on hand, and reorder quantities shown in Table 3.7.

Design the program and then create the form with the appropriate objects, including a **Print** button. Save the program as **Quantity Calculations**, test it thoroughly, and print all the elements.

13. You work for a small business that receives a lot of small change during the day. You have been asked to write a program that will let the user enter the numbers of pennies, nickels, dimes, quarters, and dollars and will show the total amount. As a bonus, you decide to let the user input the initial amount of money in the register at the beginning of the day and determine how much money was collected that day. Design the program and then create the form with the appropriate objects, including a **Print** button. Save the program as **Money Calculations**, test it thoroughly, and print all the elements.

14. You work for a manufacturing facility that sells its products in five regions of the country. You have been given the task of writing a program in which the user can enter the current sales for those five regions, along with the projected sales percentages, so that the projected sales can be calculated. Write a program that can be used to input the five sales amounts and the five projected sales percentages. Add labels for outputting the projected sales and a button to perform the calculations. Design the program and then create the form with the appropriate objects, including a **Print** button. Save the program as **Sales Forecast**, test it thoroughly, and print all the elements.

15. You work for a manufacturing facility that uses various parts in the manufacturing process. You have been given the task of writing a program that will determine how many of each part need to be reordered, and when, so that there will be enough on hand for the processes. An inventory was just performed, and you have been given a file with the counts of all the products found at the various locations throughout the plant. Your program will need to read the data from the file, add up the total count for each part, compare that against the reorder quantity, and display that reorder quantity if it is larger than the quantity on hand. If the quantity on hand is more than the reorder quantity, display a zero in the reorder quantity output label. The ten piece parts that are used, and their reorder quantities, are shown in Table 3.8. Because there are ten parts, your program will need to display the names and counts for those ten parts, and then the reorder quantities.

TABLE 3.7
The data for Exercise 12.

Product Name	Quantity on Hand	Reorder Quantity
Bezel	100	57
Bezel bracket	58	75
1-inch leader	43	90
2-inch leader	55	100
Tape	35	45
1-inch cord	15	25
2-inch cord	35	25
3-inch cord	22	45
1-inch bulb	87	50
2-inch bulb	53	80

TABLE 3.8
The data for Exercise 15.

Product Name	Reorder Quantity
Bezel	505
Bezel bracket	750
1-inch leader	900
2-inch leader	1000
Tape	450
1-inch cord	250
2-inch cord	250
Drive subassembly	450
1-inch bulb	500
2-inch bulb	800

In order to write this program, you need to know how to read a file. That requires three statements: one to open the file, one to read the data, and one to close the file. The file you need to read is on your work disk in the Ch-3 folder and is called **Inventory.Txt**. To open the file, you need to use the following Open statement:

```
Open "A:\Ch-3\Inventory.Txt" For Input As #1
```

Then, to read the data from the file, you need the statement

```
Input #1, strData_In
```

strData_In is the name of the input field. Each time you read the data, they will include the part name, a space, a slash, a space, and the quantity that was counted. A sample is

```
2-inch Bulb / 15
```

Thus, you need to scan for the slash and then use the number following it.

In order to read the data from start to finish, your program will need to use a loop, which will execute the code over and over until some condition within the program tells it to stop. We will explore loops in great detail in Chapter 4. The loop you need to use is

```
Do Until EOF(1)
    Your Code
Loop
```

This loop will execute until the end of the file is found. You need to open the file before the loop, input the data within the loop as well as your counts, and then close the file after the loop with the statement

```
Close #1
```

After the loop is complete, your program will have totaled the count of all the parts, and you will be ready to display the appropriate data.

Design the program and then create the form with the appropriate objects, including a **Print** button. Save the program as **File Reorder,** test it thoroughly, and print all the elements.

Using Loops and Arrays

4.1   Chapter Objectives

After finishing this chapter you will be able to:

- Explain the use of a Do…Loop.

- Demonstrate how to use a Do-While loop.

- Show how to use a For-Next loop.

- Explain and demonstrate how the Step command works.

- Explain the purpose of an array and demonstrate how one is used.

- Discuss what a control array is and demonstrate how one is used.

- Demonstrate how to use the MsgBox function.

- Demonstrate how to use the Graph object in your programs.

4.2   Introduction

In Chapter 3 we expanded your knowledge of variables and their use. In this chapter we will add to that knowledge by introducing **arrays.** An array is basically a series of variables that can be referred to by a common variable name. In addition to regular arrays that most programming languages use, Visual Basic also has a special type of array called a **control array,** which is essentially an array of objects such as text boxes. Both regular and control arrays will be discussed in this chapter.

When using arrays, it is common practice to use some type of looping structure so that you can reuse the code for accessing the array. We begin this chapter by examining several ways of creating loops. Along the way, we will uncover a few more Visual Basic functions that can prove useful.

4.3 A Look at the Widgets Graph Program

In Chapter 3 we created a program that calculated a sales receipt for the sale of Widgets. In this chapter you will add another program that deals with Widgets. Your boss at Widgets, Inc., wants you to create a program that can be used to show the quarterly sales along with the average of those sales. To add a bit of interest, he wants the data displayed as a graph. A sample program with these capabilities has been created for you.

1. Boot your computer, and run the **Widget Graph** program from the Ch-4 folder on your work disk to see the form shown in Figure 4.1

   This program has text boxes for the entry of sales for the four quarters for each of the three Widget products.

2. Click the **Display Graph** button and you immediately see the dialog box shown in Figure 4.2.

   This message is warning you that some of the data are not entered properly. We used a similar message in the last chapter, except that we simply displayed the message in a label. In this chapter you will learn how to display messages in a dialog box like the one shown.

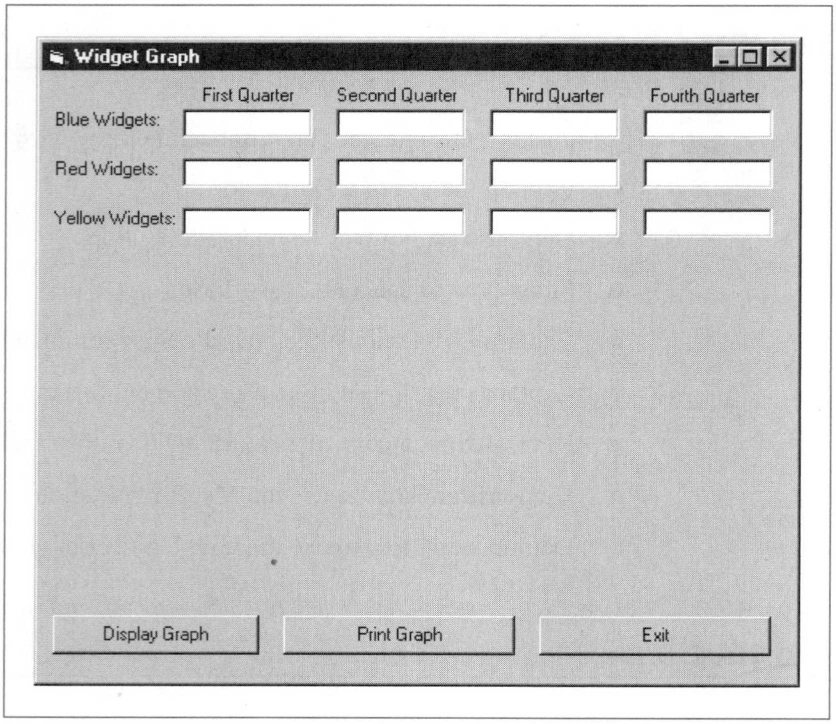

FIGURE 4.1
The Widget Graph program.

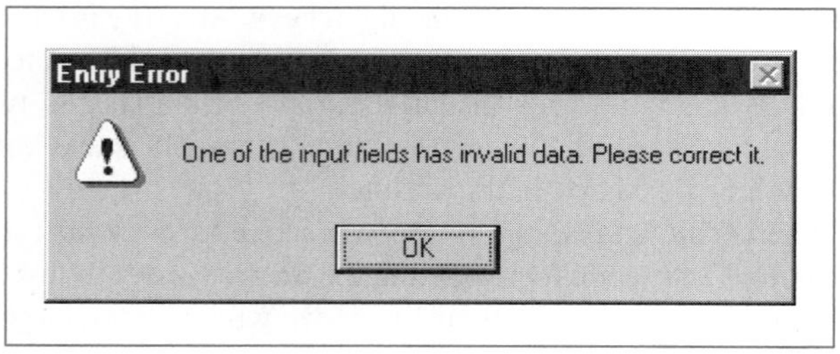

FIGURE 4.2
The dialog box indicating that you have invalid data.

There is another dialog box in the program.

3. Click the **OK** button to exit from the dialog box.

4. Click the **Exit** button to see the dialog box shown in Figure 4.3.

This dialog box asks you to confirm that you want to exit from the program. The first dialog box had just an **OK** button in it, whereas this dialog box has two buttons, one for **Yes** and one for **No**.

5. Click the **No** button to return to the program.

This program allows the user to enter data for the four quarters and the three products. It then calculates the total of the quarters for each product and displays a graph showing how the quarterly totals are related to the quarterly average. Let's see how this works.

6. Enter the data in Table 4.1 into the program.

7. Click the **Display Graph** button to see the graph as shown in Figure 4.4.

The graph shows the data in five groups, the first for the yearly average and then one for each quarter. In those groups, the first graph column is blue for the Blue Widgets, the second is red for the Red Widgets, and the last is yellow for the Yellow Widgets.

The most obvious new element in this program is the graph. The **Graph Control** object can be used to display data in a variety of formats set up through the object's properties. You will learn how to use this object. You will also learn how to use a looping structure so that you can loop through the text boxes to add up the totals. You can do the calculation because the text boxes are set up as a single **control array.** You will also learn about control arrays in this chapter.

8. Change some of the numbers in the text boxes, and click the **Display Graph** button. The graph will change.

9. Try several more samples until you are thoroughly familiar with the way the program works, and then exit the program.

FIGURE 4.3
The dialog box that appears when the **Exit** button is clicked.

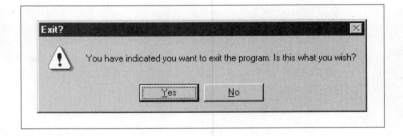

TABLE 4.1
The data for entering into the Widget Graph program.

Product	Quarter 1	Quarter 2	Quarter 3	Quarter 4
Blue Widgets	1254	2345	1879	3256
Red Widgets	2374	3487	3456	3001
Yellow Widgets	1345	1876	2392	1987

FIGURE 4.4
The displayed graph.

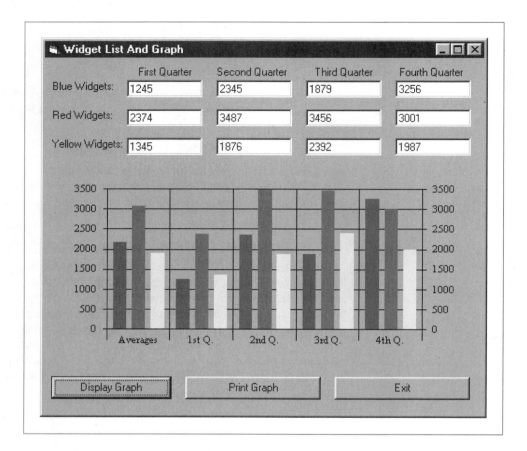

4.4   Creating a Loop

Provision for the reuse of code in a program is a vital part of any programming language. You must be able to write code so that after a section of it has executed, control in the program will return to the top of that section, allowing that same code to be executed again. If you properly use controls, Visual Basic already gives you this capability.

Let's try an example in which we will enter a series of grades and determine the average. The grades are entered and added together while the program counts the number of grades that were entered. Then, to determine the average, the accumulated total is divided by the number of grades entered.

1. Get into Visual Basic and put your work disk in drive A.

2. Create the form as shown in Figure 4.5 by doing the following:

    a. The caption of the form should be **Average Calculation** and the name should be **frmAverage_Calculation**.

    b. **Grade Entry:** is a label. You can use a control name you think appropriate.

    c. The box next to the **Grade Entry:** label is the text box in which you enter the grades. It has the control name **txtGrade_In**.

    d. The button has the caption **Average** and the control name **cmdAverage_Button**.

    e. The box next to the **Average** button is a label with a border around it. This label is where the average is displayed and has the control name **lblAverage_Out**.

FIGURE 4.5
The form for the looping experiment.

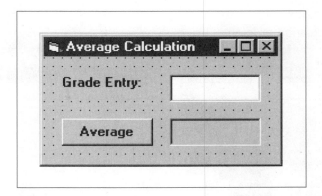

You need a variable in which to store the calculated total of the grades as they are entered. When you are accumulating a total, the standard technique is to add the keyed number to the total field and then store that total back in the total field. This requires a calculation statement using the txtGrade_In.Text property:

```
intTotal_Grades = intTotal_Grades + Val(txtGrade_In.Text)
```

3. Open the code window for the **Average** button, and key this statement into the procedure along with the appropriate comment statements. Then intTotal_Grades and int-Number_Grades (to be used shortly) need to be declared as static integers. They must be static so that they will retain their values as the program goes in and out of the procedure.

Now that we have the accumulated total, we need to divide it by the number of grades that have been input. This means we need some type of counter to determine this number. A counter is basically an accumulated total except that what you are accumulating is 1 each time. A counter statement would look like

```
intNumber_Grades = intNumber_Grades + 1
```

4. Key this statement after the other calculation statement, adding an appropriate comment.

> **HINT:** At this point, we will stop mentioning that you need to add appropriate comments. We will assume you always add the necessary comments on your own.

Now that you know the total of the grades and how many there are, you are ready to determine the average. The result of the average calculation will be displayed in the **lblAverage_Out** label box. The necessary statement is

```
lblAverage_Out.Caption = Str(intTotal_Grades / intNumber_Grades)
```

5. Key this statement after the other two.
6. Save the program as **Average Calculation**.
7. Run the program, key **100** as the first grade, and select the button.

Instantly 100 shows up as the average. Because there is only one number so far, the average is that number (intTotal_Grades / 1).

8. Key **50** as the second grade and select the button.

This time **75** appears.

FIGURE 4.6

The code for the Average Calculation program.

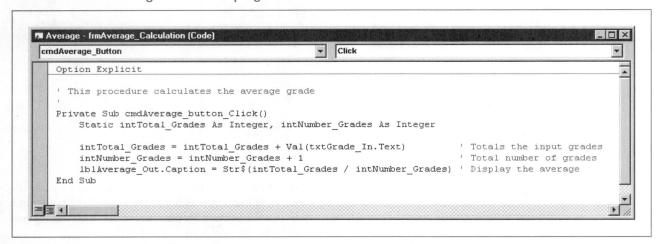

```
Average - frmAverage_Calculation (Code)

cmdAverage_Button                                          Click

Option Explicit

' This procedure calculates the average grade
'
Private Sub cmdAverage_button_Click()
    Static intTotal_Grades As Integer, intNumber_Grades As Integer

    intTotal_Grades = intTotal_Grades + Val(txtGrade_In.Text)      ' Totals the input grades
    intNumber_Grades = intNumber_Grades + 1                        ' Total number of grades
    lblAverage_Out.Caption = Str$(intTotal_Grades / intNumber_Grades) ' Display the average
End Sub
```

9. Key a few more numbers until you are satisfied that the program is working as it should, and then exit it. Your final code for the procedure should look like the code shown in Figure 4.6 (your comments will no doubt be different).

Again, the point of this exercise is to introduce the idea of a loop. You can continue to enter numbers, and the program will continue to use the same code, the button procedure, until you exit the program.

This is much better than having to enter a calculation statement for every grade that is entered. You could, for example, create a form that had 25 text boxes so that 25 grades could be entered, but then you would need 25 calculation statements (or one very long statement with 25 additions) in order to accumulate all the grades.

4.5   Looping within Procedures

Though Visual Basic handles many looping chores for you, there are times in a program when you need to reuse sections of code within a procedure without any external controls such as a click on a button. This is the type of loop we will look at now.

Looping with the Do...Loop

There are thousands of reasons why you might need a loop. For example, we use loops to read through records stored in a file on disk or to reuse any other series of statements that need to be executed multiple times. As we progress through this chapter and later chapters, you will encounter many uses of loops. We begin with some loops that use a counter to determine when the loop is finished.

In order to create a loop, we need some way of going from the bottom of the loop to the top of the loop. One way to do this in Visual Basic is with a **Do...Loop** construct. A Do...Loop is a defined structure with a starting point, the **Do-While statement** or **Do-Until statement**, and an ending point, the **Loop statement.** The only difference between the two loops is that the Do-While loop continues to execute *while the condition is true*, whereas the Do-Until loop continues to execute *until the condition becomes true*.

Because the Do-While loop tests the condition before executing the code to determine if the code should be executed, the code of a Do-While loop may never be executed. If the condition initially evaluates to false, the code within the loop is skipped and the program continues with the code after the loop.

On the other hand, the code of a Do-Until loop is always executed at least once. Even if the condition initially evaluates to false, the code is executed before the test is performed, and then the loop is exited.

Because the Do-While loop is more commonly used, we deal with it at this point. The format of the Do-While loop is

```
Do While condition
    Program code within the loop
Loop
```

Each time the loop is executed, Visual Basic checks the condition, and if it is still true, the loop code is executed again. Within the loop, you can use any valid Visual Basic code. To illustrate how a Do-While loop is constructed and used, we will create a program that uses a loop and shows us what is happening as the loop is executed.

1. Create a new form with a label box called **lblOutput** and a button as shown in Figure 4.7. The control name for the button should be **cmdDisplay**. The label box is used for display output so we can see that the loop is actually doing something. Save the program as **While Loop Testing**.

2. Open the code window for the button.

All loops must have some way to determine the end of the loop. When the user is controlling the looping process by entering data and then clicking a button, the user determines the end of the loop by exiting the program. When a Do…Loop is used, however, the condition determines the end. The condition generally takes a form similar to an If Test condition.

To determine how many times our code should loop, we can use a counter. As you will discover later, there are many other ways to control a loop: a counter is merely one of the easier ones. To see that the loop is actually doing something, we will display the value of the counter in the label box. We want the loop to execute exactly ten times and to show us what is happening. This means we need to set the value of intCounter to 1 before we start the loop so that the first time we print the counter, it will be 1. That requires a statement like

```
intCounter = 1
```

FIGURE 4.7
The form for looping practice.

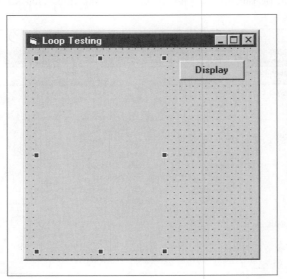

3. Key this statement as the first statement in the **Display** button procedure.

Then we will need to loop as long as the counter is 10 or less. So we need a Do-While statement such as

```
Do While intCounter <= 10
```

4. Key this statement as the second in the Display button procedure.

Within the loop, we need a statement to display the value of the counter so that we will be able to tell that something is actually happening:

```
lblOutput.Caption = lblOutput.Caption & Str(intCounter)
```

5. Key this statement as the third.

We concatenated the new counter value to what was already in the label to keep from overwriting what was there. If we simply assigned Str(intCounter) to the caption, what was previously in the caption would be replaced with the new value.

Then we need a statement to increase the value of the counter so that the loop will conclude when intCounter has increased beyond the test value:

```
intCounter = intCounter + 1   ' Increment the counter
```

6. Key this statement on the fourth line and key the Loop statement on the fifth line to close the loop.

The entire procedure should be as shown in Figure 4.8.

7. Run the program and select the button.

The display will be **1 2 3 4 5 6 7 8 9 10,** just as we wanted.

Having the program print the counter works, but it might be nicer if it printed a message with each number.

8. Exit the program and change the assignment statement to

```
lblOutput.Caption = lblOutput.Caption & "Counter =" & Str(intCounter)
```

9. Run the program and select the button.

Now the messages run into each other as shown in Figure 4.9, and they wrap to the next line at the edge of the label box. Not exactly what we want. What we need is a way to have each output line displayed on a separate line. That's not as hard as it might seem.

FIGURE 4.8
The code for the loop.

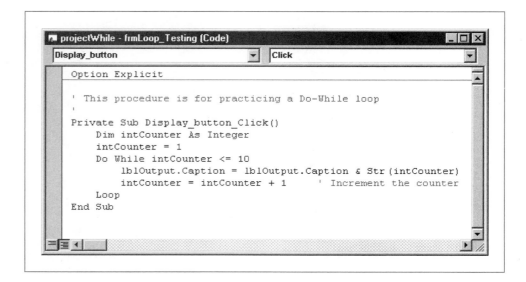

FIGURE 4.9
The initial program
output.

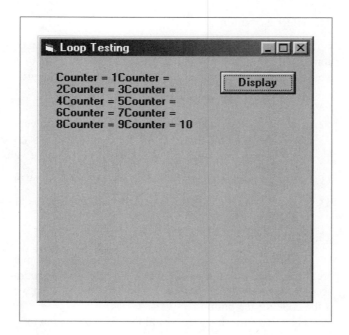

When any program divides text between lines, it places a return at the end of the first line and carries the rest of the text to the next line. Well, we can put a return in the caption at the end of each display line by using the predefined constant **vbCr**. If we want a return after each of the displayed lines in the label box, we just need to concatenate vbCr onto the end of the line:

```
lblOutput.Caption = lblOutput.Caption & "Counter =" & Str(intCounter)
 ↳ & vbCr
```

10. Exit the program, add the constant to the end of the statement, run the program, and select the button.

Now each line of output will appear on a separate line, as shown in Figure 4.10. Before we go on, let's make one final change to the program.

FIGURE 4.10
The revised program
output.

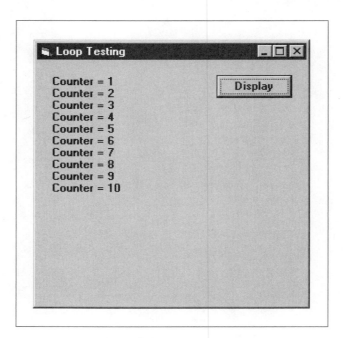

11. Select the button again.

Note that a second group of the counter lines appears as shown in Figure 4.11. We don't really want more than one group to appear in the display. How can we fix this? All we need to do is empty the caption before concatenating to it with the statement

```
lblOutput.Caption = ""              ' Empty the caption
```

12. Exit the program and add this statement to the procedure above the loop. It must be above the loop; otherwise, every time a new value is concatenated, the rest of the values will be erased, and we will end up with only one value in the display.

With this final change, we end up with the code shown in Figure 4.12.

13. Run the program and select the button twice. Now the lines appear only once, as shown in Figure 4.11.

14. Exit the program.

Before we move on to another loop, let's take a moment to discuss the design for the previous code. We won't bother to design the entire program, because you already know how to create the design for labels and text boxes. What we are concerned with right now is the code for the button.

The design for this loop would look like the following:

```
A.  cmdDisplay_Button
    1.  Click
        Erase lblOutput caption
        Do While counter is less than maximum
            Concatenate counter value to caption
            Increment counter
        End loop
```

Note that we didn't specify any particular variables or calculations in the design. We simply used words to explain the intended purpose of the code. Instead of End loop, you can use just Loop. We prefer to use End loop so that it will not look like Visual Basic code.

Now we are ready to discuss another loop.

FIGURE 4.11
The repeated output.

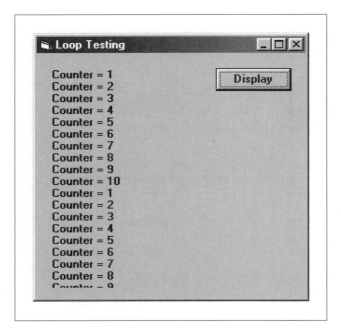

FIGURE 4.12

The completed code for the Do-While loop program.

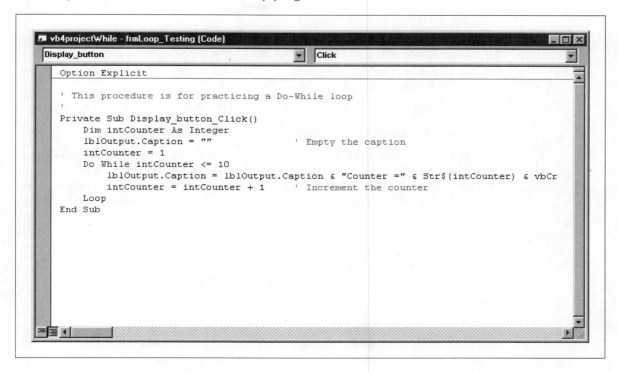

```
vb4projectWhile - frmLoop_Testing (Code)

Display_button                          ▼    Click                                  ▼

    Option Explicit

    ' This procedure is for practicing a Do-While loop
    '
    Private Sub Display_button_Click()
        Dim intCounter As Integer
        lblOutput.Caption = ""                  ' Empty the caption
        intCounter = 1
        Do While intCounter <= 10
            lblOutput.Caption = lblOutput.Caption & "Counter =" & Str$(intCounter) & vbCr
            intCounter = intCounter + 1      ' Increment the counter
        Loop
    End Sub
```

A Second Loop

Just to be sure you have the idea of how a loop is created, we will create another.

1. Using the **Save File As** option on the **File** menu, save the form file as **frmAlphabet_Loop**, and then use the **Save Project As** option and save the project as **Alphabet Loop Testing**. This will let you keep the While program and reuse the form for this new looping program. You can always use forms you have already created by loading the old program and saving it with a new name, as we've just shown.

What we are going to do is create a program that will print the alphabet in the label box, six letters per line.

Each character on the keyboard sends a unique code to the computer when that key is pressed. We can send those same codes to the computer by using the function **Chr**, which has the format

Chr(character number)

The character number in the format is the numeric equivalent of the character needed. The capital-letter alphabet begins with capital A, code 65. The other letters of the alphabet follow numerically. That is, B is 66, C is 67, and so on. If we want to display the alphabet with a loop, we can display the letters using the Chr function beginning with 65.

Currently, the loop counter starts at 1 because of the initialization statement we put in the code. We want to display the characters beginning with 65, so we must change that statement to initialize intCounter to 65.

2. Change the initialization statement.

Next, in order to be able to display only six letters on a line, we need a counter to keep track of how many have been displayed. Thus, we will need to add a line counter:

```
intLine_Counter = intLine_Counter + 1        ' Count printed letters
```

This statement must go right before the statement to display the letters in the label. The counter will also need to be declared as an integer.

3. Add the two statements to your code.

The assignment statement for the label caption needs to be modified. We put a message in the assignment statement that is not needed for this program, and the carriage return on the end should be removed as well. We will, however, display a blank between the letters. So your new assignment statement should be

```
lblOutput.Caption = lblOutput.Caption & Chr(intCounter) & " "
```

4. Change the assignment statement as shown.

The carriage return that we removed needs to be concatenated onto the caption, but only after every six letters have been displayed. Then, after the carriage return is used, the line counter should be zeroed out so that the program can begin counting again for the next group of six letters. You need to add—after the label assignment statement—a test like the following:

```
If intLine_Counter = 6 Then
    lblOutput.Caption = lblOutput.Caption & vbCr
    intLine_Counter = 0
End If
```

5. Add this code.

The last change needed is on the Do-While statement. Right now, the loop functions as long as Counter is less than or equal to 10. This won't work any more because Counter begins as 65. The exit number will have to be at least larger than 65. The question is how large the exit number should be. The loop begins with 65 and there are 26 letters, so it would seem that the proper number for ending the loop would be 91. This is correct.

6. Change your Do-While statement to

```
Do While intCounter <= 90
```

Now your entire procedure should be as shown in Figure 4.13.

7. Run the program and select the button. The program will display four lines with six letters and a final line with the two leftover letters, as shown in Figure 4.14.

8. Exit the program.

For-Next Loops

If the loop you need is a counter loop like the ones just discussed, you can use a different Visual Basic structure to take care of the loop details for you. The **For-Next** loop allows us to specify a loop that will have an automatic counter, an ending-point test, and a jump back to the top of the loop. The form of the For-Next loop is

```
For counter variable = start point To end point [Step step value]
    body of loop
Next counter variable
```

The **counter variable** can be any numeric variable and is the counter of the loop. It begins with the starting-point value and, if a Step isn't used, is increased by 1 every time the loop executes. When the counter value exceeds the ending-point value, the loop terminates and execution passes to the line following the Next statement.

The Step variable is used to specify the amount by which the loop counter is incremented or decremented if the change is to be some amount other than 1. The Step option will be discussed later.

FIGURE 4.13
The code for the Alphabet Loop Testing program.

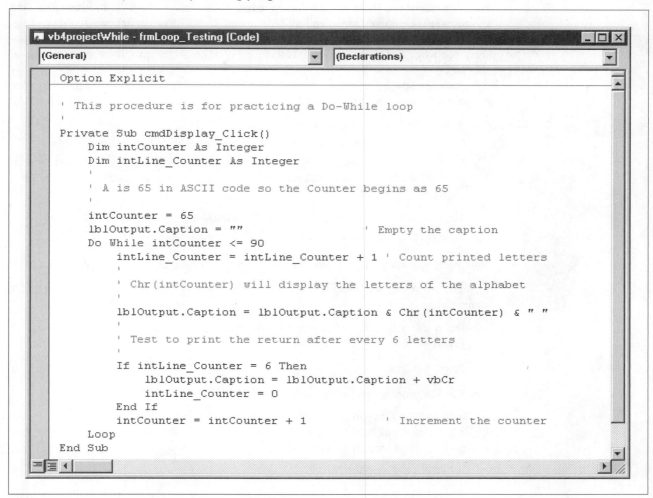

```
vb4projectWhile - frmLoop_Testing (Code)
(General)                                    (Declarations)

Option Explicit

' This procedure is for practicing a Do-While loop
'
Private Sub cmdDisplay_Click()
    Dim intCounter As Integer
    Dim intLine_Counter As Integer
    '
    ' A is 65 in ASCII code so the Counter begins as 65
    '
    intCounter = 65
    lblOutput.Caption = ""                  ' Empty the caption
    Do While intCounter <= 90
        intLine_Counter = intLine_Counter + 1 ' Count printed letters
        '
        ' Chr(intCounter) will display the letters of the alphabet
        '
        lblOutput.Caption = lblOutput.Caption & Chr(intCounter) & " "
        '
        ' Test to print the return after every 6 letters
        '
        If intLine_Counter = 6 Then
            lblOutput.Caption = lblOutput.Caption + vbCr
            intLine_Counter = 0
        End If
        intCounter = intCounter + 1          ' Increment the counter
    Loop
End Sub
```

FIGURE 4.14
The sample program
output.

The execution of a For-Next loop begins with the For statement setting the counter to the starting-point value. Then each statement in the body of the loop is executed until the Next is reached and the counter is incremented. Then control returns to the For again, and the counter is compared to the ending-point value. If it is less than or equal to that ending-point value, the loop executes again. Otherwise, control passes out of the loop to the statement following the Next statement. If there are no other statements, the procedure ends at that point.

Let's see how a For-Next loop might be constructed. We will redo the counter loop that displayed the numbers 1 through 10.

1. Reload the **While Loop Testing** program.

2. Save the form as **frmFor_Loop** and then save the project as **For Loop Testing**.

3. Open the code window, change the comment so that it mentions the For-Next loop instead of the Do-While loop, and delete lines until your code contains only the lines shown in Figure 4.15.

   The program needs to loop from 1 to 10, so the For statement should be

   ```
   For intCounter = 1 to 10
   ```

4. Insert this statement between the two lblOutput statements as shown in Figure 4.16.

   The only other statement you need is the Next statement, which follows the rest of the statements.

5. Insert the following statement after the caption assignment statement as shown in Figure 4.17.

   ```
   Next intCounter
   ```

6. Run the program and select the button.

   You will see that you get exactly the same result with this program as you did with the Do-While loop (look back at Figure 4.11). Using a For-Next loop is sometimes easier than using a Do-While loop. It depends on the purpose of the loop.

7. Exit from the program.

   We can begin a For-Next loop at any starting value we choose. The choice is usually 1, but it doesn't have to be.

FIGURE 4.15
The lines to be left for practicing the For-Next loop.

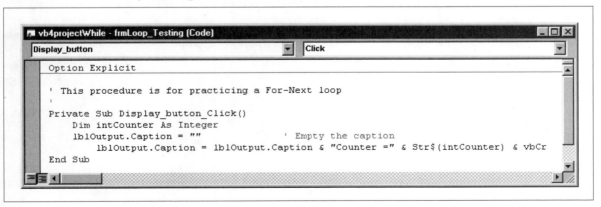

FIGURE 4.16

Where to insert the For statement.

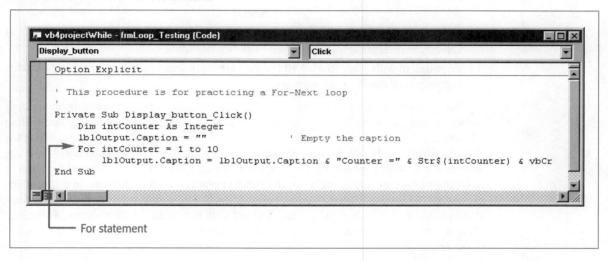

For statement

FIGURE 4.17

The placement of the Next statement.

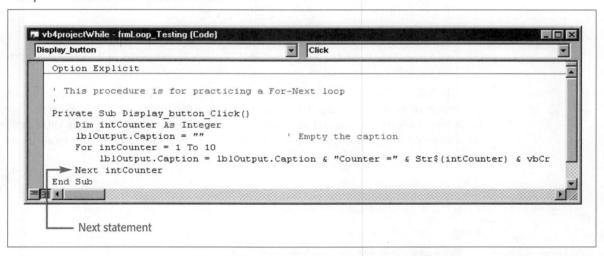

Next statement

8. Change the For statement to:

```
For intCounter = 8 To 10
```

9. Run the program and select the button.

Now the program shows only 8, 9, and 10, because it begins with 8 and ends when the counter exceeds 10. The value of intCounter is 11 when the loop finishes; that is the first number that is larger than 10.

The ending point can be any value, just as the starting point can be. Also, the starting and ending points do not have to be constants. We can use variables to allow more flexibility in our programs. Let's expand this program to use variables for the starting and ending points.

10. Add two text boxes to the form under the button. The control name for the first one should be **txtStart_Point** and that of the other should be **txtEnd_Point**.

11. Change the For statement to

```
For intCounter = Val(txtStart_Point.Text) To Val(txtEnd_Point.Text)
```

12. Run the program, key **5** as the starting point, and key **20** as the ending point. You get the numbers 5 through 20 displayed as shown in Figure 4.18.

13. Experiment with other starting and ending numbers until you have a good feel for what the loop is doing. Then exit the program.

As the loop executes, only the value of the counter changes. The starting and ending points remain the same. In fact, even if you change the values of the starting and ending variables in the body of the loop, the starting and ending points will not change. When the computer begins a For-Next loop, the starting-point value is set into the counter variable, and from that point forward, the starting value does not change. Also, when the computer reads the For statement, the value of the ending point is stored in memory in a special location that is separate from the ending variable itself. The comparison for the ending point is then made with this special location, and not with the ending-point variable. Therefore, changing the ending-point variable in the body of the loop has no effect. You will test that in the next step.

14. Insert the following line immediately after the For statement.

```
txtEnd_Point.Text = Str(10)
```

15. Run the program using 5 for the starting point and 20 for the ending point.

Note that the ending-point text box now has 10 in it but the loop runs through 20 anyway.

16. Try a few more numbers in the program until you are satisfied, and then exit the program and delete the line you just added (it adds nothing to the program).

The idea of changing the starting and ending points in the loop without changing the processing of the loop does not hold true for changing the counter variable. When the loop functions, it depends on the counter variable to know when it is finished. This value is derived strictly from the storage setup for that variable, so changing that variable modifies the loop. Let's experiment with that for a moment.

FIGURE 4.18

The output showing the count of 5 through 20.

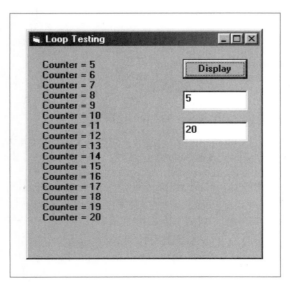

17. Insert the following line immediately after the For statement.

```
intCounter = 20
```

18. Run the program using 5 for the starting point and 20 for the ending point.

This time, you see only one number displayed: 20. Because you changed the value of the counter to 20, when the program reached the Next statement it increased the counter to 21. Then, when the program returned to the For statement and compared Counter to the ending point, it was found to be too large and the loop ended.

Changing the value of the counter variable can damage the processing of your loop. Be extremely careful with For-Next loops so that you don't change the counter variable within the loop unless you intend to. There are times when you need to modify the counter for a specific purpose, but again, be careful when you do.

19. Try a few more numbers in the program until you are satisfied, and then exit the program and delete the line you just added (intCounter = 20).

HINT: If your program is running without stopping, you have created an infinite loop. Press **Ctrl-Break** to stop the program.

The For-Next loop has a special feature that is important in certain instances. How would you write a For-Next loop if you needed the loop to count backwards, say, starting at 10 and stepping down to 1? Right now you can't. Try it.

20. Run the program and use **20** as the starting point and **5** as the ending point.

What happened? Nothing was displayed. Why? Because the counter started as 20 and the ending point was 5, the loop ended without ever executing. As you see, a regular For loop can't count backwards, but with an addition to the For statement, it will. By adding a **Step command**, you can increment your counter variable by whatever amount you choose, including a negative amount.

21. Add another text box to the form under the other two text boxes, and use the control name **txtStep_In** for this one.

22. Change your For statement to

```
For intCounter = Val(txtStart_Point.Text) To Val(txtEnd_Point.Text)
 ⤷ Step Val(txtStep_In.Text)
```

23. Run the program and use **20** as the starting point, **5** as the ending point, and **–1** as the step value. Now you see that the loop works properly and you get the numbers 20 through 5, decreasing each time by 1 as shown in Figure 4.19.

24. Use **20** as the starting point, **5** as the ending point, and **–3** as the step value. This time the counter is decreased by 3 and you see six numbers displayed.

25. Use **20** as the starting point, **50** as the ending point, and **5** as the step value. This time, the counter increased by 5 as the loop executed, as shown in Figure 4.20.

26. Try various other starting, ending, and step values until you understand exactly what the program is doing. Then exit and save the program.

You may have occasion to use one For-Next loop inside another. This is called **nesting** the loops. Each loop will work just as we have been discussing, and your only real concerns should be that you don't use the Next statements in the wrong place, that you don't use the same counter variable on both loops, and that you don't accidentally change the outside loop counter somewhere in the inside loop. A nested loop might look like this:

FIGURE 4.19
The output decreasing
from 20 to 50.

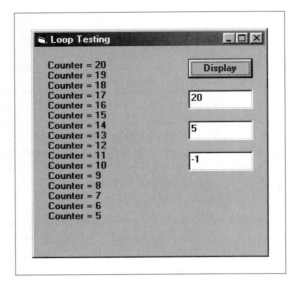

FIGURE 4.20
The counter increasing
by 5.

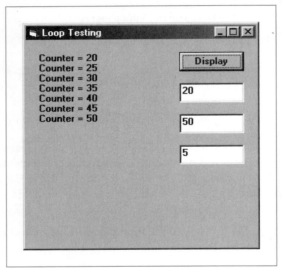

```
For intCounter = 1 to 20
    outside loop code
    For intInside_Counter = 10 to 70
        inside loop code
    Next intInside_Counter
    more outside loop code
Next intCounter
```

As you can see, you can use code in the first For-Next loop before and after the inside loop. Actually, the inside loop is a part of the code of the outside loop.

4.6   The ZOrder Method

When you have several objects of the same kind on a form, they can be hidden behind each other and then their order can be changed. That is, you can have a series of buttons, for example, that lie one behind another, and only the one at the top of the pile is active. This is known as the **ZOrder**, and we will write a program to see how it works.

1. Start a new project and change the caption on the form to **ZOrder Practice**. Save the program as **ZOrder Practice**.

2. Add a button to the form with the control name **cmdButtons**, copy it (**Ctrl-C**), and paste it (**Ctrl-V**) back two more times, answering **Y** when asked whether you want to create a control array.

3. Separate the buttons on your form so that you can work with all of them. In a moment, we will stack them on top of each other again.

4. Find the one with the index of zero and change the caption to **Button 0**. Then change the captions of the other two buttons to **Button 1** and **Button 2**, corresponding to their indexes.

5. Now stack the buttons on top of each other, add a text box (**txtOutput**), and size the form so that it looks like the one in Figure 4.21. The button you have on top may or may not be Button 2 as in the figure; that doesn't matter.

6. Open the code window for the buttons. Remember that there is only one code window for all three of the buttons, because they are a control array. Key the following statements:

```
txtOutput.Text = "Button" & Str(Index) & " was just on top"
cmdButtons(Index).ZOrder 1
```

The first statement displays a message in the text box specifying which of the buttons was on top before the button was selected. The second statement uses the **ZOrder** method to move that button (the one that was just clicked) to the back. The order of objects of the same kind on a form is called the ZOrder. The ZOrder method works with any objects of the same kind on the form. They do not have to be elements of a control array. We used a control array because that's what we are currently dealing with, but you can use ZOrder on any objects that can be placed on top of each other.

The ZOrder method is used to move the objects to the top or bottom when they are stacked. If you specify 0 as the ZOrder parameter (or if you don't specify a parameter; zero is the default), the specified object is moved to the top. 1 specifies that the object be moved to the bottom of the stack. Thus, the foregoing command will move the just-used button to the bottom of the stack.

7. Run the program and note which of the buttons is on top.

8. Click the button, and the message for the button that was just on top will appear in the text box, and a new button will be on top.

9. Click each of the buttons that appears on top until you are comfortable with the idea of order, and then exit the program.

If you want to put your stacked controls in a specific order during design time, you can use the **Bring to Front** (shortcut key **Ctrl-J**) and **Send to Back** (shortcut key **Ctrl-K**) options on the **Order** submenu of the **Format** menu.

FIGURE 4.21
The form, showing the stack of buttons and the text box.

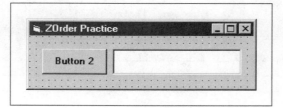

4.7   The About Dialog Box

Most professional programs have a menu system, and a Help menu with an About dialog box is usually a part of that. An **About dialog box** is usually just a dialog box that gives information about the program. In this section, you will create an About dialog box that will later be added to the major project of this book.

To show what the program is going to look like, a sample has been created for you.

1. Run the **About Dialog Box** program, found in the Ch-4 folder of your work disk, to see the form shown in Figure 4.22.

This dialog box has the standard general program information, such as copyright date and version number, but to add interest and show a little imagination, it has a scrolling marquee at the top of the form. This is not a dialog box that the user will typically keep on the desktop, so there are no **Minimize** or **Maximize** buttons on the form. You will see how to turn them off.

> **HINT:** Because of the differences in the speeds of the various computers used, your scrolling display may or may not flicker. If it does, don't let it bother you. This program is used to illustrate certain programming techniques and is not meant to represent the best way to do a scrolling display. There are other ways to do the same type of display.

2. Exit from the program.
3. Create a new project and change the caption of the form to **Personal Information Manager**.

    You will begin work on a Personal Information Manager in the next chapter.

4. Save the form as **frmAbout** and the project as **About Dialog Box**.

    All that is required to create the marquee is four labels.

5. Add the label shown in Figure 4.23. Change the background color to red. The control name of this label is unimportant, because it will not be referenced.

FIGURE 4.22
The About Dialog Box program form.

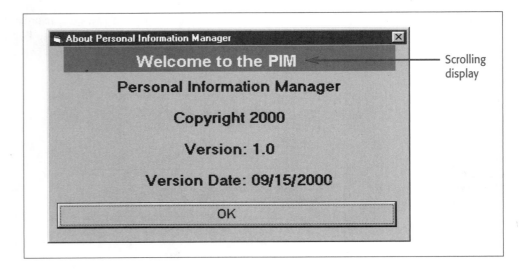

FIGURE 4.23
The first label of the
About dialog box.

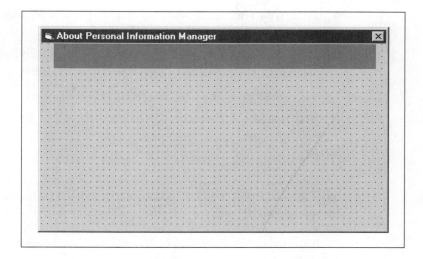

6. Create a second label and name it **lblMarquee**. Change its ForeColor property to yellow, change its AutoSize property to True, and change its **BackStyle** property to **0 - Transparent**.

The **BackStyle** property dictates whether the label is see-through (0 - Transparent) or not (1 - Opaque). We want this label to be see-through because we want the red of the other label to show through. We are going to position it on top of the other label.

7. Position the lblMarquee on top of the first label and change the caption to **Welcome to the PIM** as shown in Figure 4.24.

The problem with this label is obvious. The letters are too small. We will fix that.
A **font** is a particular style for the characters displayed. There are six font properties available:

■   **FontName** is the name of the font being used. There are many different fonts that can be used; the particular ones available are the ones previously installed.

■   **FontBold** makes the text bold.

■   **FontItalic** makes the text italic.

FIGURE 4.24
The lblMarquee label
on top of the first label.

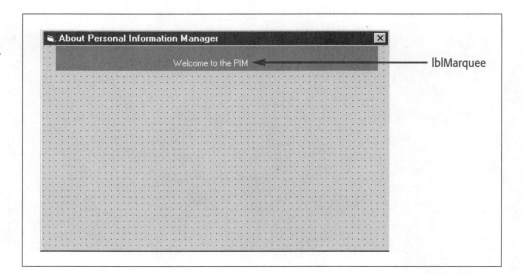

- **FontStrikeThrough** draws a dash through each text character.
- **FontUnderline** underlines the text.
- **FontSize** is the point size, a point being 1/72 of an inch. This is the font characteristic we are going to change.

8. Select the lblMarquee label and select the Font property.

You will see a small button appear to the right. This allows you to load the Font dialog box.

9. Click the button to load the Font dialog box as shown in Figure 4.25.

One machine may have more or fewer fonts installed than another. Certain fonts are automatically installed with Windows, but additional fonts can be installed and some that are not used may be deleted. The installed fonts are not related to the Visual Basic installation.

This dialog box lets you specify the Font (**FontName** method), Font style (methods **FontBold** and **FontItalic**), and Size (**FontSize** method) as well as a couple of effects: **Strikeout** (**FontStrikeThrough** method) and Underline (**FontUnderline** method). The dialog box also has a small window to show you what the font will look like as you make the changes.

In your program code, if you want to change one of the font properties, it must be done by specifying the object followed by the method for that font property (as listed above). For example, if you have a label called lblOutput and want to change the font to bold and italic, you do it with the following two statements:

```
lblOutput.FontBold = True
lblOutput.FontItalic = True
```

As you can tell, these properties are switches. Either they are on (True) or they are off (False). All font properties have False as their default. A font is bold only if you set it to bold. It will not automatically be bold.

10. In the Font dialog box, select **Arial** as the font name and then click on **Bold**. Change the size of the font to **16** and click the **OK** button.

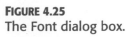

FIGURE 4.25
The Font dialog box.

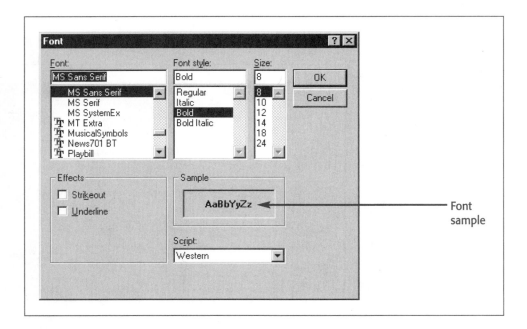

Now the font in the label is larger, as shown in Figure 4.26.

Next, we must add two more small labels at the end of the large red label. We are going to move the lblMarquee label, and it needs to move *under* the labels on the end of the red label. This will make the marquee label seem to disappear off the end of the red label. For the marquee label to go under the end labels, the end labels must be on top of the marquee label in the ZOrder. That's why we discussed the ZOrder.

As long as the labels are added to the program in the right order, their ZOrder will be correct. The newer elements are always created with a higher ZOrder than the ones before them.

11. Add two small labels, delete the captions, and position them on the ends of the large label as shown in Figure 4.27.

12. Add the rest of the labels and the button as shown in Figure 4.28. The control names of the labels are, top to bottom, **lblPIM, lblCopyright, lblVersion,** and **lblVersion_Date**. Key the appropriate copyright year and the date in the version date label caption. The rest of the captions should be as shown. Change the font size to 14 and make it bold on each of the labels. The control name of the button is **cmdOK**.

FIGURE 4.26
The About dialog box, showing the larger font.

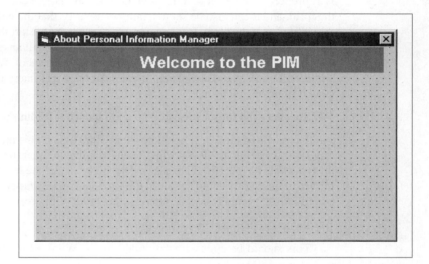

FIGURE 4.27
The About dialog box with the small labels added.

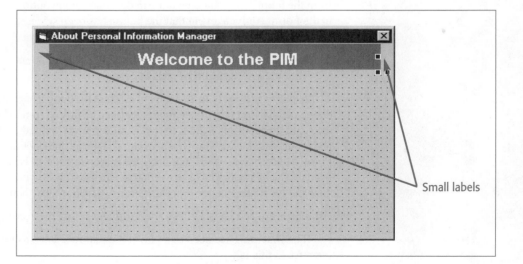

FIGURE 4.28
The About dialog box
with the final objects
added.

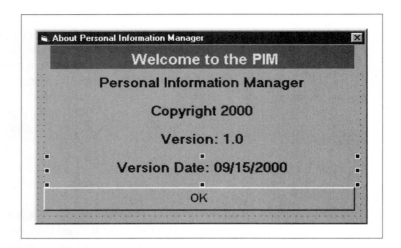

To make the marquee work, we simply move the label. We have already discussed the Left property, which specifies where the left side of an object is displayed on the form. The Left property can be set to a negative number so that the entire label is off the left side of the form, and it can also be set to a number so large that the entire label will be pushed off the right side of the form. But how far left do we want to start the label? And how far to the right do we want to move it? A couple of calculations will answer both of these questions.

To decide how far to the left we want to start the label, we merely need to know the width of the marquee label. Then, if we position it that many twips left of zero, the entire label will be off the form.

13. Switch to the form and select the marquee label Width property.

The width of the label should be about 3000 twips. This means that the label Left property needs to begin at –3000 twips. Then, to move the marquee label across the surface of the red label, we merely add to the Left property so that the left position becomes larger and farther to the right. We do this until the label has moved far enough to the right to be completely off the form. This is dictated by the width of the form.

14. Switch to the form and select the Width property.

This should be approximately 6800 twips. We need to move the label until the Left property is 6800 or larger.

This movement can be handled in a Do…Loop, but we have to have some way to exit from the loop. This should be done in the code for the button, but how do we signal the loop in the Form_Activate event that the button has been selected? One way is with a form-level variable that can be set when the button is clicked.

15. Switch to the (General) procedure on the form, and add a Dim statement for a boolean variable called **mblnOff_Right**.

Now we are ready to add the code. The **OK** button is going to be used to exit from the dialog box, so the code for the marquee has to be placed somewhere else. We have been using the Load_Form event as a place to put code that we wanted to run before anything else happens, but in this case that won't work. The form does not appear on the desktop until the Form_Load code finishes. We need the marquee code to be running after the form has appeared. The form does have an event that will work, however. The **Activate** event is executed after the form has appeared on the desktop, because only then does the form become active.

16. Open the code window for the form and select the Activate event from the event list.

The first thing we need to do is set the marquee label as far left as necessary. The statement to do this is

```
lblMarquee.Left = -3000
```

17. Key this statement into the procedure.

Boolean variables are initialized to False so that if we loop as long as mblnOff_Right is false and set the variable to True in the button code, the marquee will continue to operate until the user clicks the button. Thus the Do statement should be

```
Do Until mblnOff_Right = True
```

> **HINT:** To emphasize that the Do…Loop will always be executed at least once, some programmers put the conditional on the Loop statement instead of on the Do statements, as in the following:
>
> ```
> Do Until
>    loop code
> Loop mblnOff_Right = True
> ```
>
> This will work just as well as the method we are employing in our code—using the conditional on the Do statement. Which form to use is merely a matter of preference.

18. Key this statement into the procedure.

As we have said, to move the marquee label, we need to increase the value of the Left property. How many twips should we add to it? To answer such questions, you generally have to try one value and then adjust it until you find the value that seems to work the best. Five twips seems to work well. The statement to increase the Left property follows:

```
lblMarquee.Left = lblMarquee.Left + 5
```

19. Key this statement into the procedure.

We want the label to move to the right only until it is off the form, the edge of which is about 6800. Therefore, we need to test the Left property to discover when it is larger than 6800. Then we will need to set it back to –3000 so that it will begin moving across the form again. This is done with the following statements:

```
If lblMarquee.Left > 6800 Then
    lblMarquee.Left = -3000
End If
```

20. Key the If Test into the procedure.

Now the program runs into a problem. If we close the loop now by coding the loop statement, this procedure will continue to execute until the user clicks the **OK** button. Unfortunately, while the loop is executing, the user cannot click the button. Nothing in the program is functional except the loop.

Visual Basic has a function to handle this situation. The **DoEvents** function will release control from the program to Windows so that events such as a mouse click on a button can be detected. This function is added to the program as a single element statement.

21. Add a DoEvents statement and then the Loop statement to end the Do…Loop. This gives you a complete procedure:

```
lblMarquee.Left = -3000
Do Until mblnOff_Right = True
    lblMarquee.Left = lblMarquee.Left + 5
    If lblMarquee.Left > 6800 Then
        lblMarquee.Left = -3000
    End If
    DoEvents
Loop
```

FIGURE 4.29
The code for the entire program.

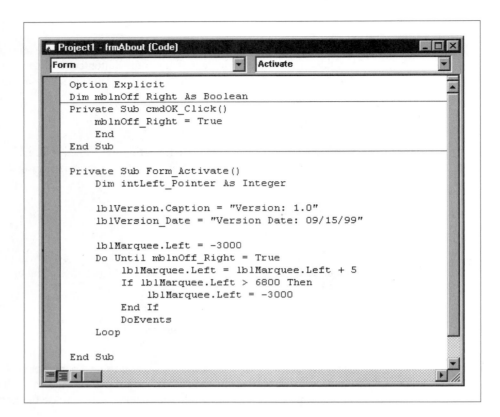

```
Project1 - frmAbout (Code)

Form                            Activate

Option Explicit
Dim mblnOff_Right As Boolean
Private Sub cmdOK_Click()
    mblnOff_Right = True
    End
End Sub

Private Sub Form_Activate()
    Dim intLeft_Pointer As Integer

    lblVersion.Caption = "Version: 1.0"
    lblVersion_Date = "Version Date: 09/15/99"

    lblMarquee.Left = -3000
    Do Until mblnOff_Right = True
        lblMarquee.Left = lblMarquee.Left + 5
        If lblMarquee.Left > 6800 Then
            lblMarquee.Left = -3000
        End If
        DoEvents
    Loop

End Sub
```

The last piece of code the program needs has to do with the **OK** button. Later, when this form is added to the PIM program as the About dialog box, the **OK** button will be used to put the form away and return to the main program form, but for now, the **OK** button needs to exit the program. And we also need to set the value of mblnOff_Right to True so that the loop will end.

22. Switch to the code window for the **OK** button and add the two statements.

Now the program is ready. The code for the entire program is shown in Figure 4.29.

23. Run the program, and the marquee should scroll across the screen. Click the **OK** button, and the program will end.

4.8   Arrays

Thus far in our study of Visual Basic, when we have needed to store a number or string other than those stored in an object, we have used a variable as a pointer to the memory location where those data were stored. Each variable could store only one item at a time, so if we needed to store two items, we had to use two different variables. The more items we needed to store, the more variables we had to use. Imagine the difficulty of using a program that has 100 variables or, worse yet, 1000. Just getting the appropriate data into 1000 variables would require 1000 assignment statements.

Visual Basic gives us a much easier way to store large amounts of similar data. We merely tell Visual Basic that we want a series of storage locations set aside; Visual Basic will then allow us to access the information stored in these locations by referencing the locations using their positional numbers. These locations are adjacent to one another in a block of memory called an **array.** The entire array is labeled with a single variable name that follows the same variable-name rules that apply to regular variables. Each of the single stored items in an array is referenced by number. Suppose, for example, that you had five grades that you wanted stored for later use by the program. You could store all five in an array called **intGrade,** and each grade would be stored in its relative location in the array. The first location or number would be referenced by calling for intGrade(1) (pronounced intGrade sub 1), the second location or number by calling for intGrade(2), and so on. If we were to look at the storage pictorially, it would look like this:

intGrade(1) = first item

intGrade(2) = second item

intGrade(3) = third item

intGrade(4) = fourth item

intGrade(5) = fifth item

It might be helpful to think of an array as similar to an apartment complex. The apartment complex has a name, but to find a particular apartment, we must know the number of the apartment. A single variable, on the other hand, is like a single-family home. For access, only the name of the house (the address) is needed.

For an array, the number within the parentheses is called the **index** or **subscript,** and it can be either a number or a numeric variable. This allows a lot of freedom in accessing an array. You can use a loop counter as the index for the array going from 1 to 100, for example. In this way, you can automatically access each element of a 100-element array in sequence.

Array items are just like other variables. You can store the items in an array either by using an assignment statement or by inputting the data with a text box or from a file stored on disk. As an example of how an array can be manipulated, we will create a program with data stored in a label that will act like a disk file for input. We will load those data into an array and then manipulate that array in several ways.

Let's take a look at your next program.

1. Run the **Array Manipulations** program from the Ch-4 folder on your work disk to see the form shown in Figure 4.30.

This program takes the data from the text box and reverses the list. It also adds up all the numbers and displays the total and the average. Then it sorts the numbers into numerical order.

2. Click the **Manipulate the Array** button to see the results shown in Figure 4.31.

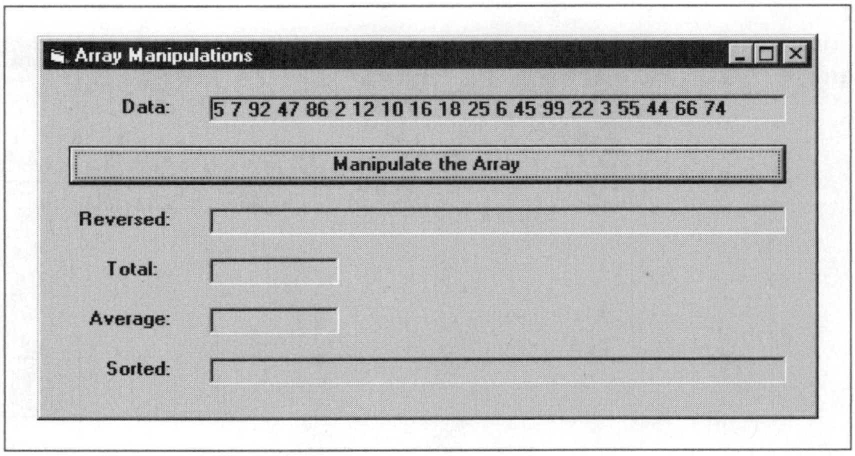

FIGURE 4.30
The form for the Array Manipulations program.

FIGURE 4.31
The results shown in the Array Manipulations program.

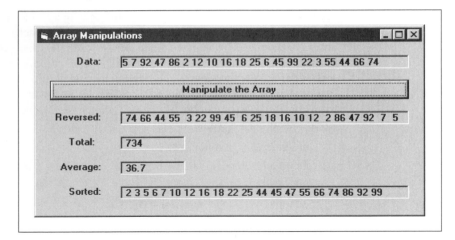

Look at the Data and Reversed labels. As you can see, the numbers are displayed in reversed sequence in the Reversed label. Now look at the data in the Sorted label. There, the numbers are in numerical sequence.

Let's see how all this is done.

Extracting the Array Elements

1. Create a new form that looks like the one in Figure 4.32.

   a. The boxes are labels with a border; use the control name **lblData_In** for the data, and the others are **lblReversed_Out**, **lblTotal_Out**, **lbl_Average_Out**, and **lblSorted_Out**. Use a label to indicate the purpose of each of these output labels as shown in the figure. You may use the default label names for these labels; they will not be referenced.

   b. Key the numeric data shown as the caption for lblData_In. Be sure to put a blank at the end of the last number, or you will get an error when you run your program.

   c. Use **cmdManipulate_Button** for the control name of the button.

   d. Store the program as **Array Manipulations**.

The first thing we need to do is see how to load the data from the caption into the array. This requires us to use some of the string manipulation functions we discussed in Chapter

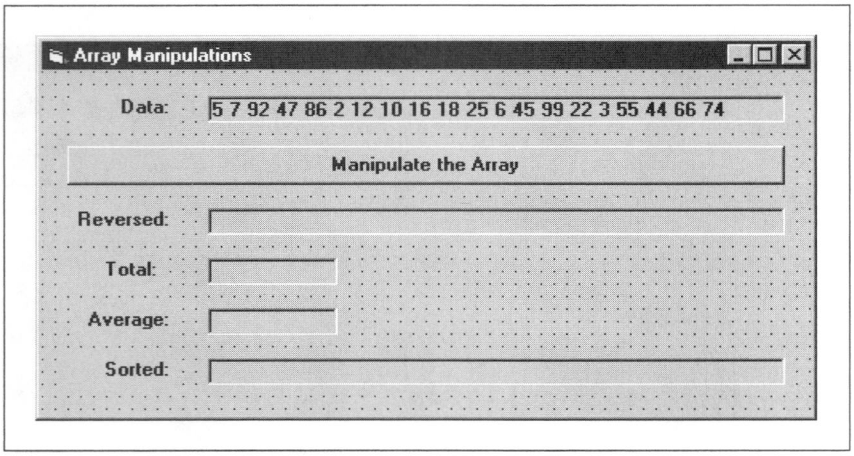

FIGURE 4.32
The form for practice using an array.

![Form titled "Array Manipulations" with a Data field showing "5 7 92 47 86 2 12 10 16 18 25 6 45 99 22 3 55 44 66 74", a "Manipulate the Array" button, and empty labeled fields for Reversed, Total, Average, and Sorted.]

3. We will use the Instr function to find the spaces between the numbers so that the numbers can be separated. The caption is text, so we will use a string array rather than converting the individual substrings to numeric values. We could do that, but later we will want to change the data to a series of words, and the conversion would have to be removed. Array manipulations work the same whether the array is string or numeric, so let's stick with text strings.

Because an array requires storage to be set aside for the number of elements in the array, you must tell the program how many elements your array is going to require. An array declaration is done the same way as a variable declaration. The only difference is that you follow the variable name with the number of elements you want to have in the array. The statement for our array is

```
Dim strData_Array(20) As String
```

As you see, arrays are declared in the same manner as variables except that you specify the number of elements. In this case, you will need 20 elements (there are 20 numbers in the caption).

You can declare an array in the (General) procedure, which would make it local to the form. You can also declare one in a module as Global, which would make the array available to all the forms and other modules in the entire program. If you declare an array with the Dim statement, you can have an array that is static in size by specifying the number of elements, or you can make it a **dynamic,** or changeable, array by leaving out the number of elements and using just the empty set of parentheses:

```
Dim strData_Array () As String
```

If you do this, then before you use the array in the program, you must use the **Redim** statement to redimension the array so that the program will know how many elements the array should have. Later in the program, if you want the array to have more or fewer elements, you can use the Redim statement again to respecify the number of elements.

2. Open the code window for the button, and key the Dim statement with 20 elements into the procedure.

There are 20 elements to be extracted from the caption, so we will use a For-Next loop.

3. Key the following For statement:

```
For intCounter = 1 To 20
```

We need to use the Instr function to determine the position of each of the array elements in the caption so that they can be extracted. We will need a statement such as

```
intPosition = Instr(intLast, lblData_In.Caption, " ")
```

This statement begins the search beyond the last extracted element by using the intLast variable.

4. Insert this statement after the For statement.

Now, because the Instr statement cannot begin its search at position zero, we need to initialize intLast to 1.

5. Insert the following statement above the For statement.

```
intLast = 1
```

After we have figured out the position of the element to be extracted from the caption, we need to extract it and assign it to the array. We will use the Mid function for that.

```
strData_Array(intCounter) = Mid(lblData_In.Caption, intLast,
 intPosition - intLast)
```

intLast will contain the position just beyond the last extracted element, and because there are two-digit and one-digit numbers, we cannot use a literal as a length. Instead, we'll use the expression intPosition – intLast, which evaluates to the correct number of digits.

6. Key the foregoing statement after the Instr statement.

Finally, we need to figure out what value should be assigned to intLast. It cannot be just intPosition, because intPosition points to the blank space following the element to be extracted. We want intLast to point to the first character of the next element, so we need to add 1 to intPosition:

```
intLast = intPosition + 1
```

7. Key this statement followed by the **Next intCounter** statement.

Now your entire procedure (thus far) should look like that shown in Figure 4.33.

Displaying the Data in Reverse Order

With the code created to store the data in the array, it is time to create the code to manipulate those data. We will begin by displaying the elements of the array in reverse order. That is, we will display the last element first, the next to last second, and so on.

> **HINT:** Keep in mind that we are going to *display* the data from the array in reverse order. We are not going to reverse the order of the data in the array. These are two distinct operations.

1. Be sure to add a separation comment between the previous routine and this next routine. Something like the following is sufficient:

```
'
' Reverse the array
'
```

FIGURE 4.33
The array manipulations code thus far.

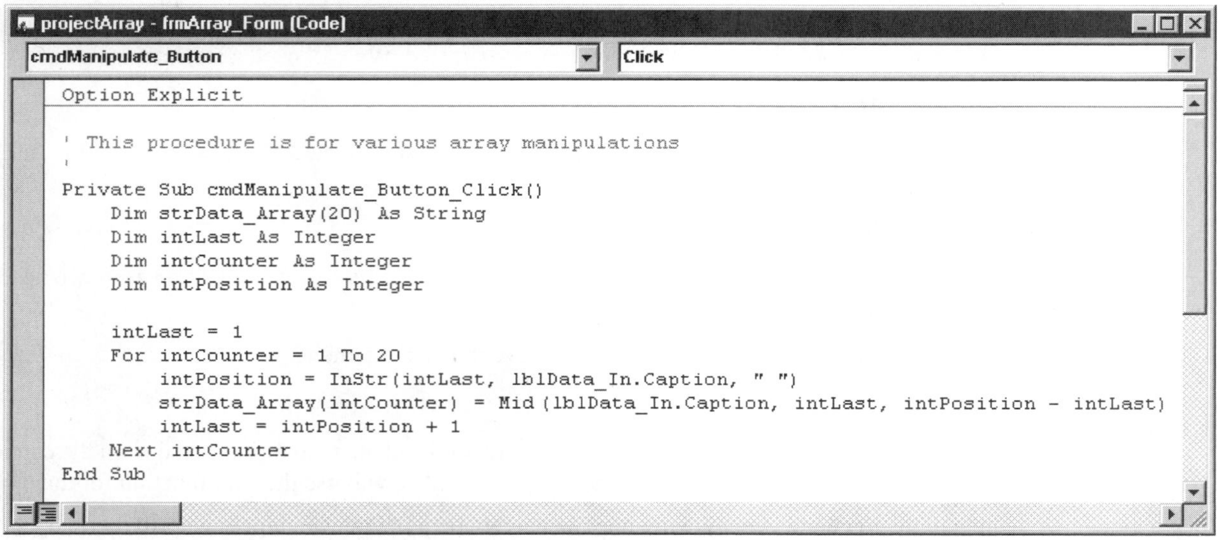

```
projectArray - frmArray_Form (Code)

cmdManipulate_Button          ▼   Click                              ▼

Option Explicit

' This procedure is for various array manipulations
'
Private Sub cmdManipulate_Button_Click()
    Dim strData_Array(20) As String
    Dim intLast As Integer
    Dim intCounter As Integer
    Dim intPosition As Integer

    intLast = 1
    For intCounter = 1 To 20
        intPosition = InStr(intLast, lblData_In.Caption, " ")
        strData_Array(intCounter) = Mid(lblData_In.Caption, intLast, intPosition - intLast)
        intLast = intPosition + 1
    Next intCounter
End Sub
```

2. Key the comments.

Before we reverse the array and display it in the label, we need to erase the label so the output is displayed there only once. This requires the statement:

```
lblReversed_Out.Caption " " =
```

3. Key this statement after the comments.

To reverse the way the data from the array are displayed, we need to display the elements of the array from the end to the beginning. The easiest way to do this is to use a For-Next loop starting at 20 and counting down:

```
For intCounter = 20 To 1 Step -1
```

4. Key this statement.

To display the elements, you need to assign them to the caption (lblData_Out.Caption) the same way you saw earlier in the chapter:

```
lblReversed_Out.Caption = lblReversed_Out.Caption & " " &
 ↳ Data_Array(intCounter)
```

That's it, except for the Next intCounter statement.

5. Add the final two statements as shown in Figure 4.34, run the program, and select the button. Instantly you see the reverse display of numbers in the lblReversed_Out box.

Calculations

Now that we have the data in the array, there are many things that can be done with it. A couple of simple things we can do are to add up the numbers and then to determine the average. We will use the next two labels we already have on the form.

FIGURE 4.34
The program code with the For-Next loop to display the array in reverse order.

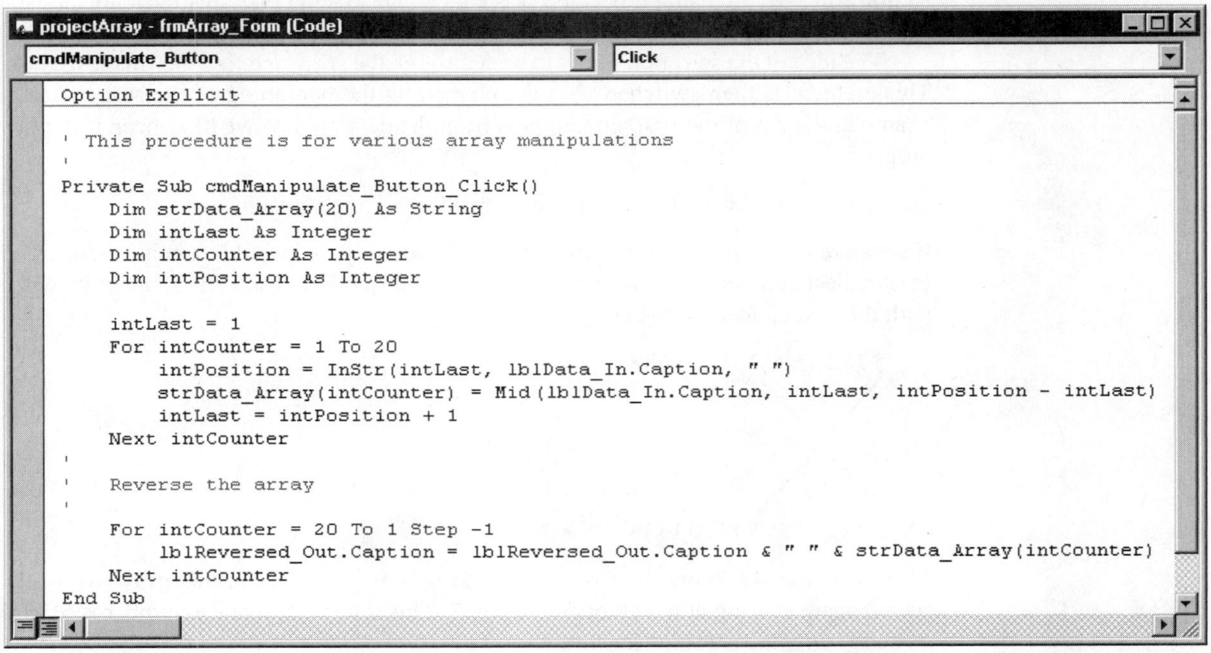

```
projectArray - frmArray_Form (Code)

cmdManipulate_Button              ▼   Click                              ▼

 Option Explicit

 ' This procedure is for various array manipulations
 '
 Private Sub cmdManipulate_Button_Click()
     Dim strData_Array(20) As String
     Dim intLast As Integer
     Dim intCounter As Integer
     Dim intPosition As Integer

     intLast = 1
     For intCounter = 1 To 20
         intPosition = InStr(intLast, lblData_In.Caption, " ")
         strData_Array(intCounter) = Mid(lblData_In.Caption, intLast, intPosition - intLast)
         intLast = intPosition + 1
     Next intCounter
 '
 '    Reverse the array
 '
     For intCounter = 20 To 1 Step -1
         lblReversed_Out.Caption = lblReversed_Out.Caption & " " & strData_Array(intCounter)
     Next intCounter
 End Sub
```

1. Change to the code window, and key the following additional code (be sure to declare all new variables).

```
'
' Calculate Total and Average
'
  For intCounter = 1 To 20
    intTotal = intTotal + Val(strData_Array(intCounter))
  Next intCounter
  lblTotal_Out.Caption = "Total =" + Str(intTotal)
  lblAverage_Out.Caption = "Average =" + Str(intTotal / 20)
```

2. Run the program and select the button. The total of 734 and the average of 36.7 appear in the new boxes.

3. Exit the program.

Sorting the Array

A commonly used array manipulation technique is **sorting.** This simply means putting a list of items into some type of sequence. As an example, suppose we have a list of people who have contributed to our favorite charity, and we need to know how long it has been since everyone on the list contributed. We could sort the list into order by date of last contribution. Then we would know who has contributed recently and who has not done so for a long time.

How does one go about putting a list in sequence? Well, many sorting techniques exist, some better than others. Probably the technique most often learned is the **bubble sort.** This sorting technique starts at the beginning of the list and moves the biggest items to the end. When you finish, the list is in sequence. Though the bubble sort is one of the most widely taught, it is by no means the best sort. It is extremely slow. Therefore, instead of using the bubble sort, we will use one that is twice as fast and just as easy to learn: the **selection sort.** Keep in mind, however, that there are many sorts that are faster than the selection sort. We are using it because it is easy to understand and illustrates how a list can be put into sequence. It will also give us practice manipulating an array.

The idea of the selection sort is to scan through the array and find the smallest element. This element is then switched with the element at the beginning of the array. Take, for example, the list of the first ten numbers from the caption data we have been using in our program:

```
5 7 92 47 86 2 12 10 16 18
```

If we were to use the selection sort on these ten numbers, we would examine them and find the smallest number in the list. In this case, 2 is the smallest. Then this element is switched with the first element in the array, 5.

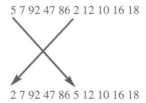

Then, because we know the first element is now the smallest in the array, we begin to search again starting at the second element, 7. This time, the smallest number is 5. This is switched with the starting element, 7.

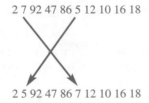

2 7 92 47 86 5 12 10 16 18

2 5 92 47 86 7 12 10 16 18

Now the search begins at the third element, 92, and 7 is the smallest. After 7 is switched with 92, the list becomes

```
2  5  7  47  86  92  12  10  16  18
```

The rest of the procedure is as follows:

Search from position 4 to find 10, switch, and the list becomes

```
2  5  7  10  86  92  12  47  16  18
```

Search from position 5 to find 12, switch, and the list becomes

```
2  5  7  10  12  92  86  47  16  18
```

Search from position 6 to find 16, switch, and the list becomes

```
2  5  7  10  12  16  86  47  92  18
```

Search from position 7 to find 18, switch, and the list becomes

```
2  5  7  10  12  16  18  47  92  86
```

Search from position 8 to find 47, and the list doesn't change.

```
2  5  7  10  12  16  18  47  92  86
```

Search from position 9 to find 86, switch, and the list is completely sorted.

```
2  5  7  10  12  16  18  47  86  92
```

Now you understand basically how the sort works. We will see how to construct one by adding it to our current program. We will use the lblSorted_Out label that we put on our form earlier for the output of the sorted array.

We have been using only text in our array manipulations thus far. We can continue doing this with the sort, but we need to realize something first. If we have two strings, one containing 6 and the other containing 19, the order in which they would be sorted is 19 first and then 6. This is because a text sort looks at the characters left to right, and 1 (the first character of 19) is less than 6. In order to use strings in our sort and get them properly ordered, we will need to put a blank at the beginning of each number with just one digit.

The single statement in the extraction routine,

```
strData_Array(intCounter) = Mid(lblData_In.Caption, intLast,
 ↳intPosition - intLast)
```

will need to be changed to the following If Test:

```
If intPosition - intLast > 1 Then
    strData_Array(intCounter) = Mid(lblData_In.Caption, intLast,
     ↳intPosition - intLast)
Else
    strData_Array(intCounter) = " " & Mid(lblData_In.Caption,
     ↳intLast, intPosition - intLast)
End If
```

This will determine which of the array elements are single-digit and will put a space before each single digit.

1. Make the foregoing change in your code (leave the original statement, and key the other statements around it).

Now the output data contain extra spaces and will not fit in the reversal output box. All you need to do is use the LTrim function in the assignment statement to remove the extra spaces. Instead of

```
lblReversed_Out.Caption = lblReversed_Out.Caption & " " &
    strData_Array(intCounter)
```

you will need to use

```
lblReversed_Out.Caption = lblReversed_Out.Caption & " " &
    LTrim(strData_Array(intCounter))
```

2. Make this change.

Now let's work on the code for the sort.

In order to find the smallest item in a list, we need to set up a save variable to store the smallest value. In the beginning, we will put in the largest possible value. Our list is made up of string numbers, so we need to pick something larger than numbers (you cannot use 99 because 99 is in the list). It turns out that letters are larger (in terms of the storage codes) than numbers, so we can use AA as our largest possible value. Using AA will ensure that all elements in the array will be less and that the first comparison for the smallest value will be less than this initial value.

We will also create another variable that will hold the index number of the smallest array element. This is necessary for switching the elements of the array.

After the item is located, the switching is done through a third temporary variable. This switch is interesting in itself. For example, suppose you have two items: strItem_One, which contains 5, and strItem_Two, which contains 10. We want to switch them so that strItem_One is 10 and strItem_Two is 5. At first it might seem as if you need to use only two assignment statements, like this:

```
strItem_One = strItem_Two
strItem_Two = strItem_One
```

The problem with this is that both variables now have the same value. The first assignment will indeed give strItem_One the value of 10, but because the second assignment assigns the value of strItem_One to strItem_Two, and the value of strItem_One is now 10, both variables end up with the value of 10. Somehow, we lost a value. The only way to do an exchange is by using a temporary storage variable for one of the numbers:

```
strTemporary = strItem_Two
strItem_Two = strItem_One
strItem_One = strTemporary
```

Now the value of strItem_Two (10) is stored in strTemporary, the second assignment puts the value of strItem_One (5) into strItem_Two, and the third assignment will take the temporary value of 10 and put it in strItem_One. This gives strItem_One the value of 10 and strItem_Two the value of 5, just as we wanted.

Now we are ready to build the sort routine. We add it on the end of the current procedure.

3. After the current code, add the following sort routine section.

```
'
' Selection Sort Routine
'
```

First we need to blank out the label so the data are displayed only once. This is the statement:

```
lblSorted_Out.Caption = " "
```

We need to use a For-Next loop to go through the elements in order to switch them, but we don't need to use the last element because it will already be the largest. Our routine will need to begin with

```
For intCounter = 1 To 19              ' To Elements -1
```

Note that we added a comment on the end of the statement clarifying where the 19 came from (20 − 1). We will add comments to most of the statements in this routine so that when you look at it later you will remember the purpose of each of the statements.

Then we need to set up the comparison value. It will need to be inside the main loop so it can be reset at the beginning of each search for the smallest element. It will be

```
strCompare = "AA"                     ' Comparison value
```

Now we need a new loop. We have established the starting point for each search using the outside loop, and now we need a loop for the actual search. It must begin at the intCounter position and search all the remaining elements. Thus, it should be

```
For intInside_Counter = intCounter To 20    ' Comparison loop
```

We need to compare each element in the array against the comparison value to find the smallest one. If we find one smaller, we change the comparison value and save that spot so that it can be exchanged with the array element where the search began. The code for this is

```
If strData_Array(intInside_Counter) < strCompare Then
    strCompare = strData_Array(intInside_Counter)    ' Store smaller
                                                     ↳ item
    intSmaller = intInside_Counter                   ' Save the array
                                                     ↳ spot
End If
```

That's the end of the inner loop, so

```
Next intInside_Counter
```

Now the items need to be switched:

```
strTemporary = strData_Array(intSmaller)              ' Store item to
                                                      ↳ switch
strData_Array(intSmaller) = strData_Array(intCounter)' Beginning item
                                                      ↳ during loop
strData_Array(intCounter) = strTemporary             ' Put in original
                                                      ↳ spot
```

And that's the end of the outside loop, so

```
Next intCounter
```

Finally, the newly sorted array must be displayed in the label box.

```
For intCounter = 1 To 20
    lblSorted_Out.Caption = lblSorted_Out.Caption & " " &
    ↳ LTrim(strData_Array(intCounter))
Next intCounter
```

The entire new routine is shown in Figure 4.35 (don't forget to declare the new variables strCompare, intInside_Counter, intSmaller, and strTemporary).

4. Add the rest of this code to your routine, run the program, and select the button. If all goes well, your caption should give the sorted data as shown in Figure 4.36.

5. Exit the program.

FIGURE 4.35
The selection sort routine.

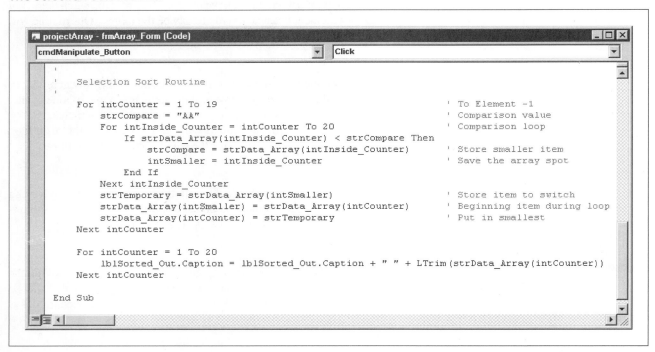

```
projectArray - frmArray_Form (Code)

cmdManipulate_Button                              Click

    '
    '   Selection Sort Routine
    '
    For intCounter = 1 To 19                              ' To Element -1
        strCompare = "AA"                                 ' Comparison value
        For intInside_Counter = intCounter To 20          ' Comparison loop
            If strData_Array(intInside_Counter) < strCompare Then
                strCompare = strData_Array(intInside_Counter)   ' Store smaller item
                intSmaller = intInside_Counter                  ' Save the array spot
            End If
        Next intInside_Counter
        strTemporary = strData_Array(intSmaller)          ' Store item to switch
        strData_Array(intSmaller) = strData_Array(intCounter)  ' Beginning item during loop
        strData_Array(intCounter) = strTemporary          ' Put in smallest
    Next intCounter

    For intCounter = 1 To 20
        lblSorted_Out.Caption = lblSorted_Out.Caption + " " + LTrim(strData_Array(intCounter))
    Next intCounter

End Sub
```

FIGURE 4.36
The output of the program, showing the sorted data.

Array Manipulations

Data: 5 7 92 47 86 2 12 10 16 18 25 6 45 99 22 3 55 44 66 74

Manipulate the Array

Reversed: 74 66 44 55 3 22 99 45 6 25 18 16 10 12 2 86 47 92 7 5

Total: 734

Average: 36.7

Sorted: 2 3 5 6 7 10 12 16 18 22 25 44 45 47 55 66 74 86 92 99

Earlier we made sure that we put a space before each number that was only one digit long so that the numbers would be sorted properly. We also could have been assured of a proper sort by sorting the numbers numerically. This would require only a couple of minor program changes. If we were sorting numerically, the initial number put into strCompare would have to be larger than the largest numeric value; we could use 100 (instead of AA). Then we would simply change the If Test that currently is

```
If strData_Array(intInside_Counter) < strCompare Then
```

to the following so that it would compare numeric values instead of string values.

```
If Val(strData_Array(intInside_Counter)) < Val(strCompare) Then
```

With these changes, the sort would work the same as it did before. You can experiment with these changes on your own. Be sure to save your code before you begin to experiment, and then switch back to this saved code before going to the next section.

Sorting Words

Now that we know how to use a sort, let's make the few changes necessary to sort words instead of numbers. Because this is a character string sort, the changes will be mostly in the number of elements.

1. Change the caption of **lblData_In** to the following words:

```
word now new next this array time sample got see string
```

> **WARNING:** Be sure to put a space at the end of **string**. Otherwise, your program will not work properly because the Instr function is looking for a blank to determine where each word ends.

There are only 11 words instead of the 20 numbers, so everywhere in the program that we previously used 20, we will need to change it to 11.

> **HINT:** If we had used a variable everywhere that we used 20, we could have corrected the program by simply changing the statement that assigned 20 to the variable rather than having to change all the individual statements.
>
> For example, if we had used
>
> ```
> intNumber_Elements = 20
> ```
>
> and then For statements like
>
> ```
> For intCounter = 1 to intNumber_Elements
> ```
>
> we could just have changed the assignment statement to
>
> ```
> intNumber_Elements = 11
> ```
>
> and the necessary For statement changes would all have been made automatically.

2. Change all the For statements that use 20 so that they use 11 instead (and 10 for the number of elements minus 1).

The comparison value of AA that we used is no longer appropriate. We need a comparison value that is larger than that of any of the words in our list. The largest value in words is all *z*s. Thus, the comparison statement should be changed to

```
strCompare = "zzzzzz"
```

3. Save the form as **frmWords_Form** and save the program as **Word Manipulation**.

   The sort routine will now look like the one shown in Figure 4.37.

4. Run the program and select the button. Your words should be sorted as shown in Figure 4.38. The words are also reversed.

> **HINT:** The total and average calculations did not cause any problems because the Val function gives a result of zero if there are no numbers to convert.

5. Exit the program.

FIGURE 4.37

The new sort routine.

```
projectArray - frmArray_Form (Code)                                    _ □ ×

cmdManipulate_Button                        ▼    Click                           ▼

    '
    '   Selection Sort Routine

    For intCounter = 1 To 10                              ' To Element -1
        strCompare = "zzzzzz"                             ' Comparison value
        For intInside_Counter = intCounter To 11          ' Comparison loop
            If strData_Array(intInside_Counter) < strCompare Then
                strCompare = strData_Array(intInside_Counter)   ' Store smaller item
                intSmaller = intInside_Counter                  ' Save the array spot
            End If
        Next intInside_Counter
        strTemporary = strData_Array(intSmaller)          ' Store item to switch
        strData_Array(intSmaller) = strData_Array(intCounter)   ' Beginning item during loop
        strData_Array(intCounter) = strTemporary          ' Put in smallest
    Next intCounter

    For intCounter = 1 To 11
        lblSorted_Out.Caption = lblSorted_Out.Caption & " " & LTrim(strData_Array(intCounter))
    Next intCounter
End Sub
```

FIGURE 4.38

The words sorted and reversed.

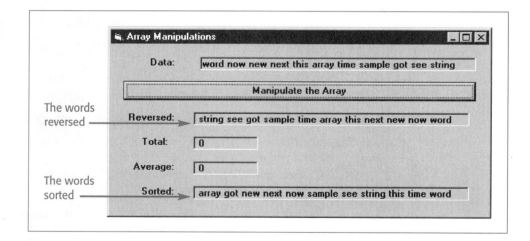

The words reversed

The words sorted

Initializing Arrays

If you are reusing an array in a program, you may want to erase all the elements before loading new data into it. Visual Basic gives you the **Erase** statement for just such a task. The form of this statement is

```
Erase Array_Name
```

and it works differently depending on how your array was declared. If you set up a static array, the elements are initialized; numeric elements are set to zero, and string elements are set to the empty string (""). If you are using a dynamic array, Erase releases the memory used by the array. Then the array must be redeclared before it can be accessed again. If you use the Redim statement in a procedure, it will erase the elements as well as specify the number of elements, so the Erase statement is not necessary.

Using Multidimensional Arrays

Now that we have had the opportunity to use single-dimension arrays and are familiar with them, it is time to turn our attention to arrays with more than one dimension. That is, we have thus far used arrays that are called one-dimensional, each with a single column. Many times, however, we need to be able to work with data that require two or more dimensions. A simple example is data found in a tax table. Such data are really better examined by using an array with two dimensions so that the storage will match the way the table is constructed. Let's use an example to help us understand this concept better. Table 4.2, a small table of costs and sales prices of items, will assist us.

Now, this table is set up to allow us to determine the cost to us, and the price to our customer, of items we are selling. For example, item 100 costs us 1.05 and we are selling it for 1.50, which yields us a profit of .45.

A two-dimensional array needs to be dimensioned just like a single-dimension array, except that two dimensions are used. Recall that the Dim statement we used earlier was

```
Dim strData_Array(20) As String
```

To use a second dimension, we simply add the second dimension as follows:

```
Dim strData_Array(20,3) As String
```

In two-dimensional arrays, the first dimension is generally used as the row of the table created by the array and the second dimension as the column. That is the normal convention. Actually, the two numbers can work either way. It depends on how the information in the table is put into the array. Our example program will put them in "row first," so the first number will represent the rows.

Now let's look at how the necessary data could be loaded into a two-dimensional array. We will use a small loop to put the data, row first, into the array. The sample routine is

```
For intCounter = 1 To 20                    ' 20 rows
    For intInside_Counter = 1 To 3          ' 3 Columns
        strData_Array(intCounter, intInside_Counter) = strData_Item
    Next intInside_Counter
Next intCounter
```

Note that we don't specify where strData_Item comes from. It might be extracted from a text box or a file, as we discussed earlier. We are not going to write a program, so where the data actually come from is not important.

The program stores the data as follows. The first time through the loops (there are two loops), intCounter is 1 and so is intInside_Counter. That means that the first strData_Item is put in strData_Array(1,1). Then intInside_Counter increases, which means that the second strData_Item, which is the item in the first row, second column of the table, is placed in array location strData_Array(1,2). Note that we have row 1, strData_Array(1,) and column 2, strData_Array(,2). The third item read is placed in strData_Array(1,3). This drops us out of the inside loop, and the outside loop is increased

TABLE 4.2
The data to be viewed as a two-dimensional array.

Item Number	Cost	Selling Price
100	1.05	1.50
105	2.25	2.69
200	3.25	5.50
207	1.25	2.05

to 2. The fourth strData_Item will then be placed in the array in strData_Array(2,1), which corresponds to row 2, column 1, and the rest of the array gets the same treatment through all 20 rows.

Now that we have the data in the array, how do we find the particular piece of data we need? For example, say we are visually examining the table and are asked, "What is the cost of item 105?" We merely scan down column 1 (the item numbers), find item number 105 (row 2), and then look in the cost column (the second column) for the cost of 2.25. We can do the same thing in our program by knowing which columns correspond to the item number, cost, and selling price. We merely scan through column 1, which consists of items strData_Array(1,1), strData_Array(2,1), and so on through strData_Array(20,1), until we find the item number we are looking for. How do we determine that we have found it? With an If Test, of course. Such a routine, assuming the item number we want is stored in a text box called **txtItem_Wanted**, would be similar to this:

```
Scan Routine
intFound = 0
Do While intCounter < 20 and intFound = 0
    If txtItem_Wanted.Text = strData_Array(intCounter,1) Then
        intFound = intCounter
    End If
    intCounter = intCounter + 1
Loop
If intFound = 0 Then
    Display Error
    txtCost_Out.Text = ""
    txtSelling_Price_Out.Text = ""
Else
    txtCost_Out.Text = strData_Array(intFound, 2)
    txtSelling_Price_Out.Text = strData_Array(intFound, 3)
End If
```

Note that we used a compound conditional on the Do-While statement. It works the same way there as on an If Test. In this case, we need to be sure we have not yet gone through all the elements (intCounter < 20) or already found the item (intFound = 0). After the loop, if intFound is still zero, we know that the item wasn't found. This means we need to display some type of error (we will see how an error can be displayed later) and blank out the displays of the cost and selling price. If the item was located, we display the cost and selling price by using intFound as the first subscript and the appropriate position in the table as the second subscript.

> **HINT:**   You can actually create arrays with up to 60 dimensions, though arrays with more than two dimensions are generally very specialized and are seldom used.

4.9   Control Arrays

Visual Basic allows you to use a special type of array that is called a **control array** because it is created from the controls used on your form. You created a control array of labels in Chapter 3 to make copying the labels easier.

The Calculator

The easiest way to understand a control array is to see an example of how one is actually used. For this, we will create a small calculator that adds the number selected to the displayed total.

1. Create a new form as shown in Figure 4.39 by doing each of the following:

   a. Create the new form and change the caption to **Calculator** and the name to **frmCalculator**.

   b. Add the label for the output at the top of the form as shown. You need to set the BorderStyle property to Fixed Single. Use the control name **lblAnswer_Out**. Change the font size to 14 and make the font bold.

   c. Add the first button, change the caption to **1**, and use the control name **cmdNumber**.

   d. Press **Ctrl-C** to copy the button to the clipboard, and press **Ctrl-V** to paste another into the form.

   Instantly the warning message shown in Figure 4.40 appears. This is the same message you saw in Chapter 3 when you created the control array of labels. It is just telling you that you are about to create a control array. The message appears so that you won't create a control array unintentionally.

2. Select **Yes** to create the control array, and add the button. Move the first "1" button out of the way and position this new "1" button in its place.

   Each element of a control array is assigned an **index** value. The first element is automatically assigned the zero index. Because we are just going to add the number of the button to the displayed total, we don't need a zero button. The first "1" button you moved out of the way has an index of zero. The copied button has an index of 1. The subsequent buttons will have indices related to the order in which they were pasted into the program.

FIGURE 4.39
The form for creating the calculator.

FIGURE 4.40
The warning box telling you that you are about to create a control array.

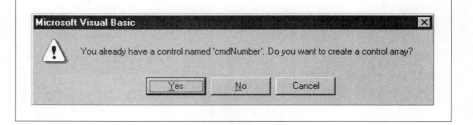

3. Paste a third button, position it as shown in Figure 4.39, and change the caption to **2**.

4. Add, position, and change the captions of the rest of the buttons as shown in Figure 4.39. Be sure to position the buttons in the sequence of the numbers on the caption. That is, the fourth button added to the form must be 3 because its index is 3, the fifth button added must be 4 because its index is 4, and so on.

5. Select the first "1" button and delete it.

6. Open the code window for any of the buttons. They will all open the same procedure.

The Sub statement for the procedure is

```
Private Sub cmdNumber_Click(Index As Integer)
```

Note that at the end of the Sub statement, "Index As Integer" appears in parentheses. This is the index number of the control array element. It is passed into the procedure as a parameter so that you can use a test to determine which of the buttons was selected. That is, if the button with the 1 on it is selected, the index will be 1. This is true because you deleted the first button with the "1" on it that had the zero index. That's why we made a second "1" button and deleted the first. Now the "1" button has an index of 1. This technique works well as long as you keep the zero-indexed object until all the objects you need have been added. If you deleted the button with the index of zero before you had added all of the other buttons, the next one you added after deleting the zero-indexed button would have been given an index of zero. But as long as you leave the zero button until you have added them all, you will end up with the indices used properly.

We want to add the index value of the clicked button to the total being displayed in the label. This can be done with the statement

```
lblAnswer_Out.Caption = Str(Val(lblAnswer_Out.Caption) + Index) & " "
```

This statement takes the caption, converts it to a number, adds the index that corresponds to the number on the button, converts the new total to a string, concatenates a blank on the end, and stores the number back in the caption. The blank on the end of the caption is just to move the caption away from the edge of the label. This makes it a bit more readable.

7. Key the foregoing statement into your procedure.

8. Save the program as **Calculator**.

9. Run the program and select a few of the buttons to see the total increase. The output will look similar to that in Figure 4.41. After determining that the program is working properly, exit it.

We mentioned that when you are adding the buttons to the form, you must be sure to add them in the proper sequence. As elements of a control array are added, Visual Basic automatically assigns their index values. If you do place various control array objects on your form in the wrong sequence, they can be renumbered. You can change the index numbers of your objects by using the **Index** property.

10. Select the button with 1 on it and change to the Index property in the Properties window.

Note that the value of this property is 1.

11. Change to the button with 2 on it. Now the Index value will be 2.

If one of the indices is incorrect, you can change it. You cannot do it directly, but we'll soon discuss that.

12. Change the index value of this button to **3**, and then change to another button. A dialog box appears telling you that there is already a control object with the index 3.

13. Select **OK** to exit the dialog box.

FIGURE 4.41
The calculator, showing the output.

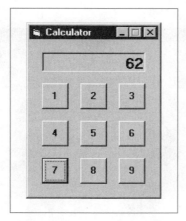

The process of changing an index is a bit more complicated than the change you just attempted. Suppose button 4 has an index of 7 and button 7 has an index of 4. This is the reverse of what it should be. You cannot just change the index of button 4 to 4, because button 7 is already using that index. What you have to do is change the index of button 4 to 14 (or some other number beyond the actual number of indices), change the index of button 7 to 7 so that it will no longer be a button with an index of 4, and then change the index of button 4 to 4. By using this technique, you can renumber the indices of any control array that needs to be rearranged for some reason.

4.10   Creating the Widget Graph Program

Now that you know something about control arrays, we will return to the Widget Graph program to get more experience with such arrays.

1. Start a new program and add all the objects shown in Figure 4.42 with the following considerations:

   ■   The row and column labels are a control array named **lblMiscellaneous**.

   ■   The top row of text boxes are a control array called **txtBlue**. The indices should be 0 through 3.

   ■   The middle row of text boxes are a control array called **txtRed**. The indices should be 0 through 3.

   ■   The bottom row of text boxes are a control array called **txtYellow**. The indices should be 0 through 3.

The Graph Control

The graph generation is done by the **Graph Control**, which we add by using the Components dialog box.

1. Select the **Components** option from the **Project** menu. You saw this dialog box in Chapter 2 when you turned on the Multimedia Control.

2. Scroll the list and select the Microsoft Chart Control item. Click the **OK** button. This will add the **Graph Control** to the Toolbox.

3. Add the Graph Control to the form, using the tool shown in Figure 4.43. Size and position the control as shown in Figure 4.44.

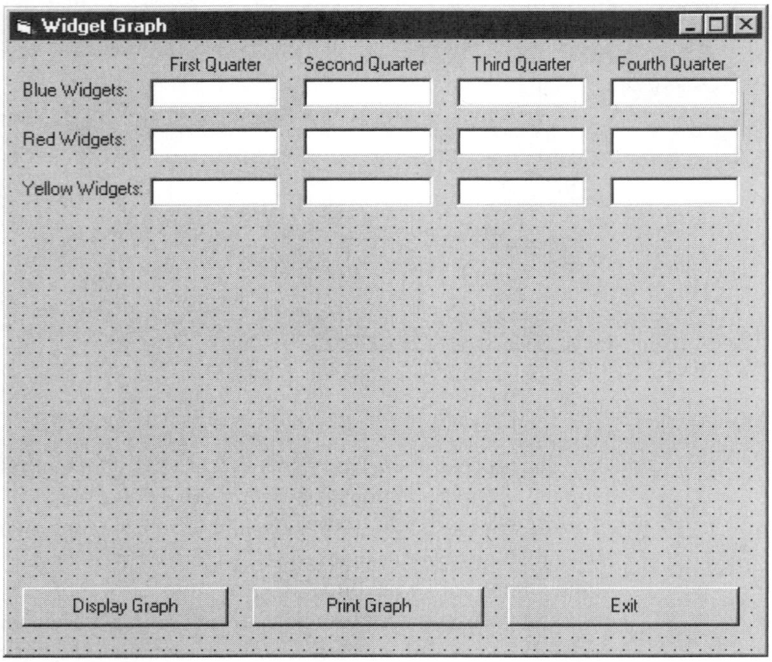

FIGURE 4.42
The form for the Widget Graph program.

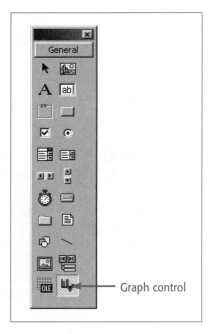

FIGURE 4.43
The Graph Control.

Graph control

4. Change the control name to **graWidget_Sales**, where the "gra" prefix stands for Graph Control.

We want the graph to display the four quarterly sales totals for each product as well as the average of these totals. That means we need five groups of three elements each. This layout is just like a two-dimensional array, and that is how Visual Basic treats it.

To have the layout set up properly, we need to tell the program how many groups there are, which is the **RowCount** property. This represents the rows in a two-dimensional array

FIGURE 4.44
The Widget Graph form with the Graph Control added.

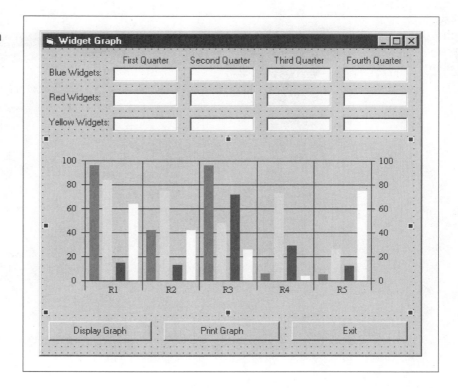

and the rows of elements in our program. The number of elements in each of those groups is set by using the **ColumnCount** property. This correlates the columns in a two-dimensional array with our program. The RowCount property is already set to 5, but we need to change the ColumnCount property to 3.

5. Change the ColumnCount property to **3**.

Now the Graph Control shows five groups with three elements in each, as Figure 4.45 illustrates.

In an array we use indices to move from one element to the next. With the Graph Control, we use two different methods to move between elements. The RowCount property sets the number of groups, so the **Row** method moves between the groups or rows. The format of the method is

```
[Form.]Graphname.Row = rownumber
```

The ColumnCount property sets the number of elements in the graphs, so the **Column** method is used to change from one element to the next. The format of this method is the same as the format of the Row method.

Setting Row to 1 and Column to 1 points to the first bar in the first group of the graph. We will represent the average of the four quarterly totals for the Blue Widgets with this bar. A Row value of 1 and a Column value of 2 point to the second bar in the first group of the graph, which we will use to display the average of the four quarterly totals for the Red Widgets. If we change Row to 2 and Column to 2, we get the second bar (Column) in the second group (Row), which we will use for the first quarterly amount for the Blue Widgets.

Because our Widget groups have the names of colors (Blue Widgets and so on), it makes sense to use the corresponding colors in the graph. This is done with the Property Pages window, which can be called up with the Custom property or by using the **Properties** option of the menu that appears when you right-click the control.

6. Right-click the control, and a small menu appears. Select the **Properties** option at the end of the menu to see the dialog box shown in Figure 4.46.

FIGURE 4.45
The Graph Control,
showing the five groups
of three elements each.

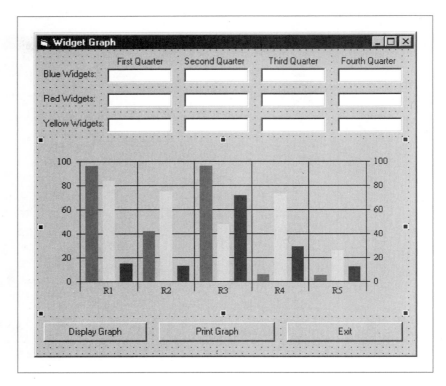

FIGURE 4.46
The Property Pages
dialog box for the graph
control.

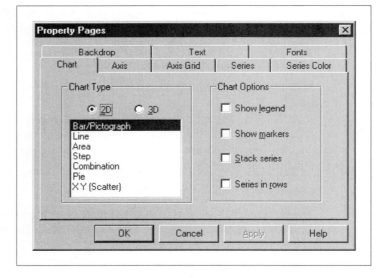

As you can see, there are several tabs on this dialog box. The one we need to use is the **Series Color**.

7. Click the **Series Color** tab to see the dialog box display shown in Figure 4.47.

To change the colors of the bars, we begin by selecting the Series. C1 refers to the first set of colors, which we want to change to blue. We don't have to change to a different series, but we do have to change the color. This requires a change to the **Color** list shown in the **Interior** group.

FIGURE 4.47
The Series Color tab on
the Property Pages
dialog box for the graph
control.

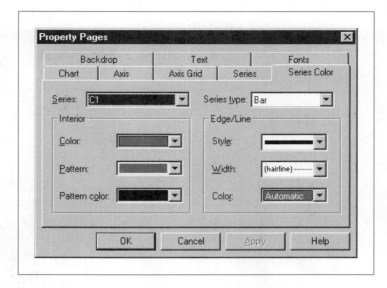

FIGURE 4.48
The list of available
colors with the
appropriate one
indicated.

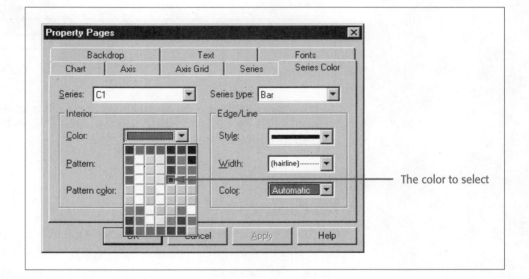

The color to select

8. Click the arrow at the end of the **Color** list to see the list of available colors shown in Figure 4.48.

9. Click the color indicated in Figure 4.48 to change the color of the element to blue.

   This selects the color for the series of bars that represents the values of the Blue Widget totals and the average of those totals. Now we need to set the other two colors.

10. Click the arrow at the end of the **Series** list to see the list show C1, C2, and C3. These represent the column groups.

11. Select C2 from the list and change the color of that column group to Red, using the red box in the same relative position as the blue box you chose.

12. Change to the C3 column group and change its color to yellow. Then click the **OK** button to exit from the dialog box. Now you will see the new graph colors shown in Figure 4.49.

FIGURE 4.49
The new colors of the graph columns.

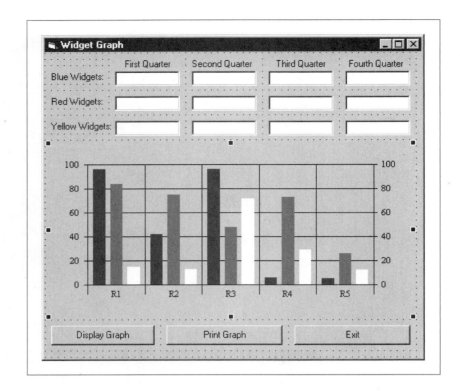

As you can see, the graph already looks as though it has been calculated and drawn. We really don't want this to give the user the wrong idea, so let's turn the graph off until the **Display Graph** button is clicked.

13. Change the Visible property to **False**.

The Code

Now that the properties are set, we are ready for the code. Let's do the easy code first. The **Print Graph** button will simply use the PrintForm statement.

1. Open the code window for the **Print Graph** button and add the appropriate statement.
2. Open the code window for the **Exit** button and add the appropriate statement.
3. Open the code window for the **Display Graph** button.

   This is where all the real work in this program will be done.

   We want the bars of the first graph group to represent the averages of the quarterly totals, so we have to total those numbers for each product. Thus, we will need three variables for those totals.

4. Declare three variables called **intTotal_Blue**, **intTotal_Red**, and **intTotal_Yellow**.

   The first thing in the code, then, is to calculate the totals of the values in the text boxes. This can be done in a For-Next loop such as

```
For intLoop_Counter = 1 To 4
    intTotal_Blue = intTotal_Blue + Val(txtBlue(intLoop_Counter))
    intTotal_Red = intTotal_Red + Val(txtRed(intLoop_Counter))
    intTotal_Yellow = intTotal_Yellow + Val(txtYellow
    ↪(intLoop_Counter))
Next intLoop_Counter
```

This loop goes through the four quarters and each of the three products. The loop counter (intLoop_Counter) is used as the index of the control arrays in the Val functions.

5. Add the foregoing loop to the procedure.

Next we need to calculate the average and assign that to the graph element. This can be done as one statement. We don't need to use another variable to store the calculated average. But to assign the average to the appropriate graph element, we need to specify which graph element that is. As we discussed earlier, we use the Row and Column methods to point to the graph element.

For the average for the Blue Widgets, the graph element is pointed to with the following two statements:

```
graWidget_Sales.Column = 1
graWidget_Sales.Row = 1
```

6. Add these statements to the procedure.

After pointing to the appropriate element, all that remains is to assign the data. This is done with the **Data** method, which has the format

```
[Form.]Graphname.Data = numeric expression
```

This statement will assign the data value to the graph element to which the graWidget_Sales.Column and graWidget_Sales.Row statements point. The statement we need for the Blue Widgets average is

```
graWidget_Sales.Data = intTotal_Blue / 4
```

We divide the total by 4 because there are four quarters.

7. Add this statement to the procedure.

We need to do the same thing for the other two averages. The Row statement will be the same for all three of the averages, because we are putting all the averages in the same group, and the first Row statement is all that is needed. The Column statement must change from 1 to 2 and then to 3. The Data statement will be similar to the one given above.

8. Add the four statements needed to change the columns and assign the Data (no Row statements).

Because the Row groups are labeled as R1, R2, and so on, we should change the labels to something more meaningful. This is done with the **RowLabel** property, which has the normal format:

```
[Form.]Graphname.RowLabel = string expression
```

For this property to be used, the Row property has to point to the proper group. Thus, to assign the label of the first group as averages, we would use the following statements:

```
graWidget_Sales.Row = 1
graWidget_Sales.RowLabel = "Averages"
```

9. Add these two previous statements.

Then we need to assign the other labels as follows:

```
graWidget_Sales.Row = 2
graWidget_Sales.RowLabel = "1st Q."
graWidget_Sales.Row = 3
graWidget_Sales.RowLabel = "2nd Q."
graWidget_Sales.Row = 4
graWidget_Sales.RowLabel = "3rd Q."
graWidget_Sales.Row = 5
graWidget_Sales.RowLabel = "4th Q."
```

10. Add the previous assignment statements.

To display the quarterly data, we need to loop through the text boxes and the data points to which those values are to be assigned. We will create three different loops. They will all begin by assigning the appropriate Column:

```
graWidget_Sales.Column = 1
```

Then they will all have the same For statement:

```
For intLoop_Counter = 1 To 4
```

Then we need to point to the proper group:

```
graWidget_Sales.Row = intLoop_Counter + 1
```

Here we increment the loop counter by 1 to offset it, because there are five data groups (the first is the totals) and the quarterly total for the first quarter needs to be assigned to the second data point, and so on.

Lastly, we need to assign the data:

```
graWidget_Sales.Data = Val(txtBlue(intLoop_Counter))
```

and close the loop:

```
Next intLoop_Counter
```

The entire loop looks like this:

```
graWidget_Sales.Column = 1
For intLoop_Counter = 1 To 4
    graWidget_Sales.Row = intLoop_Counter + 1
    graWidget_Sales.Data = Val(txtBlue(intLoop_Counter))
Next intLoop_Counter
```

11. Add the above loop to the program. Create two more loops, one for each of the other two products. Be sure the Column statement points to the correct element.

There is only one thing left to do. Remember that we set the Visible property to False so the user will not see the graph before the **Display Graph** button is clicked. Because this is the click event procedure for the button, we need to set the Visible property to True so that the graph will be displayed.

12. Add the statement required.

Well, that's it. We're ready to try the program. The entire code in the **Display Graph** procedure follows.

```
' This routine is used to display the graph
'
Private Sub cmdDisplay_Click()
    Dim intTotal_Blue As Integer
    Dim intTotal_Red As Integer
    Dim intTotal_Yellow As Integer
    Dim intLoop_Counter As Integer

    For intLoop_Counter = 1 To 4
        intTotal_Blue = intTotal_Blue + Val(txtBlue(intLoop_Counter))
        intTotal_Red = intTotal_Red + Val(txtRed(intLoop_Counter))
        intTotal_Yellow = intTotal_Yellow + Val(txtYellow
        ↳(intLoop_Counter))
    Next intLoop_Counter
```

```
              graWidget_Sales.Column = 1
              graWidget_Sales.Row = 1
              graWidget_Sales.Data = intTotal_Blue / 4

              graWidget_Sales.Column = 2
              graWidget_Sales.Data = intTotal_Red / 4

              graWidget_Sales.Column = 3
              graWidget_Sales.Data = intTotal_Yellow / 4

              graWidget_Sales.Row = 1
              graWidget_Sales.RowLabel = "Averages"

              graWidget_Sales.Row = 2
              graWidget_Sales.RowLabel = "1st Q."
              graWidget_Sales.Row = 3
              graWidget_Sales.RowLabel = "2nd Q."
              graWidget_Sales.Row = 4
              graWidget_Sales.RowLabel = "3rd Q."
              graWidget_Sales.Row = 5
              graWidget_Sales.RowLabel = "4th Q."

              graWidget_Sales.Column = 1
              For intLoop_Counter = 1 To 4
                  graWidget_Sales.Row = intLoop_Counter + 1
                  graWidget_Sales.Data = Val(txtBlue(intLoop_Counter))
              Next intLoop_Counter

              graWidget_Sales.Column = 2
              For intLoop_Counter = 1 To 4
                  graWidget_Sales.Row = intLoop_Counter + 1
                  graWidget_Sales.Data = Val(txtRed(intLoop_Counter))
              Next intLoop_Counter

              graWidget_Sales.Column = 3
              For intLoop_Counter = 1 To 4
                  graWidget_Sales.Row = intLoop_Counter + 1
                  graWidget_Sales.Data = Val(txtYellow(intLoop_Counter))
              Next intLoop_Counter

              graWidget_Sales.Visible = True
          End Sub
```

13. Run the program. The graph does not show because the Visible property is set to False.

14. Key the data given in Table 4.3, and click the **Display Graph** button to see the graph shown in Figure 4.50. These are the same data you used when you were experimenting with the sample program at the beginning of this chapter.

15. Change a couple of the numbers, and then click the **Display Graph** button again. The graph will be changed.

16. Practice with the graph a bit more before exiting the program in preparation for the next section.

TABLE 4.3
The data used in the Widget Graph program.

Product	Quarter 1	Quarter 2	Quarter 3	Quarter 4
Blue Widgets	1254	2345	1879	3256
Red Widgets	2374	3487	3456	3001
Yellow Widgets	1345	1876	2392	1987

FIGURE 4.50
The displayed graph.

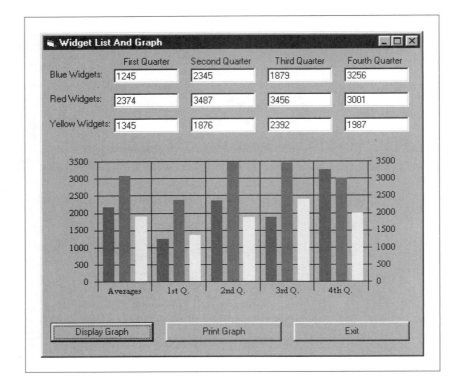

There are other features that can be added to the graph, such as additional labels and a legend. The graph can also be displayed in a number of different formats, such as three-dimensional bars and pie charts. You can experiment with these features on your own or by doing the exercises at the end of the chapter.

4.11   The MsgBox Function

There is one more function we want to add to this program to make it more professional. In the sample version of this program, when the **Exit** button is selected, a dialog box appears asking the user to confirm that the **Exit** button was selected on purpose and that the user truly does wish to exit the program. This is done with the **MsgBox** function, which can also be used to present the user with a variety of different forms of dialog boxes.

The format of the MsgBox function is

```
MsgBox(prompt[, buttons] [, title])
```

This function can be used as a stand-alone statement or as a function that returns a value based on which button the user selected. There are three parameters in the function:

- The **prompt** is the message that appears in the dialog box workspace.
- The **buttons** specify what buttons and other dialog box parameters you want it to have.
- The **title** is the title of the dialog box; it appears in the title bar.

Here is a sample of a MsgBox statement:

```
intReturned = MsgBox ("This is the message.", vbCritical, "Warning
 message")
```

This statement will display a message box like the one in Figure 4.51.

FIGURE 4.51
The message box
generated from the
MsgBox statement.

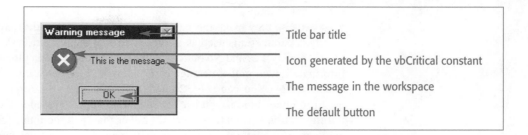

Title bar title

Icon generated by the vbCritical constant

The message in the workspace

The default button

The first parameter of the function causes "This is the message" to appear in the dialog box workspace. The second parameter can have a variety of formats. This one, "vbCritical", specifies the icon that is to be displayed in the dialog box but nothing else. Therefore, Visual Basic automatically displays the default **OK** button. The third parameter causes "Warning message" to appear in the title bar.

The uses for the first and last parameters of the function are easy to see from the figure. The second parameter requires a bit more explanation. This parameter is used to specify the icon you want to display in your message box, the type(s) of buttons you want, and which button has the initial focus. The predefined constants, values, and descriptions for this parameter are shown in Table 4.4.

You can use the numeric value of the constant instead of the predefined constant if you wish. This would change the previous statement to

```
intReturned = MsgBox ("This is the message.", 16, "Warning message")
```

TABLE 4.4
The predefined constants, values, and descriptions for the second parameter of the MsgBox function.

Predefined Constant	Value	Description
		Number and type of buttons
vbOKOnly	0	*OK* button only
vbOKCancel	1	*OK, Cancel* buttons
vbAbortRetryIgnore	2	*Abort, Retry, Ignore* buttons
vbYesNoCancel	3	*Yes, No, Cancel* buttons
vbYesNo	4	*Yes, No* buttons
vbRetryCancel	5	*Retry, Cancel* buttons
		Icon style
vbCritical	16	Critical Message icon (⊗)
vbQuestion	32	Question Mark icon (?)
vbExclamation	48	Warning Message icon (⚠)
vbInformation	64	Information Message icon (ⓘ)
		Default button
vbDefaultButton1	0	First button has initial focus
vbDefaultButton2	256	Second button has initial focus
vbDefaultButton3	512	Third button has initial focus
		Modality
vbApplicationModal	0	Application modal. The user must respond to the message box before continuing to work on the current application.
vbSystemModal	4096	System modal. All applications are suspended until the user responds to the message box.

vbCritical is simply a constant defined as 16. We recommend that the constants always be used because they make the statements much easier to understand.

This parameter is used as a combination of the numeric values in the table. For example, to display **Yes** and **No** buttons with the **No** button having the initial focus, and using the information icon in the message box, you would use the total of the three numbers, 4 + 64 + 256 = 324. You can use 324 and Visual Basic will interpret the three numbers. It is easier to understand if you use the predefined constants added together (as in vbYesNo + vbInformation + vbDefaultButton2) rather than just the total. Then, when you look at the application at a later date, you will know exactly what values you were using.

Modality is an interesting concept that we will run into again. Normally, if the program displays a message box, the user will not be able to continue working in the current program until the user responds to the message box. This is the modality number of zero (which is the default). You can make sure the user cannot do anything else in any application by setting the modality to 4096 (vbSystemModal). If the message you are displaying deals with some type of system error, such as a disk drive problem, it might be a good idea to suspend all applications until the problem is resolved. Modality cannot be turned off completely in the MsgBox function. Doing this would allow users to ignore the message box and continue to use the application as they normally would. A message box generally contains information that the user needs, so ignoring the message is not allowed.

Because the user is required to respond to the box in some way, a numeric value is returned to the program. Our statement stores that returned value in the variable **intReturned.** The constants, their values, and their meanings for the returned value are shown in Table 4.5.

If you have several buttons in your message box, you can test this returned value so that you know what button the user selected. For example, suppose your message box has **Yes** and **No** buttons in it. After the application returns the value, if **intReturned** is vbYes (or 6), the user selected the **Yes** button; if not, then **intReturned** would be vbNo (or 7), and you would know the user selected the **No** button. Your application could then do whatever was appropriate on the basis of the **intReturned** value.

In cases in which you use just the **OK** button and do not need to check for a returned value, you can use the MsgBox function without the resultant field. The previous statement becomes

```
MsgBox "This is the message.", vbCritical, "Warning message"
```

Note that the parentheses around the MsgBox parameters have been removed.
To see just how all this works, we will add a MsgBox function to our program.

1. Open the code window for the **Exit** button, and key the following MsgBox statement in front of the End statement already in the procedure.

TABLE 4.5
The constants, their values, and their meanings for the value returned from the MsgBox function.

Predefined Constant	Value	Description
vbOK	1	*OK* button was selected
vbCancel	2	*Cancel* button was selected
vbAbort	3	*Abort* button was selected
vbRetry	4	*Retry* button was selected
vbIgnore	5	*Ignore* button was selected
vbYes	6	*Yes* button was selected
vbNo	7	*No* button was selected

FIGURE 4.52
The dialog box that appears when the **Exit** button is selected.

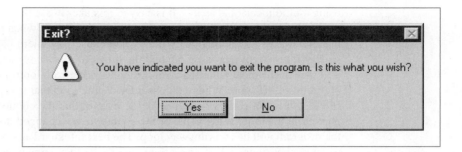

```
intResult = MsgBox("You have indicated you want to exit the program.
 ↳ Is this what you wish?", vbExclamation + vbYesNo, "Exit?")
```

Because we wish to verify that the user actually wants to exit the program, we use both the **Yes** and **No** buttons, and we store the value returned from the function. To determine what that value is and what action the program should take, we need to test the value with the following If Test:

```
If intResult = vbYes Then
```

2. Key this statement before the End statement as well.

If the user clicks the **Yes** button, the user intends to exit the program, and the End statement needs to be executed.

3. Indent the End statement and add the End If statement following it.

This makes the entire procedure appear as follows:

```
Private Sub cmdExit_Click()
    Dim intResult As Integer
    intResult = MsgBox("You have indicated you want to exit the
     ↳ program. Is this what you wish?", vbExclamation + vbYesNo,
     ↳ "Exit?")
    If intResult = vbYes Then
        End
    End If
End Sub
```

4. Run the program and select the **End** button. Immediately you see the dialog box shown in Figure 4.52.

This is the result of the MsgBox function.

5. Click the **No** button, and the program resumes as though no event had been triggered.

6. Click the **Exit** button again, and this time click the **Yes** button to exit the program.

4.12 Debugging Your Programs

One of the most common mistakes people make when working with arrays is to use an incorrect index for the element for which they are looking. The index may be calculated incorrectly, or they may use a loop that goes beyond the number of elements in the array. If your program asks for an element beyond the end of the array, Visual Basic gives you an error message. If you use the wrong index, however, you simply get the wrong results. When working with arrays, always be sure to handle the indices properly, especially when using multidimensional arrays. It is easy to mistakenly use the index for the first element as the index for the second element, and vice versa, such as when you need element (5,8) but use the indices (8,5). Obviously this would cause a problem in the program, especially if neither index were increased beyond the limits of that array element.

One of the most common errors when working with loops is never to arrive at the ending point of the loop. When you use a Do-While loop that is supposed to end on the basis of the value of a counter, you need to be careful that the counter is incremented or decremented in the loop. If the value of the counter is not changed, the loop will never end, and the program will be in a runaway loop. The best safeguard against runaway loops is always to remember to use a DoEvents statement in the loop somewhere. Then, if you do happen to create a runaway loop, at least you will be able to interrupt it by pressing **Ctrl-Break**.

When using control arrays, you need to be certain that the indices of the objects are correct for your purposes. If you have four text boxes in the control array, for example, and you have reversed objects 2 and 3, the data you input from those text boxes will not be correct for what you intend to do with those data. Also remember that the first element of any control array is always the zero element. If you want your control array to have a zero element, there is no problem, but if your objects need to start with an index of 1 or higher, you need to compensate for the elements you don't want by renumbering the indices in some way.

If you are having trouble with a program that uses a loop, remember that you can use the Debug.Print statement to help you determine what is happening. You can use it to print the value of the counter or of other variables as the loop progresses.

An important consideration with Do-Loops is that you should use the proper type. If it is important that the loop always execute at least once, you need to use a Do-Until loop rather than a Do-While loop. On the other hand, if you don't want the loop to execute even once if the condition is false, you need to use a Do-While loop.

Using the Graph Control can be tricky at times. You need to be sure you have set up the program for the proper number of rows and columns so that all the data can be displayed. Then you have to be sure to adjust the Row and Column properties properly as you assign the data.

4.13 Command and Menu Summary

In this chapter you learned to use the following keystrokes:

- **Ctrl-J** brings an element to the front of a ZOrder pile.
- **Ctrl-K** moves an element to the back of a ZOrder pile.

In this chapter you learned to use the following commands and functions:

- **Chr** lets you send a keyboard character to the computer by using the storage code for that character.

- **DoEvents** releases control from the program to Windows so that events such as a mouse click on a button can be detected.

- **Do-While** is the initial statement of a Do…Loop structure in which the loop will function as long as the condition is true.

- **Do-Until** is the initial statement of a Do…Loop structure in which the loop will function until the condition is true.

- **Erase** allows you to reinitialize an array.

- **For** is the initial statement of a For-Next loop.

- **Loop** is the ending statement of a Do...Loop structure.

- **MsgBox** is used to display a dialog box on the desktop.

- **Next** is the end statement of a For-Next loop.

- **Redim** lets you specify or respecify the number of elements of an array that was declared without specifying the number of elements.

- **Step** is the part of the For statement that specifies the increment value.

In this chapter you learned about the following properties and methods:

- **BackStyle** is used to change the background style of a label from Opaque to Transparent and back.

- **Column** specifies the current element with the current group of graph elements in the Graph Control.

- **ColumnCount** specifies how many graph elements are in each group in the Graph Control.

- **Data** assigns a data value to the graph element that is currently pointed to in the Graph Control.

- **FontBold** makes the font bold.

- **FontItalic** makes the font italic.

- **FontName** is the name of the font being used. There are many different fonts, and what particular ones are available depends on which fonts have been installed on the computer.

- **FontSize** is the point size of the font, a point being 1/72 of an inch.

- **FontStrikeThrough** draws a dash through each text character.

- **FontUnderline** underlines the font.

- **Index** specifies the location of one of the elements in a control array.

- **RowCount** specifies how many groups of graph elements are to be used in the Graph Control.

- **Row** specifies the current group of graph elements in the Graph Control.

- **RowLabel** specifies the labels that will be displayed under the groups of graph elements in the Graph Control.

- **ZOrder** lets you change the display order of objects on a form by sending them to the back or bringing them to the front.

In this chapter you learned about the following event:

- **Activate** is executed after a form appears on the desktop.

In this chapter you learned about the following object prefix:

- **gra** is used for the Graph Control objects.

In this chapter you learned about the following menu options:

- **Format:**
  - **Order:**
    - **Bring to Front** (shortcut key **Ctrl-J**) lets you send the specified object to the front of the ZOrder.

■　**Send to Back** (shortcut key **Ctrl-K**) lets you send the object to the back of the ZOrder.

In this chapter you learned about the following Toolbox tool:

■　🔲　The tool to add the Graph Control to the project.

4.14　Performance Check

1. What is the ending statement for a Do-While loop?

2. What other type of Do...Loop is there besides the Do-While loop?

3. If your code has a statement similar to C = C + 1, what type of program element is C most likely to be (besides a variable or data type)?

4. What is the purpose of a statement such as **lblInput_Field.Caption = ""**?

5. What does vbCr yield when it is displayed?

6. What is wrong with each of the following statements?

   a. For 2 To 8

   b. For intCounter = intCounter To intEnd

   c. For intCounter = 1 To 10 Step –1

7. You have created a program that has a form you want to use in a new project you are creating. How can you create a new project and use an existing form?

8. What happens to the execution of a For-Next loop when the ending value of the loop is changed within the loop?

9. In simple terms, what is an array?

10. What is another name for an array subscript?

11. What advantage does the selection sort have over the bubble sort?

12. What does the Erase statement do?

13. What is the difference between a static array and a dynamic array?

14. What is a control array?

15. Write the Dim statement for an array of 50 elements called strData_In.

16. Write the Dim statement for a two-dimensional array called intArray_Storage with 20 and 30 elements, respectively.

17. What Graph Control property can be used to tell Visual Basic to redraw the graph?

18. What event is executed after the form appears on the desktop?

19. What property is used to specify the labels displayed under the groups of graph elements in the Graph Control?

20. What is the purpose of the ZOrder method?

4.15 Programming Exercises

1. For this first exercise, you will change the word sort so that you can choose whether you want the display to be in ascending order (as it currently is) or in descending order. (We will not show the design, because we have built this program step by step and are making a minor change at this point.) At the computer, do each of the following:

- **a.** Get into Visual Basic with your work disk in drive A.
- **b.** Load the **Word Manipulations** program, save the form as **frmDescending_Words_Form**, and save the project as **Descending Words**.
- **c.** The **Manipulate the Array** button already prints the list in ascending order, so you will leave that code as is and simply change the caption of the button to **Manipulate the Array - Ascending** (it isn't necessary to change the control name).
- **d.** Center a new button, captioned **Manipulate the Array - Descending** and with the control name **cmdDescending_Button**, under the **Sort_Out** label.
- **e.** Open the code window for the **Ascending** button. Because there will be two displays into the lblSorted_Out caption, the caption will need to be emptied now, before being displayed. Add the appropriate statement before the routine to display the sorted data.
- **f.** Copy all the code from the **Ascending** button to the cmdDescending_Button procedure.
- **g.** The search in the array can be done the same way as before. The exception is that instead of looking for the smallest element, you will be looking for the largest. Thus, the strCompare variable should be aaaaaa instead of zzzzzz and the If Test should be

```
If strData_Array(intInside_Counter) > strCompare Then
```

instead of

```
If strData_Array(intInside_Counter) < strCompare Then
```

- **h.** Test the program to be sure it gives you the words in ascending order when you select the **Ascending** button and in descending order when you select the **Descending** button. Then exit the program and print the program elements.
- **i.** Exit Visual Basic and shut down the system properly.

2. Date translation is a commonly used technique in business. Your supervisor has asked you to write a program that will translate a month number, such as 12, into its written name, such as December. The design of this program is

```
Project Month - Form1
   A.  Convert_Button
       1.  Click
              Store the months in the array Month_Array
              Use the month number from the Month_In text box to put
              ↳the proper month name or an error message in the
              ↳Month_Out text box
```

```
B.  Month-in text box
    Used to input the month number
C.  Month_Out text box
    Used to output the month name
D.  Label for month entry
```

Using this design, at the computer, do each of the following:

a. Get into Visual Basic with your work disk in drive A.

b. Create a new project and do each of the following:

   1) Add a label with **Month Entry:** in it, and put a text box next to it. The text box should have the control name **txtMonth_In**.

   2) Under the label, add a button with the caption **Convert**, and use the control name **cmdConvert**.

   3) Next to the button, add a label box with a border and the control name **lblMonth_Out** to display the name of the month.

   4) Use the caption **Month Conversion** on the form.

c. Open the code window for the button. Use 12 assignment statements to assign the month names to the 12 elements of an array called **strMonth_Array**. Don't forget to declare the array.

d. Next you need a statement to display the month name in the **lblMonth_Out** label caption, using the number of the month from the text box. This needs to be put within an If Test and an error must be displayed if the number entered is outside the 1-to-12 range.

e. Run the program and try entering each of the months to be sure the conversion is done correctly.

f. Exit the program, save it as **Month Conversion**, and print the code and form.

g. Exit Visual Basic and shut down the system properly.

3. You have been assigned to code part of a larger program being created by your programming team. Your part is to allow a user to input a code, verify it against the allowable codes, and then display a message if the entered code is not an allowable code. For example, the allowable codes are A15, B17, G97, R22, and C87. Each time the user enters a code, you will need to match it against these and display a message if it doesn't match any of them. Before you create the routine that will be added to the actual larger program, you decide to create a sample program to test the routine. At the computer, do each of the following:

   a. Design the program using the information given above, which you get from the form shown in Figure 4.52, and the clues given in step d, below.

   b. Get into Visual Basic with your work disk in drive A.

   c. Create a new program with the form shown in Figure 4.53 by doing each of the following:

      1) The label with the border and the codes keyed in should have the control name **lblAllowable_Codes**.

      2) The text box used to input the code to be checked should have the control name **txtCode_In**.

      3) The label beside the text box is where the message is going to be displayed and should have the control name **lblMessage_Out**.

      4) The button should have the control name **cmdVerify_Button**.

      5) Save the program as **Code Test**.

FIGURE 4.53
The form for
Programming Exercise
3.

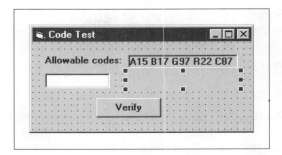

d. Open the code window and key the needed code, given the following clues:

1) The For-Next loops will need to go from 1 to 5 because there are five allowable codes.

2) The routine to extract the data from the caption needs to use the Mid function Mid(lblAllowable_Codes.Caption, intCounter * 4 – 3, 3)

3) The easiest way to determine whether the input code is correct is to use a "Found" variable (as in the scan routine in the discussion of multidimensional arrays) to determine after the loop whether the code matched or not.

4) The message to be displayed if the code does not match any of the allowable codes should be something like "**Code Incorrect**".

5) You will need to initialize the lblMessage_Out box before the routine, because if you don't, after a message has been displayed, it will continually be displayed and all the codes entered will appear to be incorrect.

e. Test the program by entering correct codes and incorrect codes. Note that an entry of "a15" will be interpreted as incorrect, whereas "A15" will be interpreted as correct, because, to the computer, "a" and "A" are different characters.

f. Exit the program and print the program elements.

g. Exit Visual Basic and shut down the system properly.

4. You have been assigned the job of adding sort routines to several programs that already exist. To be sure you thoroughly understand how the sort works, you decide to create a sort routine that sorts 100 numbers that range from 1 to 10,000. You want the numbers to be random, so you decide to use the **Rnd** function to generate them. At the computer, do each of the following:

a. Get into Visual Basic with your work disk in drive A.

b. Load the **Array Manipulation** program you created in this chapter, and copy the sort routine from it to the clipboard. (There is no sense in rekeying the entire sort routine, though you will want to change the variable names that begin with str to int.)

c. Create a new project and do each of the following:

1) Use the caption **Random Number Sort** on the form.

2) Add a large label box in which to display your sorted output. You will display the output with ten numbers across on ten different lines, so the box needs to be large enough to hold ten five-digit numbers. Make the box whatever size seems appropriate. You can always adjust the size later. Name the label **lblSort_Out**.

3) Add a button with the caption **Sort** and the control name **cmdSort_Button**.

4) Save the program as **Random Sort**.

d. Open the code window for the button. Copy the sort routine into the code window.

e. Before the sort routine, you need a routine to generate the random numbers. Begin by keying the statement **Randomize**. This will make the program generate a different list of random numbers every time the button is selected.

f. Now you need a For-Next loop from 1 to 100 with the following statement within:

```
intData_Array(intCounter) = Int(10000 * Rnd + 1)
```

The **Rnd** function will generate a random number between 0 and 1. Multiplying it by 10,000 gives you a number from zero to 9999, and by adding 1, you can ensure that you will get a number from 1 to 10,000. The number will not yet be an integer, so you should use the **Int** function to change it to an integer.

g. You will need to modify the sort routine to use a numeric array. Change the compare field to be initialized to 10,001, which will ensure that it is larger than the largest possible number being generated. Also change the ending points of the For-Next loops so that they are appropriate for the number of numbers being sorted.

h. Create a loop so that after the numbers are generated and sorted, they will be displayed in the label caption. Display ten numbers on each of ten lines (use **vbCr** to create the carriage returns).

i. Run the program several times to be sure it is sorting the numbers properly.

j. Exit the program and print the program elements.

k. Exit Visual Basic and shut down the system properly.

5. You have a friend who is a programmer, and you help each other out occasionally. This time he has come to you with a program he has been creating that he just cannot get to work properly. You have agreed to help him debug the program. At the computer, do each of the following:

a. Get into Visual Basic with your work disk in drive A.

b. Load the **Widget Debug** program from the Ch-4 folder.

c. Run the program and enter **1**, **2**, **3**, and **4** into the text boxes, respectively. Click the **Display Graph** button. You get an error. Click the **Debug** button. Look carefully at the highlighted statement. Remember that the Column property refers to the item within the group. This program only has one item in each group. Fix the statement and restart the program.

d. The program finishes executing, but the graph doesn't appear. What statement is missing? Exit from the program and add the appropriate statement.

e. You probably noticed that the **Exit** button doesn't work properly. Fix this too before running the program again.

f. Run the program and enter **1**, **2**, **3**, and **4** into the text boxes. Click the **Display Graph** button. Now the graph is displayed, but there is something seriously wrong. Pause the program and examine the For statement. How many groups are there? Fix the statement, restart the program, and click the **Display Graph** button.

g. Run the program again and enter **1**, **2**, **3**, and **4** into the text boxes. Click the **Display Graph** button. Note that the graph bars don't represent the numbers properly. Examine the data in the text boxes and the bars on the graph and find the correlation. Then exit from the program and fix this error. (Hint: Look at the Index property.)

h. Run the program again and enter **1**, **2**, **3**, and **4** into the text boxes. Click the **Display Graph** button. Now the program displays the graph correctly. Thoroughly test the program and then print the elements.

4.16 Performance Mastery

1. You have been asked by your supervisor to write a program that will sort a list of product numbers with the associated quantities on hand. This will require you to sort two arrays in tandem. Design and then create a program that will extract the product numbers from one label caption and the quantities from another and store them in two arrays. Use product numbers of different lengths, such as 12 and 1255. Modify one of the sort routines we used in this chapter to sort the two arrays at the same time. Sort the arrays twice, once in product number order and once in quantity order. Then display the sorted lists in labels as two columns with the product number in the first column and the quantity in the second column. Test the program, save it as **Twinsort**, and print the program. (Hint: To help the columns align properly, change the Font Name to Courier.)

2. You decide to write a program that will have ten text boxes for input of the values to be sorted. Use a separate text box to display the list that is sorted using the sort routine given in this chapter. Design your program, create it, save it as **Text Sort**, test it, and then print the program elements.

3. You work for a manufacturing firm that uses various raw materials to create its products. Table 4.6 gives you the amount of raw materials and the number of prefabricated parts needed for each of the products your company creates.

    Design and then create a program that stores the information in either a two-dimensional array or six one-dimensional arrays. Use a control array of labels to store each of the rows of the table, one label of the control array for each row of the table. Then input the data from the labels and store these data in the array(s).

    On the form, put two text boxes that will allow the user to input the product number and the quantity needed. With that quantity, determine how much of each raw material and how many of each part are needed to produce the specified quantity, and display those five results on the form. For example, suppose you needed to produce 5 of product 1597. You would need 50 of Raw A, 100 of Raw B, 25 of Part A, 15 of Part B, and 5 of Part C. Format the output to use commas so that it is more readable and does not show anything in the output box if the result is zero. Save the program as **Raw Materials**, test it, and then print it.

4. You showed your boss the Widget Graph program you created in this chapter. When she used it, she pressed the **Display Graph** button without entering all the data, and the graph was misleading. She has requested that you make the program verify that an entry has been made in each of the text boxes before the graph is displayed. If one of

TABLE 4.6
The data for Performance Mastery Exercise 3.

Product	Raw A	Raw B	Part A	Part B	Part C
1597	10	20	5	3	1
1246	3	2525	2	4	6
1334	115	35	5	0	0
1289	1133	22	4	0	6
1987	22	2319	0	3	0
8276	0	12	2	0	1
8273	12	0	0	3	4

the pieces of data has not been entered, a warning message should be displayed. Make the necessary additions to the program, save it as **Widget Graph Updated**, and print it.

5. You work for a fruit wholesaler and have been assigned to write a program to calculate invoice amounts. You are to create a form that will allow the input of a product code and the number of cases ordered. With those data, you are to translate the product code into the product name and calculate the total price from the price per crate, given the information in Table 4.7.

   Put **Calculate** and **Print** buttons on the form. Store the data in one two-dimensional array (the two strings) and a one-dimensional array (the price) or in three separate arrays. Load the data into the array in the Form_Load event procedure. Design your program, create it, save it, as **Fruit Calculations**, test it, and then print the program elements.

6. You work for a company that sells products all over the United States. Your boss has asked you to write a program that will allow the input of the four quarterly sales amounts and will present a pie chart of those data. Design your program, create it, save it as **Pie Chart**, test it, and then print the program elements. (Hint: Use a RowCount of 1 and a ColumnCount of 4.)

7. You work for a company that sells products all over the United States. Your boss has asked you to write a program that will allow the input of the four quarterly sales amounts and will present those data as a two-dimensional bar chart, a three-dimensional bar chart, or a pie chart. Use a text box to input the type of chart to be presented. Design your program, create it, save it as **Three Charts**, and test it, then print the program elements.

8. For practice, you decide to write a program that will have a text box for entry of data to be sorted. Each time the sort button is clicked, the data from the text box are put in the next available element at the end of an array, and then that array is sorted and displayed in an output text box. Design your program, create it, save it as **Single Sort**, and test it, then print the program elements.

TABLE 4.7
The data for
Performance Mastery
Exercise 5.

Product	Code	Price per Crate
Jonathan apples	App	3.75
Bartlett apples	Bap	3.43
Delicious apples	Dap	3.22
Granny Smith apples	Gap	2.95
Peaches	Pea	2.77
Bartlett pears	Prs	3.56
Hansen pears	Hpr	3.22
Delta oranges	Dor	5.96
Hammond oranges	Hor	4.22
German oranges	Gor	3.45
Apricots	Apr	6.75
Lemons	Lem	2.22

9. You work for a hardware company that has stores throughout the United States. Every day your office receives the daily sales from each of the stores, and these are combined into one set. You have been given the task of writing a program that can input the data for the ten stores and graph them in a bar graph. Design your program, create it, save it as **Store Graph**, test it, and then print the program elements.

10. You have been assigned the task of dividing a large list of words into three groups A–G, H–O, and P–Z, so that the related paperwork can be properly filed. Each of the three lists is to be sorted. Using a text box for input of a new word, the program should use a button to process the word into the proper list and then sort that list. Design your program, create it, save it as **Triple List Sort**, test it, and then print the program elements.

11. You have a friend who is a science teacher in a local high school. She has been teaching her students the periodic table of the elements. She has asked you to help her out by creating a program that will show the user the name of the element and then allow entry of the abbreviation and weight of the element. The program should then check to see whether these are correct. If they are correct, display an appropriate message. If they are incorrect, display a message indicating which of the answers is incorrect. The program should have two buttons: one for a new prompt and one to be used after the answers have been entered. You should use three arrays: one for the name of the element, one for the abbreviation, and one for the weight. You will have to look up the data needed for the program in a periodic table. Design your program, create it, save it as **Periodic Table**, test it, and then print the program elements.

12. A member of the payroll department has asked for your help. You need to write a program that will store job class codes in an array with the rate of pay associated with each job class. Then the program will allow a name, job class, and number of hours worked to be entered and will calculate the gross pay. Then, using a tax rate of 22% and a FICA rate of 6.75%, it will calculate the net pay. The form should display the gross pay, the tax, the FICA, and the net pay. Design your program, create it, save it as **Payroll Calculations**, test it, and then print the program elements.

13. You have a friend who is a teacher. He has a program that he has been using all semester to store grades in a file. He has asked you to write a program to read that file, total the four grades for each name, and display a list of the names and total grades. You decide to improve on his idea for the program and graph the total grades.

    To create this program, you will have to be able to read a sequential file from disk. This requires three commands: one to Open the file, one to Input the data, and one to Close the file. The file you have to read is in the Ch-4 folder on your work disk, and you will need the following Open statement:

    ```
    Open "A:\Ch-4\Student Grades.Txt" For Input As #1
    ```

    Because there are ten lines of data in the file, you can use a For-Next loop to input the data. Within the loop, you will need to input the data one line at a time with the statement

    ```
    Input #1, strData_Input
    ```

    This will give you the data with the name first, followed by the four grades separated by commas. Parse out the appropriate data.

    After the loop, you have to close the file with the statement

    ```
    Close #1
    ```

    Design your program, create it, save it as **Grades From File**, test it, and then print the program elements.

14. You have been assigned the task of reading a file of names with last name, a comma and space, and first name, sorting them on last name, and then presenting them in a list with first name first.

To create this program, you will have to be able to read a sequential file from disk. This requires three commands: one to Open the file, one to Input the data, and one to Close the file. The file you have to read is in the Ch-4 folder on your work disk, and you will need the following Open statement:

```
Open "A:\Ch-4\Names.Txt" For Input As #1
```

Because the number of names in the file is unknown, you will want to use a **Do-Until EOF(1)** loop. EOF(1) tests for the end of the file, which is the point beyond the last piece of data stored in the file. A special marker is placed at that point when the file has been written, and the EOF(1) function tests for that marker. The file number, shown in parentheses, is the number of the file from the Open statement. Within the loop, you will input the data one line at a time with the statement

```
Input #1, strData_Input
```

After the loop, you will close the file with the statement

```
Close #1
```

Design your program, create it, save it as **Names From File**, test it, and then print the program elements.

More Labels, Buttons, and Text Boxes

After finishing this chapter you will be able to:

- Understand how to use the text selection properties in an application.
- Explain the SetFocus method.
- Show how a button is disabled and enabled.
- Explain and demonstrate how to create access keys on the buttons.
- Show how to capture keystrokes for editing.
- Demonstrate the use of a **Timer** and **Option** buttons.
- Demonstrate how to change the icon used for an application and how to compile an application.

We have only scratched the surface of the useful applications that can be created with labels, buttons, and text boxes. There are, however, other properties that we need to examine before we can create some of the more complicated applications you may find useful.

In this chapter we will add a new tool to the tool box, explore **multiline** text boxes, and create a notepad complete with cut and paste capabilities. We can do this easily because Visual Basic will handle most of the details of the notepad automatically. The notepad will use multiple buttons, and we will look at how to assign access keys (or keyboard shortcuts) to these buttons.

You will occasionally run into an application that needs a timer. Visual Basic has a timer object that can be added to your form just like any other object. With it you can keep track of the passage of time and set off alarms. To explore the use of timers, we will create an alarm clock. While creating the alarm clock, we will uncover another couple of objects that can prove useful.

We begin this chapter, as usual, with a brief look at what we will have accomplished by the end of the chapter.

5.3 Your First Look at the PIM

We have mentioned before that the main project throughout this book will be a **personal information manager (PIM)**. This is an application that has tools for managing your personal needs, such as an address list, a notepad, an appointment scheduler, and an alarm clock. These are the types of applications that we are going to add to our PIM. In this chapter we will add a notepad and an alarm clock.

1. Get into Visual Basic with your work disk in drive A.
2. Run the **PIM** program in the Ch-5 folder on your work disk to see the form shown in Figure 5.1.

The first thing you will notice about this program is that there are three tabs. This **Tabbed Control** will be introduced in the next section. It works like tabs you have seen in other programs.

3. Click the **Alarm Clock** tab, and the display changes to the one shown in Figure 5.2.

FIGURE 5.1
The first look at the PIM.

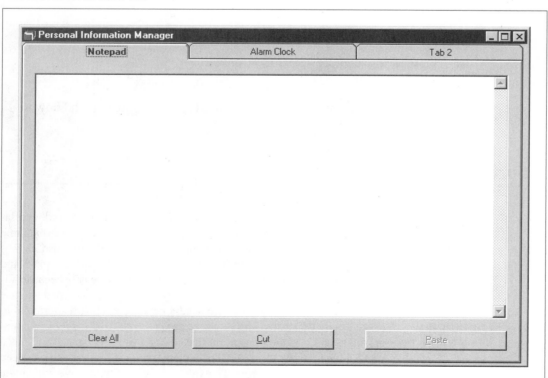

FIGURE 5.2
The **Alarm Clock** tab.

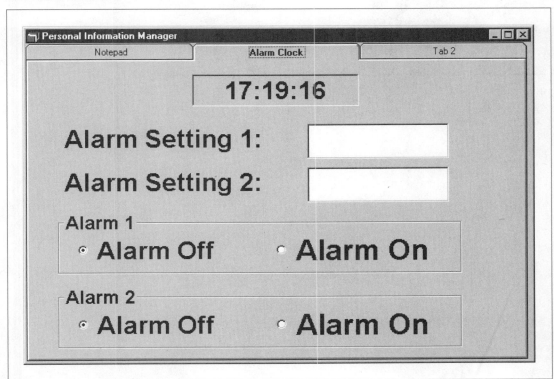

The content of this tab is not related to that of the other two tabs. On the first tab there is a notepad, and here there is an alarm clock. Currently there is nothing on the third tab. We will be adding more functionality to the tabs in future chapters. For now, however, let's take a look at the two functions that are currently in the program.

4. Click on the **Notepad** tab to switch back to the Notepad as shown in Figure 5.1.

This portion of the program is a notepad. It will allow you to enter information into the large text box that makes up the workspace of the program.

5. Key **This is a sample** into the workspace text box.

6. Press **Enter** and then key **This is the second line**.

Now you have two lines of text in the text box as shown in Figure 5.3.

Keying multiple lines into a text box will be introduced in this chapter. You will also learn how to copy selected text to the clipboard.

7. Highlight part of the text in the workspace and click the **Cut** button.

That text disappears, but it is not gone. It is merely cut from the workspace and placed on the clipboard.

8. Click the **Paste** button and the text reappears. Click the **Paste** button again and the text appears again. Each time you press the **Paste** button, the text is copied from the clipboard to the workspace where the insertion point happens to be.

9. Move the insertion point to the middle of the first line and click the **Paste** button. The text is pasted there.

FIGURE 5.3

The text in the workspace text box.

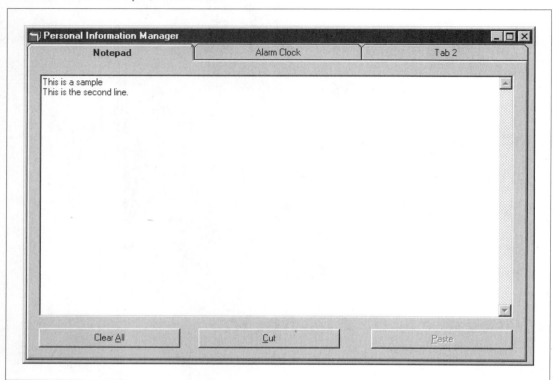

10. Move the insertion point to the end of the last line in the text box, press **Enter** three times, and click the **Paste** button. The text is pasted there now.

11. Click the **Clear All** button, and all the text in the workspace disappears.

   This function is pretty easy to understand. You probably already know the code behind the **Clear All** button. It simply assigns the empty string to the Text property of the text box. But enough of the notepad for the moment. Let's check out the alarm clock.

12. Click the **Alarm Clock** tab to see the display shown in Figure 5.2.

   This alarm clock allows two alarms to be set independently. When the time in the display, which is obtained from the computer, moves past the time set in the text box for one of the alarms, that alarm will be set off. The noise the alarm makes can be set to a beep, for which Visual Basic has a command, or to a sound if you have a sound card and speakers and choose to do it that way.

13. Set the time in the first alarm text box to a minute or so beyond the time in the display, and then click the **Alarm On** option button for that alarm (see Figure 5.4). The option button is another tool you will learn how to use in this chapter.

   You will have to set the time in **military time.** If your display is similar to the one in Figure 5.4, your time will be a number of hours past 12:00. For example, the time in the display is 42 minutes past 5 o'clock in the afternoon.

14. Wait until the displayed time exceeds the time in the text box. The computer should start beeping. It will beep once every second until the alarm is turned off. Click the **Alarm Off** option button for the first alarm, and the beeping stops.

FIGURE 5.4
The alarm set and turned on.

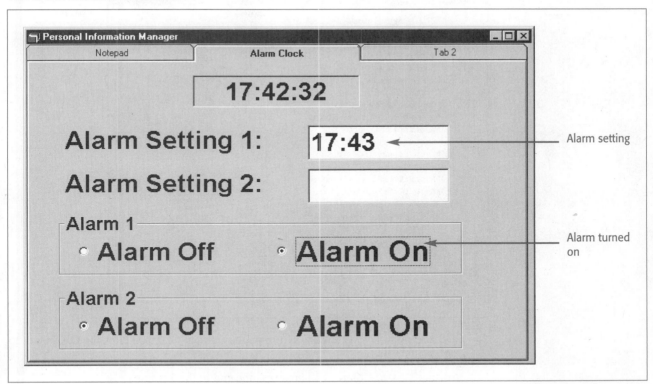

Now that we have explored the tools you will be learning about in this chapter, it is time to begin working with them.

5.4 The Tabbed Control

One of the nicest features of Visual Basic is the ease with which you can make the simplest program look professional. You have already seen several examples of this with the standard tools. The next tool we want to explore is not considered one of the "standard" tools. There are so many tools available that the designers of Visual Basic decided to give you initially only the tools they felt everyone would want to use, the "standard" tools that you have already seen in the toolbox. All the other available tools must be added to the toolbox.

The tool we want to add is the **Tabbed Control**, and it is found in the dialog box displayed using the Components option of the Project menu.

1. Get into Visual Basic with your work disk in drive A.

2. Click the **Project** menu and select the **Components** option (shortcut key **Ctrl-T** or right-click the toolbox and then click the **Components . . .** option) to see the dialog box shown in Figure 5.5.

The elements are listed alphabetically, and the component we want is not shown.

3. Scroll the list until you find the **Microsoft Tabbed Dialog Control 6.0**.

FIGURE 5.5
The Components dialog
box.

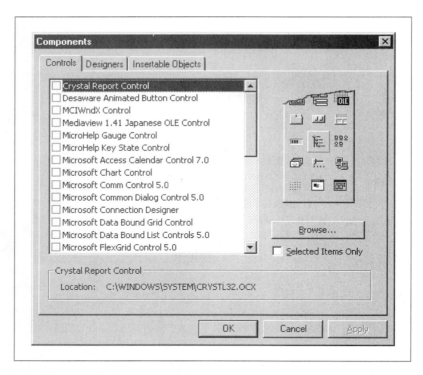

4. Click the small box on the left to turn on the element, and then click the **OK** button to exit the dialog box.

   Now the Tabbed Control will appear at the end of the Toolbox.

5. Double-click the Tabbed Control as shown in Figure 5.6.

   This will add the control to your form as shown in Figure 5.7.

   Note that the control appears as a series of tabs similar to ones you have seen in other Windows applications, including your first look at the PIM application. The nice thing about this control is that it's easy to use, just like most other Visual Basic tools.

FIGURE 5.6
The Tabbed Control.

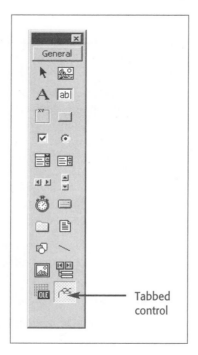

Tabbed control

FIGURE 5.7
The Tabbed Control
added to the form.

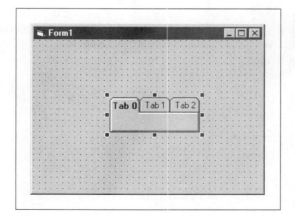

The first thing we need to do, of course, is adjust the size of the control to fit the other objects for which we want to use the control. You saw earlier that we are going to use this control for the notepad and alarm clock, but that didn't tell you how big the form should be, and there really isn't any good way to decide that until you have added to the form whatever elements you will need. Thus, we will simply tell you how big the control should be.

6. Change the height of the form to 6555 and the width to 9600.

This will leave room enough for all the tools we are going to add to the control. It also makes the form the right size so it will fit on a screen that is set at 640 by 480, which is the minimum screen resolution, though you probably use a higher-resolution setting on your monitor.

Now you need to adjust the size of the Tabbed Control to fit the form.

7. Move the Tabbed Control to the top of the form and expand it to fill the form as shown in Figure 5.8.

The first thing we need to do with the Tabbed Control is to specify what captions we want on the tabs. As you have seen, we are going to create a notepad, so we will want the

FIGURE 5.8
The form with the
resized Tabbed Control.

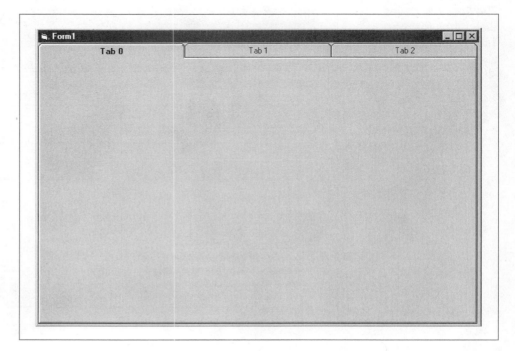

first tab to say Notepad. To change the captions on the tabs, you need to get to the Properties dialog box for the control, which is different from the Properties window. Although they often contain the same properties, the Properties dialog box is often easier to use when one is available. Not all controls have a Properties dialog box. You load the Properties dialog box by right-clicking the control.

8. Right-click the control to see a small menu. Select the **Properties** option, and you see the dialog box shown in Figure 5.9.

Note that this dialog box has tabs on it. The tabs here are all related to the tabs of the Tabbed Control. You can specify a variety of changes for the elements of the control:

- The captions of the tabs (TabCaption)
- The number of tabs in the control (Tab Count)
- The number of tabs per row (TabsPerRow)
- The height of the tabs (TabHeight), which may need to be adjusted to compensate for the size of the font you are using (the Font tab)
- The placement of the tabs (Orientation)

Currently the only thing we want to change on the control is the caption for the tabs. Because we are going to put a notepad on the first tab, we want the tab to be called Notepad.

9. Highlight **Tab 0** in the TabCaption text box, and key **Notepad**.

As long as we're here, we might as well change the TabCaption for the alarm clock.

10. Click the right arrow on the **Current Tab** as indicated in Figure 5.9 to change to the second tab.

11. Highlight **Tab 1** in the TabCaption text box, and key **Alarm Clock**.

12. Click the **OK** button to exit the dialog box; your first tab will now say Notepad and the second will say Alarm Clock as shown in Figure 5.10.

FIGURE 5.9
The Property Pages dialog box for the Tabbed Control.

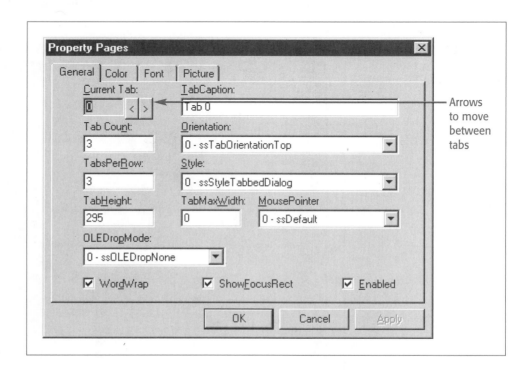

FIGURE 5.10
The form showing the captions on the tabs.

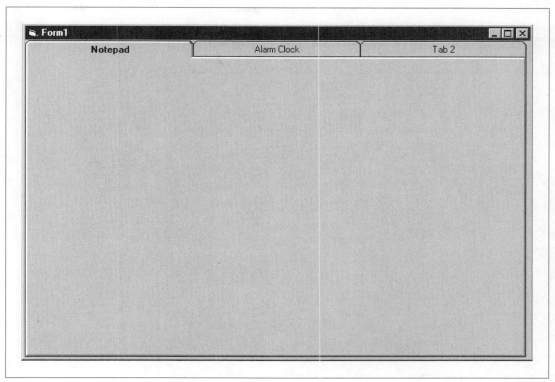

Before we continue, we should name all the elements of the program and save it.

13. Change the name of the form to **frmPIM** and the caption to **Personal Information Manager**.

14. Change the name of the Tabbed Control to **tabPIM** and save the form as **frmPIM** and the project as **PIM**.

With the Tabbed Control set up and the project saved, we are now ready to add the notepad to the program.

5.5 Creating a Notepad

The text boxes we have been using up to this point have all been single-line boxes with a maximum line length of 255 characters. To create a notepad, all we need to do is use the **Multiline** property.

1. Switch to the Notepad tab, click the Text Box control in the Toolbox, and draw it on the Tabbed Control as shown in Figure 5.11.

You need to draw it on the control because if you simply double-click the control, it will be added on the form even though it may look as if it is on the control. Be sure to leave the space shown at the bottom of the text box, because we are going to put some buttons there.

2. Change the control name of the text box to **txtNotepad** and delete the default text from the text box.

FIGURE 5.11
The notepad text box added to the Tabbed Control.

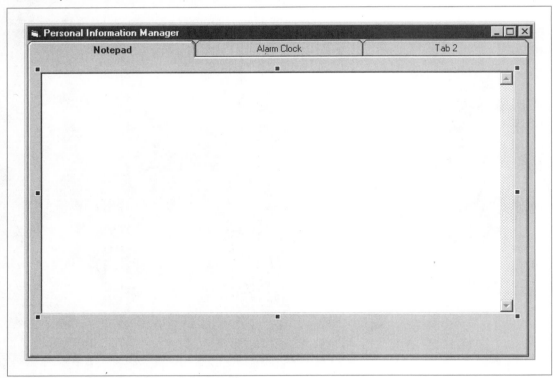

3. Select the **Multiline** property.

   Note that the current value is False. This means that the text box will allow you to key on only one line.

4. Run the program, click in the text box, key **This is a sample**, and then press **Enter**.

   Nothing happens. The insertion point does not even appear on the next line down. That's because you can't use the **Enter** key to create a second line. The Multiline property is False, so this is a single-line box. We need to change the Multiline setting to True.

5. Exit the program, switch to the form, select the text box, change to the Multiline property, and press **T**.

6. Run the program again. Click in the text box, key **This is a sample**, and press **Enter**. This time the insertion point will go to the next line down. Key **This is on the second line**.

   Now you can have more than one line. As a matter of fact, there is virtually no limit to the number of lines that the user can add in the text box.

7. Continue to press **Enter** until the text at the top of the workspace scrolls off the top.

   The text is not gone, of course. It has simply been scrolled off the top of the workspace.

8. Press **Ctrl-Home**, and the text reappears with the cursor in the home position.

9. Press **End** to move to the end of the first line, press **Spacebar**, key enough text so that the text will reach the edge of the text box, and then key one more word.

   The text automatically wraps when the text reaches the edge of the workspace. Visual Basic adds the word wrap capability automatically as long as you don't use a horizontal scroll bar. But because the text will scroll off the top (or bottom) of the workspace, you will probably want to have a vertical scroll bar so that you can easily get to the particular section of text that you want. **Ctrl-Home** and **Ctrl-End** will move the insertion point to the top or bottom of the text in the text box, but without a scroll bar, there is no way to move the insertion point to a particular position except by using the arrow keys. If there are many lines, using the arrow keys is a poor method.

Scroll bars can be added by using the **ScrollBars** property. You can use a vertical scroll bar, a horizontal one, or one of each.

10. Exit the program and switch to the form.

11. Click the text box and select the **ScrollBars** property. Note that it is currently set to 0 - None. Change it to **2 - Vertical**, and notice that a vertical scroll bar now appears as shown in Figure 5.12.

FIGURE 5.12
The Notepad, showing the vertical scroll bar and the ScrollBars property in the Properties list.

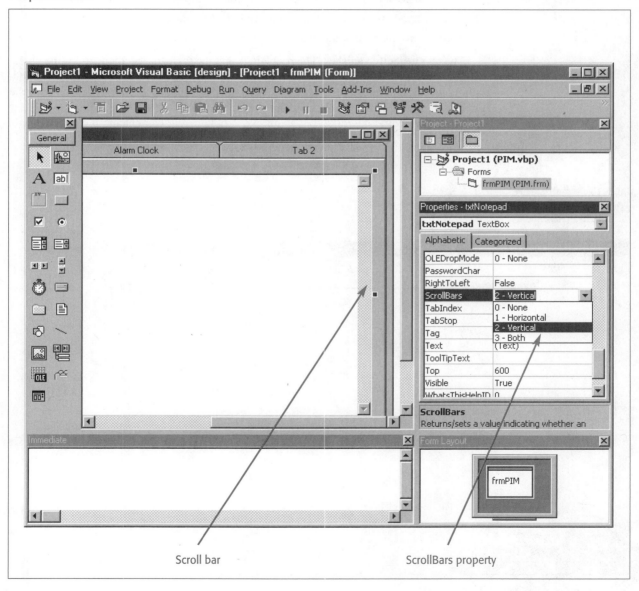

Scroll bar   ScrollBars property

We briefly used **Ctrl-Home** to jump to the top of the text box and the **End** key to jump to the end of a line of text. If you recall, we have already mentioned that Visual Basic automatically adds most of the keystroke functionality of Windows to text boxes. **Ctrl-Home, Ctrl-End, Backspace, Home,** and **End** are a few examples of this.

Manipulating the Text

One of the first things we want to be able to do in our notepad is delete all the text that is currently in the text box by selecting a button. We already know we can erase the contents of a text box by setting its Text property to the empty string. All we need to do to empty the entire text box is use the command

```
txtNotepad.Text = ""
```

For this function, we will add a **Clear All** button.

1. Add a button with the caption **Clear All** and the control name **cmdClear_Button** to your form as shown in Figure 5.13. The width of the button should be 2655.

2. Open the code window for the button, and key the statement we just discussed.

3. Run the program, click the text box, key **This is a sample**, and then select the button.

The text instantly vanishes. The problem is that the **focus** of the application (the object currently active) is still the button, and if you begin keying right after clicking the button, nothing will be entered in the text box because the program is not currently focused on the text box. It would be nice if the program would automatically shift focus back to the text box so that we could begin keying again. No problem. We can change the application's focus.

FIGURE 5.13
The notepad with the **Clear All** button added.

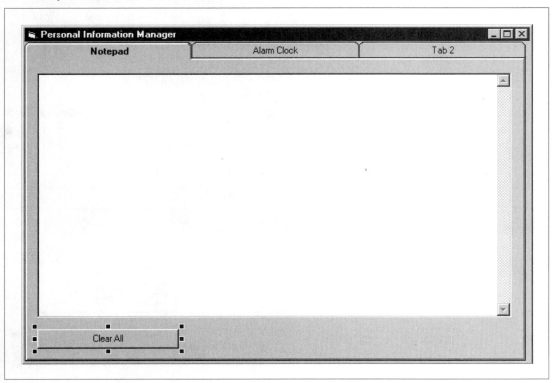

To do this, we need the **SetFocus** method, which allows us to change the application's focus from one object to another. The format of the method is the normal format:

```
Object name.SetFocus
```

To change the focus from the button back to the text box, the statement would be

```
txtNotepad.SetFocus
```

4. Exit the program, change to the code for the cmdClear_Button, and key this statement after the assignment statement.

5. Run the program, click the text box, key **This is a sample**, and then select the button.

This time the insertion point will automatically reappear in the text box.

The other problem is that the focus does not start in the text box. The Tabbed Control was the first item added to the form, so the focus starts there because the **TabIndex** property of the Tabbed Control is zero, indicating that it is the first element to have the focus. The TabIndex property of objects tells Visual Basic what object to move to when the **Tab** key is pressed. If the focus of the program is currently a text box with a TabIndex of 3, the object that has the TabIndex of 4 will be the next object to gain the focus when the user presses the **Tab** key.

If we change the TabIndex of the Notepad text box, we can make it have the focus of the program when the form first appears on the desktop.

6. Exit the program, click the text box, and change the TabIndex property to 0.

7. Run the program, and note that this time the focus starts in the text box.

It is interesting to note that the TabIndex property is not like the Index property of a control array. When you change the Index property of a control array element, the Index properties of the other elements in that control array are not automatically changed. That is not true of the TabIndex property. If you change the TabIndex property of one object, the TabIndex properties of all the objects that have a TabIndex numerically following the one you changed will automatically be adjusted. For example, if the TabIndex of one object is 5 and you change it to 3, whatever object had the TabIndex of 3 will now have a TabIndex of 4, and the one that had a TabIndex of 4 will now have a TabIndex of 5. Any object that had a TabIndex of 6 or more would not be affected by this change.

> **HINT:** The other thing you can do to specify what object has the initial focus is to specify the Setfocus statement for that object in the Form_Load procedure.

Text Selection   You have already seen many times that you can highlight (select) text in text boxes and cut and paste that text. Visual Basic handles all these details automatically in your notepad in response to the same keystrokes and mouse movements you have been using all along. But what if you want your application to have buttons that can control the cut and paste functions for those users unfamiliar with the cut and paste keystrokes that are already part of Visual Basic?

Visual Basic has three properties set up to allow you to handle selected text. **SelStart** is the starting location of the selection. If no text is selected, SelStart will indicate the insertion point. If SelStart is zero, the text selection begins on the first character in the text box. If it is the same as or larger than the number of characters in the text box, the start of the selection is after the last character in the text box. You should note that because SelStart is declared as a long integer, it can handle numbers up to 64K.

SelLength, another long integer, is used to keep track of the length of the selected text. If it is zero, no text is selected. If it is equal to or is larger than the value of the length of the Text property, all the text in the text box has been selected from the point specified by SelStart, and if SelStart is zero, all the text has been selected.

The third property, **SelText**, will actually contain the selected text. If no text has been selected, SelText will be the empty string (" ").

Even though these are properties, their values can be set only during program execution. The format for assigning to SelStart and the others is the normal format for assigning to a property:

```
Text Box name.SelStart = numeric value
```

Being able to set the starting position of a text selection allows you initially to highlight text in a text box. For example, the following two statements select and highlight all the text in the text box called **txtInput**:

```
txtInput.SelStart = 0
txtInput.SelLength = Len(txtInput.Text)
```

Cutting the Text   Now that we know how to access the selected text, we want to add a button that will allow us to cut that text.

1. Add the button shown in Figure 5.14 with the caption **Cut**, and use the control name **cmdCut_Button**.

When this button is selected, the highlighted text is cut from the text box. We could set up a temporary storage variable as a place to put the cut text, but Windows already has such a temporary storage location called the clipboard, and we can put the cut text there. For that we will need a special object, **Clipboard**, and another method, **SetText**.

The format of the statement for using the Clipboard object is a bit different from that of the statements we have been using. It is essentially an assignment statement without the equals sign:

```
Clipboard.SetText txtNotepad.SelText
```

FIGURE 5.14
The notepad with the **Cut** button added.

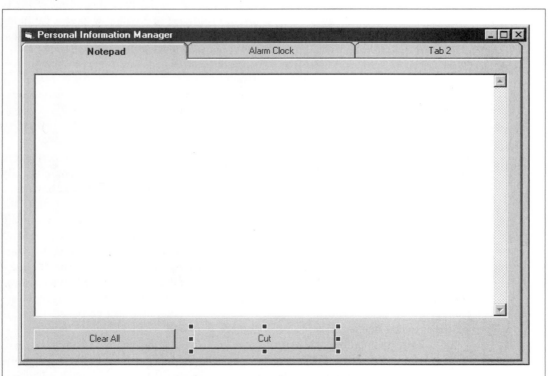

2. Change to the code window in the procedure for cmdCut_Button, and key this statement.

This statement will copy the selected text in the text box to the clipboard. It will not, however, remove the text from the box. To do that, we will need to empty the string ourselves with the statement

```
txtNotepad.SelText = ""          ' Erase the text
```

3. Key this statement after the previous statement.

Finally, we will want the focus to be given back to the text box after this button is used.

4. Key the same focus statement we used earlier (or simply copy the other one).

This gives you the code shown in Figure 5.15.

5. Run the program and key **This is a sample**. Now highlight part of the sentence and select the **Cut** button.

The highlighted text disappears, and the insertion point returns to the text box. Let's make sure that the removed text is indeed on the clipboard.

6. Switch to the System Tools subgroup of the Accessories subgroup of the Programs group in the computer's Start menu and launch the **Clipboard Viewer**. (If your computer doesn't have the Clipboard Viewer installed, skip this step.) The text you cut should be on the clipboard. Exit from the clipboard application.

Pasting the Text   Our last step is to paste the text back into the text box. For this, we will add another button.

1. Add the **Paste** button as shown in Figure 5.16 with the control name **cmdPaste_Button**.

2. Change to the code section for the cmdPaste_Button.

To get the text back from the clipboard, we need to use the clipboard method **GetText**, and the statement necessary is more like a conventional assignment statement:

```
txtNotepad.SelText = Clipboard.GetText()
```

The parentheses in the method are to enable you to specify the type of data you are retrieving; in the case of text, it is unnecessary. We will see in a later chapter that the parameter is sometimes necessary when we are retrieving graphics data from the clipboard.

FIGURE 5.15
The code of the PIM program so far.

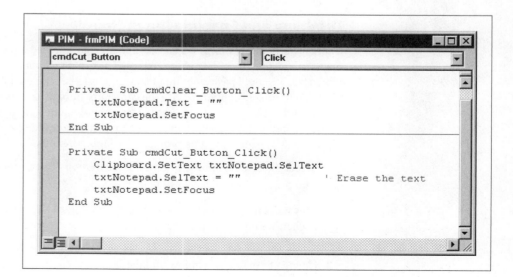

FIGURE 5.16
The notepad after the **Paste** button has been added.

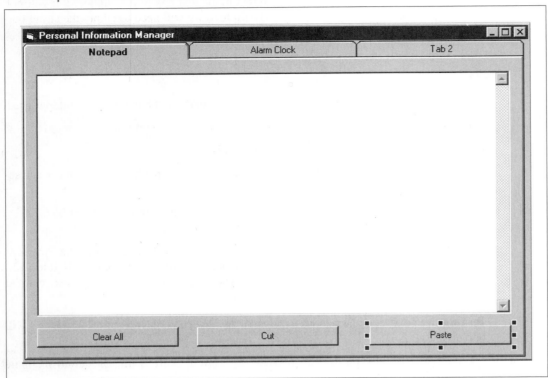

3. Insert the previous statement into the procedure and add the focus statement after it.

4. Run the program and select the **Paste** button. The text you cut earlier should appear.

5. Key some text of your choosing, highlight some of it, cut it, and paste it back in a different location. Move to another location and paste it again. As you can see, you can paste the text in as many times as you wish. Continue playing with the three buttons until you are sure you thoroughly understand what is happening. Then exit the application and save it.

Disabling and Enabling the Buttons

There are still a few things we can do to make our notepad a bit better. For one, before we have cut any text, there is nothing to paste back into the text box. Because we are using the clipboard, we could paste anything that happens to be on the clipboard, but we want this application to be self-contained with the capability of pasting only what we have cut. Thus, if we haven't cut anything, the **Paste** button should not be available.

You saw in an earlier chapter how to disable a text box with the **Enabled** property. Virtually all objects have this property, including buttons.

1. Select the Enabled property of the **Paste** button. The current value is True.

2. Key **F** to change the value to False.

This will initially disable the button. Now we need a way to re-enable it. We want it enabled when we cut some text, so we need to add a statement to the procedure for the **Cut** button.

3. Change to the code window and the procedure for the **Cut** button.

4. Key the following statement at the end of the others (see Figure 5.17):

```
cmdPaste_Button.Enabled = True        ' Turn on the Paste button
```

> **HINT:** You could also disable the **Paste** button after the text had been pasted into the text box by adding, to the cmdPaste_Button procedure, the statement
>
> ```
> cmdPaste_Button.Enabled = False
> ```
>
> This, however, would mean that you could paste the cut text only once. There will be many times when you want to paste the same text in several different locations, so you will not want to disable the **Paste** button in this manner.

5. Run the application and note that the **Paste** button is dimmed and unavailable.
6. Key in some text and select the **Paste** button. Nothing happens because the button will not function.
7. Highlight some of the text and cut it. Now the **Paste** button becomes enabled.
8. Select the **Paste** button to be sure the text appears as it is supposed to; then exit the application and save it again.

Using Access Keys

We will make one final change to our notepad in this chapter. You have seen that on many buttons in Windows applications, one of the letters of the caption is underlined. This **access key** allows you to select the button by holding **Alt** and pressing the underlined key. You can easily add this capability to your buttons by putting an ampersand (&) in front of the letter you want for the access key.

1. Select the Caption property of the **Clear All** button.
2. Key **&** in front of the "A" in "All."

FIGURE 5.17
Where to insert the new statement.

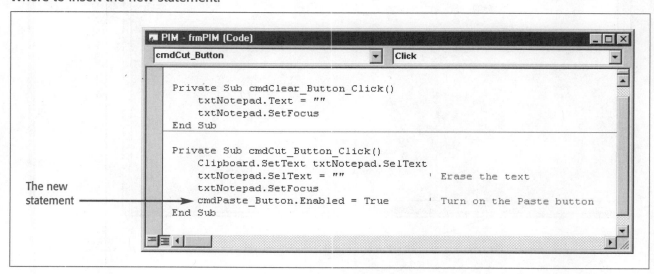

Note that the "A" on the button is now underlined (Figure 5.18).

3. Switch to the **Cut** button and add **&** in front of the "C."

4. Switch to the **Paste** button and add **&** in front of the "P."

> **HINT:** When adding access keys, be careful not to add the same key twice. If you do, then when you use the access key as the application is running, the application will shift the focus to the first of the buttons in the tab order but will not execute it. This is a convenience for the user to keep the program from executing a button in error.

5. Run the program, key in some text, and press **Alt-A** (for Clear All). The text disappears.

6. Key some more text, highlight some of it, and press **Alt-C** (for Cut). The text is cut and the **Paste** button is enabled.

7. Press **Alt-P** (for Paste). The text is pasted back in the text box.

As you can see, the access keys allow you to select the buttons from the keyboard, without using the mouse to click them.

FIGURE 5.18
The access key for the **Clear All** button.

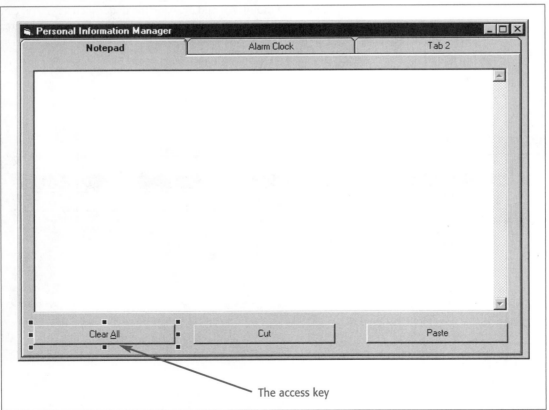

> **HINT:** You can also use access keys on the Tabbed Control by the method just discussed. We won't do that, because access keys on the tabs have a tendency to get in the way of other uses for the access keys.

Well, that's it for the notepad portion of the PIM application for now. It's time to move on to another application for the PIM to discover some more properties and objects.

8. Exit the program and save it.

> **HINT:** Though we added buttons for the Cut and Paste functions, Visual Basic will actually handle cutting and pasting of text box text automatically with the **Ctrl-C** (Copy), **Ctrl-X** (Cut), and **Ctrl-V** (Paste) keys. We added the functions because it is better for the user to be able to access such functions from a menu, and we will switch our text manipulation functions to a menu in the next chapter.

5.6   Creating an Alarm Clock

Thus far, when you have keyed information into a text box, Visual Basic has handled the reception and placement of the keystrokes. That is, if the program focus is on a text box and the user presses a key, that key is registered in the text box. This is handled automatically, but with the proper techniques, you can intercept those keystrokes. You might want to do this if you needed to edit these keystrokes for some reason. This is one of the things we will do as we create the alarm clock. You will also learn about two new objects: the timer and the option button.

Adding the Alarm Clock

1. Click the Alarm Clock tab on the Tabbed Control to switch to the second tab area of the Tabbed Control. Note that it is empty. The notepad is on the first tab area, and we have yet to add anything to this area.

2. Add the alarm clock elements to the Tabbed Control as shown in Figure 5.19 with the following adjustments:

   a. The large box on the top is a label with the control name **lblTime_Out**. Change the font to **Arial**, make it bold, and change the font size to **24**.

   b. The box on the right is a text box with the control name **txtAlarm_In_1** and the font **Arial**, **bold**, and **24 points**.

   c. **Alarm Setting:** is a label that you can name as you please.

If we are going to have an alarm clock, it makes sense to have a text box to input the time when the alarm is to be sounded. That's what the **txtAlarm_In_1** text box is for. It has the 1 appended because we will add a second one later.

Monitoring the Keystrokes

Time is generally input in a specific format with colons between the hours and minutes, as in 03:15. No problem. Text boxes will allow you to key any data you wish, including letters.

FIGURE 5.19

The beginnings of the alarm clock form.

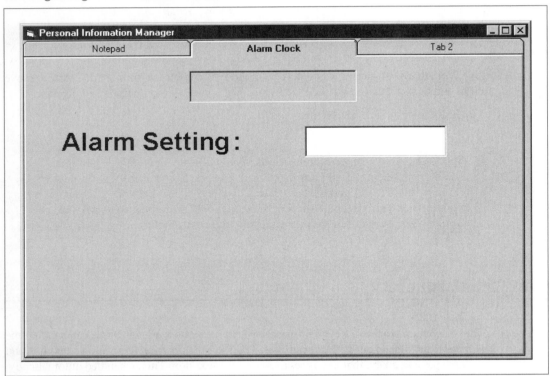

But letters can be a problem. In our programs thus far, either the specific input in the text box was not important or we simply assumed that the user would be smart enough to enter the proper type of data. Such an assumption is not valid when you are working with users. You must always assume the worst: that they don't know what they are supposed to key in or that they will make lots of errors. Thus, when the specific type of data is important, as in time entry, it is a good idea to verify the data as they are being input. Visual Basic enables you to monitor every keystroke.

Almost every time a user presses a key in a text box, Visual Basic receives the key code and the **KeyPress** event is activated. Certain keys, such as the **Home** and **End** keys, are ignored by Visual Basic, so they function in the normal fashion.

> **HINT:** There are also **KeyUp** and **KeyDown** events. They handle the keyed input a bit differently than does the **KeyPress** event. You can check the Visual Basic Programmer's Guide or the help system for information on those events.

1. Open the code window for the text box and select the KeyPress event (the default event is Change) as shown in Figure 5.20.

As you can see from the parameter passed, the key code is received in KeyPress as KeyAscii. We can use KeyAscii to determine whether the proper key was pressed by the user. KeyAscii will contain the numerical equivalent code for the key that was pressed.

As we have discussed before, every key that is pressed generates a code. The coding scheme used in Visual Basic is the ASCII coding standard. That standard dictates the

FIGURE 5.20
The code window for the KeyPress event.

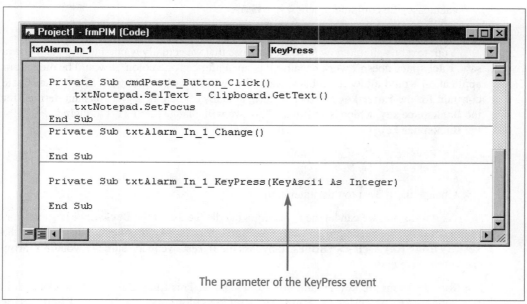

The parameter of the KeyPress event

numerical equivalent for every character. It is this numerical equivalent that is stored in KeyAscii.

Because the user is supposed to be entering a time, all the numeric digits would be valid input, but the user should also be able to enter a colon. Rather than look up all the key codes for the numbers and the colon, we will change the numeric KeyAscii to its string equivalent using the Chr function. Then we can compare for regular characters rather than their ASCII equivalents. Our If Test can look for a colon (:) rather than the ASCII code for a colon, which is 58. Thus, our If Test should look something like

```
' This procedure inputs the alarm setting
'
    Sub txtAlarm_In_1_KeyPress (KeyAscii As Integer)
        Dim strKey_In As String
        strKey_In = Chr(KeyAscii)
        If (strKey_In < "0" Or strKey_In > "9") And strKey_In <>
        ⮑ ":" Then
            Beep
            KeyAscii = 0
        End If
    End Sub
```

Note the use of the compound If Test. The parentheses tell the application to try the two Or conditionals first, and then the And relational test is carried out. If the key is not in the range 0 to 9 and is not a colon, the key is not accepted. If the key is not accepted, the computer beeps (the **Beep** statement) and the keystroke is erased by setting KeyAscii to zero.

HINT: You can use a sound file instead of the Beep statement if you have a sound card and speakers. There is an exercise at the end of the chapter for this change.

2. Key the given code and then run the program.

3. Key **1:a**. The computer beeps when you press **a** and nothing appears in the text box. Press a few more keys, including **Backspace**, other than numbers and the colon. In each case, the computer beeps.

4. Exit the program and change to the code window.

Your text box should now have **1:**. Suppose that we actually wanted to key **10:**. As you saw, **Backspace** doesn't work because it is not a number or a colon. It would be nice if our application would allow us to backspace. We learned earlier that vbCr is a Visual Basic constant for the **Enter** key (carriage return, actually). There is also a constant defined for the **Backspace** key, which is **vbBack**. Thus, we will change the If Test to include a test for the **Backspace** key.

```
If KeyAscii <> vbBack And (strKey_In < "0" Or strKey_In > "9") And
 ↳strKey_In <> ":" Then
```

5. Change the If Test to this statement.

As it turns out, we can let the application handle the use of the **Backspace** key as it normally does. All we needed to do was make sure our keystroke routine did not intercept the key. By using **KeyAscii <> vbBack** to bypass the If Test, we made sure we wouldn't throw the keystroke away.

6. Run the program, key **1:**, and press **Backspace**. This time, **Backspace** works as it is supposed to. Try using the **Home** and **End** keys along with the **Del** and **Right Arrow** and **Left Arrow** keys.

Note that these keys work just as they should. Visual Basic does not pass these keys to your routine. The only ones you can control are 8 for **Backspace**, 9 for **Tab**, 10 for **Linefeed** (which works like the carriage return except that it doesn't return the cursor to the left column), and 13 for **Enter** (or carriage return).

7. Exit the application.

What we used the KeyPress event for is only one of many uses for the routine. Another thing you can do with the KeyPress event is sense when the user has pressed the **Enter** key. The defined constant for a carriage return, which is what the computer sends when the user presses the **Enter** key, is vbCr. Since this constant is a string, however, to use it we have to change KeyAscii to a character by using the Chr function you learned about in Chapter 4. Being able to sense this is useful in programs that have a series of text boxes. Users like the capability of pressing the **Enter** key to move from field to field rather than having to use the **Tab** key. When you sense that the user has pressed the **Enter** key, you can use the SetFocus method to move the focus to the next text box that is to be entered. This can be done with an If Test like the following:

```
If Chr(KeyAscii) = vbCr Then
    txtBox_2.Setfocus
End If
```

If any other key is pressed, this test is skipped and nothing is done.

User-Defined Functions

You can also use the KeyPress event for things like making sure that the input in a text box consists entirely of capital letters. This is handy in programs in which codes or the like are used and they need to be entered only in uppercase. This can be done with the following statement in the KeyPress event:

```
KeyAscii = Asc(UCase(Chr(KeyAscii)))
```

This statement begins by changing the KeyAscii variable to a string with the Chr function. Then the UCase function makes that character uppercase. If the key pressed is something other than a letter, such as a dollar sign ($), the UCase statement doesn't do anything because UCase is used only to capitalize letters. Lastly, the **Asc** function changes the string character back to its character code equivalent. This statement sets the KeyAscii variable to the uppercase equivalent of a lowercase keystroke for letters of the alphabet.

In applications that have a lot of text boxes in which you need the input in uppercase, there is a slight problem with the foregoing KeyAscii statement: this grouping of functions is a bit difficult to remember. It would be much easier if we had a single function that we could use to change KeyAscii to its uppercase equivalent. Well, we can create one by defining our own function. Functions defined in our code are called **user-defined functions**, and they have the format

```
Function functionname (declared parameters) As function type
```

The keyword **Function** defines this procedure as a function that differs from a regular procedure in that a function returns a value to the procedure that called the function. It is followed by the name of the function, which must reflect all object-naming conventions, such as beginning with a letter. We will also observe the standard variable-naming convention of using the type of the variable as a prefix, because the function name has to be declared as a type (an issue to be discussed soon). We will call this function **intReAscii**. The function name is followed by whatever parameters you want to pass to the function. In the case of this function, you will want to pass the KeyAscii code to the function, so your parameter will be something like

```
(KeyAscii as Integer)
```

This is the same way the parameter is defined in the KeyPress event.

Finally, the function itself must be defined as a type. Since the purpose of the function is to return a value to the statement that calls the function, Visual Basic must know what type of value to return. Because we want to return an integer to the KeyPress event procedure, we will declare the function as an integer type. That makes the entire function declaration

```
Function intReAscii (KeyAscii As Integer) As Integer
```

Again, we are using the "int" prefix on the function name because this function is declared as an integer function. The prefix helps us easily recognize the data type.

This is only the declaration of the function, similar to the first statement of a subroutine procedure. That means you must add the code for the function just as you add code within a Sub procedure. The only code we need in this function is the translation statement to change the KeyAscii code to uppercase. We used KeyAscii for the parameter name in our function, so we can use a statement almost exactly like the one we used before. Again, the statement from before is

```
KeyAscii = Asc(UCase(Chr(KeyAscii)))
```

The only change we need to make to this statement is to use the name of the function as the result of the statement. This way, the function will return the result to the calling statement. Therefore, we change the above statement to

```
intReAscii = Asc(UCase(Chr(KeyAscii)))
```

In the KeyPress event, the statement using this function would be

```
KeyAscii = intReAscii(KeyAscii)
```

This statement sends KeyAscii to the function and stores the returned value in KeyAscii.

There are literally thousands of uses for functions. We will see many more uses as we progress through this book.

Adding a Timer

Now that we can enter the time when we want the alarm to go off, we need to be able to determine when that time has occurred. Visual Basic's **Timer** control is an object designed specifically for such instances.

1. Double-click the **Timer** control as shown in Figure 5.21, and a timer is added to your form as shown in Figure 5.22.

The position of the timer on the form is of no importance, because it will not appear when the application is running. You can move it to wherever on the form you think it will be least intrusive. The current control name of the timer is **Timer1**, and we want to change it to conform to the naming standards we used with the other objects we added to our project.

2. Change the name of the timer to **tmrAlarm_Timer**.

The fact that a timer has been added to the form does not mean that the timer is active. To activate the timer, you need to set the **Interval** property.

3. Select the Interval property.

Note that the value is 0. The interval is the number of milliseconds (thousandths of a second) that the application will wait between times it runs the timer code. If that number is 0, it will not look at the code at all. The interval must be at least 1 to activate the timer, but it is best to set the interval well above 1. Otherwise, since the application will activate the timer code every time the specified interval has elapsed, continually accessing the code once every millisecond might make the computer slow down. A meaningful time interval is one second, so we will use an interval of 1000.

FIGURE 5.21
The Timer control.

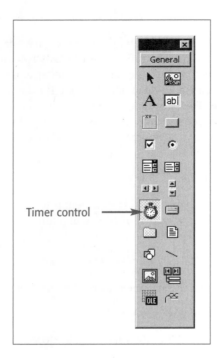

Timer control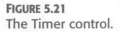

FIGURE 5.22
The PIM with the timer added.

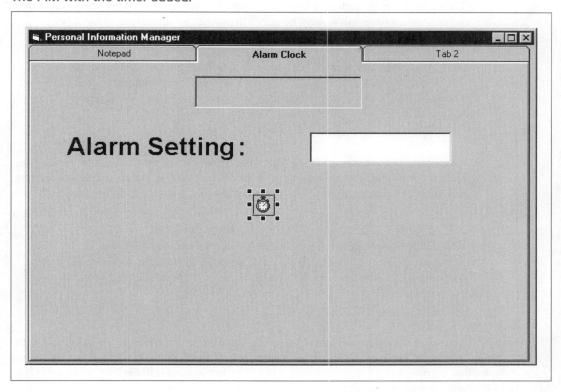

4. Change the value to **1000**.

   Now the application will execute the code in the timer procedure every second. But we don't have any code there yet.

5. Open the code window for the timer.

   What is it we want in here? First, we want to check our entered alarm setting against the current time. We can get that with the **Time$** function. A bonus is that Time$ gives us the time already formatted as hh:mm:ss. We need to compare Time$ against our input setting:

```
If Time$ >= txtAlarm_In_1.Text Then
    Beep
End If
```

> **HINT:** **Date$** will give you the date already formatted as mm-dd-yyyy, whereas **Date** will format the date as mm/dd/yy. **Time** will give you the time already formatted as hh:mm:ss AM/PM, such as 2:45:15 PM.

6. Key the foregoing If Test. It will cause the computer to beep when the current time is beyond the time entered for the setting.

   We also need to display the current time in the label. That requires the statement

```
lblTime_Out.Caption = Time$
```

7. Add this statement after the If Test and run the application.

The application immediately begins to beep. Because you have not entered an alarm setting, the current time will always be larger than what is currently in the text box.

> **HINT:** As we mentioned at the beginning of this chapter, if you are in the lab after 12 noon, you will note that the time is displayed in military format, wherein 2:00 P.M. is shown as 14:00. There are ways around this, but for now, we will work with the application as is.

8. Key a time in the setting that is about a minute larger than the current time being displayed in the label. The beeping stops. Wait until the displayed time exceeds the setting, and the beeping starts again. Now you know the alarm works. Exit the program.

> **HINT:** On some computers the Beep command can scarcely be heard. If you wish, you can put the Beep command within a loop from 1 to 100 so it will beep 100 times. Doing this will cause the computer to buzz rather than beep, and that sound is much more noticeable.

The alarm clock is ready now; we can set the time, and the alarm will go off. Unfortunately, you cannot stop the alarm without exiting the program. We can fix this by adding another object—two of them, actually, called **Option** buttons—to the form after a brief exploration of date formatting.

Date Formatting

Even though the PIM program displays the time directly out of the Time$ function, often when using dates and times, you will need to format the output. We have mentioned that the Time$ function extracts the time from the computer and the Date$ function extracts the date, but there is also the **Now** function, which extracts the date and the time.

For formatting dates, you can use the special formatting characters **m** (month), **d** (day), and **y** (year), and for times you can use **h** (hours), **n** (minutes), and **s** (seconds). Some of the more common uses follow.

> **d**, **m**, **y**, **s** (single character) will display a number without a leading zero (such as 1, 5, and 9), but if the element has two digits, both will be displayed (such as 15).
>
> **dd**, **mm**, **yy**, **ss** (two characters) will display a one-digit number with a leading zero or a two-digit number normally (such as 01, 05, 09, 12, and 15).
>
> **ddd** will display the day as an abbreviation (Sun–Sat).
>
> **mmm** will display the month as an abbreviation (Jan–Dec).
>
> **dddd** will display the day as a full name (Sunday–Saturday).
>
> **mmmm** will display the month as a full name (January–December).
>
> **yyyy** will display the year as a four-digit number (1900–2040)
>
> **ddddd** will display a complete date, including day, month, and year.
>
> **ttttt** will display a complete time, including hour, minute, and second.
>
> **AM/PM**, **am/pm**, **A/P**, or **a/p** will display the AM or PM or A or P following the time in caps or lowercase and with one or two characters depending on the pattern.

The easiest way to understand the methods of formatting dates is to see some examples:

Format(Now, "m-d-y") = "7-6-93" (using dashes and single digits)

Format(Now, "m/d/y") = "7/6/93" (using slashes and single digits)

Format(Now, "mm/dd/yy") = "07/06/93" (using slashes and double digits)

Format(Now, "ddddd") = "10/16/93" (full date)

Format(Now, "ttttt") = "10:22:03" (full time)

Format(Now, "dddd hh:nn:ss AM/PM") = "Saturday 10:02:04 AM" (day as full name and time)

Format(Now, "dddd, mmmm, d yyyy") = "Saturday, October, 16 1993" (day and month as full name)

Format(139, "mmmm") = "May" (the month is interpreted from the serial number of the day—commonly known as the Julian date—January 1 being day 1, February 1 being day 32, and December 31 being day 365 or 366)

Adding Option Buttons

To use an alarm properly, we need a way to turn it on and off (without exiting the program) and to indicate whether it is on or off. An easy way to do this is with **Option Buttons** (also called **radio buttons**). Option Buttons (Figure 5.23) work as a group. When one of the group is on, the rest of the group is off. Visual Basic handles this automatically. This on-or-off setting is set in the **Value** property of the Option Button object. When the button is on, the Value property is True; when it is off, the Value property is False.

1. Add two Option Buttons to the form, position them as shown in Figure 5.24, change the captions as shown with the font **Arial**, **bold**, and **24 points**, and give them the control names **optAlarm_Off_1** and **optAlarm_On_1**. You will see why we put the 1s at the ends of the control names shortly.

FIGURE 5.23
The Option Button control.

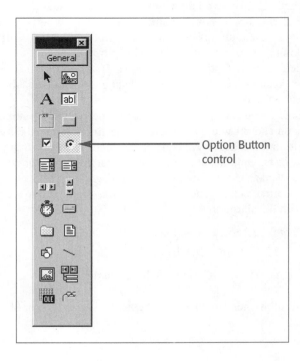

Option Button control

FIGURE 5.24
The form with the Option Buttons added.

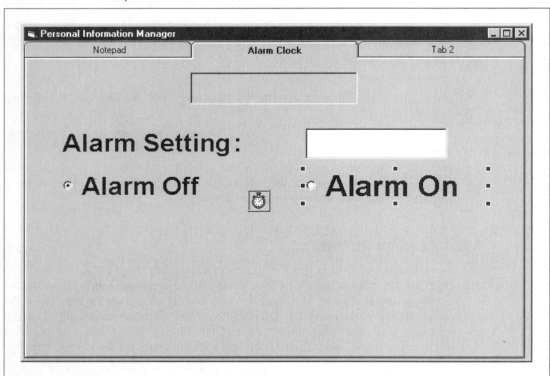

Note that the button for the Option Button is rather small compared to the size of the font. Unfortunately, there is nothing that you can do about this. The size of the button is not adjustable.

Together, these two buttons make a group. Visual Basic will handle turning them on and off. If you turn one on, the other is automatically turned off. When there is a black dot in the circle, the button is on; without the dot, the option is off. The buttons are turned on by clicking them or by setting the Value property.

Clicking on an Option Button that is off not only turns it on and sets the Value to True but also executes the Click event for that button. Clicking a button that is on does not turn it off, nor does it execute the Click event.

Because you can change the Value property in code, you can actually turn the Option Buttons on and off without the user's selecting them. If the user clicks the Option Button to turn it on, the Click event code is executed. The same thing occurs if you set the Value property of an Option Button to True in your code. You are turning the Option Button on, so it is treated as if the button were clicked, and the Click event code is executed.

An alarm clock is generally off until it is turned on, so we will want our application to begin with the alarm off.

2. Select the **Alarm Off** button and the Value property. It is currently set to False.

3. Press **T** (or double-click it) to change the value of the property to True.

Now the **Alarm Off** button will have a dot in the circle. This signifies that it is on, or True.

Now all we need to do is test whether the alarm is on or off. We will do this in the timer code.

4. Change to the Timer code.

The If Test is currently

```
If Time$ >= txtAlarm_In_1.Text Then
```

We need to change it so it will also test to be sure the alarm is on. The test will become

```
If Time$ >= txtAlarm_In_1.Text And optAlarm_On_1.Value = True Then
```

With this final addition, your program code for the alarm clock should look like that shown in Figure 5.25.

5. Run the program.

Note that the **Alarm Off** button is currently turned on (the black dot in the circle) and the application is not beeping.

6. Select the **Alarm On** button. As you do, the **Alarm Off** button turns off, and the application begins beeping (because there is no alarm setting).

7. Practice keying a couple of different times in the alarm setting with the alarm on to be sure the application is working properly. Also try turning the alarm on and off a few times. When you are satisfied that everything is working properly, exit the program.

We added the Option Buttons as separate objects, but Option Buttons can be used as a control array. This feature can be helpful when you are using a series of buttons. If you use Option Buttons as a control array, they still work as a group. When you turn one on, the others are automatically turned off.

To see the possible advantage of using a control array of Option Buttons, suppose you have a program in which you need to use five Option Buttons whose captions indi-

FIGURE 5.25
The code for the alarm clock timer.

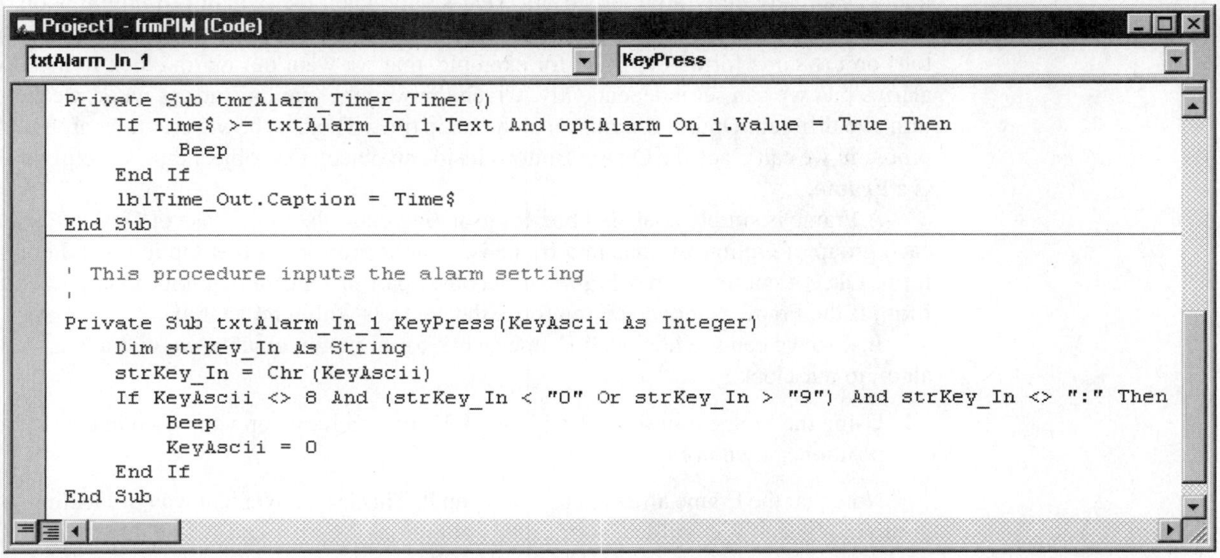

```
Project1 - frmPIM (Code)

txtAlarm_In_1                                    KeyPress

Private Sub tmrAlarm_Timer_Timer()
    If Time$ >= txtAlarm_In_1.Text And optAlarm_On_1.Value = True Then
        Beep
    End If
    lblTime_Out.Caption = Time$
End Sub

' This procedure inputs the alarm setting
'
Private Sub txtAlarm_In_1_KeyPress(KeyAscii As Integer)
    Dim strKey_In As String
    strKey_In = Chr(KeyAscii)
    If KeyAscii <> 8 And (strKey_In < "0" Or strKey_In > "9") And strKey_In <> ":" Then
        Beep
        KeyAscii = 0
    End If
End Sub
```

cate a percentage that you are to use in a calculation. You could use an If Test like the following:

```
If optButton_1.Value = True Then
    Do Calculation using optButton_1.Caption
ElseIf optButton_2.Value = True Then
    Do Calculation using optButton_2.Caption
ElseIf optButton_3.Value = True Then
    Do Calculation using optButton_3.Caption
ElseIf optButton_4.Value = True Then
    Do Calculation using optButton_4.Caption
ElseIf optButton_5.Value = True Then
    Do Calculation using optButton_5.Caption
End If
```

Or you could use just an Else at the end for optButton_5, such as

```
Else
    Do Calculation using optButton_5.Caption
End If
```

This is not a good idea, because all the Option Buttons can be off at the same time. And you cannot assume that the fifth Option Button is on just because the first four are off—it might also be off.

The code shown will work fine, but there is a lot of duplication of effort. If you set up the Option Buttons as a control array, you can use a loop like the following:

```
For intCounter = 1 to 5
    If optButton(intCounter).Value = True Then
        Do Calculation using optButton(intCounter).Caption
    End If
Next intCounter
```

Adding a Frame

We mentioned that the Option Buttons work as a group. That is, if you have five buttons on your form, only one of them can be turned on at a time. If you select another one, the one that was already on will be turned off. That's why when the **Alarm On** button is on, the **Alarm Off** button is off. But what happens when you want to use two sets of Option Buttons on the same form? Suppose, for example, that we want our alarm clock to have two alarms that we can set independently. Given the way the Option Buttons work, we cannot turn two different Option Buttons on at the same time. There is, however, a way around this problem: we can place the Option Buttons inside an object. One object that is useful for this is a **Frame.**

A Frame is simply a labeled box for grouping controls. In the case of Option Buttons, each group of Option Buttons in a frame is separate from any other Option Button on the form. Once a control is in a Frame, it becomes part of the Frame rather than part of the form. If the Frame is moved on the form, the controls within move, too.

Just so we can see how well Frames work for grouping objects, we will add a second alarm to our clock.

1. Using the Frame tool shown in Figure 5.26, draw a frame on your form in the size and position shown in Figure 5.27.

   Note that the Frame already has a label on it. This is a convenient way of labeling your group of objects. We will label our groups of buttons Alarm 1 and Alarm 2.

2. Change the Caption of the Frame to **Alarm 1**, change the name to **fraAlarm_1**, and change the font to **Arial**, **bold**, and **18 points**.

FIGURE 5.26
The Frame control.

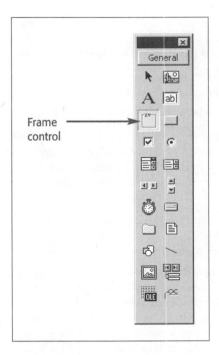

Frame control

FIGURE 5.27
The alarm clock, showing the added Frame.

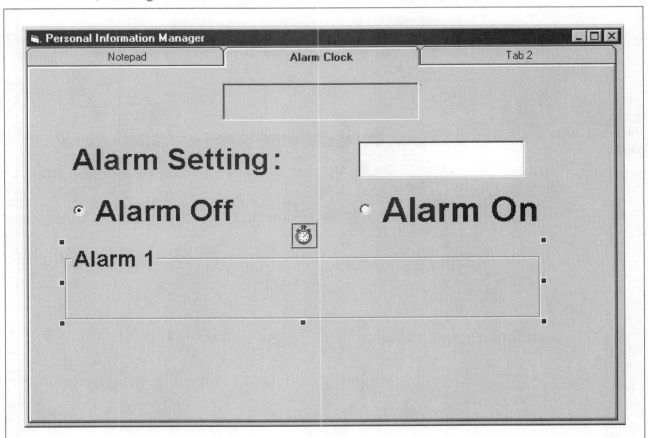

Now we are ready to move the buttons into the Frame. This is not a difficult process, but it is a bit tricky. To put an object into the Frame, we must add the object to the form, cut it from the form, and then insert it into the Frame or draw it directly into the Frame.

3. Select the **Alarm Off** button, cut it, select the Frame, and paste the button. This will paste it inside the frame. Move it to the position shown in Figure 5.28.

4. Cut and paste the **Alarm On** button and position it as shown in figure 5.28.

Now we have a group of Option Buttons inside the frame. If the frame is moved, both of the Option Buttons move with (or inside) the frame. As you will see, these buttons will act separately from any other buttons we add to the form. Because we need another set of Option Buttons that are virtually identical to the ones we already have, the simplest thing to do is copy the entire Frame.

5. Select the Frame, copy it to the clipboard, and paste it back to the form. As you do, Visual Basic will ask you whether you want a control array for each of the three elements. Answer No to each of the prompts.

6. Move the second Frame to the position shown in Figure 5.29, change the caption of the Frame to **Alarm 2**, and change the name to **fraAlarm_2**. Change the control name of the **Alarm Off** button to **optAlarm_Off_2** and the control name of the **Alarm On** button to **optAlarm_On_2**. Note that the value of the new **Alarm Off** button was automatically set to True, because when you copy an object, you also copy all the property settings of that object. That's why all the fonts in the new objects match the fonts in the copied object.

Next, we change the label to Alarm Setting 1: instead of just Alarm Setting:, and we add another alarm setting label.

7. Change the Label to **Alarm Setting 1:**, and select, copy, and then paste the label and the text box (do not make them a control array). Position them as shown in Figure 5.30, change the Caption to **Alarm Setting 2:**, and change the control name of the text box to **txtAlarm_In_2**.

FIGURE 5.28
The alarm buttons
pasted in the Frame.

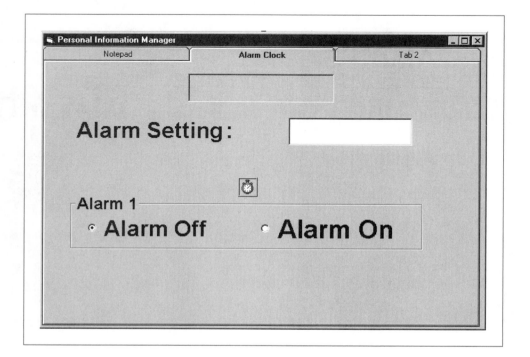

FIGURE 5.29
The alarm clock with
the second Frame
added.

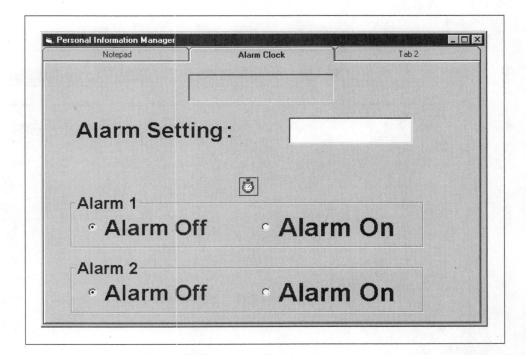

Now we add the code for the new alarm and alarm setting. The code for the two alarm settings will be virtually the same, so the easiest thing to do is copy the code.

8. Copy the code from the KeyPress input procedure for the first text box into the procedure for the second text box.

Finally, we change the timer code so that it sets off the alarm for the second alarm setting. Again, the necessary code is virtually the same as for the first timer. The only difference is the name of the text box.

FIGURE 5.30
The alarm clock with
the second text box and
label added.

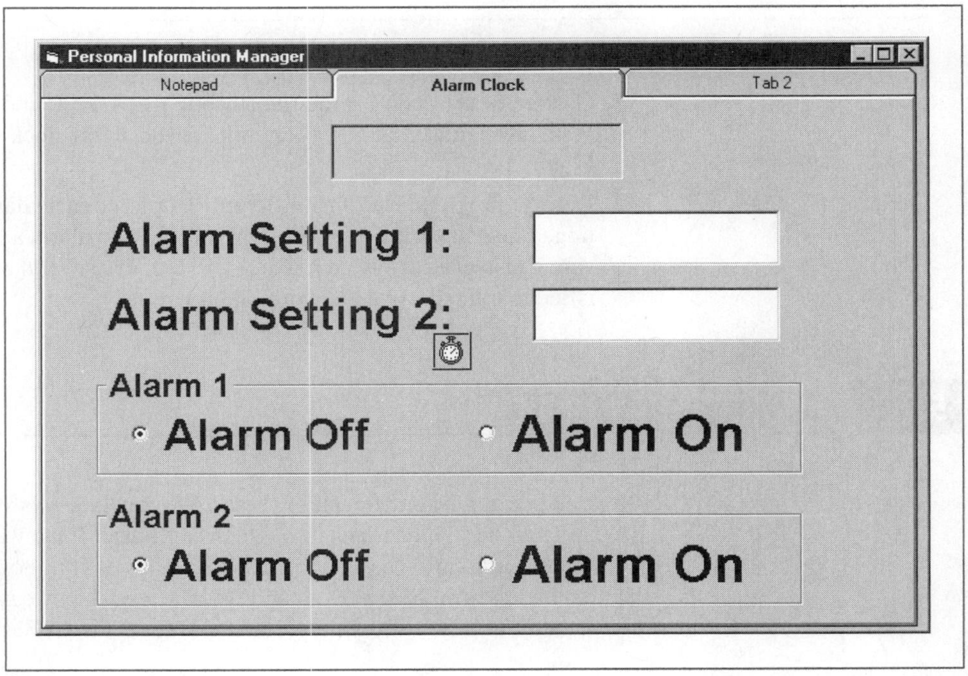

FIGURE 5.31
The completed code for the alarm clock timer.

```
Project1 - frmPIM (Code)                                          _ □ X
txtAlarm_In_2                        ▼   KeyPress                    ▼

    Private Sub tmrAlarm_Timer_Timer()
        If Time$ >= txtAlarm_In_1.Text And optAlarm_On_1.Value = True Then
            Beep
        End If
        If Time$ >= txtAlarm_In_2.Text And optAlarm_On_2.Value = True Then
            Beep
        End If
        lblTime_Out.Caption = Time$
    End Sub

    ' This procedure inputs the alarm setting
    '
    Private Sub txtAlarm_In_1_KeyPress(KeyAscii As Integer)
        Dim strKey_In As String
        strKey_In = Chr(KeyAscii)
        If KeyAscii <> 8 And (strKey_In < "0" Or strKey_In > "9") And strKey_In <> ":" Then
            Beep
            KeyAscii = 0
        End If
    End Sub
    ' This procedure inputs the alarm setting
    '
    Private Sub txtAlarm_In_2_KeyPress(KeyAscii As Integer)
        Dim strKey_In As String
        strKey_In = Chr(KeyAscii)
        If KeyAscii <> 8 And (strKey_In < "0" Or strKey_In > "9") And strKey_In <> ":" Then
            Beep
            KeyAscii = 0
        End If
    End Sub
```

9. Change to the code for the timer, copy the If Test, and make the necessary changes. With these final changes, your code for the alarm clock should look like that shown in Figure 5.31.

10. Run the program. Key in a different setting for each alarm, turn on the first alarm setting, and wait until it goes off. Turn off the first alarm and turn on the second one to be sure it also goes off when it is supposed to. Try several alarm settings until you are satisfied that the program is working properly.

5.7   Making an EXE File

We need to examine one final thing before we conclude this chapter. Thus far, we have been executing all our applications through Visual Basic. If we wanted to run an application we had written earlier, first we had to load Visual Basic. This, however, is not always necessary. We can have Visual Basic create an **EXE file**, and then we will be able to run that application directly in Windows without having to load Visual Basic first, just as you have been doing with the sample programs you have been running before actually creating them yourself. After creating such a program, we can give other people copies of it, and they can run it whether they have Visual Basic on their machine or not. Visual Basic even has a special program called the **Setup Wizard** that helps you set up programs for distribution to others.

This process of creating an EXE file from your keyed code and forms is, in most computer languages, called **compiling** the application. Essentially, the computer translates the code and forms into a special set of instructions that the computer can understand better and faster than the English code and graphical forms that make up your application.

There are essentially two steps in creating an EXE file: assigning an icon to the application and making the EXE file. You don't actually have to assign an icon to the application, because all Visual Basic applications are automatically assigned a generic icon. But if you have several compiled programs, all with the same generic icon, it becomes difficult to tell one application from another when they are minimized onto the Windows taskbar.

Actually, you can assign a different icon to every form and module in your application and then use whichever of those icons you want when making the EXE file. We have only one form at present, so this isn't an issue.

1. Run and then minimize your PIM application.

You will see an icon similar to ⬜. This is the generic icon automatically assigned to all new applications. This application will keep this icon, even after it is made into an EXE file, unless you assign a different icon to the application. Fortunately, assigning an icon to an application is not difficult.

> **HINT:** Icons were provided with installation in previous versions of Visual Basic. In version 6.0, Microsoft decided not to provide the icons. To help you, we have included a folder of icons on the Web site for your use.

2. Exit the application. Remove your work disk from drive A and insert a new disk you can use to store icons. Copy the Icons folder (mentioned above) from wherever it is stored on your system onto a new work disk.

3. Change to the **Icon** property for the PIM form.

4. Select the pull-down box (...) at the end of the property value box, and a dialog box similar to the one shown in Figure 5.32, appears. Change the folder to the Icons folder on your work disk, and you see a list of Icon folders appear in the workspace (Figure 5.32).

5. Change to the Office folder to see a list of icons.

Each of the icons is a separate file, and we have created one for use on a Personal Information Manager. The one we will use for our application is called PIMIcon (📁). It seems appropriate; our PIM uses the Tabbed Control, which is designed to look like file folders. We simply added a bit of color to the icon for interest.

6. Double-click the PIMIcon.ico icon image file to add it to the program.

That gives our application an icon. Now we are ready to make an EXE file. This is done with a **File** menu option.

7. Select the **File** menu and select the **Make PIM.exe...** option to see the dialog box that allows you to create the EXE file.

The default name for the EXE file will be the name you used for the project. In our case, and indeed in most cases, it is what you will want to use. Your folder, brought up in

FIGURE 5.32
The dialog box for loading an icon.

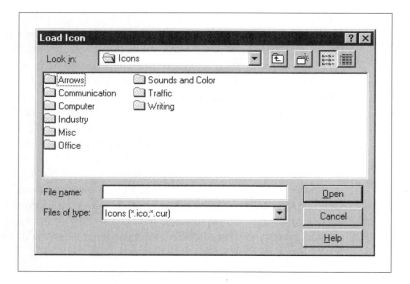

the dialog box, should be the one where your PIM project was stored. If not, change to that folder on drive A.

8. Select **OK** to make the EXE file. It will take Visual Basic only a few seconds to finish.

To be sure the program was created properly, we will run it using Windows.

9. Minimize Visual Basic.

10. Open the Explorer and change to the Ch-5 folder on drive A.

11. Double-click the PIM application to run it. Your new PIM application should appear on the desktop exactly as it did before.

12. Minimize the application.

The icon for the minimized application should be the folder icon you assigned earlier. If you were to add the PIM as an icon on the desktop or in one of the Start button menu sub-groups, the folders icon would be the default icon for the application in those displays.

13. Exit from the application.

14. Restore Visual Basic and save your application.

There is still one minor change to the program that we have to deal with. You have already changed the name of the project as stored on the disk and the form as displayed and stored on the disk. You can also change the name of the project as shown in the Visual Basic display.

15. Switch to the project display as shown in Figure 5.33.

16. Select the project name, and the Properties dialog box changes so that it holds only the project name.

17. Highlight the project name in the Properties dialog box, key **PIM**, and press **Enter** to change the name of the project. You see the new project name in all the places where the project name is displayed. These places are indicated in Figure 5.33.

18. Put your work disk back in drive A, save the program, and then recompile it.

19. Exit from Visual Basic and shut down the system properly.

FIGURE 5.33

The Visual Basic display, showing the name of the project.

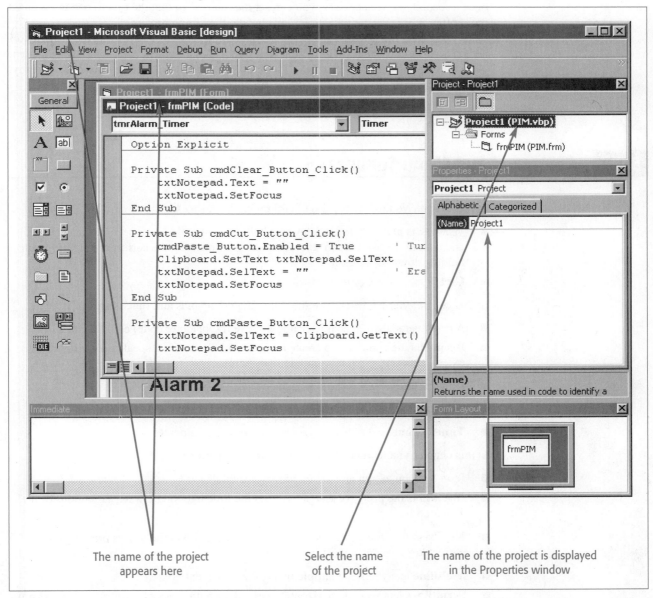

The name of the project
appears here

Select the name
of the project

The name of the project is displayed
in the Properties window

5.8   Debugging Your Programs

One thing you can do in your programs that your users will appreciate is to make sure the focus is always in the appropriate place. When you use the SetFocus method, however, it is easy to put the focus on the wrong object. You must test your programs carefully to be sure the focus moves from object to object properly.

In addition to the SetFocus method, the TabIndex property for the objects needs to be set carefully. Remember that focus will automatically move among objects when the user presses the **Tab** key, and the order that dictates that movement is set in the TabIndex property.

When using the Timer Control, you need to be sure the Interval property is set properly for the purpose of the timer. The Interval doesn't generally have to be set shorter than once a second, but if necessary, you can set the Interval so that the timer code is executed more often. It is important that your code handle the timing properly.

When using the Enabled property on objects, you need to be sure to set the property off and back on at the proper times in your program. If you disable a button and then enable it in the wrong place in your code, the user may click the button before your code is ready. Test your program to be sure the objects are enabled and disabled properly.

5.9 Command and Menu Summary

In this chapter you learned to use the following keystrokes:

- When **&** is placed before a letter in a button caption, the letter becomes underlined, and then the user is able to select the option by pressing the corresponding key while holding down the **Alt** key.
- **Ctrl-T** loads the Components dialog box.

In this chapter you learned to use the following commands and functions:

- **Asc** converts a string character into its ASCII (character code) equivalent.
- **Beep** tells the computer to create a sound with the internal speaker (or with the external speakers if your computer has them).
- **Date$ (Date)** extracts the system date from the computer.
- **Now** extracts the system date and time from the computer.
- **Time$ (Time)** extracts the system time from the computer.

In this chapter you learned about the following properties:

- **Icon** lets you assign an icon to a form or module.
- **Interval** is the property that determines the time interval between executions of the Timer code.
- **KeyPress** lets you capture keystrokes for verifying that the user is pressing the correct keys for entry in a text box.
- **Multiline** lets you key multiple lines of text in a text box.
- **ScrollBars** lets you add horizontal, vertical, or both types of scroll bars to a text box.
- **SelLength** is the length of selected text in a text box.
- **SelStart** is the starting location of selected text in a text box.
- **SelText** contains the text selected in a text box.
- **TabIndex** tells the program which object to move the focus to when the **Tab** key is pressed.
- **Value** tells the program whether an Option Button is on (True) or off (False).

In this chapter you learned about the following methods:

- **GetText** lets you paste text from the clipboard (which is a special object).
- **SetText** lets you store text on the clipboard (which is a special object).
- **SetFocus** lets you change the active object while the application is running.

In this chapter you learned about the following prefixes:

■   **fra** is for Frames.

■   **opt** is for Option Buttons.

■   **tab** is for the Tabbed Control.

■   **tmr** is for the Timer Control.

In this chapter you learned about the following menu options:

■   **File:**

  ■   **Make (Project Name).exe…** lets you make an EXE file that can subsequently be run using Windows with no need to load Visual Basic first.

■   **Project:**

  ■   **Components…** (shortcut key **Ctrl-T**) loads the Components dialog box for adding new tools to the program.

In this chapter you learned about the following Toolbox tools:

■   adds a Frame to the form. A Frame allows you to group objects on the form.

■   adds an Option Button to the form. Option Buttons work as a group so that when one is turned on, all the rest are automatically turned off by Visual Basic.

■   creates a Timer that you can use in your program to determine how often the timer code should be executed.

■   adds a Tabbed Control to the form. A Tabbed Control is a tool that has a defined number of tabs where different objects can be placed.

5.10   Performance Check

1. Which object is the Multiline property for?

2. What is the purpose of the TabIndex property?

3. What is the default value of the Multiline property?

4. What do you know about your application if you test SelLength and find it to be zero?

5. What are two possibilities if SelStart is 10?

6. What statement can be used to erase all the contents of a text box called txtInput_Text?

7. What is the focus?

8. What command can be used to change the focus to the cmdClear_Button while the application is executing?

9. If you have a text box called txtInput_Text, what statement can be used to copy its entire contents to the clipboard?

10. Why might you want to disable a button?

11. What character is used in a button caption to assign an access key?

_____

12. What is the major purpose of the KeyPress event?

_____

13. What does the Beep statement do?

_____

14. What property is used to activate a Timer object?

_____

15. What is true of two Option Buttons that is not true of two other objects of the same kind?

_____

16. What is another name for an Option Button?

_____

17. What property is used to turn an Option Button on?

_____

18. Why do programmers normally assign icons to their programs before making the EXE file?

_____

19. What is another name for the process of making an EXE file?

_____

20. What is the Asc function used for?

_____

21. What is the ASCII code for the **Enter** key?

_____

22. What ASCII code does the **Backspace** key translate into?

_____

5.11   Programming Exercises

1. You decide to write a program to try out date formatting. At the computer, do each of the following:

   a. Get into Visual Basic with your work disk in drive A.

   b. Create a new program, and change the caption of the form to **Date Display** and the name to **frmDate_Display**. Save the project as **Date Display**.

   c. Add a button with the caption **Show Date,** the name **cmdDate_Button,** and a label with the name **lblDate_Out**.

   d. Add a text box called **txtFormat** that will be used to input the format used to display the date.

   e. Change to the code window for the button and key the following:

   ```
   lblDate_Out.Caption = Format(Now, txtFormat)
   ```

   f. Run the program, key **dddd, mmmm, d yyyy — hh:mm:ss** in the text box, and click the button. You should see a display similar to **Wednesday, April 5, 2000 — 10:15:03**.

   g. Try several more formats until you are satisfied that you understand the way each format is handled, and then exit from the program. Print all the program elements.

   h. Use the **DateEdit** icon and then compile the program. Exit Visual Basic, and shut down the system properly.

2. You are pleased with the alarm clock portion of the PIM, but you don't like its military time display. You decide to change the application so that it will display the time as am and pm. Go into the lab and do each of the following:

a. Get into Visual Basic with your work disk in drive A.

b. Load the PIM application.

c. Open the code window for the Timer and do each of the following:

　1) Change the If Test so that it checks the lblTime_Out.Caption instead of Time$. This is necessary because you will have to use the Format statement to display the time.

　2) Change the assignment statement to use the Format statement for the Time$ function. The appropriate format is "HH:MM:SS am/pm".

d. Change to the code for the text box. You need to check against the time with am or pm on the end, so your key input routine will have to allow "a," "p," "m," and blank to be entered. Make the appropriate changes on the If test. (Hint: Check the am-pm portion with a separate portion of the If Test.)

e. Save the form and then the project as **PIM Update**.

f. Run the application to make sure it now works with am and with pm.

g. Make an EXE file from your application, and run the program directly in Windows. Then exit the application and, using Visual Basic, print the program elements.

h. Exit Visual Basic and shut down the system properly.

3. The alarm clock portion of the PIM was a nice application, but you just want a clock that will do one of the following:

a. Display the date with slashes

b. Display the date with dashes

c. Display the time

d. Switch between the date with slashes and time displays

e. Switch between the date with dashes and time displays

You want to control this changeable display with the use of Option Buttons, because if there is only one output area, only one type of display can be shown at any one time. The design for this program is

```
Project Clock - frmClock
    A. lblDisplay_Time label box
        Used to display the date or time based on the setting of
        ⮑the Option Buttons
    B through F are the Option Buttons for the display choices of
        B. display the date as MM/DD/YY
        C. display the date as MM-DD-YY
        D. display the time
        E. switch between the date as MM/DD/YY and time
        F. switch between the date as MM-DD-YY and time
    G. Timer tool
        If Date as MM/DD/YY option button is on Then
            Display date with MM/DD/YY format in display label box
        Else If Date as MM-DD-YY option button is on Then
            Display date with MM-DD-YY format in display label box
        Else If Time option button is on Then
            Display the time
        Else If Switch between Date as MM/DD/YY and Time option
        ⮑button is on Then
            Switch between the displays in the display label box
        Else (the Switch between Date as MM-DD-YY and Time option
        ⮑button is on)
            Switch between the displays in the display label box
        End If
```

Using this design and the design for the form shown in Figure 5.34, go into the lab and do each of the following:

a. Get into Visual Basic with your work disk in drive A.

b. Create a form like the one shown in Figure 5.34 with the following considerations:

1) The five Option Buttons should be made into a control array called **optDate_Option**.

2) The display box at the top is a label with a control name of **lblDisplay_Time**. Center the caption.

c. Open the code window for the timer and do the following:

1) You will need a multipart If Test to determine which of the Option Buttons is turned on. Because the Option Buttons are a control array, the first few lines of your test should be similar to

```
If optDate_Option(0).Value = True Then
    lblDisplay_Time.Caption = Format(Now, "m/d/yy")
ElseIf optDate_Option(1).Value = True Then
```

2) To switch between the date and the time, you will need a special variable (generally called a flag) to determine which of the two you just displayed. Declare the flag as Static so that it will not be initialized each time through the code. Using the flag in the If Test should be similar to

```
ElseIf optDate_Option(3).Value = True And intFlag = 1 Then
    lblDisplay_Time.Caption.Caption = Format (Now, "m/d/yy")
    intFlag = 0
ElseIf optDate_Option(3).Value = True Then
    lblDisplay_Time.Caption.Caption = Format(Now, "h:m:ss am/pm")
    intFlag = 1
```

d. After you have finished your code entry, save the program as **Clock**.

e. Run the application to make sure that each of the Option Buttons displays what it is supposed to display.

f. Exit the application and print the program elements.

g. Using the **Clock** icon, make an EXE file from your application and run the program directly using Windows.

h. Exit Visual Basic and shut down the system properly.

FIGURE 5.34
The form for the digital clock.

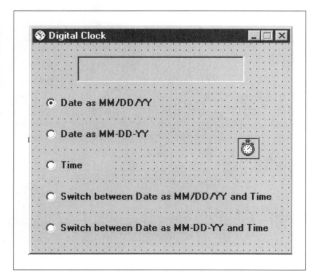

4. When you cut text in most word processors, it is saved in a special storage area and can be pasted back from that area. You can usually cut several different groups of data and paste back any of them. The trouble is that in most word processors, you cannot see what you have cut. You are going to create a notepad to solve that problem. You will be able to cut three items, see the items, and paste any or all of them back into the word processor. Using the above information (reading through the programming steps may also help) and the form design shown in Figure 5.35, design the program. Then go into the lab and do each of the following:

a. Get into Visual Basic with your work disk in drive A.

b. Create a form like the one shown in Figure 5.35 with the following considerations:

    1) The Tabbed Control should have the control name **tabMulticut**.

    2) The main notepad should have the control name **txtNotepad**.

    3) The cut text boxes placed in the tabs of the same names should have the control names **txtStorage_1**, **txtStorage_2**, and **txtStorage_3**.

    4) The **Paste** buttons should have the control names **cmdPaste_Button**, **cmdPaste_Button_1**, **cmdPaste_Button_2**, and **cmdPaste_Button_3**.

    5) The rest of the buttons should be given appropriate control names.

c. Open the code window for the **Cut** button and create code for the following:

    1) When the text is cut, copy the text from txtStorage_2 to txtStorage_3, then from txtStorage_1 to txtStorage_2, and finally from SelText to txtStorage_1. This will make the text in txtStorage_1 the most current, and the old text in txtStorage_3 will be lost.

    2) Enable the cmdPaste_Button and cmdPaste_Button_1 and enable the other two buttons only if there is text in them.

d. Change to the cmdPaste_Button code. When this button is selected, the text from all three storage areas will need to be pasted into the text box.

e. When the other three **Paste** buttons are selected, the text stored in the corresponding storage box should be pasted into the text box.

FIGURE 5.35
The form for the multi-cut notepad.

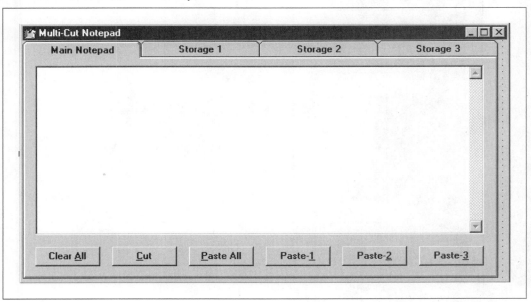

 f. Change to the **Clear All** button code. Empty not only the text box but also all three of the storage boxes, and disable all the paste buttons when this button is selected. Because the text is not on the clipboard any longer, there is no longer anything to paste when **Clear All** has been selected.

 g. Save the form as **frmMulticut** and the application as **Multicut**.

 h. Thoroughly test your program, making sure that

  1) The text is shifted between the storage boxes properly.

  2) The buttons are enabled and disabled properly.

  3) All the text is erased when the **Clear All** button is selected.

 i. Exit from the program and print the program elements.

 j. Use the MultiCut icon, make an EXE file from your application, and then run the program directly within Windows.

 k. Exit Visual Basic and shut down the system properly.

5. You have been asked to help out at the next track meet by tabulating the top eight times in the races. You will need an application that displays the elapsed time and then, upon selection of a button, stores that elapsed time in one of eight different labels. Using this information, the hints given in the steps, and the design of the form shown in Figure 5.36, design the program. Then go into the lab and do each of the following:

 a. Get into Visual Basic with your work disk in drive A.

 b. Create a form like the one shown in Figure 5.36 with the following considerations:

  1) The label at the top should have a font size of 18 and a control name of **lblTime_Display**.

  2) The eight labels for displaying the times should be a control array called **lblTime_Label**.

FIGURE 5.36
The form for the stop watch.

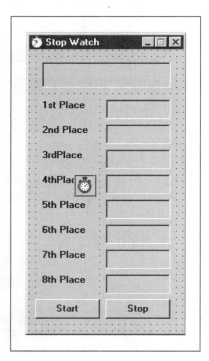

3) The buttons should have the control names **cmdStart_Button** and **cmd-Stop_Button**.

c. Write code for the buttons and the timer, keeping in mind the following hints:

1) In the cmdStart_Button code, you should extract the current time and determine how many **Total** seconds are in the current time (there are 3600 seconds in an hour and 60 in each minute). Then save that number in a (general) variable that can be picked up by the other procedures.

2) In the timer code, you should use the number of seconds that have passed to determine the elapsed time from the start time to the current time. Then that time should be displayed in the lblTime_Display caption.

3) Every time the **Stop** button is selected, you need to determine the elapsed time and then display that time in the next available lblTime_Label box.

d. Thoroughly test your program. Use the **StopWatch** icon, make an EXE file from your application, and run the program directly within Windows. Save the form as **frmStopwatch** and the project as **Stopwatch**, and print the program elements.

e. Exit Visual Basic and shut down the system properly.

6. You have a friend who has been experimenting with the Setfocus method and the TabIndex property. He has written a program but cannot seem to make things work the way he wants. He has asked for your help in debugging the program. At the computer, do each of the following:

a. Get into Visual Basic with your work disk in drive A.

b. Load the **SetFocus Practice** program from the Ch-5 folder.

c. Run the program. Position the cursor in the text box in the upper left corner and press **Tab**. The cursor moves to the proper text box. Continue to press **Tab** from text box to text box. They are all in the proper sequence. You wonder what your friend's problem was.

d. Position the cursor in the upper left corner text box and press **Enter**. Immediately you get an error. One of the elements of the control array is missing. Now you see at least one problem with the program.

e. Add the appropriate element to the control array, deleting the highest one because you would otherwise have one too many. Arrange the text boxes in the proper sequence. This means you have to adjust the TabIndex properties on all the text boxes as well.

f. Test the program again. When you press **Enter**, nothing happens. The SetFocus statement is supposed to move the cursor from one text box to another.

g. Exit the program and open the code window. Before you examine the code, note what event opened in the code window. This is not the proper event. Cut the code from this event and paste it into the proper event.

h. Run the program. Position the cursor in the first text box and press **Enter** in each of the text boxes. You get an error again. Examine the statement that caused the error and the code in the routine. Find and fix this error.

One thing that many programmers do in programs that use a lot of input text boxes is to change the background color of the text box that currently has the focus. This way, the users are never confused about which text box to use for keying. This can be done with the **GotFocus** event, which is executed when the object gets focus. There is also a **LostFocus** event that is executed when focus leaves the object.

i. In the GotFocus event for the text boxes, change the background color of the current text box to cyan. Then, in the LostFocus event, change the background color of the text box to white.

j. Test the program and then print all the elements.

5.12   Performance Mastery

1. You like the idea of being able to move the focus from one text box to the next as the user presses the **Enter** key, and you decide to write a program to test the KeyPress event. Create a program that has four text boxes, and write KeyPress procedures to move the focus from one text box to the next. When the cursor reaches the fourth text box, change the focus back to the first text box. Design your program, create it, save it as **Text Box Practice**, and test it, and then print the program elements.

2. You work for a painting company and need to create an About dialog box for a program you are creating. Because your company paints houses, you decide to write a program that will change the color of the dialog box once every second. It will loop through the colors and, when finished, start at the beginning of the colors. Create the program with labels that are related to the business, and add a button that allows the user to exit the dialog box. Save the program as **About Colors** and then test the program. Using the **PaintBrush** icon, compile the program, and test it again. Finally, print the program elements.

3. You work for a sound company that specializes in sound effects for radio stations. You need to create a program that can be used to demonstrate the sound effects your company offers. Create a program that uses Option Buttons properly labeled with the names of the sound files you want to demonstrate. In the Click event for the Option Button, play the sound file. Add a button that will allow the user to exit from the program. Save the program as **Sound Test** and then test the program. Using the **Sound** icon, compile the program, and test it again. Finally, print the program elements.

4. To get more practice using Option Buttons, you decide to write a program that will have a control array of eight Option Buttons, each labeled with one of the predefined colors (vbBlack, vbRed, vbGreen, vbYellow, vbBlue, vbMagenta, vbCyan, and vbWhite). Don't use the constant's name as the label, only the color. That is, the label should be "Blue," not "vbBlue." The Click event should be used to change the background color of the form to the color selected. Save the program as **Option Colors** and then test it. Using the **Color** icon, compile the program, and test it again. Finally, print the program elements.

5. You work at an office where salespeople come in at infrequent intervals. You need a program in which the display will tell you at a glance who is in the office and who is not. Design and then create a program that has six sets of Option Buttons, where one button in each set is labeled **In** and the other button is labeled **Out**. Initially have all the button sets display that the person is out. Be sure to label each Frame with the person's name. There should be a **Print** button so that the current status of the form can be printed. Save the program as **In-Out** and then test it. Using the **PushPin** icon, compile the program, and test it again. Finally, print the program elements.

6. You like to listen to music as you work. You decide to create an application that will play music files for you. Create an application with five Option Buttons. The caption of each button should represent the name of the music file that is to be played (with or without the pathname). In the code for the Click event, start the music for that file playing. The Multimedia Control has a **Done** event. Within the code for that event, close the music file and play it again. Save the program as **Option Music** and then test it thoroughly. Using the **Sound** icon, compile the program, and test it again. Finally, print the program elements.

7. You work at an office with salespeople who come into the office several times a day, and a computer in the front office is used to post notes to these salespeople. You need to design and then create a program that has six text boxes (two rows of three) where notices can be posted and seven Option Buttons, each of which can be used to activate

a particular text box. One Option Button turns off all the text boxes, and each of the other buttons turns on the corresponding text box. The buttons that turn on individual text boxes should use the Visible property to make all the text boxes invisible (False value) except the particular one that is selected. Label each of the Option Buttons with the name of a salesperson; the extra button should be labeled **Hide Messages**. Save the program as **Messages**, test it, and print the program elements. Using the **PushPin** icon, compile the program, and test it again.

8. A local high school teacher is teaching his students about Fahrenheit and Celsius temperatures and has asked you to write a program in which one of the temperatures can be entered and the program will calculate the other. The formula is **Fahrenheit = (9/5)Celsius + 32**. The user should be able to enter a temperature and use Option Buttons to indicate the current temperature scale. Then your program should display the translated temperature in an output label. Design and then write the program, saving it as **Option Temperature Changes**. Using the **Thermometer** icon, compile the program, test it, and then print all the elements.

9. You work for a company that sells products all over the United States. Your boss has asked you to write a program that allows input of the four quarterly sales figures and presents those data as a two-dimensional bar chart, a three-dimensional bar chart, or a pie chart. Use three Option Buttons to indicate the type of chart to be presented. There should also be a **Print** button so that the graphs can be printed. Design your program, create it, save it as **Option Button Charts**, and test it, and then print the program elements. Choose an appropriate graph icon and compile the program.

10. You work for the Moon Mortgage Company. You are in the process of creating a large application and want to create an About dialog box for the program. You want it to reflect the name of the company. To write this program, you need to add a series of **Image** ( ) controls to the form. Add a large Image control in the upper left corner, and change the **Stretch** property to True. This allows Visual Basic to increase the size of the picture put in the control to expand to fill the control. Then add a control array of eight Image controls. The **Picture** property is used to put the picture into the Image control. Load the **Moon-1.BMP** through **Moon-8.BMP** files into the control array. The control array should not be visible, because the user should see only the larger image.

Using a Timer control and a loop, change the Picture property of the large Image control to the images stored in the control array, one at a time. After you have loaded the last image, start with the first one again. You can assign the Picture property just like any other property. You will have to adjust the Interval property on the Timer control until the sequencing of the images seems to go by at the proper speed.

Add the appropriate labels to the form and a button that allows the user to exit from the dialog box. Design the program, create it, and save it as **About Moon**. Using the **MoonIcon** icon, compile and test your program, and then print the program elements.

Using Menus and Related Features

6.1   Chapter Objectives

After finishing this chapter you will be able to:

- Demonstrate how to add menus to applications.

- Demonstrate how to use access keys and shortcut keys on the menus.

- Demonstrate how to enable, disable, and add check marks to menu items during creation and runtime.

- Demonstrate how to modify a menu system by moving, inserting, and deleting items.

- Demonstrate how to add, delete, and change items in a menu during runtime.

- Demonstrate how to sense the press of the **Ins** key and create an overtype mode in a text box.

6.2   Introduction

As a Windows user, you are familiar with menus. Visual Basic uses many menus. In this chapter you will learn how to add menus to your programs. Before we begin, however, you need to be sure the terminology of a menu system is fresh in your mind. Figure 6.1 shows an example of a Visual Basic menu with the various parts labeled.

At the top of the figure is the menu bar highlighting (by indenting it) the name of the menu that is currently pulled down. The first item on the menu is automatically highlighted and ready for the user to select by pressing **Enter.** The arrow keys (or the mouse movement) can be used to move the highlighter down to select a different item, the item can be selected

FIGURE 6.1

The File menu of Visual Basic.

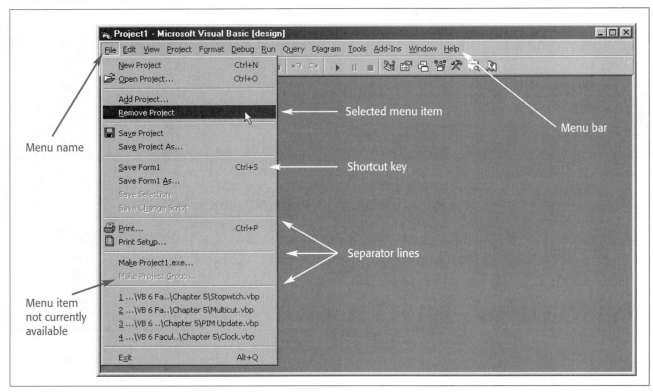

via the access key (the underlined letter in conjunction with the **Alt** key), or the item can be selected by clicking the mouse button. Groups of related items are separated from the other menu items by **separator lines**. Some items have **shortcut keys** assigned to them. These keys can be used to select the menu item without the user's having to pull down the menu. The menu items with an **ellipsis** (…) will call up a dialog box for the user to enter more in-formation, whereas those without an ellipsis will execute immediately.

Like most design elements in Visual Basic, many of the details of menu operation are handled automatically by Visual Basic. This makes menu creation much easier. You will see how to set up menus with all the features we just discussed in addition to other program elements that are related to menus. The only exceptions are items with an ellipsis. You will also see how to put an ellipsis on menu items, but you won't learn about the dialog boxes they call up until Chapter 7. You will put in your menus a few menu items related to files, although you will not be able to use these items until we discuss files in a later chapter. We begin by looking at the additions to the PIM application we started working with in the last chapter.

6.3   A Quick Look at the PIM

1. Get into Visual Basic with your work disk in drive A.

2. Run the compiled **PIM** program from the Ch-6 folder to see the form as shown in Figure 6.2.

As you can see, you will make a number of changes to the form in this chapter. First, we have removed the **Clear All**, **Cut**, and **Paste** buttons and moved their functions to the menus, of which there are three.

FIGURE 6.2
The PIM form.

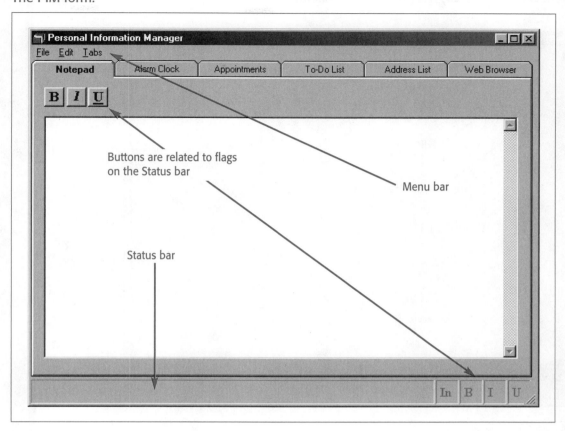

3. Pull down the **Edit** menu to see the menu display as shown in Figure 6.3.

    In this menu you see the options from the removed buttons, along with the new Copy option.

4. Click outside the menu to close it.

    Next, we have added three buttons for **Bold**, *Italics*, and <u>Underline</u>. On the status bar, at the bottom of the form, are markers to indicate whether the font functions have been turned on (see Figure 6.2).

5. Put the insertion point in the workspace and key **This is a sample**. Click the **Bold** button to turn on boldfacing. The **Bold** flag on the status bar is now darker than the other markers, and all the text becomes bold (darker).

6. Click the **Italics** button, and the text will now be italicized as well as bold. The Italics flag on the status bar is now darker. Click the **Bold** button. The text is no longer bold, and the Bold flag character on the status bar is lighter again.

    The status bar at the bottom of the form not only has the flags for various keys, but is also used to display messages about the element of the program over which the mouse pointer is positioned.

7. Position the cursor over the **Bold** button.

    A message appears in the status bar that explains the **Bold** button (see Figure 6.4). Note that a **ToolTip** box appears under the button as well. These are two different methods of displaying information about the tools in your program. We produce the messages in the status bar

FIGURE 6.3

The **Edit** menu, showing the **Cut, Copy, Paste,** and **Clear All** options.

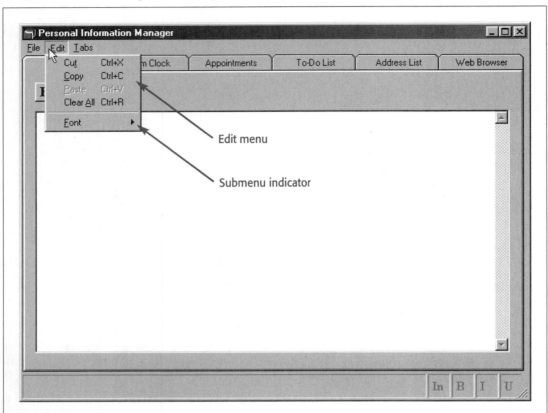

by using a mouse-type event. The ToolTips, however, are displayed automatically by Visual Basic on the basis of text we put in one of the properties of the control.

8. Move the cursor over the **Italics** button, and the message in the status bar changes and a different ToolTip appears.

There is also a flag on the status bar for the Insert (**Ins**) key. It is turned on and off when the **Ins** key is pressed.

A text box is automatically in insert mode, in which new text is inserted and existing text is moved aside. Normally there is no overtype mode in a text box, but in this chapter you will learn how to add one to your notepad text box. In steps 9 and 10 you will discover how the overtype mode you will create later works.

9. Move the insertion point in front of the **a,** and key **replaced**. The letters to the right of the insertion point are deleted as you key the new letters. In effect, you are keying over the old letters, allowing **replaced** to replace **a sample.**

10. Press the **Ins** key. The Insert flag becomes darker on the status bar. Reposition the insertion point before **replaced.** Key **inserted**, and you will see that now the letters are being inserted as the other letters are pushed to the right.

In addition to the **Edit** menu, there is a menu for the Tabs of the Tabbed Control.

11. Pull down the **Tabs** menu to see that the **Notepad** item is checked. Click the **Appointments** tab and pull the **Tabs** menu down again. Now the **Appointment Calendar** is checked.

As you see, selecting the Tab in the Tabbed Control to switch tabs causes the menu item to be checked. Clicking the menu item will also allow you to switch tabs.

FIGURE 6.4
The ToolTip and status bar message.

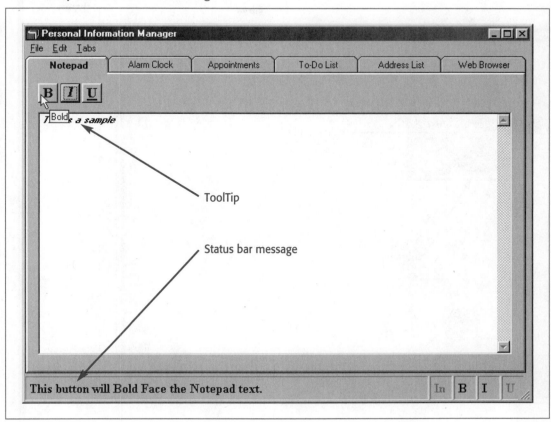

12. Click the **To-Do List** item in the menu. The program switches to the **To-Do List** tab.

   Because the menu items have shortcut keys assigned to them, you can perform the menu item function by using the shortcut key rather than pulling down the menu.

13. Press **Ctrl-N** and the program will switch to the **Notepad** tab.

   The **Edit** menu also has a **submenu.** Look back at Figure 6.3 to see the submenu indicator.

14. Pull down the **Edit** menu and highlight the **Font** item to see the submenu appear as shown in Figure 6.5.

   This submenu has items for **Bold**, *Italics*, and <u>Underlining</u>, which, of course, correspond to the buttons and the status bar flags. The **Bold,** *Italics*, and <u>Underline</u> options are checked to indicate that they are turned on. The functions can also be set and turned off here.

15. Click the **Italics** item. The text in the workspace is no longer italicized, and the **Italics** flag is now lighter, as are the others.

   One final feature is worth exploring.

16. Pull down the **Edit** menu and highlight the **Font** item to see the submenu again. Click on the **Options...** option to see the dialog box shown in Figure 6.6.

   This dialog box is what is called a **Common Dialog Control.** It shows you which font was selected in the notepad, that the Bold feature was turned on, and the size of the font. To change any of these features, you select them in the dialog box.

FIGURE 6.5
The Font submenu.

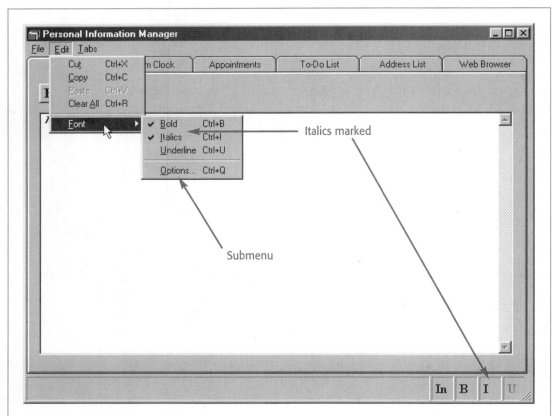

FIGURE 6.6
The Font dialog box.

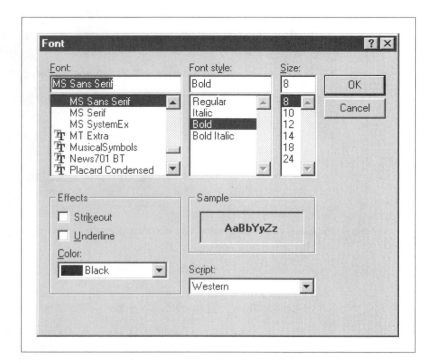

FIGURE 6.7
The notepad, showing the font changes.

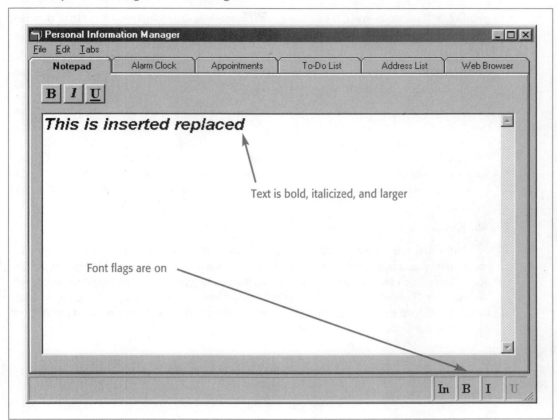

17. Change the Font to **Arial**, the Font Style to **Bold Italic**, and the Size to **16**. Then click the **OK** button to see the text in the notepad like that shown in Figure 6.7.

The changes you specified are represented by the changes to the font, and the status bar flags are set.

We have made a lot of changes to the PIM program, so let's move on to see how all these new features are added.

18. Minimize the PIM application, because you will probably want to refer to it as you progress through this chapter.

6.4　Adding Menus to the PIM

If we are going to add menus to the PIM, we will have to load it first.

1. Get into Visual Basic with your work disk in drive A.

2. Load the PIM application (or the PIM Update application if you did Programming Exercise 2 in the previous chapter).

Because we are going to modify this application and we don't want to erase the original one, we will save this application in the Ch-6 folder.

3. Save the form and project in the Ch-6 folder (as **PIM**).

We have been adding controls to our forms through the use of the toolbox since the beginning of this book. Well, menu items are basically a different type of control: they are added to the form through the **Menu Editor** option on the **Tools** menu.

4. Switch to the form display if necessary; then pull down the **Tools** menu, and select the **Menu Editor** option (shortcut key **Ctrl-E**) to see the dialog box shown in Figure 6.8. You can also use the Menu icon (⬚) on the Tool bar.

The first thing we want to specify is the name of the menu. This is done with the Caption entry box at the top of the dialog box.

The first menu we are going to create is the **File** menu. One of the applications in the PIM is a notepad, so it makes sense to be able to store on disk the notes we create. Though we will not learn how to save the data to disk in this chapter, we can at least put the entries in our menu so that we will be ready to add the options when we learn how to access files.

5. Key **&File** and press **Tab**.

Note that the "&File" entry appears in the workspace. This is where each of your menu names and menu items will appear. The ampersand (&) in front of "File" is for the access key. You can use access keys in your menus just as you learned how to do on button captions. They also work on menus in conjunction with the **Alt** key. On the menu items themselves, once the menu is called up, simply pressing the access key without the **Alt** key selects the menu item.

FIGURE 6.8
The Menu Editor dialog box.

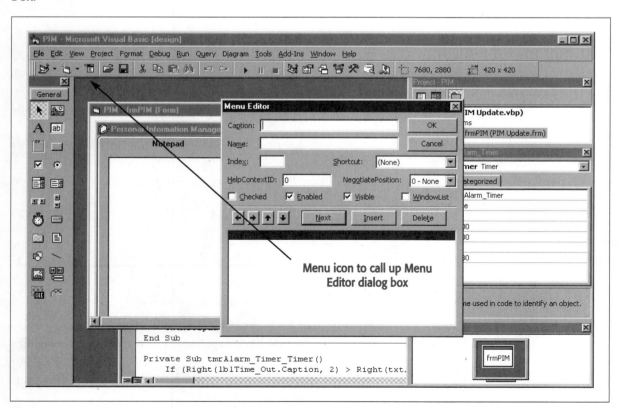

Because the menu items are essentially controls, we have to assign control names to them so that they can be accessed.

6. Key **mnuFile_Menu** and press **Enter**. Note the mnu prefix, which we will use for all our menu items.

This finishes the name of the menu (see Figure 6.9 for the appearance of the dialog box before you pressed **Enter**). Now you are ready to add the menu items. By pressing **Enter**, you told Visual Basic to clear the Caption and Name entry boxes in preparation for the next entry.

> **HINT:** You need to be careful not to put spaces before or after your control names in the Menu Editor. Because spaces are not allowed in variable or control names, Visual Basic will tell you that you have an illegal object name.

The first **File** menu item we will add is to load a file. When a file is loaded, it is done through the use of a dialog box so that you can specify the name of the file you want and the disk location of the file. Because this action involves the use of a dialog box, the standard practice, which we will follow, is to use an ellipsis on the menu item.

7. Key **&Open File...**, press **Tab**, and key **mnuOpen_File** as the control name.

Note that the item is on the same level (even on the left) in the workspace as the menu name. In order for Visual Basic to know which of your entries are menu names and which are menu items, the menu items must be indented. You control this with the large arrow buttons just above the workspace.

8. Click the right arrow (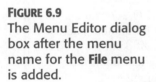), and the &Open File... entry is indented as shown in Figure 6.10.

By indenting the entry, Visual Basic will use it as an item in the menu shown by the menu name above it.

FIGURE 6.9
The Menu Editor dialog box after the menu name for the **File** menu is added.

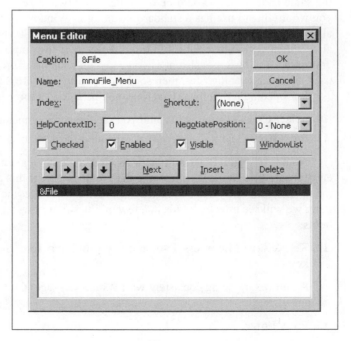

FIGURE 6.10
The Menu Editor dialog
box, showing how the
menu item is indented.

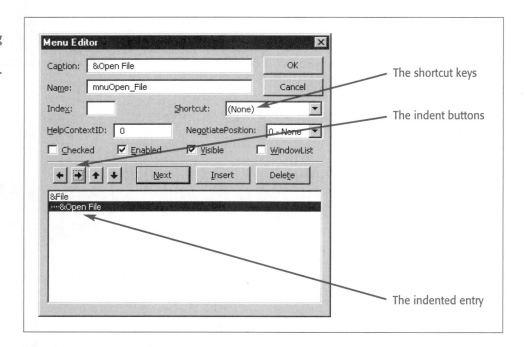

FIGURE 6.10
The Menu Editor dialog
box, showing how the
menu item is indented.

Before we move to the next menu item, we want to put a **shortcut key** on our menu item. Having access keys on the menu items is fine for menu users, but others prefer shortcut keys. With a shortcut key, it is not necessary to pull the menu down at all. Let's add shortcut keys.

The shortcut keys are added with the Shortcut entry box (as indicated in Figure 6.10).

9. Select the Shortcut box and pull the list down (Figure 6.11).

This list is made up of all the alphabetic keys with **Ctrl**, the function keys, the function keys with **Ctrl**, the function keys with **Shift**, and the function keys with both **Ctrl** and **Shift**. When you are assigning shortcut keys, it is best to use a meaningful key. Sometimes the same shortcut key would be meaningful for two different options or the shortcut key you would like to use has a standard meaning in Windows. Ctrl-O, for example, is generally used for opening a file. You wouldn't want to use Ctrl-O for another purpose if you also had an option to open a file in your program. An important point in Windows programming is to be as consistent as you can with what other programs do. If most programs use Ctrl-O for opening files, then so should you in your programming.

For opening a file, then, **Ctrl-O** would be a good choice for the shortcut key.

10. Select **Ctrl-O** from the list, and you see the updated menu item shown in Figure 6.12.

11. Press **Enter** and you are ready for the next menu item.

Note that Visual Basic automatically indented the next entry. It assumed that the next entry would be a menu item just like the previous one. If this entry happens to be the next menu name, the entry can be pushed back to the left to become a menu name rather than an item; we will see how to do this in a few minutes. For now, let's just add a few more menu items.

12. Key **&Save File**, press **Tab**, and key **mnuSave_File**. Select **Ctrl-S** for the shortcut key.

Again we are being consistent with Windows usage; **Ctrl-S** is commonly used for file saving options.

13. Press **Enter**.

FIGURE 6.11
The list of shortcut keys.

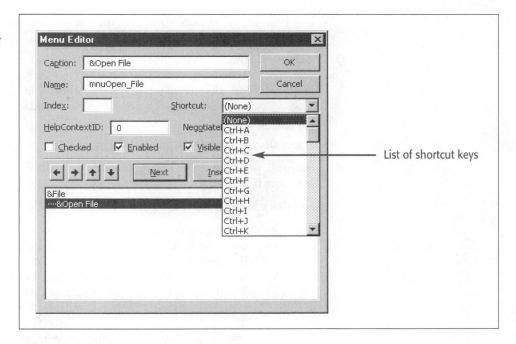

List of shortcut keys

14. Key **Save File &As...**, press **Tab**, key **mnuSave_File_As**, select **Ctrl-A** for the shortcut key, and press **Enter**.

Now we are ready to put in a separation line because the next menu item will be to exit the program, and we want to separate this item from the ones dealing with files. This is done by simply keying a dash.

15. Key **-**, press **Tab**, key **mnuDash**, and press **Enter**.

We used mnuDash as the control name. Even though the separation line is essentially a dummy entry, it still must have a control name. When there are multiple lines, you can use control names such as mnuDash_1, mnuDash_2, and so on.

FIGURE 6.12
The added shortcut key.

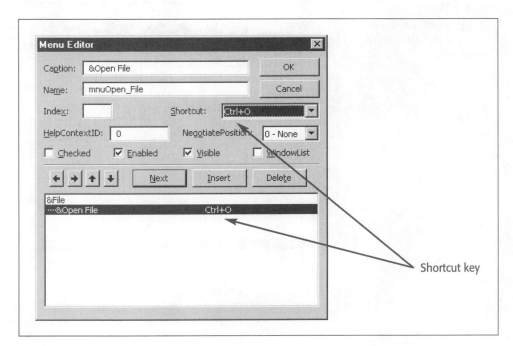

Shortcut key

16. Key **Exit**, press **Tab**, key **mnuExit_Application**, and press **Enter**.

There is no shortcut key for the **Exit** option. This is so that the user will not accidentally exit the program. If you chose not to exit, you could continue and call any other option you want with the appropriate shortcut key.

We aren't finished with the menu system yet, but it might be helpful to see what our work looks like at this point. Your menu currently should look like the one shown in Figure 6.13.

17. Select **OK** to exit the dialog box and go back to the program.

Note that your application now has a menu bar and the form has grown a bit vertically to allow room for it. Let's see what the menu looks like.

18. Pull down the **File** menu to see the menu shown in Figure 6.14.

There are four items on the menu and the separator bar, just as we wanted. Note that all the options have access keys and all but the **Exit** option have shortcut keys.

We aren't finished with the menu yet. We have more menus and menu items to add. Next, we want to have a menu to replace the buttons we used before. This menu, as is generally the case in Windows applications, will be called Edit.

19. Call the Menu Editor dialog box back to the desktop.

The current item in the menu is always the first item when you reload this dialog box. To put new items at the bottom of the list, you must select the line below the last item in the list.

20. Click the line below the **Exit** menu item.

21. Select the Caption entry box, key **&Edit**, press **Tab**, key **mnuEdit_Menu**, and press **Enter**.

FIGURE 6.13
The Menu Editor dialog box with the File menu completed.

FIGURE 6.14
The **File** menu we just created.

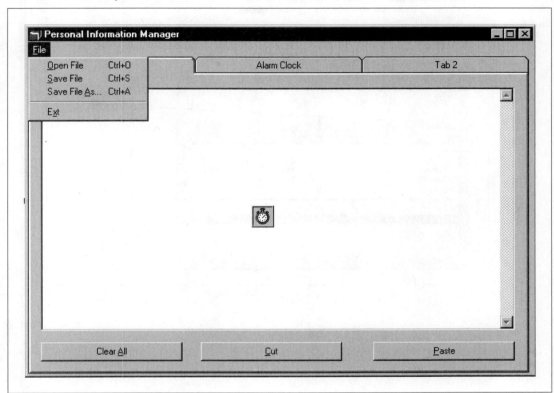

22. Key **Cu&t**, press **Tab**, and key **mnuCut_Text.** Use **Ctrl-X** for the shortcut key. This is, again, the commonly used shortcut key for the Cut option.

    This entry needs to be indented so that it is an item.

23. Select the right-pointing arrow (as shown in Figure 6.15) and the entry will become indented. Then press **Enter**.

    Next, even though we didn't have a button for copying text, we will add a menu item for it.

24. Key **&Copy**, press **Tab**, and key **mnuCopy_Text.** Use **Ctrl-C** for the shortcut key and press **Enter**.

25. Key **&Paste**, press **Tab**, and key **mnuPaste_Text.** Use **Ctrl-V** for the shortcut key and press **Enter**.

26. Key **Clear &All**, press **Tab**, and key **mnuClear_All.** Use **Ctrl-R** for the shortcut key and press **Enter**. We can't use **Ctrl-A** for this menu option because we used it for the **Save File As** option on the **File** menu.

    Note that we used **A** as the access key on the first menu and on this one too. Access keys can be used only when the menu is pulled down, so the two **A** access keys do not conflict.

27. Select **OK** and pull down the **Edit** menu to verify that it looks just as it should (see Figure 6.16).

FIGURE 6.15
The Menu Editor, indicating the indent button to use to indent the menu item.

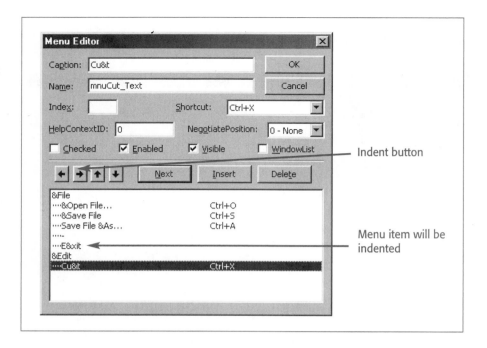

FIGURE 6.16
The **Edit** menu.

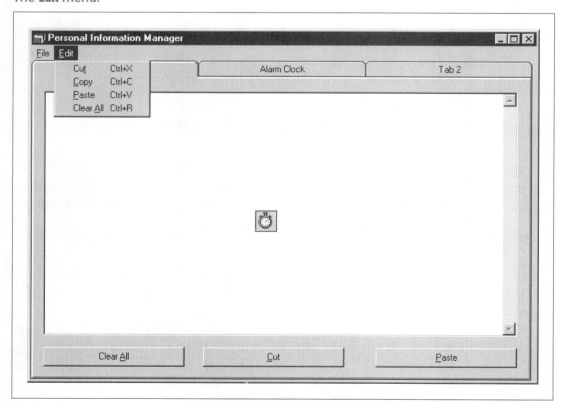

6.5 Adding Code for the Menu Items

Because the menu items are basically objects, code is added to them essentially the same way as for other objects.

1. Pull down the **File** menu and select the **Exit** option. The code window for that option will open up.

We would like this option to prompt the user, verifying that this option was not chosen by accident. We will use a message box for this as we have done previously.

2. Key the appropriate code for a verification message box in which the code will exit the program if the user selects the **Yes** button.

We can't add any code to the other three options on this menu, because we haven't covered techniques for using files yet. We can, however, add code to the **Edit** menu items.

3. Switch to the cmdCut_Button_Click code. Highlight all the code (not the Sub statements) and cut it (see Figure 6.17).

4. Switch to the mnuCut_Text_Click code and paste the cut code there.

The **Cut** option on the **Edit** menu is going to replace the **Cut** button, so it stands to reason that the same code can be used for the menu item as is used for the button. The one exception is the code to enable the **Paste** button. This will have to be changed so that it will enable the **Paste** menu item instead. The line of code is currently

```
cmdPaste_Button.Enabled = True       ' Turn on the Paste button
```

It will have to be changed to

```
mnuPaste_Text.Enabled = True ' Turn on the Paste menu item
```

FIGURE 6.17
The code to cut from the cmdCut_Button_Click event.

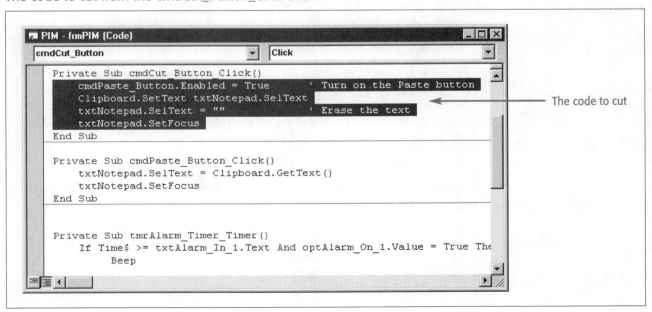

```
PIM - frmPIM (Code)

cmdCut_Button                        Click

Private Sub cmdCut_Button_Click()
    cmdPaste_Button.Enabled = True        ' Turn on the Paste button
    Clipboard.SetText txtNotepad.SelText
    txtNotepad.SelText = ""               ' Erase the text
    txtNotepad.SetFocus
End Sub

Private Sub cmdPaste_Button_Click()
    txtNotepad.SelText = Clipboard.GetText()
    txtNotepad.SetFocus
End Sub


Private Sub tmrAlarm_Timer_Timer()
    If Time$ >= txtAlarm_In_1.Text And optAlarm_On_1.Value = True The
        Beep
```

The code to cut

5. Change the code accordingly.

6. Move the code from the **Paste** button to the mnuPaste_Text_Click procedure.

7. Move the code from the **Clear All** button to the mnuClear_All_Click procedure.

Now we have added a new menu item for copying the text rather than cutting it. This code will be identical to that for the **Cut** button except that we will not erase the selected text.

8. Copy the code from the **Cut** button, paste it in the mnuCopy_Text_Click procedure, and delete the line of code that is not needed.

9. Run the application, key some text, and select the **Clear All** option from the **Edit** menu. Key some more text, highlight a portion of it, select the **Cut** option from the **Edit** menu, and then press **Ctrl-V**, which is the shortcut key for the **Paste** option. The cut text should be pasted back into the workspace.

10. Highlight some more text and press **Ctrl-C** to copy it. Move the insertion point to a different location and press **Ctrl-V** to paste the copied text.

11. Continue to experiment with the application until you are satisfied that the menu options are working as well as the buttons did. Then exit the application.

6.6   Enabling and Disabling Menu Items

1. Delete the three buttons and expand the notepad workspace appropriately.

The buttons are no longer necessary because we now have menu items for the same purposes. Also, there is now no code behind the buttons, so they wouldn't do anything anyway.

2. Pull down the **Edit** menu.

The **Paste** option is currently enabled. We don't want it to be enabled when the program is first run. We have code in the **Cut** and **Copy** menu item events to enable the **Paste** item. If it is already enabled, we don't need that code. But, just as with the buttons, we don't want to be able to paste until we have put something on the clipboard by cutting or copying.

Can we enable and disable menu items the same way as we did buttons? The answer is yes, and it is done in a similar fashion.

3. Call up the Menu Editor again.

Remember from Chapter 5 that if we wanted a button to be unavailable when the application started, we turned it off with a property. Menu items don't have properties, so the necessary changes are made through the Menu Editor dialog box.

4. Highlight the **&Paste** menu item.

5. Select the **Enabled** option to turn it off by removing the check mark in the box (as indicated in Figure 6.18), and select **OK**.

It's just that easy. The **Paste** option is now disabled.

6. Pull down the **Edit** menu and you will see that the **Paste** option is disabled.

7. Run the program and pull down the **Edit** menu. The **Paste** option is disabled.

8. Key some text, highlight a portion of it, cut it, and pull down the **Edit** menu. Now the **Paste** option is available. Select it and the cut text appears. Remember, we already have the code to turn the menu option on since it was in the copied code and we changed it so it is now appropriate for the menu item.

9. Experiment a bit more with the application until you are satisfied that everything is working properly.

FIGURE 6.18
The Enabled check box.

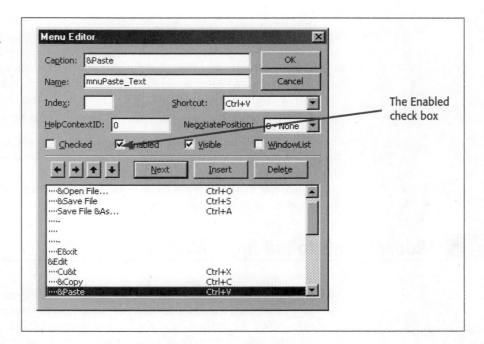

The Enabled check box

6.7   Putting Menus in Your Design

Because we now know how to put menus in our programs, we should look at how to specify menus in our designs. The easiest way is to specify a single element that we will call the Menu Bar and put all the elements under it. For example, the design for the menu of the Notepad program would look like this:

```
Project PIM - frmPIM
    A. Menu Bar
        1. File
            a) Load File… (Ctrl-L)
               Unknown at this point
            b) Save File (Ctrl-S)
               Unknown at this point
            c) Save File As… (Ctrl-A)
               Unknown at this point
            d) Exit
               Exit the program
        2. Edit
            a) Cut (Ctrl-X)
               Copy the highlighted text to the clipboard and erase
               ↳it from the workspace
            b) Cut (Ctrl-C)
               Copy the highlighted text to the clipboard without
               ↳erasing it from the workspace
            c) Paste (Ctrl-V)
               Copy the text from the clipboard into the workspace
               ↳at the current position
            d) Clear All (Ctrl-R)
               Erase the workspace
```

Note that each of the options specifies its shortcut key. Although this is not mandatory, specifying them in the design may reduce confusion about what shortcut key is the most appropriate for what option. These decisions should have already been made.

To make your design as clear as possible, you might also want to list the shortcut keys as separate program elements and then refer them to the menu item:

```
B. Ctrl-R
   The shortcut key for the Clear All option on the Edit menu
```

Shortcut keys are already listed with the menu item itself, so it isn't really necessary to list them separately. Also, because the keystroke is not a program element, it does not seem to fit the design pattern when done this way.

The Menu Bar is generally listed as the first object in the design, because it is always the first element at the top of the form.

6.8   Adding Fonts to the Application

One of the features common to applications such as the notepad is the capability to change the font and the font size. You have already seen how to change the font size by using the properties before the application is run, but like most properties, the font properties can also be changed during runtime. There is one drawback to changing fonts when using a text box: all the text in the text box is changed. You cannot change just some of the text and leave the rest in the previous font. Changing the font properties will, however, give us the opportunity to explore a few more Visual Basic techniques.

> **HINT:** You can create a text box that will allow you to use several different fonts by using the **Print** method, which will be covered in a later chapter. The problem with this technique is that Visual Basic will no longer handle the text details, and you will have to write routines for things such as scrolling and text selection.

We want to be able to change the font in the Notepad, so we should have a menu item for that change.

1. Open the Menu Editor window and add an **&Font** item to the Edit menu after using a separator line. Use **mnuFont_Change** for the control name and **Ctrl-F** for the shortcut key.

The fonts available in Visual Basic are the same fonts that are available in Windows, because Windows handles all the display functions of Visual Basic. To access the fonts in our program, we will add another tool to the Toolbox.

2. Open the Components dialog box by using the **Components** option on the **Project** menu or by pressing **Ctrl-T**.

3. Find and select **Microsoft Common Dialog Control. 6.0.**

Note that you now have a new control in your Toolbox, as shown in Figure 6.19.

The Common Dialog Control was created to give Visual Basic programmers an easy way to add commonly used dialog boxes to their programs. With this control you can add dialog boxes for opening and saving files, printing, changing colors, and selecting fonts. We're going to use it to select fonts.

To use a common dialog box, you first add the tool to your form. Then you add the appropriate command in your code to call up the dialog box. You need only one tool on your form to use as many dialog boxes as are required.

FIGURE 6.19
The Common Dialog
Control.

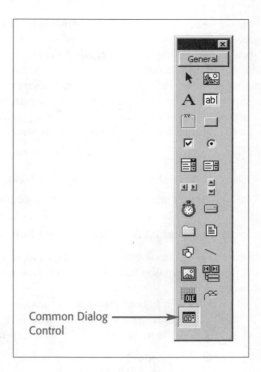

Common Dialog
Control

4. Add the Common Dialog control to your form and change the control name to
cdgPIM.

This control is like the timer control in that it will not appear when the program is being
run and cannot be resized (though it can be positioned anywhere on the form).

Because the common dialog box is a control much like other controls, there are a number of properties that can be changed. What we are concerned about at this point, however,
are the methods necessary to get the appropriate dialog box. To tell Visual Basic what dialog box you want to use, you employ the **Showname** method as in the following format:

```
Object.Showname
```

This method uses the method names (shown in Table 6.1) to give the various dialog
boxes.

If we wanted to use a Font dialog box, we would use the command

```
cdgPIM.ShowFont
```

TABLE 6.1
The dialog boxes
displayed by the various
Showname methods.

Showname Method	Dialog Box Displayed
ShowOpen	File Open dialog box
ShowSave	File Save As dialog box
ShowColor	Color dialog box
ShowFont	Font dialog box
ShowPrinter	Print or Print Options dialog box
ShowHelp	Calls Windows Help program for displaying Windows Help files

This isn't all we need, however. There are two types of fonts available, printer and screen, so we need to specify to the dialog box which type we want to use. This requires the use of a special predefined constant: **cdlCFScreenFonts**, **cdlCFPrinterFonts**, or **cdlCFBoth**. The use of each constant is indicated by its name. If you wanted to use only the screen fonts, for example, you would use the **cdlCFScreenFonts** constant. Then, if you wanted such effects as underline to appear in the dialog box, you would use a second constant, **cdlCFEffects**. These constants are assigned to the property **Flags**, and because there are two constants to use, they must be combined in one statement as follows:

```
cdgPIM.Flags = cdlCFScreenFonts Or cdlCFEffects
```

5. Call up the code window for the **Font** option of the **Edit** menu.

6. Key the Flags and ShowFont statements into the procedure (the Flags statement must come first).

7. Run the program and select the **Font** option on the **Edit** menu.

This will cause the Font dialog box to be displayed as shown in Figure 6.20. Note that this dialog box is just like the dialog box you use to change the font properties of an object, and it works the same way.

After the font properties have been changed on the dialog box and the **OK** button has been selected, control returns to the procedure that called up the dialog box. Then we need to assign the user's choices to the notepad font. This is done with the following commands:

```
txtNotepad.FontName = cdgPIM.FontName
txtNotepad.FontSize = cdgPIM.FontSize
txtNotepad.FontBold = cdgPIM.FontBold
txtNotepad.FontItalic = cdgPIM.FontItalic
txtNotepad.FontUnderline = cdgPIM.FontUnderline
txtNotepad.FontStrikethru = cdgPIM.FontStrikethru
txtNotepad.ForeColor = cdgPIM.Color
```

You don't actually need to use all of the commands if you are interested in only a few of the options, such as the fontname, but because the dialog box allows the user to change all these options, it makes sense to allow all the changes in the notepad.

FIGURE 6.20
The Font dialog box.

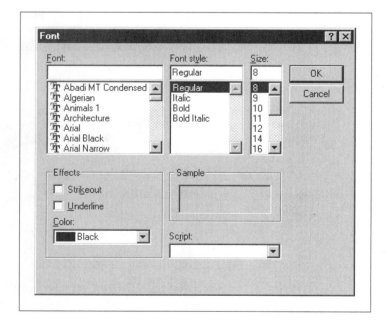

8. Exit from the dialog box and then from the program.

9. Open the code window for the Font menu item and key the foregoing statements after the ShowFont statement.

10. Run the program and key some text in the notepad. Then select the **Font** option, change some of the font properties, and select the **OK** button.

Note that the text in the notepad automatically changes to reflect the choices made in the dialog box.

11. Call up the dialog box several more times, making various changes each time, until you are confident that the program is working properly. Then exit and save the program.

HINT: When using a group of statements that need to be classified as to the form they are on, you can use the **With** construct to make it easier. For example, the last section of code could be changed to the following:

```
With txtNotepad
    .FontName = cdgPIM.FontName
    .FontSize = cdgPIM.FontSize
    .FontBold = cdgPIM.FontBold
    .FontItalic = cdgPIM.FontItalic
    .FontUnderline = cdgPIM.FontUnderline
    .FontStrikethru = cdgPIM.FontStrikethru
    .ForeColor = cdgPIM.Color
End With
```

Note that you begin the grouping by specifying the object following the keyword With, and then use the End With statement to end the construct.

6.9   A Control Array of Menu Items

One of the things we want to add to our menu is the capability to switch tabs by using the menu instead of the tabs. This is much appreciated by users who are uncomfortable with the mouse. When we assign shortcut keys to the menu items, the user can switch tabs by using the shortcut keys instead of the mouse. Later we are going to add an appointment calendar, To-Do list, and name and address list to our PIM application, so we will change the tabs to reflect this. Then we will have five tab entries to add to the menu.

1. Load the dialog box for the Tabbed Control.

2. Change the Tab Count entry to **6** so you will have six tabs, and then change the TabsPerRow to **6** so all the tabs will be on the same row.

3. Change the Tab Caption of the third tab to **Appointments**, the Tab Caption of the fourth tab to **To-Do List**, the Tab Caption of the fifth tab to **Address List**, and the Tab Caption of the sixth tab to **Web Browser**. Exit from the dialog box.

Now your Tabbed Control should look like the one in Figure 6.21.
Next you need to add the menu items for changing tabs.

4. Open the Menu Edit dialog box and add a new menu called **&Tabs** with the control name **mnuTab_Menu**.

FIGURE 6.21

The updated Tabbed Control.

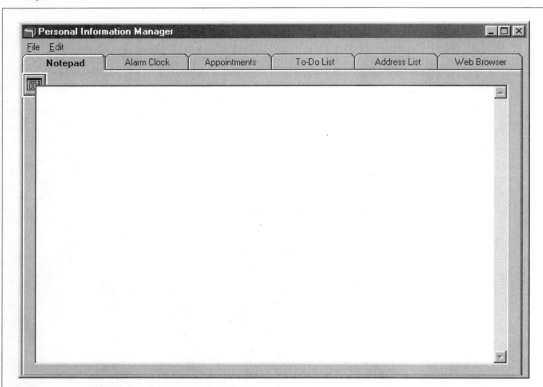

Now we need an item for each of the tabs. We could create six separate items, but because the tabs in the Tabbed Control are basically part of an array in that the particular tab is pointed to by number (the Notepad is tab 0, the Alarm Clock is tab 1, and so on), it makes more sense to use a control array of menu items. Remember that a control array is a grouping of like controls that are selected in code by their index numbers. Setting up a control array of menu items makes it possible to use the number of the menu item to point to the appropriate tab.

5. Under the **Tabs** menu, add **&Notepad** with the control name **mnuTab_Item** and the shortcut key **Ctrl-N**.

Note that under the entry box for the control name there is an entry box for the index. When you copy objects and paste them back onto the form, Visual Basic will automatically assign the index number. Such is not the case in the menus. You have to decide what the appropriate index numbers are and assign them yourself. The first mnuTab_Item should have the index 0 (zero) and the second the index 1 (one).

6. Key **0** in the index entry box.

7. Add another item called **Alar&m Clock** with the control name **mnuTab_Item**, the index **1**, and the shortcut key **Ctrl-M**.

8. Add the other four items as **A&ppointments** (shortcut key **Ctrl-P**), **&To-Do List** (shortcut key **Ctrl-T**), **A&ddress List** (shortcut key **Ctrl-D**), and **&WebBrowser** (shortcut key **Ctrl-W**), all with the same control names and appropriate indices.

9. Exit the dialog box.

Note that the program accepted the indices you used. That means that you have just created a control array of menu items.

10. Pull down the **Tabs** menu as shown in Figure 6.22.

11. Select one of the tab items. It doesn't matter which one; they are a control array and will all open the same code.

The code for the procedure shows the index as a parameter, as did the other control arrays you have worked with. When the program is executing and the user selects one of the menu items, Index will contain the number of the menu item selected.

Now we need to be able to switch between the tabs by using the index number given when the user selects the menu item. All we need to know is what property is used to change the current tab in the Tabbed Control. That just happens to be **Tab**. So to change the current tab on the Tabbed Control, we would use a statement such as

```
tabPIM.Tab = 3
```

This changes the tab to the fourth tab because the first tab is actually Tab = 0. This means that to use the mnuTab_Item parameter called Index, we need the statement

```
tabPIM.Tab = Index
```

12. Enter this statement in the procedure.

13. Run the program and select one of the items from the **Tabs** menu. The system will switch to the appropriate tab in the Tabbed Control.

14. Exit the program.

FIGURE 6.22
The **Tabs** menu.

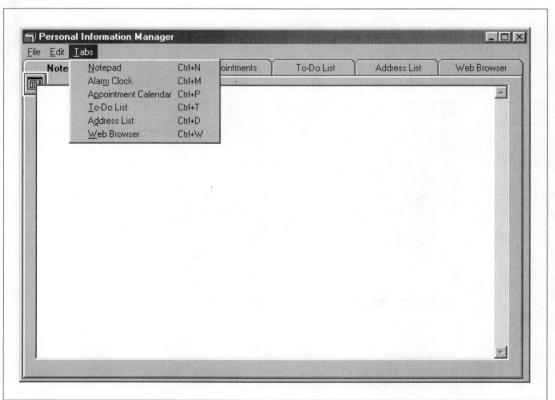

6.10   Adding Check Marks to the Font Menu

When you have a menu in which only one of the items is active at any time, it is customary to indicate the active item by displaying a check mark beside it. Adding a check mark
is merely a matter of setting another property.

1. Open the Menu Editor dialog box and select the Notepad item under the **Tabs** menu as
   shown in Figure 6.23.

   Note the Checked option on the left side of the dialog box (Figure 6.21). If this is
   turned on (selected or checked), the menu item will automatically be checked when the program is executed.

2. Click the check box to turn on the **Checked** option.

3. Exit the dialog box and run the program. Pull down the **Tabs** menu and note that
   Notepad is checked as shown in Figure 6.24.

   So far, this is only a partial solution because we have no code to be sure that the item
   checked is the one that is selected in the Tabbed Control. For example, you may have
   already selected a tab other than **Notepad,** even though the menu indicates that **Notepad** is
   the one selected.

4. Click the **Address List** tab and then pull down the **Tabs** menu. The **Notepad** item is
   still checked.

   This means that we actually have to change two things. In the Tabs item procedure, we
   need to be sure the proper menu item becomes checked while all the others are unchecked.
   Because menu check marks are not like option buttons in that you can have as many items
   as you wish checked, we need to turn off all the ones currently checked before we turn on
   the one that needs to be checked. Also, we must do the same thing to the menu when the
   user clicks one of the tabs to change function.

FIGURE 6.23
The checked option.

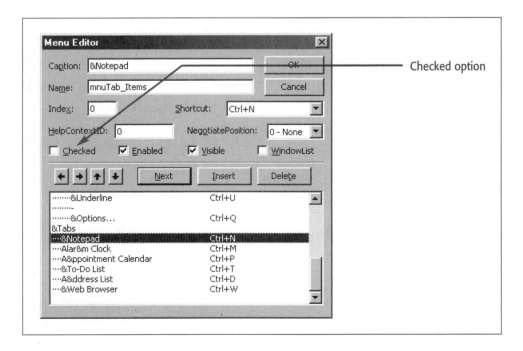

FIGURE 6.24
The checked **Notepad** item.

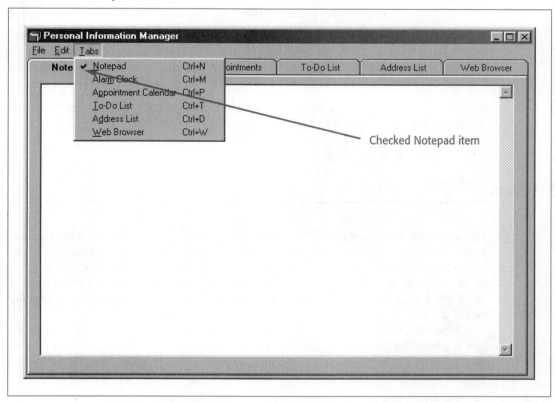

You might think that to turn off the check mark on the menu item, we would need to know which one is on. This isn't necessary. We can simply turn them all off. This will ensure that the one that needs to be turned off will be turned off.

The property we need to turn off is the one you might suspect, **Checked**, and the code to do this is a simple loop.

```
For intCounter = 0 to 5
    mnuTab_Item(intCounter).Checked = False
Next intCounter
```

Now, we could enter this code to turn off the menu items and enter an additional statement to turn on the proper one in the procedure for the menu items. But we already have code there that will cause the Click procedure of the Tabbed Control to execute. If we put the code to check the appropriate menu item in that Click procedure, it should serve both purposes.

5. Switch to the code window, pull down the objects list, and select the tabPIM object.

6. Pull down the Events list and select the Click event.

7. Key the previous loop into the procedure.

This unchecks all the menu items. Now we need a statement to check the one that should be on. To do this we need the number of the tab that was selected. Remember that to select the appropriate tab by using the menu item, we set the Tab property of the Tabbed Control to the index of the menu item. This will work in reverse. That is, we can use the Tab property as the pointer in the control array of the menu items. Thus, we need a statement similar to

```
mnuTab_Items(tabPIM.Tab).Checked = True
```

8. Key this statement after the loop.

9. Run the program and click one of the tabs. Pull down the menu to verify that the menu item is now checked. Click a few more tabs and menu items until you are satisfied that the program is working properly. Be sure to try a few of the shortcut keys.

This leaves us with only one more thing to add. We need to be sure that **Notepad** is the first tab selected when the program is executed, because this is the item we checked. All that is required is a statement to set the Tab property to 0 in the Form_Load procedure.

10. Add the statement in the Form_Load procedure and then retest the program. When you are satisfied, exit from the program.

6.11 Submenus

The next subject we want to look at is **submenus.** Earlier, you saw how to indent an item under a menu to create a menu item. You may have been wondering what happens if you indent an item twice. What happens is that you create a **submenu** under the immediate predecessor, which would be indented once. You can't indent a menu item twice under a menu that is not indented. To see how this works, we will add a few more items to the **Font** menu.

Although we can change the font to bold, italics, and so on by using the Font dialog box, it would be nice to be able to do it directly from the menu so that it could be done with shortcut keys as is normally the case in a word processor or text editor. We will want to add, under the Font menu item, additional items that will make the Font item a submenu.

1. Open the Menu Editor dialog box and add a new item under the Font menu item by selecting the Tab menu entry and clicking the **Insert** button (Insert). A blank entry appears after the Font entry, but it is not indented.

2. Add a new item with the name **&Bold**, the control name **mnuBold**, and the shortcut key **Ctrl-B**. Be sure to indent the Bold item twice so that it will be an item under the **Font** menu as shown in Figure 6.25.

3. Click the **OK** button and you get an error.

Because the **Font** item is now a menu, you cannot use a shortcut key to access it. Visual Basic will not allow a menu or submenu to be selected with a shortcut key. Access keys are fine for menus and submenus, but not shortcut keys.

4. Click **OK** in the error box and remove the shortcut key from the **Font** submenu by changing it to **(None)**.

5. Click **OK** and then pull down the **Edit** menu. Note that the **Font** item now has a large arrow on it, indicating that there are items within. Highlight the **Font** submenu, and you see the Bold entry appear as shown in Figure 6.26.

6. Open the Menu Editor dialog box and insert three more items under the Bold entry, indenting them properly. The entries should be

   a. **&Italics** with the control name **mnuItalics** and the shortcut key **Ctrl-I**.

   b. **&Underline** with the control name **mnuUnderline** and the shortcut key **Ctrl-U**.

   c. **&Alignment** with the control name **mnuAlignment** and no shortcut key; this one will be a submenu.

You can also create submenus within submenus, which is why we used no shortcut key on the Alignment item.

FIGURE 6.25
The **&Bold** item.

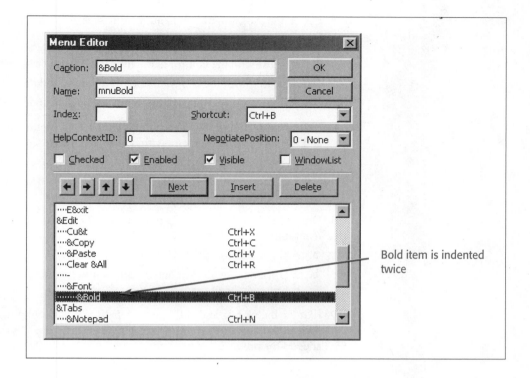

Bold item is indented twice

FIGURE 6.26
The **Edit** menu, showing the **Font** submenu with the **Bold** item.

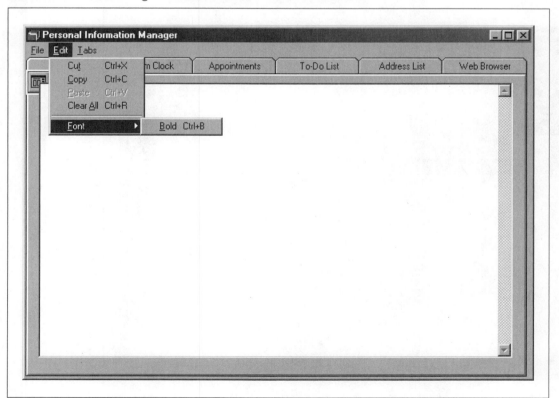

7. Under the **Alignment** submenu, insert three more items, which should be indented three times and named as follows:

   a. **&Right** with the control name **mnuRight** and the shortcut key **F2**.

   b. **&Center** with the control name **mnuCenter** and the shortcut key **F3**.

   c. **&Left** with the control name **mnuLeft** and the shortcut key **F4**.

8. Exit from the dialog box and pull down the **Edit** menu. Highlight the **Font** submenu and the **Alignment** submenu within to see the menu structure shown in Figure 6.27.

After just one more entry, we will be finished with the **Font** submenu. Originally, the **Font** item called up the Font dialog box, but no longer, because it is now a submenu, not an item. So we need a menu item for font options.

9. Open the Menu Editor dialog box and insert the following two entries after the Alignment item:

   a. A separator line.

   b. **&Options…** with the control name **mnuOptions** and the shortcut key **Ctrl-Q** (O has already been used).

10. Exit the dialog box and pull down the **Edit** menu. Highlight the **Font** submenu and the **Alignment** submenu within to see the menu structure shown in Figure 6.28. Note the added **Options…** submenu item.

FIGURE 6.27
The new menu structure.

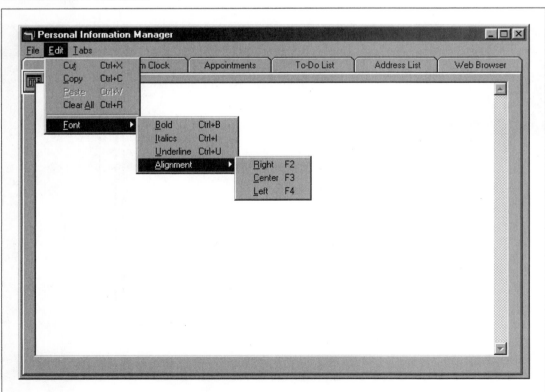

FIGURE 6.28
The menu structure after the **Options...** item is added.

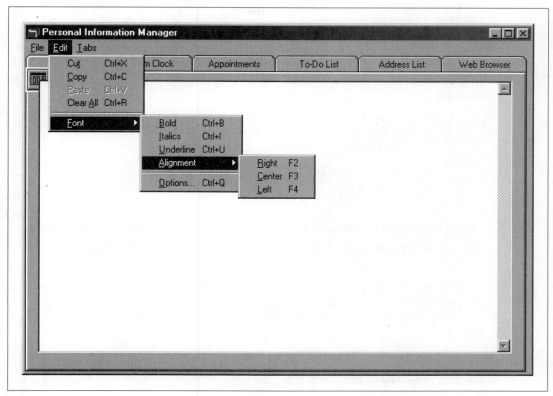

Now that the Font portion of the submenu is complete, we need to add some code so that the menu items will cause the appropriate things to happen. Because there is currently code on the **Font** submenu item, we need to move that code to the **Options...** submenu item.

11. Select the code for the **Font** submenu and move that code to the **Options...** menu procedure.

Now we need the code for the rest of the submenu items. They are all done in a similar fashion by setting the Font properties. For example, the Bold property is set with the statement

```
txtNotepad.FontBold = True
```

12. Open the code for the **Bold** menu item and insert this statement.

13. Add similar statements to the **Italics** and **Underline** menu items.

Now we have a slight problem. We cannot change the alignment of a text box during runtime, because the alignment properties can only be set during design time. That's okay, because we added the **Alignment** menu just so we could see how a submenu would look within another, and now you can get practice deleting menu items.

14. Open the Menu Editor dialog box, select the **Alignment** menu items, and click the **Delete** button.

15. Delete the **Right, Left,** and **Center** menu items the same way.

16. Exit the Menu Editor dialog box and run the program. Key some text in the notepad and then select the **Bold** menu item. The text should become bold. Try **Italics** and also **Underline.**

Now it would be nice if, as we turned on one of the font properties, the submenu became checked. It would also be good to be able to turn off the property from the submenu item. All we need to do is test whether the property is on. If it is on, we turn it off and turn off the check. If it is not on, we turn it on and check it. This requires an If Test like the following:

```
If txtNotepad.FontBold = True Then
    txtNotepad.FontBold = False
    mnuBold.Checked = False
Else
    txtNotepad.FontBold = True
    mnuBold.Checked = True
End If
```

17. Add this code and add similar code for the **Italics** and **Underline** submenu items.

18. Test the program again to be sure that the properties are turned on and off and that the submenu items become checked properly.

One final thing needs to be added. If we are going to mark the submenu items when the font property is turned on, we will need to add similar code so that if the property is turned on with the Font dialog box, the submenu item is checked. For example, the FontBold statement is

```
txtNotepad.FontBold = cdgPIM.FontBold
```

To change the code so that it will check the submenu item, we need to add code similar to the previous If Test. It is

```
If txtNotepad.FontBold = True Then
    mnuBold.Checked = True
Else
    mnuBold.Checked = False
End If
```

Note that we turned the logic of the previous If Test around. Now we need to check the submenu item if the font property is already turned on, because we are not using the If Test to turn the property on or off, but simply to check or uncheck the submenu item.

19. Open the code window for the **Options...** menu item and add the foregoing code. Add similar code for the Italics and Underline commands.

Also, because the Font dialog box allows changes to the FontName and the FontSize, we should use those values already assigned to the notepad text box and assign them to the Font dialog box properties. This requires the following two statements:

```
cdgPIM.FontName = txtNotepad.FontName
cdgPIM.FontSize = txtNotepad.FontSize
```

20. Add these statements to the procedure.

21. Test the program to be sure it is working properly. Be sure to test the **Options...** item and the Font dialog box. Exit the program.

HINT: You can use up to four submenu levels, and then the entries on the fifth level must be commands. You simply keep indenting the items as we practiced.

6.12   Pop-Up Menus

Pull-down menus work fine for most applications, but there may be times when you do not want the pull-down menu to obscure whatever is being displayed in the workspace, and then a **Pop-up menu** may be a better choice. Or you may want a pop-up menu of various options to be available when the user right-clicks a workspace. A pop-up menu is similar to a pull-down menu, except that the pop-up menu can appear anywhere on the desktop, whereas the pull-down menu always appears below the menu name.

With just a few exceptions, you create pop-up menus the same way as you create pull-down menus. To call forth a pop-up menu, you use the method **PopupMenu** followed by the name of the menu you want to display.

To see how this works, we will set up a new menu name and call up the **File** menu.

1. Save the PIM form and project as **Popup**. This way you won't overwrite your current version.

2. Call up the menu system, and insert in front of the other menu items a new menu item. Call the new item **Sample** with the control name **mnuSample_Menu** by highlighting the **&File** item and clicking the **Insert** button.

3. Exit from the menu system and call up the code window for the **Sample** menu.

4. Key **PopupMenu mnuFile_Menu** as the code for the procedure.

5. Exit the code window, execute the program, and click the **Sample** menu to see the pop-up menu appear as shown in Figure 6.29.

FIGURE 6.29
The **File** menu as a pop-up menu.

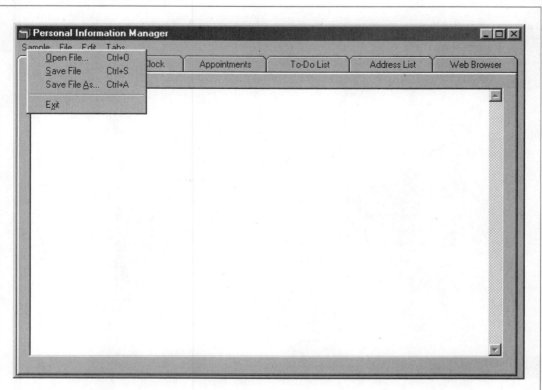

Note that the pop-up menu appears right under the mouse pointer. This is the default location. To have the menu appear elsewhere, you must tell Visual Basic where to put it. You do this with the three parameters that can be added to the PopupMenu command. The first parameter tells Visual Basic where to align the menu: left (value of 0, which is the default), center (value of 4), or right (value of 8). The second and third parameters designate the X and Y positions for that alignment.

6. Select **Exit** from the menu, open the code window for the **Sample** menu, and add **0, 2800, 2400** to the end of the PopupMenu command so that it becomes **PopupMenu mnuFile_Menu, 0, 2800, 2400.**

7. Run the program again and select the **Sample** menu. The menu now appears near the middle of the workspace as shown in Figure 6.30.

This is nice, but we probably don't want the **File** menu to be popped up from a **Sample** menu name. We would prefer that the **File** menu pop up when the **File** menu name is selected. This is, however, a more difficult proposition than it might seem. You cannot simply put the PopupMenu command in the code for the menu name already found on the menu bar. The menu on the menu bar is designed as a pull-down menu, so trying to switch it to a pop-up menu disturbs the logic of the system, and the menu will neither pop up nor pull down. If you want to be able to pop up the **File** menu by clicking on the **File** menu name in the menu bar, you will have to turn off the original **File** menu so that it does not appear in the menu and then set up a new **File** menu with no items under it.

8. Exit the program and call up the menu system.

9. Change the **Sample** menu caption to **&File** and change to the other **&File** menu item.

FIGURE 6.30

The pop-up menu in the center of the workspace.

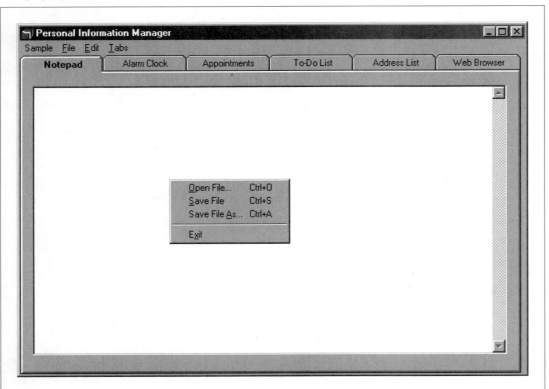

10. On this menu item, click the Visible check box to turn off the visibility of this **File** menu and then exit the menu system.

Now you will note that the menu bar looks the same as it did before you began your manipulations.

11. Run the program and select the **File** menu.

Now the menu pops up in the middle of the workspace as it did before, and there is no longer a pull-down **File** menu.

12. Try changing the position of the menu by changing the three parameters until you are thoroughly familiar with the way each of them works. Then exit the program.

6.13   Adding Font Buttons

This next topic doesn't actually deal with menus, but we have been experimenting with ways to let the user choose options, and most Windows applications have custom buttons for making such selections. In this section, we will add buttons that allow changes to the font properties, such as those you might find in a word processor.

We want three buttons: one for **Bold**, one for *Italics*, and one for <u>Underline</u>. We will put a **B** (boldfaced), an *I* (in Italics), and a <u>U</u> (underlined) on the buttons.

1. Reload the PIM program, change to the Notepad tab if necessary, and change the Height property of the Notepad workspace to 4695 and the Top property to 1080. This will give you room for the buttons you are going to add.

2. Add a button to the Tabbed Control. Change the Left property to **240**, and change the Top property to **520**. Change the Height and Width properties to 375. Change the caption to **B**, and change the font to **Bold,** the font type to **Times New Roman** and the size of the font to **14**. Give the button the name **cmdBold**. Your button should now be as shown in Figure 6.31.

Now we want the button to show a ToolTip hint. This is done by entering the desired text in the **ToolTipText** property.

3. Key **Bold** in the ToolTipText property.

4. Copy the button and paste it twice, positioning the new buttons beside the first as shown in Figure 6.32. Do not create a control array. The middle button's Left property should be **660** (the normal spacing puts the buttons too close together), and the Left property of the right button should be **1065**. Change the caption of the middle button to **I** and bold and italicize the font. The name of the button should be **cmdItalics**. Key **Italic** in the ToolTipText property.

5. Change the name of the right button to **cmdUnderline**, change the caption to **U**, and underline it. Key **Underline** in the ToolTipText property. Your three buttons should now look like the ones in Figure 6.32.

Let's see if the ToolTips work.

6. Run the program and position the mouse pointer over the **Bold** button. The tool tip will appear under the button as shown in Figure 6.33.

7. Move the mouse pointer over the **Italics** button. The ToolTip will change.

8. Move the mouse pointer over the **Underline** button. The ToolTip will change again.

Now let's add code for the **Bold** button so that the text will become boldfaced when the button is clicked.

FIGURE 6.31
The **Bold** button.

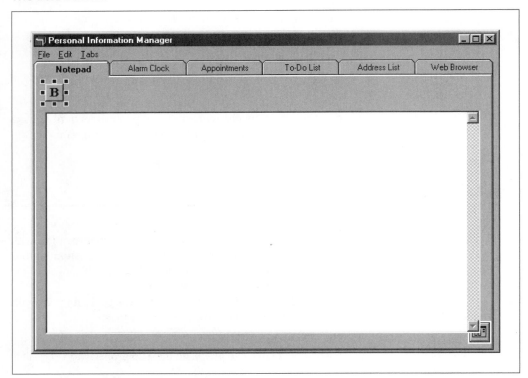

FIGURE 6.32
The buttons on the notepad.

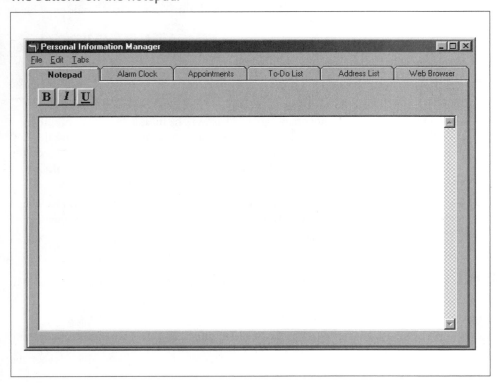

FIGURE 6.33
The tool tip for the **Bold** button.

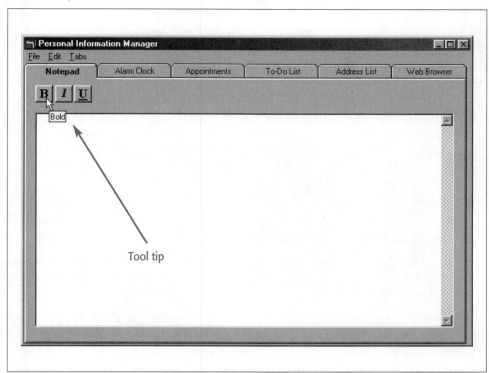

9. Exit the program and open the code window for the **Bold** button.

We have the code we need to determine whether the font is already boldfaced or bold needs to be turned on. We have that code in the menu. All we need to do is execute the menu item click procedure with the statement

```
mnuBold_Click
```

This causes control of the program to switch to the mnuBold_Click procedure and execute the code there, just as though the item on the menu had been selected. Then control of the program switches back to the next statement after the procedure call statement, where execution of the code continues normally.

10. Key the foregoing statement into the procedure.

11. Run the program, key some text in the text box, and click the **Bold** button. Note that the text becomes darker.

12. Pull down the **Edit** menu and display the **Font** menu. Note that the **Bold** menu item is checked.

13. Practice a bit more and then exit from the program.

This takes care of boldfacing, but remember that in addition to code for boldfacing the text, we need code for the **Italics** and **Underline** buttons. These changes are left as an exercise at the end of the chapter.

6.14   Adding a Status Bar

We aren't finished yet. At the bottom of the Notepad, we're going to add a **status bar** for displaying hints about the use of the buttons. That is, we are going to add a window that will display the functions of the buttons as the mouse passes over them as well as the status of the buttons we added. As a bonus, it will also show the status of the **Ins** key.

> **HINT:** As you might suspect, having all these different ways to turn the properties on and off and to display their status is actually overkill. Most applications won't have all these options, but you are learning about the variety of techniques available, and the only way to learn how to use them is to use them!

To create a status bar, we will add a new control to the Visual Basic toolbox.

1. Call up the Components dialog box and turn on the **Microsoft Windows Common Controls 6.0**. Exit the dialog box, and you see that a number of new controls have been added to the toolbox.

   The tool we want to use is shown in Figure 6.34. It is called a **status bar,** though we are also going to use it as a hint bar. To make room for it, we need to expand the form.

2. Expand the form as shown in Figure 6.35.

3. Add a StatusBar to the form under the Tabbed Control as shown in Figure 6.36. Change the name of the control to **staPIM_Status**.

FIGURE 6.34
The StatusBar control.

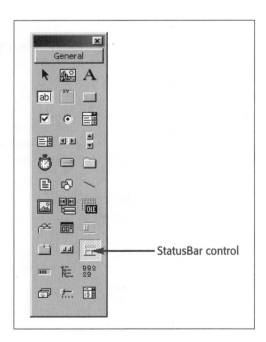

StatusBar control

FIGURE 6.35

The larger form making room for the status bar.

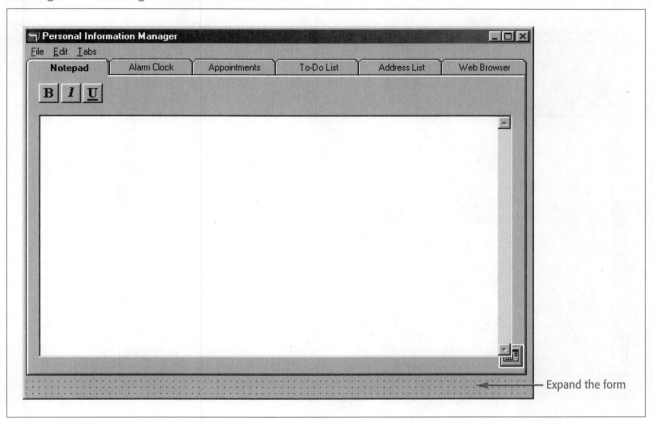

— Expand the form

Note that there is, by default, one inset panel in the status bar. The number and size of the panels are adjustable. This tool has a properties window similar to the one for the Tabbed Control where the panel properties are specified.

4. Right-click the panel, select **Properties** from the menu, and click the Panels tab to get to the portion of the dialog box shown in Figure 6.37.

The first thing we need to do is add four more panels. We want one panel for the Hint panel, and then we want four more for the button status indicators.

5. Click the **Insert Panel** button four times to add four more panels.

Each of the panels is the same size. We want the first one to be much larger than the other four, however. You can change the panel that the dialog box is pointing to by changing the number in the index box, which is done by clicking the small arrows or keying the index you want to use. We will adjust each of the panels as we go.

6. Change to the first panel, which has an index of 1.

7. Change the Minimum Width to **7560** and click the **Apply** button. This will push the other panels far to the right, and you will lose sight of some of them. That's okay, because we will change their sizes soon.

8. Change to the second panel (index of 2) by clicking the right arrow on the right side of the Index box and change the Minimum Width to **440**. Do the same to the other three panels and click the **Apply** button.

FIGURE 6.36

The PIM showing the new status bar.

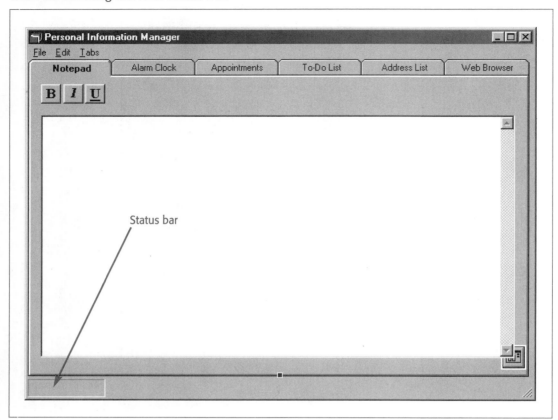

FIGURE 6.37

The StatusBar properties for the panels.

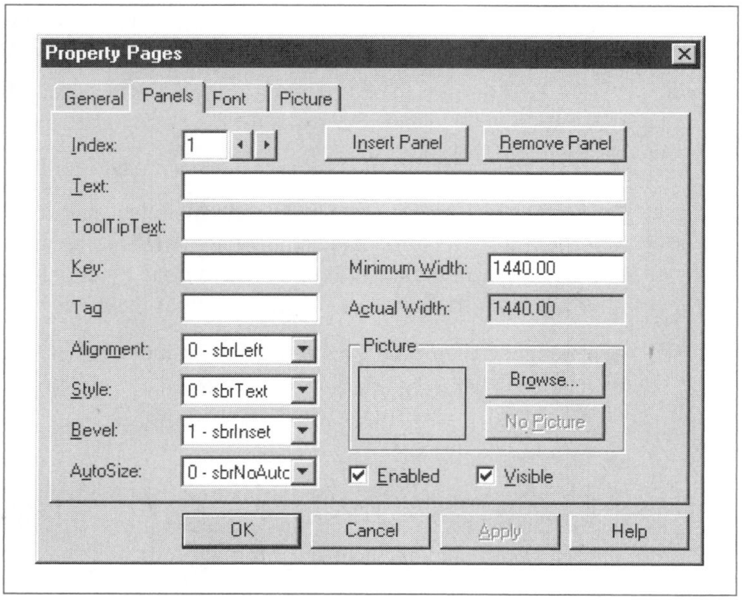

Now your panels should look like the ones on the status bar in Figure 6.38.

9. Key **U** in the Text entry box for the fifth panel, and then click the Enabled check box to turn it off. This will make the letter in the panel appear dimmed, which indicates that the text in the Notepad is not underlined. We will enable the panel when the text underline function is turned on.

10. Change to the fourth panel, key **I**, and turn off the Enabled check box.

11. Change to the third panel, key **B**, and turn off the Enabled check box.

12. Change to the second panel, key **In**, and turn off the Enabled check box.

Note that the font in the panels is not very large, but we can adjust it.

13. Click the **Font** tab to see a fonts display similar to those you have seen in the past. Change the font to **Times New Roman**, **12** points, **Bold**.

Unfortunately, you will not be able to make the font for the two indicators italicized or underlined as you did on the buttons. All the panels in the status bar use the same font, so if you made the font italicized, all the display elements would be italicized.

14. Exit the dialog box. The status bar now looks like the one shown in Figure 6.39.

To add text to the panels and to change the Enabled properties, you must use the **Panels** property of the status bar. This allows you to point to the particular panel by index. To change the Enabled property of the Bold indicator would require a statement like

```
staPIM_Status.Panels(3).Enabled = True
```

FIGURE 6.38
The status bar with the five panels.

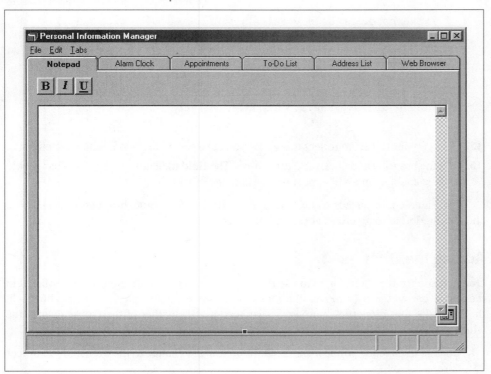

FIGURE 6.39

The status bar with the font properties indicators.

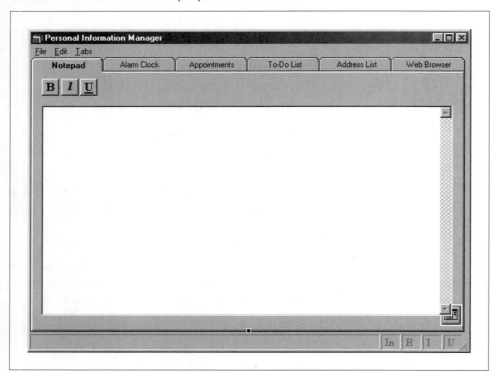

This statement needs to be added to the Bold menu procedure so that it will be enabled and disabled as the button is used. The updated If Test would look like

```
If txtNotepad.FontBold = True Then
    txtNotepad.FontBold = False
    mnuBold.Checked = False
    staPIM_Status.Panels(3).Enabled = False
Else
    txtNotepad.FontBold = True
    mnuBold.Checked = True
    staPIM_Status.Panels(3).Enabled = True
End If
```

15. Change your If Test to reflect this code (you need to add the two Enabled statements).

16. Run the program and click the **Bold** button. The Bold indicator on the status bar should now be enabled and will appear darker than the others.

The same coding needs to be done for the **Italics** and **Underline** buttons, but those changes are left as an exercise at the end of the chapter.

Adding the Hints

One purpose for the status bar is to use it as a hint bar. We want the hint to be displayed in the status bar as the user moves the mouse over the element that the hint is about—in this case, the font properties buttons. So we need to use another of the mouse events, the **MouseMove**.

1. Change to the code window for the **Bold** button and change to the MouseMove procedure.

The only code we need here is to display an appropriate message in the first panel of the status bar. The code would be

```
staPIM_Status.Panels(1).Text = "This button will bold face the
↳Notepad text."
```

2. Key this statement into the procedure.

This will display the message as the mouse pointer passes over the button, but there is nothing to erase the message from the box when the mouse pointer is no longer on one of the buttons. What we need is code in the MouseMove procedure of the Tabbed Control to erase the caption.

3. Change to the MouseMove procedure of the Tabbed Control and key the appropriate code.

4. Run the program and move the mouse pointer so that it is over the button. The message should appear in the label at the bottom of the Notepad. Now move the mouse pointer off the button. The message should disappear.

5. Exit the program.

Creating an Overtype Mode

A text box has only one mode, insert mode. That is, if you position the insertion point in the middle of an existing word and key new text, the existing text is pushed to the right in the text box. Because we want our notepad to be more like a word processor, we want to have an insert mode and an overtype mode in which, as you type, the characters after the insertion point are removed, one for one, as the new characters are input.

To turn the insert mode on and off, the program needs to sense when the user presses the **Ins** key. We want the program to do this regardless of what object in the program has the focus, so the form needs to see the keystrokes before the object that has the focus. We can cause this to occur by setting the **KeyPreview** property of the form to True. Then the form will see all the keystrokes first.

1. Change the KeyPreview property of the Form to **True**.

That is only part of it. Now we need to add the code so that the intercepted keystroke for the **Ins** key is used to set the flag. For this we need to use the **KeyDown** event of the form.

2. Switch to the form and change to the Keydown event procedure.

The first parameter here is **KeyCode**. This is similar to the KeyAscii parameter used in the KeyPress event procedure. It contains the numeric key code, but in this procedure we can see all keystrokes, including the **Ins** key. To sense the **Ins** keystroke, we will need to compare KeyCode against its numeric key code, but it is easier just to use the predefined constant for the **Ins** key: **vbKeyInsert**. To do this, we will need an If Test like the following:

```
If KeyCode = vbKeyInsert Then
```

3. Key this statement.

If this statement is true, we need to test the status of the insert flag. If it is already on, it needs to be turned off. If it is off, it needs to be turned on. This will require a nested If Test:

```
If staPIM_Status.Panels(2).Enabled = False Then
    staPIM_Status.Panels(2).Enabled = True
Else
    staPIM_Status.Panels(2).Enabled = False
End If
End If
```

4. Key this code.

As we mentioned, a text box really has no overtype mode. It is always in insert mode. Thus, if we want an overtype mode, we have to create it ourselves. An overtype mode simply means that as the user presses a key, the character where the cursor is must be erased and the new key character put in its spot. So all we have to do is delete the current character before the new character is put in the text box.

We can do this easily by highlighting the current character with the SelLength function. If we don't reset the pointer with the SelStart function, the SelLength function will select the specified number of characters from the current insertion point position. The number of characters we want to highlight is just one. This can be done with the statement

```
txtNotepad.SelLength = 1
```

This statement has to be put in the KeyPress event procedure, but we need more than just the one statement. We must test the status of the Insert flag, because if it currently indicates insert mode, we don't want to delete the character. In addition, we need to be sure that the key the user pressed is not **Backspace.** If it is and we don't ignore it, two characters are deleted: one because of the backspace and another because of the selection. Thus, we need an If Test like the following:

```
If staPIM_Status.Panels(2).Enabled = False And KeyAscii <>
    ↳ vbBack Then txtNotepad.SelLength = 1
End If
```

5. Open the code window for the KeyPress event of the Notepad text box, and key the previous code in the event procedure.

6. Run the program and key some text in the Notepad text box.

7. Press **Backspace.** It functions as it is supposed to.

8. Move the insertion point to the middle of the text you keyed. Key some different letters. Note that the newly keyed characters replace the ones that are already there.

9. Press the **Ins** key. Key some more letters. Now the letters already there are moved as they normally are in a text box. This means that the SelLength highlight is no longer deleting the character.

10. Continue to test the program until you are sure everything is working correctly.

11. Exit the program and shut down the system properly.

We are finished with the Notepad application, at least for the time being. We will continue to add to it as we progress through the book, however. We will also add functions to the various other tabs, and add more items to the menus.

6.15　Debugging Your Programs

There are a few things to watch out for when you are using menus. If you are enabling and disabling menus and menu items, be sure to disable them in the proper routine and at the proper time. And don't forget to enable them again in whatever procedure is appropriate.

You can turn menus and menu items on and off using the Visible property, just as you can other objects. During design time, the Visible property is a check box in the Menu Editor, as is the Enabled property. During runtime, it is a normal property and is handled in the normal fashion using assignment statements.

Making menu items and especially menus invisible is not generally a good technique. It can be distracting for a user to click the menu bar where a menu usually is and click another menu by mistake. If you simply disable the menu instead of making it invisible, the rest of the menus will continue to occupy the same physical locations, and the users will be happier with your program.

Also, even though it is allowed, you should not use menus without menu items. When a menu with no items is selected, the code for the menu item Click event is executed as though it were a menu item. So the menu acts like a button. When users are accustomed to seeing items under a menu and then suddenly find a menu that functions automatically when selected, it can be confusing. If you don't have any items to put under a menu, that menu should become a menu item under another menu.

You cannot have two menus with the same shortcut key. When you are creating large menus, it is helpful to create a list of the shortcut keys that have already been used so that you will know which ones are still available. Then, as you use the shortcut keys, remove them from the list or add them to the list of used ones, whichever way you create your list.

Remember that when you are creating a control array of menu items, Visual Basic doesn't automatically number your array elements for you. You must assign the index numbers yourself, and you must be careful. Visual Basic will let you skip index numbers. That is, you can give the first object the index 1 and the second the index 3. If you try to use such a scheme, you will have to be sure your code is written to exclude the missing indexes; otherwise, you will get an error when your code tries to use the missing index. The best thing is not to skip indexes deliberately or by accident.

You can use the same access key for two or more menu items on the same menu. If you do this, however, the user will not be able to generate the Click event for the menu item by just using the access key. Visual Basic will move the highlight to each of the elements with the same access key, one after the other. Then, to select the item, the user must press **Enter**. Though this is allowed, it certainly reduces the utility of the access keys and is not a recommended technique.

6.16 Command and Menu Summary

In this chapter you learned to use the following keystrokes:

- **&** is used to add an access key to a menu item.
- **Ctrl-E** calls up the **Menu Editor** option of the **Tools** menu.

In this chapter you learned to use the following event procedures:

- **KeyDown** lets you add code to determine which key is pressed.
- **MouseMove** lets you add code for when the mouse pointer passes over your object.

In this chapter you learned to use the following commands:

- **PopupMenu** is used to change pull-down menus to pop-up menus (or to add new pop-up menus).

In this chapter you learned about the following properties:

- **Checked** lets you check (True) or uncheck (False) a menu item.
- **Color** gives you the color that was set in the Font Common Dialog box.
- **Enabled** lets you enable (True) or disable (False) a menu item during runtime.
- **Flags** lets you specify what is to be displayed in the Font Common Dialog Control.
- **FontBold** lets you boldface the font being used to display the text in an object.
- **FontItalic** lets you italicize the font being used to display the text in an object.
- **FontName** lets you change the font being used to display the text in an object.

- **FontSize** lets you change the size of the font being used to display the text in an object.

- **FontStrikethru** lets you cause a line to be drawn through the font being used to display the text in an object.

- **FontUnderline** lets you underline the font being used to display the text in an object.

- **KeyPreview** lets a form intercept keystrokes before they are passed on to the object with the focus.

- **Panels** lets you point to a specific panel in a status bar.

- **Tab** lets you change the current tab in a Tabbed Control.

- **ToolTipText** causes the program to display a ToolTip when the mouse pointer is positioned over the control.

In this chapter you learned about the following prefixes:

- **cdg** is for the Common Dialog Control.

- **mnu** is for menus and menu items.

- **sta** is for the StatusBar control.

In this chapter you learned about the following menu option:

- **Tools:**

  - **Menu Editor** (shortcut key **Ctrl-E**) opens the dialog box that allows you to create a menu for the application.

In this chapter you learned about the following button:

- ▥ (shortcut key **Ctrl-E**) calls up the Menu Design window.

  In this chapter you learned about the following tools:

- ▥ lets you add a Common Dialog Control to the form.

- ▥ lets you add a status bar to the form.

6.17 Performance Check

1. What does it mean when a menu item is gray rather than black?

2. What does an ellipsis on the end of a menu item mean?

3. How do access keys differ from shortcut keys?

4. Why must all the menu items be assigned a control name?

5. What is true of a menu item when there is an index value?

6. What kind of menu entry is a dash?

7. How do you add an access key to a menu item?

_____

8. What do you do to access the code window for a menu item?

_____

9. What property is used to change a menu item so that it is not available?

_____

10. What is true of the text of a text box when the font is changed?

_____

11. What function did we use to create the Insert mode in the Notepad?

_____

12. What property is used to add a check mark to a menu item?

_____

13. What property is used to hide a menu item so that it cannot be seen?

_____

14. Why must a pull-down menu always have at least one item?

_____

15. What is on a menu item to indicate that the item is a submenu name?

_____

16. How do you create a submenu?

_____

17. How many levels deep can a submenu be?

_____

18. What is the command used to cause a menu to be popped up on the screen rather than pulled down?

_____

19. What property of the Form was it necessary to turn on to let the form sense the press of the **Ins** key?

_____

20. What is the prefix for a menu item?

_____

6.18 Programming Exercises

> **HINT:** If your instructor wants you to compile your exercises, you may use any of the furnished icons.

1. To get more practice using menus, you decide to create a small Tic Tac Toe game with menus. The game will be for two players rather than for one player against the computer (which is a great deal more difficult to program). The design for the program is

```
Project TicTac - Form1
A.  Menu Bar
    1.  Game
        a)  New Game
            Erase the X's and O's off the game buttons
        b)  Exit
            Exit the program
```

```
2. Control array of nine buttons
    1. Click
        If it is X's turn Then
            Change the button to X
        Else
            Change the button to 0
        End If
```

Using this design, at the computer do each of the following:

a. Get into Visual Basic with your work disk in drive A.

b. Create a form like the one shown in Figure 6.40, with the buttons as a control array called **Game_Button**. The buttons will be used to mark the players' choices.

c. Open the Menu Design window and add

1) A menu called **&Game** with the control name **mnuGame_Menu**.

2) A menu item called **&New Game** with the control name **mnuNew_Game**.

3) A menu item called **E&xit** with the control name **mnuExit_Game**.

d. Open the code window for the New Game menu item. This option will erase the captions of all the buttons so that the game can begin anew. Key a loop to go through all the buttons (0 through 8), emptying their captions.

e. Change to the code window for the Exit menu item, and enter the appropriate code.

f. Change to the code window for the buttons. Here you need code to determine whose turn it is and to put an **X** or an **O** in the selected button on the basis of whose turn it is. To know whose turn it is, set up a variable called **intTurn** as static. For example, if Turn is 0, change the caption to **O** and set Turn to 1. Reverse the process in the Else.

g. Save the program as **Tic Tac Toe**, test it, and print it out.

h. Exit Visual Basic and shut down the system properly.

2. To get more practice with submenus, you decide to change the menu of the PIM so that the three properties (Bold and so on) appear in a submenu called **Properties** on the **Font** menu. At the computer, do each of the following:

a. Get into Visual Basic with your work disk in drive A.

b. Load the **PIM** application.

c. Open the Menu Editor dialog box and do the following:

1) Add a new menu item called **&Properties** (with control name mnuProperties) below **Font,** indented to the same level as **Bold**.

FIGURE 6.40
The form for the Tic Tac Toe game.

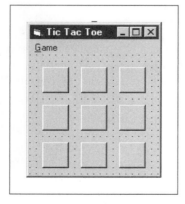

2) Indent the three properties once more so that they are items within the **Properties** submenu.

d. Save the form and project as **Properties**. Test the program, making sure the properties still work as before. Then print out the program.

e. Exit Visual Basic and shut down the system properly.

3. You decide to change the application you created in Programming Exercise 3 in Chapter 5 so that it will work with menus instead of buttons. If you didn't do Exercise 3, you can get a copy of the program from your instructor. You should refer to that exercise for information on how the application is supposed to function. At the computer, do each of the following:

a. Get into Visual Basic with your work disk in drive A.

b. Load the **Multicut** application.

c. Open the Menu Design window and add each of the following:

1) The menu name **&File** with the control name **mnuFile_Menu**.

2) The menu item **&Load File...** with the control name **mnuLoad_File** and the shortcut key **Ctrl-L**.

3) The menu item **&Save File** with the control name **mnuSave_File** and the shortcut key **Ctrl-S**.

4) The menu item **Save File &As...** with the control name **mnuSave_File_As** and the shortcut key **Ctrl-A**.
(Note that you will not add any code for these first four **File** menu options. They are added just for practice.)

5) A separator line called **mnuDash_1**.

6) The menu item **E&xit** with the control name **mnuExit_Item** and the shortcut key **Ctrl-X**.

7) The menu name **&Edit** with the control name **mnuEdit_Menu**.

8) The menu item **Clear &All** with the control name **mnuClear_All** and the shortcut key **F4**.

9) The menu item **&Cut** with the control name **mnuCut** and the shortcut key **F5**.

10) The submenu name **&Paste** with the control name **mnuPaste_Menu**.

11) The submenu item **Paste &All** with the control name **mnuPaste_All** and the shortcut key **Ctrl-P**.

12) The submenu item **Paste &1** with control name **mnuPaste_1** and the shortcut key **F1**.

13) The submenu item **Paste &2** with control name **mnuPaste_2** and the shortcut key **F2**.

14) The submenu item **Paste &3** with control name **mnuPaste_3** and the shortcut key **F3**.

d. Copy the code from and to each of the following:

1) From cmdClear_Button to mnuClear_All

2) From cmdCut_Button to mnuCut

3) From cmdPaste_Button to mnuPaste_All

4) From cmdPaste_Button_1 to mnuPaste_1

5) From cmdPaste_Button_2 to mnuPaste_2

6) From cmdPaste_Button_3 to mnuPaste_3

e. You need to change the code that refers to the **Paste** buttons so that it refers to the menu items instead.

f. Add the appropriate code to the mnuExit_Item.

g. Save the program as **Menu Multicut**. Test the application, being sure to try the access keys and the shortcut keys. Then exit the program and print it out.

h. Exit Visual Basic and shut down the system properly.

4. You have a friend who is learning how to program in Visual Basic. He has been experimenting with control arrays, buttons, and menus but can't get his program to work properly. He has asked for you help. At the computer, do each of the following:

a. Get into Visual Basic with your work disk in Drive A.

b. Load the **Color Buttons** program from the Ch-6 folder.

c. Run the program. It was designed to change the form background color when either a menu option or one of the buttons is selected. Click the **Red** button and the program generates an error that tells you control array element 8 doesn't exist. Click the **Debug** button. The statement in error is trying to remove a check mark from the control array item. This must mean there is something wrong with the menu indices. Exit the program and examine the menu indices. Fix the one that is incorrect.

d. Run the program again. Click the **Red** button. You get a similar error. Click the **Debug** button. This time the index problem is with the buttons themselves. Fix them.

e. Run the program again. Click the various buttons, and note that they change the color of the form properly. Click the **Cyan** button. Pull down the menu. The **Yellow** menu item is selected. Examine the menu closely. You will see a problem. Correct this problem.

f. Run the program and check each of the menu items and buttons to be sure they work properly. When you are satisfied that the program is working properly, print it out.

6.19 Performance Mastery

1. To get more practice with custom buttons and related properties, you decide to go back to the PIM program and add the appropriate code for the **Italics** and **Underline** buttons, menus, and Options dialog box. Be sure to add code before the ShowFont statement so that the appropriate options in the Font dialog box are selected. These commands will essentially be the reverse of the statements that set the font properties for the notepad text box after returning from the Font dialog box. Save the program, and then test and print it.

2. To get more practice with menus and the ZOrder method, you decide to create a program with a control array of eight buttons, each labeled as a different color. Create a control array of menu items, one for each of the colored buttons. When the option is selected, bring the selected button to the top, check the menu item, and change the background color. For example, if the **Blue** menu option is selected, bring the **Blue** button to the top and check the menu option. When one menu option is checked, the one that was previously checked should be turned off. Save the program as **Colored ZOrder**, and then test the program and print it.

3. To get more practice using pop-up menus, you decide to finish the work we began in the chapter and make all the menus in the **Popup** program pop-ups. Save the program as **PopDone**, and then test it and print it out.

4. You like being able to change the font in a text box, but you don't like the Font dialog box. You decide your users would prefer to be able to pick their font characteristics in a menu. Create a program with a multiline text box and four menus:

■ **FontName,** with the font names of at least four fonts

■ **Size,** with at least six font sizes appropriate for the four fonts you have chosen

■ **Color,** with the eight standard colors

■ **Options,** with Bold, Italics, Underline, and Strikeout

As the user selects the menu items, the status of the text box should change to reflect the chosen option, and the option on the menu should be checked. The program should begin with the first menu item of each menu checked and used as the default in the text box. Save the program as **Text Box Fonts**, and then test it and print it out.

5. You like the message board program you created in the previous chapter, but you decide you would like the names to be in a menu rather than displayed as **Option** buttons. Change the program so that there is one menu with seven options instead of seven **Option** buttons. Save the program as **Menu Messages**, test it, and print it out.

6. You learned how to use the Common Dialog Control in this chapter. You have decided to experiment with this control a bit. Create a program with a text box, and add the Common Dialog Control to the form. Add a menu with three options: one for the foreground color, one for the background color, and one for the font options. Use the Common Dialog Control commands to call up the Font dialog box and the Color dialog box (twice, once for each of the two menu items). Then use the values returned from the dialog boxes to set the appropriate properties in the text box. If you need any help using the Color dialog box, look it up in the Help system. Save the program as **Common Dialog Controls**, test it, and print it out.

7. You work for a company that creates music and sound effects for computers. You have been assigned the job of creating a program that can be used to sample the music and sound effects. Create a program with three menus: one for the sound effects, one for the music files, and a **File** menu with an **Exit** option and one to turn off the sound. You should use a separator bar between the items on the **File** menu. The menus should be control arrays with the menu name the name of the file without the pathname. When the menu item is selected, check it, and then use the name of the menu appended to the appropriate pathname to play the sound or music file. Save the program as **Sound Menus**. Test it and then print it out.

8. You like the message board program you created in the previous chapter, but you decide you would like the names to be displayed on buttons rather than as **Option** buttons. Change the program so that there are seven buttons instead of seven **Option** buttons. Save the program as **Button Messages**. Test it and then print it out.

9. You work for a company that creates sound effects for computers. You have been assigned the job of creating a program that can be used to sample the sound effects. Create a program with a series of buttons to play the sounds. You will need to add a **File** menu with an **Exit** option and one to turn off the sound. You should use a separator bar between the items on the **File** menu. The name of the sound file should be displayed on the button, and when the button is selected, use the name on the button appended to the appropriate pathname to play the sound file. Save the program as **Sound Buttons**. Test it and then print it out.

10. You work for a company that creates short animation files for computers. You have been assigned the job of creating a program that can be used to sample the animation files. Create a program with a series of buttons to play animations. You will need to add a **File** menu with an **Exit** option and one to turn off the animation. You should use a separator bar between the items on the **File** menu. The name of the animation file should be displayed on the button, and when the button is selected, use the name on the

button appended to the appropriate pathname to play the animation file. Save the program as **Animation Buttons**. Test it and then print it out.

11. You work for a company that creates short animation files for computers. You have been assigned the job of creating a program that can be used to sample the animation files. Create a program with a control array of menu items labeled with the animation file name. The menu item should be checked while the animation plays and should be unchecked when it is finished or is stopped. The Multimedia Control has a **Done** event that is executed when the animation file is finished. You will need to add a **File** menu with an **Exit** option and one to turn off the animation. You should use a separator bar between the items on the **File** menu. When the menu item for an animation file is selected, use the name of the menu appended to the appropriate pathname to play the animation file. Save the program as **Animation Menu**. Test it and then print it out.

12. You work for a company that creates music and sound effects for computers. You have been assigned the job of creating a program that can be used to sample the music and sound effects. You decide to write a program that will read the filenames from the disk and display each of the names in one of two menus. If the file is a sound file, it should be put in a **Sounds** menu, and the music files should be put in a **Music** menu. There should also be a **File** menu with an **Exit** option and one to turn off the sound or music. You should use a separator bar between the items on the **File** menu. The menus should be control arrays with the menu name the name of the file without the pathname. When the menu item is selected, check it, and then use the name of the menu item appended to the appropriate pathname to play the sound or music file. When the file is finished playing, you should uncheck the menu item. The Multimedia Control has an event called **Done** that is executed when the file being played finishes.

This program will require you to read the directory of the folder to get each of the filenames to be displayed and played. This will require you to use a new statement.

To read the directory of a folder, you need to use the **Dir** function, which has the format

```
Dir[(pathname[, attributes])]
```

Here, **pathname** refers to the pathname where the file is to be found, along with the type of file you are looking for. For example, the WAV files you want to play are probably found in the **C:\Windows\Media** folder, so this would be the first part of the pathname. But you also need to specify the type of file. This is done with a specification like **"*.WAV"**. Put together, the pathname would be **C:\Windows\Media*.WAV**. In this case, however, we want to imput all the file types, so the specification would be *.* instead of *.WAV. Then you will need to use an If Test to determine the type of file and the menu in which the file name belongs.

The attributes in the function indicate the type of element for which you are looking. In this case you want the directory of a folder, which is a value of 16. This can also be specified by using a predefined Visual Basic variable called **vbDirectory**. When this is done, the entire function looks like

```
Dir ("C:\Windows\Media\*.*", vbDirectory)
```

This being a function, Visual Basic executes the command and then returns something to the program. In this case, it returns the name of the file that is found.

This format of the command is the one to be used for reading the first file in the folder. To read subsequent ones, you use only the Dir function by itself. You should use the entire command before a loop that will be used to read the rest of the file names into the program. You should make the loop end when the result of the Dir function is null (empty), which means there are no more file names that match the criteria of the Dir function.

To add menu items in code, you need to begin with a control array of menu items with only one entry. You can assign the caption of that entry before the loop. Then you can add new menu items in the loop (items 2 and so on) using the **Load** method, as in

```
Load mnuFile_Array(intCounter)
```

This will create the menu item. After this, you need a statement to put the file name in the menu caption.

Add to this all the rest of the statements needed to play a file in the menu item Click event, along with the appropriate code for the menu items on the **File** menu, and your program should be ready. Save the program as **Menu and File Sounds** and thoroughly test it. When you are satisfied, print all the elements.

7

Using Dialog Boxes and Multiple Forms

7.1　Chapter Objectives

After finishing this chapter you will be able to:

- Demonstrate how to use the InputBox function.
- Demonstrate how to add more forms to a project and how to load and unload the extra forms in the application.
- Demonstrate how to use list and combo boxes.
- Demonstrate how to use scroll bars.

7.2　Introduction

We learned in a previous chapter the usefulness of the MsgBox function for displaying message boxes to prompt or warn the user. There are many other uses for additional windows in a program besides just displaying messages. The Common Dialog Control advances program capabilities, but only in a limited way. We need to be able to load additional forms in our programs to input additional data from the user or simply to give our programs more information.

In this chapter we will learn how to add more forms to our applications. Along the way, we will look at several new properties and Toolbox tools that can prove useful for working with such windows.

We begin, as usual, with a brief look at the features we will be adding to the PIM program.

7.3   Looking at the PIM

We added menus to the PIM in Chapter 6. In this chapter we will add a few more functions to the menu; most of them load additional forms.

1. Launch Visual Basic and Windows Explorer.

2. Copy the folders for Chapters 7 through 9 (Ch-7 through Ch-9) from wherever they are located on your system onto a blank disk. This disk will be your new work disk. Leave this disk in the disk drive.

3. Run the PIM program from the Ch-7 folder. The new version of the program has the new **Controls** menu shown in Figure 7.1.

4. Pull down the **Controls** menu to see the menu shown in Figure 7.1.

   The first option is to change the size of the workspace.

5. Click **Change Workspace Size...** to see the dialog box shown in Figure 7.2.

   Not only did you call up the form you see, but the PIM moved to the upper left corner of the desktop. This is done so that as you resize the form, you will have the entire desktop to work with. Though this dialog box is labeled **Change Workspace Size...**, it would make little sense to change the workspace size without also changing the size of the form

FIGURE 7.1
The new **Controls** menu.

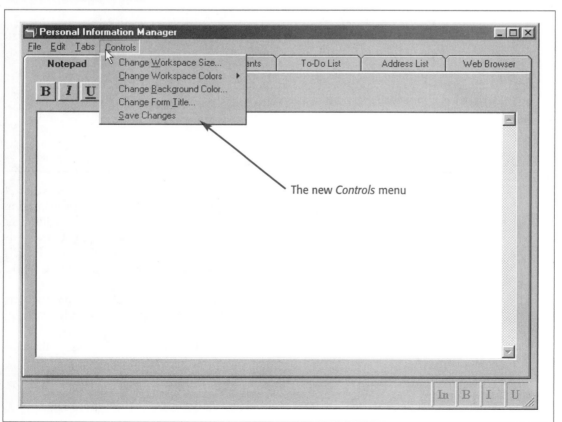

The new *Controls* menu

FIGURE 7.2
The dialog box that will allow you to change the size of your form.

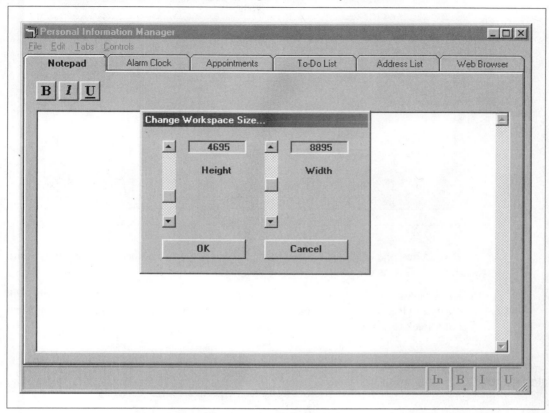

and related objects. Thus, as you change the size of the workspace, many of the program elements will change in size as well.

You adjust the width and height of the form using the scroll bars.

6. Click the **Height** scroll bar twice above the scroll box. Click the **Width** scroll bar once above the scroll box. This will change the width and height of the form to what you see in Figure 7.3.

These scroll bars function just like other scroll bars. As you have just seen, they can be adjusted by clicking the scroll bar. They can also be adjusted by clicking the up or down arrow or by dragging the scroll box.

7. Practice adjusting the scroll bar. As you do that, the size of the form will change.

If you were to click the **OK** button, the form would be left the size you set it. By clicking the **Cancel** button, you cancel all the changes you have made.

8. Click the **Cancel** button, and the form reverts to the size it was.

There are three menu items that can be used for color changes. The **Change Workspace Colors** submenu has two options, and then there is the **Change Background Color...** option. This option uses the Common Dialog Control Color dialog box to change the background color of the workspace. The other two options call up custom dialog boxes that you will construct. Let's look at the **Change Background Color...** option first.

9. Select the **Controls** menu, and select the **Change Background Color...** option to see the dialog box shown in Figure 7.4.

FIGURE 7.3
The form with the
height and width
changed.

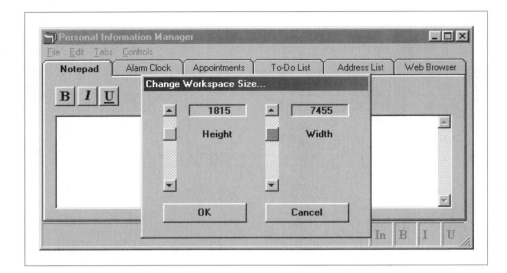

If you click one of the colors and then click the **OK** button, the dialog box will return the selected color as the result of the function call.

10. Click one of the colors and then click the **OK** button. The workspace background will change to the color you selected. Use the same dialog box to change the background color back to white.

FIGURE 7.4
The Common Dialog Control Color dialog box.

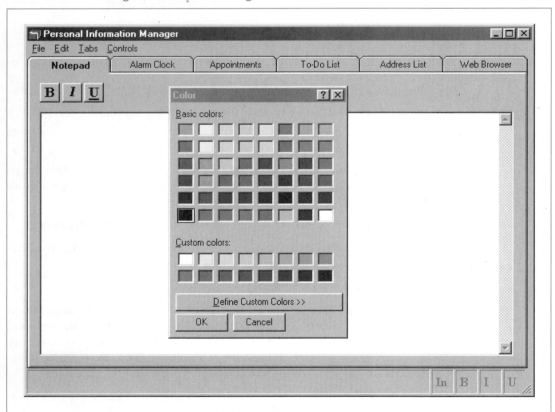

The problem with this dialog box is that you can change only one color at a time. What if you wanted to change the foreground color and the background color of an object such as the workspace text box? You would have to call the Color dialog box twice, once for the foreground color and once for the background color. A better solution is to create your own color form where the background and foreground colors can be changed. We've done this with both of the **Change Workspace Colors** submenu options.

11. Pull down the **Change Workspace Colors** submenu of the **Controls** menu, and select the **By Color Selection Boxes** option to see the dialog box shown in Figure 7.5.

Using this dialog box, you can change the foreground color by clicking a color box and the background color by right-clicking a color box.

12. Click the Red color box and then right-click the Yellow color box. The small box under the color selection boxes will display the colors you have chosen.

13. Click the **OK** button to exit the dialog box and change the colors of the text box.

14. Key **This is a sample** in the text box. The background of the text box is yellow and the text is red. Use the same dialog box and change the background color back to white.

This dialog box is only one of many ways to change both colors. The other option of the **Change Workspace Colors** submenu provides another way, using lists.

15. Pull down the **Change Workspace Colors** submenu of the **Controls** menu, and select the **By Lists of Colors** option to see the dialog box shown in Figure 7.6.

FIGURE 7.5

The Change Workspace Colors… dialog box that allows the colors to be changed with color selection boxes.

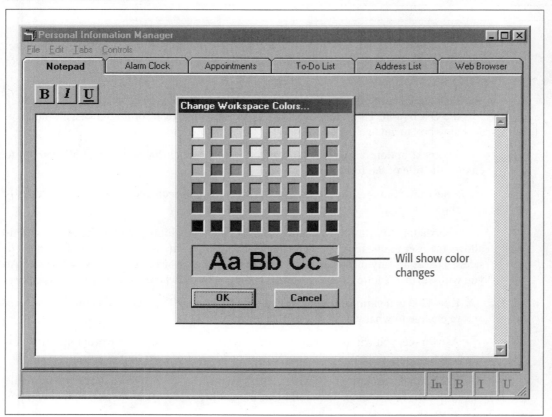

FIGURE 7.6
The dialog box to change the workspace colors with list selections.

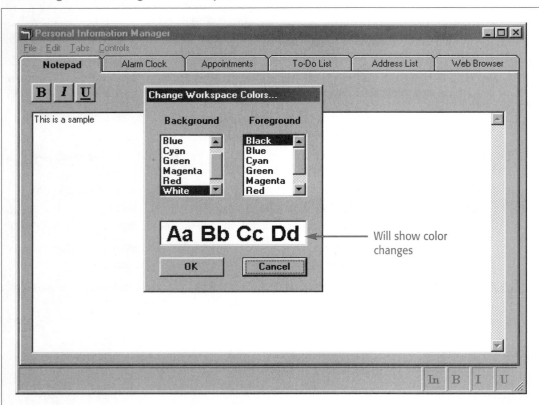

This dialog box has two lists, one for the background color and another for the foreground color. The form has the same box as the previous dialog box to illustrate your color
choices.

16. Pick Green as the Background color and Black as the Foreground color, and then click
    the **OK** button. The colors of your text box will change accordingly. Use the same di-
    alog box to change the background color back to white.

    The next option on the **Controls** menu is for a small dialog box that allows you to
    change the title of the form.

17. Select the **Change Form Title...** option on the **Controls** menu to see the dialog box
    shown in Figure 7.7.

    This dialog box shows the caption of the title already highlighted in the text box. This
    allows the user to change the text box entry by keying something new without the need to
    select what is already in the text box. Note that this dialog box does not have a title bar. As
    you will see, this feature can be turned off on dialog boxes where it is not deemed necessary.

18. Key **This is a sample title** and click the **OK** button. This causes the title of the form
    to change to what was keyed in the text box.

    As you see, you will be adding a lot of different dialog boxes to the program and learn-
    ing how to use other tools such as scroll bars and lists. Let's get to it.

19. Play with the program for a while, trying all the new options until you are comfortable
    with their functioning. Then minimize the sample PIM so you can refer to it later if you
    wish.

FIGURE 7.7

The dialog box to change the form title.

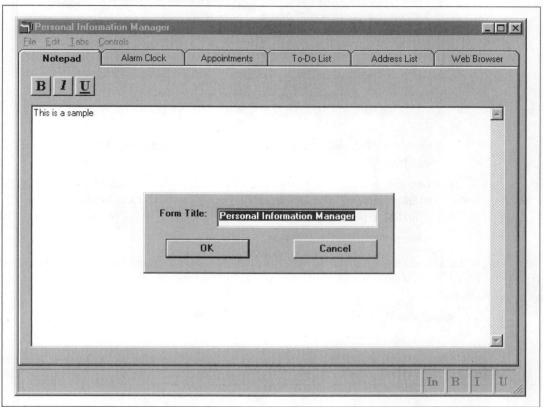

7.4   Using MsgBox to Display a Message

We introduced the **MsgBox** function in a previous chapter, so you are already familiar with it. Because we are dealing with forms and dialog boxes in this chapter, a brief review of the MsgBox function seems to be in order.

Though functional and easy to use, MsgBox is rather limited. It will only display a message and let the user respond through the use of buttons. Many times, that's all that is needed. Such windows are perfect for warning messages and the like.

Many programs display a warning message when you save a file if the file is already on the disk. It warns you that the file already exists and that saving the file again will erase the original copy of the file. We will add a message box with this type of warning to the **Save File** option on the **File** menu.

1. Load the **PIM** application from your Chapter 6 folder, and save the form and project in your Chapter 7 folder.

2. Open the code window for the **Save File** option, and key the following statements:

```
Dim intReturned As Integer
intReturned = MsgBox("File already exists. Saving the file will
↳ overwrite the original. Is this what you wish?", vbYesNo +
↳ vbExclamation + vbDefaultButton2, "Save File Warning")
```

FIGURE 7.8
The message box for
the Save File option.

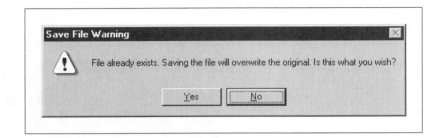

3. Run the application, pull down the **File** menu, and select the **Save File** option to see the message box shown in Figure 7.8.

The box has the **Yes** and **No** buttons (**vbYesNo**), with the initial focus on the **No** button (**vbDefaultButton2**), and the exclamation sign icon (**vbExclamation**).

After the user responded to the message box, we would use an If Test like the following:

```
If intReturned = vbYes Then
```

If the user selected the **Yes** button, the procedure would execute and the file would be saved. If **No** were selected, the If Test would fail and the routine to save the file would be skipped.

4. Respond to the prompt and then exit the program.

7.5   The InputBox Function

Using the previously discussed type of message box in your applications can make them look more professional, but the user is limited in the amount of input that can be sent to the program. The selection of a button doesn't help much if a textual response, such as a file-name, from the user is needed. In such cases we will need to use a second form.

There are many reasons why you might need to get information from the user. We will add an information box to our current application by using the **Open File...** option. When the user wants to open a file, the name of the desired file must be entered. For this we will use the **InputBox** function, which has the format

```
InputBox (prompt [, dialog box title] [, default] [, xpos] [,ypos] )
```

The prompt is the text that shows up in the main part of the dialog box, and the dialog box title is just that, the title of the dialog box. If you have a value you want the dialog box to display for the user to accept as the default, you can specify that as the third parameter. The fourth and fifth parameters are used to specify the X (horizontal) and Y (vertical) positions of the dialog box on the desktop. If these are omitted, the dialog box is centered and the top is placed about one third of the way down on the desktop.

This is a function and will return a string value. This means that you must use a statement like

```
strFilename = InputBox("Please input the pathname and the name of
⤷the file you want to open.", "Filename Input")
```

1. Open the code window for the **Open File...** option. Key the foregoing statement and declare the strFilename variable.

2. Run the program and select the **Open File...** option to see the dialog box shown in Figure 7.9.

FIGURE 7.9

The input box for the *Open File...* option.

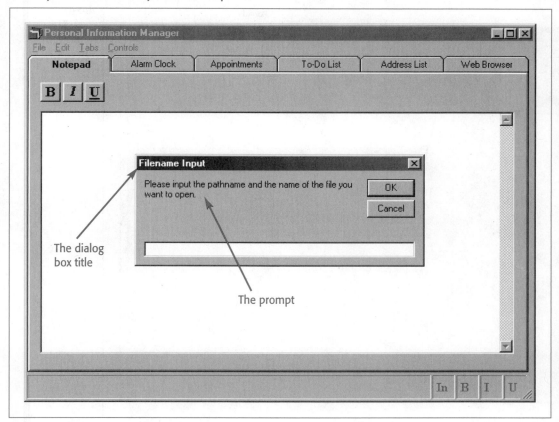

The result of the function, strFilename, contains the text that the user entered into the entry box in the input box window. If the user clicks the **Cancel** button instead of the **OK** button, the function returns an empty string. You can test the result for an empty string to be sure the user entered something into the dialog box.

When entering a filename, you use strFilename in an appropriate statement to open the file and load the data into the text box. We are not yet ready for this functionality, but we can use the data returned from the function.

A common technique, which we'll use, when loading files into a text editor is to change the title of the program to display the name of the program and the name of the open file.

3. Respond to the dialog box and then exit the program.

4. Add the following statement after the InputBox function statement:

```
frmPIM.Caption = frmPIM.Caption & " - " & strFilename
```

This will take the caption of the form and append the input filename to it.

5. Run the program and select the **Open File...** option from the **File** menu.

6. Key **Sample Filename** into the entry box in the dialog box and then click the **OK** button.

Now you will see that the title of the PIM form has become **Personal Information Manager - Sample Filename** as shown in Figure 7.10.

FIGURE 7.10

The changed title on the title bar.

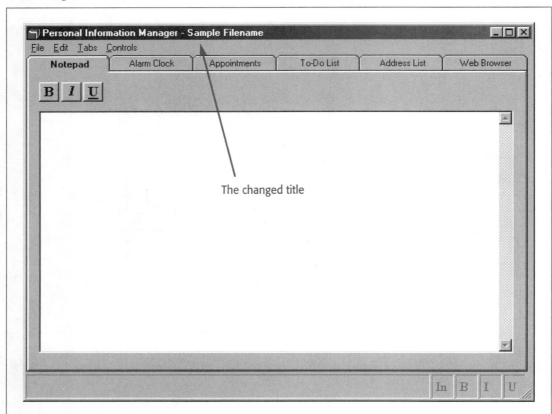

The changed title

The InputBox function is useful and easy to use, but just like the MsgBox function, it is limited. It allows only one input field. You cannot use scroll bars or lists as we did on the forms called up by the sample PIM program you ran at the beginning of this chapter. We simply need more functionality. One option is creating your own input box by using a second form. We will examine this possibility next.

7. Exit the program.

7.6   Adding a Second Form to Your Application

Adding more forms to our application is no more difficult than adding more controls to a form. We simply select the **New Form** option from the **File** menu.

1. Pull down the Visual Basic Project menu, and select Add Form or use the **New Form** button ( ).

Now you see a dialog box asking you to choose the type of form you want. You want just the ordinary type of form, which is the default type.

2. Click the **Open** button to add the form to your project.

Instantly, a second form appears in the desktop workspace as shown in Figure 7.11. Note that the caption of this form is Form1. The name of the form (the name, not the cap-

FIGURE 7.11
The second form that we added to the project.

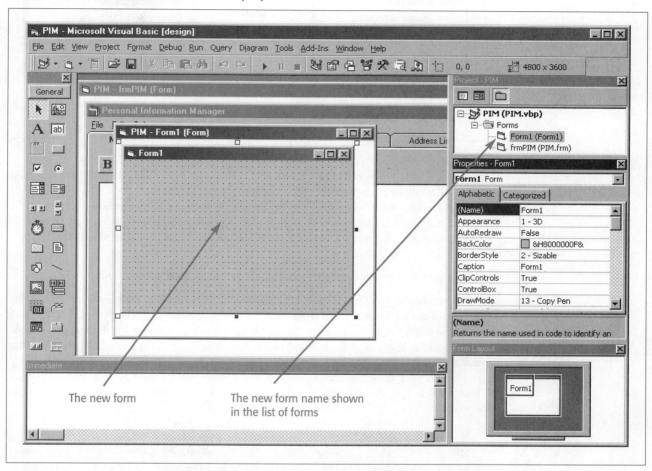

The new form

The new form name shown
in the list of forms

tion) is also Form1. Because this is the second form in the project, if you had not renamed the original Form1, this form would have been named Form2, but as long as each new form is renamed, the next form will always be called Form1.

> **HINT:** You can change the workspace so that it displays both the form and the code window by clicking the Restore button for the form, which is below the Restore button of the Visual Basic window.

In the Form Layout window (lower right corner), you can see that a second form has been added to the project. This form can be positioned on the desktop, just as the first form can, by simply moving it around in the Form Layout window as illustrated in Figure 7.12.

3. Position the mouse pointer over the new form on the display. The shape changes to a four-sided pointer as indicated in Figure 7.12.

4. Drag the new form's indicated shape so it is more toward the center of the screen. This will be the new position of the form.

You can always change the position of one of the program forms by simply dragging it as you have just done. Secondary forms should generally appear in the center of the original form, though there are situations in which this is not the best position. If a form is

FIGURE 7.12
Illustration of adjusting a forms position in the Form Layout window.

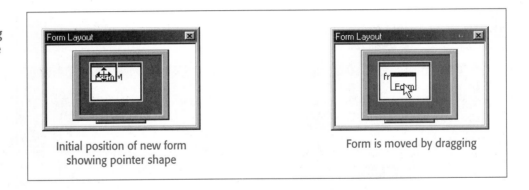

Initial position of new form showing pointer shape

Form is moved by dragging

related to a pull-down button, for example, perhaps it would be better if the new form appeared directly beneath the pull-down button.

As you saw when you looked at the sample PIM, one of the features we want to add to the program is a dialog box with which the user can change the name of the form title. That's how we are going to use this form. We will give the form the name **frmChange_Title**.

5. Select the Name property and change the value to **frmChange_Title**.

Because there are two forms, which are essentially separate windows, you can switch between them just as with other windows, by clicking the one you want active. Alternatively, you can switch forms through the Project Window, which you can see docked in the upper right corner of the Visual Basic window (indicated in Figure 7.11). Note that the new form now shows the new form name that we gave it and that the other form is called frmPIM.

To switch forms, you can highlight the one you want and then press **Enter**, or you can double-click it in the Project window. Then the selected form will appear on top in the workspace.

> **HINT:** If you have a form that was created in another program and that you now wish to use in your current program, it can be added using the **Add File** option of the **Project** menu.

Displaying a Form

When you are working with multiple forms, the first thing you need to know is how to switch between forms when the application is running. There are four methods (remember that a method is a runtime-only property) for this purpose: two to display the form and two to remove the form from the desktop.

- **Show** loads and displays the named form.
- **Load** puts the form into memory without displaying it.
- **Hide** removes the form from the desktop and leaves it in memory.
- **Unload** removes the form from the desktop and from memory.

When you display the form, Show is generally used, though Load is available for specialized purposes. If you use Hide to remove the form from the desktop, many of the elements of the form that have been changed will remain changed when the form is put back on the desktop. If you Unload the form, the next time it is brought to the desktop will be like the first and any changes to the forms settings, such as the width or height, will revert to the original settings.

We are going to add a number of new forms to the PIM program. Probably the easiest one to work with is the one to change the title of the form. This is called up with the **Change Form Title...** option of the **Controls** menu. To add this form, we need to add the **Controls** menu, and if we do that, we might as well add all the menu options at the same time.

1. Open the Menu Editor dialog box, go to the end of the menu system, and add a new menu called **&Controls** with the control name **mnuControl_Menu**.

2. Add menu items under the Controls menu as follows:

   a. **Change &Workspace Size...** with the control name **mnuChange_Size**.

   b. **&Change Workspace Colors** with the control name **mnuChange_Colors**.

   c. **By Color &Selection Boxes...** with the control name **mnuColor_Selection,** with an extra indent to make it an item under **Change Workspace Colors**.

   d. **By &List of Colors...** with the control name **mnuColor_Lists** as an item under **Change Workspace Colors**.

   e. **Change &Background Color...** with the control name **mnuChange_Background_Color**. Bring this item back a level so that it is a menu item under the **Controls** menu. The next two will stay on this level.

   f. **Change Form &Title...** with the control name **mnuChange_Title**.

   g. **&Save Changes** with the control name **mnuSave_Changes**.

The last menu item will let users save the changes they have made to the form through the use of the other menu items. This information is saved to a file on the disk so that the next time the PIM is run, the form appears as it was set up by the user. We don't know how to do this yet, but we'll learn in a future chapter.

As mentioned, to display the form on the desktop, you need to use the Show method. The format of the method is

```
Form name.Show Style
```

Style refers to whether the from will be modal or not. We talked about modality earlier when we discussed the MsgBox function. If we specify the Style as 1 or use the predefined constant for 1, **vbModal**, the form will be program modal. This means the user will not be able to do anything in the program until the form is responded to in some way. Other programs can continue to be used. Program modality affects only the program where the form is modal. If the Style is left off or set at 0 or **vbModaless**, the form is not modal and the user can click a button or select a menu item while the form is on the desktop.

When we use the Show method, the statement to show the **frmChange_Title** form is

```
frmChange_Title.Show vbModal
```

Note that we made the form modal.

3. Switch to the code window for the **Change Form Title...** option of the **Controls** menu, and add the foregoing statement to your code.

4. Run the program, and select the **Load File** option from the **File** menu, and the program will display your new form.

This form has the control box and **Minimize** and **Maximize** buttons on it. Often you will not want the user to be able to minimize or maximize the dialog boxes in your programs. Because that is the case for this form, we want to remove these options. This is easy to do. All you need to do is delete the value of the caption and change the **ControlBox** property to False.

5. Exit the program. Change to the new form. Delete the value of the **Caption** property of the frmChange_Title form, and change the value of the ControlBox property to False.

As you do these things, you will see that the title bar of the form disappears. Now that the window itself is set up, it is time to add the controls to the form.

6. Add controls to the form to make it look like the one in Figure 7.13 with the following considerations:

a. The control name for the text box is **txtTitle_Input**. Be sure this control has the TabIndex property set to 0 so that it will have the initial focus when the form is loaded.

b. The control names for the buttons are **cmdOK** and **cmdCancel**.

> **HINT:** When you start working with many forms, the Visual Basic workspace can become crowded. It is sometimes easier to work in the one or two windows necessary. To accomplish this, you can close or minimize the ones you do not need at the present time. You can also open them again when you need them.

Adding Code for and to a Second Form

Adding code to a second form is no different from adding code to the first form. All the code in the controls of the form is automatically local to the form. You can have cmdOK buttons on ten different forms if you need to, and each will be attached only to the form it is on. The Click event code behind each of those buttons will be executed by the user only when the button on that form is clicked. That doesn't mean you can't reference something on frmChange_Title from code for a control on frmPIM or reference a control on frmPIM from event code on the frmChange_Title form. To do that, all you do is use the name of the form as a qualifier in front of the control or property. A sample would be

```
txtTitle_Input.Text = frmPIM.Caption
```

This statement assigns the Caption property on the frmPIM form to the Text property of txtTitle_Input on the current form, which is frmChange_Title, using the form and object names in our current program.

We are actually going to use this statement in our code. Because this form allows the user to change the form title, it makes sense to show the current title as the initial entry in the text box. If the user has changed the title previously but misspelled it, there is no reason to require the entire title to be keyed again. If we put the current title in the text box, the user can simply make a correction to what was already keyed. And so we will want to determine what the current caption of the form is and display it in the text box.

We can do this from two different places in the program. We can put the caption of the frmPIM form into the text box on the frmChange_Title form by using the following statement in the menu item Click event:

```
frmChange_Title.txtTitle_Input = frmPIM.Caption
```

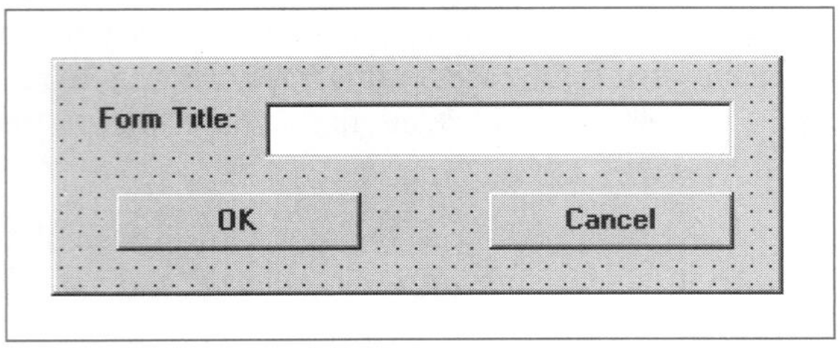

FIGURE 7.13
The second form with the controls added.

which could also be used as

```
frmChange_Title.txtTitle_Input = Caption
```

because the frmPIM form is the default reference.

If we want to put the code in the event code on the frmChange_Title form instead, we can still use the first statement because it specifically mentions each of the forms:

```
frmChange_Title.txtTitle_Input = frmPIM.Caption
```

or we could remove the reference to the frmChange_Title form to make the statement

```
txtTitle_Input = frmPIM.Caption
```

because the frmChange_Title form is now the default form.

If we are going to use the code in the menu item Click event of the frmPIM form, we need to be sure we use the statement before the Show statement. If the form is to be modal, as it is in our Show statement, code execution in the application switches to the new form, and any code that follows the Show statement waits to be executed until after the user exits the new form.

If the form is not modal, the code in the procedure that Shows the new form runs to completion before execution switches to the new form. The Show statement we specified earlier is

```
frmChange_Title.Show vbModal
```

If we were to put the assignment statement after the Show statement, as in

```
frmChange_Title.Show vbModal
frmChange_Title.txtTitle_Input = frmPIM.Caption
```

then the assignment statement would not be executed until after the user exited the frmChange_Title form. If the Show statement were not modal, as in

```
frmChange_Title.Show
frmChange_Title.txtTitle_Input = frmPIM.Caption
```

then execution of the assignment statement and of any other statements in the procedure would be completed before execution switched to the frmChange_Title form, and the caption would be displayed in the text box.

If you want the form to be modal and need to make such an assignment, the assignment statement must be put before the Show statement:

```
frmChange_Title.txtTitle_Input = frmPIM.Caption
frmChange_Title.Show vbModal
```

Now it doesn't matter whether the form is modal or not, because the assignment statement is executed before the Show statement.

This assignment statement is actually not sufficient for our program. If you recall, we added an InputBox statement to add the name of the current file to the end of the Caption on the title bar with the statement

```
frmPIM.Caption = frmPIM.Caption & " - " & strFilename
```

Therefore, if we are going to display the caption, we need to remove the filename from it first. This will require an InStr statement like

```
intSearch = InStr(frmPIM.Caption, " -")
```

which searches for the space and dash we put between the caption and the filename.

1. Open the code window for the **Change Form Title** menu option. Key this statement into the procedure.

Then we will need to make sure there is a filename by seeing whether intSearch was assigned a value (remember that intSearch will return zero if it doesn't find the dash):

```
If intSearch = 0 Then
```

2. Key this statement into the procedure.

If the dash is not found, we can assign the entire caption to the text box:

```
    frmChange_Title.txtTitle_Input.Text = frmPIM.Caption
Else
```

3. Key these statements into the procedure.

If the dash is found, we need to assign just the caption. Because intSearch will point to the space, if we assign to the position in the caption one less than intSearch, we will get only the caption without a trailing space. Given this, the end of the If statement becomes

```
    frmChange_Title.txtTitle_Input.Text = Left(frmPIM.Caption,
      ↳ intSearch - 1)
End If
```

4. Key these statements.

This makes the code for the mnuChange_Title_Click event procedure as you see in Figure 7.14.

If we are going to change the title of the main window, we generally want to erase what is in the entry box before we begin to key the new information. This is done quickly by highlighting the current contents of the box. Then when we key the new information, it replaces the text that was already there. We can make this easier for the user by automatically

FIGURE 7.14

The entire mnuChange_Title_Click event procedure.

```
Private Sub mnuChange_Title_Click()
    Dim intSearch As Integer

' Search for the dash on the Caption

    intSearch = InStr(frmPIM.Caption, " -")

' Assign the caption to the Text Box on the Change Title form

    If intSearch = 0 Then
        frmChange_Title.txtTitle_Input = frmPIM.Caption
    Else
        frmChange_Title.txtTitle_Input = Left(frmPIM.Caption, intSearch - 1)
    End If

' Show the form

    frmChange_Title.Show vbModal
End Sub
```

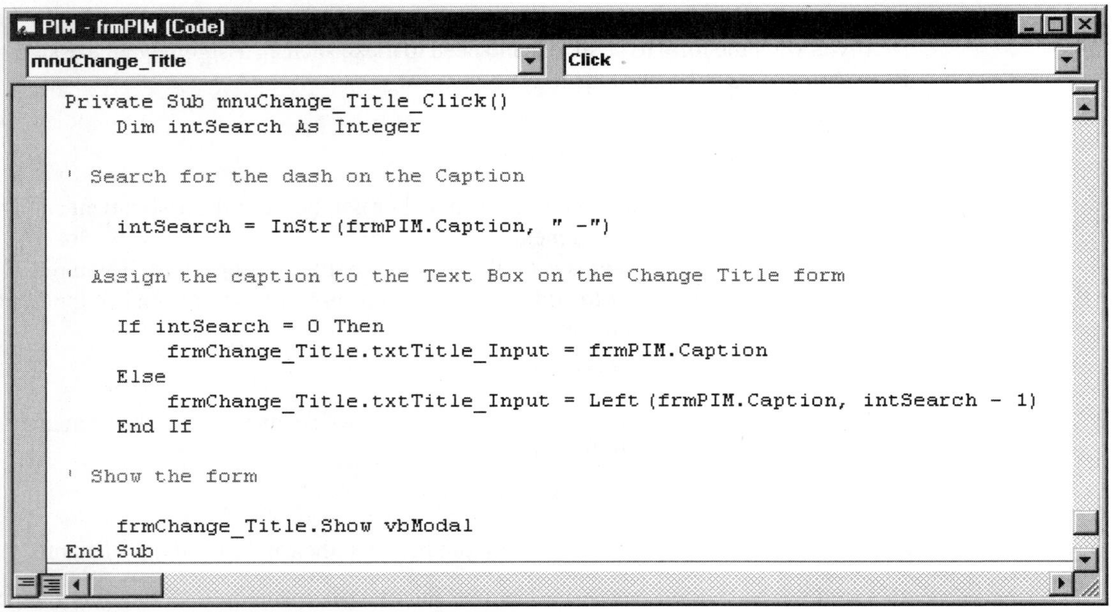

highlighting the initial text using the SelStart and SelLength methods we learned about in an earlier chapter. The code we need is

```
txtTitle_Input.SelStart = 0
txtTitle_Input.SelLength = Len(txtTitle_Input.Text)
```

The first statement sets the starting point of the selection at the beginning of the text, and the next statement sets the length of the selection to the length of what is already in the text box. We didn't qualify the text box references because we are going to put this code in the Form_Activate procedure of the frmChange_Title form, which is executed whenever the form is selected rather than just when it is loaded. We could have added it to the code of the mnuChange_Title_Click event procedure, but this code doesn't make reference to the frmPIM form, so it makes more sense to put it on the form with which it deals.

This code needs to be put in the Form_Activate procedure instead of the Form_Load procedure, because we are going to hide the form rather than unload it. We don't want to unload the form, because if we do, we won't be able to read the Text property of the text box. You cannot use any of the object properties from a form that has been unloaded. Instead, if you want to use the properties without the user's being able to see the form, the form must be hidden. If we are going to use the Text property to change the title of the frmPIM form, we need to be able to assign the Text property to the Caption property of the frmPIM form.

5. Switch to the frmChange_Title form. Open the code window for the Form_Activate procedure, and key the two previous statements.

We mentioned that when a form is hidden rather than unloaded, and then redisplayed, all the objects on the form will be in precisely the same state they were in when the form was hidden. This means that after the user has selected either the **OK** or the **Cancel** button to exit the form, that button will retain the focus even while the form is hidden. But we want the text box to have the focus every time the form is displayed, so we need to add another statement to the Form_Activate procedure before we are finished with it.

6. Add a Setfocus statement after the other two statements in this procedure.

> **HINT:** The Setfocus method will not work on any objects on a form if the statement is placed in the Form_Load procedure, because until the Form_Load procedure is complete, the form is not displayed, and you cannot set the focus to any objects on that form. If you try to, you will get an error. In addition, if the form is hidden and not unloaded, the Form_Load event is not triggered when the form is shown. In such cases the Form_Activate event must be used. It is triggered when the form is activated or switched to, not when it is loaded.

Because we assigned the caption to the text box in the Click event of the menu, we will also do the reverse. We will use the menu item Click event to assign the text box entry to the caption. That means that the **OK** and **Cancel** buttons on the frmChange_Title form don't require much code.

The only statement we need for the **OK** button is the Hide statement.

7. Open the code window for the **OK** button and add the following Hide statement:

```
frmChange_Title.Hide
```

The **Cancel** button requires an additional statement. When users click the **Cancel** button, we can assume they don't want to change the title to whatever they have keyed into the text box. To make sure that this is the case, we will delete whatever is in the text box. Then, in the menu item click procedure, we will simply check to see whether there is anything in the text box. If there is, we change the caption; if there isn't, we don't.

8. Open the code window for the **Cancel** button, and key the following two statements:

```
txtTitle_Input.Text = ""
frmChange_Title.Hide
```

We aren't finished yet. We need to go back to the menu item click procedure to assign the text in the text box to the caption. We first need to verify that the user didn't click the **Cancel** button by checking to see if the text box has anything in it. This requires the statement

```
If frmChange_Title.txtTitle_Input.Text <> "" Then
```

Within this If Test we need to use an If Test similar to the one that we used to assign the caption to the text box:

```
If intSearch = 0 Then
    frmPIM.Caption = frmChange_Title.txtTitle_Input.Text
Else
    frmPIM.Caption = frmChange_Title.txtTitle_Input.Text &
    ↳Mid(frmPIM.Caption, intSearch)
End If
End If
```

Just as before, if there is no dash (we know this from the previously used Instr statement), we assign the text box to the caption without worrying about the filename. If there is a value in intSearch, we assign the text box text and append to that the rest of the caption from the point of the space in front of the dash.

9. Key the foregoing code into the mnuChange_Title_Click procedure after the Show statement.

This completes the code for the mnuChange_Title_Click event procedure as shown in Figure 7.15.

10. Run the application, select the **Open File...** option from the **File** menu. Key **Sample** as the filename and click the **OK** button. This will cause Sample to be displayed at the end of the title in the title bar.

11. Select the **Change Form Title...** option on the **Controls** menu, and note that the initial entry **Personal Information Manager** is highlighted. This is the caption of the title bar without the filename, just as we wanted.

12. Key **Practice** and select the **OK** button.

Now the PIM form will have Practice followed by the "Sample" filename as the window title, as shown in Figure 7.16.

13. Select the **Change Form Title...** option on the **Controls** menu again. This time the highlighted entry in the text box is Practice.

14. Key **This will not appear** as the caption, and click the **Cancel** button. The caption of the form does not change.

15. Practice with the program a bit more until you are certain it is working properly and then exit it.

Setting Up a Default Button

When using the dialog box you just created, the user will key the new title and then select the **OK** button. It might be nice to have the **OK** button already selected so that after

FIGURE 7.15
The completed code for the mnuChange_Title_Click event procedure.

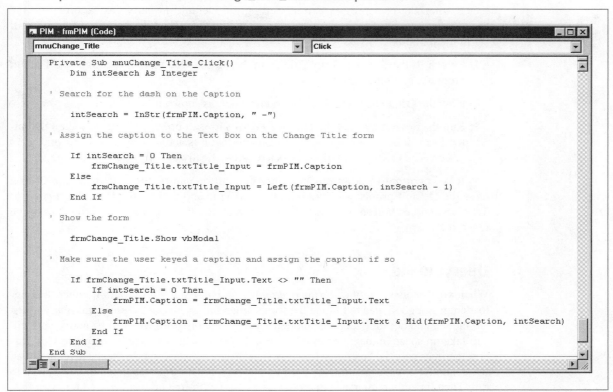

```
PIM - frmPIM (Code)

mnuChange_Title                              Click

    Private Sub mnuChange_Title_Click()
        Dim intSearch As Integer

    ' Search for the dash on the Caption

        intSearch = InStr(frmPIM.Caption, " -")

    ' Assign the caption to the Text Box on the Change Title form

        If intSearch = 0 Then
            frmChange_Title.txtTitle_Input = frmPIM.Caption
        Else
            frmChange_Title.txtTitle_Input = Left(frmPIM.Caption, intSearch - 1)
        End If

    ' Show the form

        frmChange_Title.Show vbModal

    ' Make sure the user keyed a caption and assign the caption if so

        If frmChange_Title.txtTitle_Input.Text <> "" Then
            If intSearch = 0 Then
                frmPIM.Caption = frmChange_Title.txtTitle_Input.Text
            Else
                frmPIM.Caption = frmChange_Title.txtTitle_Input.Text & Mid(frmPIM.Caption, intSearch)
            End If
        End If
    End Sub
```

FIGURE 7.16
The form, showing the changed title.

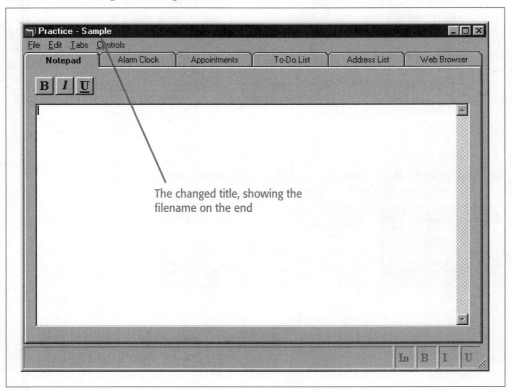

The changed title, showing the
filename on the end

keying the name, the user can just press **Enter** to select **OK**. This can be done with the **Default** property that each button has. When this property is set to True, the button is selected when the user presses **Enter**. Setting the Default property has no effect on the focus. That is, one of the buttons can be set as the default while the initial focus is still set in the text box.

1. Switch to the Change Form Title form, select the **OK** button, highlight the Default property, and set it to **True**.

   Now the **OK** button will have a darker border, as shown in Figure 7.17.

2. Run the program, select the **Change Form Title...** option, and note that the **OK** button has a dark border around it, suggesting that it is active. Key a new title and press **Enter**. The **OK** button will be selected automatically and the title will change.

It is important to point out that only one button can be the default button. If you have the Default property of one button set to True and you set the Default property to True on another button, the Default property on the first button will automatically be reset to False.

QueryUnload

When you are using a lot of forms that are being hidden in your program rather than unloaded, it is a good idea to unload the forms when the user exits the program. If any forms are hidden and not unloaded, the hidden forms of the program will still be active and will still take up space in the computer's memory, even though you won't be able to tell. This is sometimes called a "memory leak." If your programs cause such a "leak," eventually all the computer's resources may be used up and additional programs may not be allowed to run. Then the only recourse is to reboot the computer to free up this "wasted memory."

If the user exits the program using an exit button or an exit option on a menu, you can use the Click event to unload all the forms. If the user clicks the title bar **Close** button or uses the **Control** menu to exit the form, your Click event will not be executed. Visual Basic does, however, notify you in such situations. The **QueryUnload** event is executed when the user selects the title bar **Close** button or uses the **Control** menu to exit. If you want to query the user for verification of the intention to exit the program, this event is the place to do it. In this routine you can also close all the forms your program uses. There is no harm in unloading a form that has not been loaded, so your unload routine can unload all the forms without checking whether they have been loaded or not.

FIGURE 7.17
The difference between the look of the default button and that of an ordinary button.

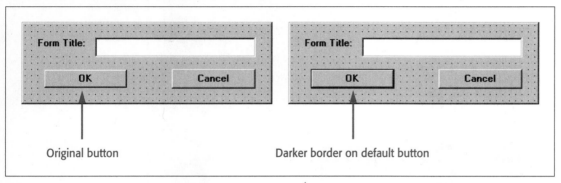

7.7   Adding New Forms in Your Designs

Now that we know how to add new forms to our programs, we should pause to look at how we would expand our design to include these new forms. Because the forms are called up (in this case, at least) by menu options, they should be shown under the menu selections. If you recall, in Chapter 6 we looked at the menu setup for the program, which was

```
Project PIM - frmPIM
    A. Menu Bar
        1. File
            a) Open File… (Ctrl-O)
               Unknown at this point
            b) Save File (Ctrl-S)
               Unknown at this point
            c) Save File As… (Ctrl-A)
               Unknown at this point
            d) Exit
               Exit the program
        2. Edit
            a) Cut (Ctrl-X)
               Copy the highlighted text to the clipboard and erase
               ⤷ it from the workspace
            b) Copy (Ctrl-C)
               Copy the highlighted text to the clipboard without
               ⤷ erasing it from the workspace
            c) Paste (Ctrl-V)
               Copy the text from the clipboard into the workspace
               ⤷ at the current position
            d) Clear All (Ctrl-R)
               Erase the workspace
```

We weren't sure at the time what to do for the **File** menu options (except Exit, of course), so we simply said they were "Unknown at this point." Well, now we know what to put there and on one of the options of the **Controls** menu. Furthermore, we added to the design in the last chapter before we put the **Tabs** menu in the program, so we need to add that to the design too. Thus, the new design would look like the following:

```
Project PIM - frmPIM
    A. Menu Bar
        1. File
            a) Open File… (Ctrl-O)
               Show InputBox to input Filename
               Display Filename as part of caption
            b) Save File (Ctrl-S)
               Unknown at this point
            c) Save File As… (Ctrl-A)
               Unknown at this point
            d) Exit
               Exit the program
        2. Edit
            a) Cut (Ctrl-X)
               Copy the highlighted text to the clipboard and erase
               ⤷ it from the workspace
            b) Copy (Ctrl-C)
               Copy the highlighted text to the clipboard without
               ⤷ erasing it from the workspace
            c) Paste (Ctrl-V)
```

```
                              Copy the text from the clipboard into the workspace
                            ↳ at the current position
                      d)  Clear All (Ctrl-R)
                          Erase the workspace
               3.  Tabs
                   Switch tabs on the Tabbed Control, checking and
                 ↳ unchecking menu items
               4.  Controls
                      a)  Change Workspace Size…
                          Unknown at this point
                      b)  Change Workspace Colors (submenu)
                          1)  By Color Selection Boxes…
                              Unknown at this point
                          2)  By List of Colors…
                              Unknown at this point
                      c)  Change Background Color…
                          Unknown at this point
                      d)  Change Form Title…
                          1)  Display form to let user enter new form title
                              a)  Text box used to input new form title
                              b)  OK button
                                  1)  Hide form
                              c)  Cancel button
                                  1)  Delete contents of text box
                                  2)  Hide form
                          2)  Use new title to change caption of PIM form
                      e)  Save Changes
                          Unknown at this point
```

Now we are ready to add more forms to the program and fill in many of the "Unknown" portions of the design.

7.8   Adding Adjustment Dialog Boxes to the Notepad

A nice feature that is available in many programs like the PIM is a way to control the look of the workspace. We have already added a menu that allows the user to do just that in the PIM program, and you saw how these options function when you experimented with the completed program at the beginning of this chapter. Now it is time to work with some more of those functions by adding more dialog boxes to the program.

Because we have already created the dialog box to let the user change the title of the form, we will move on to the option to let the user change the workspace size.

Changing the Workspace Size

Visual Basic automatically allows a window such as a form to be resized by moving the window border, but that doesn't change the size of the workspace. That is not under Visual Basic's direct control, but it is under the programmer's control by virtue of the Height and Width properties.

We worked hard to get our notepad workspace, Tabbed Control, and form border spaced properly, so we don't want them to be adjusted incorrectly if we change the size of the workspace. If we are going to adjust the size of the workspace in the application, we will need to adjust the size of the form and the other elements at the same time and maintain the same relative spacing. We need to know the current size of each in order to keep the same relative spacing when we change the size of the workspace. The height and width of the workspace (txtNotepad), Tabbed Control (tabPIM), status bar (stsPIM_Status), and form (frmPIM) in the figures are given (in twips) in Table 7.1.

We listed the height of the status bar as "not needed" because we are not going to change it. Changing the height of the status bar would probably require us to change the size of the font and might end up making it difficult to read. Besides, most applications don't adjust the height of their status bars but only the width, which we will do in our application.

If your screen resolution is 640 by 480, the given dimensions will yield a form that fills the desktop, and in order to experiment with changing the element sizes, you will need to use different dimensions or change to a higher screen resolution so that your form will be smaller on the desktop.

We have the following differences between the given dimensions:

Form width minus Workspace width yields 9600 – 8895 = 705.

Tabbed Control width minus Workspace width yields 9405 – 8895 = 510.

Status Bar Panel 1 width minus Workspace width yields 7560 – 8895 = –1335.

Form height minus Workspace height yields 7350 – 4695 = 2655.

Tabbed Control height minus Workspace height yields 6135 – 4695 = 1440.

Note that the status bar panel is actually smaller than the width of the workspace. This is because we are going to adjust only the first panel; we want the other six panels to remain the same size. Because it is smaller, as we adjust the elements, we will need to subtract from the size of the workspace rather than add to it.

1. Adjust any of your elements (if necessary) so that they are the same sizes as the dimensions given. If you wish to use different sizes for your elements, you will have to modify the calculations we are going to present in this section.

Now we need to add another dialog box for adjusting the workspace size.

2. Add another form with the form name **frmAdjust_Size** and the caption **Change Workspace Size…**. Size the form as shown in Figure 7.18 (Height = 3180, Width = 4335). Turn off the ControlBox, MaxButton, and MinButton properties. This will give you a title bar with just a title on it (Figure 7.18). All the control buttons will be gone.

We know that twips are the default measuring system in Visual Basic and that to adjust the size of the workspace, we can just change the number of twips in the width and height of the workspace and form. The problem is that most users don't really have a good feel for the size of a twip, which is 1/1440 of an inch. Just having them key the new height and width sizes into a text box is probably not the best idea. Instead, we can employ a commonly used Windows graphical tool for smoothly converting a numeric value into a numeric range: a **scroll bar**.

You've seen scroll bars many times while working in Windows applications. We even used them ourselves in the workspace of the notepad. When we use scroll bars in a text box workspace, Visual Basic handles all the details of how the scroll bar functions. Now, however, we will be in control of what it does.

TABLE 7.1
The relative sizes of the program elements.

	Width	Height
Workspace	8895	4695
Tabbed Control	9405	6135
Status bar (Panel 1)	7560	not needed
Form	9600	7350

FIGURE 7.18
The frmAdjust_Size form, showing the title bar with just the title.

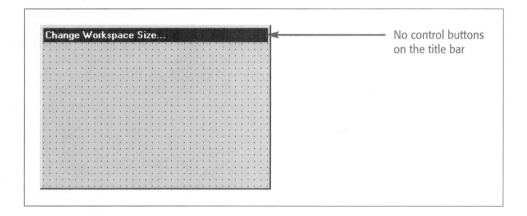

No control buttons on the title bar

When using scroll bars, we will be concerned with five primary properties: **Min**, **Max**, **Value**, **LargeChange**, and **SmallChange**. The values of all of these properties can range from 0 to 32,767. **Min** is the value assigned to the top or the left end (depending on whether we place the scroll bar vertically or horizontally on the form) of the scroll bar and is the minimum value that can result from scroll bar movements. **Max** is the value assigned to the bottom or the right end of the scroll bar and is the maximum value available. **Value** is the current value corresponding to the relative position of the scroll box on the scroll bar. If the scroll box is all the way to the top or the left, Value contains the minimum value; if the scroll box is at the bottom or all the way to the right, Value contains the maximum value. Value will always be between the Min and Max values.

LargeChange is the change in Value created when the scroll bar is clicked above or below the scroll box, and **SmallChange** is the change in Value generated when the scroll arrows are clicked. With the exception of Value, these values are generally set at design time, although, because they are properties, they can also be changed during runtime.

To begin with, we need to decide what minimum and maximum values we want to use. We should allow the user to shrink the workspace a little, without shrinking it so much that it is unusable or the captions on the tabs are unreadable (remember that we are going to shrink the Tabbed Control at the same time as we shrink the workspace).

If you were to adjust the size of the workspace yourself, you would discover that anything narrower than about 6890 would cause the Appointments tab to be as narrow as the words will permit, and a height less than about 615 would be of little use. In this case we will use a minimum width of 6890 and a minimum height of 615.

For the maximum value, we would like to be able to use all the available desktop space. This will vary according to the screen resolution you are using. If you were using 800 by 600, the maximum sizes of the workspace would be 11390 for the width and 6015 for the height. These values leave enough room for appropriate spacing between the workspace, the Tabbed Control, and the form border.

The values for LargeChange and SmallChange are largely a matter of preference. Because there are 1440 twips per inch, if we made LargeChange 1440, then each large change would be an inch; 140 twips for a SmallChange would yield approximately 1/10 of an inch.

Now that we understand these properties and know what values we want to use, it is time to add the scroll bars to the form.

3. Add two scroll bars to the form, using the Vertical Scroll Bar tool as shown in Figure 7.19. Size and position them until they appear as shown in Figure 7.20. Use the control names **vsbHeight_Bar** and **vsbWidth_Bar** for the scroll bars (the vsb prefix is for Vertical Scroll Bar).

4. Add the labels, label boxes, and buttons as shown in Figure 7.20 with the following provisions:

FIGURE 7.19
The Vertical Scroll Bar tool.

Vertical Scroll Bar tool

FIGURE 7.20
The finished form for changing the workspace size.

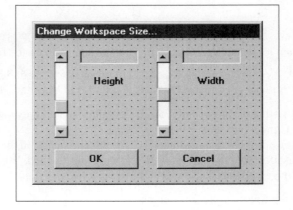

a. The control names of the label boxes are **lblHeight_Out** and **lblWidth_Out**. These boxes will be used to display the height and width of the workspace as they are adjusted with the scroll bars.

b. The buttons use the control names **cmdOK** and **cmdCancel**.

5. Change to the Max property of the Height scroll bar, and change the value to 6015. Change the value of the Min property to 615, the LargeChange to 1440, and the SmallChange to 140.

6. Change to the Max property of the Width scroll bar, and change the value to 11390. Change the value of the Min property to 6890, the LargeChange to 1440, and the SmallChange to 140.

Now we are ready to add the code necessary to make the scroll bars work. Because we are going to allow the user to increase the size of the workspace and the form window to their maximums, we should probably move the form up to the top left corner of the desktop before the size adjustments are made. This should be done in the menu option code that loads the dialog box.

7. Change to the PIM form, pull down the **Controls** menu, and select the **Change Work-space Size...** option to open the code window.

8. Key the following three statements. The third statement will cause the form to appear on the desktop.

```
frmPIM.Top = 0
frmPIM.Left = 0
frmAdjust_Size.Show 1
```

This will cause the form to be loaded. There are a few things we need to do as the form is loading. We are allowing users to cancel, with the **Cancel** button, the changes they have made, so we will need to know the size of the workspace before they made the adjustments on this form. We need a couple of fields to save the current values of the width and height of the workspace.

9. Change to the **frmAdjust_Size** form and open the code window for the form. Then add the following to the (General) procedure:

```
Dim mintSave_Workspace_Height As Integer
Dim mintSave_Workspace_Width As Integer
```

> **HINT:** Remember that the "m" prefix is to indicate that the variable is module-level (form-level).

10. Switch to the code for the Form_Load event, and key the following two statements:

```
mintSave_Workspace_Height = frmPIM.txtNotepad.Height
mintSave_Workspace_Width = frmPIM.txtNotepad.Width
```

This will save the current workspace values so that they can be restored if the user selects the **Cancel** button.

Next we need to display the current width and height in the label boxes on the form so that the user can see the current values as they are changed. We also need to set the current value of the scroll bars.

11. Key the following four statements:

```
lblHeight_Out.Caption = Str(frmPIM.txtNotepad.Height)
vsbHeight_Bar.Value = frmPIM.txtNotepad.Height
lblWidth_Out.Caption = Str(frmPIM.txtNotepad.Width)
vsbWidth_Bar.Value = frmPIM.txtNotepad.Width
```

Visual Basic will automatically handle the adjustments to the value of the scroll bar as the scroll box is moved. But we do need to change the height of the workspace and other elements, the caption in the label box in the code of the scroll bars, and the code of the scroll bars so it will correctly report the size of the workspace.

12. Change to the code for the vsbHeight_Bar, and key the following statements:

```
frmPIM.txtNotepad.Height = vsbHeight_Bar.Value
frmPIM.Height = vsbHeight_Bar.Value + 2655
frmPIM.tabPIM.Height = vsbHeight_Bar.Value + 1440
lblHeight_Out.Caption = Str(vsbHeight_Bar.Value)
```

Note that the second of these statements changes the height of the form itself. If we are going to change the size of the workspace and want the workspace to maintain its relative position in the form, we will have to change the size of the form, too. 2655 is the difference between the two sizes, as we discovered earlier (see Table 7.1, at the beginning of this section). The same adjustment is used for the height of the Tabbed Control. We don't list the status bar, because we decided that it would stay the same height.

We need to use similar code for the vsbWidth_Bar.

13. Change to the code for the vsbWidth_Bar, and key the following statements:

```
frmPIM.txtNotepad.Width = vsbWidth_Bar.Value
frmPIM.Width = vsbWidth_Bar.Value + 705
frmPIM.tabPIM.Width = vsbWidth_Bar.Value + 510
frmPIM.stsPIM_Status.Panels(1).Width = vsbWidth_bar.Value - 1335
lblWidth_Out.Caption = Str(vsbWidth_Bar.Value)
```

Note that we subtracted 1335 from the width of the workspace to come up with the width of the status bar panel. This is necessary because the panel is narrower than the workspace.

Now we are ready for the button code. The **OK** button is simple. All we need to do is unload the form. Earlier in this chapter we mentioned that a form is usually unloaded with the Hide statement. Well, this is true only if you don't have any Load event code. If you are using code in the Load event for the form, just hiding the form does not unload it, and it will not be loaded with the Show command. Thus, instead of the Hide command, we will use the Unload command, which will really unload the form so that Show will load it again and the Load event code will be executed.

14. Change to the cmdOK code and key the following statement:

```
Unload frmAdjust_Size
```

The **Cancel** button requires more code because it will need to change the workspace and other elements back to the sizes they were when the dialog box was loaded. First we merely need to restore the scroll bars to their original values; if we do so, the program will automatically run the change events that contain the code to change the size of the workspace:

```
vsbHeight_bar = mintSave_Workspace_Height
vsbWidth_bar = mintSave_Workspace_Width
```

Then we will need to unload the form:

```
Unload frmAdjust_Size
```

15. Change to the code for the **Cancel** button and key the foregoing statements.

16. Run the application, pull down the **Controls** menu, and select the **Change Workspace Size...** option. The dialog box appears, and the PIM form jumps to the upper left corner.

17. Click the **Height** scroll bars twice above the scroll box. Click the **Width** scroll bar once above the scroll box. This will change the width and height of the form to what you see in Figure 7.21.

18. Click the **Cancel** button and the form reverts to its original size.

19. Practice with the changes until you are comfortable with the way the application is working. Then exit the application.

Changing the Workspace Background Color

One thing that users sometimes want to be able to do is change the colors of the various elements of the program. We will experiment with changing the colors of the workspace, using three different techniques. We will start with the color Common Dialog Box.

FIGURE 7.21
The form with the
height and width
changed.

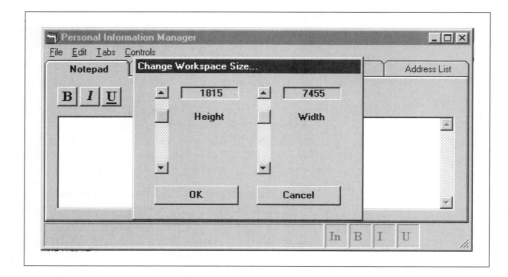

Because we have already added the Common Dialog Box tool to the program, we don't need to do it again. We merely need to use the appropriate code to access the color dialog box.

If you recall, when we used the Font version of the Common Dialog Box before, we used the statement

```
cdgPIM.ShowFont
```

to access it. Now we need to access the color version of the Common Dialog Box and will use the following statement:

```
cdgPIM.ShowColor
```

1. Call up the code window for the **Change Background Color...** option of the **Controls** menu, and key the foregoing statement into the procedure.

   This will cause the dialog box to be displayed. After the user chooses the color for the background, the dialog box will disappear, and it is up to us to use the color returned to us. We do this by assigning the returned color to the background with the command

   ```
   txtNotepad.BackColor = cdgPIM.Color
   ```

2. Add this command.

   That's all we need.

3. Run the program and select the **Change Background Color...** option of the **Controls** menu to see the dialog box shown in Figure 7.22 appear.

   To pick the color you want, you simply click it.

4. Click the color you want for the workspace background and then select **OK**.

The background color of the workspace will now be the color you selected.

5. Change the background color a few more times until you are comfortable with the way the dialog box works. You may even want to try defining a custom color by clicking the **Define Custom Colors >>** button. When you're finished, exit the program.

Changing Both Colors of the Workspace

Changing the colors of the workspace normally requires changing both the foreground and the background colors. It could be done by simply using the Common Dialog Box once for

FIGURE 7.22
The color dialog box.

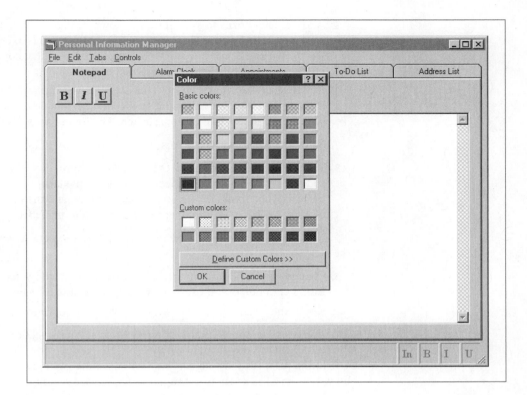

each of the colors. We prefer to select both the foreground and the background colors at the same time and to see samples of them. This means we need to create our own dialog box.

1. Add a new form with the form name **frmWorkspace_Colors** and the caption **Change Workspace Colors…**. Turn off the control box and the **Maximize** and **Minimize** buttons.

2. Change to the BackColor property, and pull down the color selection box as shown in Figure 7.23. If your color selection box is set to System, click the Palette tab.

You have seen a color selection box similar to this before (such as the color version of the Common Dialog Box). It is generally used when a color is to be changed. We are going to create a dialog box with a color selection box similar to this one (leaving out the bottom two rows because they are all white). In ours, however, we will be able to set the background and foreground colors at the same time on the basis of which button we use to click the color.

FIGURE 7.23
The color selection box.

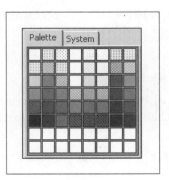

3. Add 48 label boxes to your form as shown in Figure 7.24. They should be a control array called **lblColors**. The easiest way to create them is to create the first one, change the control name, copy it, and then continually paste that copy back to the form, moving the new one to where it is supposed to be.

4. Add the label box under the color labels as shown Figure 7.24. It should have the name **lblSample_Out**. We will use it to display the sample colors for the foreground and background colors as they are selected. The font is **Arial, Bold,** and **24** points.

Now we need to add the colors to the control array of label boxes.

5. Select the first label box, select the BackColor property, show the color selection box, and select the Palette tab. Select the color for the label box, representing the same position in your form and the color selection box, and then exit the color selection box (see Figure 7.25). Repeat the process for each of the labels.

Now we need to add the code to make our color selection box work. First we must get the form loaded.

6. Change to the PIM form and call up the code window for the **By Color Selection Boxes...** option of the **Change Workspace Color** submenu on the **Controls** menu.

7. Key a Show statement to show the frmWorkspace_Colors form.

There are, essentially, three controls on this color selection box: the two buttons and the color boxes. We will begin with the color boxes.

In the past, for most objects we have used the Click event in our code. In this case, however, the Click event is not suitable. The Click event registers only the left mouse button. We want to change the background color with a click of the right mouse button and the foreground color with a click of the left mouse button (this technique is used in many applications). Instead of Click we will use the **MouseDown** event.

8. Open the MouseDown event procedure. The Sub statement for the procedure is

```
Private Sub lblColors_MouseDown(Index As Integer, Button As
  Integer,Shift As Integer, X As Single, Y As Single)
```

Note the Button parameter. The value of this parameter represents the button that was clicked. **vbLeftButton** (or 1) represents the click of the left button, and **vbRightButton** (or 2) represents the click of the right button. If you also have a middle button, clicking it gives you a value of **vbMiddleButton** (or 4).

You know that the Index parameter points to the element of the control array the user selected, but what do the parameters X and Y represent? They are the X and Y positions within the object where the mouse pointer is when the button is clicked. This can be useful when you are using a large bitmap (image) that has several different objects in it and you want to know which of the objects the user clicked. Knowing where the objects are in the bitmap, and letting the MouseDown event tell you where in the bitmap the user clicked, you can determine which of the objects the user selected. One of the exercises at the end of this chapter introduces this technique.

The first thing we need to do in the MouseDown event procedure is set up an If Test to determine which mouse button was clicked:

```
If Button = vbRightButton Then
```

9. Key this statement into the procedure.

Because the Button value **vbRightButton** represents the right button, we will want to set up the background color in the sample box we created to show it, **lblSample_Out**. This is done with the statement

```
lblSample_Out.BackColor = lblColors(Index).BackColor
```

FIGURE 7.24
The form for changing the colors of the workspace.

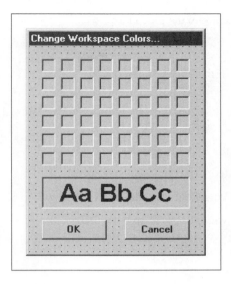

FIGURE 7.25
Which colors to select for the lblColors control array.

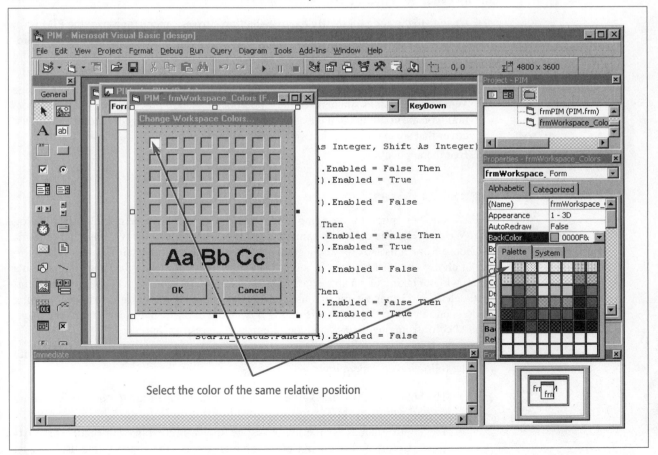

10. Key this statement into the procedure.

   Now comes the Else part of the If Test, which will change the foreground color. This occurs if the user clicks the left button. The statement needed here is essentially the same (along with the rest of the If Test statements):

   ```
   Else
       lblSample_Out.ForeColor = lblColors(Index).BackColor
   End If
   ```

11. Key the rest of the If Test as given.

   The **Cancel** button will simply hide the form.

12. Change to the **Cancel** button code, and key the appropriate Hide statement.

   The **OK** button will hide the form but will also change the background and foreground colors of the workspace, using the background and foreground colors of the sample label as the template. You will need three statements:

   ```
   frmPIM.txtNotepad.BackColor = lblSample_Out.BackColor
   frmPIM.txtNotepad.ForeColor = lblSample_Out.ForeColor
   frmWorkspace_Colors.Hide
   ```

13. Change to the **OK** button code, and key these three statements.

   Since we are going to change the background and foreground colors of the notepad workspace, it is a good idea to display those colors in our sample text box when the dialog box is first displayed. We can do that by adding the appropriate assignment statements in the **By Color Selection Boxes...** menu option code.

14. Change to the code for the **By Color Selection Boxes...** menu option on the PIM form and key the appropriate assignment statements to change the background and foreground colors of the sample label to the colors used in the notepad workspace. These statements can be either before or after the Show statement since it is not modal.

15. Run the application, select the **By Color Selection Boxes...** option of the **Change Workspace Colors** submenu of the **Controls** menu, and practice changing the colors until you are confident that the application is working as it is supposed to. You will discover that some color combinations work better than others.

16. Exit the application.

Using List Boxes

There is another option for changing the foreground and background colors using a dialog box. We could list the colors by name in a **list box.** Any time you have a number of items to choose from, a list box may be a good idea. List boxes can have scroll bars, so the number of choices in a list box can be significantly greater than the number you can have in a menu without taking up an appreciable amount of space on your form. Though you can insert, delete, and change items in a list during runtime, for our application all we are going to do is add items to the list in this dialog box. We will allow the user to select the background color from one list box and the foreground color from another.

1. Create a new form with the form name **frmColor_Lists** as shown in Figure 7.26 with the following considerations:

   a. The boxes under the Background and Foreground labels are the list boxes and are created with the List Box tool as shown in Figure 7.27.

   b. The control names for the list boxes are shown in the boxes in Figure 7.26: **lstBack_Colors** and **lstFore_Colors**. Though you see the names of the list boxes in

FIGURE 7.26
The form for changing colors by name using a list box.

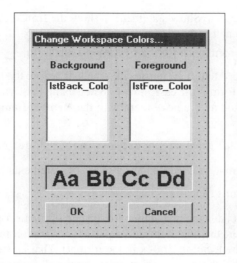

them as they are created, the names will not appear in the list boxes when the application is running.

c. The sample label box has the control name **lblSample_Out**. The font is **Arial, Bold,** and **24** points.

d. The two buttons should have the standard control names of cmdOK and cmdCancel.

e. Turn off the control box and the **Maximum** and **Minimum** buttons so that the title bar will only have a title.

2. Switch to the code for the **By List of Colors...** option on the **Change Workspace Colors** submenu on the **Controls** menu of the PIM form.

FIGURE 7.27
The List Box tool.

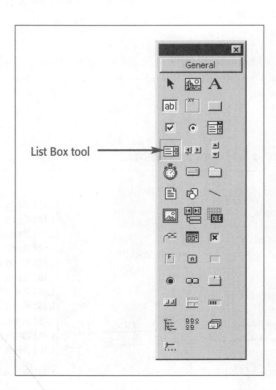

List Box tool

3. Add the appropriate Show statement to show the frmColor_Lists form along with the statements to change the colors of the sample text box.

4. Change to the form code for the frmColor_Lists form.

Because we need to put the entries into the lists before the lists are displayed, using the Load event for the form is the easiest way. When using lists, you put items into the list with the **AddItem** method and remove them with the **RemoveItem** method. The format of the AddItem method is

```
Objectname.AddItem stringexpression [, index]
```

To employ this format, you need to use a series of statements like

```
lstBack_Colors.AddItem "Black"
```

This statement adds the new item onto the end of the list of items already in the list. If you wanted to insert the new item into a particular location in the list, you could use the index number of the location (**index** in the format). That is, suppose your list already has 10 items (0 through 9, because the first index number is automatically zero). If you wanted to put one item in position 8, you could use the statement

```
lstBack_Colors.AddItem "Black", 8
```

This will cause the new item "Black" to be placed at position 8, the original 8 to become 9, and the original 9 to become 10 (see Figure 7.28).

If you want your list to be in alphabetical order, you can add the items in alphabetical order as we will do, or you can turn on the **Sorted** property and Visual Basic will automatically alphabetize (sort) the list for you.

When you want to remove an item from the list, it must be removed with the RemoveItem method, which has the format

```
Objectname.RemoveItem stringexpression, index
```

This time the index is not optional. An item must be removed by referencing its index number. A sample statement is

```
lstBack_Colors.RemoveItem 8
```

This would remove item 8 from the list. Then item 9 would become the new item 8, item 10 would become item 9, and so on. We will not use the RemoveItem method in our application.

FIGURE 7.28

Illustration of adding a new item to a list by index number.

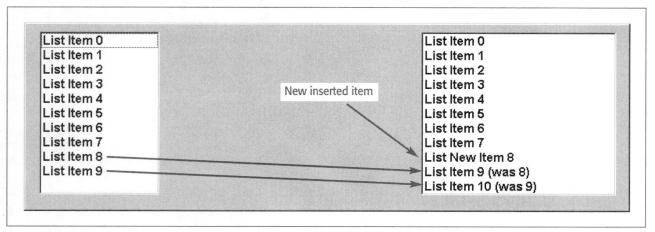

5. Add code using statements like lstBack_Colors.AddItem "Black" for adding eight colors to the selection list of the lstBack_Colors and eight for the lstFore_Colors. The eight colors are **Black, Blue, Cyan, Green, Magenta, Red, White,** and **Yellow.**

We will also set up the initial display value for each of the lists. A list box is made up of a string array called **List**. The index into that array is a method called **ListIndex.** If we tell the application what the current ListIndex should be, it will automatically highlight the proper entry in each list. If we wanted to highlight the fifth item in a list, we would use a statement such as (remember, the first index is zero)

```
lstBack_Colors.ListIndex = 4
```

Because the default background color is white and the default foreground color is black, we will start our lists with those selections. Black is item 0 and white is item 6 in the List array (the first item is item 0). We can use that knowledge to create the following two statements:

```
lstBack_Colors.ListIndex = 6
lstFore_Colors.ListIndex = 0
```

6. Add these two statements to the code.

The Case Construct

Now we need to add code to the Click event of the lists. Here, we must determine what color has been selected in the list and what to do with it. The **Text** property will contain the text of the item currently selected in the list.

To assign the colors that are picked from the lists, we need to determine the value in the list and then use that to assign the variable of that color to lblSample_Out.BackColor. The way we would normally do something like this is with an If Test such as

```
If  lstBack_Colors.Text = "Black"  Then
       lblSample_Out.BackColor = vbBlack
    ElseIf lstBack_Colors.Text = "Blue"  Then
       lblSample_Out.BackColor = vbBlue
```

And so on. There is a different Visual Basic construction that can be used here that requires a bit less keying and will prove useful in other instances. The **Case construct** (it is called a construct since it generally is made up of many statements) can be used to test a field for a particular value and then execute one or more statements based on the value of that field. In this situation, the entire case construct we need looks like the following:

```
Select Case lstBack_Colors.Text
    Case "Black"
        lblSample_Out.BackColor = vbBlack
    Case "Blue"
        lblSample_Out.BackColor = vbBlue
    Case "Cyan"
        lblSample_Out.BackColor = vbCyan
    Case "Blue"
        lblSample_Out.BackColor = vbBlue
    Case "Green"
        lblSample_Out.BackColor = vbGreen
    Case "Magenta"
        lblSample_Out.BackColor = vbMagenta
    Case "Red"
        lblSample_Out.BackColor = vbRed
    Case "White"
        lblSample_Out.BackColor = vbWhite
    Case Else ' Yellow
        lblSample_Out.BackColor = vbYellow
End Select
```

The Case construct begins with the statement:

```
Select Case lstBack_Colors.Text
```

"Select Case" is among the Visual Basic reserved words, and is followed by the variable you are testing, "1stBack_Colors.text" in this situation. This field can be either numeric or text (as in this example). Then each value of the field is listed in a separate statement following the word "Case." Under each Case statement is one or more statements that you want carried out when the field matches the specified value. In our code, we want the color constant assigned to the text box BackColor property for each specified value. After all the Case statements are used, you tell Visual Basic that the construct is finished with the **End Select** statement.

When lstBack_Colors.Text contains the text literal "Black," that case option is selected and lblSample_Out.BackColor will be assigned vbBlack. If 1stBack_Colors.Text does not contain "Black", then the next case, "Blue", is checked. This continues until a match is found or the End Select Statement is found and executed. If no case is matched, control simply falls through the entire construct and execution continues following the End Select Statement. If you want to be sure some section of code is always executed, you can use the special statement Case Else and if no other Case values are matched, the code of the Else is executed. In our sample, we used the Case Else statement to default to Yellow. We could have used "Yellow" as the text to check for, but Case Else was useful as an example.

1. Change to the code for the lstBack_Colors_Click procedure and key the code given above.

The lstFore_Colors_Click procedure is done with the same type of Case construct the lstBack_Colors_Click procedure used. As a matter of fact, you can copy the lstBack_Colors_Click code, change "Back" to "Fore", and be essentially finished with the procedure.

2. Copy the code for the lstBack_Colors_Click Case construct, switch to the lstFore_Colors_Click procedure and paste the code in there.

3. Use the **Replace** option on the **Edit** menu (the Visual Basic Edit menu) to replace "Back" with "Fore." Note that you need to select the Current Procedure for the scope of the replace operation or you will end up changing code unintentionally.

The Rest of the Code

The code for the two buttons is the standard code that we have created many times in this chapter. The **OK** button will need the following code:

```
frmPIM.txtNotepad.BackColor = lblSample_Out.BackColor
frmPIM.txtNotepad.ForeColor = lblSample_Out.ForeColor
frmColor_Lists.Hide
```

1. Change to the code for the **OK** button and key the above statements.

2. Change to the code for the **Cancel** button and key just the **frmColor_Lists.Hide** statement.

In most lists like this, if you double-click one of the list elements, the element is selected and you exit the dialog box. We can also set up our application like that because the List box has a double-click event.

3. Change to the code for the **DblClick** event for the lstBack_Colors list.

All we really need to do is execute the same code that we used on the **OK** button. But we don't need the code. We can simply execute the cmdOk_Button code by calling the CmdOK_Button_Click procedure with the statement

```
cmdOk_Button_Click
```

When you call a procedure like this, execution of the program simply switches to the called procedure, executes that procedure, and then jumps back to the procedure it came from. Then execution continues with the next statement in the calling procedure.

4. Key this statement into the procedure and do the same for the DblClick event of the lstFore_Colors.

5. Run the application, select the appropriate option, and thoroughly test the new dialog box. When you are satisfied, exit the application.

Using Combo Boxes

There is another tool similar to a list box called a **combo** box. It is essentially a list box that allows users to key their choices as well as select from the list. If you want the list of choices to be limited to those you give the user, you should use a list box. If the list of choices is only a sample and you want users to be able to key their own choices, a combo box is necessary. We will learn how to use a combo box by changing the box in our frmColor_Lists.

There are three combo box styles available (see Figure 7.29). When you add a combo box to the form, you must choose the style you want. Style 0 is a pull-down list where users can key an entry as well as select from the list. Style 1 is not a pull-down list. It is expanded at design time like a list box. The difference is that the user can also key an entry that is not in the list. Style 2 is basically a list box that uses a pull-down list rather than showing the list on the screen. This style is basically what we have been using, so we will begin with Style 2.

1. Change to the frmColor_Lists and delete the lstBack_Colors box.

2. Add a combo box to the form, using the tool shown in Figure 7.30. Give the box the control name of **lstBack_Colors**, and the code created earlier will still work. Change the Style property to 2.

3. Turn off the option that automatically saves your programs by selecting the **Options...** option of the **Tools** menu, selecting the Environment tab, and clicking the **Don't Save Changes** option button. Run the application, select the proper option, and

FIGURE 7.29
The three combo box styles.

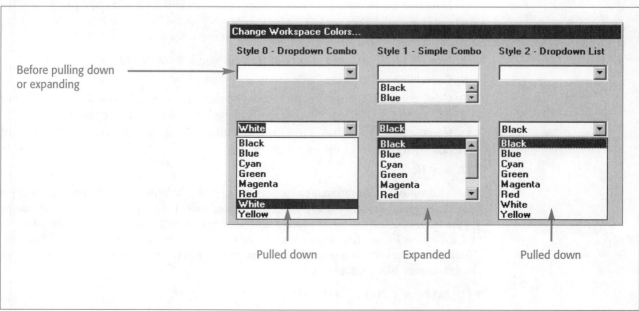

FIGURE 7.30
The Combo Box tool.

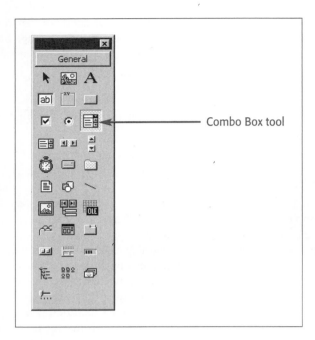

Combo Box tool

note that where there was a list of background colors, there is now a pull-down list. Select a few of the colors from the pull-down list until you are satisfied that the application is still working properly, then exit the application (but don't save it).

Now we will see what the other combo styles look like.

4. Change to frmColor_Lists, and change the style of the combo box to 0. This is the pull-down list where you can also key an entry.

5. Run the application and select the proper option, and you will see a pull-down list similar to the previous one. The difference is that you can key an entry here.

6. Pull down the list and select one of the colors (not Red). The pull-down list still works the way it did before.

7. Key **Red**.

Note that the background color did not change to red. As it turns out, using the Click event to change the color works fine for the entries selected from the list, but it does not register the keyed entry. We need to use a different event for that.

8. Exit the application and change to the code window for the list.

9. Copy all the code in the Click event procedure.

10. Change to the **Change** event procedure and paste the code here. You don't need to make any changes to the code because the Text method still contains the selected entry.

11. Run the program, pull down the list, and select one of the colors (not Red). The pull-down list still works the way it did before.

12. Key **Red**.

This time the background color does change to red. When using boxes like this, you need to be careful to key the entry precisely; "red" won't work if the entry being tested for in the Case construct is "Red". Many programmers solve this problem by using either the **UCase** or the **LCase** function to convert the entry to either all uppercase or all lowercase. Then there is never any question that the entry is correct. You can use one of the functions in a statement like the following:

```
lstBack_Colors.Text = UCase(lstBack_Colors.Text)
```

All the entries in the list must now be in capital letters or, once again, the entry will not match the elements in the list.

13. Select a few more colors by keying them and selecting them from the list. Then exit the application (without saving).

There is one more style to try. Style 1 is not a pull-down list at all. You expand it like a list box.

14. Change to the frmColor_Lists, and change the style of the combo box to 1. Expand the box to the approximate length of the list box.

15. Run the application and select the proper option. Now the list will already show in the box.

16. Select a color from the list to verify that list selection still works. Then key a different color. Note that this method still works (because of the code in the Change event).

The decision as to what style, combo box to use, or whether or not a list box is better, is largely a matter of preference and the input needs of the program. If, however, your dialog box needs to be compact or is already too large to contain a list, a pull-down combo box may be a reasonable choice.

17. Save the frmColor_Lists as **frmCombo** and then save the project as **Combo**. This will save all the rest of the forms and modules with the names they had before, but the next time you load the COMBO program, the combo boxes will be part of it.

A List Sample

The way we used the list in the PIM program covers only a small portion of what lists can be used for. To expand your knowledge of lists, we will create another program for practicing with lists. Let's look at the finished application first.

The Sample Program

1. Run the Personnel Numbers program in the Ch-7 folder on your work disk to see the form shown in Figure 7.31.

FIGURE 7.31
The form of the Personnel Numbers program.

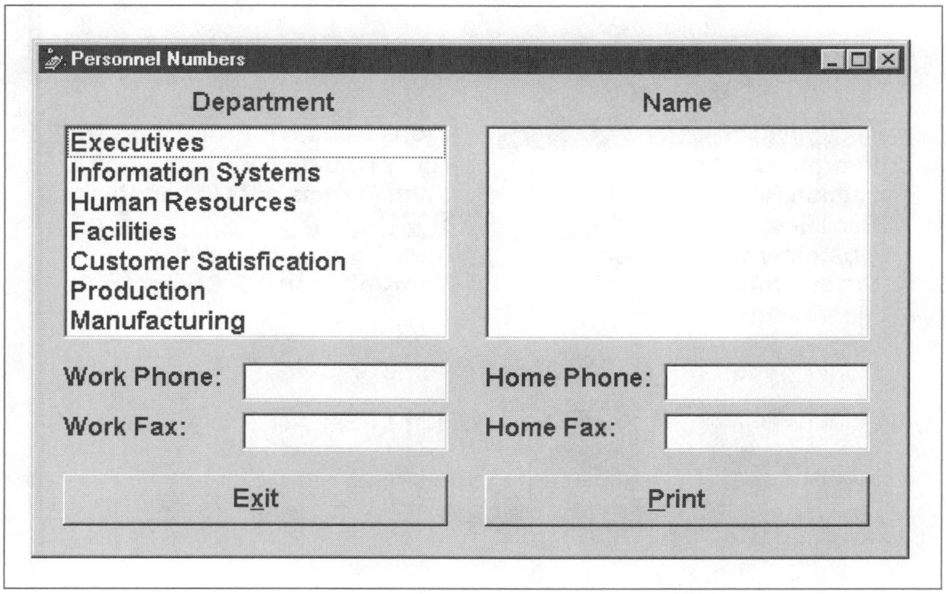

This program was written because of a request by the head of the Human Resources Department. She wants everyone to be able to look up the phone and fax numbers of all the personnel in the company. To make this possible, the names are broken up by departments in the first list. When the Department list is selected, all the personnel in that department are shown in the Name list. When an item in that list is selected, the four numbers are displayed.

2. Click **Executives** in the **Department** list to see the names for the personnel of that department displayed in the second list as shown in Figure 7.32.

3. Click **John Smith, President** in the Name list to see the numbers appear in the labels as shown in Figure 7.33.

4. Click **Facilities** in the **Department** list. The list of names changes and the numbers are erased.

FIGURE 7.32
The list of names for the Executives department.

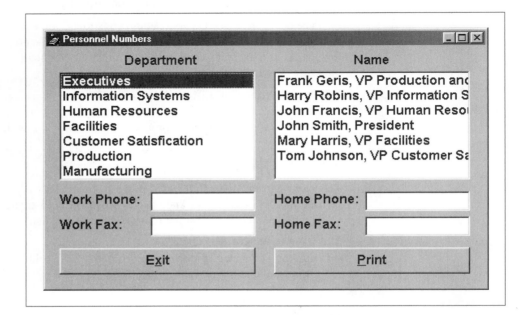

FIGURE 7.33
The numbers for John Smith.

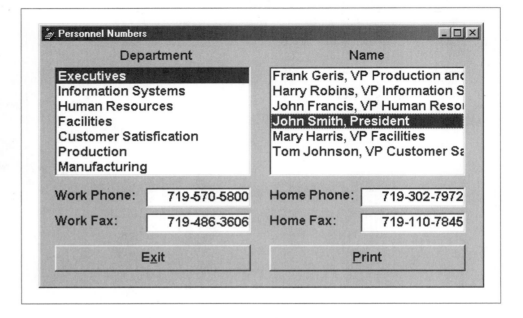

5. Click one of the names in the list, and that person's numbers are displayed.

6. Select a different name, and the numbers change.

7. Practice with the program a bit more until you are familiar with the way the lists work.

8. Minimize the program.

Writing the Program   Now it's time to write the program and learn more about manipulating lists. Some of the work of writing this program has already been done for you.

1. Load the Personnel Numbers project from the Ch-7 folder on your work disk. As you can see, all the objects are already on the form, and some of the code is already written.

2. Open the code window for the (General) procedure to see the code shown in Figure 7.34.

FIGURE 7.34
The code already written.

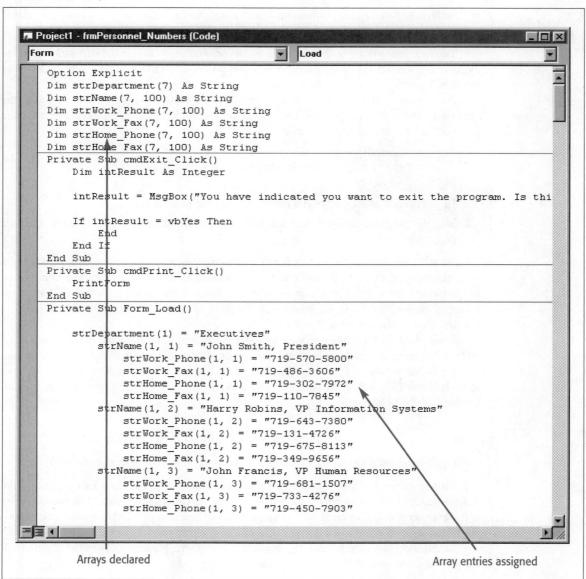

```
Project1 - frmPersonnel_Numbers (Code)

Form                                          Load

Option Explicit
Dim strDepartment(7) As String
Dim strName(7, 100) As String
Dim strWork_Phone(7, 100) As String
Dim strWork_Fax(7, 100) As String
Dim strHome_Phone(7, 100) As String
Dim strHome_Fax(7, 100) As String
Private Sub cmdExit_Click()
    Dim intResult As Integer

    intResult = MsgBox("You have indicated you want to exit the program. Is thi

    If intResult = vbYes Then
        End
    End If
End Sub
Private Sub cmdPrint_Click()
    PrintForm
End Sub
Private Sub Form_Load()

    strDepartment(1) = "Executives"
        strName(1, 1) = "John Smith, President"
            strWork_Phone(1, 1) = "719-570-5800"
            strWork_Fax(1, 1) = "719-486-3606"
            strHome_Phone(1, 1) = "719-302-7972"
            strHome_Fax(1, 1) = "719-110-7845"
        strName(1, 2) = "Harry Robins, VP Information Systems"
            strWork_Phone(1, 2) = "719-643-7380"
            strWork_Fax(1, 2) = "719-131-4726"
            strHome_Phone(1, 2) = "719-675-8113"
            strHome_Fax(1, 2) = "719-349-9656"
        strName(1, 3) = "John Francis, VP Human Resources"
            strWork_Phone(1, 3) = "719-681-1507"
            strWork_Fax(1, 3) = "719-733-4276"
            strHome_Phone(1, 3) = "719-450-7903"
```

Arrays declared   Array entries assigned

Normally this type of program loads the lists by reading data from a file. You will learn how to do this in the next chapter, but for now, we have simply assigned all the necessary data to arrays.

There are six different arrays:

- **strDepartment** contains the department names to be put in the Department list.

- **strName** is a two-dimensional array that contains the names of the personnel in each department that are to be displayed in the Name list when the Department list is clicked. The first dimension refers to the department, the second to the name itself.

- **strWork_Phone** is a two-dimensional array that contains the work phone numbers related to the names selected from the Name list. The dimensions of this array and the next three are the same as the dimensions of the strName array.

- **strWork_Fax** is a two-dimensional array that contains the work fax numbers related to the names selected from the Name list.

- **strHome_Phone** is a two-dimensional array that contains the home phone numbers related to the names selected from the Name list.

- **strHome_Fax** is a two-dimensional array that contains the home fax numbers related to the names selected from the Name list.

The next thing that needs to be done in this program is to assign the departments to the Department list. This is done in the Form_Load procedure, and the code can be added after the existing array assignment statements.

As you saw earlier, the method used to add elements to a list is AddItem. Because the data are stored in an array, we merely have to loop through that array to add the items to the list. Such a loop would look like this:

```
For intCounter = 1 To 7
    lstDepartment.AddItem strDepartment(intCounter)
Next intCounter
```

3. Key this code at the end of the Form_Load event procedure.

4. Run the program, and you will see that the departments show up in the list. Exit the program.

Now we need to put the names for the appropriate department in the Name list when a department is selected. As it turns out, that's not difficult either. The items are entered into the list in the same order in which we assigned them to the array, so when an item is selected in the list, the ListIndex number of that item points to the array, offset by 1 because the first element in the list is 0, not 1.

If you look through the array assignments, you will note that each array group has a different number of names. When the Department is selected, the program will need to load into the Name list only those items that have been assigned. To determine that, all we have to do is check for a null entry (empty). The code for the Click event procedure for the Department list should begin

```
intCounter = 1
Do Until strName(lstDepartment.ListIndex + 1, intCounter) = ""
```

5. Open the code window for the Department list Click event, and key this code.

This is creating a loop until the strName entry is blank. The first index is using the index pointer of the Department list, which is **lstDepartment.ListIndex**. The second index is the counter itself. This code will loop through all the items pointed to by the index number of the item selected in the Department list until a null entry is found.

In this loop, the item pointed to should be added to the Name list. Then the counter will need to be incremented. This will take the following code:

```
        lstName.AddItem strName(lstDepartment.ListIndex + 1, intCounter)
        intCounter = intCounter + 1
Loop
```

6. Key the above statements to complete the loop.

7. Run the program and select **Human Resources** in the Department list. The entries should show up in the Name list.

8. Click **Human Resources** again, and the names will show up in the Name list twice.

The problem is that the entries are still in the list from the first time the Department list entry was selected. Before the items are displayed in the Name list, the list should be emptied. This is done with the **Clear** method, which has the following format:

```
Listname.Clear
```

The statement we need is

```
strName.Clear
```

9. Exit the program, switch to the Department list Click event code, and key this statement before the loop.

10. Run the program and click **Human Resources** in the Department list twice. This time the names appear only once in the Name list.

11. Exit the program.

Next, we need to display the phone and fax numbers when the Name list is selected. This code must be added in the Click event procedure for the Name list. Four assignment statements are needed:

```
lblWork_Phone = strWork_Phone(lstDepartment.ListIndex + 1,
 ⮑ lstName.ListIndex + 1)
lblWork_Fax = strWork_Fax(lstDepartment.ListIndex + 1,
 ⮑ lstName.ListIndex + 1)
lblHome_Phone = strHome_Phone(lstDepartment.ListIndex + 1,
 ⮑ lstName.ListIndex + 1)
lblHome_Fax = strHome_Fax(lstDepartment.ListIndex + 1,
 ⮑ lstName.ListIndex + 1)
```

Here, both array indices use the ListIndex pointers into the lists. The ListIndex for the Department list is the first index, and the ListIndex for the Name list is the second.

12. Open the code window for the Name list and key the foregoing code.

13. Run the program. Select **Human Resources** in the Department list and **Greg Baker** in the Name list to see the display shown in Figure 7.35.

14. Experiment with the program a bit more until you are comfortable with the way it works. Then exit the program.

You may have noticed that the numbers at the bottom are not changed when a new entry in the Department list is selected. This is misleading for the user, so let's take care of it.

All you have to do is empty the labels when the Department list is selected. The code should be inserted into the existing code before the items are added to the list.

15. Make this change and test the program before exiting it.

Sorting the Lists We mentioned that a list can be sorted just by changing the **Sorted** property to True.

1. Select the Sorted property of the Department list, and change the value to True.

2. Run the program. Note that the elements in the Department list are now sorted.

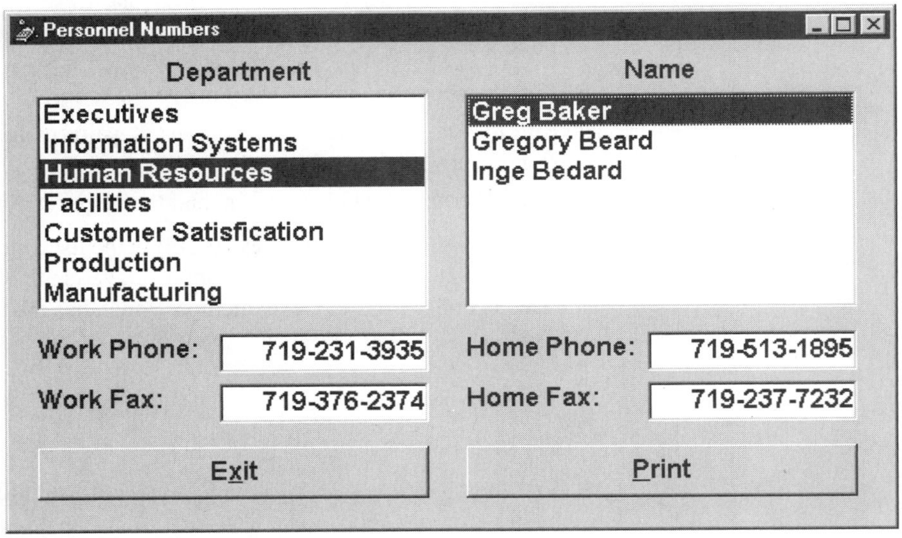

FIGURE 7.35
The numbers displayed
in the Personnel
Numbers program.

3. Select **Human Resources** in the Department list.

Earlier there were just three names in the Name list for the Human Resources Department. The problem is that because the list is sorted, the ListIndex property no longer points to the proper element in the array. The items in the list no longer correspond to the order in which they are stored in the array. Sorted lists are commonly used, so we have to discover a way to allow the program still to point to the proper item in the array. That is done with the **ItemData** property, which has the format

```
Listname.ItemData(index) [= number]
```

Because the items in the list are indexed, it stands to reason that the related ItemData properties also need to be pointed to by index. The number assigned to the ItemData property is optional, as you can see in the format. If you were retrieving the ItemData property value to assign to something else, you would not assign a number to the property.

To use the ItemData property, you assign to it the proper number of each of the items as it is added to the list. The original code for adding the elements to the Department list is

```
For intCounter = 1 To 7
    lstDepartment.AddItem strDepartment(intCounter)
Next intCounter
```

As the items are added to the list, intCounter points to the proper index number in the array. Therefore, if we assign intCounter to the ItemData property, the property will then point to the corresponding array element. The statement to do this is

```
lstDepartment.ItemData(lstDepartment.NewIndex) = intCounter
```

We have used a new property called **NewIndex**. This property contains the ListIndex number of the latest item added to the specified list. By using lstDepartment.NewIndex as the index of the ItemData property, we are assigning the counter to the ItemData property of the last item added to the Department list.

4. Insert the ItemData statement into the loop after the AddItem statement.

These are only half the changes required to make the code work with the ItemData property. Now we need to change the assignment to the Name list so that it uses the ItemData property. That code is currently

```
lstName.Clear
intCounter = 1
Do Until strName(lstDepartment.ListIndex + 1, intCounter) = ""
    lstName.AddItem strName(lstDepartment.ListIndex + 1, intCounter)
    intCounter = intCounter + 1
Loop
```

To use the ItemData property, you need to change the AddItem statement to

```
lstName.AddItem strName(lstDepartment.ItemData(lstDepartment.
⤷ListIndex),intCounter)
```

Now the statement will add the array item that is pointed to by the ItemData property whose index is the ListIndex property.

5. Change the AddItem statement to the foregoing.

6. Run the program and select **Human Resources** in the Department list. This time, the three entries in the Name list are those that you saw before.

You can change the Name list so that it is also sorted by making the same types of changes so that the ItemData property is used. This is left as an exercise at the end of the chapter.

7. Exit the program.

Other List Properties

Normally lists allow the user to select a single item. If you want your users to be able to select multiple items in a list, you have to change the setting of the **MultiSelect** property. The available settings are

- **0 - None** is the normal, single-item selection mode.
- **1 - Simple** allows selection of multiple items by clicking on them or moving through the list with the arrow keys and pressing **Spacebar.**
- **2 - Extended** allows multiple selection by clicking, by moving the arrow key and pressing **Spacebar,** or by dragging the highlight.

The default mode for the list is **None.** This is the normal mode in which the user can select only a single item. If a second item is selected, the first item becomes deselected automatically. Lists for which the MultiSelect property is set to Simple allow the user to select multiple items, but only one item at a time; each item must be selected separately by clicking it or moving the focus and pressing **Spacebar.** Lists that use the Extended multiple selection option allow the user to select items the same way as with the Simple option, but items can also be selected by dragging the highlight to select multiple items. If the user does highlight the list items by dragging the highlight, the Click and MouseUp events are executed when the mouse button is released.

When using lists that allow multiselections, you need to use the **Selected** property to determine which items are selected. This property has the following format:

```
Listname.Selected(index) [= boolean]
```

If the Selected property is True, the item is selected; if False, it is not. This property, like most properties, can be used in an assignment statement to assign a boolean value to the property. That is, the user can select the items, or your code can do it by setting the property of the appropriate item in the list to True. The following statement would highlight the third item of the lstName list (remember that the first item of a list has index 0):

```
lstName.Selected(2) = True
```

To find the selected items, you generally use a loop to search through all the list items. For this, the **ListCount** property is useful. It contains the number of elements in the list. For example, suppose you have a multiselection list called lstDog_Types that contains the names of all the types of dogs in the local dog show. After the user has selected one or more items in the list, you can determine which items have been selected by using a loop such as

```
For intCounter = 0 To lstDog_Types.ListCount - 1
    If lstDog_Types.Selected(intCounter) = True Then
        Code for whatever you are doing with the selected items
    End If
Next intCounter
```

In this loop, the code begins with the 0 item in the list, which is the first item, and goes through all the items. Because lstDog_Types.ListCount contains the number of items in the lstDog_Types list, if the loop goes until 1 less than ListCount, it will have examined every item in the list. Then the If Test checks the Selected property of the list, using the loop counter as the index.

7.9   Debugging Your Programs

Using multiple forms can cause problems in your programs if you are not careful. You need to remember a few things about using forms. If you use a modal Show statement, program execution switches to the new form at the Show statement. Code execution in the code of the calling form is stopped and resumes only after the user exits the called form. If the Show statement is not modal, code execution continues until the end of the calling procedure, and then execution switches to the called form. Thus, if you need to set any properties on the form being called with a modal Show statement, the statements to set these properties must be executed before the Show statement.

If you want to retain settings on a form, that form must be removed from the desktop with the Hide method rather than the Unload method. If a form is unloaded, then when it is reloaded, it will always be in its initial state, and whatever changes were made to the form the last time it was on the desktop will be lost.

Code on one form can be executed from any other form by simply qualifying the procedure call. If you have two procedures with the same name on two different forms, be sure to qualify the call to the procedure if the call is supposed to be executing the procedure on the other form. Without qualification, all calls refer to the procedures on the current form. Normally it is bad practice to have two procedures, on different forms, with the same name. However, it is also a good idea to be consistent with the names of objects that are the same on different forms. That is, if you have **OK** buttons on several forms, it is better always to use a name like cmdOK for all the **OK** buttons than to give each of the buttons a different name. In such cases, however, when you qualify any calls to these objects, you have to be extremely careful that they are done correctly. Otherwise the wrong code may be executed.

If you need to set the focus to an object on a form, that form must be loaded, although it doesn't have to be active. The SetFocus statement cannot be used in a Form_Load procedure, because the form is not loaded until after the Form_Load procedure has been completed. If you need to set the focus every time a form is brought back to the screen, that code should be in the Form_Activate procedure; it cannot be in the Form_Load procedure.

When you are adding items to a list, you need to be careful always to clear the list if the procedure to add the items can be executed more than once. If the routine to add the items is in a Form_Load procedure, the list doesn't need to be cleared, because any lists on that form will be in their initial states when a Form_Load is executed. If you are adding to a list by selection of a button or an item in another list, the items added to the list will be added with the current items unless the list is cleared.

7.10   Command and Menu Summary

In this chapter you learned to use the following events:

- **DblClick** registers when the mouse is double-clicked.
- **MouseDown** registers when a mouse button is pressed.
- **QueryUnload** executes any time the user uses the title bar **Close** button or the **Control** menu to exit from the program.

In this chapter you learned about the following properties:

- **Color** allows you to access the color returned from the color Common Dialog Box.
- **ControlBox** turns the control box on a form on or off.
- **Default** specifies which of the buttons on a form is the default button.
- **ItemData** allows the program to store a number with each item added to a list.
- **LargeChange** sets the change in the value of the scroll bar when the user clicks on the scroll bar above or below the scroll box.
- **ListCount** indicates the number of items in a list box or a combo box.
- **Max** sets the maximum value of a scroll bar.
- **Min** sets the minimum value of a scroll bar.
- **MultiSelect** allows the user to select multiple items in a list.
- **NewIndex** contains the index of the latest item added to a list.
- **Selected** is True if the list item is selected and False if not.
- **SmallChange** sets the change in the value of the scroll bar when the user clicks on a scroll arrow.
- **Sorted** automatically sorts the items in a combo box or list box.
- **TabIndex** allows you to change the order of the tabs that take the user from object to object on the form.
- **Text** contains the text of the item currently selected in a list.
- **Value** is the current value corresponding to the relative position of the scroll box on a scroll bar.

In this chapter you learned about the following methods:

- **AddItem** adds items to a list box or a combo box.
- **Clear** empties the contents of a list.
- **Hide** allows you to remove a form from the desktop without unloading it.
- **ListIndex** is the index number of an item in a list box or a combo box.
- **Load** loads the form without showing it.
- **RemoveItem** removes items from a list box or a combo box.
- **Show** allows you to place a form on the desktop. If it is not yet loaded, Show loads it.
- **Unload** removes a form from the desktop and from memory until it is loaded again.

In this chapter you learned about the following commands and functions:

- **InputBox** allows you to display a message and lets the user key some information as a response.

- **LCase** is used to convert text to all lowercase.

- **MsgBox** allows you to display a message in a dialog box and lets the user respond through the use of buttons.

- **ShowColor** causes the color Common Dialog Box to be displayed.

- **UCase** is used to convert text to all uppercase.

In this chapter you learned about the following prefix:

- **vsb** is for a vertical scroll bar.

In this chapter you learned about the following menu option:

- **Project:**
  - **Add Form** allows you to add an additional form to your program.

In this chapter you learned about the following button:

- ⬛ lets you add an additional form or module to the application.

In this chapter you learned about the following Toolbox tools:

- ⬛ The tool to add a combo box to the form.

- ⬛ The tool to add a list box to the form.

- ⬛ The tool to add a vertical scroll bar to the form.

7.11   Performance Check

1. How many parameters are used in the MsgBox function and what are they?

2. What is returned to the application from the MsgBox function?

3. What is the Clear method used for?

4. How many combo box styles are there?

5. What method gives you the number of items in a list box?

6. What menu option is used to add an additional form to a project?

7. What is the initial form name for the second form added to a project?

8. Why do we change the names of the forms we use?

9. What is the method to cause a form to be displayed?

10. When we are using the method to display a form, what is the purpose of the parameter that can follow the name of the form?

11. What is the difference between the Hide and Unload methods?

12. What is a modal form?

13. What property contains the index number of the latest item added to a list?

_____

14. What object is the Min property related to?

_____

15. When is LargeChange used?

_____

16. What is the purpose of the button parameter of the MouseDown event?

_____

17. Which of the combo boxes is basically a list box?

_____

18. What method is used to add items to a list box?

_____

19. What is the ListIndex method for?

_____

20. What is the smallest value that ListIndex can contain?

_____

21. What property gives a list multiple selection capabilities?

_____

22. What object has the QueryUnload event?

_____

7.12 Programming Exercises

1. You decide you need more practice using the InputBox function. At the computer, do each of the following:

    a. Get into Visual Basic with your work disk in drive A.

    b. Start a new project called **InputBox Practice**. Call the form **frmInputBox**.

    c. Add a **File** menu to the form with an option to exit the program and another to print the form.

    d. Add five labels to the form: one each for name, address, city, state, and zip code. Create five additional labels so that each of the output labels can be a label of what is being displayed.

    e. Use the InputBox function to input each of the five data items. Display the InputBox when the user clicks on the associated label.

    f. Test the program and then print it out.

    g. Exit Visual Basic and shut down the system properly.

2. You like the Tic Tac Toe application you created in Programming Exercise 1 in Chapter 6 and decide you want to be able to change the background color of the form. At the computer, do each of the following:

    a. Get into Visual Basic with your work disk in drive A.

    b. Load the **Tic Tac Toe** application from Chapter 6. If you didn't create the Tic Tac Toe application in Chapter 6, you can get a copy of the application from your instructor.

    c. Save the form and project in your Chapter 7 folder.

    d. Update the menu to include the entry **&Change Form Color...** with the control name **mnuChange_Form_Color** between the other two menu items.

    e. Call up the code window for the new menu item, key the appropriate statements to load the color Common Dialog Box, and use the color received to change the background color of the form.

    f. Add the Common Dialog Box control to the program.

    g. Run the application to be sure the dialog box appears and the color changes work. Try several colors. Then exit the application and print it.

    h. Exit Visual Basic and shut down the system properly.

3. You like the Menu Multicut application originally created in Chapter 5 and updated in Programming Exercise 4 in Chapter 6. You decide you would like to be able to change the background and foreground colors of each of the workspaces. At the computer, do each of the following:

a. Get into Visual Basic with your work disk in drive A.

b. Load the **Menu Multicut** application from your Chapter 6 folder, and resave the form as **frmColor_Multicut** and the project as **Color Multicut** in your Chapter 7 folder. If you don't have the appropriate application, you can get a copy of it from your instructor.

c. Add the Common Dialog Box tool to your application.

d. Using the **Add File...** option from the **Project** menu, load the **frmWorkspace_Colors.frm** file, and resave the file as **frmMulti_Workspace_Colors.frm**. This will be used to change all the workspace colors.

e. Add a section of menu items at the bottom of the Edit menu with a separation line between them and the Paste item. There should be a menu item for each workspace (four of them). Make the menu items for the workspaces into a control array.

f. Change the code of the **OK** button of the frmMulti_Workspace_Colors form so that it only unloads the form.

g. Add code so that the color variables can be used in the menu item procedure (control array) to change the colors of the workspaces.

h. Run the application to be sure the color changes work properly. Be sure to try several colors and all workspaces. Then exit the application and print it.

i. Exit Visual Basic and shut down the system properly.

4. You work at a used car lot. Your boss has asked you to create an application that will display a list of the cars currently on the lot. When one of the items in the list is selected, the asking price should be displayed. The program should have a button that will bring up a form where a new list entry can be made. The dialog box will need to allow entry of the name of the car and the asking price. When the dialog box is exited, the new item needs to be added to the list. Another button on the form should allow the currently selected item in the list to be removed from the list. (These are the cars that have been sold.) A third button should be available to exit the program. At the computer, do each of the following:

a. Get into Visual Basic with your work disk in drive A.

b. Start a new program and add a sorted list and three buttons as described above.

c. Create two arrays: one for the car names and the other for the prices. The list needs to be sorted, so you will have to use the ItemData property when the items are added to the list and the prices are displayed.

d. Add a second form to the program that can be used to add new cars to the list as described above. Don't forget to add the item to the arrays when it is added to the list.

e. The code for the **Sold** button should use the RemoveItem method to remove the item from the list. The items (the name of the car and the price) will have to be removed from the arrays also. All you need to do is blank out the item in the array, because the ItemData property will no longer point to those items in the array when the item is removed from the list.

f. Save the program as **Car List**, test it, and then print it out.

g. Exit Visual Basic and shut down the system properly.

5. You work for an organization that sponsors the local dog show. A colleague has been working on a program that visitors to the dog show can use to access information about the entries, but she can't get the program to work and has asked for your help. At the computer, do each of the following:

a. Get into Visual Basic with your work disk in drive A.

b. Load the **Dog Show** program.

c. Run the program.

The program is supposed to allow the user to click one of the dog types shown on the initial form and to load the secondary form, which will display information about the particular dog.

d. Click **Cocker Spaniel** in the list, and the second form appears.

Now when you click an item in the list of names, the data for that dog should appear in the labels.

e. Click **Bitmap** in the list, and the data will show up in the labels. Click **Fluffy** and information is in the labels. Examine the labels carefully. Where the Owner was listed, the program now shows the Latest Win.

f. Stop the program and examine the code in the Click event procedure for the list of names on the second form. Look at the second line in the If Test. It is incorrect. Correct it and then run the program again.

g. Click **Cocker Spaniel** in the list. When the second form loads, click the **Done** button. Click **Cocker Spaniel** again. As you can see, the items in the list are duplicated. Exit the program and correct this problem.

h. The second form is actually supposed to be modal. Check the code for the dog type list Click event. Note that the statement to show the form has the modal portion commented out. Make the code active again. When you do this, you create another problem in this same procedure. Run the program, if necessary, to discover the problem, and then correct it.

i. Test the program thoroughly to be sure it is working properly, and then print it out.

7.13   Performance Mastery

1. You like the message board application you first created in Chapter 5 and then updated in Chapter 6 with the menus (saved as **Menu Messages**). The problem is that anyone can read anybody else's messages by simply selecting the name from the menu. You decide it would be better if each message board were password-protected. Update the program so that the application asks for a password the first time each message board is accessed and prompts for that password each subsequent time. Test the application. Then save it in your folder for Chapter 7 and print it out.

2. You have been asked by a personnel officer to create a program that will have a list of personnel from which one can be selected and various information about that person will be displayed. She wants to be able to see the date of hire, whether the person is salaried or hourly, and how many days of vacation the person has accumulated. Write the program, assigning the data to arrays that can be displayed using techniques similar to the ones presented in this chapter. Save the program as **Personnel Info**, test it, and then print it out.

3. Your boss liked the IN/OUT board you created back in Chapter 5. The problem is that not everybody should be allowed to leave the office at the same time. He wants you to change the program so that all three people on either of the two rows of buttons will not be able to be out of the office at the same time. In other words, if two of the people on the top row of buttons have checked out, the third should not. Add to the program the appropriate tests and an error message to take care of this problem. Test the application, save it in your Chapter 7 folder, and print it out.

4. You will soon be working on a large project in which you will be using a lot of lists and multiple forms. To get practice, you decide to write a program to practice using lists where multiple selections are allowed. Your program should have a button that, when selected, will take all the items selected in the list and put them in a list on another form. Your program should begin with a selection of entries for the list but should also have a text box where the user can key entries to be added to the list with a button to cause the addition. You will also need to have a button that will allow the user to delete from the list whatever items are selected. Use the MsgBox function to generate error messages if the user tries to remove a record without selecting the appropriate item in the list or tries to add an item to the list without keying anything in the text box. The text box should be erased after it has been added to the list. Use whatever data you wish in the list. A good method for testing programs is to use list items that are numbered, such as List item 1, List item 2, List item 3, and so on. Design and create the program, save it as **MultiSelection Lists**, test it, and then print it out.

5. You work for Widgets International and have been given the assignment of writing a program that will display various information about the products that your company sells. The program should display the Widget products in a list so that when the user selects an item, the program will display the cost of the product, the quantity on hand, the selling price, and the total profit that should be arrived at when all the products are sold (the difference between the cost and the selling price). Use a combo list so that the user can key the name of the product as well as select it by clicking the item in the list. Use the data shown in Table 7.2 in the program. Save the program as **Widget Product List**, test it, and print it out.

6. You work for Widgets International. Your boss has asked you to write a program that will display a list of the various products that the company sells. When an item is selected from the list, the program should display in a bar graph the quarterly sales for the three sales areas. The data to be used for the program are shown in Table 7.3. Create the program, and then save it as **Widget List and Graph**. Test the program and then print it out.

7. You have decided to finish the work on the **Personnel Numbers** program that you worked on in this chapter. It needs to have the Name list sorted, so the ItemData property will have to be used to properly display the numbers. Change the program, test it, and then print it out.

TABLE 7.2
The data for Performance Mastery Exercise 5

Product	Quantity on Hand	Cost	Selling Price
Red widget	150	15.25	30.25
Blue widget	125	16.27	30.25
Yellow widget	235	18.24	30.25
Widget holder	147	5.24	9.95
Extra blades	321	2.16	3.45
Strap	12	1.25	4.15
Cleaning kit	76	7.65	12.50

TABLE 7.3
The data for Performance Mastery Exercise 6

Product	Southern Area	Western Area	Eastern Area
Red widget	15,225	17,897	16,435
Blue widget	12,345	32,456	16,543
Yellow widget	14,567	19,423	12,456
Widget holder	9,357	12,983	6,231
Extra blades	1,346	2,984	6,534
Strap	5,245	6,298	3,490
Cleaning kit	6,298	4,298	4,991

8. The personnel staff of the company you work for has asked for your help. They need an application that will allow them to view lists of active and inactive employees. The program should allow them to select an employee in the active list and move that item to the inactive list. The user should also be able to reactivate employees by moving the names from the inactive list to the active list. Finally, the user should be able to remove from the inactive list employees who are no longer under consideration for rehire and delete them permanently. Use the MsgBox function to generate error messages if the user tries to move or remove a record without selecting the appropriate item in the list. Make up names that can be used in the lists. Design and create the program, and then save it as **Active and Inactive Lists**. Test the program and then print it out.

9. You work for a local dentist. He has asked you to write a program that can be used to look up the previous appointment, the next appointment scheduled, and the balance that the patient owes. You will need to have a list of patient names sorted in alphabetical order by the patient's last name. Use corresponding arrays to store the data. Use the data shown in Table 7.4 in the program. Design and create the program, and then save it as **Dentist List**. Test the program and then print it out.

10. You work for Widgets International. One of your colleagues has been working on a program that can be used to display various information about the products the company sells. He has created the arrays for the data and the form with the lists, buttons, and output labels, but he doesn't have time to finish the program and has asked for your help. The program should allow the user to select a color in the Widget list and then an accessory in the Accessories list. Then it should calculate the results when the **Calculate** button is selected. The program needs to check to be sure an item in each list has been selected before the calculations are done and, if not, should display an appropriate message. The three costs are to be totaled to come up with the Total Cost. The Total Cost is then multiplied by the quantity on hand to come up with the Total Cost of QOH. The program is called **Widget Lists** and can be found in the Ch-7 folder on your work disk. Add the necessary code to the program, and test it to be sure it is working properly. Then print it out.

11. You like the way your PIM application can automatically adjust the various program elements, but you want the program to adjust the elements automatically as the user changes the size of the form with the form border. This is done using the **Resize** event on the form. Change the PIM application so that this is done, save the program, test it, and then print it out. (Hint: When the program uses the Resize event to change the size of elements on the form, you must not resize the elements on the form when it is

TABLE 7.4
The data for
Performance Mastery
Exercise 9

Patient Name	Last Appointment	Next Appointment	Balance Due
Frank Tack	2/15/98	8/16/98	124.56
Fran Nedel	3/12/98	7/14/98	12.32
Gena Smith	1/15/98	9/12/98	456.98
Mary Reed	6/01/98	1/19/99	75.00
Harry Sanchez	3/4/98	2/16/99	85.00
Tom Parent	5/13/98	7/19/98	125.00
Fernando Maglia	4/9/98	8/1/98	16.00
Joseph Wachtler	4/8/98	8/12/98	12.45
Ed LaBorde	5/1/98	7/22/98	15.97

minimized or an error will occur. Use the **WindowState** property to determine when the form is minimized.)

12. You are soon to be given an assignment working with bitmaps in which you have to allow the user to click on various portions of the bitmap as though they were buttons. To practice the technique, you decide to use a bitmap that you have captured. Load one of the programs you have created in the past with buttons on it and run it to display the form on the desktop. Capture a bitmap image of the display by pressing **Alt-PrintScreen**. Run the Windows Paint program, paste the bitmap there, and use the Copy To option to save the bitmap to a file.

   Create a program with a text box and add an Image object to the form. Load the captured bitmap into the Image using the Picture property. Using a MouseDown procedure and the Debug.Print statement (or **Stop** if you prefer), determine the X and Y dimensions of the buttons on the form. Then, using an If Test to test for the boundaries of the objects, display the name of the object on the bitmap that is clicked in the text box. Save the program as **Bitmap Clicking**, test the program, and then print it out.

13. You are working on a project with other programmers in your company. One of the tasks you have been assigned is to create a password entry dialog box that can be used in the other applications. Create a program that will have a button whose only purpose is to call up the Password Entry dialog box. That dialog box should have two text boxes, one to allow users to enter an ID, which will consist of their first initial and their last name, and the other for their password. Create two arrays, one containing IDs and a corresponding array with the passwords. When the user selects the **OK** button, the entries need to be checked for validity. If the entry is wrong, display an error message. Give the user three chances to enter the correct data, and then display an error message and exit the program. If the password is verified, the password form should be unloaded.

   There should be a second button that will allow users to change their password. If this button is selected, the program should display another dialog box with a text box for entry of the original password, and two more text boxes for double entry of the new password. When the user selects the **OK** button, the program should check the two new entries to be sure the password has been properly entered. If not, an error message should be displayed, all three text boxes emptied, and the focus set in the first text box. If the entries are verified, the new password should be substituted for the original one in the array and the form unloaded.

   Normally such programs display asterisks or some other character as the password is keyed so that someone else will not be able to read it. This is done in the KeyPress routine by changing the KeyAscii character to the substitute character. However, the KeyAscii character must first be saved. Thus the entire password is stored in a temporary variable rather than being read from the text box. This means that if the user presses **Backspace,** a character must also be removed from the temporary variable. This portion of the program is not a requirement of the assignment, but you can add it to the program if you want more of a challenge.

   Design and create the program, and then save it as **Password Practice**. Test the program and then print it out.

Saving and Loading Files

8.1   Chapter Objectives

After finishing this chapter you will be able to:

- List and describe the three types of files that Visual Basic can use.

- Explain the process of accessing data in each of the types of files.

- List and explain the use of the three different access methods for sequential files.

- Demonstrate the use of the appropriate statements to open, read data from, write data to, and close each of the three types of files.

8.2   Introduction

We have written many applications in the past in which it would have been useful to be able to save the data to disk so that they could be used at a later time. When we exit the applications we have created up to this point, whatever data we have entered are lost. In anticipation of this need, when we began to add menus to our applications, we added menu choices to support files. Now is the time to add file processing to these applications.

    Most applications use three functions: Open File… (or Load) to retrieve data previously saved to disk, Save File As… to save the file and tell the application what the filename is and where to save the file (what drive and folder), and Save File to resave a file that has been saved in the past. If Save File is selected for a file that has not been saved previously, most applications automatically call up the Save File As… dialog box to allow the user to give the application the information it needs to save the file properly. In this chapter, we will learn how to add each of these functions to our applications. We will also learn some of the ways in which files are processed by the operating system.

8.3   Looking at the PIM

We will begin, as always, with a brief look at the PIM as it will be when we have completed the chapter.

1. Boot the system with your work disk in drive A.

2. Launch the PIM program from the Ch-8 folder.

> **HINT:** The file references used in the PIM are hardcoded to point to the Ch-8 folder on the floppy disk in drive A. If the files that the application uses on your system are placed elsewhere, you will have to have a version of the application that has been modified by your instructor so that it points to a different, proper location for its files.

The look of the program has not changed except for "[Untitled]" in the title bar, but the functionality of the menu has. "[Untitled]" refers to the name of the file currently being used in the notepad. Because there is currently no file there, the file has no title.

3. Pull down the **File** menu. There is now a **New** option. It is used to erase the current file loaded into the notepad and allows the user to start from scratch.

You have learned that one type of dialog box that the Common Dialog Control will display is the Open File dialog box. We will take advantage of this in the **Open File...** menu option.

4. Select the **Open File** option to see the dialog box shown in Figure 8.1.

This dialog box is just like the Open dialog box that is normally found in Windows applications.

5. Open the Ch-8 folder and you will see the **Sample Document.txt** file. Double-click the filename in the list to open the file and display it in the PIM notepad as shown in Figure 8.2.

In Chapter 7, we put in the name of the file as a suffix of the title bar caption. In this chapter, we will continue doing so when we actually load files as shown in Figure 8.2.

In many programs, when a file is loaded, a list of recently used files is displayed in the File menu. We are going to do this too.

6. Pull down the **File** menu to see that the name of the file just loaded is shown in the menu as in Figure 8.3.

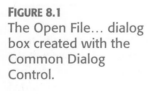

FIGURE 8.1
The Open File... dialog box created with the Common Dialog Control.

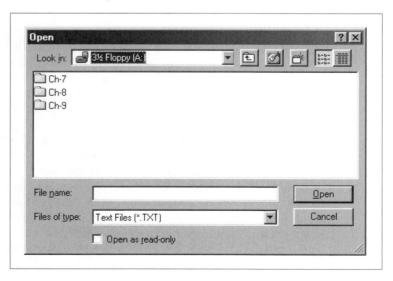

FIGURE 8.2
The file loaded into the notepad with the file name showing on the title bar.

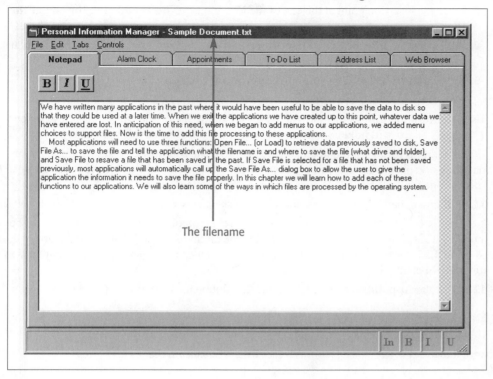

The filename

FIGURE 8.3
The **File** menu, showing the file name list.

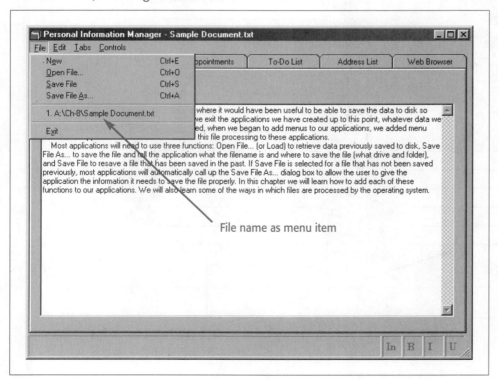

File name as menu item

If you change the text in the notepad and save the file, it can be reloaded later. You can also use the **Save As...** option to save the file with a different file name.

7. Place the insertion point at the end of the text and key **This is added to the end of the file**.

8. Pull down the **File** menu and select the **Save As...** option to see a dialog box similar to the Open File dialog box.

9. Key **Updated** as the file name and click the **Save** button.

Now the file name shown on the title bar reflects the new file name (Updated).

10. Pull down the **File** menu, and you will see that the list of file names now has two entries. The list will hold up to four file names with the most current at the top.

In addition to saving the notepad file, the program will now also save the font information, workspace colors, and any other changes you might make to the program settings. This is done with the **Save Changes** option of the **Controls** menu.

11. Pull down the **Controls** menu and you will see a new option, **Set Alarm Offset**.

This is to specify the amount of time before an appointment that the alarm is to be sounded. That is, if the alarm is set at 5:00 and the alarm offset is 5 minutes, the alarm will go off at 4:55. Perhaps, on the basis of this option, you can surmise that in this chapter we are going to create the Appointment calendar.

12. Click the **Appointments** tab to see the Appointments display shown in Figure 8.4.

FIGURE 8.4
The Appointments display.

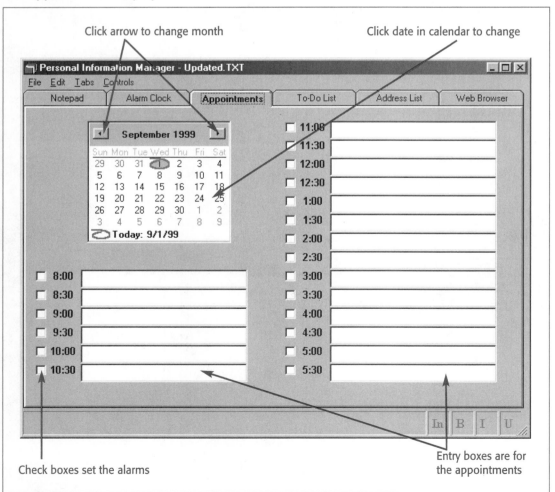

Click arrow to change month

Click date in calendar to change

Check boxes set the alarms

Entry boxes are for the appointments

As you can see, the program has a small calendar that lets you choose the date for which you want to record appointments. To pick a day, you merely click that day in the calendar. If you wish to change months, you can use the small arrows on either side of the month name or you can click the month name and a list of months for you to choose from will appear. The date shown as the current date (Today) is automatically set when the program first loads, so the current date displayed in the figure will certainly not match the one in your program. This tab has a set of appointment entry boxes as well as check boxes that are used to set the alarms. The timer control continually checks whether there is an appointment set for the current time, and if there is, it sets off the alarm. When the date in the calendar is changed, if any of the data on the display have been changed, those data are stored before the data for the newly chosen date is displayed.

13. Key **This is the 8:00 sample** in the 8:00 text box and click the check box to turn on the alarm for that time as shown in Figure 8.5.

14. Change the date. The display will clear and almost immediately you will see the dialog box shown in Figure 8.6. This is the alarm message indicating that you have an appointment.

15. Click the **OK** button on the dialog box and then reselect the previous date. The entry will be redisplayed (**This is the 8:00 sample**) but the alarm check box will be turned off because the alarm has been triggered.

If you exit the program and then rerun it, the appointment will still be associated with the date. This is because the information you put in the appointment calendar is stored in a file on the disk so it is "remembered" from one use of the program to the next.

FIGURE 8.5
The entered appointment comment and the checked alarm check box.

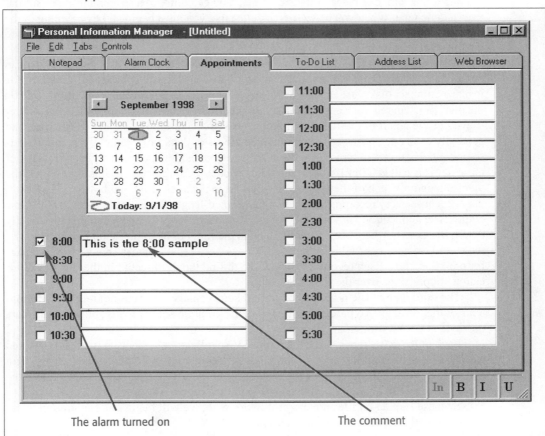

FIGURE 8.6
The alarm dialog box.

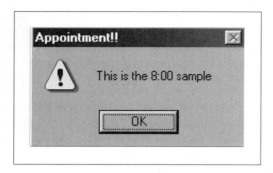

16. Play with the program a bit more until you have experienced the new features. Be sure to try the **New** option on the **File** menu. When you are finished, minimize the program; you will probably want to view it as you work through this chapter.

8.4   About Files

Three types of files are used in Visual Basic: **sequential, random,** and **binary.** With these three basic files, you can use any number of special-purpose file access methods, such as **index, linked list,** and **binary trees.**

A **sequential** file is one where the data are read from or stored in the file from the beginning to the end, one piece of data at a time. You can think of a sequential file as similar to a cassette tape. When you listen to a cassette tape, you must begin at the beginning of the tape and either listen or fast-forward to any other point on the tape. If you want to listen to the third song on the tape, you have to move past the other two songs first.

Random files, on the other hand, are considered direct-access files, because you can directly access any point in the file. If a sequential file is like a cassette tape, a random file is like a compact disk. Just as you can tell the CD player to go directly to the third song on the disk, you can tell your application to go directly to a particular point in the file and retrieve or save a part of the file at that point. These parts of the file are called **records,** and generally each one consists of several related pieces of data. For example, a record of personnel information will typically have at least a name, address, city, state, and zip. Each of these items is called a **field,** and all the fields make up a single record. In random files, the precise length of each of these fields is specified in the application, and the length doesn't vary. Because every record is made up of these fixed-length fields, every record is the same length. The application knows just how long the entire record is, and it can mathematically determine exactly where each record will be in the file. For example, suppose the length of the record we have been talking about is 60 bytes (recall that a byte is enough storage space for one character). Each record is 60 bytes, so to find the third record in the file, the application simply skips over the first 120 bytes.

The third type of file is a **binary** file, and here Visual Basic does not interpret the contents of the file at all. To process a binary file, the program simply reads and writes the data one byte at a time without any groupings.

Each of these file types has its own set of Visual Basic statements to process the stored data. We will discuss the various commands for sequential and random files as we begin and we will work with an example of each of these files. If necessary, you can explore the use of a binary file on your own; this is beyond the scope of this book.

Because sequential files are easier to work with, we will begin our exploration there. Later, we will look at accessing a random file.

8.5 Opening a Sequential File

Before any file can be processed in Visual Basic, it must be opened, and there are three ways to do that, depending on how the file will be used. We can open a sequential file for **Input**, **Output**, or **Append**. We open a file for input if we want to read from it, for output if we want to write to it, and for append if we want to write to the end of it. Remember that a sequential file must be worked with from beginning to end, so if we want to write data in a file that already has data in it, the only way to do it is write the new data at the end of the old data, which is referred to as *appending* the data.

When Visual Basic tries to open an Output file, if the file already exists, it will erase the data contained in the file and subsequently write the new data in place of the old. If the file is not found, Visual Basic will automatically create it for us. If we open a file for input and the file cannot be found on the disk, we will receive an error because we cannot read data from a nonexistent file.

A summary of the file modes is shown in Table 8.1.

The format of a Visual Basic **Open** statement for a sequential file is

```
Open Pathname For Mode As # Filenumber
```

The Pathname in the format specifies the file name and the path where the file is to be found on the disk. The Mode is Input, Output, or Append, as we have said. The Filenumber is a number that is assigned to the file. All files in Visual Basic are referred to by the number that is assigned to them in the Open statement. We can use many different files at the same time in an application, so to process one of the files, Visual Basic needs to know which one we are trying to process. That's what the Filenumber is for.

The Filenumber used for a file is associated with that particular file for as long as that file is open. If your program tries to use the same Filenumber again before the file is closed, you will get an error. Once the file that is associated with the Filenumber is closed, the Filenumber is freed and can be used again.

You should be careful when reusing a Filenumber for a different file or a different purpose. It is easy to get confused about which file the Filenumber is referring to at present. Because you can use many different Filenumbers, it is better to use a different Filenumber for each file you are processing.

Table 8.2 shows several uses of the Open statement.

TABLE 8.1
The summary of the Open statement modes for sequential-access files.

Open Statement Mode	Use to:
Input	Read data from an existing sequential-access file. If the file specified in the Open statement does not exist, Visual Basic will generate an error.
Output	Create a sequential-access file and write data into it. If the file specified in the Open statement already exists, the data in the file are erased before the new data are written.
Append	Add data to the end of a sequential-access file. If the file specified in the Open statement does not exist, it is automatically created.

TABLE 8.2
Uses of the Open
statement.

Open Statement	Result
Open C:\Work Files\Sample.txt for Input as #1	Opens a sequential-access file called Sample.txt for Input. The file is found in the Work Files folder on drive C, and the Filenumber assigned to the file is 1.
Open A:\Ch-8\Data.txt for Output as #4	Opens a sequential-access file called Data.txt for output. The file is found in the Ch-8 folder on drive A, and the Filenumber assigned to the file is 4.
Open D:\Practice.doc for Append as #2	Opens a sequential-access file called Practice.doc for Append. The file is found in the root directory on drive D, and the Filenumber assigned to the file is 2.

The Save As Form

Now that we know how to open a file, it is time to add that part to the Notepad portion of the PIM application.

Let's learn how to use the various Visual Basic tools available for file manipulation, because they can be used for all types of file access.

1. Get into Visual Basic with your work disk in drive A.

2. Load the **PIM** application from your Ch-7 folder, and save each of the forms and the project in your Ch-8 folder.

3. Create a new form and modify it so that it looks like the one in Figure 8.7 with the following provisions:

   a. The form name is **frmSave_As**.

   b. The control name of the text box is **txtFilename**.

FIGURE 8.7
The beginnings of the
Save File As... dialog
box.

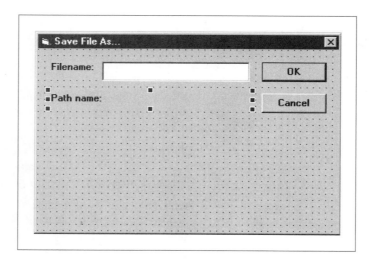

    c. The control names of the buttons are the standard ones. Make the **OK** button the default.

    d. Turn off the **Maximize** and **Minimize** buttons.

    e. The label that shows "Path name:" is called **lblPathname**.

We left room on the form for the addition of the file controls that Visual Basic needs to determine where the file is to be stored. This requires the use of a few new tools. There are three tools that can be combined to get the necessary file information. There is one to determine the disk drive to be accessed, one for the folder location, and one that gives you a list of the filenames found there so that you can pick the file you are after from the list. We will add two of these tools to this form and the third to the form that will load a file from disk.

  4. Select the **DriveListBox** control shown in Figure 8.8 and position it on the form as shown in Figure 8.9, giving it the control name of **drvSave_As**.

As you can see, this is a pull-down list box, which is the only way this box will appear, as we cannot control it. The other two tools also have a predetermined form although not pull-down lists. When the application is executed, the required drive can be chosen from this pull-down list.

Next we need to add the folder tool.

  5. Select the **DirListBox** control shown in Figure 8.10 and size and position it on the form as shown in Figure 8.11. The default control name of **Dir1** should be changed to **dirSave_As**. Note that this is a normal list box, not a pull-down list.

Now that we have finished the form, we are ready to add the form to the menu item.

  6. Switch to frmPIM, open the code window for the **Save File As…** option on the File menu, and key the appropriate Show statement. Such dialog boxes are generally modal, which disables the rest of the program until the user is finished with the dialog box.

FIGURE 8.8
The DriveListBox control.

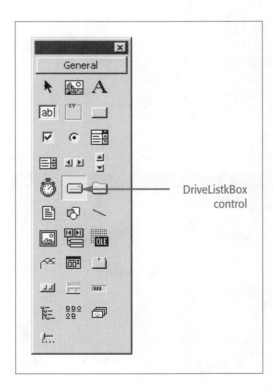

DriveListkBox control

FIGURE 8.9
The form with the
DriveListBox control
added.

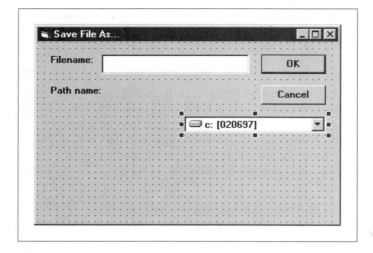

FIGURE 8.10
The DirListBox control.

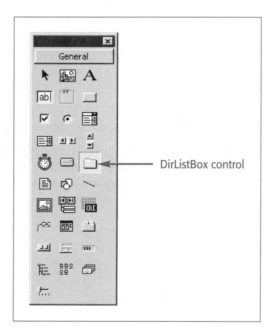

DirListBox control

FIGURE 8.11
The form with the
DirListBox control
added.

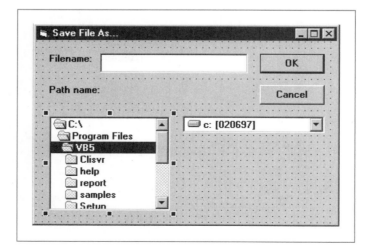

Now we are ready to add the code to open the file. Before we can create the Open statement, however, we need to get the pathname data from the two new tools so that these data can be combined with the keyed file name to have a valid file name.

We will start with the drive box.

7. Switch to the frmSave_As form and open the code window for the drive box.

Normally we would use the Click event when working with a list, but this list is special, and we need to use the Change event instead. As you see, the code window for the drive box opens with the Change event.

The property of the drive box that contains the drive designation is **Drive**. To be able to use this drive designation, we assign it to a special property of the directory box called **Path**. Thus, to change the drive in this change procedure, we use the statement

```
dirSave_As.Path = drvSave_As.Drive
```

8. Key this statement in the procedure.

Because we set up a special label on the form that displays the current pathname, we want to put our new pathname there with the statement

```
lblPathname.Caption = "Path name: " & dirSave_As.Path
```

9. Key this statement after the dirSave_As.Path statement.

This same statement needs to be placed in the Change event procedure for the Directory list box.

10. Change to the code for the directory list box (**dirSave_As**), and key the statement as above.

The same statement needs to go in one more place. When we first load the form, the path name will not be shown. We need to add the statement to the Load event for the form. If you're wondering what the path name will be when the form is first loaded, it will be whatever drive and directory the application was in when Visual Basic was launched or whatever it currently is if you have been using Windows to change drives or directories since Visual Basic was launched.

11. Open the code window for the Form_Load event of the frmSave_As form, and key the lblPathname.Caption statement.

Now we need to open the file for the file name the user keys into the file name entry box. We can do that by combining the dirSave_As.Path with the file name from the entry box. Ordinarily the Open statement would be

```
Open dirSave_As.Path & txtFilename.Text For Output As #1
```

There is, however, a problem with this statement. A full pathname contains the drive designator followed by a colon and a backslash; then each folder in the path is separated by a backslash from the previous folder, and the file name at the end from the last folder, so that the operating system can follow the path directly to the file location. Using this statement, if the pathname happened to be for the root directory, such as C:\, everything would work fine. The trouble arises when the pathname is for a folder such as C:\VB. Now there is no trailing backslash to separate the folder from the filename, and if we combine the file name with the pathname, we will get something like C:\VBSample, where Sample is the file name. This will not work, because the program would attempt to open a file in the root directory of drive C, called VBSample. We need a backslash between the pathname and the file name, as in C:\VB\Sample. Thus, we need to determine when there is already a trailing slash and when there isn't. We require an If statement such as

```
If Right(dirSave_As.Path, 1) = "\" Then
    gstrFilename = dirSave_As.Path & txtFilename.Text
Else
```

```
         gstrFilename = dirSave_As.Path & "\" & txtFilename.Text
      End If
      Open gstrFilename For Output as #1
```

12. Open the code window for the **OK** button, and key the foregoing code.

Creating a Module

We mentioned modules several chapters ago, but we never had a need for one. Now, however, we need to declare the gstrFilename variable so that we can access it from the Save As form. To do this, we must declare it as Global, and that is done only in a module.

Remember that modules are designed to hold only code and variables and do not contain any objects. They are added to the program using the **Add Module** option of the **Project** menu or the **Module** option of the list of forms shown when you select the new form button (🖻▾) on the tool bar.

1. Click the down arrow on the new form button (🖻▾) and select the **Module** option. A dialog box appears. Click the **Open** button, and a new code window opens up. Modules contain only code, so the only thing you will see for a module is a code window.

2. Declare the **gstrFilename** variable as a global string in the module so that it can be used and passed between the various forms. To do this, key the following statement:

```
Global gstrFilename as String
```

Thus far, we have only opened the file. Now we need to write the data into it.

8.6   Writing Data into the Sequential File

We can write to a sequential file with two different statements: **Write #** and **Print #**. The Write # statement will insert commas between the fields and put quotation marks around string fields as they are put into the file. This creates what is known as a **delimited** file. This type of data is suitable to be input into other applications such as spreadsheets and databases. The Print # statement will simply write the data into the file as we specify, without any formatting. In the case of the Notepad, we have only one string to put into the file, so we don't need any delimiting. If we were to use the Write # statement, our text would come back with quotation marks around it. So we will use the Print # statement. The Print # and Write # statements have the same format:

```
Print #Filenumber, [output item] [, output item …]
Write #Filenumber, [output item] [, output item …]
```

The Filenumber in the statements must be the same Filenumber that was used in the Open for Output statement that opens the file into which you want to print or write the data. If you don't put any output items (or data) on the statement, you must still use the comma, and a blank line is printed into the file. You can put as many output items on the statements as you need, using a comma, a space, or a semicolon to separate them. A few sample Print # statements are shown in Table 8.3.

The Print # statement we need in this instance is

```
Print #1, frmPIM.txtNotepad.Text
```

This copies the text from the Notepad workspace into the file. Because the file was opened as #1, we also use #1 in the Print # statement. If we have several files open at the same time, we can write to whichever one we wish by using the file number for that particular file.

1. Switch back to the code window for the **OK** button on the **Save As** form and add this Print #1 statement after the Open statement.

TABLE 8.3
Examples of the Print #
statement for
sequential-access files.

Print # Statement	Result
Print #1, txtNotepad.Text	Writes the contents of the text property of the txtNotepad control to the sequential-access data file opened as #1.
Print #3, intCounter, strOutput	Writes the values of both of the variables intCounter and strOutput into the sequential-access data file opened as #3.
Print #2, intCounter; lstColor.ListCount	Writes the values of the variable intCounter and the ListCount property of the lstColor list into the sequential-access data file opened as #2.

After we have finished writing the data into a file, we need to close the file. The data in the file are not really safely written until the file is closed. Also, suppose we want to copy this same document into two separate files. All that is required is to select the **Save File As...** option again, and we can save the same document to another disk, in another folder on the same disk, or in exactly the same place with a different file name. But the Open statement uses #1 for the Filenumber, and if we have already used that number, it cannot be used again until the file is closed. If we use the same Open statement twice without closing the file in between, we will get an error. Closing the file releases the Filenumber so that it can be used again.

Given all this, we must add a **Close** statement to our code after the Print statement. The format of the statement is simply

```
Close #Filenumber
```

and the statement we need is

```
Close #1
```

because the file we are currently using is #1.

2. Add this statement after the Print # statement.

3. Run the application, key some information in the notepad workspace, select the **Save File As...** option of the **File** menu, change the drive to A and the folder to Ch-8, key **Sample** as the file name, and select the **OK** button.

We will be able to get the data back from the disk by loading the file as soon as we have looked at a few more things.

4. Exit the application.

This takes care of the **Save File As...** option, but what of the **Save File** option? We mentioned earlier that if the file has not been previously saved, we have to open the **Save File As...** option dialog box so that the user can specify the proper file name. We need some way to determine whether this particular file has already been saved. There are a number of ways to do this. One of the easiest is to display the file name and store it appended to the end of the title bar caption, as we did in the previous chapter. This way we can check for the file name on the title bar, and if it is [Untitled], we know the file hasn't been saved. By putting the file name on the title bar, we ensure that the user will always know the name of the current file, and we will have something we can test for to determine whether the file has been saved previously.

Remember that in Chapter 7 we gave the user an option that could be used to change the form title. That means we don't know what the title on the title bar will be and we don't know how long the title will be. What we do know is that there will always be a dash between the name of the form and the name of the file. We can search for this dash with the following code:

```
intDash_Found = InStr(frmPIM.Caption, " - ")
```

After the dash is found, we need to write the title and file name with the statement

```
frmPIM.Caption = Left(frmPIM.Caption, intDash_Found + 2) &
↳ txtFilename.Text
```

This displays just the file name. You could use the pathname in the caption as well, but since pathnames can get rather long, it is safer to display the file name alone.

5. Add the foregoing statements just after the Close statement. Then add an appropriate Hide statement.

   The final addition is for the **Cancel** button. Just hide the dialog box.

6. Open the code for the **Cancel** button and add the appropriate statement.

   The code for all the procedures of the new form should be as shown in Figure 8.12.
   The other change we need to make is to the original caption of the title bar. If the current file hasn't been saved yet, we need to reflect that on the title bar. In most applications this is done with something similar to

```
Formname - [Untitled]
```

7. Switch to the code for the Form_Load procedure of the frmPIM, and add a statement to append the foregoing default file name to the form title with a dash between them.

   Now we are ready to test the application.

8. Run the application. "[Untitled]" should follow the program name on the title bar.

9. Key some text in the workspace, pull down the **File** menu, select **Save File As...**, key **Sample** as the file name, change the drive to A, change to the Ch-8 folder, and select the **OK** button. This will save the file in the Ch-8 folder of drive A.

   Look at the title bar of the window. It should have the file name Sample after the program title, and unless there is an error of some kind in the application, the program should have created a file called Sample with the keyed text stored in it.
   Now if the title bar has "[Untitled]" appended to the caption, we will know that this is the first time the file has been saved, and if the user selects the **Save File** option, we will need to bring up the **Save File As**... option window.

10. Exit the application and open the code window for the **Save File** option.

    Note that there are already two statements in this procedure (counting the Dim statement that we inserted in Chapter 7). We could leave them there, but when the user selects the **Save File** option, it is assumed that the file will be saved on top of an existing file, so this warning merely indicates something the user already knows. The warning is not really necessary, and we will delete it (we put it there only for practice).

11. Delete the existing statements and key the following:

```
intDash_Found = InStr(frmPIM.Caption, " - ")
If Mid(frmPIM.Caption, intDash_Found + 3) = "[Untitled]" Then
    frmSave_As.Show vbModal
Else
```

FIGURE 8.12
The code of the frmSave_As form.

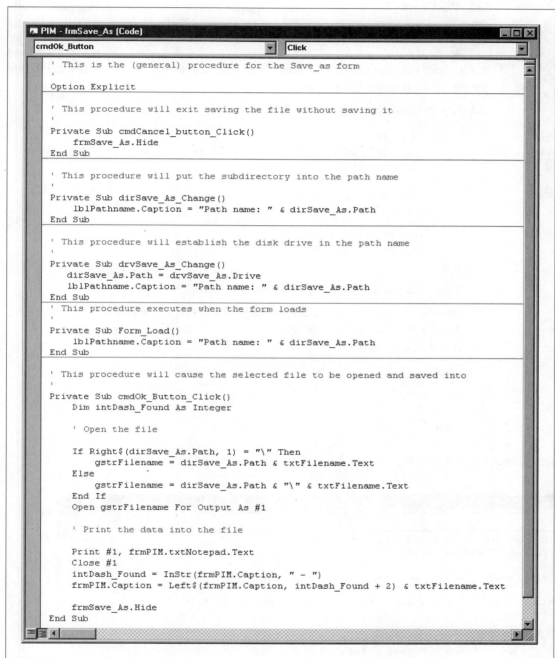

```
PIM - frmSave_As [Code]                                              _ □ ✕
cmdOk_Button                    ▼      Click                              ▼
' This is the (general) procedure for the Save_as form
'
Option Explicit

' This procedure will exit saving the file without saving it
'
Private Sub cmdCancel_button_Click()
        frmSave_As.Hide
End Sub

' This procedure will put the subdirectory into the path name
'
Private Sub dirSave_As_Change()
    lblPathname.Caption = "Path name: " & dirSave_As.Path
End Sub

' This procedure will establish the disk drive in the path name
'
Private Sub drvSave_As_Change()
  dirSave_As.Path = drvSave_As.Drive
  lblPathname.Caption = "Path name: " & dirSave_As.Path
End Sub
' This procedure executes when the form loads
'
Private Sub Form_Load()
        lblPathname.Caption = "Path name: " & dirSave_As.Path
End Sub

' This procedure will cause the selected file to be opened and saved into
'
Private Sub cmdOk_Button_Click()
    Dim intDash_Found As Integer

    ' Open the file

    If Right$(dirSave_As.Path, 1) = "\" Then
        gstrFilename = dirSave_As.Path & txtFilename.Text
    Else
        gstrFilename = dirSave_As.Path & "\" & txtFilename.Text
    End If
    Open gstrFilename For Output As #1

    ' Print the data into the file

    Print #1, frmPIM.txtNotepad.Text
    Close #1
    intDash_Found = InStr(frmPIM.Caption, " - ")
    frmPIM.Caption = Left$(frmPIM.Caption, intDash_Found + 2) & txtFilename.Text

    frmSave_As.Hide
End Sub
```

Note that the If Test is checking the title to find out whether it has been changed. If not, we use the Save File As... dialog box. Otherwise, we will want to save the file without a dialog box.

Now we want to save the file by using the current dirSave_As.Path, which we could do here. Shortly, however, we will create an Open File dialog box that we will use to open files and copy them into the notepad. If the file is brought into the notepad by using the

Open File dialog box, the dirSave_As.Path will not be available because the **Save File As...** option will not have been used. Therefore, we need to get the path from somewhere else. The **CurDir** function is set up for just such needs. It retrieves the current path directly from Windows. Then we can combine this pathname with the file name we put in the title bar caption to form the complete path to the file.

We have the same problem with the backslash at the end of the path name that we had before, and will need to check for it as before. We have to use a nested If Test in the Else portion of the If Test already begun.

12. Key the following as the rest of the If Test:

```
If Right(CurDir, 1) = "\" Then
        gstrFilename = CurDir & Mid(frmPIM.Caption, intDash_Found + 2)
    Else
        gstrFilename = CurDir & "\" & Mid(frmPIM.Caption,
        ↳ intDash_Found + 2)
    End If
    Open gstrFilename For Output As #1
    Print #1, txtNotepad.Text
    Close #1
End If
```

This gives you the entire If Test shown in Figure 8.13.

13. Run the application, and select the **Save File** option to be sure the Save File As... dialog box comes to the desktop.

14. Exit the application.

FIGURE 8.13
The code in the mnuSave_File_Click event procedure.

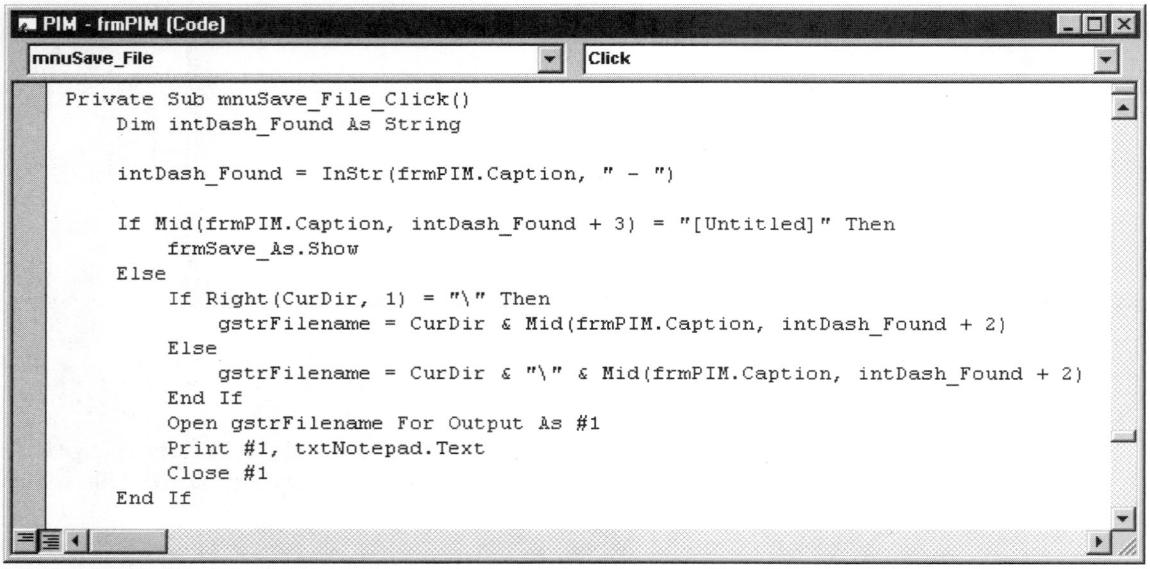

```
PIM - frmPIM (Code)                                              _ □ ×

mnuSave_File                    ▼    Click                            ▼

    Private Sub mnuSave_File_Click()
        Dim intDash_Found As String

        intDash_Found = InStr(frmPIM.Caption, " - ")

        If Mid(frmPIM.Caption, intDash_Found + 3) = "[Untitled]" Then
            frmSave_As.Show
        Else
            If Right(CurDir, 1) = "\" Then
                gstrFilename = CurDir & Mid(frmPIM.Caption, intDash_Found + 2)
            Else
                gstrFilename = CurDir & "\" & Mid(frmPIM.Caption, intDash_Found + 2)
            End If
            Open gstrFilename For Output As #1
            Print #1, txtNotepad.Text
            Close #1
        End If
```

8.7 Loading a Sequential File

Now that the file has been saved to disk, our next concern is loading that file (or any other file) from disk into the application. In order to verify that the data loaded from disk are what was saved, it is always a good idea to erase the workspace before loading the file. We could erase the data in the workspace with the **Clear All** option, but this would not (nor would we want it to) clear the file name on the title bar. We need a new option to clear the workspace and remove the file name from the title bar. This brings up a menu option that we didn't put on the file menu before, **New**. We will use it to erase everything from the workspace. Let's add it now.

The New Option

1. Call up the menu design window for frmPIM, insert a new line before the **Open File...** option, and add **N&ew** with the control name **mnuNew_File** and the hot key **Ctrl-E**.

   It would be more logical to use the access key **N** and the hot key **Ctrl-N,** but we have already used **Ctrl-N** on the **Tab** menu for the **Notepad** option. So we will use **E**.

2. Open the code window for the **New** item on the **File** menu, and key the statement to erase all the text in the workspace and another statement that will change the caption of the title bar so that it will again reflect an [Untitled] document.

3. Run the application and key some text into the workspace.

4. Select the **New** option to verify that it works as it is supposed to. The workspace should be empty, and the title bar caption should again contain [Untitled] after the program name.

The Open File Form

With that addition we can now create a form for opening the file. We need to be able to change the drive, change the directory, and select the file we want from a list of available files, which is done with a new control called a **FileListBox** (see Figures 8.14 and 8.15).

FIGURE 8.14
The Open File form with the FileListBox added.

The FileListBox control

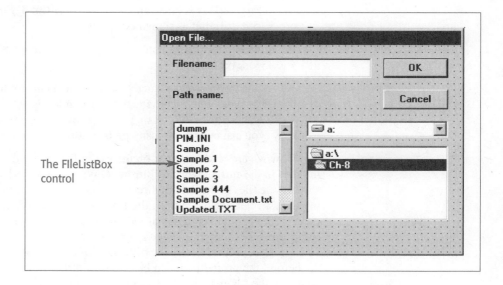

FIGURE 8.15
The FileListBox control.

FileListBox
control

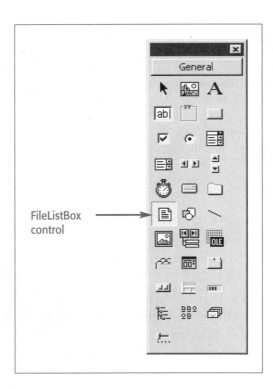

1. Add a new form called **frmOpen_File**. Add the objects shown in Figure 8.14 with the following considerations:

   a. The control name of the text box is **txtFilename**.

   b. The control names of the buttons are the standard ones.

   c. Make the **OK** button the default.

   d. Turn off the **Maximize** and **Minimize** buttons.

   e. The label that shows "Path name:" is called **lblPathname**.

   f. The directory box should be **dirOpen_File**.

   g. The drive box should be **drvOpen_File**.

2. Add a **FileListBox** control with the name of **filLoad_File**, using the tool shown in Figure 8.15. Position it as shown in Figure 8.14.

We already know how to create many of the code elements that we need to make this new form work properly.

3. Add to the Form_Load event the proper statements for the form, the directory box, and the drive box. Note that the text box for entering the filename on this form is called TxtFilename, just as it was on the other form. This makes entering the necessary code easy (you can even copy many parts of it from the other form if you wish).

Now we are ready to work on the use of the FileListBox control. It will always show the files in the current working directory. When you added the box to your form, it already showed the files in the default directory. There are three properties of concern when working with a FileListBox control: the **FileName**, the **Path**, and the **Pattern**. The FileName property holds the filename that the user has selected from the list. This is essentially the same as the Text property that a normal list uses.

The Path property holds the path name of the directory whose files you want to display. As before, the proper path can be found in dirOpen_File.Path, and it will need to be assigned to the filOpen_File.Path in the directory box and drive box code.

The Pattern property holds the specification for the type of files you want to appear in the list. The default pattern is "*.*" but for our application we want to display the files without an extension, so our pattern will need to be "*." We could, of course, have decided to assign to our files an extension such as TXT (which is what most notepad-type programs use), and then we would want our default pattern to be something related to that, such as "*.TXT." Most applications show this pattern in the file name entry box, and we will do this too. We will also highlight the pattern so that if the user chooses to key a file name or a different pattern, the current pattern will automatically be erased. The code to add the pattern should be put in the Form_Load event, and the **OK** and **Cancel** buttons will need to unload the form rather than just hide it.

4. Open the code window for the drive object and add the following statement between the other two you should already have there:

```
filOpen_File.Path = dirOpen_File.Path
```

which will give you the three statements shown here:

```
dirOpen_File.Path = drvOpen_File.Drive
filOpen_File.Path = dirOpen_File.Path
lblPathname.Caption = "Path name: " & dirOpen_File.Path
```

The inserted statement follows the assignment of the drive to the path. This assignment sends all the drive and directory information to the part of the application that controls the display of the file list, and the file list will reflect that change.

5. Switch to the code window for the directory object and add the filOpen_Fil.Path statement on the end.

Now we need to add a bit of code to the Load event for the form so that it will put the pattern in the file name entry box and highlight it.

6. Switch to the code window for the Open File form, and key the following in the Form_Load event:

```
txtFilename.Text = "*."
txtFilename.SelStart = 0
txtFilename.SelLength = Len(txtFilename.Text)
filOpen_File.Pattern = "*."
```

There are two events for the file list that are of interest. If the user clicks one of the file names in the list, that file name should be placed in the file name entry box. If the user double-clicks one of the file names, then we need to exit from the dialog box and use that file name. For this double-click event we can simply call on the **OK** button code.

7. Switch to the code window for the file list Click procedure (single click action), and key the following:

```
txtFilename.Text = filOpen_File.FileName
```

This will place the file name in the entry box.

8. Switch to the code window for the file list DblClick procedure , and key the following:

```
cmdOk_Click
```

We must make sure a file name has been entered into the text box. If it hasn't, we need to change the Pattern property so that a new list of files appears, on the off chance that a new pattern was entered into the box rather than a file name. For example, the user might enter S*.* to see all the files that begin with S. In such a case, we need to redisplay the file list without exiting the dialog box. We can discover such a pattern by checking for an asterisk or question mark; these are the only valid wildcard characters. As in most other Windows-type dialog boxes, an asterisk matches any characters from the place of the asterisk to the right, while a question mark matches any single character.

9. Switch to the code window for the **OK** button and key the following:

```
Dim intAsterisk As Integer
Dim intQuestion_Mark As Integer

' Determine if the filename pattern has been changed or a filename
↳ has been entered

intAsterisk = Instr(txtFilename.Text, "*")
intQuestion_Mark = Instr(txtFilename.Text, "?")
If intAsterisk <> 0 Or intQuestion_Mark <> 0 Then
    filOpen_File.Pattern = txtFilename.Text      ' Change the pattern
Else
```

Note that we are checking for an asterisk and then a question mark. If either of these is found, we change the pattern and then exit the procedure, because the rest of the procedure is the Else part of the If Test. If neither the asterisk nor the question mark is found, what is in the text box must be a file name, not a pattern, and we can go ahead and read the file.

As when a file is saved, the first thing we must do when reading a file is open that file. The Open statement is the same as before, except that the mode is Input rather than Output. We also need the same type of If Test that we used before, because we are still inputting the pathname the same way.

10. Key the following after the Else statement (in this case, we do want to have the If following the Else rather than using an ElseIf).

```
' Open the file

If Right( dirOpen_File.Path, 1) = "\" Then
    gstrFilename = dirOpen_File.Path & txtFilename.Text
Else
    gstrFilename = dirOpen_File.Path & "\" & txtFilename.Text
End If
Open gstrFilename For Input As #1
```

Reading from the File

Now that the file is opened, we are ready to read the data. There are three different statements that can be used to input data from a file:

■ **Input #** is used when the file to be read is delimited (with commas separating each item and quotation marks around text strings).

■ **Line Input** reads text strings and quits when it finds a carriage return.

■ **Input** is designed specifically to read text strings. It ignores carriage returns and just inputs the data.

We are going to input data that were stored as text and quite likely may have commas and quotation marks imbedded as part of the data. We don't want the input to stop when it finds a delimiter such as a comma, so we will not be able to use the Input # function.

We also can't use the Line Input function because it will stop reading the file when it encounters a carriage return. The user will probably use a carriage return between paragraphs, so the Line Input function would read the data only until the end of the first paragraph. If we are using the Line Input function to read a file that contains a series of strings, we need to use the Line Input statement as many times as there are strings in the file. For this type of processing, a loop is generally used. It can end when the end of the file is found, which is tested with the **EOF(Filenumber)** function. A sample of such a loop is

```
Do Until EOF(1)
    Loop statements
Loop
```

This loop will continue to function until the program senses the end of the file.

Because we can't use either the Input # or the Line Input function, we need to use the Input function. When using the Input function, you must tell the function exactly how many bytes it is to read. The format of this function is

```
Input (Length of data, # Filenumber)
```

The first parameter is the length of the data you are accessing, and the second parameter is the Filenumber. If the first input of data from the file you are processing contained 30 bytes, the Input statement would be

```
strInput_Data = Input (30, #1)
```

In the case of the notepad, we don't know how many bytes of data there are, but we want to read it all. We want to read the entire file. To do this, we can use the Visual Basic function **LOF(Filenumber)**, which stands for **Length Of File**, to tell the function how long the file is. A sample of this statement for inputting the notepad text is

```
frmPIM.txtNotepad.Text = Input(LOF(1), #1)
```

This tells the application to read LOF(1) bytes from file #1, where LOF(1) is the length of file number 1.

1. Key the foregoing statement after the Open statement in the code for the **OK** button.

   Next, the file needs to be closed because we have read all that it holds.

2. Key the necessary Close statement.

   We have just input a new file, so change the filename on the title bar caption.

3. Key the statements required to change the name on the title bar caption, (Try it yourself and then check your code against that shown in Figure 8.16.)

Changing the Drive and Directory

Our application will work fine now, except for one thing. When we change the drive and/or directory, we can load a file from there. Unfortunately, the next time we use the **Open File...** option, the drive and directory will revert to the original ones, because those are still the ones that Windows knows about. What we need to do is actually change the drive and directory in Windows, not just in our forms. Visual Basic has two functions, **ChDir** and **ChDrive**, that are designed for this purpose.

The **ChDir** function has the following format:

```
ChDir pathname
```

This pathname is the pathname of the directory to which we want to change. In our program, this is stored in dirOpen_File.Path. This means the statement we need is

```
ChDir dirOpen_File.Path
```

The format of the ChDrive function is similar:

```
ChDrive drive letter
```

The drive letter is simply the letter of the drive to which we want to change. In our program the first character of dirOpen_File.Path contains the drive letter. So we use a statement like

```
ChDrive Left(dirOpen_File.Path, 1)
```

1. Add these statements, as well as an Unload statement, to the procedure and key the End If statement at the end. This will give you a procedure that looks like the one in Figure 8.16.

FIGURE 8.16
The code for the **OK** button on the Open Form dialog box.

```
PIM - frmOpen_File [Code]                                          _ □ ×

cmdOK                              ▼   Click                               ▼

' The procedure for the OK button
'
Private Sub cmdOK_Click()
    Dim intAsterisk As Integer
    Dim intQuestion_mark As Integer
    Dim intDash_Found As Integer

    ' Determine if filename pattern is changed or a filename is entered

    intAsterisk = InStr(txtFilename.Text, "*")
    intQuestion_mark = InStr(txtFilename.Text, "?")
    If intAsterisk <> 0 Or intQuestion_mark <> 0 Then
        filOpen_File.Pattern = txtFilename.Text    ' Change the pattern
    Else

        ' Open the files

        If Right(dirOpen_File.Path, 1) = "\" Then
            gstrFilename = dirOpen_File.Path & txtFilename.Text
        Else
            gstrFilename = dirOpen_File.Path & "\" & txtFilename.Text
        End If
        Open gstrFilename For Input As #1

        ' Input the data

        frmPIM.txtNotepad.Text = Input$(LOF(1), #1)
        Close #1

        intDash_Found = InStr(frmPIM.Caption, " - ")
        If intDash_Found = 0 Then
            intDash_Found = Len(frmPIM.Caption) + 1
            frmPIM.Caption = frmPIM.Caption & " - "
        End If
        frmPIM.Caption = Left(frmPIM.Caption, intDash_Found + 2) & txtFilename.Text

        ' Change the drive and directory in Windows

        ChDir dirOpen_File.Path
        ChDrive Left(dirOpen_File.Path, 1)

        Unload frmOpen_File
    End If
End Sub
```

Because we also change the drive and directory in the Save File As... dialog box, it would be a good idea to make the path changes there as well.

2. Add the two statements to change the drive and directory to the **OK** button code on the Save File As... dialog box.

With this final addition, the application is ready.

3. Run the application, select the **Open File...** option, and change to the Ch-8 folder on drive A to see the dialog box display shown in Figure 8.17.

FIGURE 8.17
The Open File dialog box.

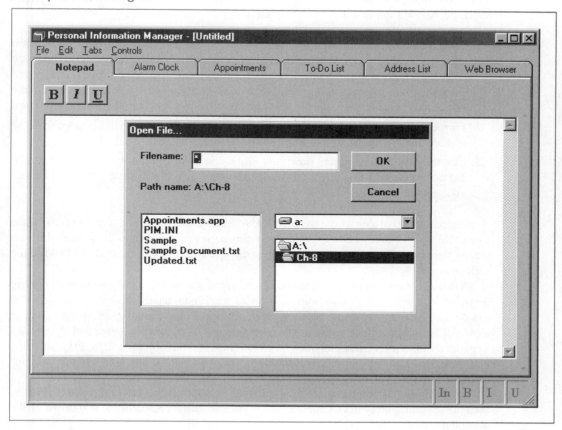

4. Double-click the **Sample Document.txt** file. The application reads the file and displays it in the Notepad workspace. This is the same data you saw at the beginning of this chapter. The title bar shows the name of the current file.

5. Change the data in the workspace and use the **Save File As...** option and a different file name to save the data. Use the New option to erase the data and then reload that file with the **Open File...** option. Continue to try various combinations of the options until you are fully convinced that the application is working properly. Then exit the application.

8.8   Adding Menu Items

When we looked at the sample PIM program at the beginning of this chapter, you saw how, when a file is loaded or saved for the first time or with a new name, the program will list the name of that file in the list of recently used files. In order to do this, we have to be able to add menu items to an existing menu. This is done with the **Load** statement, which has the format

```
Load menuitem
```

HINT: We won't need to delete menu items in the PIM program; we will only add them. But in programs where it is necessary, you can delete menu items with the **Unload** statement.

For us to use the Load statement, what we are manipulating must be part of a control array. We must add the first element of the control array to the file menu above the mnuExit_Application item.

1. Open the Menu Editor dialog box and add two entries above the mnuExit_Application item. The first should have a blank caption, because we are not ready to give the menu a name yet, and a control name of **mnuFile_Array** with the index 1 (one). The second entry should be a separator line because we want the filenames to be separated from the exit item. You should call the separator line mnuDash_2, as we will use that name later.

2. Turn off the Visible property of both menu items so that they will not appear in the menu when the program first runs.

3. Exit the dialog box and pull down the **File** menu to verify that it looks the same as it did before the two new items were added. It should, because these two items are not visible.

There are two places where we will need to add an item to the list of recent files: when a new file is saved and when a file is opened. Since the updating of the list is needed in two places, we can create a subroutine to perform the updating so that we only have to write the code once.

The Load statement can be used to create additional elements of any type of control array. That is, you can add additional text boxes, additional labels, or any other object that can be used as a control array. This means that you must have an original object set up as a control array from which to create the other objects. As these objects are added, they automatically inherit the characteristics of the original. All the objects will be the same size, will have the same font name, size, and so on, and will even be positioned in the same location. All the new ones will be under the original one in terms of the ZOrder.

For example, if you have a text box in your program called txtOutput and it is index zero in the control array of txtOutput objects, you can create an additional text box with the statement

```
Load txtOutput(1)
```

This text box would be element 1 in the control array of txtOutput objects.

When the new objects are created, they are not visible because the Visible property is set to False. For these objects to be seen, the Visible property must be set to True. Also, these new objects are directly underneath the original objects, so either the new or the original objects must be moved for the new objects to be viewed. The Top and/or Left properties must be adjusted so that the new object is no longer directly under the original. Such manipulation is generally done in a loop of some type.

When you've finished using these dynamically added objects, the Unload statement can be used to erase them from the program.

User-Defined Procedures

We have made calls to procedures in our code before, but we have yet to create our own procedure. The ones we have used up to this point have all been event procedures. Because we now have a module in our program, we will put the new procedure to add menu items there so that it can be shared on all the forms, though we only need to see the procedure from the frmOpen_File form and the frmSave_As form.

We are going to add a procedure called **Add_Menu_Item**. The format of a **Sub** statement is

```
[Public | Private] [Static] Sub procedurename ([argument list])
```

A procedure can be public or private. As you recall, if a procedure is private, it can be seen only on the module or form where it resides. When a procedure is public, it can be seen on all forms and modules. If Static is specified, then the values of all the procedures' local variables are preserved between calls regardless of how they are declared. The argument list is placed inside parentheses and has the following format:

```
[Optional] [ByVal | ByRef] variablename [As type] [= default value]
```

If the parameter is specified as optional, it can be left out of the calling statement. If one parameter is optional, all the parameters in the argument list must be optional. A default value can be specified for optional parameters so that they will always have a value in the procedure.

A parameter can be specified as **ByVal** or **ByRef**. If a parameter is specified as ByVal, the variable in the procedure is a copy of the value sent by the calling procedure. Any change to the variable in the procedure doesn't affect the original variable in the calling procedure. If a parameter is specified as ByRef, the variable in the procedure is a representation of the original value sent by the calling procedure. If the value of the variable is changed in the called procedure, the value of the variable is also changed in the calling procedure.

Generally to call a procedure, you simply use the name of the procedure. For example, to call the cmdOK_Click procedure, you would use the statement

```
cmdOK_Click
```

When there are parameters to be passed, they follow the calling statement

```
cmdOK_Click strPassed
```

This statement sends the value of the variable strPassed to the cmdOK_Click procedure.

> **HINT:** The calling statement can actually begin with the keyword **Call,** though this is not required. If Call is used, the parameters must be enclosed in parentheses. This would make the previous calling statement
>
> ```
> Call cmdOK_Click (strPassed)
> ```

An example will be helpful here.

1. Minimize the copy of Visual Basic where you are working on the PIM program and launch a new copy of Visual Basic. As you may already know, you can have several copies of Visual Basic running at the same time.

2. Add a button called **cmdOK** to the form.

3. Key the following code in the Click event procedure for the button.

```
Dim strValue as string
strValue = "Test"
Try_Out_The_String strValue
Debug.Print "Returned = "; strValue
```

This procedure will simply establish a variable called strValue, pass it to the Try_Out_The_String procedure, and then print the value of what is in strValue when it comes back from the Try_Out_The_String procedure.

The Try_Out_The_String procedure looks like this:

```
Public Sub Try_Out_The_String (ByRef strInput_Value As String)
```

```
        Debug.Print strInput_Value
        strInput_Value = "Changed"
End Sub
```

As you see, the variable name used in the called procedure does not have to be the same as the variable name in the calling procedure. It can be (and in many cases it is a good idea) but it doesn't have to be.

4. Key the foregoing Sub statement under the End Sub statement of the cmdOK_Click procedure and press **Enter**, and the new procedure will be created.

5. Key the two statements into the procedure.

6. Run the program and click the button. The output in the immediate window will be the two lines

```
Test
Returned = Changed
```

This shows that the value of the variable in the cmdOK_Click procedure was changed by the assignment statement in the Try_Out_The_String procedure. Because it was coded as ByRef, and by reference points to the storage location of the original variable, the change to the variable in the Try_Out_The_String procedure was a change to the same variable referred to in the cmdOK_Click procedure.

7. Exit the program. Change the ByRef in the Try_Out_The_String Sub statement to ByVal and run the program again.

This time the output is

```
Test
Returned = Test
```

Because the variable is now declared ByVal in the Try_Out_The_String procedure, the change to the value of the variable there did not cause any change to the value of the variable in the cmdOK_Click procedure. Only a copy of the variable was used in the Try_Out_The_String procedure and the original variable was left unchanged.

8. Exit the program. You can save the program if you wish, but it isn't necessary. Exit this copy of Visual Basic.

9. Restore the PIM copy of Visual Basic to the desktop and switch to the code for the module. Key the following statement and press **Enter**. When you press **Enter**, Visual Basic automatically adds the End Sub statement.

```
Public Sub Add_Menu_Item (gstrFilename As String)
```

We need to start this procedure with some declarations:

(General Procedure)

```
Global gstrPathnames(4) As String
```

(Add_Menu_Item procedure)

```
Dim intFilename_Count As Integer
Dim intCounter As Integer
```

The gstrPathnames declaration needs to be put in the (General) procedure. We will need to use it later in one of the forms. The other two declarations are for this procedure.

10. Switch to the (General) procedure, and key the gstrPathnames declaration statement; then switch back to the Add_Menu_Item procedure, and key the other two declaration statements.

gstrPathnames is to be used to keep track of the file names displayed on the menu items. The menu items don't exist until they are needed, so we cannot just check to see how many are used. Instead, we need an array to keep track of them. We defined the array with four items, because that is all we want the menu to show. This is arbitrary but common. We could have used eight or ten or even more, but most Windows programs use only four, so we will, too.

intFilename_Count will be used to count the number of active menu items by counting the number of gstrPathnames elements that are not empty. This is the first thing we will do. It requires the following code:

```
For intCounter = 1 To 4
    If gstrPathnames(intCounter) > "" Then
        intFilename_Count = intFilename_Count + 1
    End If
Next intCounter
```

11. Key this loop.

When this procedure is executed, the program has just established a new file name. The new file name needs to become the first item in the gstrPathnames array, which means we need to move the others down in the array. That is, we have to move element 1 to 2 to make room for 1, element 2 to 3, and so on. It needs to be done from the bottom of the list to the top, though, as shown here:

```
For intCounter = 3 To 1 Step -1
    gstrPathnames(intCounter + 1) = gstrPathnames(intCounter)
Next intCounter
```

12. Key this loop.

Now element 1 is available, and we need to copy the new file name there:

```
gstrPathnames(1) = gstrFilename
```

13. Key this assignment statement.

Now we are ready to assign the file names to the menu items. Since the first item in the mnuFile_Array control array of menu items already exists, we don't want to use the Load statement. If we do, we will get an error. So we need to assign the file name to the menu item and then make it and the separator bar visible. This is done as follows:

```
frmPIM.mnuFile_Array(1).Caption = "1. " & gstrPathnames(1)
frmPIM.mnuFile_Array(1).Visible = True
frmPIM.mnuDash_2.Visible = True
```

Note that we assign the number 1 to the file name that is stored in the first element of the gstrPathnames array. The numbers are used just so that there will be an ordering scheme to the filenames. This is the most common method. Note that the separator bar in your program may not be mnuDash_2. You will need to change the statement to correspond to whatever you named the separator bar. We specified the form name (frmPIM) on all these statements because this procedure is in the module and the menu is on the frmPIM form.

14. Key the foregoing statements into the procedure.

The intFilename_Count variable was used to determine how many menu items have already been used. We will use the variable again to assign file names to the menu items that don't need to be loaded. This code is

```
For intCounter = 2 To intFilename_Count
    If gstrPathnames(intCounter) > "" Then
        frmPIM.mnuFile_Array(intCounter).Caption =
            ↳ Trim(Str(intCounter)) & ". " & gstrPathnames(intCounter)
```

```
      End If
Next intCounter
```

We start the loop at element 2 because we have already set up element 1. Then we check to see if the array item is not empty. If it isn't, we assign the file name to the menu item with the appropriate number in front.

15. Key the loop into the procedure.

Now we know there may be an additional active menu item, so we increase the counter:

```
intFilename_Count = intFilename_Count + 1
```

16. Key this statement into the procedure.

The last step is to see whether or not we have used all the menu items. We want to use only four items, so we need to check to be sure they are not all used already:

```
If intFilename_Count < 5 And intFilename_Count > 1 Then
    Load frmPIM.mnuFile_Array(intFilename_Count)
    frmPIM.mnuFile_Array(intFilename_Count).Caption =
    ↳ Trim(Str(intFilename_Count)) & ". " &
    ↳ gstrPathnames(intFilename_Count)
End If
```

In this If Test, we have used the Load statement we discussed earlier. Since we need to move a Filename down in the list, we need a menu item on which to store this item. The Load statement creates this menu item.

17. Add the new code. This completes the code for this procedure, which is shown in Figure 8.18 (some of the lines extend beyond the edge of the figure).

Next, we need to set up the statements to call this procedure. As we have said, this needs to be done anywhere a new file name is entered, which happens in two places: the cmdOK_Click event procedure on the Open File dialog box and the cmdOK_Click event procedure on the Save File As dialog box.

18. Open the code window for the cmdOK_Click event on the Open File dialog box.

The statement we require will call the Add_Menu_Item procedure with the file name specified as the parameter. But where is the file name? That's easy. In this and the other cmdOK_Click procedure, it is in the gstrFilename variable. Thus, we need the following statement in both places:

```
Add_Menu_Item gstrFilename
```

19. Insert this statement just above the Unload statement in the procedure, as shown in Figure 8.19.

20. Open the code window for the cmdOK_Click event procedure on the Save File As dialog box, and put the same statement in the same location in this procedure.

21. Run the program and open the Sample Document file in the Ch-8 folder on your work disk.

22. Pull down the file menu to see the file name in the list as shown in Figure 8.20.

23. Use the **Save File As...** menu option to save the file as **Sample 1**. Pull down the **File** menu and you should have two entries, the first one "Sample 1.TXT" and the second "Sample Document.TXT."

24. Use the **Save File As...** option twice more, using Sample 2 and Sample 3 as the filenames. Then use the **Open File...** option and open the Updated file that you created in the beginning of this chapter. This will give you a file name list as shown in Figure 8.21.

FIGURE 8.18
The code for the Add_Menu_Item procedure.

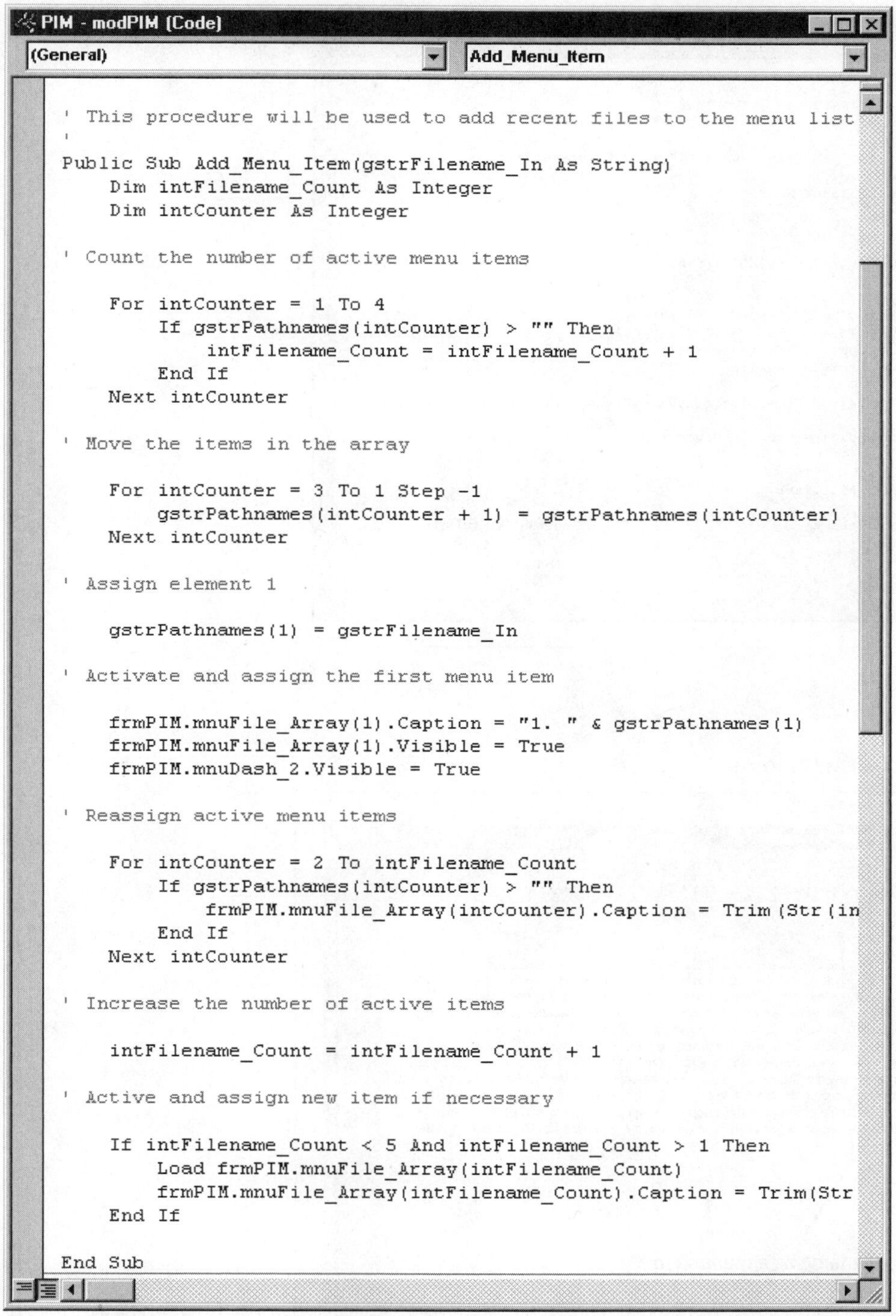

```
PIM - modPIM (Code)                                          _ □ ✕
(General)                           ▼   Add_Menu_Item                ▼

   ' This procedure will be used to add recent files to the menu list
   '
   Public Sub Add_Menu_Item(gstrFilename_In As String)
       Dim intFilename_Count As Integer
       Dim intCounter As Integer

   ' Count the number of active menu items

       For intCounter = 1 To 4
           If gstrPathnames(intCounter) > "" Then
               intFilename_Count = intFilename_Count + 1
           End If
       Next intCounter

   ' Move the items in the array

       For intCounter = 3 To 1 Step -1
           gstrPathnames(intCounter + 1) = gstrPathnames(intCounter)
       Next intCounter

   ' Assign element 1

       gstrPathnames(1) = gstrFilename_In

   ' Activate and assign the first menu item

       frmPIM.mnuFile_Array(1).Caption = "1. " & gstrPathnames(1)
       frmPIM.mnuFile_Array(1).Visible = True
       frmPIM.mnuDash_2.Visible = True

   ' Reassign active menu items

       For intCounter = 2 To intFilename_Count
           If gstrPathnames(intCounter) > "" Then
               frmPIM.mnuFile_Array(intCounter).Caption = Trim(Str(in
           End If
       Next intCounter

   ' Increase the number of active items

       intFilename_Count = intFilename_Count + 1

   ' Active and assign new item if necessary

       If intFilename_Count < 5 And intFilename_Count > 1 Then
           Load frmPIM.mnuFile_Array(intFilename_Count)
           frmPIM.mnuFile_Array(intFilename_Count).Caption = Trim(Str
       End If

   End Sub
```

FIGURE 8.19
Where to insert the new statement.

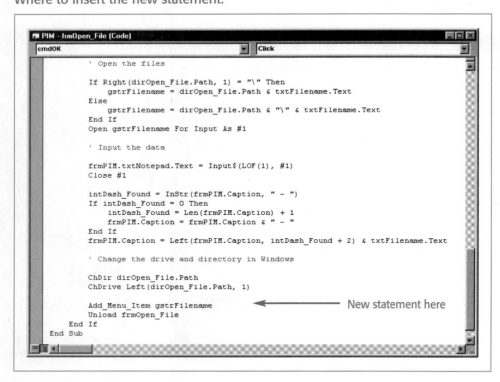

FIGURE 8.20
The file name appearing as a menu item.

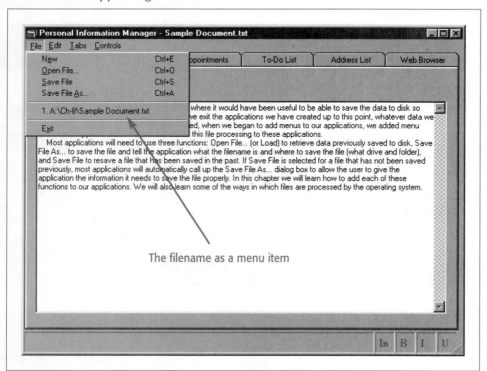

The filename as a menu item

FIGURE 8.21
The recently added files as shown in the **File** menu.

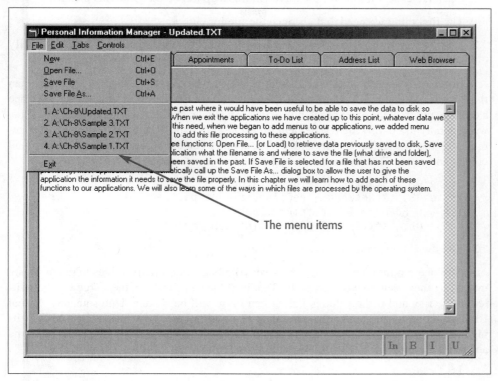

The menu items

25. Practice a bit more with the program to be sure it is working properly. When you are satisfied, exit the program.

8.9   Saving Multiple Fields in a File

Reading one field out of a file is easy. Many times, however, you want to read several fields out of one file. For example, one of the menu items we added previously was to save the settings (font name, size, bold, etc.) for the notepad. Also, we would like to maintain the list of the four previously used files and display them on the menu. This will require saving many different fields into one file.

Generally, files that have information pertinent to the starting of a program are set up as **initialization** files, and the **INI** extension is used. You may have seen some INI files on your hard disk. We will use this idea for the initialization data for our PIM program. In it we will store the settings data and the names from the menu listing of the last four files accessed.

Let's begin by listing all the data we will need to store in our INI file:

- The height and width of the workspace.
- The foreground and background colors of the workspace.
- The form title (caption).
- The Bold, Italics, and Underline settings.
- The size and name of the font.
- The four most recent files stored on the menu.

Now we need to create the routine to store these data in the INI file on the disk.

1. Open the code window for the **Save Changes** option on the **Controls** menu.

   The first thing we need to do is open the file for output.

2. Key the appropriate Open statement using **PIM.INI** as the file name. Be sure to specify the path properly, storing the file in the Ch-8 folder. Use #2 as the Filenumber.

Because these data need to be delimited, we will use the Write # statement rather than the Print # statement. When writing sequential files using the Write # statement, we place a carriage return at the end of each line of data, and when storing the foregoing type of data, we generally use one Write # statement for each set of data. That is, we will use one statement for the worksheet height and width, another for the foreground and background colors, and so on. That means we need the following statements:

```
Write #2, txtNotepad.Height, txtNotepad.Width
Write #2, txtNotepad.ForeColor, txtNotepad.BackColor
intDash_Found = InStr(frmPIM.Caption, "._.")
Write #2, Left(frmPIM.Caption,intDash_Found)
```

3. Key these statements into the procedure.

Now we run into a problem. When we write boolean property values (True or False) into a file, they seem to work properly. That is, if the value is True, then True will be written in the file, and if the value is False, then False will be written. Unfortunately, Visual Basic cannot read and use such output data as a boolean property. Instead of simply writing the font properties, we will test them and then write a 1 in the file if the property is True and a 0 if the property is False. This requires the following If Tests:

```
If txtNotepad.FontBold Then
    Write #2, 1
Else
    Write #2, 0
End If
If txtNotepad.FontItalic Then
    Write #2, 1
Else
    Write #2, 0
End If
If txtNotepad.FontUnderline Then
    Write #2, 1
Else
    Write #2, 0
End If
```

4. Key these If Tests.

We also have the font size and name to store. This will require the next statement:

```
Write #2, txtNotepad.FontSize, txtNotepad.FontName
```

5. Key this statement.

This brings us to the recent files from the menu. Remember that the names are actually stored in the gstrPathnames array. All we need to do is loop through the array and write them into the file. If there is a file name in the array element, that is written into the file. If not, an empty string is written, which means nothing is actually written into the file. This requires the following loop:

```
For intCounter = 1 To 4
    Write #2, gstrPathnames(intCounter)
Next intCounter
```

6. Key this loop.

Finally, we need to close the file.

7. Key the appropriate Close statement.

This gives us the code shown in Figure 8.22.

Now that the properties and file names are stored in the file, we need to read and set them when we run the program. This is done in the Form_Load procedure. You might think that to read the properties and set them, all you would need would be a statement such as

```
Input #1, txtNotepad.Height, txtNotepad.Width
```

FIGURE 8.22

The code in the mnuSave_Changes_Click procedure.

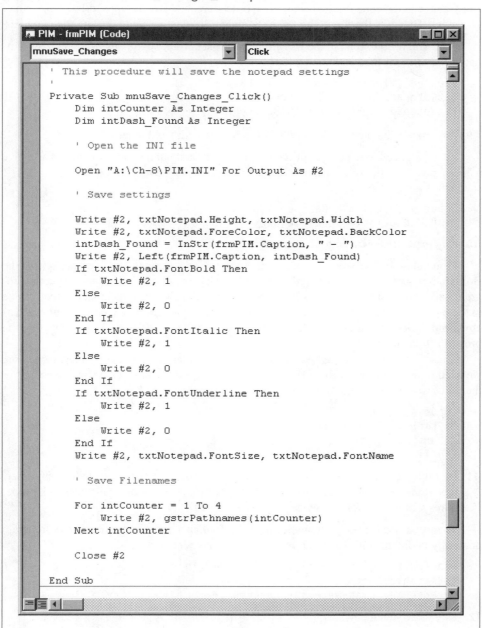

```
PIM - frmPIM (Code)

mnuSave_Changes                    Click

' This procedure will save the notepad settings
'
Private Sub mnuSave_Changes_Click()
    Dim intCounter As Integer
    Dim intDash_Found As Integer

    ' Open the INI file

    Open "A:\Ch-8\PIM.INI" For Output As #2

    ' Save settings

    Write #2, txtNotepad.Height, txtNotepad.Width
    Write #2, txtNotepad.ForeColor, txtNotepad.BackColor
    intDash_Found = InStr(frmPIM.Caption, " - ")
    Write #2, Left(frmPIM.Caption, intDash_Found)
    If txtNotepad.FontBold Then
        Write #2, 1
    Else
        Write #2, 0
    End If
    If txtNotepad.FontItalic Then
        Write #2, 1
    Else
        Write #2, 0
    End If
    If txtNotepad.FontUnderline Then
        Write #2, 1
    Else
        Write #2, 0
    End If
    Write #2, txtNotepad.FontSize, txtNotepad.FontName

    ' Save Filenames

    For intCounter = 1 To 4
        Write #2, gstrPathnames(intCounter)
    Next intCounter

    Close #2

End Sub
```

The problem here is that even though you can simply write the properties into the file when storing them, you cannot simply read them back into the properties to set them. If you use a statement like the foregoing, you will get an error. You need to read all the properties into temporary variables and then assign them to the properties themselves. This requires the above Input statement to be changed into three statements such as the following:

```
Input #1, intHeight_In, intWidth_In
txtNotepad.Height = intHeight_In
txtNotepad.Width = intWidth_In
```

Note that we read the two properties in on one statement. Because we saved them using one statement, it makes sense that we would want to read them back in with one statement. Then we assign the temporary variables (intHeight_In and intWidth_In) to the txtNotepad properties.

8. Change to the code for the Form_Load procedure, and key the appropriate Open statement. Then key the foregoing three statements, remembering to declare the variables.

Next you need to read in the foreground and background colors using statements similar to the ones for the height and width as in:

```
Input #1, lngForecolor_In, lngBackcolor_In
txtNotepad.ForeColor = lngForecolor_In
txtNotepad.BackColor = lngBackcolor_In
```

9. Key these statements following the ones for the width and height.

Then you need to read the caption for the title bar and put it there. Remember, we have a dialog box that allows the user to change the caption and have stored that in the file. The statements are:

```
Input #1, strTitle_Bar_Caption
frmPIM.Caption = strTitle_Bar_Caption & " - [Untitled]"
```

10. Key these statements into the procedure.

Remember that we stored the boolean properties as a 1 or a 0, and if we are setting the Bold, Italics, and Underline properties, it would be wise to set our indicators so that the program will show which of the properties are set. This setting of the indicators is already done in the button routines, so all we need to do is execute the appropriate Click routine, such as **cmdBold_Click,** for indicating that the Bold property has been turned on and setting the property in the notepad.

Thus, if one of the properties was stored in the file as having already been turned on, we need to discover that with an If Test and call the appropriate Click event. The code for the Input statement and the If Test for the Bold property would be:

```
Input #1, blnBold_In, blnItalics_In, blnUnderline_In
If blnBold_In = 1 Then
    cmdBold_Click
End If
```

11. Key the previous statements and add the If Test for the Italics and Underline properties. Remember, you don't have to turn on the properties themselves; the Click procedures will do that for you when they are executed.

Then you need the statements to input the font size and font name. These are again done as you did the width and height input. The statements would be:

```
Input #1, sngFontsize_In, strFontname_In
txtNotepad.FontSize = sngFontsize_In
txtNotepad.FontName = strFontname_in
```

12. Key these statements.

Now we need to read the file names out of the file so they can be stored as menu items. There are four of them, so we can begin this portion of the code as

```
For intCounter = 1 To 4
    Input #1, gstrPathnames(intCounter)
```

13. Key these two statements.

If the file name isn't null, we need to add it as a menu item. Remember, however, that the first menu item already exists, so it isn't loaded, but we will need to turn on the separator line. All subsequent items (2 through 4) do need to be loaded (created). This gives us a nested If Test as follows:

```
If gstrPathnames(intCounter) <> "" Then
    If intCounter = 1 Then
        mnuDash_2.Visible = True
    Else
        Load mnuFile_Array(intCounter)
    End If
```

14. Key these statements.

With the menu item created, whether it is the first one that was already there or a newly created one, we need to make the item visible and then assign to it. That requires the following statements:

```
        mnuFile_Array(intCounter).Visible = True
        mnuFile_Array(intCounter).Caption = Trim(Str(intCounter)) &
            ↳ "."& gstrPathnames(intCounter)
    End If
Next intCounter
```

15. Key these statements into the procedure.

16. Key the command to close the file.

Because you ran the sample PIM program at the beginning of this chapter, it stands to reason that there is already a PIM.INI file in your Ch-8 folder. You can look at the current contents of the file by loading it with your program.

17. Run the program. Select the **Open File...** option from the **File** menu.

The program is looking for files with no extension, but the PIM.INI file has an INI extension. Therefore, the PIM.INI file will not show up in the file list. But you can load the file by keying the file name in the file name entry box.

18. Key **PIM.INI** in the file name entry box and click the **OK** button to see a file display similar to that shown in Figure 8.23.

Because you have probably practiced with the program on your own, the values of the entries may not correspond to those shown in the figure. On the lines that have multiple entries, the entries are separated by commas. Also, the strings such as the file names are enclosed in quotation marks. The last two entries in the file are the empty file names. The commas and quotation marks are created automatically by the delimiters that the Write # statement creates.

The entries in the file in the figure are

- Workspace height = 4695 and workspace width = 8895
- Workspace foreground color = –2147483640 (white) and background color = –2147483643 (black)
- Form title = "Personal Information Manager"
- Bold, Italics, and Underline settings all = 0

FIGURE 8.23
The contents of the PIM.INI file.

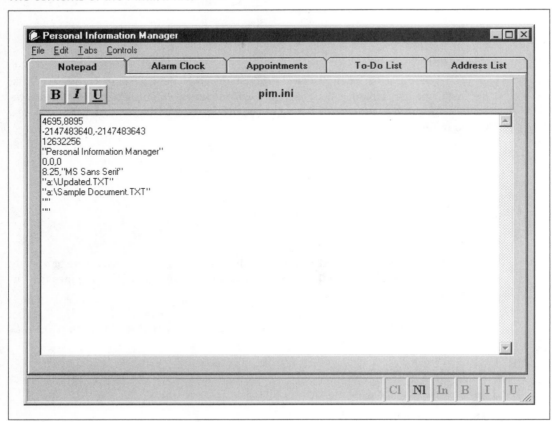

■   Font size = 8.25 and font name = "MS Sans Serif"

■   The two file names used at the start of the chapter and two null entries (" ")

19. Record the information in your PIM.INI file and then change some of the settings. Save the changes and then reopen the PIM.INI file. The data in the file will have changed.

20. Experiment with the program until you are satisfied that everything is working properly. Exit the program.

Updating the Filenames

Now we have a problem. The program saves the filenames when you use the **Save Changes** option, but the filenames are updated in the menu when a file is saved with a new name (Save File As...) or when a new file is loaded. The program should automatically update the INI file in those instances. To do this, we will set up another procedure in the module.

This is a sequential file, so we can't simply replace the data at the end of the file. We could append the current file names, but the others would still be there and they would be the ones read first. What we must do is read the current settings and then rewrite the entire file with the new file names at the end. We don't want to use the settings; we just want to read them. If we used the settings in the file, we might change the current settings that the user set up for properties such as bold and so on. Thus, we will simply read them and write them back into the file.

The first thing to do is open the file.

1. Create a new procedure in the modPIM module called **Rewrite_Filenames.** It doesn't need any parameters, because this procedure will use the file names stored in the gstrFilenames array.

2. Key the appropriate Open statement for input of the PIM.INI file.

   Now we need to read the values of the various settings.

3. Key the appropriate Input statements. You will need to set up temporary variables for each of the settings to be read into so they can be used subsequently to write the settings back into the file. You don't need to input the file names from the INI file; the procedure will simply write the proper ones at the end of the other data written into the file.

4. Key the statement to close the file and then the statement to open the file for output.

5. Using the variables that you previously used for input, key Write # statements to write the data back into the file.

   Finally, you need a loop to write the elements of the gstrPathnames array into the file.

6. Key the appropriate loop and then close the file.

   This procedure needs to be called from the cmdOK_Click event procedures on the Save As and Open File forms. But both of these procedures call the Add_Menu_Item procedure. We can add the call to the Rewrite_Filenames procedure to the end of the Add_Menu_Item procedure, and both of the cmdOK_Click events will then automatically call the Rewrite_Filenames procedure.

7. Open the code for Add_Menu_Item and insert the call statement for the Rewrite_Filenames procedure as shown in Figure 8.24.

FIGURE 8.24
The call statement for the Rewrite_Filenames procedure.

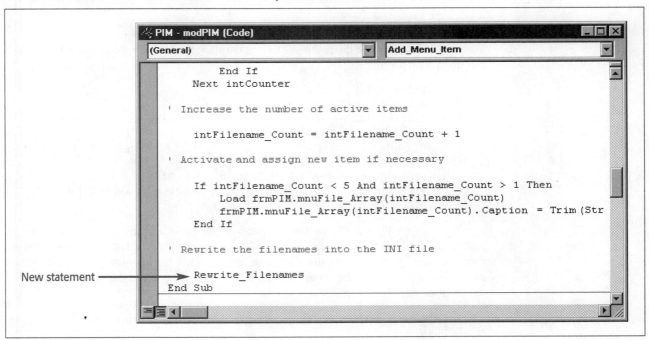

8. Test the program by loading a file, saving it with a different file name, and then opening the PIM.INI file. The file names of the files you just used should be in the list of file names at the end of the file.

9. Exit the program when you are certain it is working correctly.

Opening the Files from the File List

We listed the filenames in the **File** menu so we could see what files had been used recently and so the user would be able to load the files by simply clicking the file names. We already know how to load the file, so this step is not too difficult.

1. Open the code window for the mnuFile_Array_Click event. You cannot open it by selecting the menu item, because the first menu item is not visible and the others do not yet exist. Instead, open the code window for any procedure and select the mnuFile_Array procedure from the pull-down list.

To load the file, we need to extract the pathname and file name from the item listed in the menu. This requires a statement like the following:

```
gstrFilename = Mid(mnuFile_Array(Index).Caption, 4)
```

We skip the first three characters of the array item since they are the sequential numbers before the pathname.

2. Key this statement into the procedure followed by an Open statement, using gstrFilename as the name of the file to be opened.

3. Key the appropriate statement to input the data from the file, and store it in the notepad workspace. Then key the statement to close the file.

Now the file name needs to be displayed on the title bar. To do this we need to find the file name without the pathname, because we are displaying only the file name on the title bar. This means we need to scan through gstrFilename until we find the last backslash between folders. Suppose the pathname is

```
a:\Practice Folder\Chapters\Ch-8\Filename.txt
```

We need to scan through the pathname to find the slash between Ch-8 and Filename.txt. We can use a loop for this:

```
intPointer = 1
intCounter = 1
Do Until intCounter = 0
    intPointer = intCounter
    intCounter = InStr(intCounter + 1, strFilename, "\")
Loop
intDash_Found = InStr(frmPIM.Caption, " - ")
frmPIM.Caption = Left(frmPIM.Caption, intDash_Found + 2) &
Mid(gstrFilename, intPointer + 1)
```

This loop will look for the last instance of the backslash and save that position in intPointer. We have to use a second variable to keep track of it (the last use of InStr will return a value of zero into intCounter because InStr will not find any backslash past the last one). Then we use the same statements we have used before to put the name at the end of the program name on the title bar.

4. Key the foregoing loop into the procedure. This gives you a procedure like that shown in Figure 8.25.

FIGURE 8.25
The complete code for the mnuFile_Array_Click procedure.

```
PIM - frmPIM (Code)                                                    _ □ ×

mnuFile_Array                           ▼   Click                          ▼

    Private Sub mnuFile_Array_Click(Index As Integer)
        Dim intCounter As Integer
        Dim intPointer As Integer
        Dim intDash_Found As Integer

        gstrFilename = Mid(mnuFile_Array(Index).Caption, 4)

        Open gstrFilename For Input As #1

        frmPIM.txtNotepad.Text = Input(LOF(1), #1)

        Close #1

        intPointer = 1
        intCounter = 1
        Do Until intCounter = 0
            intPointer = intCounter
            intCounter = InStr(intCounter + 1, gstrFilename, "\")
        Loop
        intDash_Found = InStr(frmPIM.Caption, " - ")
        frmPIM.Caption = Left(frmPIM.Caption, intDash_Found + 2) & Mid(gstrFilename, intPointer + 1)
    End Sub
```

5. Run the program and click the first menu item. The file should load.

6. To be sure you are loading the correct file, key something you will recognize at the end of the document, save the file with a new file name, and then select the **New** option of the **File** menu to erase the current contents.

7. Select the latest saved file from the **File** menu list. Be sure that the file is properly loaded and the message you added is at the end.

8. Exit the program.

8.10 About Random-Access Files

Using sequential files is only one aspect of using files in Visual Basic. They are fine as long as you are saving only a few data items as we just did. If, on the other hand, you are saving many records with multiple fields, accessing the records can be a slow process because they can be accessed only sequentially. Consider a file with 10,000 records. If you use a sequential file, then every time you want to look at any of the 10,000 records, you have to read through all the records from the beginning of the file until you locate the record of interest. This is simply unmanageable.

Another method would be to read all 10,000 records into memory when the file is first opened and then continue to process them there. This would mean that the application could not begin to work until all 10,000 records were stored in memory. This delay would render the program useless for most purposes. Also, as we modified the records, we would want the new data to be stored back into the file. If we simply continued to process the records from memory and then the computer lost power, whatever changes we had made to the data would be lost.

A much more practical solution is to leave the data on the disk and simply read in the data we need as we need them. By using random access, we can fetch any specific record among the 10,000 records by simply knowing which one it is. There are many ways to determine which record to input, but one of the easiest is to use an **index**.

About Indices

An index is generally a file or list separate from the main file of data. This list is made up of the data from a particular field in the records. That field, generally called the **key** or **index**, must either be unique (in some applications) or have very few duplicates for us to use it to differentiate one record from another. Along with the key, we store a pointer to the regular record in the random-access file that contains all the data of the record. For example, suppose our file contains company name, contact person, address, several numeric fields, and other data. If the key for our file were the company name, the index file or list would consist of the company name of each of the records, along with the record pointer to the rest of the data in the random-access file. This concept is illustrated in Figure 8.26.

The index file is sorted because it is quicker to look something up in a sorted list than in a list of random elements. When we look up the key in the index, we use the record pointer to go to the original file to retrieve all the data in that record.

If we don't want to use a file for the index, we can load all the keys into a list in memory with the record pointer appended to it. The program can pick the key for the record needed from the list. Then we can use the record pointer stored with the key to access the actual data record from the random file.

We are going to use a random-access file for the Appointment calendar. For this application, we are going to go one step farther when working with the index. We will load all the data from the file into memory and process the data from there. To be safe, however, we will also automatically write any updated records back into the file. Because there will not be many records in the file (we will limit the number of records to 400), the amount of memory required to store the data will not be excessive. As you will see, each of our 400 records will require only about 410 bytes, which means that in total we will store only about 16K in memory—not much by comparison with the amount of memory in the typical computer.

To keep the number of records manageable, we will save only the appointments for the month before the current date (we will delete the ones older than that).

Considering that we will be deleting the old records, 400 records will probably be sufficient for most users. For some people, however, it may not be enough. If 6 to 10 appointments are made per day, there may only be two or three months' worth of records. If later on you decide 400 records is not sufficient, you can always increase that number. That's what's nice about writing the program yourself. It can always be adjusted to fit your changing needs.

FIGURE 8.26
The look of a random-access file index.

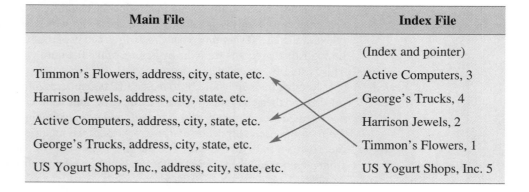

Main File	Index File
	(Index and pointer)
Timmon's Flowers, address, city, state, etc.	Active Computers, 3
Harrison Jewels, address, city, state, etc.	George's Trucks, 4
Active Computers, address, city, state, etc.	Harrison Jewels, 2
George's Trucks, address, city, state, etc.	Timmon's Flowers, 1
US Yogurt Shops, Inc., address, city, state, etc.	US Yogurt Shops, Inc. 5

About Records

When we wrote data into the sequential file, we stored one long string for the notepad and several separate fields for the settings, but there was no breakdown of the data into separate groupings like names and addresses. Random-access files, on the other hand, most often are created using small fields like names and addresses grouped together into records. For example, for every customer there will be a company name (or maybe just a customer name), an address (street address, city, state, zip code), a phone number, and the balance currently owed. Each of these items is considered a separate piece of data and is known as a **field.** Grouping all the fields for a particular company together gives us a **record,** and a record is the standard access element for a random file.

All the records must be the same length, and they are stored one after the other. This gives Visual Basic an easy way to determine where each of the records is stored. The particular record that is needed can be found by adding up the lengths of the records that need to be bypassed.

Creating a Record

Thus far, when we have set up fields, we have used the predefined field types such as string or integer. Visual Basic will, however, let you create your own data types using the **Type** structure. Records are a perfect candidate for a self-defined data type. To create a record for a file similar to the one we have been discussing requires a type statement like the following:

```
Type udtRecord
    strName As String * 20
    strAddress As String * 20
    strCity As String * 15
    strState As String * 2
    strZip_Code As String * 5
    strPhone As String * 10
    sngBalance As Single
End Type
```

Note that the structure begins with a Type statement; udtRecord itself is simply what we have chosen to call our structure (the **udt** prefix is for the user-defined type designation). We could have called it udtDatabase_Record, udtCompany_Data, or any other legal Visual Basic name. Then, within the record, we define the seven fields we need. Normally, the length of a string is automatically adjusted to fit the data being stored there. A random file record must have a fixed length, so we have to tell Visual Basic how long each of the strings is going to be by using the "* 20" or a similar designation. For example, this means that the strName string is always 20 characters long. This is an important designation, because if we let each string be only as long as necessary for the data, the length of each record would be different, and the structure would not be suitable for a Visual Basic random file.

The Type structure simply sets up a type of data. It does not specify a variable for data storage. A declaration statement must still be used, such as

```
Global udrCompany_Data As udtRecord
```

This sets up a variable called udrCompany_Data (**udr** stands for user-defined record) as a udtRecord type, which means that udrCompany_Data is actually made up of strName, strAddress, and so on. To access a particular field in udrCompany_Data, we classify the field the same way we have been classifying object properties, with a decimal. To access the strName field, for example, we would use a statement such as

```
udrCompany_Data.strName = txtFilename.Text
```

Fields in this type of structure can be arrays, and the record itself can be an array. In the case of our appointment calendar, we will use both, as you will see in the next section.

8.11 Reading and Writing the Appointments

Because of the advantages of using random-access files when processing large amounts of data, we will use a random-access file for storing the records for the appointment calendar that we are going to add in this chapter. The record structure for the appointment calendar will need 20 time periods for each of the days (8:00 through 5:30 with periods on the half hour, as shown in Figure 8.27) for which we want appointments stored and wish to know whether we have set alarms. We will allow each appointment message to contain up to 30 characters and will need a record structure as follows:

```
Type udtAppointment_Record
    dtmRecord_Date As Date
    intFile_Pointer As Integer
    strComment(20) As String * 30
    blnAlarmon(20) As Boolean
End Type
```

Note that we made the comment and alarm fields into arrays. As we mentioned, a type structure can contain any type of field, including an array.

Note also that we placed a field for the record pointer in our record (intFile_Pointer). This just allows us to store the file pointer to where the record is stored in the file. Then there will never be any question where this particular record is stored on the disk when we need to write it back on the disk.

The records will be stored into the main file sequentially, so the file pointer or record number will be a sequential number. That is, the first record stored in the file will be record 1, and the tenth record in the file will be record 10. Each time a new record is stored into the file, we will capture the file pointer (record number) and save that in the field in the record (intFile_Pointer). We will also use a counter to keep track of how many records are currently stored in the file so that we will know where the next record is to be written. Each time a new record is stored, we will simply increment the counter.

We will open and close the file each time a new record is accessed. If anything ever happens to the program while we are processing one of the records, the file itself will not be damaged. This is the way such applications normally operate.

As you can tell by looking at Figure 8.26, we are going to add a new control called the MonthView to the Appointments tab.

1. Switch to the Appointments tab.

   The **MonthView** control is part of the Microsoft Windows Common Controls-2 6.0.

2. Press **Ctrl-T** to call up the Components dialog box, then scroll to and click the Microsoft Windows Common Controls-2 6.0. Click the OK button.

   Now your Toolbox will have several new controls. The MonthView control is the one indicated in Figure 8.27.

3. Add the MonthView control and position it as shown in Figure 8.28. Change the name of the control to **mnvAppointments_Date**.

4. Next, add the rest of the tools on the tab as shown in Figure 8.28, with the following considerations:

   ■ Add a control array of text boxes with the name **txtAppointment_Comments** and the ToolTipText entry **Appointment Comment**.

   ■ Add a control array of option buttons labeled as shown in Figure 8.28. Use ToolTipText entries of **Appointment Alarm**.

FIGURE 8.27
The MonthView control.

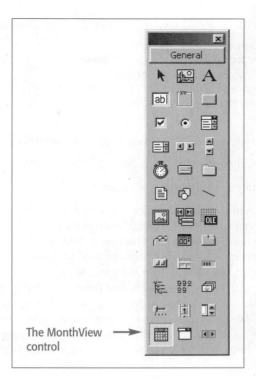

The MonthView ——→
control

FIGURE 8.28
The Appointments display.

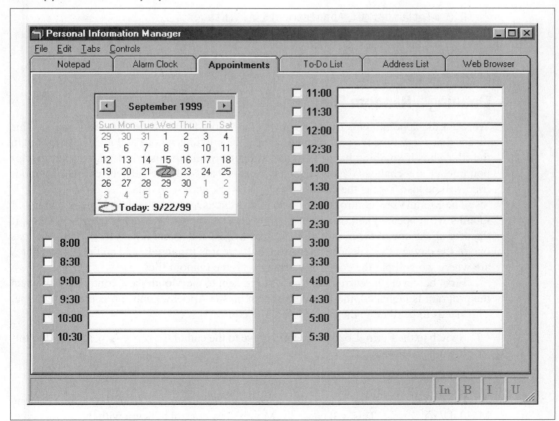

5. Change to the modPIM module and key the Type structure that we discussed earlier:

```
Type udtAppointment_Record
    dtmRecord_Date As Date
    intFile_Pointer As Integer
    strComment(20) As String * 30
    blnAlarmon(20) As Boolean
End Type
```

Then you will need to define the record array as follows:

```
Global gudrAppointment_Records(400) As udtAppointment_Record
```

6. Key this statement after the type structure.

Now we need a variable to keep track of the current record number for each of the records as they are stored in the file and another variable to keep track of how many records there are in the file. This is used to give new records that are added to the file their assigned sequential numbers. A third variable is needed to keep track of the previously displayed record after the month, day, or year list value is changed to bring in a new date. This will allow any changed data to be saved before the new record is displayed. Finally, we need a boolean variable that we can use to determine when the displayed record has been changed. Using this variable enables us to know when to save a displayed record. If we saved every record that was displayed, we might end up saving blank records, because not every record displayed will have appointments added. These variables don't need to be global, only form-level.

7. Open the code for the (General) procedure on the frmPIM form, and key the following four declaration statements.

```
Dim mintNumber_Of_Appointments As Integer
Dim mintCurrent_Record As Integer
Dim mdtmPrevious_Date As Date
Dim mblnWas_Changed As Boolean
```

Opening a Random File

We want the appointments file to be opened and closed every time a record is saved. This means that every time the user changes a date, the previous record will need to be stored in the file. Thus if anything happens to the computer while the user is working with the appointments, any changed data will already be saved and only the data currently being modified will be lost. This is the customary way to work with such data.

The MonthView control is set up so that if the user clicks the month name, the list of months will appear. Then, if one of them is chosen, the Click event is triggered. Also, if the user clicks one of the month-change arrows, the Click event is set off. If the user clicks one of the days in the calendar, the **DateClick** event is triggered. And so these procedures are where we will put the code for working with the random file.

First, however, the current date needs to be sent to the MonthView control so that when the program is launched, the first date shown on the Appointments tab is the current one. This needs to be done in the Form_Load procedure.

1. Switch to the Form_Load procedure, move to the end of the procedure, and key the following statement:

```
mnvAppointments = Date
```

Date, of course, is the function for retrieving the current date from the computer in the MM/DD/YY format. This will cause the MonthView control to begin with the current date.

Next we need to load all the existing data into our record structure. We will do this in the Form_Load procedure so that the data will be ready when the user switches to the Appointments tab.

There are only two differences between an Open statement for a random-access file and one for a sequential file. Obviously, we have to tell Visual Basic that the file is random, but we also have to show how long the records in the file are. Remember that every record in a random-access file must be the same length, so Visual Basic can determine where each record begins and ends. The format of the new type of Open statement is

```
Open Pathname For Mode As # Filenumber Len = Recordlength
```

As you can see, the addition to the Open statement is the Recordlength on the end. In order for Visual Basic to calculate the record offset, it must know how long the records are. But we don't need to calculate the length. We can let Visual Basic do that for us with an open statement such as

```
Open "A:\Ch-8\Appointments.app" For Random As #1 Len =
 ↳ Len(gudrAppointment_Records(1))
```

Here the Len function is used to automatically calculate the record length as the length of the first element of the array. Note that we specified the first record in the array. Because our array is a collection of records, not a single record, Visual Basic cannot determine the length of the records by using just the name of the array. We have to specify a particular record so that it can get the length of one record. We could have used any index we wished; our choice of 1 is arbitrary.

2. Key the foregoing statement after the date assignment statement.

Reading a Random-Access File

Next we need to read the records from the file. Records in a random file are accessed by number. That is, we specifically tell the application that we want record 15 or record 20. It is important that we know the record number of each record in the file so that we will know which one we want to access. That's why we have made arrangements to store that number in the record itself. To know that record number, we simply count them with a loop counter as we read the existing records in. Then each new record that is added to the file will simply be assigned the next number. We added the declaration of the counter earlier, and it is time to start using it by initializing it:

```
mintNumber_Of_Appointments = 0
```

1. Key this statement into the procedure after the Open statement.

Because we don't know how many records are in the file, as we are reading the data from the file into the array, we need to test to be sure we haven't run off the end of the file. There is a special marker at the end of every file, called the **end-of-file marker,** that the application reads to determine when there are no more records. We can test whether the end-of-file marker has been found with the EOF() function, which has the following format:

```
EOF(Filenumber)
```

As you can see, we specify the Filenumber so that Visual Basic will know for which file we are checking the end-of-file. The Do-Until statement we need is

```
Do Until EOF(1)
```

2. Key this statement into the procedure.

Now, as we read the data in, we need to increment the mintNumber_Of_Appointments variable so that it will point to the next record by number. This requires the statement

```
mintNumber_Of_Appointments = mintNumber_Of_Appointments + 1
```

3. Key this statement into the procedure.

To read the data from a random file requires a **Get #** statement, which has the following format:

```
Get # Filenumber, [Recordnumber], Variablename
```

If we want just to read the records sequentially, we can use the Get statement without specifying the record we want, and the application will merely read the next record in the file. We want to read all the records in this procedure, so we will use the Get statement without the record number.

4. Key the following statement (the extra comma is necessary because the record number is left out, and Visual Basic must be informed of the missing parameter).

```
Get #1, , gudrAppointment_Records(mintNumber_Of_Appointments)
```

This will input the record into the array of records, pointing to the appropriate one by the mintNumber_Of_Appointments variable. In the loop, we continually read the records into the array until the end-of-file is found.

Next we need to end the loop and then close the file. Remember that we always close the file when we are through processing, whether we have read all the records or just saved a single one.

5. Key the two statements needed.

One final statement is required before we are finished with this routine. We are incrementing mintNumber_Of_Appointments before trying to read a record from the file, so mintNumber_Of_Appointments will always be one more than the number of records in the file. After the loop is finished, we need to reduce mintNumber_Of_Appointments so that it matches the number of records that were read.

6. Add the statement to reduce mintNumber_Of_Appointments by 1.

7. Save the application.

Viewing the Appointments

Because we now have the code to load any existing data into the program, we are ready to learn how to cause those data to be displayed. Right now, of course, there aren't any data in the file. As a matter of fact, there isn't even a file. It will be created automatically when we first save a record.

As we mentioned, we are going to set up the MonthView Click procedures to process the data. This is to be done with two procedures, the **Save_Appointments** procedure, which will save the appointments into the file and the **Get_Appointments** procedure, which will retrieve the appointments from the file and put the data in the controls on the Appointments tab. We will begin by looking at the Get_Appointments procedure.

1. Create a new procedure called **Get_Appointments**.

The first thing we need to do is to erase any data that may still be in the controls on the tab. This is necessary since if there are no data for the date changed to, no data will be written in the controls. This requires a loop like the following:

```
For intCounter = 1 To 20
    txtAppointment_Comments(intCounter) = ""
```

```
        chkAlarm(intCounter).Value = vbUnchecked
Next intCounter
```

We loop from 1 to 20, since there are 20 sets of controls. The vbUnchecked constant has a value of zero, which represents the value to which a check box is set to turn it off.

2. Key the above code into the procedure.

The next thing we need to do is save the newly selected date as the previous date so that when a new date is selected in the MonthView control, we will be able to save the previous data in the array and file before the new data are displayed. We created a form-level variable in which to store this date, so the statement we need is

```
mdtmPrevious_Date = mnvAppointments.Value
```

mnvAppointments.Value is the date that is currently displayed in the MonthView control.

To display the record data, we need to determine whether there is a record for the date that was selected. Because mintNumber_Of_Appointments tells us how many records are currently stored in the file, we can loop through them until we find the one we are looking for. If there is not one for the particular date, we need to know that too. Thus, we will need a Do-While statement and counter initialization like the following:

```
intCounter = 0
Do While gudrAppointment_Records(intCounter).dtmRecord_Date <>
↳mnvAppointments.Value And intCounter
↳<= mintNumber_Of_Appointments
```

3. Key the previous statements.

The first thing we need inside the loop is a statement to increase the value of the counter. This way, the counter will be 1 when the first record is processed.

4. Key a statement to increment the intCounter by 1.

Next we need the statement that will allow us to see whether any of the records we have processed match the selected date. Looking back, you will recall that the dtmRecord_Date field is where we intend to store the date for the records. This means we need a statement like

```
If gudrAppointment_Records(intCounter).dtmRecord_Date =
↳mnvAppointments.Value Then
```

5. Key this statement into the procedure.

We are checking the date in the record (dtmRecord_Date) against the value of the date that was selected in the MonthView control.

Within this If Test we will need a loop to display all the data of the comments field array in the control array of text boxes. This loop will be

```
For intInside_Counter = 1 To 20
    txtAppointment_Comments(intInside_Counter) = Trim(gudrAppointment_
    ↳ Records(intCounter).strComment(intInside_Counter))
```

6. Key these statements into the procedure.

We also need to turn on the alarm check boxes for any alarms that were set on when the record was saved. Because the boolean we are using to save the status of the alarms has a value of True or False and a check box has a value of checked or unchecked, we need an If Test to turn the alarms on or off. This If Test is

```
If gudrAppointment_Records(intCounter).blnAlarmon(intInside_
↳ Counter) = True Then
```

```
        chkAlarm(intInside_Counter).Value = vbChecked
Else
        chkAlarm(intInside_Counter).Value = vbUnchecked
End If
```

7. Key this If Test into the procedure.

That's it, except for ending the inside For-Next loop, the If Test, and the outside For-Next loop.

8. Key the appropriate statements.

Note that we trimmed the spaces off the record before we stored it in the text box. This is necessary because the comment field in the record will automatically be 20 characters long; that's how the field is specified in the record. If we simply copied the data into the text box, we would be copying 20 blanks and each text box would start with 20 blanks. Then, when the cursor appeared in the text box, there would already be 20 blanks there. This would make the user's job more complicated. By removing the blanks, we make things easier for the user—something that's always a good idea.

If none of the records that we retrieved from the file matches the date, intCounter will be larger than mintNumber_Of_Appointments. We can check to determine whether we have a record for the selected date by checking the value of intCounter. If the record exists, intCounter will point to the current record number. And what if no record exists? We want to assign zero to intCounter so that when the user changes the date, we can either create a new record if intCounter is zero or save the current record back to the file if intCounter is not zero. This requires the following If Test:

```
If intCounter > mintNumber_Of_Appointments Then
    mintCurrent_Record = 0
Else
    mintCurrent_Record = intCounter
End If
```

9. Add this If Test to the procedure.

The final thing we need in the procedure is a statement to tell the program that nothing was changed on the tab. Remember that we use the mblnWas_Changed variable to indicate that something was changed. Thus, we need to set this variable to False.

10. Key the appropriate statement to yield the code shown in Figure 8.29.

Adding or Saving a Record to the Random File

The next procedure we need to be concerned about is the one that adds a new record or saves a currently existing record to the file. We will set up the Save_Appointments procedure for this.

1. Create a new procedure called **Save_Appointments** on the frmPIM form.

The first thing we need to do is to determine whether there have been any changes to the data in the displayed record. Since mblnWas_Changed was set up to signify a change to the data, if we test that variable, we can determine if any of the displayed data were changed. This requires an If Test like the following:

```
If mblnWas_Changed = True Then
```

2. Key this statement into the procedure.

Within the If Test, we need to begin by opening the file so that we can save the data into the file on disk at the same time as we save it in the array record.

FIGURE 8.29
The code for the Get_Appointments procedure.

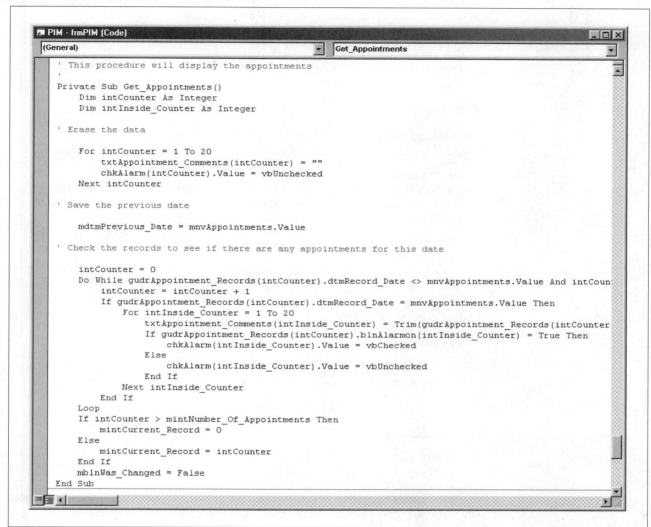

```
PIM - frmPIM (Code)
(General)                                              Get_Appointments

' This procedure will display the appointments
'
Private Sub Get_Appointments()
    Dim intCounter As Integer
    Dim intInside_Counter As Integer

' Erase the data

    For intCounter = 1 To 20
        txtAppointment_Comments(intCounter) = ""
        chkAlarm(intCounter).Value = vbUnchecked
    Next intCounter

' Save the previous date

    mdtmPrevious_Date = mnvAppointments.Value

' Check the records to see if there are any appointments for this date

    intCounter = 0
    Do While gudrAppointment_Records(intCounter).dtmRecord_Date <> mnvAppointments.Value And intCoun
        intCounter = intCounter + 1
        If gudrAppointment_Records(intCounter).dtmRecord_Date = mnvAppointments.Value Then
            For intInside_Counter = 1 To 20
                txtAppointment_Comments(intInside_Counter) = Trim(gudrAppointment_Records(intCounter
                If gudrAppointment_Records(intCounter).blnAlarmon(intInside_Counter) = True Then
                    chkAlarm(intInside_Counter).Value = vbChecked
                Else
                    chkAlarm(intInside_Counter).Value = vbUnchecked
                End If
            Next intInside_Counter
        End If
    Loop
    If intCounter > mintNumber_Of_Appointments Then
        mintCurrent_Record = 0
    Else
        mintCurrent_Record = intCounter
    End If
    mblnWas_Changed = False
End Sub
```

3. Key the same Open statement we used earlier, because there is only one form of an Open statement for a random file. By definition, all random files open as both input and output.

Earlier, we put either a value of zero or the current record number in the mintCurrent_Record variable. Now, to determine whether the record being displayed already exists or needs to be added to the file, we must check the value of mintCurrent_Record with a statement such as

```
If mintCurrent_Record = 0 Then
```

4. Key this statement.

If this statement is true, this record did not previously exist and we need to add it to the file. This requires the use of the mintNumber_Of_Appointments counter, which tells us how many records are currently in the file. To come up with the number for the next record, we need to add 1 to this counter with the following statement:

```
mintNumber_Of_Appointments = mintNumber_Of_Appointments + 1
```

5. Key this statement.

Then we will use this counter as the record pointer in the array record and store the date that we previously saved in the mdtmPrevious_Date field:

```
gudrAppointment_Records(mintNumber_Of_Appointments).intFile_
↳Pointer = mintNumber_Of_Appointments
gudrAppointment_Records(mintNumber_Of_Appointments).dtmRecord_
↳Date = mdtmPrevious_Date
```

6. Key these statements.

Next, we need to assign the comments from the text boxes to the comments array in the record and the check box values for the alarms into the boolean fields in the record.

```
For intInside_Counter = 1 To 20
    gudrAppointment_Records(mintNumber_Of_Appointments).strComment
    ↳(intInside_Counter) = txtAppointment_Comments(intInside_Counter)
    If chkAlarm(intInside_Counter).Value = vbChecked Then
        gudrAppointment_Records(mintNumber_Of_Appointments).
        ↳blnAlarmon(intInside_Counter) = True
    Else
        gudrAppointment_Records(mintNumber_Of_Appointments).
        ↳blnAlarmon(intInside_Counter) = False
    End If
Next intInside_Counter
```

7. Key this loop.

With all the data stored in the record, we are ready to save the record into the file. This is done with the **Put #** statement, which has the format

```
Put # Filenumber, Variablename
```

The statement we need is

```
Put #1, mintNumber_Of_Appointments,
    ↳gudrAppointment_Records(mintNumber_Of_Appointments)
```

We use the same file number and then use the (**mintNumber_Of_Appointments**) variable to indicate the particular record in the gudrAppointment_Records array that we want to put into the file.

8. Key the Put # statement into the procedure.

Then, since we have increased the number of appointments, the mintCurrent_Record will also need to be updated with the following statement:

```
mintCurrent_Record = mintNumber_Of_Appointments
```

9. Key the assignment statement.

For the Else portion of the If Test, we simply need to assign values of the 20 text boxes and the 20 check boxes to the arrays, as we did before, and then store the record into the file with the same Put # statement, using the current record pointer (intCurrent_Record) instead of the counter. Then we need to end the inside If Test, close the file, and end the outside If Test. Following that, we need to turn off the mblnWas_Changed variable since any changed data was just saved.

10. Key the appropriate statements as specified. This gives you a complete procedure like the one shown in Figure 8.30.

FIGURE 8.30

The code for the Save_Appointments procedure.

```
PIM - frmPIM (Code)                                                    _ □ ×
(General)                              ▼   Save_Appointments              ▼
' This procedure will save the appointments if they were changed
'
Private Sub Save_Appointments()
    Dim intCounter As Integer
    Dim intInside_Counter As Integer

' Save the records

    If mblnWas_Changed = True Then

        ' Open the Appointments file

        Open "A:\Ch-8\Appointments.app" For Random As #1 Len = Len(gudrAppointment_Records(1))

        If mintCurrent_Record = 0 Then
            mintNumber_Of_Appointments = mintNumber_Of_Appointments + 1
            gudrAppointment_Records(mintNumber_Of_Appointments).intFile_Pointer = mintNumber_Of_Appo
            gudrAppointment_Records(mintNumber_Of_Appointments).dtmRecord_Date = mdtmPrevious_Date
            For intInside_Counter = 1 To 20
                gudrAppointment_Records(mintNumber_Of_Appointments).strComment(intInside_Counter) =
                If chkAlarm(intInside_Counter).Value = vbChecked Then
                    gudrAppointment_Records(mintNumber_Of_Appointments).blnAlarmon(intInside_Counter
                Else
                    gudrAppointment_Records(mintNumber_Of_Appointments).blnAlarmon(intInside_Counter
                End If
            Next intInside_Counter
            Put #1, mintNumber_Of_Appointments, gudrAppointment_Records(mintNumber_Of_Appointments)
            mintCurrent_Record = mintNumber_Of_Appointments
        Else
            For intInside_Counter = 1 To 20
                gudrAppointment_Records(mintCurrent_Record).strComment(intInside_Counter) = txtAppoi
                If chkAlarm(intInside_Counter).Value = vbChecked Then
                    gudrAppointment_Records(mintCurrent_Record).blnAlarmon(intInside_Counter) = True
                Else
                    gudrAppointment_Records(mintCurrent_Record).blnAlarmon(intInside_Counter) = Fals
                End If
            Next intInside_Counter
            Put #1, mintCurrent_Record, gudrAppointment_Records(mintCurrent_Record)
        End If
        Close #1
    End If
    mblnWas_Changed = False
End Sub
```

Indicating That the Data Were Changed

We have reset the mblnWas_Changed variable to False in the Get_Appointments and Save_Appointments procedures, but we have yet to set the mblnWas_Changed variable to True. There are two procedures that will be handy for this function, the Click event procedure of the check boxes and the Change event procedure of the comments entry boxes.

1. Change to the Click event procedure for the check boxes and key the statement to set the mblnWas_Changed variable to True.

2. Change to the txtAppointment_Comments_Change event procedure and key the same statement.

Now, when the user changes an alarm setting on one of the comments, the mblnWas_Changed variable will so indicate.

The Date Procedures

Now that we have created the procedures to save and get the data, we need to tell the program when to do it. As we mentioned earlier, we are going to use the Click procedures of the MonthView control for doing this.

We also mentioned that there are actually two events that are set off by a selection on the control. If you click the month name, the list of months will appear and then when you click one of the list items, the mnvAppointments_Click procedure is set off. This same procedure is triggered when you click one of the month selection arrows. On the other hand, if you click one of the days in the calendar, the DateClick event is used. We need to be sure something happens in each event.

1. Open the code for the Click event of the MonthView control.

The code we need here is pretty basic. Save the current data in the controls for the previous date and then read the data for the new date. This means we need to call the Save_Appointments procedure and then immediately call the Get_Appointments procedure.

2. Key the two procedure call statements.

That leaves us with the DateClick procedure. Again, this is easy. All we need here are the same two statements to save the previous data and then get the new data.

3. Change to the DateClick event procedure and key the same two call statements.

Additional Use of the Save and Get Procedures

This completes the code for the MonthView control, but not for the use of the save and get procedures. When you have a program like the PIM, it is easy for the user to switch to the Appointments tab, make changes, switch to another tab, and then exit the program without saving the changes that were made. We could make use of the QueryUnload event to be sure the data is saved if the user exits the program. This would be fine except for one thing: If the program or computer happens to crash before the user exits the program, the changed data will be lost. Thus, we want to save the changes when the user switches tabs.

1. Switch to the tabPIM_Click event procedure.

Notice that this procedure has PreviousTab as a parameter. This indicates which tab was displayed before the change was made to the new tab. We will use this as well as the Tab property for the currently selected tab.

If the program had previously been on the Appointments tab when the change was made, the PreviousTab variable will contain the number of that tab, which happens to be 2. To save the appointments when the user switches from the Appointments tab will take the following code:

```
IfPreviousTab = 2 Then
    Save_Appointments
End If
```

2. Key this If Test in the procedure.

8.12   Setting Off the Alarms

We set up check boxes to allow the user to set an alarm on each of the appointments. It is time to do something with those settings.

The first thing of concern is the alarm offset. This is the time prior to the scheduled event when we want the alarm to go off. That is, if you have a meeting scheduled at 3:00 p.m., you want to be notified of the meeting not at 3:00 p.m. but a few minutes before so you have time to get to the meeting. How long before the meeting you want to be notified is generally a matter of preference, and we allow the user to set this preference. There is an option in the menu to call up a dialog box for the user to change that offset. Since we are going to allow the offset to be changed, we need a variable in which the offset can be saved.

1. Switch to the module and add a global declaration for the **gintAlarm_Offset** integer.

   Now we want this variable to have a default value.

2. Switch to the Form_Load procedure for the PIM form and add an assignment statement to initialize the gintAlarm_Offset variable to 15.

   Now let's move on to the form to let the user change this default value.

3. Create a new form as shown in Figure 8.31 with the following considerations:

   a) The name of the form is **FrmAlarm_Offset**.

   b) The name of the text box is **txtMinutes_Input**.

   c) The name of the button is **cmdOK**.

   The only code needed on the form is for the **OK** button, and all that is needed is to hide the form.

4. Open the code window for the **OK** button and key the appropriate statement.

   Now we need to work with the menu item.

5. Open the code window for the **Set Alarm Offset...** menu item on the **Control** menu.

   The first thing we need to do is to put the current alarm offset into the text box and highlight it. Remember that to highlight a text box entry we use the SelStart function to set the beginning point of the highlighted portion and SelLength to indicate the length of the highlighted portion. This requires the following statements.

   ```
   FrmAlarm_Offset.txtMinutes_Input = Str(gintAlarm_Offset)
   FrmAlarm_Offset.txtMinutes_Input.SelStart = 0
   FrmAlarm_Offset.txtMintues_Input.SelLength = 99
   ```

6. Key the previous statements. Note that we used a SelLength of 99 since we don't know how long the text box entry is.

   Next we need to show the form.

FIGURE 8.31
The new alarm offset form.

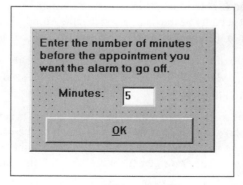

7. Key the modal Show statement.

Then we need to reassign the value from the form with the following statement:

```
gintAlarm_Offset = Val(FrmAlarm_Offset.txtMinutes_Input)
```

8. Key the statement.

Now that we have the offset established, we need to use it to determine if any of the alarms for the current day should be set off. As you might expect, this is done in the code for the Timer control.

9. Change to the tmrAlarm_Timer_Timer procedure and move the cursor below the code already in the procedure.

To check for the alarms, we need to loop through all the appointments and find the record for the current day. If the user has not used the program for a few days, it might be nice to be notified of any appointments that were forgotten. Thus, the loop statement is

```
For intCounter = 1 To mintNumber_Of_Appointments
```

10. Key this statement.

Next we need to check for the current day with the following If Test:

```
If gudrAppointment_Records(intCounter).dtmRecord_Date = Date Then
```

11. Key the statement.

Now we need to loop through the 20 alarms to determine if any of them are on and are prior to the current time plus the alarm offset. Thus, we need to loop from 1 to 20:

```
For intInside_Counter = 1 To 20
```

12. Key this statement.

Now we need to test the alarms to see if they have been turned on. The problem is that the first eight check boxes are a.m. and the other twelve are p.m. If we are to use the captions of the check boxes, which is the easiest thing to do, we need to add a.m. to the first eight and p.m. to the last twelve so we can compare them against the current time. This time must be assigned to a temporary variable that we have declared as a Date. If we simply appended an a.m. on a string variable, a comparison against a date variable would not work. Thus, we need the If Test shown here (and remember, dteAlarm_Time needs to be declared as a Date):

```
If intInside_Counter < 9 Then
    dteAlarm_Time = chkAlarm(intInside_Counter).Caption & "AM"
Else
    dteAlarm_Time = chkAlarm(intInside_Counter).Caption & "PM"
End If
```

13. Key this If Test.

Now we need to determine if the alarm represented by the counter is on. Since the current date may not actually be the date selected in the MonthView control, we need to process the array instead of the check boxes:

```
If gudrAppointment_Records(intCounter).blnAlarmon
↳(intInside_Counter)= True Then
```

14. Key the previous statement.

Now we have to determine if the date plus the offset is beyond the time represented by the alarm check box caption that we have assigned to the dteAlarm_Time Date variable. Though we haven't yet learned how to add the offset to the current time, there is a Visual Basic function for it. The **DateAdd** function has the following format:

```
DateAdd(internal,number,date)
```

where the **interval** is specified by using the same string expression used in the Format statement ("n" for minutes in this case), the **number** is the number of intervals to be added to the third parameter, the **date** to be increased. The function we need is

```
DateAdd("n", gintAlarm_Offset, Time)
```

which we will put in the following If Test:

```
If DateAdd ("n", gintAlarm_Offset, Time) >= dteAlarm_Time Then
```

15. Key the statement.

When we created the alarm clock, we made the program beep to signal that the alarm was going off. In this case, it makes more sense to have a message box appear on the screen, showing the appointment message itself. This leads us to the following statement.

```
MsgBox gudrAppointment_Records(intCounter).strComment
 ↳(intInside_Counter), vbExclamation, "Appointment!!"
```

16. Key the MsgBox statement into the procedure.

Next, we need to turn off the alarm both in the array and in the check box if the current date is the one being displayed. The first statement is

```
gudrAppointment_Records(intCounter.blnAlarmon(intInside_Counter)
 ↳ = False
```

Then, to determine if we need to turn off the check box, we need to check the MonthView date against the current date as in the following If Test:

```
If mnvAppointments = Date Then
    chkAlarm(intInside_Counter).Value = Unchecked
End If
```

17. Key the If test.

Now we need to tell the program we have made a change and then save the appointments:

```
mblnWas_Changed = True
Save_Appointments
```

18. Key these statements and then close the two inside If Tests, the inside loop, the outside If Test, and the outside loop.

Now we are ready to test the program.

19. Run the program. Switch to the Appointments tab, key some data into a couple of the text boxes, and then change the date.

20. Change the date back to the original one. The appointments you entered should show up.

21. Set a couple of the alarms. Exit the program and then rerun it. Switch to the Appointments tab. The data and alarm setting should show up automatically, because you are working on the current date. This means that the data were properly stored in and retrieved from the file.

22. Experiment with the program a bit more to be sure that everything is working properly. Be sure to set some alarms prior to the current time plus offset to test that the alarms work. Change the offset and try it again.

23. Exit the program when you are satisfied that everything is working properly.

Though it's not necessary because the record structure specifies that each of the fields is 20 characters long, if we needed to be certain we had 20 characters in the text boxes, we could ensure that the field was always 20 characters long by adding the appropriate number of blanks to the end. Visual Basic has a function for that. The **String** function has the following format:

```
String(number of characters, character)
```

This function will return a string of the specified length filled with the specified character. To be sure the text box is always 20 characters long, we could use a function like

```
txtAppointment_Comments(intCounter).Text =
↳ txtAppointment_Comments(intCounter).Text & String(20 -
↳ Len(txtAppointment_Comments(intCounter).Text)," ")
```

This subtracts the actual length of the field from 20 and then creates a string of that many blanks (" "). That string is appended to the end of the current comment. For example, if txtAppointment_Comments(intCounter).Text is Fred, then 20 – Len(Fred) would be 16 and the String function would give us 16 blanks.

We don't have to fill with blanks using the String function. We can fill the string with any character, such as the asterisk:

```
txtOutput = String(20 - Len("Fred"), "*")
```

This would yield a string containing Fred followed by 16 asterisks.

8.13   Using the Common Dialog Control for Files

We have mentioned that there are common dialog boxes for opening and saving files, but we chose to create our own file dialog boxes so that we would understand the process and learn about the various file tools. Before we leave this chapter, however, we need to understand how to use the common dialog boxes for file processing; they can save a lot of time.

To begin with, we will need to make the Show statement in the current Open File code window a comment. This will allow us to leave the statement in the program while making sure that Visual Basic doesn't execute it. We don't need this statement because it loads the dialog box we created and we are going to replace our dialog box with the common dialog box.

1. Open the code window for the **Open File...** option and make the Show statement into a comment.

Before we begin creating the new code, we need to briefly examine the dialog box that we want the Open File option to bring to the desktop (see Figure 8.32). Note that this window has the elements that should, by now, be familiar. There is one element, the list of file types, that we did not put in our dialog box. Its purpose is to allow users to specify what types of files, by type pattern, they want displayed in the file list. For example, you might want to display all the text files (*.TXT) or batch files (*.BAT).

To use this file type list, you must tell Visual Basic what those file types are. The statement to do this uses a common dialog property called a **Filter**. The format of the Filter property is

```
object.Filter [= Description1 | Filter1 | Description2 | Filter2…]
```

The Description (1, 2, etc.) is a string expression describing the filter to be used. The Filter (1, 2, etc.) is the actual filter to be used. The description is separated from the filter by the pipe (|) symbol, and each Description | Filter combination is separated from the other sets by another pipe symbol. You can specify as many Description | Filter combinations as you wish. The filter statement we will use is

```
cdgPIM.Filter = "All Files (*.*)|*.*|Text Files (*.TXT)|*.TXT|Batch
↳ Files(*.BAT)|*.BAT|No Extension (*.)|*."
```

FIGURE 8.32
The Open dialog box.

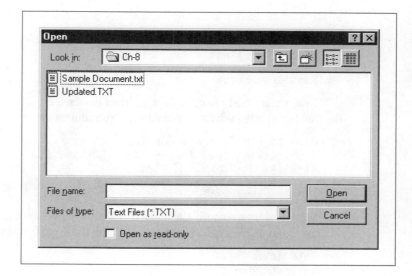

The text portion (the right side) of this statement consists of a list of four different filter patterns. The descriptions are as shown in Table 8.4.

2. Key the Filter statement given above.

Following the Filter statement, we need to tell Visual Basic which of the filter patterns we want to be the one that is used initially. This is done with the **FilterIndex** statement, which has the format

```
Object.FilterIndex = Indexnumber
```

The Indexnumber is the pointer to the specific Description | Filter combination we want to use initially. The statement we want to use is

```
cdgPIM.FilterIndex = 2
```

This specifies using the second filter in the list, so the initial filter will be for text files (*.TXT).

3. Key the foregoing statement.

Next we need to specify the command to load the dialog box. The method for the Open dialog box is **ShowOpen**, so the next statement should be

```
cdgPIM.ShowOpen
```

4. Key this statement.

Because this statement causes the dialog box to be displayed, the next statement in the procedure should begin the ones that are needed when the user exits the dialog box. The dialog box **Cancel** button is set up so that if it is selected, the file name returned will be null.

TABLE 8.4
The breakdown of the Filter statement.

Description	Filter
All Files (*.*)	*.*
Text Files (*.TXT)	*.TXT
Batch Files (*.BAT)	*.BAT
No Extension (*.)	*.*

So we need to verify that the file name that is returned is not null before we attempt to open the file.

```
If cdgPIM.Filename <> "" Then
```

5. Key this statement.

Now we are ready to open the file, input the data, close the file, and change the title of the title bar to reflect the new file name. This requires the following statements:

```
Open cdgPIM.filename For Input As #1
frmPIM.txtNotepad.Text = Input(LOF(1), #1)
Close #1
```

6. Key these statements.

We just want to put the file name on the title bar. Therefore, we just need to select the file name and display it. This can be done with the same type of loop we used earlier.

```
intPointer = 1
intCounter = 1
Do Until intCounter = 0
    intPointer = intCounter
    intCounter = InStr(intCounter + 1, cdgPIM.filename, "\")
Loop
```

7. Key this loop.

To make the title bar assignment statement, we need to discover where on the title bar to put it and then select just the file name from the point of the last instance of the slash that is stored in intPointer. We need a routine such as

```
intDash_Found = InStr(frmPIM.Caption, " - ")
If intDash_Found = 0 Then
    intDash_Found = Len(frmPIM.Caption) + 1
    frmPIM.Caption = frmPIM.Caption & " - "
End If
frmPIM.Caption = Left(frmPIM.Caption, intDash_Found + 2) &
    ⤷Mid(cdgPIM.filename, intPointer + 1)
```

8. Key these statements.

That's all we need to be able to load a file but we still need to save the file name in the menu by calling the Add_Menu_Item procedure with

```
Add_Menu_Item cdgPIM.Filename
```

9. Key the previous statement.

10. Run the program and verify that it will load a file. Save the file under a different name, select the **New** option, and then reload the file you just saved. Do this several times until you are certain that everything is working properly. Exit the program.

The **Save File As...** option needs virtually the same code to load the common dialog box for saving files.

11. Copy all the code that you created in this procedure, change to the code window for the **Save File As...** option, and paste the code there.

Only a few changes need to be made.

- The Show statement needs to be ShowSave instead of ShowOpen.

- The Open statement needs to open the file for output rather than input.

- The Input statement needs to be changed to a Print # statement:

```
Print #1, frmPIM.txtNotepad.Text
```

11. Make these changes. Then run the program and thoroughly test both the open and the save functions to be sure the program still operates as it is supposed to. Then exit the program.

8.14 Debugging Your Programs

There are a number of potential problems that you may encounter when using files in your programs. The most common of these arises when you are not careful with the file numbers you are using on your Open statements. If you try to open a second file using the same file number that you used on the first Open statement, before the first file is closed, you will get a "File already open" error. As we have mentioned in this chapter, the easiest way to avoid this type of problem is to use a different file number for each of the files you use in your program.

That's not to say that you can then be careless about closing your files. You should always close a file when you are finished processing it. You shouldn't simply change the file number on the statement that gives you the "File already open" error so that the error will go away. You need to determine why you have the problem in the first place. Somewhere prior to the Open statement causing the error, the file has been opened, and it should be closed properly. It is possible, however, that you need to have several files open at the same time. This is perfectly acceptable and is sometimes necessary.

It is important to close your files properly. Though Windows will automatically close all open files when you exit the program, you should always close them yourself as soon as you are finished with them. Windows uses a special storage area in the computer called a **buffer** to store the data written into a file before actually writing the data to the file. It does this to save processing time. It writes the data to the buffer rather than to the disk because this is faster. Then, when the data accumulated are deemed sufficient, which depends on the size of the buffer and several other considerations, the data are written to the disk. If the system goes down between the time the data are written into the buffer and the time when they are written to the file, the data still in the buffer are lost. When you close the file, the buffer is automatically written to the file. As soon as you close your file, the data are safely stored on the disk. That's why you should always close a file as soon as you are finished with it.

When using sequential files, you need to be careful to use the appropriate input statement for the type of output that was written to the disk. If you write a delimited file, you should use the input statement designed to read delimited files. The wrong type of input statement may produce confusing or erroneous results. Also, don't try to read random data with anything but a Get # statement. The data are not written into the file with the Put # statement the way they are with the Write # statement. If you write a number into the file with a Write # statement, the number appears as a number when the file is viewed in the notepad. A number written into a random-access file, however, is written in a compressed format. If you view a random-access file with the notepad, the numbers are not readable. You must be sure to read the data back with the appropriate input statement, or the data will not be interpreted correctly. The next steps will illustrate this.

1. Launch the Notepad application from the **Accessories** submenu of the **Programs** submenu of the **Start** menu on the Taskbar.

2. Load the Appointments.app file from the Ch-8 folder on your work disk.

3. Turn on the **Word Wrap** option of the **Edit** menu.

The data will look something like Figure 8.33.

You can read the comments that have been keyed in the text boxes, but the dates (dtmRecord_Date) and file pointers (intFile_Pointer) are unreadable.

FIGURE 8.33

The data from the Appointments.app file.

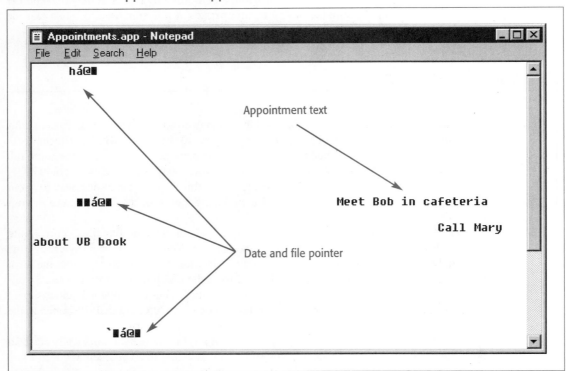

4. Exit from Notepad, exit from Visual Basic, and shut down the system properly.

One final note. When creating sequential files using a word processor or other program that can save text files, it is important not to leave extra carriage returns at the end of the data. If your program is reading the data until the end of the file is found (EOF()), the carriage returns may be interpreted as additional pieces of data. If that happens, your program may not generate the proper results. Always be careful to remove any excess carriage returns from the end of the data file by backspacing to remove them.

8.15   Command and Menu Summary

In this chapter you learned about the following properties:

- **Drive** is a property of a pull-down drive list that contains the drive designation for the current disk drive.
- **FileName** is a property of the file list that contains the current file name highlighted in the list.
- **Filter** is a property of the Open or Save File Common Dialog Control that allows the program to specify the filters to be shown in the list in the dialog box.
- **FilterIndex** is used on the common dialog command to specify the default file types that the file dialog box is to use.
- **FileName** is the file name that is returned from the common dialog file access box.

- **Path** is a property of the drive, directory, and file lists that holds the pathname of the file location.
- **Pattern** is a property of the file list that contains the pattern that will be used to display the files in the file list.

In this chapter you learned about the following functions and commands:

- **ChDir** changes the current directory in the operating system.
- **ChDrive** changes the current drive in the operating system.
- **Close** is the command needed to stop access to a file by closing the file and releasing the file number so that another Open command can use it.
- **CurDir** retrieves the current pathname from Windows.
- **DateAdd** allows you to add an integer value to a date variable.
- **EOF()** checks to determine whether the end-of-file marker has been read in the file designated by the file number in the parentheses.
- **Get #** is the command to read a record from a random-access file.
- **Input #** reads data from a delimited sequential file.
- **Input** reads the data in an entire sequential file.
- **Line Input** reads a sequential file until a carriage return is found.
- **Load** adds a new menu control array item.
- **LOF()** calculates the length of the file designated by the file number in the parentheses.
- **Open** opens a file for access.
- **Print #** is used to write sequential files without any formatting.
- **Put #** is the command to write a record into a random-access file.
- **String** is the function that can be used to create strings of a specified length and filled with a specified character.
- **Type** lets the programmer define new file structure types.
- **Unload** deletes a menu control array item.
- **Write #** is used to write sequential data with delimiters.

In this chapter you learned about the following method:

- **ShowOpen** displays the File Open Common Dialog Box.

In this chapter you learned about the following prefixes:

- **dir** is for the Directory List box.
- **drv** is for the Drive List box.
- **fil** is for the File List box.
- **udr** is for user-defined records.
- **udt** is for user-defined types for defining user-defined variables.

In this chapter you learned about the following Toolbox tools:

- The tool to add a directory list that allows the user to change the directory.
- The tool to add a pull-down list of available drives that allows the user to change drives.
- The tool to add a file list that allows the user to pick the needed file from the list.
- The tool to add a MonthView control that allows the user to pick a date from the calendar.

8.16   Performance Check

1. What are the three types of files mentioned in this chapter?

   _____ ,

   _____ ,

   and _____

2. How are the data in a binary file read?

   _____

3. Explain how Visual Basic determines where a particular record in a random file is located.

   _____

4. What are the three sequential file access methods?

   _____ ,

   _____ ,

   and _____

5. Create an Open statement for a sequential file called File_In so the data in the file can be read.

   _____

6. What is the purpose of the file number in the Open statement?

   _____

7. What does the statement dirSave_As.Path = drvSave_As.Drive accomplish?

   _____

8. What is a delimited file?

   _____

9. What file processing statement writes a delimited file?

   _____

10. Why might we want to create a delimited file?

    _____

11. What is the CurDir function for?

    _____

12. Which object uses the Pattern property?

    _____

13. What is the Pattern property used for?

    _____

14. What type of sequential file is the Input command designed to be used on?

    _____

15. What information must be given to the Input command that is not needed for the other two sequential input statements?

    _____

16. What is the ChDir command for?

    _____

17. What advantage does a random-access file have over a sequential file?

    _____

18. What is the field that is used to create an index called?

    _____

19. Besides the field from the data file, what else is stored in an index file?

    _____

20. What is the Type statement used for?

    _____

21. What is added to the Open statement for a random file that is not used on the Open statement for a sequential file?

    _____

22. What is the EOF() function for?

    _____

23. What is the LOF() function for?

    _____

24. What does the String function do?

_____

25. If you use a Get # statement without specifying the record number, what record is read?

_____

26. Give two reasons why we wrote the filename in the title bar caption.

_____

and _____

8.17 Programming Exercises

1. In past chapters you have worked on an application that has six message boards. The last update of the application was in Chapter 7, and it was saved as **Menu Messages**. You have decided that the application needs to be updated so that the data in the six workspaces can be saved if the user exits the application. Also, the data will automatically be loaded when the application is loaded. There will be no load and save options on the menu, just an exit option, but to be consistent with other applications, you will add a **File** menu even though it will have just the one **Exit** option. This exercise will give you practice in saving and loading multiple sequential files. At the computer, do each of the following:

   a. Get into Visual Basic with your work disk in drive A.

   b. Change to your Ch-7 folder and load the Menu Messages application. If you haven't created the Menu Messages application, you can get a copy of it from your instructor.

   c. Save all the program elements in the Ch-8 folder.

   d. Open the frmMessages form, and insert a **File** menu with the one **E&xit** option with the control name **mnuExit_Application** and the shortcut key **Ctrl-X** in front of the Whose Message menu.

   e. Open the code window for the **Exit** option.

   f. This procedure will open a separate file for each of the six workspaces and save the data found within. Each of these files will have the name of a person and will have an extension of Mes (for message). Because the same pathname will be needed for each file, setting it up first is the easiest way. Key the following:

   ```
   strPath = "A:\CH-8\"
   ```

   g. Now key the six Open statements:

   ```
   Open StrPath & "Bob.Mes" For Output As #1
   Open StrPath & "Sam.Mes" For Output As #2
   Open StrPath & "Sara.Mes" For Output As #3
   Open StrPath & "Fred.Mes" For Output As #4
   Open StrPath & "Heidi.Mes" For Output As #5
   Open StrPath & "Joanne.Mes" For Output As #6
   ```

   h. The six workspaces are in a control array (named txtText_Boxes), so they can be written to the files using a loop:

   ```
   For intCounter = 0 To 5
       Print #intCounter + 1, txtText_Boxes(intCounter).Text
   Next intCounter
   ```

   i. Only one Close statement is needed:

   ```
   Close #1, #2, #3, #4, #5, #6
   ```

j. We are also going to save the entered passwords in another file. Key

```
Open strPath & "Password.Mes" For Output As #1
For intCounter = 0 To 5
    Write #1, strPasswords(intCounter)
Next intCounter
Close #1
```

k. Add the End statement.

l. Now we need to open the files when the application is loaded. Change to the code for the Load event for the Form. The code is virtually the same as the code in step g. Key

```
strPath = "A:\CH-9\"
Open strPath & "Bob.Mes" For Input As #1
Open strPath & "Sam.Mes" For Input As #2
Open strPath & "Sara.Mes" For Input As #3
Open strPath & "Fred.Mes" For Input As #4
Open strPath & "Heidi.Mes" For Input As #5
Open strPath & "Joanne.Mes" For Input As #6
For intCounter = 0 To 5
    txtText_Boxes(intCounter).Text = Input(LOF(intCounter + 1),
    ↳#intCounter + 1)
Next intCounter
Close #1, #2, #3, #4, #5, #6
Open strPath & "Password.Mes" For Input As #1
For intCounter = 0 To 5
    Input #1, strPasswords(intCounter)
Next intCounter
Close #1
```

m. Before you can execute this program, you have to create the seven files that the program expects to find on the disk. You can put anything (or nothing) into each of the text box files, but the password file will need to have six delimited passwords. You can use the notepad in your PIM application to create the files.

n. Run the application and enter a password and message in several of the boxes; then exit it. Run it again and make sure that all the keyed messages are still in the boxes and that the application still has the passwords.

o. Exit the application.

p. Exit Visual Basic and shut down the system properly.

2. In past exercises you have created and updated a notepad application with three extra workspaces for storage of the data cut from the original workspace. This application was updated in Chapter 7 and is now called **Color Multicut**. When it was created, the same file save and load options of our regular notepad were put in the menus. It is now time to add those functions to this program. This exercise will give you practice working with multiple sequential files. At the computer, do each of the following:

a. Get into Visual Basic with your work disk in drive A.

b. Change to the Ch-7 folder on drive A, and load the **Color Multicut** application. If you did not work on the exercise where Color Multicut was created, you can get a copy of the application from your instructor.

c. Save each of the forms and the module in the Ch-8 folder. This is a new folder, so it is not necessary to change the names of the elements. You should, however, change the name of the project to **File Multicut** before saving it in the Ch-8 folder.

d. Add the frmLoad_File form, resave it as **frmMulti_Load_File**, add the frmSave_As form, and resave it as **frmMulti_Save_As**. Resave the project.

e. Change the loading function so that it will load four files when the file is selected from the list. The four files all have the same file name, with extensions of NP, NP1, NP2, and NP3 for the original workspace and each of the three cut workspaces, respectively.

f. Change the saving function so that each of the four files is saved with the proper extension.

g. Change the save and load options on the menu, adding the statements necessary to load the dialog boxes. Also make sure you change the Notepad title in the appropriate places in the code.

h. Run the program, key some data into the main workspace, and cut it several times so that each of the other workspaces has some data. Save the file and clear all the workspaces. Reselect the file you saved to check that the data are replaced in each of the workspaces.

i. Exit the application, exit Visual Basic, and shut down the system properly.

3. To gain a bit more practice with adding and deleting menu items during runtime, you decide to create a simple phone book database that will add names to the menu and display the name and the phone number when the name in the menu is selected. Using this information, the information given in the steps of the problem, and the design for the form, design the program and then, at the computer, do each of the following:

a. Get into Visual Basic with your work disk in drive A.

b. Create a form like the one shown in Figure 8.34. The two boxes are text boxes with the control names **txtName_Input** and **txtPhone_Input**.

c. Open the Menu Design Window and add each of the following:

1) The menu name of **&Entries** with the control name **mnuEntry_Menu**.

2) The menu item of **&Add Current Entry** with the control name **mnuAdd_Item** and the shortcut key **Ctrl-A**.

3) The menu item of **&Delete Current Entry** with the control name **mnuDelete_ Item** and the shortcut key **Ctrl-D**.

4) A separator line called **mnuDash_1**.

5) A blank menu item with the control name **mnuMenu_Names** and an index value of 0. Turn off the Visible box so that the item will not show in the menu (this is okay this time because there are other items in the menu).

6) Another separator line called **mnuDash_2**.

7) The menu item of **E&xit** with the control name **mnuExit_Item**.

d. When the Add Current Entry menu option is selected, the data in the txtName_ Input entry box will be put in the menu, and the text in the txtPhone_Input entry box will be put in an array called **strStored_Phones**. Set up **strStored_Phones** with a maximum of 10 items (there has to be some limit). Also set up a variable called **intNumber_Names** to be used to keep track of how many names have been

FIGURE 8.34
The form for the Phone Book.

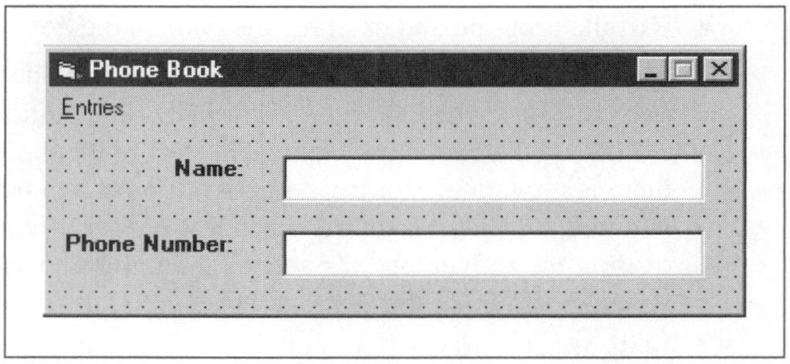

put in the menu. When mnuAdd_Item is selected, increase **intNumber_Names** by 1, add the menu item (**mnuMenu_Names**), put the text in the caption, make the item visible (this is necessary because the menu items will inherit the false visible value from the 0 control array element), and store the phone number in the array. Then set the text boxes to null.

e. Essentially, you reverse the process used for adding menu items for the **Delete Current Entry** menu option.

f. Switch to the code for the menu items. In this code you display the text from the selected menu item in the txtName_Input box and the phone number from the array in the txtPhone_Input box.

g. To improve the look of the menu, you can make one of the dashes invisible when creating the menu and then make it visible when the items are added to the menu. That way the menu initially shows only one separator line.

h. When the user exits the program, the data should be saved to a file on the disk that will automatically be loaded when the program is run again. Depending on how you create this program, you may need to create an empty file for the program to open when it is first run.

i. Save the application as **Phone Book**. Test the program, and then print it out.

j. Exit the program, exit Visual Basic, and shut down the system properly.

4. Harold, a fellow programmer working for a library, has been trying to get a program of his to work and has asked for your help. The program is supposed to read sets of data from a sequential file and display a list of authors. Then, when one of the authors is selected from the list, the names of the books the author wrote are to be displayed in a series of text boxes. The text boxes are a control array that will display only as many text boxes as are needed for the data.

Harold created a small file of data with which to test the program. These sample data from the Authors.txt file found in the Ch-8 folder on the work disk are shown in Figure 8.35.

The first line of each set of author information has the name of the author followed by the number of books that are listed next in the file. The program should read the first two fields and then loop through the number of books that follow. Knowing this, let's work on the program. At the computer, do each of the following:

a. Get into Visual Basic with your work disk in drive A.

b. Load the **Authors** program from the Ch-8 folder on your disk.

c. The form will show a list, one text box, and **Exit** and **Print** buttons. The text box is element 1 of a control array.

d. Run the program.

Immediately you can see that there is a problem. The list has the name of the author, followed, on the same list element, by the number of books. Then the next few elements of the list are the books by that author. Obviously this isn't correct.

e. Exit the program and examine the code in the Form_Load event procedure.

The first input statement in this procedure is supposed to input the author's name (strName) and then the number of books the author has written. As you can see, Harold used a Line Input statement storing the input in the strName variable, and there is no variable for the number of books. If you examine the loop just below, you will see that it goes from 1 to intNumber. We see that the program should be reading the intNumber variable as the number of books. But the input statement should be an Input # statement instead of Line Input.

f. Make these changes and run the program again.

FIGURE 8.35
The data in the Authors.txt file.

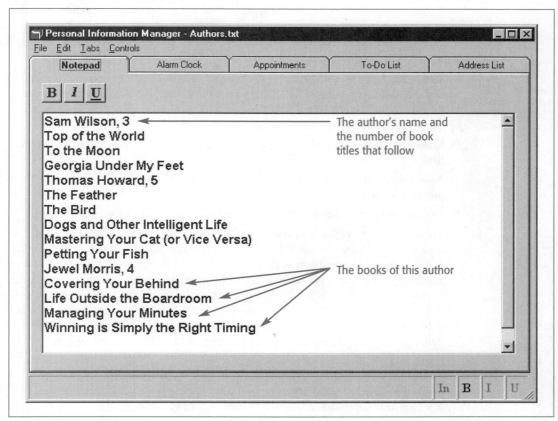

Now you get an "Input past end of file" error. Stop the program and examine the statement causing the error. It is the input statement you just corrected.

g. Move the mouse pointer over the intAuthor_Count variable in the code.

This variable has a value of 4. It is the variable that is counting the number of author/book groups that are being read, and if you look back at the data, you will see that there are only three groups in the file. Think a minute. Think of what you read earlier in the chapter about sequential files. What could the problem be? That's right. There are extra carriage returns at the end of the data in the file.

h. Exit the program. Launch a new version of Visual Basic and run the PIM program. Open the Authors.txt file from the Ch-8 folder on your work disk. Remove the carriage returns from the end of the data, and save the file back on the disk.

i. Run the program. Now the list shows the three authors' names.

j. Click the first author in the list. The first book shows up in the text box, but the other text boxes do not appear. Exit the program.

Remember that when new elements of a control array are loaded, the new elements are not visible. The Visible property must be set to True. Harold forgot this.

k. Add the appropriate statement in the lstAuthors_Click event procedure.

l. Run the program and click the first element of the list.

Here you can see a couple of things wrong. First, there is a blank text box at the end. Second, if you look back at the data in the file, you will see that the books shown do not belong to Sam Wilson. Third, Sam Wilson is credited with only three books, whereas this listing shows four. These four books actually belong to Jewel Morris. This error is a bit difficult to locate, so we will help you.

m. Exit the program. Explore the code in the Form_Load procedure again.

The ItemData statement is

```
lstAuthors.ItemData(lstAuthors.NewIndex) = intNumber
```

The problem is that intNumber is the number of books, not the sequential number of the author as that line of data was read from the file. The ItemData pointer needs to point to the Author/Books set of data, not to the number of books. The statement should use intAuthor_Count instead.

n. Make this correction and run the program again. Select each of the authors in the list.

Now there is only one error. An extra Text box shows up each time. This error must be in the lstAuthors_Click event procedure.

o. Exit the program. Examine the code in the lstAuthors_Click event procedure.

The first element of the list is put in the first text box and then, within the loop, the counter is incremented so that the next text box is created and the text from the array is put in there. The problem is that the loop checks the value of the array element using the counter as it is incremented in the loop. Because it is incremented at the beginning of the loop, it is used before it is tested to see whether there are any data in that element of the array. This is backwards. It needs to be tested first and then used if it is valid to do so. The increment statement needs to be at the end of the loop rather than the beginning. But this means that the next element the loop will try to create will be element 1, because the counter will be 1 when the loop begins. We need to increment the counter before the Do-Until statement.

p. Make the correction and addition, and run the program again. Now the program works as it is supposed to.

q. Exit the program and print it out.

r. Exit Visual Basic and shut down the system properly.

8.18 Performance Mastery

1. You like the message board application that you saved as Menu Messages in your Ch-7 folder. You decide to update the program so that the passwords and messages are saved in a file when the program is exited and are automatically loaded when the program is executed. You will need to add a menu option to allow the program to be exited so that you can put the save routine in it. Load the application and make the appropriate changes. Then test the application, save it in your folder for Chapter 8 as **File Messages**, and print it out.

2. You have been talking to a friend who works in the payroll department. She has asked you to write an application that she can use to display personnel salaries. Use the notepad portion of the PIM program to create a sequential file that has a name followed by a salary amount, as in

Fred Smith, 25000

John Jones, 32000

and so on.

Write a program that can be used to read this file from disk and to display the names in a list. When a name in the list is selected, the salary amount should be displayed in a label. Add a **Print** button to print the form and another button to exit the program. Design and create the program, and save it as **Salary File**. Test and then print the program.

3. The personnel officers of the company you work for have asked for your help. They need an application that will allow them to view lists of active and inactive employees. The program should allow them to select an employee in the active list and move that item to the inactive list. The user should also be able to "reactivate" employees by moving the names from the inactive list to the active list. Finally, the user should be able to permanently delete from the inactive list employees who are no longer under consideration for rehire. Use the MsgBox function to generate error messages if the user tries to move or remove a record without selecting the appropriate item in the list. Make up names that can be used in the lists, and create two files from which the names can be read. One file should be called **Active**, the other **Inactive**. Each time the elements in one of the lists change, the file that the list came from should be rewritten. Design and create the program, and then save it as **Active and Inactive Files**. Test the program and then print it out.

4. You work for Widgets International. One of your colleagues has created a sequential data file with product specifications. You have been assigned the task of reading the file and displaying the data. The data are divided into the five Widget colors and the seven products. Each line of data in the sequential file has the color, the product name, and four numbers, which are quantity on hand, materials cost, production cost, and indirect cost. Your program must display a set of five option buttons for the colors and another set of seven option buttons for the products. When the user selects one of each set of option buttons and presses the calculate button, the three costs are to be totaled to yield the Total Cost. The Total Cost is then multiplied by the quantity on hand to come up with the Total Cost of QOH (quantity on hand).

Have your program read all the data and store them in an array that can be used to display the data and do the calculations. There should be labels to display the data and a **Print** button to print out the results. Save the program as **Widget Files** in the Ch-8 folder. Test the program to be sure it is working properly. Then print it out.

5. You have been asked by the personnel officer of your company to create a program that will have a list of personnel from which an individual can be selected and then certain information about that person will be displayed. She wants to be able to see the date of hire, whether the person is salaried or hourly, and how many days of vacation the person has accumulated. Create a program that will use a random-access file. As the records are read from the file, the name should be put in a sorted list and its relative number in the ItemData property. When the user selects the name from the list, the program should access the appropriate record in the file and display the rest of the data. The program will need to allow the addition of records to the file and the deletion of records from it. Design the program, write it, and then save it as **Random Personnel**. Test the program and then print it out.

6. You work for a company that creates sound effects and music files for computers. You have been assigned the task of creating a program that can be used to allow your customers to sample your files. The program should use the appropriate disk access tools to allow the user to change folders on the disk to find the appropriate files, which should be shown in the File List box. When the user clicks the element in the File List box, the program should play the file. There should also be a button to turn off the sound. Design and write the program, and then save it as **Sound Disk**. Test the program and then print it out.

7. You work for a company that creates animations that can be played on computers. You have been assigned the task of creating a program that can be used to allow your customers to sample your files. The program should use the appropriate disk access tools to allow the user to change folders on the disk to find the appropriate files, which should be shown in the File List box. When the user clicks the element in the File List box, the program should play the file. There should also be a button to turn off the animation display. Design and write the program, and then save it as **Animation Disk**. Test the program and then print it out.

8. You work for the In Your Ears production company, which puts on plays and concerts. They need a program that can be used to keep track of which seats have been booked for each of the nights of the production. Create a program that uses a sequential file to display and store the status of the seating for each night. The theater has 200 seats: 20 rows of 10 seats each. Use a display of text boxes to display the seat status. When a seat is booked, the text box should have a B put in it. If a seat is unoccupied, the text box should be empty. Clicking the seat text box should open a dialog box where the name and phone number of the patron booking the seat can be entered or displayed if the seat is already booked. These should be saved in a separate file with the date of the production and the seat number. (Hint: This file can have a record for each date and seat. When they are not booked, the name and phone number can be null.) The dialog box should have a button to allow the user to cancel the reservation, which should change the status of the seat. The dates of the seating should be displayed in a list, and the appropriate check boxes in the seating display should be checked when the user selects a date from the list. The check boxes for the seating chart should not be visible until a date is chosen from the list. The program should have a button to print the display and another to exit the program. The exit procedure should save the data in the file. Design and write the program, and then save it as **In Your Ears**. Test the program and then print it out.

9. Sam teaches math at a local high school. He has asked you to write a program for him that can be used to store and display the grades his students receive in his classes. He teaches four classes and has up to 30 students in each class. The program should display the names of the classes in one list, and when that list is selected, the names of the students in the class should appear in a second list. When a student is selected from that list, the grades for that student should then be displayed in text boxes so that they can be changed or entered. There should be up to 10 grades for each student. The program should store the data in a random-access file. Each record should have the name of the class, the name of the student, and the 10 grades (in an array). When the program begins, the file should be read and the record number saved with the student name. Then, when the name is chosen from the list, the record should be accessed and the current grades displayed. There should be a **Save** button to save changes to the grades. These should immediately be saved in the file. There should also be an **Add** button that will bring up a new dialog box to allow the entry of a student name and the current grades (up to 10). There should also be **Print** and **Exit** buttons. Design and write the program, and then save it as **Random Grades**. Test the program and then print it out.

10. You work for a company that creates bitmapped graphics (files with a BMP extension). You have been assigned the task of creating a program that can be used to allow your customers to view your files. The program should use the appropriate disk access tools to allow the user to change folders on the disk to find the appropriate files, which should be shown in the File List box. When the user clicks the element in the File List box, the program should display that file in an **Image** box ( ). The property used to specify the file being displayed is the **Picture** property. You cannot, however, simply assign the file name to the property. It must be loaded with the **LoadPicture** function as shown here:

```
imgGraphic.Picture = LoadPicture("C:\Windows\Metal Links.bmp")
```

In your program, you will need to use the results of the selection from the File List box in the function rather than a literal as shown above. Design and write the program, and then save it as **Image Sampler**. Test the program and then print it out.

11. You work for a company that creates bitmapped graphics (files with a BMP extension). You have been assigned the task of creating a program that can be used to allow your customers to view your files in a slide show. The program should use the appropriate disk access tools to allow the user to change folders on the disk to find the appropriate files, which should be shown in the File List box. These lists should be on a second form, which is loaded with a menu item. When the user clicks the **Show** button on the dialog box, the program should display the items that are found in the folder one at time. Use a timer to delay the displaying of the images such that one, two, or three seconds elapse between them. The delay choice should be selected from option buttons on the dialog box. The bitmaps should be displayed on the initial form. The property used to specify the file being displayed on the form is the **Picture** property. You cannot, however, simply assign the file name to the property. It must be loaded with the **LoadPicture** function as shown here:

```
frmSlide_Show.Picture = LoadPicture("C:\Windows\Metal Links.bmp")
```

In your program, you will need to use the List items from the File List box in the function rather than a literal as shown above. You can read through the list one element at a time just as though it were a normal List box using the List properties such as List and ListIndex. Design and write the program, and then save it as **Image Slide Show**. Test the program and then print it out.

12. You work for a company that creates bitmapped graphics (files with a BMP extension). You have been assigned the task of creating a program that can be used to allow your customers to view an array of small images of the files. The program should use the appropriate disk access tools to allow the user to change folders on the disk to find the appropriate files, which should be shown in the File List box. These lists should be on a second form, which is loaded with a menu item. When the user clicks the **Show** button on the dialog box, the program should display the items that are found in the folder in an array of **Image** boxes. The property used to specify the file being displayed in the Image box is the **Picture** property. You cannot, however, simply assign the file name to the property. It must be loaded with the **LoadPicture** function as shown here:

```
imgDisplay.Picture = LoadPicture("C:\Windows\Metal Links.bmp")
```

In your program, you need to use the List items from the File List box in the function rather than a literal as shown above. You can read through the list one element at a time just as though it were a normal List box using the List properties such as List and ListIndex.

The Image boxes will need to be a control array. You need only create the first element, because you can use the Load statement to create the rest of the elements. You will always have to have one element, but the other elements in the array should be unloaded when a new folder is chosen. This way, only the files in the currently selected folder will be shown. Also, the procedure to display the Image boxes will start with only one control array item loaded. If the first one were already created and the rest of the time any number were created, the procedure to display the images would be much more difficult. You will need to size the Image box to whatever you deem appropriate. When the new ones are loaded, they will inherit the property specifications of the original except that they are not visible. You will change the Visible property to True to have the new images appear. Your form should display five or six images across and as many rows as are necessary to display all the images until the form is filled. If you want a bit more work, you can add a button so that the user can move forward and backward in the images when the form is filled.

The menu should have an item to print the form and another to exit the program. Design and write the program, and then save it as **Multiple Image Display**. Test the program and then print it out.

Error Handling and Debugging

9.1   Chapter Objectives

After finishing this chapter you will be able to:

- Discuss the four types of errors that can occur in applications.

- Demonstrate the use of the On Error statement in detecting runtime errors.

- Demonstrate the use of the various debugging tools available in Visual Basic.

9.2   Introduction

Regardless of the experience or expertise of the programmer, programming errors occur. And the longer and more complex the application, the more likely there will be errors in it. Throughout this book, we have been discussing possible errors and what you can do about them or do to avoid them. Each chapter has had a debugging section and at least one debugging exercise to help you discover potential trouble spots in your programs. Even so, a number of points have yet to be discussed.

    In this chapter you will learn about the different types of errors that can occur and what you can do about them. You will learn how to trap certain computer-generated errors so that they won't make your application crash, and we will discuss many user-generated errors and what to do about them.

9.3   Four Types of Errors

There are four different types of errors that you will run into: **design-time errors, runtime errors, logic errors,** and **user-generated errors. Design-time errors,** which are also known as **syntax errors,** are those you make as you are keying the code. The syntax of a language such as Visual Basic consists of the methods and rules for writing the code. Visual Basic will catch syntax errors for you and will not let you run the application until they are fixed. You are even offered guidance in the form of error message dialog boxes, many of which have **Help** buttons to allow you to call up a Help window for additional assistance. You have no doubt seen many of these dialog boxes while creating your practice programs. We will look at an example of this.

1. Get into Visual Basic, and put your work disk in drive A.

2. Open the code window for the form, and key the following statement precisely as given:

```
intAmount = Val((strAmount)
```

3. Press **Enter**.

An error will be displayed, indicating that a list separator or ending parenthesis was expected (see Figure 9.1). Actually, the problem is that you have entered one too many beginning parentheses, so Visual Basic is a bit confused. It counted the opening parentheses and then expected to find the same number of closing parentheses. This shows that not all the errors generated tell you exactly what's wrong, but at worst, they will give you an indication of what's wrong.

FIGURE 9.1

The error that occurs on the assignment statement.

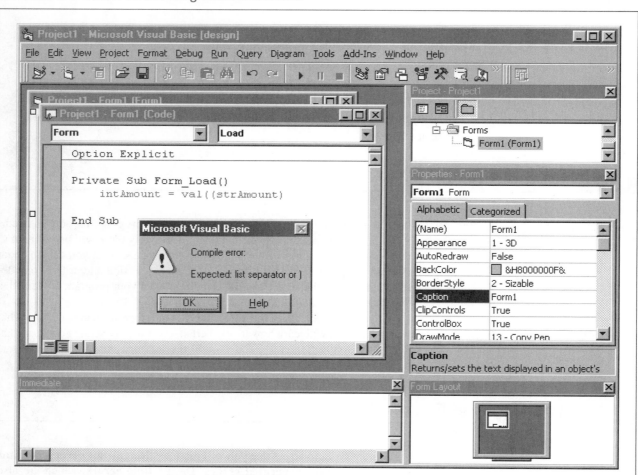

Notice also that the incorrect line is shown in red (if you have a color monitor). This is simply another helpful indication that there is something wrong with the statement.

> **HINT:** If you did not see the error message, the automatic syntax checker has been turned off. To turn it on you need to do the following:
>
> a) Pull down the **Tools** menu and click the **Options...** menu to view the Options dialog box.
>
> b) Click the Auto Syntax Check check box on the Editor tab.
>
> c) Click the **OK** button to exit the dialog box.
>
> d) Move the cursor to the end of the line of code, delete the opening parenthesis, key it again, and press **Enter**.

If the error you see doesn't tell you enough to figure out what you have done wrong, you can press **F1** or click the **Help** button to get a bit more information.

4. Press **F1** and a MSDN Library window opens, further explaining the error as shown in Figure 9.2.

> **HINT:** You may need to insert the MSDN Library CD in your CD-ROM drive.

Note that this window tells you that you are missing some part of your code and that the error is usually to the left of the selected item. Help windows such as this one can help clarify the error so that you will be able to correct it.

FIGURE 9.2
The Help window for the error generated by the assignment statement.

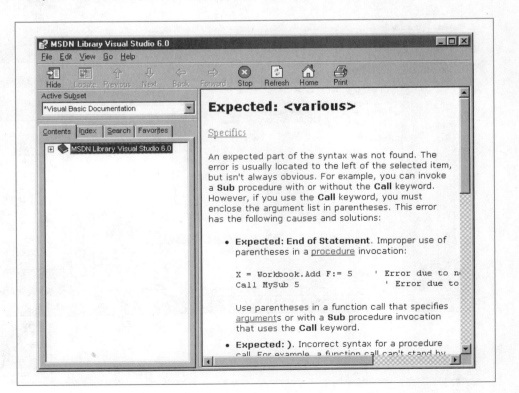

5. Exit the Help window and select **OK** on the error box.

   Runtime errors occur when the application is executing. These are referred to as **trappable errors,** or errors that Visual Basic will allow you to trap or intercept and display an error message to the user so that whatever is wrong can be corrected and allow the application to continue. We can find trappable errors easily because Visual Basic catches them. It knows exactly when they occur, and it allows us to take some action. We can easily generate a trappable error that Visual Basic has caught.

6. Eject the disk in drive A, select the **Open Project...** option from the **File** menu, click No when asked whether you want to save the program changes, and select drive A. You will see an error like the one shown in Figure 9.3.

   Because the system cannot access the drive if there is no disk inserted, Visual Basic traps the error and displays an error message. Once again, this error doesn't really tell you what is wrong. It would be better if the error message told you that the disk isn't properly inserted in the drive, but all the operating system knows is that it cannot access the drive.

7. Select Cancel on the error box and Cancel in the Open Project dialog box.

   The third type of error is a **logic error,** which is more commonly called a **bug.** This is an error that Visual Basic will not recognize, so it will not interfere with the operation of the application, but the application will not generate the proper results. Logic errors take

FIGURE 9.3
The error caused by the missing disk.

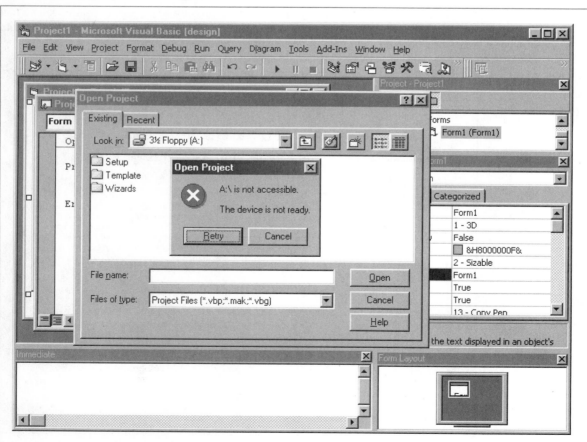

many forms, and many can be very difficult to find. A simple example is an application that is reading numbers from a file, totaling them, and calculating the average of the numbers. Suppose the routine were written like the following:

```
intAmount = 0
intCounter = 1
Do While Not EOF(1)
    intCounter = intCounter + 1
    Input #1, intAmount
    intTotal = intTotal + intAmount
Loop
intAverage = intTotal / intCounter
```

Do you see the problem in this code? That's right, when the first number is read from the file, intCounter is already 2. If five numbers were read from the file, the total of those five numbers would be divided by 6, and the average would not be correct. There is no way that Visual Basic can discover errors like this, because there is nothing syntactically wrong with the code. Such errors must be located by the programmer, and sometimes that can be difficult. To find such errors, we'll want to use Visual Basic's debugging capabilities to help us. We may have to go through the entire program, perhaps line by line, to locate some logic errors. We will look at these error-locating tools a bit later.

The final type of error is one that the user creates by entering data incorrectly or failing to enter necessary data. We have already trapped many of these errors in previous programs and printed error messages for the user. For example, we have checked text boxes to be sure data that are supposed to be there are actually there. We will have more to say about this type of error at the end of this chapter.

9.4   Handling Runtime Errors

As we mentioned earlier, Visual Basic will catch runtime errors and give you an opportunity to do something about them. For example, if an application tries to write to disk but there is no disk in the drive, we can intercept the error before it crashes the application. Let's see how.

The On Error GoTo Statement

The primary method of trapping runtime errors is with the **On Error GoTo** statement. This statement has the following format:

```
On Error Goto Label
```

Label refers to a label put into your code so that the program has somewhere to go when the error occurs. A sample procedure using the On Error Goto statement follows.

```
Sub cmdOk_Click ()
    On Error GoTo Open_Error  ←———————— On Error statement
    Open strFilename For Input As #1
    :::
    More Code
    :::
    Exit Sub  ←——————————————— Will exit from the procedure
Open_Error:  ←———————————————— Label
    MsgBox "An error occurred upon opening the file. Please correct
    ⮡the problem and try again.", vbCritical, "Open File Error"
    Resume
End Sub
```

The first statement in this procedure is the On Error GoTo statement. The On Error part of the statement looks for any error that Visual Basic can recognize. Then the GoTo part of the statement causes control to branch to the part of the routine specified by the **label** following GoTo. The GoTo simply serves to change the processing order of the routine. The specified label must be given somewhere else in the same procedure and is created by using the label name followed by a colon. You can see the Open_Error label in the sample code.

The **Exit Sub** statement is needed to keep the execution of the procedure from continuing into the error routine when the rest of the code is complete. The Exit Sub statement does just what it says; it exits from the subroutine (procedure) at the point where the statement is found. The error routine will have code in it that is to be executed if there is an error, so that code should not be executed if there is no error. By using the Exit Sub statement, we make sure that if the procedure code functions normally, without an error, the error routine will not be executed because the procedure will be exited before the error routine code is reached.

In the given procedure, when Visual Basic attempts to open the file and discovers that the disk is not accessible (remember, there is no disk in the drive), it will branch down to the Open_Error label, as specified on the On Error GoTo statement, and the MsgBox statement will be executed. After the user exits the dialog box, the **Resume** statement is executed. This causes the application to go back to the statement that originally caused the error. In this case, that's the Open statement. This procedure assumes that upon seeing the error dialog box, the user will correct whatever is wrong, in this case by putting the disk in the disk drive. If the user exits the dialog box without correcting the problem, the Open statement will have the same problem again and will again go to the error routine. If the user corrects the problem and the Open statement functions properly, the procedure will continue normally. Having an On Error GoTo routine executed will not affect the rest of the code. Once the problem has been corrected, the application can function normally.

The On Error GoTo does not have to be the first statement in the procedure. It merely has to be before any statement that might cause a trappable error.

If you do not want the On Error GoTo statement to be active at some point in your procedure, it can be turned off with the statement

```
On Error GoTo 0
```

0 is a dummy label. When Visual Basic sees it, it knows you do not want the On Error GoTo statement to be active any longer.

The label that the On Error Goto statement is to branch to must be in the same procedure as the On Error Goto statement. If it is not, you will get an error when you try to run the program. This is called a **compile-time error,** and is a syntax error. Visual Basic cannot find such errors as the statements are keyed into the procedure, because it doesn't look for that type of connection until it compiles the program, which it does when you run the program. We discussed compiling the program in a previous chapter. When we compile the program ourselves, we get an executable (EXE) version of the program. In order for Visual Basic to execute the program as we create it, the program must still be compiled. It is compiled every time we run it. As Visual Basic does this, it looks for the types of errors that it cannot see until it ties all the program components together by compiling it. It is then that compile-time errors are found and the programmer is notified. Visual Basic will find only one of the errors at a time, so if you have several in your program, you will have to fix them one at a time as you continue to attempt to run the program.

Though the label has to be in the same procedure as the On Error Goto statement, the statement continues to be in force if you call other procedures for the original procedure. Suppose you have the cmdOK_Click procedure with an On Error Goto statement that calls the Calculate_The_Result procedure if a trappable error occurs in the Calculate_The_Result procedure. Program execution returns to the labeled error routine in the cmdOK_Click procedure. Then, when the Resume statement in the error routine is executed, control returns to the statement in the Calculate_The_Result procedure.

If there are different types of routines in your procedure that might cause different types of errors, you can use several different On Error GoTo statements in the same procedure. That way, each potential error can have its own error routine to branch to. This is sometimes necessary, but it can be complicated, and as you will soon see, there is generally a much easier way to accomplish the same thing. For the moment, however, let's see how a routine similar to the one we just created might work.

The Error Function

When you want to test an error routine in a program, you can actually generate an error by using the **Error** function, which has the format

```
Error Errornumber
```

The Error command is followed by the number of the error you want to generate. For now, we don't care what the error is, so we will just use 76.

1. Start a new project and add a button called **cmdOK**.

2. Key the following code into the button procedure:

```
On Error GoTo Open_Error
Error 76  ◄─────────────────────────── Error function
Exit Sub
Open_Error:
    MsgBox "An error occurred upon opening the file. Please correct
    ⤷the problem and try again.", vbExclamation, "Open File Error"
    Resume
```

3. Run the program and select the button. Immediately the error dialog box shown in Figure 9.4 appears.

4. Select the **OK** button, and the dialog box reappears.

Because the Resume statement continues sending the program back to the statement that caused the error, the program continually executes the Error statement and continually executes the error routine.

5. Select the **OK** button a few more times, and then press **Ctrl-Break** and click the End icon to exit from the program.

We mentioned that if a procedure that has an On Error Goto error routine calls another procedure and there is an error in that called procedure, execution of the program returns to the calling procedures error routine. Let's see how that works.

6. Create a new procedure called **Called_Procedure**. In that procedure, key the following single-function statement:

```
Error 76
```

7. Switch back to the code for the cmdOK_Click event procedure. Remove the Error function statement there, and key **Called_Procedure** for a call to the procedure. The code you have should look like the code in Figure 9.5.

8. Run the program and click the button.

The error dialog box shows up again, just as it did before. This means that the On Error Goto statement was used in Called_Procedure to send the program execution back to the Open_Error error routine in the cmdOK_Click procedure. We know this because that's the only place in the program where the MsgBox statement is.

9. Select the **OK** button a few more times, and then press **Ctrl-Break** and click the End icon to exit the program.

FIGURE 9.4

The error that occurs because of the Error statement.

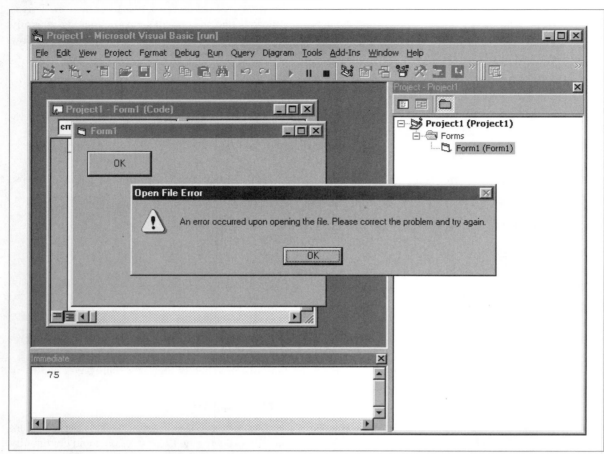

FIGURE 9.5

The current code in the sample program.

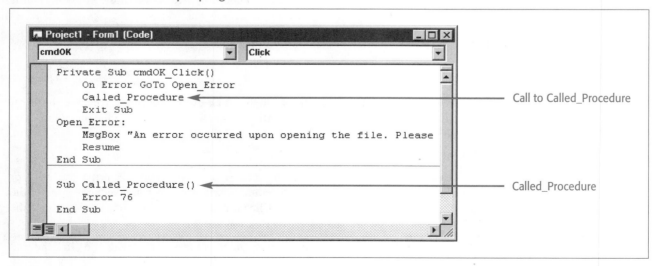

The Err Object

This error-trapping routine is fine if you want to display a generic error box. If, on the other hand, you want your error to be more indicative of the problem, you can use the **Err** object to specify the error number. Err is a special object that is internal to Visual Basic. It is not an object like a button or text box that is added to a form.

The error numbers are predefined in Visual Basic, and the most common ones are shown in Table 9.1.

You will notice that a number of these errors are ones that should be uncovered during testing of the application, long before the user ever gets the application. Errors such as "Type mismatch" and "Illegal property value" are compile-time errors that are likely to occur the first time the application is executed. Many other errors, however, will occur only when the user does something incorrect ("Bad file name") or is having trouble with the hardware ("Device I/O error").

With these error numbers, we can change our error routine so that it will display the error number. We could change the MsgBox statement to

```
MsgBox "An error occurred upon opening the file (Error number " &
  ↳ Str(Err) & "). Please correct the problem and try again.",
  ↳ vbCritical, "Open File Error"
```

1. Change the MsgBox statement in your cmdOk_Button procedure to the foregoing, rerun the program, and select the button to see the error dialog box shown in Figure 9.6.

Now your error message will tell you that the error is error number 76. This makes sense; 76 is the error number that we put in the program.

2. Press **Ctrl-Break** and click the End icon to stop the program.

The problem here is that the error numbers will mean nothing to the typical user. It would be much better if we could display some type of message instead. We can do that with the **Description** property of the Err object. This will display the error messages in Table 9.1 rather than the error numbers. To use this function, we can change our MsgBox statement to

```
MsgBox "Upon opening the file, the error '" & Err.Description & "'
  ↳ occurred. Please correct the problem and try again.", vbCritical,
  ↳ "Open File Error"
```

Now when the error routine is executed, the error message will be displayed right in the error box. It's almost like having Table 9.1 built into the application, always ready to display the appropriate message. Let's try it.

3. Change the MsgBox statement in your cmdOk_Button procedure to the foregoing.

4. Run the program and select the button to see the new error shown in Figure 9.7.

Note that your message will specify the "Path not found" error. This is what error 76 is.

5. Press **Ctrl-Break** and click the End icon to exit the program. Change the error number in the Error statement to **71** and run the program again to see the new message shown in figure 9.8.

Now the error will specify "Disk not ready," which is what error 71 is.

6. Exit the program and try a few more of the error numbers on your own.

This is an improvement over just displaying the error number, but many of the messages, such as "Disk not ready," are a bit cryptic. Such a message really doesn't say what is wrong or what the user is expected to do about it. Without knowing precisely what error has occurred, however, the application cannot display anything beyond a generic message with the Error function. There is still one more step we can take to clarify matters.

TABLE 9.1
The list of trappable errors.

Error Number	Means	Error Number	Means
5	Illegal function call	340	Control array element does not exist
6	Overflow	341	Illegal control array index
7	Out of memory	342	Not enough room to allocate control array
9	Subscript out of range		
10	Duplicate definition	343	Object is not an array
11	Division by zero	344	Must specify index when using control array
13	Type mismatch		
14	Out of string space	360	Object is already loaded
19	No RESUME	362	Controls created at design time cannot be unloaded
20	RESUME without error		
28	Out of stack space	380	Illegal property value
51	Internal error	381	Illegal property array index
52	Bad file name or number	384	Property cannot be modified when form is minimized or maximized
53	File not found		
54	Bad file mode		
55	File already open	420	Invalid object reference
57	Device I/O error	421	Method not applicable for this object
58	File already exists		
59	Bad record length	422	Property not found
61	Disk full	423	Property or control not found
62	Input past end of file		
63	Bad record number	424	Object required
64	Bad file name	425	Illegal object use
65	File previously loaded	427	Object is not the printer object
66	Tried to load file with duplicate procedure definition	428	Object is not a control
		429	Object is not a form
67	Too many files	430	There is no currently active control
68	Device unavailable		
70	Permission denied	431	There is no currently active form
71	Disk not ready		
72	Disk-media error	461	Specified format does not match format of data
75	Path/File access error		
76	Path not found	480	Unable to create AutoRedraw bitmap
		481	Invalid picture

FIGURE 9.6
The error that occurs, showing the error number.

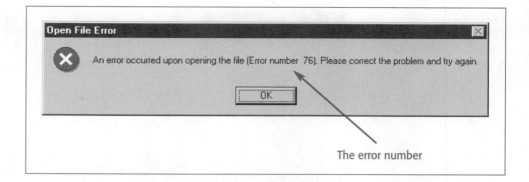

The error number

FIGURE 9.7
The error that occurs, showing the error description.

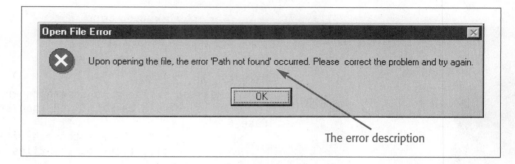

The error description

FIGURE 9.8
The error that occurs when Error 71 is used.

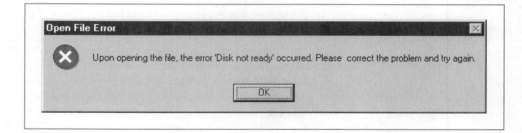

Specific Error Messages

Remember that Err will tell us specifically what has occurred in the application to cause the error (though some of the errors are still rather indeterminate). Using the error number, we can create an error routine that can have a specific message depending on the type of error. For example, suppose we checked Err after a save operation and found the error number to be 61. This means the disk is full. Knowing that, the user would realize that some of the files on the disk should be deleted before trying to save the file again.

Many of the errors listed in Table 9.1 can be categorized as to the application function that causes them. For example, the errors in Table 9.2 are related to loading a file.

Knowing these errors, we might construct our error routine to be more helpful. An example follows.

```
Load_Error:
    strMessage = Err.Description
    Select Case Err
        Case 7
            strMessage = "The file is too large to open with the
            ↳available memory. Close some applications and try
            ↳again."
```

TABLE 9.2
The errors that might be caused by trying to load a file.

Error Number	Means
7	Out of memory
55	File already open
57	Device I/O error
61	Disk full
67	Too many files
68	Device unavailable
70	Permission denied
71	Disk not ready
72	Disk-media error

```
        Case 57, 68, 71, 72
            strMessage = "There is something wrong with the disk
              ⮑drive. Please check it and then try again."
        Case 67
            strMessage = "There are too many files open. Close some
              ⮑of the applications so the files will be closed and
              ⮑try again."
    End Select
    MsgBox strMessage, vbCritical, "Open File Error"
    Resume
```

In this routine we begin by assigning the original error message to strMessage. That way, if any error has occurred other than the ones we are testing for, some error message will still be displayed in the message box. The three example error messages are just that, examples. You might want to add additional messages for additional error numbers or for subdividing the message we created using the four error numbers (57, 68, 71, and 72). You might also want to change the wording of some of the messages to fit more closely the precise errors that have occurred.

We can try this routine by substituting it for the other routine with which we have been practicing.

1. Replace the original error routine with this new code. You can use the original label of Open_Error if you wish, or you can make the appropriate change to the GoTo statement.

2. Put **71** on the Error statement.

3. Run the program and select the button. You will see the disk drive error appear as shown in Figure 9.9.

4. Try a couple of other numbers, being certain to use **7** and **67** to be sure the other two messages will appear. Then exit the program.

FIGURE 9.9
The error message for error 71.

The Resume Statement

We briefly mentioned the Resume statement earlier. It will automatically return to the statement that sent the application to the error routine in the first place. If the error occurred on an Open statement, we assume that the user has fixed whatever problem caused the error and then the application jumped back to the Open statement. But what if the user can't fix the problem? Suppose, for example, that the error is caused because of a hardware problem that has just occurred, such as a mechanical problem that prevents the disk drive from reading the disk. Now, if the application re-executes the Open statement, the error will simply recur. What we need is a way to let the user out of this situation gracefully.

Well, our MsgBox statement can be set up with the intReturned variable so that it can be checked to see which of several buttons was selected. In our current MsgBox statement, we have used only the **OK** button, but we know the statement will allow us to use several. We will need to change the dialog box so that it has both **OK** and **Cancel** buttons and returns a value, and then we can test the result to determine whether the Open statement should be tried again. It's actually pretty easy. We just need to change the message box statement to something like the following:

```
intReturned = MsgBox (strMessage & " (Select OK to Open the file
↳ or Cancel to exit.)", VbOKCancel + VbExclamation, "Open File
↳ Error")
If intReturned = 1 Then
    Resume
End If
```

If the user selects the **Cancel** button, the procedure will simply end without trying the Open statement again. At least that's what we would like to happen. If you look back at the list of errors in Table 9.1, however, you will see a No RESUME error. This occurs when the application exits an error routine without a Resume statement being executed. If we just let the procedure end with the End Sub statement as shown, we will get this No RESUME error. To avoid getting the error, we don't actually have to use a Resume statement; we just have to force the application out of the procedure rather than letting it end on its own. That is, we must use an Exit Sub statement such as

```
intReturned = MsgBox (strMessage & " (Select OK to Open the file
↳ or Cancel to exit.)", VbOKCancel + VbExclamation, "Open File
↳ Error")
If intReturned = 1 Then
    Resume
End If
Exit Sub
```

Now everything will work as it is supposed to.

1. Replace the MsgBox statement in the Case statement for error 7 with the foregoing code as shown in Figure 9.10. Then change the Error number to 7 and run the program.

2. Select the button and notice the "Out of memory" error comes up (Figure 9.11).

3. Select the **OK** button and the error will reappear. Select **Cancel** and the dialog box will vanish.

Sometimes returning to the statement that caused the error will not work for a particular error. If this is the case, Visual Basic allows two variations of the Resume statement, **Resume Next** and **Resume Label**. The Resume Next statement causes Visual Basic to return to the line following the one that caused the error that sent the application to the error routine. In our example, instead of returning to the Open statement, the application would skip the Open statement and return to the next statement in the code. Simply skipping the

FIGURE 9.10
The current code.

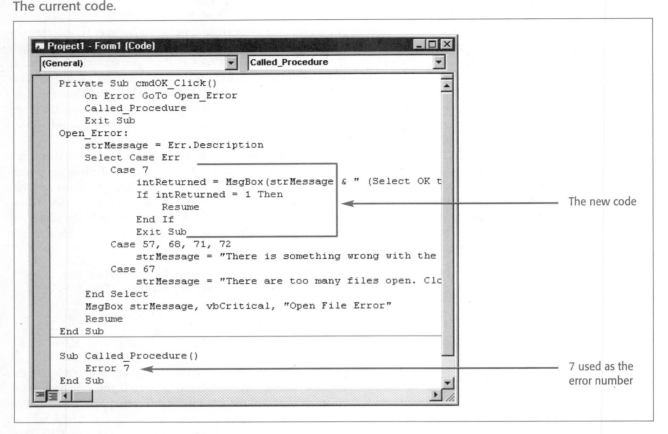

The new code

7 used as the
error number

FIGURE 9.11
The error that now
occurs.

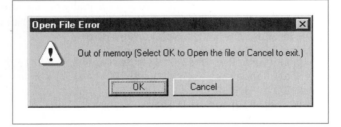

offending statement to continue executing the rest of the code is usually not a good idea. If the problem occurred because the file could not be opened for input and the application continued after that point, presumably the next statement in the code (or one shortly thereafter) would be one that read data from the file. But if the file had not been opened, no data could be read from it, and we would get another error. There just aren't many uses for the Resume Next statement.

If you are going to use the Resume Next statement, it is sometimes just as convenient to use a special form of the On Error Goto statement:

```
On Error Resume Next
```

This functions just as though you had a normal On Error Goto statement where the error routine used only a Resume Next statement. Once again, there aren't many uses for this statement.

There are times, however, when going back to a particular line in the procedure, other than the one that caused the error, is exactly what we want to do. Purposely creating a trappable error is a common programming technique to determine whether a file already exists. When a file is opened for output, the file is created automatically if it's not there. When a file is opened for input and is not there, however, a trappable error occurs, and the file is not created (it wouldn't make any sense to read from a file that was just created). When our application is creating a new file, if we want to warn the user that a new file is being created, we can try to open the file for input and then, if an error occurs, display a warning message for the user. Let's see how such code could be constructed.

```
        On Error GoTo Open_Error
        Open strFilename For Input As #1
        Close #1
Create_File:
        Open strFilename For Output As #1
        :::
        More Code
        :::
Open_Error:
        intReturned = MsgBox ("The file does not exist. It will be
        ↳created. Is this what you want?", vbOKCancel + VbExclamation,
        ↳"Open File Warning")
        If intReturned = 1 Then
            Resume Create_File
        End IF
        Exit Sub
```

Initially we try to open the file for input. If the file is not there, the application will create error 53, "File not found," and the application will branch to the error routine. A message box is displayed, letting the user decide whether the file should be created. If the user selects the **Yes** button, the Resume Label statement returns to the Create_File label, and the file is opened for output. If the user selects the **No** button, the entire procedure is exited without the file being created.

If, in the original Open statement that opens the file for input, the file is found, the application continues normally, the next statement closes the file, and then it is opened again, this time for output.

Because there are many reasons why a file might not be able to be opened besides the file's not being there, this routine should actually test the error number to be sure it is error 53, rather than just assuming that the file doesn't exist. It would be much safer to have two error messages: the one given and a generic one for any error number but 53. Here the program would give the user a chance to fix the problem and then retry the Open statement or exit the routine without trying to open the file.

9.5 Debugging Your Applications

Thus far we have discussed syntax errors and runtime errors. Now we are ready to look at logic errors, otherwise known as bugs. You will spend a good deal of your time as a programmer hunting for bugs. In fact, you have probably already done so while creating your exercise programs. Along the way, we have tried to help you find troublesome errors and avoid them by using proper techniques, but invariably they sneak in. They can sometimes be frustratingly difficult to find. One bug buried in a long chain of complex statements requiring pages and pages of code can sometimes take hours or even days to find. But, just as it's a relief when the pain of a headache finally goes away, it feels wonderful to uncover a bug you have been seeking for hours.

In this section you will learn about some Visual Basic tools and techniques that can be used to help you find, locate, and exterminate these pesky bugs. To help us with this discovery, we will use an application with some deliberate errors that Visual Basic helps you uncover. If you spot any errors as you examine the code, you should not correct them at that time. The text assumes that all imbedded errors are there, and eliminating any of them may make the flow of the text more difficult to follow.

Loading the Buggy Code

The code you are going to debug is that of a common programming procedure, a sort. If you recall, you learned how to write a selection sort back in Chapter 4. This time you will learn how a **bubble sort** works. We will use a bubble sort because it is easy to write and easy to understand.

1. If it is turned on, turn off automatic saving of your programs as they are executed. You may want to run through the information given in this chapter again, and you will need an unrepaired program to do it.

2. Load the **Debugging Practice** application from the Ch-9 folder on your disk.

   This application will execute its sort when the form is clicked.

3. Double-click the form to open the code window for the Form_Click procedure, and maximize the window so that you can see most of the code as shown in Figure 9.12.

FIGURE 9.12
The code of the Form_Click procedure.

```
Debugging_Practice - frmDebugging_Practice (Code)

Form                                          Click

Private Sub Form_Click()
    Static strNames(10) As Integer

    strNames(1) = "Fred"
    strNames(2) = "Sam"
    strNames(3) = "Al"
    strNames(4) = "Harrold"
    strNames(5) = "Alice"
    strNames(6) = "Joan"
    strNames(7) = "Jose"
    strNames(8) = "Carmilita"
    strNames(9) = "Chang"
    strNames(10) = "John"

    intPointer = 10
    Do While intSwitch_Counter <> 0
        intSwitch_Count = 0
        For intCounter = 1 To intPtr
            If strNames(intCounter) > strNames(intCounter + 1) Then
                strTemp = strNames(1)
                strNames(intCounter) = strNames(intCounter + 1)
                strNames(intCounter) = strTmp
                intSwitch_Counter = intSwitch_Counter + 1
            End If
        Next intCounter
        intPointer = intPointer - 1
    Loop
    For intCounter = 1 To 10
        Print strNames(intCounter)
    Next intCounter
End Sub
```

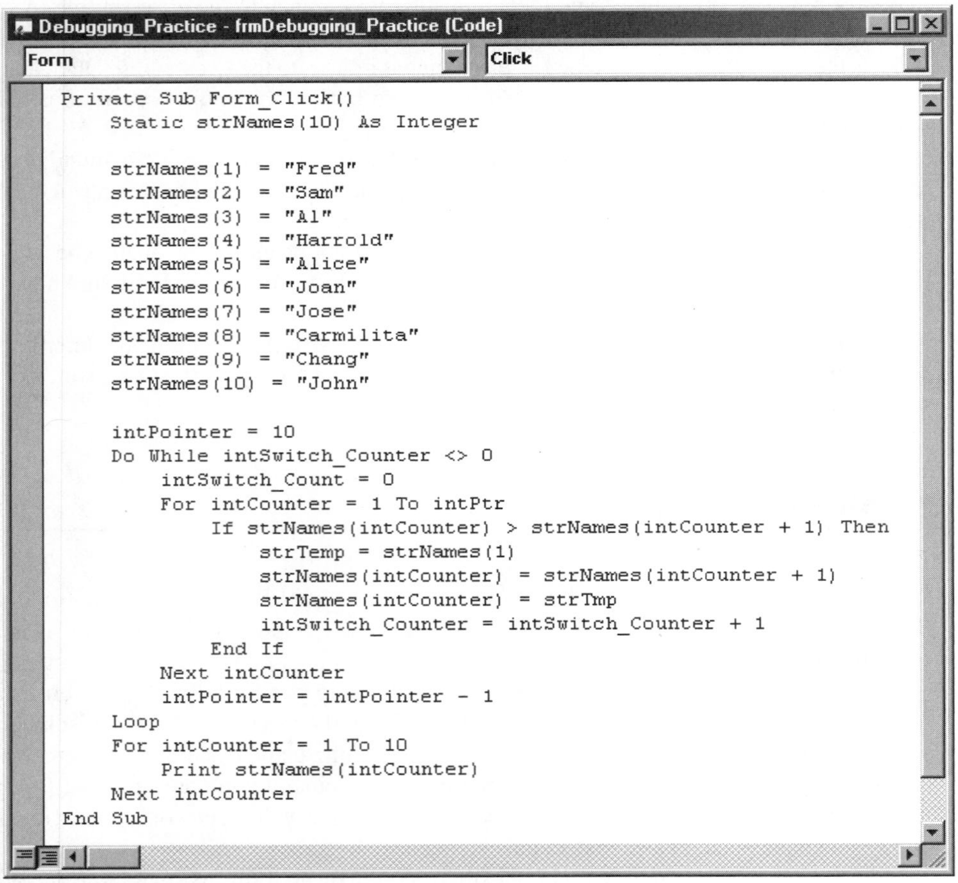

The Sort

Upon examining the code, the first thing you will see is the setup of the array to be sorted. That code is

```
Static strNames(10) As Integer
strNames(1) = "Fred"
strNames(2) = "Sam"
strNames(3) = "Al"
strNames(4) = "Harold"
strNames(5) = "Alice"
strNames(6) = "Joan"
strNames(7) = "Jose"
strNames(8) = "Carmilita"
strNames(9) = "Chang"
strNames(10) = "John"
```

Now comes the code to arrange the names in order. A bubble sort starts at the bottom of the array and compares the current item with the next item. If the next item is less than the current item, the items are switched; that is, the larger item is put one step higher in the array. The larger items will "bubble" their way to the top of the array. As we go through the array, we keep a count of the number of switches we have done. After we are through the array, if no switches have been done, we know that the array is sorted. Otherwise, the bubbling begins again at the bottom of the array. Each time we progress through the array, we go through one item less than the last time through, because the largest item will already be at the top of the array. Let's take the list of names in our array and see how the bubble sort would work on them. The names are

```
Fred, Sam, Al, Harold, Alice, Joan, Jose, Carmilita, Chang, John
```

The bubble sort used on these ten names first compares the first two elements, Fred and Sam. Sam is already the larger, so no switch is made. Next, Sam is compared against Al, and because Sam is larger, they are switched to make the following array:

```
Fred, Al, Sam, Harold, Alice, Joan, Jose, Carmilita, Chang, John
```

Next, Sam is compared to Harold and they are switched:

```
Fred, Al, Harold, Sam, Alice, Joan, Jose, Carmilita, Chang, John
```

Sam is compared to Alice and they are switched:

```
Fred, Al, Harold, Alice, Sam, Joan, Jose, Carmilita, Chang, John
```

Sam is compared to Joan and they are switched:

```
Fred, Al, Harold, Alice, Joan, Sam, Jose, Carmilita, Chang, John
```

Sam is compared to Jose and they are switched:

```
Fred, Al, Harold, Alice, Joan, Jose, Sam, Carmilita, Chang, John
```

Sam is continually switched with the other three items to make the array

```
Fred, Al, Harold, Alice, Joan, Jose, Carmilita, Chang, John, Sam
```

The array is not yet sorted. All that has happened is that the largest element has been put on the end. The process must begin again, and the process is

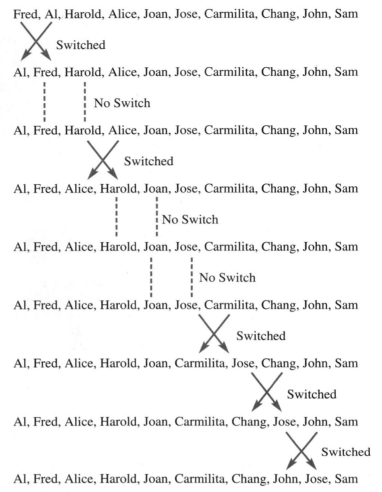

Jose is not compared to Sam because it isn't necessary. Once again, the largest item is now at the top of the portion of the array looked at (the last item is not compared), and once again, the search will begin at the beginning of the array.

This process continues until either no switches are made during a pass through the array or the pointer to the last item to switch has dropped all the way to the bottom of the array. If no switches are made, the array is sorted, and no further examination is needed. If the pointer is at the bottom of the list, the entire list has been switched and is sorted.

The first thing we need to do in the sort is establish a variable to hold the array pointer. It will be used to point to the last element of the array we need to look at in the next pass. Because there are 10 items in the array, the pointer should be set to 10.

```
intPointer = 10
```

Next we need to set up a variable to count the number of times a switch is performed during a pass through the array. We must reinitialize this counter after each pass, so we will need to loop back to the top of the process, in front of the counter initialization.

```
Do While intSwitch_Counter <> 0
    intSwitch_Count = 0
```

Now we need a loop for the scanning process, which will begin by comparing the first and second items.

```
For intCounter = 1 to intPtr
    If strNames(intCounter) > strNames(intCounter + 1) Then
```

Note that we are comparing the first item against the next item by adding 1 to the counter. In the beginning, that means that strNames(intCounter) points to item 1 and strNames(intCounter + 1) points to item 2.

If item 1 is the larger of the two, they must be switched, which takes the following routine:

```
strTemp = strNames(1)
strNames(intCounter) = strNames(intCounter + 1)
strNames(intCounter) = strTmp
intSwitch_Counter = intSwitch_Counter + 1
```

Then we end the If Test and the For-Next loop.

```
    End If
Next intCounter
```

Now, because a pass has been made and the largest item has been moved to the end, we will need to go through one less item in the array on the next pass, so we need to reduce the pointer:

```
intPointer = intPointer - 1
```

Finally, the loop ends. If any switches have been made, the Do While test will fail, we don't need to continue the scanning (because the array is sorted), and we can display the results on the form.

```
Loop
For intCounter = 1 to 10
    Print strNames(intCounter)
Next intCounter
```

Note that we used the Print statement to display the array. This will simply display the names on the form so that we can see if the array was properly sorted. We could have used a text box as we did back in Chapter 4, but displaying on the form will work just as well.

Runtime Errors

1. Run the application and click the form.

   Immediately you get a "Type mismatch" error.

2. Exit from the error by clicking the Debug button.

   Note that the following statement is highlighted:

```
strNames(1) = "Fred"
```

This is what offended Visual Basic. The problem is that "Fred" is a string and we have defined the array as integers. Because we are assigning names to the array, it obviously should be a string array. The Static statement is incorrect.

3. Change the Static statement and then run the application again.

   Visual Basic tells you that this change requires you to restart your program. That's okay; this change is required for the program to function at all.

4. Click OK and then run the program again.

Setting a Breakpoint

1. Click the form and you see the list shown in Figure 9.13.

   What's wrong with the list? That's right, it's not sorted at all.

FIGURE 9.13
The results of the
Form_Click event
procedure.

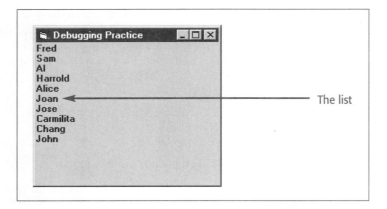

The list

2. Click the form again and the list appears again.

We didn't put an End statement in the code, so there is no exit in the code. This was deliberate, because if the program ends, whatever was displayed on the form will be erased. When we eventually fix the application and want to exit after we see the sorted list, we will need to use the control menu box, the **End** option on the **Run** menu, or the end icon on the tool bar.

But back to the problem at hand. Why isn't the list sorted? To find out, we will begin exploring some of the Visual Basic tools to help with the debugging process.

The first thing we want to do is set a **breakpoint** to make Visual Basic stop executing at a particular point in the application. That way, we can do a bit of exploring before letting the application continue executing. To set a breakpoint, you call the code window to the desktop, position the cursor on the line where you want the breakpoint to be, and press **F9** (shortcut key for the **Toggle Breakpoint** option on the **Debug** menu) or the breakpoint icon ( ) on the Debug toolbar that can be added to the desktop with the **Toolbars** option of the **View** menu.

3. Pull down the **View** menu and highlight the **Toolbars** option to see the submenu shown in Figure 9.14.

4. Click the **Debug** toolbar in the submenu to see the Debug toolbar as shown in Figure 9.15.

This toolbar appears as an independent element rather than as a part of the integrated Visual Basic display. It can be docked like the other toolbar already visible in the display.

5. Double-click the title bar of the toolbar, and it becomes docked as you see in Figure 9.16.

Okay, we can set breakpoints. Now we need to decide just where a breakpoint should be placed. It's generally a good idea to place it after all the code you are reasonably certain is not causing the problem you are trying to solve. In our case, that would be after the array and intPointer assignments, which are not likely to be causing any problems.

6. Exit the program, switch to the code window, position the cursor on the Do-While statement, and press **F9**.

The line of code will become highlighted and a large dot will appear in the left column next to the code window; see Figure 9.17. This is Visual Basic's indication that the line is a breakpoint. Now you can resume execution of the code by pressing **F5**.

7. Run the program and click the form.

Now the code window appears with the Do-While statement highlighted as shown in Figure 9.18. There are actually two highlights on the line, and in the left column there is an

FIGURE 9.14
The **Toolbars** submenu.

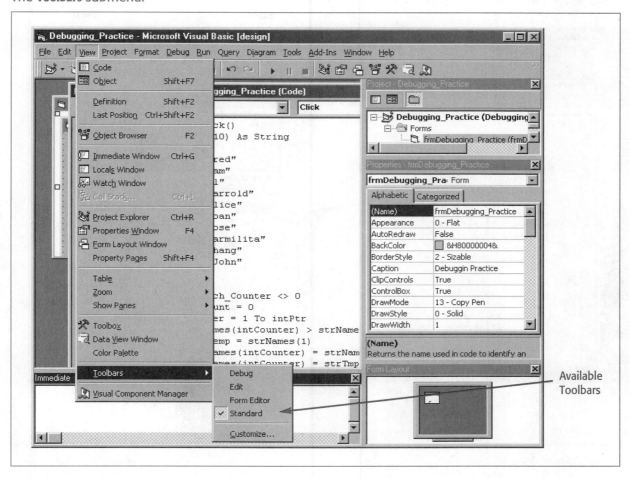

arrow in the dot. The second highlight, which is yellow, and the arrow indicate the line on which that execution is stopped. This is known as the **current line**. As you continue execution of your program, the current line will change.

> **HINT:** If you have set several breakpoints that you no longer want in your code, they can be turned off individually with **F9** or turned off all at the same time with the **Clear All Breakpoints** option on the **Debug** menu.

Single-Stepping through the Code

Just stopping the code avails us nothing by itself. We need to do something to help us determine what's wrong with our application. One thing that might help is to **single-step** through the code. Making Visual Basic go through the code one line at a time can help us follow what the application is doing. Perhaps it is not doing something we think it is doing, such as executing a loop that we think it should be executing. Let's find out.

FIGURE 9.15
The Debug toolbar with the Breakpoint icon.

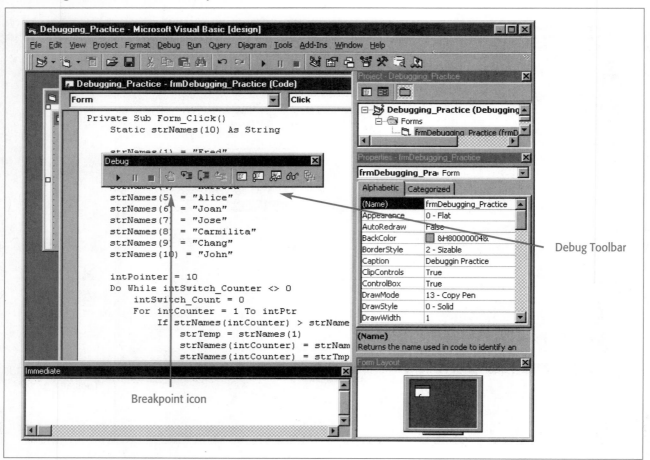

1. Press **F8** (the shortcut key for the **Step Into** option on the **Debug** menu) or select the single-step (Step Into) icon ( ) on the Debug toolbar. The current statement box will jump to the line *following* the Do-While loop, just as in Figure 9.19.

   This isn't right! It's supposed to go through the loop. Obviously there is something wrong here.

   Note the Do-While statement, which is

   ```
   Do While intSwitch_Counter <> 0
   ```

   The problem is that the intSwitch_Counter is always zero unless we give it a value. So the program will never get into the loop. We need to initialize the variable before the loop.

2. Key the following statement before the Do-While statement.

   ```
   intSwitch_Counter = 1
   ```

3. Exit the program and run it again.

4. Single-step through the program until the current line is the For statement. Then single-step again and note that the current line jumps past the loop. We missed another loop.

   Upon close examination of the For statement, we discover that we used the variable name intPtr instead of intPointer for the ending point of the loop. Misspelling variable names

FIGURE 9.16
The Debug toolbar docked.

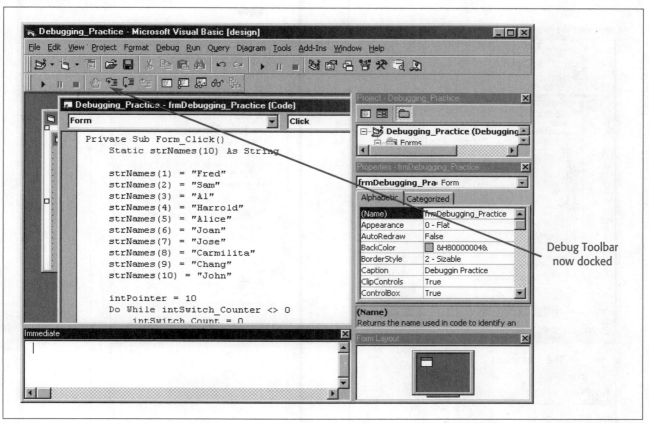

is one of the most common programming errors. That's why, earlier in this book, we introduced the Option Explicit statement. It helps you avoid this type of complication. For the purpose of this exercise, however, we will not use the Option Explicit statement.

5. Exit the program (it is important to exit the program now) and change the For statement so that intPointer replaces intPtr.

Using the Immediate Window

1. Run the program again, click the form, and press **F5** to continue the program.

Now you get a "Subscript out of range" error. That means you are trying to access an element outside the bounds of the array.

2. Click the Debug button.

The error is on the If Test, but on examining the statement, we see nothing wrong. This brings us to the use of another debugging tool to which you have already been introduced, the **immediate window**.

3. Switch to the immediate window, key **Print strNames(intCounter)**, and press **Enter**.

Immediately under the line you keyed, you will see the name "John." This, of course, is the value currently in strNames(intCounter). You can also see the name by simply positioning the cursor over strNames(intCounter) in the code window.

FIGURE 9.17
The placement of the breakpoint.

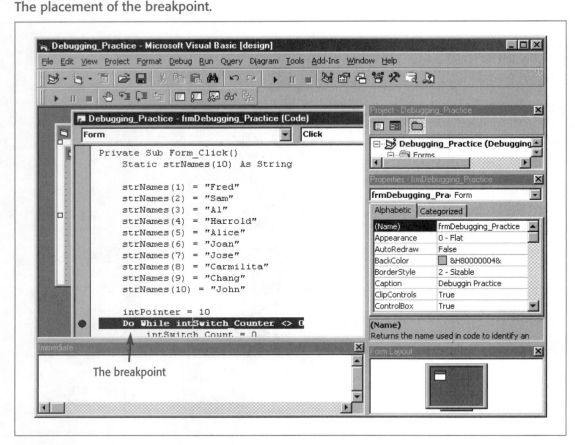

The breakpoint

FIGURE 9.18
The breakpoint and current line.

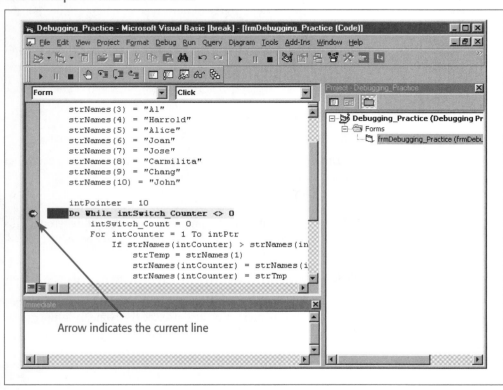

Arrow indicates the current line

FIGURE 9.19
The new current line.

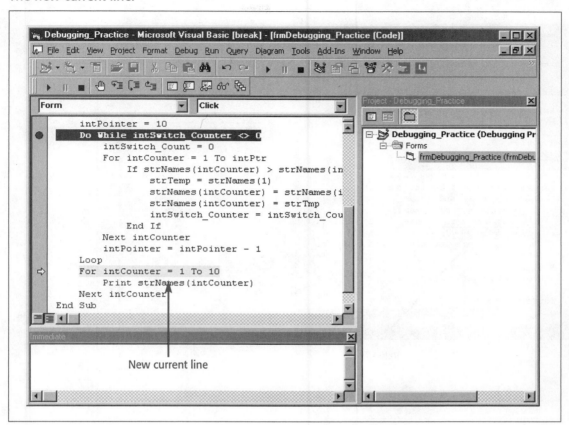

New current line

4. Position the cursor over strNames in the code window, and you see a small window called **Value Tips** appear underneath, showing the value (Figure 9.20).

5. Move the cursor over intCounter and you see that its current value is 10.

The problem is that "John" is the last element in the array. Now let's try to look at the next element in the array, which is what strNames(intCounter + 1) is asking for.

6. Switch back to the immediate window, key **?strNames(intCounter+1)**, and press **Enter**. You get the subscript error again.

You have discovered what's causing the problem. You are asking the application to access array element intCounter+1, but that element is larger than the maximal size of the array. The problem is that we set our pointer value to 10, thinking that we needed to go through the entire array. Indeed, we do need to go through the entire array, but if strNames(intCounter) looks at the end element, no elements are left for strNames(intCounter+1). Thus, intPointer needs to be 9, not 10, and then strNames(intCounter+1) will point to the last item.

7. Exit the error box, switch to the code window, and change the initial intPointer assignment statement to 9.

Now if you try to continue the execution by pressing **F5**, you will get the subscript error again. There is, however, a way around this problem without restarting the application. If you want your application to continue from a statement other than the current one, you can change the current statement.

FIGURE 9.20
The value of strNames(intCounter) in the immediate window and the Value Tips window.

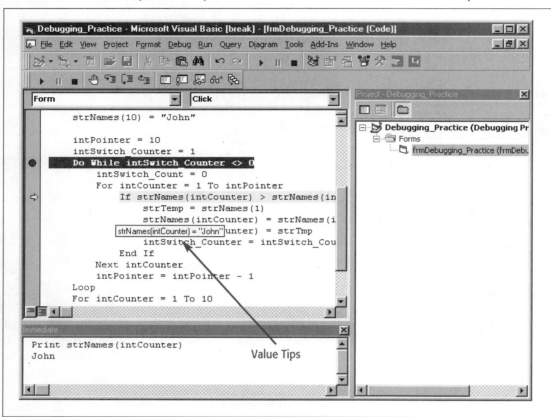

8. Move the cursor to the intPointer = 9 statement, pull down the **Debug** menu, and select **Set Next Statement** (shortcut key **Ctrl-F9**). Immediately the assignment statement will become the current line.

   Now that we have corrected several coding errors, we probably don't need the breakpoint any more, so let's turn it off.

9. Position the cursor on the Do While statement, and press **F9**. The highlighting is removed, which means that the line is not a breakpoint any longer.

10. Press **F5** to continue the execution.

    Nothing is showing up on the form. It looks as if there are more problems.

11. Click the form again. Still nothing. Try to change to the code window. Nothing. Click the **Exit** button. Nothing again.

    Now what? Don't panic. You have put the execution into a nonending loop, and because the application is executing, you can do nothing else until you stop the runaway application.

12. Press **Ctrl-Break** and the execution will stop.

    To avoid having programs that you cannot stop in the conventional fashion, you can use the DoEvents statement. As we have discussed in the past, the DoEvents statement releases system control back to Windows between operating cycles so that if some other application needs control, it can get it. This includes user input such as a mouse click on the end icon in this application.

Maybe we had better put the breakpoint back in. But let's not do that yet. Let's check a few things first and see if we can discover what's wrong by exploring the code. Besides, we've already stopped the execution, and that's all the breakpoint would do.

13. Switch to the immediate window, key **?intPointer**, and press **Enter**.

You get a negative number. That means the loop is continuing to execute long after it should have been finished, because intPointer should never have gotten any lower than 1 without exiting the routine. Let's single-step for a minute and see what's going on in the loop.

14. Press **F8** until your current statement is on the intSwitch_Count assignment statement just below the Do-While statement. Press it a few more times, and you see that execution skips over the For-Next loop without executing it.

15. Press **F8** until the current statement is the Loop statement.

Because the For-Next loop was not executed, and because intSwitch_Counter is initialized before the For-Next loop, it should still be zero and we should exit from the loop on the basis of the Do While test.

16. Press **F8** and you see that the program goes right back into the loop. What's up?

17. Press **F8** until your current line is the Loop statement again.

18. Switch to the immediate window, key **?intSwitch_Counter**, press **Enter**, and you see it has a value.

What? Didn't we just initialize the counter to zero before the loop? Look very carefully at the initialization statement and the If Test, and you will notice that we are using intSwitch_Count in one place and intSwitch_Counter in the other. One is obviously wrong, but which one? To determine that, we have to check the code. Inside the loop we are using intSwitch_Counter, which is also used on the Do-While statement. Therefore, we need to change the initialization statement to conform to the other two statements.

19. Switch to the code window and change intSwitch_Count to intSwitch_Counter.

> **HINT:** When a particular form is active, you can print, or display in the Value Tip window, the values of any of the form-level variables or object properties of that form. You can also display variables or object property values of other forms by using the form name qualification, as in Form_Name.Object_Name.

Changing Values during Runtime

The pointer value is now totally incorrect, so the application will never function correctly unless we restart it or change the current line. That's true as long as the pointer value remains negative. As you know, however, we can change its value in the immediate window.

1. Switch back to the immediate window, key **intPointer = 9**, and press **Enter**.

2. Press **F5** to start the execution again.

Now three names show up on the form: Carmilita, Chang, and John. We have lost some of our list. It's time for single-stepping again.

> **HINT:** In addition to assigning values to variables using the immediate window, you can also change the values of properties. If you entered the statement **BackColor = vbRed** in the immediate window, the background color of the form would become red.

Using the Debug Statement

1. Press **Ctrl-Break**, switch to the code window, set a breakpoint on the For statement, press **Shift-F5**, and click the form.

We could single-step through the code again, but if we did, we would discover that it seems to be working okay now. The problem is in the code statements themselves, and another debugging tool that we discovered earlier can be useful here. The Debug.Print statement sends its output directly to the immediate window.

We want to see what's happening to the array as the loop processes, so let's put a Debug.Print statement in the loop that will print the elements of the array.

2. Insert a blank line before the intSwitch_Counter assignment statement in the loop, and key the following statements as shown in Figure 9.21.

```
For intTest_Counter = 1 to 10
    Debug.Print strNames(intTest_Counter)
Next intTest_Counter
```

Now we are ready to single-step through the code to see what happens to the array.

3. Exit the program and run it again. Click the form and then single-step the program until "Fred" appears in the immediate window (will take several steps).

4. Press **F8** four times, and you see a blank line appear between "Fred" and "Al" (Figure 9.22).

FIGURE 9.21
The new code.

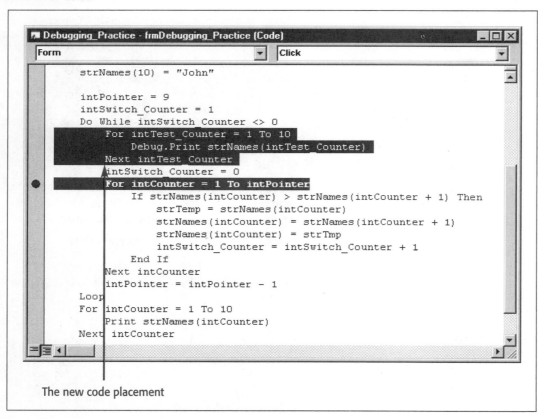

The new code placement

FIGURE 9.22

The problem statement.

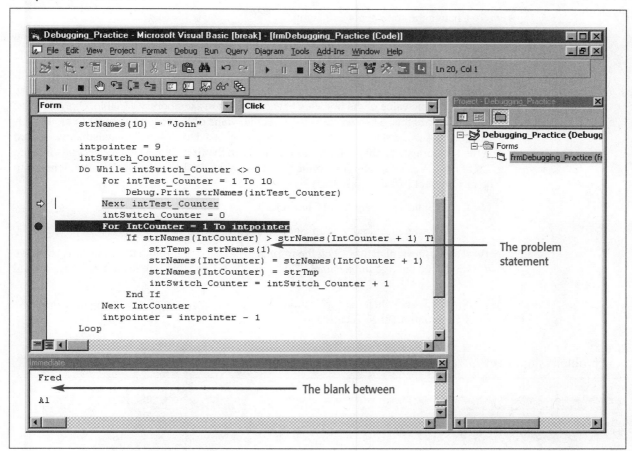

That means that the second element in the array is not there any more. Something has already gone wrong. Let's examine the statements within the loop to see if we can find anything wrong. Right away on the first statement, we see that we are saving strNames(1) as indicated in Figure 9.22. We don't want the statement to always save element 1. We want the code to be able to save whatever element is the current one. The statement needs to have strNames(intCounter) instead.

5. Fix the statement, and exit and restart the application. You need to restart the application because the array is "messed up" and restarting will reset it.

6. Click the form and single-step your way through the code until you have displayed several names in the immediate window.

The second element is still missing. We will have to examine the code again. The first statement in the loop is the one we just changed, and we believe it is correct. It takes the value of the first element of the comparison and puts it in a temporary variable called strTemp. The second statement takes the value of the second compared element and stores it in the first element. That seems okay. The third statement takes what is stored in the temporary variable and puts it in the first compared element. That seems okay too, but on closer examination, we notice that we have again misspelled a variable name. We have strTmp instead of strTemp. That's why the second element appeared empty. Because strTmp is a new variable, it is empty, and when we assign this empty value to the second compared element, instead of what was stored from the first compared element, we will assign an empty string, which, in effect, erases the item value.

7. Change the statement to strTemp.

8. Restart the application again, click the form, and single-step through the code until you have displayed the first three names.

The loop was executed, so "Sam" and "Al" should have been switched. There is still something wrong. Within the loop we are trying to switch the two elements. That means we need to take the value of the first element and store it to a temporary variable. Okay, the first statement does this. Then we need to assign the value of the second element to the first element. The second statement does this. Finally, we need to assign the value that was stored in the temporary variable, which was originally in the first element, to the second element. There it is! We are assigning it to the first element again. Instead of intCounter, it needs to be intCounter+1 (see Figure 9.23).

9. Change the statement to **intCounter +1**.

Now you should finally be finished correcting the errors.

10. Restart the application, click the form, and single-step through the code until you have displayed the first three names. This time, "Sam" and "Al" are reversed, as they should be.

11. Press **F5**, and when the application stops, press **F9** to turn off the breakpoint and press **F5** to continue the execution.

FIGURE 9.23
The next problem statement.

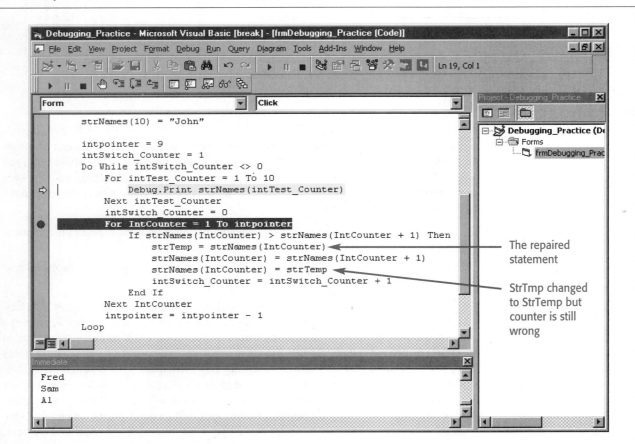

The application executes for quite a while, displaying the names every time it goes through the loop. Eventually, however, it displays the names in the proper order.

12. Exit the program, and save the form and the project as **Debugging Practice Repaired**.

When your Debug.Print statements are going to be displaying a lot of values and you are reasonably certain you no longer need the information they are giving you, you can turn them off without deleting the statements by putting an apostrophe in front of each of them, making comments out of them. Then, if you decide you need them again, you can always remove the apostrophes so that the statements will execute again.

> **HINT:** It doesn't even hurt anything to leave the statements in the code permanently just in case you need them at some other time, because when Visual Basic compiles the code, it leaves out any comments (they are not executable). The size of the compiled program will be exactly the same with or without the commented Debug.Print statements.

Stepping Over

Thus far we have only been single-stepping through our procedure, and that is all that has been necessary. There are times, however, when you need to **step over** certain sections of code. For example, suppose you are looking for an error in a procedure, and that procedure calls another procedure such as an error routine. You are sure that there is no error in the called procedure, but if you are single-stepping, you will need to step your way through this additional procedure even though you don't want to. If that procedure is long or is called frequently (such as one of the statements in a loop), this additional single-stepping may require a good deal of time. There are actually two ways around this problem. You can set up a breakpoint on the first line after the called procedure and then single-step to the procedure call and run the program from that point, whereupon it will automatically stop at the breakpoint. Then you can begin single-stepping again. Take the following code, for example:

```
Sub cmdPractice_Code_Click ()
    Lines of code
    : : : : :
    Last line before the procedure call
    Second_Procedure        ← This is the procedure call that you don't want to single-step.
    Next line of code        ← Set the breakpoint here.
```

As you can see, you could set the breakpoint after the procedure call, and then the program execution would automatically stop after the procedure had been executed.

This process works, but there is actually an easier way to do the same thing. When you have single-stepped until the current line is the call to the procedure, instead of single-stepping, you can use the **Step Over** option from the **Debug** menu (shortcut key **Shift-F8**) or use the Step Over icon from the Debug Toolbar (⬚). Then the entire called procedure is treated as a single statement, and the next statement stepped to is the next statement in the current procedure. If you select stepping over and the current statement is not a procedure call, Visual Basic processes the statement as though you had selected single-stepping.

> **HINT:** If you accidentally enter into a called procedure when single-stepping and you don't want to bother single-stepping through that procedure, you can move the cursor to the end of the procedure and press **Ctrl-F8** (or use the **Run to Cursor** option on the **Debug** menu), which will cause the program to run to the cursor. Then you can single-step back into the original procedure.

Using a Watch

A very useful debugging tool is called a **watch.** We were using the Debug.Print statement to display the values found in the Names array, and if we want to print groups like arrays, the Debug.Print statement is still the best way. But if we have single variables that we want to keep an eye on, we can use the watch.

You can add a watch to a program by using the **Add Watch** option on the **Debug** menu.

1. Pull down the **Debug** menu and click the **Add Watch...** option and you see the dialog box shown in Figure 9.24.

As you can see in the figure, you can choose the Procedure or Module (form) for which you want to add the watch. The default procedure is the one you are currently in and the default module is also the one you're in. One of the options on the Procedure list is to select all the procedures and one of the choices in the Module list is to select all the modules. That way the watch can be set up for the entire program. You need to be sure to define the watches properly. That is, if you want to watch the value of a variable declared in a particular procedure, you must select that procedure from the list, because that variable is not defined outside the procedure. If you try to use a watch for a variable outside the scope of the variable, Visual Basic lets you know.

There are three watch types. If you want just to see the value of a variable or object property, you use **Watch Expression. Break When Value Is True** will stop the execution of the program when the expression you use is true. For example, if you use an expression such as

```
intPointer = 5
```

the program will stop when intPointer becomes 5.

If you use **Break When Value Changes**, then whenever the value of the expression changes, the program will stop. If your expression is **intPointer**, then whenever intPointer changes, the program will stop.

The easiest way to understand fully how these watches work is to try them. We will add a few watches to our current program. We will use the Form_Click procedure, because it is the only one we have. Let's begin with a watch on intPointer.

2. Key **intPointer** as the expression, select **OK**, and then run the program and click the form.

FIGURE 9.24
The Add Watch dialog box.

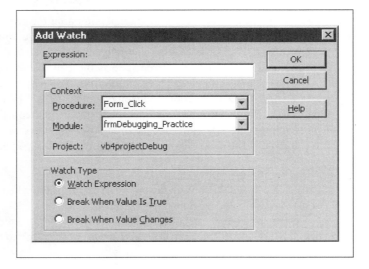

Note that the immediate window is now smaller and that the Watches window has appeared (see Figure 9.25). In the Watches window you can see the watch you set up. The glasses icon ($\widehat{\sigma\sigma}$) on the far left side indicates that this entry is a simple watch. It also tells you that the expression is "<Out of context>". This is because the program is not running and Visual Basic doesn't know the context of the variable yet.

3. Set a breakpoint on the first intPointer assignment statement (as shown in Figure 9.25) and then run the program. It will stop on the assignment statement. Single-step one line so that intPointer will be assigned.

Note that the Watches window now shows the value of intPointer as 9 as in Figure 9.26.

4. Set a breakpoint on the intPointer assignment statement following the Do-While loop. Single-step and then check the Watches window. You will see that the value of Pointer is now 8 rather than 9.

5. Continue the program so that it will stop on the intPointer assignment statement again. Single-step and note that the value of intPointer is now 7.

FIGURE 9.25

The immediate and Watches windows.

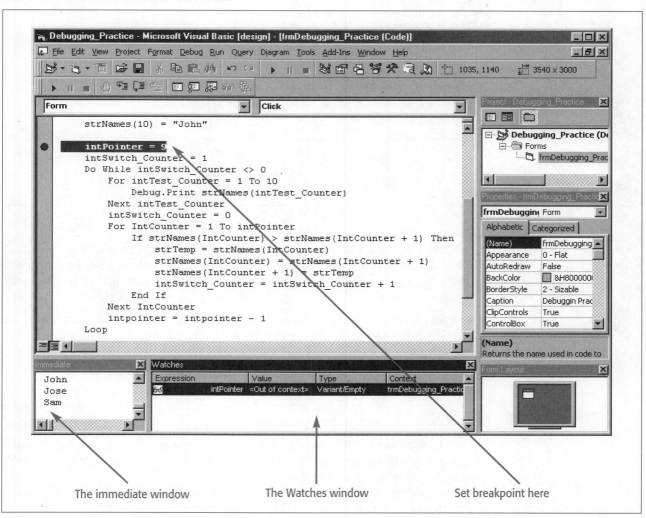

The immediate window   The Watches window   Set breakpoint here

FIGURE 9.26
The value shown in the Watches window has changed.

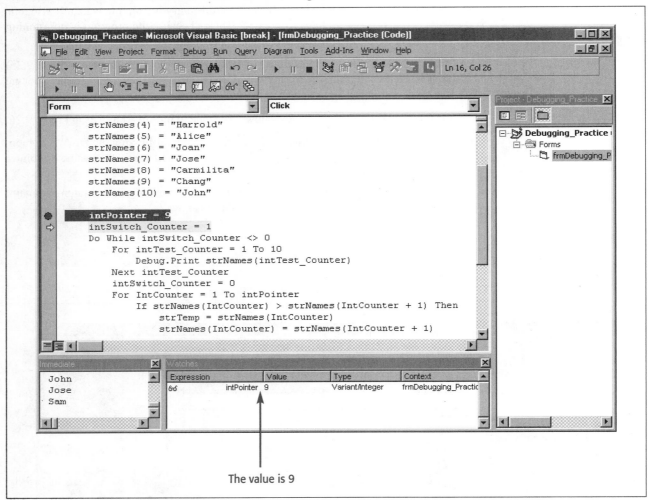

The value is 9

Using a watch is a handy way to keep track of the value of a variable, but you don't have to use a breakpoint to check its value. There is a special watch that you can use to stop the program automatically when the value of the given expression (or variable, in this case) changes.

6. Turn off the breakpoint, right-click the watch expression in the Watches window, and select **Edit Watch** from the menu that appears [or use the **Edit Watch** option on the **Debug** menu (shortcut key **Ctrl-W**)]. The Edit Watch window appears.

7. Click Break When Value Changes and then click **OK**.

8. Continue the program and it will automatically stop on the Loop statement just after the intPointer assignment statement. The Watches window will be active, and the value of the pointer will be changed (see Figure 9.27).

This watch stopped the program when intPointer changed. Note (Figure 9.27) that this watch has a different icon (🔧) from the first watch (👓). This difference in icons helps you remember which type of watch you are using.

The final type of watch is one that will break when the expression is true. We can easily try this one out, too.

FIGURE 9.27
The Watches window after the program has stopped.

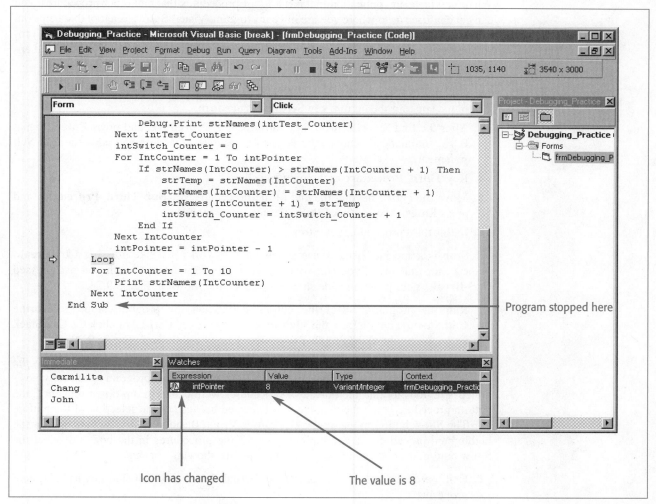

```
Debug.Print strNames(intTest_Counter)
Next intTest_Counter
intSwitch_Counter = 0
For IntCounter = 1 To intPointer
    If strNames(IntCounter) > strNames(IntCounter + 1) Then
        strTemp = strNames(IntCounter)
        strNames(IntCounter) = strNames(IntCounter + 1)
        strNames(IntCounter + 1) = strTemp
        intSwitch_Counter = intSwitch_Counter + 1
    End If
Next IntCounter
intPointer = intPointer - 1
Loop
For IntCounter = 1 To 10
    Print strNames(IntCounter)
Next IntCounter
End Sub
```

Program stopped here

Icon has changed

The value is 8

9. Open the Edit Watch window, key **intPointer = 4** as the expression, select Break When Value Is True, and select **OK**.

   Look in the Watches window, and you see that the icon for the watch has changed again ( ). Again, this icon difference allows you to tell at a glance what type of watch you have.

10. Continue the program and it will stop when the value of intPointer becomes 4. Note that the watch no longer shows the value of intPointer but tells you that the expression is true.

   You should note that watches are only temporary, as are breakpoints. If you save your program, exit Visual Basic or load another program, and then reload the original program, any watches or breakpoints that were in the program will no longer be there.

> **HINT:** You can automatically add a variable watch by highlighting the variable of interest and selecting the **Quick Watch...** option from the **Debug** menu (shortcut key **Shift-F9**) or clicking the Quick Watch icon ( ) on the Debug toolbar.

The Call Stack Dialog Box

When you have an application that has a lot of procedures that call other procedures, you can get confused as to where you are in your program. Visual Basic has a tool that helps out in such instances. The **Call Stack dialog box** shows a list of the nesting order of the procedures that are currently in use. To understand how this works, we will create a small application with several nested procedures.

1. Start a new project and add a button to the form.
2. In the code for the button, key **Second_Procedure**.
3. After the End Sub statement, key **Sub Second_Procedure**, and press **Enter**. Visual Basic automatically moves the code to a separate procedure and adds the End Sub statement.
4. Key **Third_Procedure** as the only code here.
5. Move the cursor beyond the end of the procedure, key **Sub Third_Procedure**, and press **Enter**. Again, Visual Basic creates a new procedure.
6. In this third procedure, key **Stop**.

Stop is a special Visual Basic statement that works just like pressing **Ctrl-Break**. After a Stop statement, you can continue your program just as though you had pressed **Ctrl-Break**. Your program code should look like that shown in Figure 9.28.

7. Run the program, select the button, and when the program stops, select the **Call Stack...** option from the **View** menu (shortcut key **Ctrl-L**) or click the Call Stack icon () on the Debug toolbar to see the dialog box shown in Figure 9.29.

This box lists the most current procedure first. In our example, Third_Procedure is the procedure that was called last, because it is the one in which the program is currently positioned. Previous to that, the other two procedures were called in top-down sequence, the bottom procedure being the one that was executed because of the selection of the button.

The **Show** button in the dialog box causes Visual Basic to show you the code for the highlighted procedure. If you highlight one of the procedures in the box and select the **Show** button, the code window with that procedure showing appears.

8. Exit the dialog box, the program, and Visual Basic, and then shut down the system properly.

FIGURE 9.28
The program code.

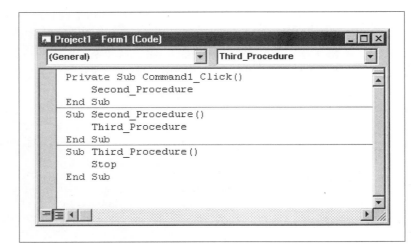

```
Project1 - Form1 (Code)

(General)                              Third_Procedure

    Private Sub Command1_Click()
        Second_Procedure
    End Sub
    Sub Second_Procedure()
        Third_Procedure
    End Sub
    Sub Third_Procedure()
        Stop
    End Sub
```

FIGURE 9.29
The Call Stack dialog box.

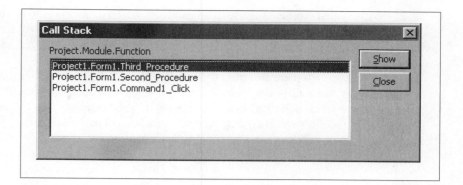

9.6　User-Generated Errors

We have learned how to use message boxes to display errors and warnings to the users who key something wrong, forget to key something that is needed, or simply press an incorrect key. Rather than allowing the users to do anything they like and then penalizing them with an error message when what they have done will not work in the application, it is better to force users to work within the defined parameters of the application and display errors and warnings only when it is necessary. For example, if you have a field where numeric data should be entered, such as an amount field, you should allow the user to key only data appropriate to the numeric field. Earlier you learned how to create a procedure to read every keystroke and accept only appropriate ones. This technique should be used any time there is a numeric field.

In addition, many fields may be valid only within specified value ranges. That is, a field may need to be set up so that it will accept only an entry of a certain type. For example, if you are creating a program to calculate grades, the allowable range for the grades is probably 0 to 100. Here a grade of 101 would be an error, and you should inform the user that the entry is incorrect. Other fields may have only certain values that are allowed. Suppose you are creating an application for a flower shop where there are codes for every type of flower arrangement available. After the user enters the code, you need to check the code entered against the list of available codes and inform the user if the one entered is not correct.

> **HINT:** Another Visual Basic tool, the **Microsoft Masked Edit control 6.0**, can come in handy for editing user data. This custom control is added from the Components dialog box. It allows you to create a mask into which the data are keyed, and unless the keyed data match the defined mask, the keystroke is ignored. This can be used for date fields as well as a number of others. You can experiment with this tool on your own.

9.7　Testing Your Applications

When testing your applications, you need to test them in every conceivable situation that might come up as they are used. The idea is to uncover the errors during the testing process rather than after the application has been delivered to the user.

If there are numbers to be entered, try to enter letters and other characters to see what will happen. Enter numbers outside the normal range that the field should have (such as negative numbers). If there are several numbers that are interdependent, such as quantity and reorder quantity (the quantity at which a product is to be reordered automatically), try various combinations to make sure that the application will function properly. "Properly" may mean that the data are accepted or that an error is generated, depending on the construction of the program and the data being entered.

If there are string fields to be entered that are codes that must have certain values, enter many different codes that are not among the accepted ones. If an acceptable code is A15, whereas B15 is not acceptable, try B15 and make sure your program doesn't accept it. If the code is specified as uppercase, see what will happen if the user enters the code in lowercase, or, better yet, automatically change the entry to uppercase (UCase statement) so that errors concerning lowercase will simply not be allowed to occur. If the field must be within a certain range, be sure to try values outside the acceptable range.

If your application uses special keys such as shortcut keys, be sure they all function as they are supposed to. Many shortcut keys are handled automatically by Visual Basic, so it is unlikely that any of the shortcut keys for menu options, for example, would not function properly, but you need to test them anyway.

If there are certain fields where the user must enter something, test the application without anything in the fields to be certain that the error checking is working properly. And be sure you do have error checking for empty fields into which the user is required to enter something.

You should attempt to duplicate every possible runtime problem that may occur to see how your application will react. File operations are primary culprits for runtime errors. For example, what happens in your application if the disk you are trying to write to is full? What happens if there is no disk in the specified disk drive? What happens when the disk is removed from the drive between the time the file is opened and when it is closed? What happens if the specified input file is not on the disk? What happens if you ask the application to write a record that is beyond the range of the file, such as record 25 when the file only has 15 records in it? As you might imagine, it is next to impossible to generate every conceivable error in every possible circumstance, but the closer you get to this ideal, the more polished your application will be.

After you have spent many hours making sure your application functions in every possible situation, you can rest assured that the user will never have any problems, right? Wrong! No matter how much time you spend refining your application, if it is of any size at all, there will still be bugs in it that some industrious user will uncover someday. Sometimes it is months or even years before a particular error shows up. This is one reason why major software companies send their new applications out to users for testing before they release them to the rest of the user public. The users of these **beta copies** are asked to use the software in their normal day-to-day operations and report any problems they have. These problems are then collected and repaired before the software is released. The philosophy is that the users will do what users are prone to do and try every possible wrong combination, thus uncovering those problem areas that the programmers were unable to locate, didn't think of, or didn't see as a problem during testing.

Debugging and testing time is virtually always in direct proportion to the size of the application. The larger the application, the longer you should expect to spend testing it. We cannot emphasize enough, however, the importance of the testing process. Regardless of how long it takes, you must be careful and thorough. Otherwise, the errors you did not take the time to find will show up, and you will have unhappy users.

9.8   Command and Menu Summary

In this chapter you learned to use the following keystrokes:

- **Ctrl-Break** stops the execution of your application.
- **Ctrl-F8** is the shortcut key for the **Run to Cursor** option on the **Debug** menu.

- **Ctrl-L** is the shortcut key for the **Call Stack...** option on the **View** menu.
- **Ctrl-W** is the shortcut key for the **Edit Watch** option on the **Debug** menu.
- **F5** lets you execute or continue the execution of your application.
- **F8** is the shortcut key for the **Step Into** (Single Step) option on the **Debug** menu.
- **F9** is the shortcut key for the **Toggle Breakpoint** option on the **Debug** menu.
- **Shift-F5** restarts the execution of your application.
- **Shift-F8** is the shortcut key for the **Step Over** option on the **Debug** menu.
- **Shift-F9** is the shortcut key for the **Quick Watch** option on the **Debug** menu.

In this chapter you learned about the following property:

- **Description** contains the description of an error that has occurred. It is a property of the Err object.

In this chapter you learned about the following functions and commands:

- **Err** (which is actually an object) contains information about the error that occurred to execute an On Error GoTo statement.
- **Error** can be used to cause an error in your program so that you can test an error routine.
- **Exit Sub** causes Visual Basic to exit a procedure (subroutine) without executing any additional statements.
- **On Error GoTo** is used to trap certain runtime errors so that an error routine can be executed.
- **Resume** is the statement used at the end of an On Error GoTo error routine. It causes execution to continue on the line that had the error. **Resume Next** continues execution on the line following the one with the error, and **Resume Label** continues execution from the specified label.
- **Stop** causes the program to halt temporarily.

In this chapter you learned about the following menu options:

- **Debug:**
  - **Add Watch...** is used to give Visual Basic an expression to keep track of and show you the result of in the immediate window.
  - **Call Stack...** (shortcut key **Ctrl-L**) is used to display the Calls dialog box.
  - **Clear All Breakpoints** removes all breakpoints previously set.
  - **Edit Watch** (shortcut key **Ctrl-W**) allows you to modify a watch already created. This can be called up by double-clicking the watch in the immediate window.
  - **Quick Watch...** (shortcut key **Shift-F9**) lets you automatically add a variable watch by selecting the variable in code and then selecting this option.
  - **Run to Cursor** (shortcut key **Ctrl-F8**) causes the program to continue to execute from the current line to the cursor location.
  - **Set Next Statement** can be used to change the current line in your application execution.
  - **Step Into** (shortcut key **F8**) lets you execute your program one statement at a time (single step).
  - **Step Over** (shortcut key **Shift-F8**) lets Visual Basic treat a procedure call as a single step.
  - **Toggle Breakpoint** (shortcut key **F9**) lets you turn a breakpoint on or off.

In this chapter you learned about the following buttons:

- This icon on the Debug Toolbar adds a breakpoint.
- This icon on the Debug Toolbar calls the stack list.
- This icon on the Debug Toolbar allows you to single-step (Step Into) through your program.
- This icon on the Debug Toolbar allows you to treat a procedure call as a single step or Step Over the called procedure.
- This icon on the Debug Toolbar allows you to add a Quick Watch.

9.9 Performance Check

1. What are the four types of errors that can occur in your applications?

2. What type of error is also known as a bug?

3. Which type of error is also known as a syntax error?

4. Explain what a syntax error is.

5. Which type of error is called a trappable error?

6. Which type of error is the easiest to find?

7. Which type of error is the most difficult to find?

8. What statement is used to turn off error checking with the On Error GoTo statement?

9. Which form of the Resume statement is the least useful?

10. What tool is available to help you edit user input?

11. What function is used to display the text error message the system produces?

12. Which shortcut key is used to set a breakpoint?

13. Why do we set breakpoints?

14. What shortcut key is used to single-step through the application?

15. What happens if you use an assignment statement in the immediate window?

16. What does the Debug.Print statement do?

17. What is a beta copy and what is it used for?

18. What is the purpose of a variable watch?

19. Which of the three types of watches do you think will be the most valuable to you and why?

20. What does the Call Stack dialog box show you?

9.10 Programming Exercises

1. You have a friend who is just learning Visual Basic. He has been working on an application with a workspace from which he wants to be able to cut the first ten words and then store those words in ten labels. The problem is that he can't get all the errors out of the application, and he has come to you for help. This exercise will give you practice finding and correcting coding errors. At the computer, do each of the following:

   a. Get into Visual Basic with your work disk in drive A.

   b. Load **Cut Program** from the Ch-9 folder.

   c. Execute the application and select the **Cut** button. The first error is because Text is not the correct type of property for this statement. Correct it and continue the application.

   d. Press **F5** to continue the program. Now you get a control array error. The problem is that the loop went too far (past the end of the array). There must be an error in the looping process. Look at the Do While statement carefully, and you notice a misspelling (again, Option Explicit would point these out to you).

   e. Fix the error, exit the program, and run it again. You will have a similar problem. This time, however, the problem is that the ending point on the Do While test is too large. Change it to 10.

   f. Exit and restart the program.

   g. Now the program works, but the data are not placed in the cut boxes properly. Exit the application, put a breakpoint on the Do While statement, run the application, key some data, and select Cut. Single-step until you are past the assignment to the control array, and then print the first value of the control array (element zero) using the immediate window. It should be the first word of the workspace text. As you see, it is okay.

   h. Single-step through the code until you get to the same assignment statement again, and print the value of the second control array element. This one is not correct, so something is wrong in the code that assigns to the control array. Study the code carefully until you discover the error and correct it. (Hint: Check the Left function.)

   i. With this last error, the program works properly except for the fact that the cut words appear in a sort of random sequence in the cut boxes. The boxes need to be ordered. Do this so that the words appear top to bottom in the first column and then the second.

   j. The application also needs a scroll bar in the workspace. Add one.

   k. Test the application one more time to be sure it is functioning properly, and then save it as **Cut Program Repaired**.

   l. Exit Visual Basic and shut the system down properly.

2. You have been asked to write an application for a local supply store that sells a large number of products. One of the things your application is supposed to do is accept an inventory item number from the user and display the appropriate item description. You decide to prepare yourself for creating the application by practicing just that part of the application. This exercise will give you practice checking an array for a coded item. At the computer, do each of the following:

   a. Get into Visual Basic with your work disk in drive A.

   b. Create a new application, and add a label specifying the entry of the item number and a text box where the item number may be entered. Under that, put two labels: one that says "Description" and another that will be used to display the description. Use **txtItem_In** as the control name for the text box and **lblDescription_Out** for the label. Add one button with the caption **Get Description** and an appropriate control name.

   c. Open the code window for the button and dimension, and key a ten-element static array with the item numbers A15, B19, G44, C12, R32, D16, G12, H01, J33, and T05.

   d. Create a second array and make up ten descriptions, one for each of the item numbers.

   e. Your code will have to get the data from the txtItem_In box and check each data item against the elements in the array. If it doesn't match any of them, display a message box for the user and then exit the procedure. If it does match, display the description in the description box.

f. Test the application to be sure it is functioning properly, and then save it in the Ch-9 folder on your work disk as **Item Check**.

g. Exit Visual Basic and shut the system down properly.

3. A colleague has been working on a small application to create a phone number list that can be accessed from a menu. She is new to Visual Basic and has asked you to help her finish debugging it. This exercise will give you practice debugging an application with unfamiliar code, much like your own code will be several months after you have written any application. At the computer, do each of the following:

a. Get into Visual Basic with your work disk in drive A.

b. Load **Phone List** from the Ch-9 folder.

c. The application has one menu where the items are added with the Add Item option. Then they can be retrieved by clicking on them. Debug the application.

d. Test the application to be sure it is functioning properly, and then save it as **Phone List Update**.

e. Exit Visual Basic and shut the system down properly.

4. A colleague has been working on a simple alarm clock application but is having trouble debugging it. She is new to Visual Basic and has asked you to help her make it work. This exercise will give you practice debugging an application with unfamiliar code, much like your own code will be several months after you have written any application. At the computer, do each of the following:

a. Get into Visual Basic with your work disk in drive A.

b. Load **Alarm Error** from the Ch-9 folder.

c. The application displays the current time, using a timer to determine what that is; compares the keyed alarm setting against that time; and, if the alarm has been turned on, beeps to alert the user. Debug the application. There are six errors in it. You will note that this user did not follow the conventional prefix-naming scheme.

d. Test the application to be sure it is functioning properly. Save it as **Alarm Error Updated**.

e. Exit the system.

9.11   Performance Mastery

1. Your boss has been wanting to learn how to program in Visual Basic for a long time. Finally he splurged and spent the weekend reading and experimenting with the language. Unfortunately, he became frustrated when he could not finish debugging a stopwatch program he tried to write. He has asked you to help him finish debugging the application. The application is called **Watch Error** and is in the Ch-9 folder on your practice disk. As you work with the program, you note that your boss did not follow the normal conventions for naming program elements. After you get the program working, save it as **Watch Error Updated** and print all the elements.

2. Your boss has been wanting to learn how to program in Visual Basic for a long time. Finally he splurged and spent the weekend reading and experimenting with the language. Unfortunately, he became frustrated when he could not finish debugging his program. He was experimenting with a multiselection list. The program is supposed to read product names, with their associated prices, from a file and to display the product names in a list. Then, when the user selects a single item in the list, the program displays the price of that product. If multiple items are selected, the program is supposed to display the total cost of all the selected products. The application is called **MultiList** and is in the Ch-9 folder on your practice disk. It uses a file already stored in the Ch-9 folder. After you get it working, save it as **MultiList Updated** and print all the elements.

3. One of the programmers who worked at your shop just quit without finishing a program for which the boss has been waiting. You have been assigned the task of finish-

ing the application. It is a message board that will display one of six different messages for the person whose name is chosen from a menu. The application is supposed to ask the user for a password and to verify that it is correct before the message is displayed. The application is called **Message Error** and can be found in the Ch-9 folder on your disk. As you work with the program, you will note that the programmer did not follow the normal conventions for naming program elements. After you get it working, save it as **Message Error Update** and print all the elements.

4. One of the programmers who worked at your shop just quit without finishing a program for which the boss has been waiting. You have been assigned the task of finishing it. It is a program that is supposed to read a file and display a list of products, while storing the quantity on hand, purchase price, and sales price. Then, when the user clicks one of the products in the list, the program is to display the quantity on hand, the purchase price, the extended purchase price (purchase price times quantity on hand), the sales price, the extended sales price, and the proposed profit. The application is called **Extended Sales** and can be found in the Ch-9 folder on your disk. It uses a file already stored in the Ch-9 folder. After you get the program working, save it as **Extended Sales Update** and print all the elements.

5. One of the programmers who worked at your shop just quit without finishing a program for which the boss has been waiting. You have been assigned the task of finishing it. It is a program that is supposed to read a file and display a list of workers' names. When a name is selected, the program is to display whether the person is on salary or hourly and what that salary or hourly wage is. Then a second file is to be read that contains the number of hours that person worked last week. If the person is on salary, the program is to display the amount of the check as 1/52 of the salary. If the person is hourly, the amount of the check is to be calculated from the hourly wage. The amount of the check is then to be displayed. The application is called **Wages** and can be found in the Ch-9 folder on your disk. It uses two files already stored in the Ch-9 folder. After you get it working, save it as **Wages Update** and print all the elements.

6. You have just been hired at a new company to take over the program of a programmer who had to go to another company location to work on a program he wrote for that location. The program you have been assigned works with three separate sequential files. The first file comes from the warehouse and contains the product name and the quantity on hand. The second file comes from the sales force and contains the product name and the sales price. The last file comes from the purchasing department and contains the product name and the purchase price. The program was designed to display the products in a list. Then, when the user selects a product from the list, the program is to display the quantity on hand, the purchase price, the extended purchase price (purchase price times quantity on hand), the sales price, the extended sales price, and the proposed profit. The application is called **Profit Potential** and can be found in the Ch-9 folder on your disk. It uses files already stored in the Ch-9 folder. After you get it working, save it as **Profit Potential Update** and print all the elements.

Accessing Databases

10.1 Chapter Objectives

After finishing this chapter you will be able to:

- Describe a relational database, explaining the terms **table, record, field,** and **index**.
- Demonstrate how to use the Visual Data Manager.
- Demonstrate how to use a data control tool to access a database table.
- Create a program to update, add records to, and delete records from a database.
- Demonstrate how to access an external database.

10.2 Introduction

In the past, we have examined many types of files that required us to do all the data manipulation. In this chapter, we will look at file systems called **databases** that handle much of the needed data manipulation for us automatically. We will thoroughly explore the prevailing concepts of databases and learn how to access them through Visual Basic. We will learn that most databases are **relational** and that a number of relational database programs create database files that Visual Basic can access directly. Visual Basic even has a tool called the **Visual Data Manager** that lets you create and manipulate databases. We will explore that tool in this chapter.

Many people believe the real strength of languages like Visual Basic is that they can act as "front ends" to databases and similar programs. In this chapter you will see how easy it is to create these "front ends."

10.2   What Is a Database?

As we just mentioned, most databases currently in use are designed around a **relational interface** to their files. In simple terms, a relational database is one that stores its data in tables of data, each table being made up of rows and columns of data. In Visual Basic, the rows are referred to as **records** and the columns are called **fields.** As you probably already know, a field is simply an item of data such as a name, address, or phone number. A group of related fields (such as all the fields for Fred) are stored together, and this grouping is a record. When all these related records are stored together in a database, you have a **table.** Each record is made up of a number of fields, and the entire group of records constitutes a table. A database can have many tables with a variety of information in them. What makes such databases "relational" is the capability to connect one table to another through a relationship between a field in one table and a field in another. This relationship can be as simple as having the same field in both tables, or it can be much more complex.

When we create a database, we specify the names of the fields that make up each record, as well as the type of data each field is to contain and the amount of space that is needed for the data the field is to hold. For example, if we want to store a name, the type of data would be text (or string), and about 20 bytes would have to be set aside to store each name. If we needed to store something like an amount of money, the type of the data might be currency or single-precision, which allows us to use decimals. Most database programs have many different data types that can be used to specify the ways the data are to be stored and manipulated.

As mentioned, a database is not limited to one table of data. Many databases have a series of tables. Take a database for student records at a college, for example. Such a database might begin with a table of information about each student. It would contain the student's name, address, city, state, zip code, status (year in school), and perhaps major and total hours taken. Then, in order to differentiate one student from another, we would want to use some unique code to identify each of them (because there could always be more than one John Smith in the school). This identification code is generally the student's social security number, though it could be any other unique number assigned to the student. This unique key field is known as an **index.** By using an index, we can gain access to the information for any particular student quickly, and these indices can give us access to information in multiple tables.

This table structure would give us the beginning of our School database as shown in Figure 10.1.

As we have said, this table is only the beginning of our sample database. To maintain school records, we need a lot more information on each student than is given in this one table. For example, we need to maintain the class records for each of these students. That is, we need to keep track of what classes the students are currently taking (the current semester) and what classes they have taken in the past. We could store the data for the classes in this same table by adding more fields, but how many fields would we need to add? Some students will have taken 30 or 40 classes; others may be in their first semester, and for them, we would need to store only 6 or 7 classes for this semester. Next semester, of course, the number of classes for each of the students would increase (except for those who have graduated). Because each of the fields exists and takes up storage space in each record regardless of whether the field is used in that particular record, we would have a lot of empty space in most of the records. That is, if we reserved 50 fields in each record for storing class information, and a particular student's record needed only 6 of them, the other 44 would be empty—a waste of space. And what would we do when a student needed 51 fields and we had only 50 reserved? It is a much more sensible approach to set up a separate table of information and then tie the two tables to-

FIGURE 10.1
The Student table of the School database.

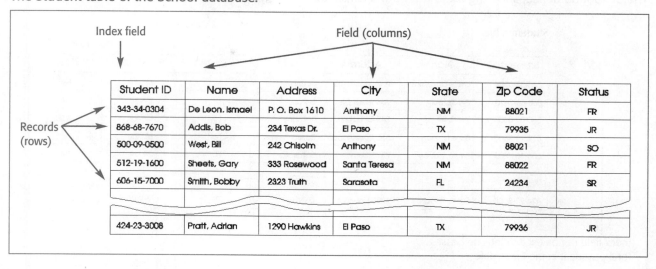

gether in some way. That's another purpose of having an index. The student ID is unique, so it points to only one student in the student table. This means that every class record with a particular student ID in it would belong to that student.

We would set up a second table in our database to contain the classes. We would probably want fields for the student ID, the course ID, the semester and year the class was taken, and the grade received. The current semester's classes would not have been given a grade, so the grade field would remain empty for a time. This table has no index because there are no fields that are unique.

When we add this second table, the picture of our database looks like the one shown in Figure 10.2. Note that the grades for the fall semester (F) of 2000 are blank. That's because the semester is not yet complete and the grades have not been recorded.

In addition to these two tables, we would probably need

■ A table of courses that contains the information about the courses themselves, such as the department, the number of hours, the class frequency (every semester, once a year, and so on), and a description of the course. This table could be indexed by the class ID so that information here could be connected to the list of classes taken by the student. That way, you could find out additional information about the classes taken by any particular student.

■ A table of the courses that are taught each semester, containing the time, instructor (just an ID), semester, and year. This table would also be indexed by the class ID.

■ A table of instructors, containing the typical name and address information along with department, degree attained, and any other information pertinent to instructors. This would be indexed by instructor ID so that instructor information could be connected to the table of courses.

As you see, a database structure can rapidly become quite complicated. When you employ such a structure, however, a huge number of possible groupings of data are available with a minimum of wasted storage space.

FIGURE 10.2
The School database, showing the Student and Class tables.

Student table

Student ID	Name	Address	City	State	Zip Code	Status
343-34-0304	De Leon. Ismael	P. O. Box 1610	Anthony	NM	88021	FR
868-68-7670	Addis, Bob	234 Texas Dr.	El Paso	TX	79935	JR
500-09-0500	West, Bill	242 Chisolm	Anthony	NM	88021	SO
512-19-1600	Sheets, Gary	333 Rosewood	Santa Teresa	NM	88022	FR
606-15-7000	Smith, Bobby	2323 Truth	Sarasota	FL	24234	SR
424-23-3008	Pratt, Adrian	1290 Hawkins	El Paso	TX	79936	JR

Index field can be used to look up classes
for the student in the Class table

Class table

Student ID	Class ID	Semester	Year	Grade
343-34-0304	CIS-1035	S	99	C
343-34-0304	ENG-1022	F	00	
424-23-3008	ENG-1022	U	99	B
512-19-1600	HIS-2044	S	99	A
606-15-7000	PE-1001	F	00	
424-23-3008	ECN-3055	F	98	B

10.4   Looking at the PIM

As always, before beginning to explore the new tools and techniques that will be introduced in this chapter, we will look at the changes you will make to the PIM.

1. Launch Windows Explorer. Copy the Ch-10 and Ch-11 folders from wherever they are stored on your system to be used as your new work disk. Then create a new folder called Ch-8. Copy the Appointments.App and PIM.ini files as well as any text documents your PIM program may expect to be there (Sample Document.txt, for example) from the work disk you used in Chapter 8. The PIM program needs these files to work properly and expects to find them in the Ch-8 folder.

2. Switch to the Ch-10 folder on your work disk. There you will see a file called **Addresses.mdb**. This is the database you will work with in this chapter. Make a copy of this file. You will revert to this backup copy of the database file when you are through with this section.

3. Run the PIM program, and switch to the **Address List** tab to see the display shown in Figure 10.3.

In addition to a filled-in **Address List** tab, the program has three new menus that are database-related. On this display, there is one new tool, the **Data Control tool**. This tool allows you to access database information without having to write any code. It will let you

FIGURE 10.3
The **Address List** display.

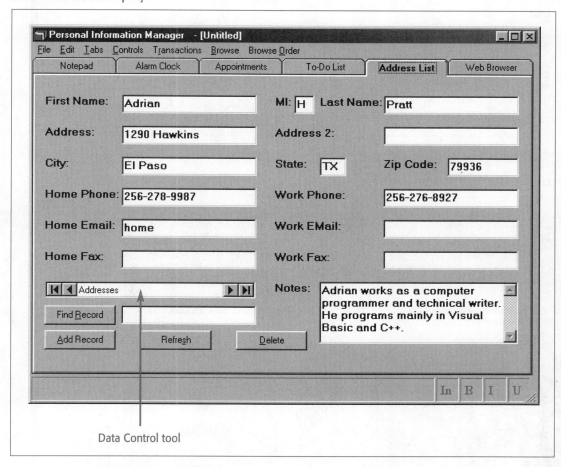

Data Control tool

move from record to record and will automatically cause the data to be placed in the other controls in the display. The data movement with the control is done by clicking the arrows as shown in Figure 10.4.

5. Click the arrow to move to the next record (▶), and the data in the display change to the record for Bobby Smith.

6. Click the arrow to move to the last record (▶|), and the data change to the record for William West. This is the last record in the database.

7. Click the arrow to move to the previous record (◀), and the data change to the record for Robert Addis.

8. Click the arrow to move to the first record (|◀), and the data change to the record for Adrian Pratt again as shown in Figure 10.3.

Not only will the Data Control tool allow you to move from record to record in the database, but it will also allow you to update the data automatically. But you can control that by turning update capabilities on and off. Right now they are turned off.

9. Key **Home** in the Home Email entry box, and click the next record arrow (▶). You will get the error shown in Figure 10.5.

FIGURE 10.4
The record movement controls on the Data Control.

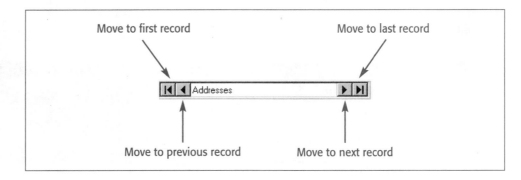

FIGURE 10.5
The error that occurs because the database is locked.

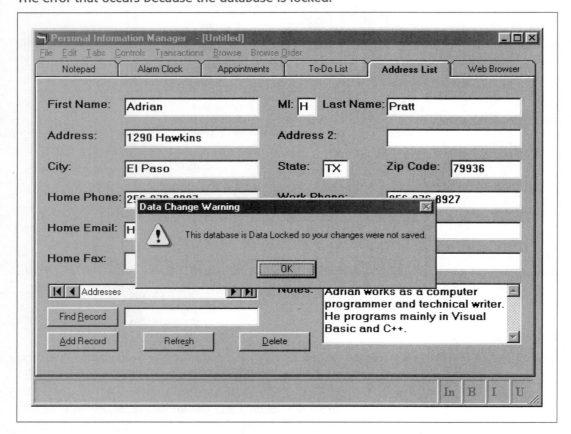

10. Click the **OK** button, and the database display moves to the next record. Click the previous record button (◀), and you see the record for Adrian Pratt again. The Home Email field is blank because the record was not updated.

You can turn on the updating capabilities by turning off Data Locking.

11. Pull down the **Edit** menu to see the **Address List Data Locked** option. It is checked, which means that it is currently turned on, so the database cannot be updated.

12. Click the **Address List Data Locked** option to turn off data locking, key **Home** in the Home Email entry box, and click the next record arrow (▶).

This time no error will occur. The data were updated. You can see this by moving back to the previous record.

13. Click the previous record button (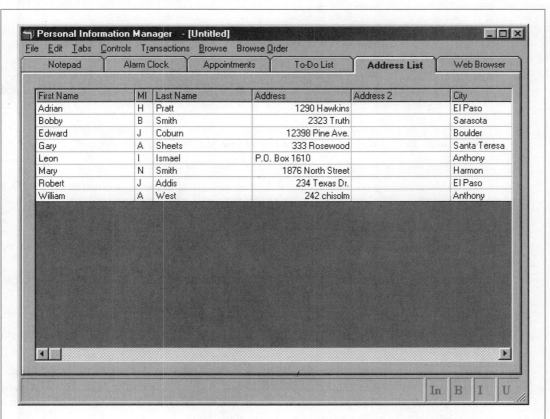), and you see the record for Adrian Pratt. The Home Email field now has Home in it. The data in the database were updated.

Not only can you look at the records one by one, but you can also **Browse** them, which simply means you can see multiple records in a list.

14. Pull down the **Browse** menu and select the **Browse Address Database** option to see the Browse display shown in Figure 10.6.

Browsing the database is not handled automatically as using the Data Control tool is. You have to write the code to browse the database yourself, but this is not difficult. It's just a matter of reading the data from the database, much as you read data from a sequential file.

Just as you can switch to the browse mode, you can switch back to the single-record display.

15. Pull down the **Browse** menu and select **Return to Single Record Display**. The display will revert to the display you saw before.

Because we will be displaying the database in browse mode, we can also cause that display to be shown in various alphabetical orders, such as by last name.

16. Pull down the **Browse Order** menu, select the **Ascending** submenu, and select **Last Name** to see the display in last-name order as shown in Figure 10.7.

17. Change back to the single-record display.

On this display, you see that there are buttons for finding a particular record, adding a new record, and deleting a record.

FIGURE 10.6
The Address database in browse mode.

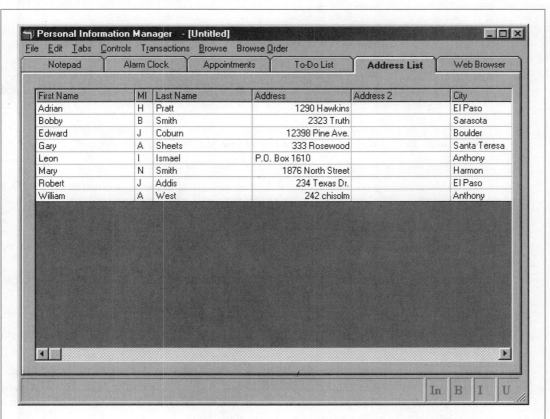

FIGURE 10.7
The browse mode sorted in last-name order.

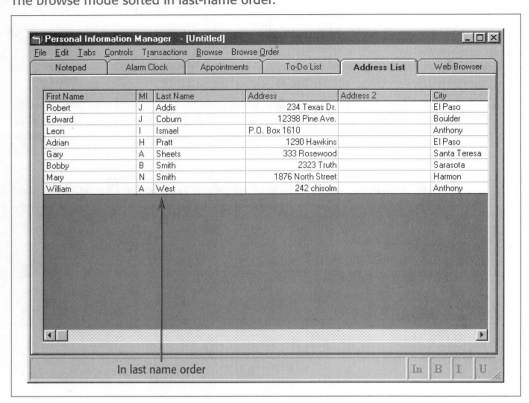

18. Click the **Add Record** button, and the display becomes blank.

19. Key **AASample** in the first-name field, **A** in the MI (middle-initial) field, and **Record** in the last-name field; then click the next record arrow (▶).

   You have just added a new record to the database. The first name begins with AA, so you would think it was the first record in the file. But that is not the case.

20. Click the first record arrow (◀◀). The Adrian Pratt record shows up.

   As new records are added to the database, they are automatically put at the end. To put them in the proper sequence, you need to **Refresh** the database.

21. Click the **Refresh** button. Now you see the record you just added.

22. Move to the last record and then back to the first record. The new record is the first one in the database now.

23. Click the **Delete** button. You will see a verification prompt. Click the **Yes** button. The record is now deleted.

24. Move to the last record and then back to the first record. There is no AASample record.

   The last button on the form, **Find**, is used to search for a particular record. You can experiment with this on your own.

25. Continue to experiment with the program until you are familiar with its processes. Then exit the program. You will have to exit in order to delete the database and rename the one you copied, because Windows will not let you rename, delete, or replace a database that is currently opened by an application.

26. Switch to Explorer and delete the Addresses.mdb database file. Copy the database file again and change the name of the new copy of the database to **Addresses.mdb**. Now you have a fresh copy of the database to work with in the remainder of the chapter and a backup copy just in case you make a mistake and need to recover the original database.

10.5 Accessing a Database in Visual Basic

Now that you understand what a database is and have looked at the changes you are going to make to the PIM program, it is time to learn how to make those changes in your current copy of the PIM.

As we have mentioned, Visual Basic has a built-in database access tool called the **Data Control** tool that allows you to access database information without having to write any code at all. It will even allow the data in a database to be updated automatically.

Setting Up the Data Control

To see how to use a data control, we will use the Address List portion of the PIM.

1. Get into Visual Basic with your work disk in drive A.

2. Load the PIM application from the Ch-8 folder (we did not use the PIM application in Ch-9), and save all the forms and the project in the Ch-10 folder (or you can simply copy all the forms, the module, and the project into the Ch-10 folder and then run that version).

3. Switch to the **Address List** tab and add the labels and text fields shown in Figure 10.8. The control names of the fields should be as follows:

    a. First Name: **txtFirst_Name**

    b. MI: **txtMiddle_Initial**

    c. Last Name: **txtLast_Name**

    d. Address: **txtAddress_1**

    e. Address 2: **txtAddress_2**

    f. City: **txtCity**

    g. State: **txtState**

    h. Zip Code: **txtZip_Code**

    i. Home Phone: **txtHome_Phone**

    j. Work Phone: **txtWork_Phone**

    k. Home EMail: **txtHome_EMail**

    l. Phone EMail: **txtWork_EMail**

    m. Home Fax: **txtHome_Fax**

    n. Work Fax: **txtWork_Fax**

    o. Notes: **txtNotes**

4. Make the Notes text box multiline and add a vertical scroll bar.

5. Using the tool shown in Figure 10.9, add a data control to your form and position it as shown in Figure 10.10. Give the data control the control name **datAddresses_Database** and the caption **Addresses**.

Now we are ready to connect the control to the Addresses database. One has already been created for you using the Access database program; it can be found in your Ch-10 folder.

FIGURE 10.8
The Address list.

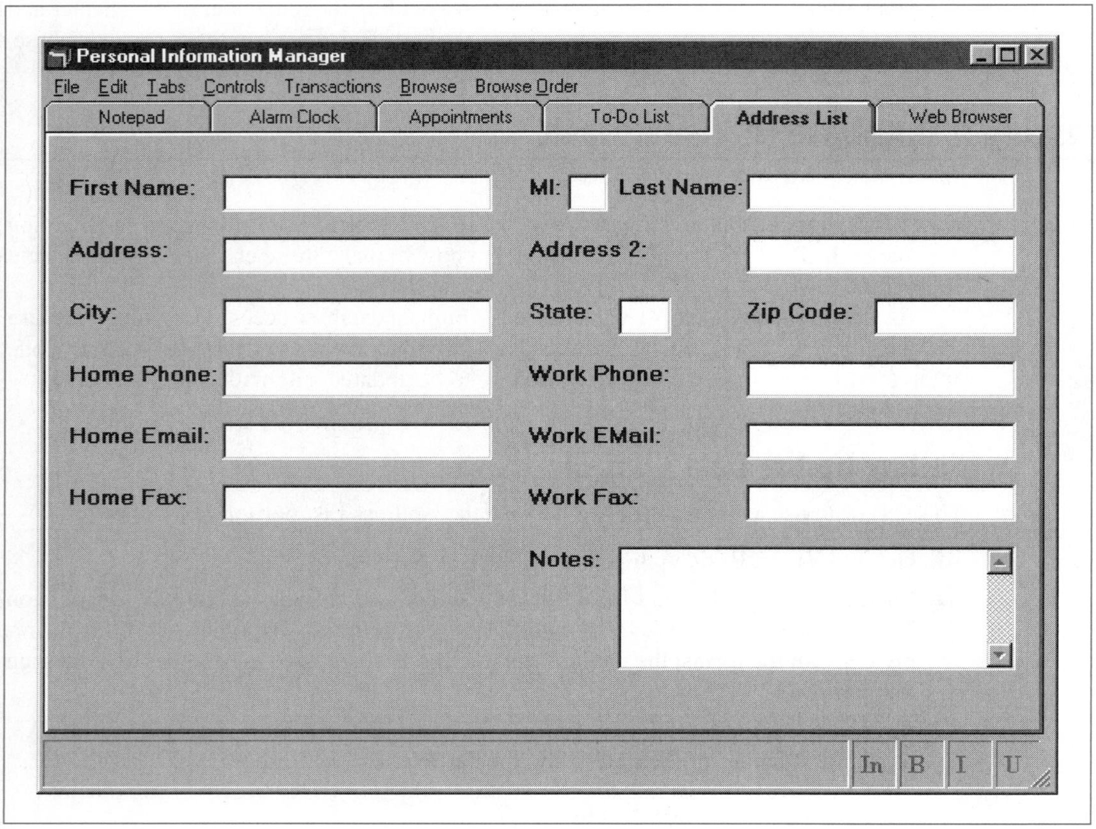

Personal Information Manager

File Edit Tabs Controls Transactions Browse Browse Order

| Notepad | Alarm Clock | Appointments | To-Do List | **Address List** | Web Browser |

First Name: [   ]   MI: [ ]   Last Name: [   ]

Address: [   ]   Address 2: [   ]

City: [   ]   State: [ ]   Zip Code: [   ]

Home Phone: [   ]   Work Phone: [   ]

Home Email: [   ]   Work EMail: [   ]

Home Fax: [   ]   Work Fax: [   ]

Notes: [   ]

In B I U

FIGURE 10.9
The Data Control tool.

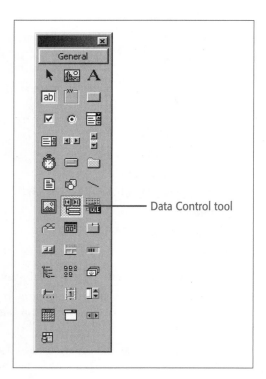

Data Control tool

FIGURE 10.10
The Address List tab with the Data Control added.

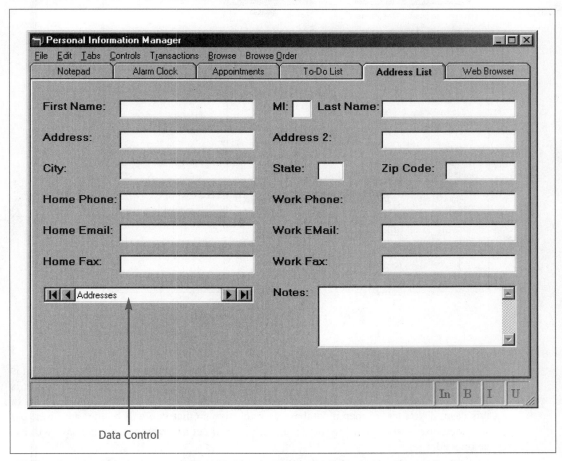

Data Control

To gain access to the database, you will need to set two properties for the data control: **DatabaseName**, which tells Visual Basic which database to use, and **RecordSource**, which indicates from which table within the database the data will be extracted.

6. Select the data control and then select the DatabaseName property. Select the ellipse button on the right to see the access dialog box for the database name. This dialog box is similar to all the other file-open dialog boxes you have seen before. Change to the Ch-10 folder on your work disk and double-click the Addresses database that shows up in the workspace of the dialog box.

7. Select the RecordSource property for the data control, and pull down the list of available tables as shown in Figure 10.11.

Note that only one table is available in this database. Though most databases will have many tables, for this application we need only the one table. Therefore, only one will show up in the list.

8. Select **Addresses** from this list.

The Exclusive Property

An important property that doesn't directly have anything to do with the actual access to the data is the **Exclusive** property. This allows you to specify to Visual Basic whether or not

FIGURE 10.11
The list of available
tables (RecordSource).

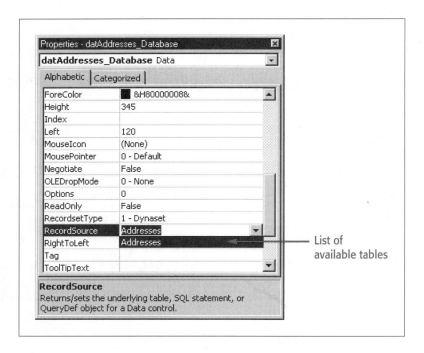

List of
available tables

your program is to be the only one allowed access to the database while your application is executing. If you want exclusive access to the database, this property is set to **True**. If it is set to **False**, which is the default mode, other users will also have access to the database. In this case, if you try to open a database as Exclusive so that you will be the only user, but someone else is already using the database, you will get an error and the database will not be opened.

You may need to have exclusive access to a database at times when you are doing things like building a report. If someone else changes a record in the database as you are building the report, the results of the report won't reflect the current state of the database. If you do set the property to True, access is restricted to the application currently running, and all other applications are locked out. A bonus when access is exclusive is that access to the database is considerably faster, because the system doesn't have to look constantly for other applications trying to access the database.

This is your own copy of the database, and no one else should be needing access to it. Therefore, you can set the Exclusive property so that your access can be as fast as possible.

1. Change to the Exclusive property of the Data Control.
2. Pull down the list and click True.

Setting Up Bound Controls

Now we are ready to specify the particular fields from this table that we want to have displayed. We are going to display the data in the text boxes we placed on the form. These text boxes are called **bound controls**. That is because they are (or soon will be) "bound" to the data control. Then, because the data control is connected to the database we selected, data will be displayed in the bound controls automatically. These controls are also called **data-aware controls**. Other data-aware controls are check boxes, picture boxes (to allow you to use graphics, such as photos, in your databases), image controls, and labels.

HINT: Because graphics require so much storage space, there are no exercises in this chapter that deal with storing graphics in a database. With the knowledge you gain in this chapter, however, you will be able to add graphics such as photos to your databases without difficulty.

To connect the bound controls to the data control, we use two properties: **DataSource,** to allow you to specify which data control you want to use (which already specifies the table to be used), and **DataField**, which lets you specify which of the fields in the table you want displayed.

1. Select the DataSource property of the First Name text box, and pull down the list of available data controls. There is only one in this list because there is only one data control on the form.

When we select the data control, it directs the program to send the data from the database and table represented into the bound control (the First Name text box) we are working with.

HINT: When a database file is constructed, each of the fields put into the database must have several parameters specified, including the length and type (such as numeric or text) of the field itself. For example, if the field is to hold a name, the data would be text and would probably require 20 bytes. Because objects in Visual Basic allow the data to flow to fill up (or exceed) the visual size of the object, and because the data are always text, there is no provision for specifying the size or type of the data to be displayed in the control.

2. Select datAddresses_Database from the list.
3. Select the DataField property of the First Name text box, and pull down the list of available fields as shown in Figure 10.12.

FIGURE 10.12
The list of available fields.

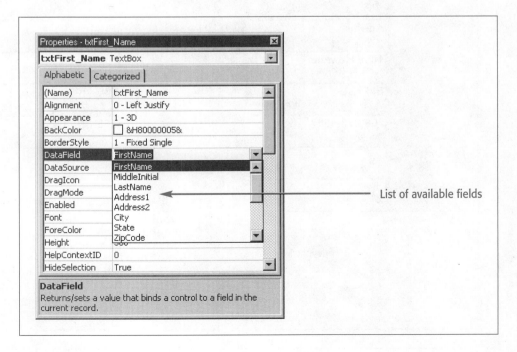

List of available fields

This particular table is made up of a lot of fields. There is one field for each of the text boxes you created on the tab. Selecting one of these causes the data in that field in the database to be copied into the bound control as the program is executing.

4. Select the First Name field.

5. Follow the same steps just given to set up the fields for the rest of the text boxes, and then save the program.

Now that the text boxes are set up, we are ready to run the program.

6. Run the program and select the **Address List** tab. The text boxes will immediately be filled with data. Your form should look like the one shown in Figure 10.13.

Note that there are no data in some of the fields. When you are creating an application such as this one, not every record will necessarily have data for all the fields. When there are no data for the field, it is merely left blank (or empty).

Changing from One Record to Another

The record you see on your form is the first one in the file. You will always get the first record in the file when the file is first opened. The record displayed is called the **current record** because it is the one currently being displayed. The data control lets you change the current record by moving from one record to the next and jumping to the first or last record. Record movement is controlled by the arrows on the ends of the data control, as you saw at the beginning of this chapter.

FIGURE 10.13
The data extracted from the database.

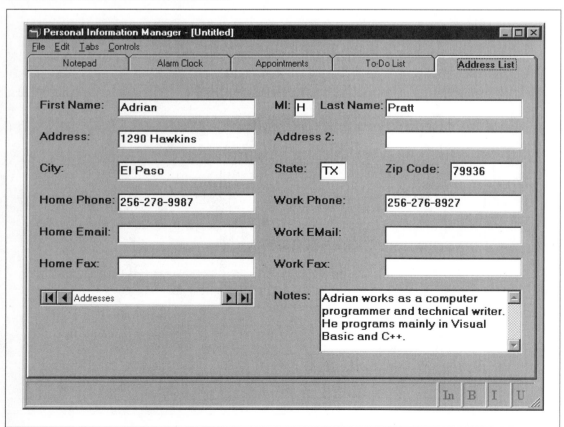

The arrows at the ends of the control move the current record to either the first or the last record in the file, whereas the inside arrows move to the next or previous record. If the current record is already the first or last record, the arrows to move further in that direction will do nothing.

1. Click the next record arrow (▶) to move to the record for Bobby Smith.
2. Click the last record arrow (▶|) to move to the last record in the file, and the record for William West will appear. This is the last record in the file.
3. Try all four of the movement controls until it is clear to you what is happening.

Changing the Data in the Database

The data control not only gives you access to the records in the database but also lets you change them.

1. Change to the first record in the table. Note that the Home Email field is empty.
2. Key **APratt@YYY.Com** and then select another record.
3. Return to the first record, and you see that the Home Email field is still **APratt@YYY.Com**.

This means the data in the record were changed when you moved to the next record. When you move from a changed record to another one, the changed data are automatically written into the database.

4. Change a few other pieces of data until it is clear what is happening, and then exit the program. Don't be afraid of making changes to the database. After all, you can always recopy the database file to have a fresh copy if you need to.

The ReadOnly Property

If you are creating a program in which the users should not be able to change the data in the database, you can set the **ReadOnly** property to True (it defaults to False). Then, when the program is used and the user tries to change the data, the changes will simply be ignored. Though Visual Basic does not give the user any indication that the changes were not saved, you can set up a routine of your own to give the user some type of warning message indicating that the changes have not been saved.

> **HINT:** You can also specify access rules, such as read-only, during runtime by using the **Options** property.

1. Select the data control and change the ReadOnly property to True.
2. Run the program, switch to the **Address List** tab, change the data in the First Name field in the first record, and then move to another record.
3. Change back to the first record, and you see that the First Name is back to what it was before you changed it. That is, the changes you made were not used to update the database.

Note that you didn't receive any type of notice that you cannot update the data. We can fix that easily. Each bound control has a special runtime property called **DataChanged** that you can test to see if the data in the control were changed. If DataChanged is True, the data were changed. Otherwise, DataChanged will be False.

To check the value of DataChanged as we move from one record to the next, we need to use one of the available events for the data control.

4. Exit the program, call up the code window for the **Validate** property of the Data Control, and key the following If Test:

```
If txtFirst_Name.DataChanged = True Then
   MsgBox "This database is Data Locked so your changes were not
   ↳ saved.", vbExclamation, "Data Change Warning"
End If
```

Now if you change the data in the First Name field and then move the database to another record, you will get an error.

5. Run the program, change the value of the First Name, and select another record. The warning dialog box appears as predicted.

6. Exit the dialog box, change one of the other fields, and move to a new record.

This time the warning message did not appear. That's because the given code checks for changes only to the First Name field. Changes to any other field will not produce the warning. If you want the message to appear when any of the fields is changed, which is the proper thing to do, you need to modify the If Test so that it will check for changes to all the fields.

7. Change the If Test statement to (remember that the underline (_) tells Visual Basic that the statement continues on the next line)

```
If datAddresses_Database.ReadOnly = True And _
   (txtFirst_Name.DataChanged = True Or _
   txtMiddle_Initial.DataChanged = True Or _
   txtLast_Name.DataChanged = True Or _
   txtAddress_1.DataChanged = True Or _
   txtAddress_2.DataChanged = True Or _
   txtCity.DataChanged = True Or _
   txtState.DataChanged = True Or _
   txtZip_Code.DataChanged = True Or _
   txtHome_Phone.DataChanged = True Or _
   txtWork_Phone.DataChanged = True Or _
   txtHome_EMail.DataChanged = True Or _
   txtWork_EMail.DataChanged = True Or _
   txtHome_Fax.DataChanged = True Or _
   txtWork_Fax.DataChanged = True Or _
   txtNotes.DataChanged = True) Then
```

8. Change the data in one of the fields and move to another record. This time the warning message does appear.

We changed the If Test to test for **ReadOnly** because not only can you specify that the database is read-only during design time, but you can also do it during runtime by using the ReadOnly property. On the datAddresses_Database.ReadOnly part of the If Test, "datAddresses_Database" refers to the particular data control (and database table) we want to protect. We used the datAddresses_Database.ReadOnly test because we don't want the warning message to appear if the file is no longer read-only. To set up the program so that we can change the read-only status, we will add a menu item.

9. Open the Menu Editor and add a separator line under the **Font** submenu of the **Edit** menu. Then add an **&Address List Data Locked** item with the control name **mnuData_Locked**. Make sure it is checked, because we will leave the ReadOnly property turned on in the beginning.

10. Exit the menu system and open the code window for the **Data Locked** menu item.

To change the state of the ReadOnly property, we first have to discover whether it is currently on. That will require the following If Test statement:

```
If datAddresses_Database.ReadOnly Then
```

11. Key this statement into the procedure.

Now, if it is read-only, we will need to change the ReadOnly property to **False**. We will also need to uncheck the menu item. This will give us the following two statements:

```
datAddresses_Database.ReadOnly = False
mnuData_Locked.Checked = False
```

12. Key these statements into the procedure.

If a database file is opened as read-only, just changing the value of the ReadOnly property is not enough. Visual Basic cannot change the status of an open file. The file needs to be closed and then reopened. This is not as difficult as it sounds, however, because both steps can be done with the **Refresh** method:

```
datAddresses_Database.Refresh
```

13. Key this statement into the procedure.

For the Else part of the If Test, we need to turn on the ReadOnly property and check the menu item (as well as refresh the file):

```
Else
    datAddresses_Database.ReadOnly = True
    mnuData_Locked.Checked = True
    datAddresses_Database.Refresh
End If
```

14. Key this statement into the procedure. This will give you the procedure shown in Figure 10.14.

That's all there is to it. Now we can test the program to make sure the changes worked properly.

15. Run the program, switch to the **Address List** tab, change one of the fields, and move to another record. The warning message should appear. Exit the message and move back to the first record. The data should be as they were originally (not changed).

FIGURE 10.14
The code for the mnuData_Locked_Click event procedure.

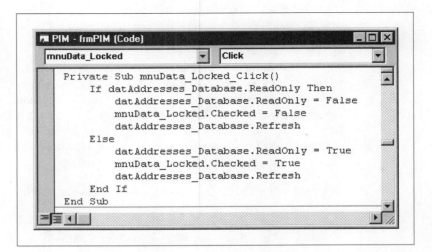

16. Pull down the **Edit** menu and select the **Address List Data Locked** item so that the file can be updated.

17. Change the Home Fax number and move to the next record. The warning message did not appear.

18. Move back to the first record, and the Home Fax number should be the one you just changed it to.

19. Change the program back and forth from ReadOnly, and change (and do not change) some records until you are sure the program is functioning properly; then exit the program.

10.6   Searching for a Record

There are only a few records in this sample database, but most databases contain a lot of data, and finding the particular record you are interested in can sometimes be a real chore. In such cases you want to be able to look up a record by one of the fields in the database. Because our database contains names and addresses, we would probably want to look up a record using the name. If we enter a name in the First Name field and then tell the program to find the record with that entry in the First Name field, and the program finds the record, it will automatically move to that record. Then, if we have the program set to ReadOnly, the program will not be able to move to the found record because it cannot change the data in the First Name field. Furthermore, if we don't have it set as ReadOnly, the first name of the current record will be changed to the name we keyed as the program shifts to the found record. Thus, if we want to give the program a name to search for, we must do it with a separate field.

1. Add the button and text box (control name **txtFind_First_Name**) to your display as shown in Figure 10.15.

There are a large number of methods and statements you can use with databases, and we will cover a number of them in this chapter. The one we need right now is the **FindFirst** method, which has the following format:

```
Object.Recordset.FindFirst Searchcriteria
```

RecordSet is the method that lets you access the records that the data control points to. **FindFirst** tells Visual Basic to find the first instance of whatever is specified in the **Searchcriteria**.

What we need to find is a first name that is the same as the one found in the new text box. We will need a statement like

```
datAddresses_Database.Recordset.FindFirst "FirstName = '" &
 txtFind_First_Name.Text & "'"
```

"FirstName = '" represents the field in the database that you are looking up. Note the single quote within the quotation marks. It is necessary to put the element you are looking for inside quotes, and the easiest way is to use single quotes within the quotation marks around the field name. Then **txtFind_First_Name.Text** is the particular data item you are looking for in the field. If txtFind_First_Name.Text contains "Fred", the above Searchcriteria would look like this after being translated:

```
FirstName = 'Fred'
```

We are looking for the first record in the database in which the FirstName field is Fred.

> **HINT:** Visual Basic also has the **FindLast**, **FindNext**, and **FindPrevious** commands.

FIGURE 10.15
The Address list with the new button and text box.

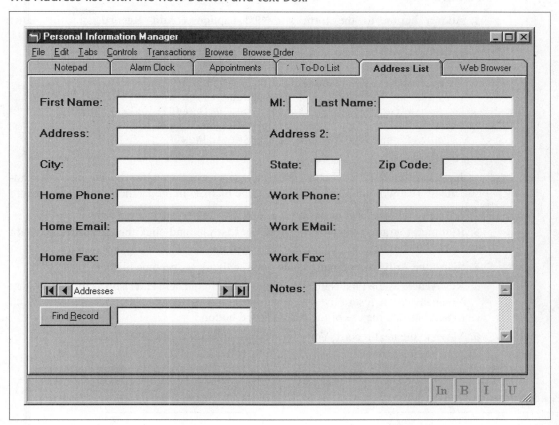

2. Key the FindFirst statement specified earlier.

Now, if everything works as it should, a new record should show up in the text boxes when we key a first name in the entry box and click the button.

3. Run the program, switch to the **Address List** tab, key **Mary** in the entry box, and click the button. The record for Mary Smith shows up.

4. Key **Tom** in the entry box and click the button.

Note that the display changes back to the record for Adrian. Because you asked for the first record that had "Tom" in it and there aren't any, the program automatically gives you the first record.

Adding New Records

One of the more important features of a database program is its capability to let us add new records to the file. This is done in Visual Basic by first creating a blank record to put the new record into and then saving that new record. The blank record is created with the **AddNew** method, which has the format

```
Object.Recordset.AddNew
```

This method does two things. It moves from the current record, saving any changes made to that record if changes are allowed, and then blanks all the bound controls so that you can input the data for the new record. After the new record is keyed, you simply move to another record with the data control, as you have been doing, and the new record is added to the end of the file.

1. Add a button to the form with the caption **&Add Record** and the name **cmdAdd_Button** as shown in Figure 10.16.

2. Open the code window for the button, and key the following If Test:

```
If datAddresses_Database.ReadOnly Then
    MsgBox "This database is Locked so you are unable to add any
    ↳new records.", vbExclamation,"Data Addition Warning"
Else
    datAddresses_Database.RecordSet.AddNew
End If
```

Just as we warn the user who tries to change a record when the database table is read-only, this If Test will not allow the record to be blanked in preparation for the new record if the setting is read-only.

3. Run the program, switch to the **Address List** tab, and click the **Address List Data Locked** menu item so that the file isn't read-only.

4. Select the **Add Record** button, and you see the fields become blank.

5. Key **Acacia** as the First Name, **H** as the Middle Initial, and **Harrison** as the Last Name. You can add the rest of the data if you wish, but the three name fields are all we need to demonstrate the use of the **Add Record** button.

6. Move to the next record. Your new record has been added to the file.

FIGURE 10.16
The tab with the **Add Record** button added.

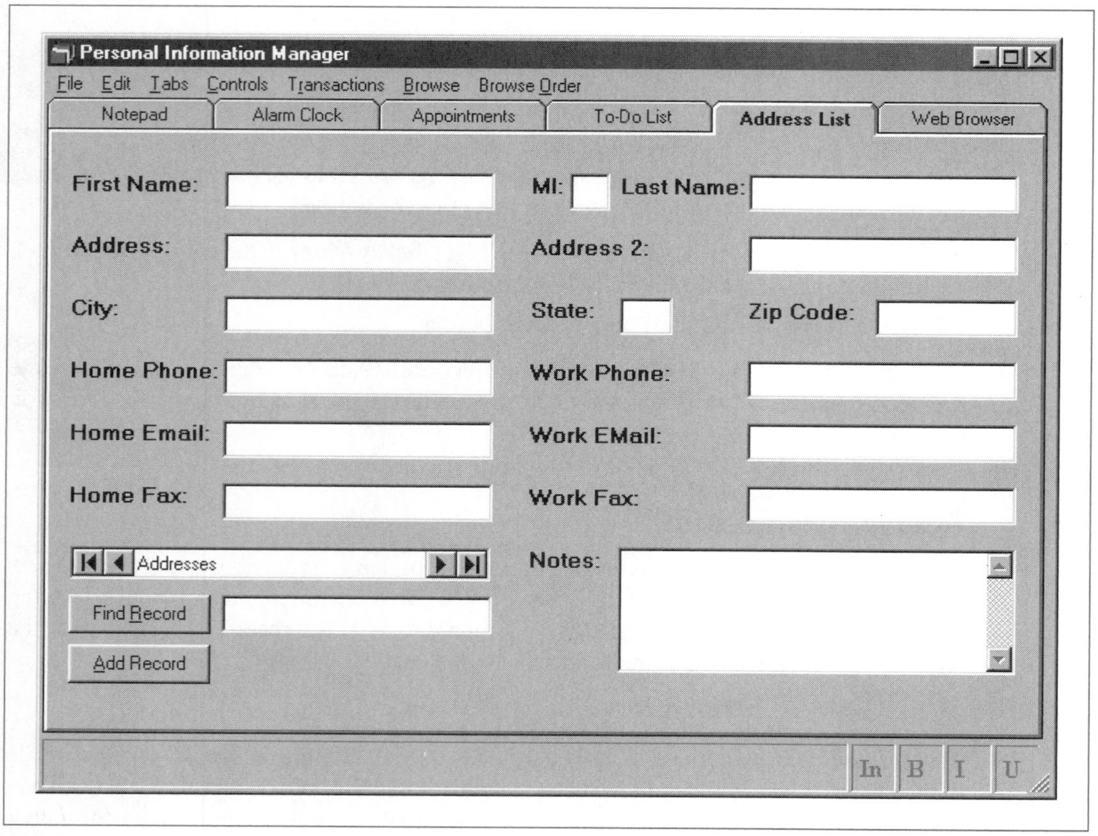

The table is indexed by the First Name, Middle Initial, and Last Name. That means the data are ordered by the First Name because this is the first field of the index, and because Acacia is lower than any other First Name in the file (Adrian was the first before), our new record should be the first record in the file.

7. Move to the first record in the file.

This isn't the Acacia record you just added. If you remember, it was stated earlier that the new record is stored at the end of the file.

8. Move to the last record in the file.

Now you have located the new record. But if the records are supposed to be in the order of the names, and the name on the new record is the lowest in the file, why isn't the new record at the beginning of the file? Visual Basic doesn't take the time to reorganize database files as new records are added. This is done only when the file is closed, and the file is closed only when the program is exited or you close the file in code.

9. Exit the program and run it again, and you see the new record at the beginning of the file.

Refreshing the File

Suppose you don't want to have to exit and restart the program just to put the records in their proper places. Well, earlier we learned about the Refresh command, which opens and closes the file. Here is another instance where this command can be useful.

1. Exit the program and add a second button next to the first one with the caption **Refre&sh** and the control name **cmdRefresh_Button**. Figure 10.17 shows the addition of this button.

2. Open the code window for the new button, and key the following statement:

```
datAddresses_Database.Refresh
```

3. Run the program, switch to the **Address List** tab, and change the **Address List Data Locked** menu item so that the file isn't read-only.

4. Click the **Add Record** button. Key **Able** as the First Name, **P** as the Middle Initial, and **Andrews** as the Last Name.

5. Move to the next record and then move to the last record in the file, and you see the record you just added.

6. Select the **Refresh** button. You will automatically be back at the first record in the file as a consequence of the Refresh command. Note that your record is now the first one.

7. Exit the program and save it.

Deleting Records

If you are going to be able to add new records, it stands to reason that you will also want to be able to delete them. All it takes is the **Delete** method, which has a format similar to that of the AddNew method:

```
Object.Recordset.Delete
```

Because deleting records is not something you want the user to do by accident, we will use a dialog box to verify that the user actually intends to delete the record. We will begin by adding the button.

1. Add a third button to the form with the caption **&Delete** and the control name **cmdDelete_Button** as shown in Figure 10.18.

FIGURE 10.17
The form with the **Refresh** button added.

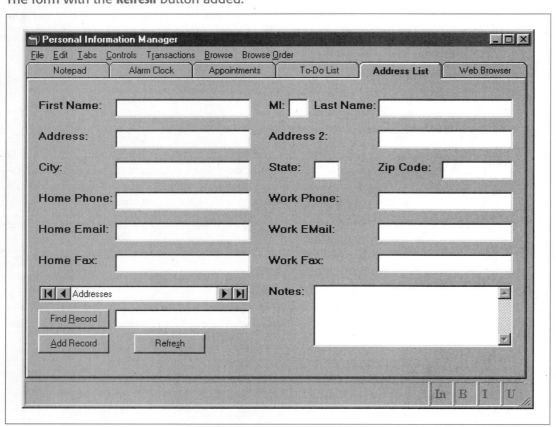

2. Open the code window for the new button, and key the following statements:

```
intResult = MsgBox("You have indicated you want to delete the
↳ current record. Is this what you intended?", vbYesNo +
↳ vbQuestion, "Record Deletion Warning")
If intResult = vbYes Then
    datAddresses_Database.Recordset.Delete
```

Just executing this statement will only delete the record. It will not change the current record, and even though the current record is now deleted, the data will remain in the bound controls. What you need to do is move to the next record so that the deletion will be registered. This can be done by the user with the data control, of course, but in this case we will want to move to the next record in the code with the **MoveNext** method, which has the same format as the other methods:

```
Object.Recordset.MoveNext
```

HINT: Visual Basic also has the **MovePrevious**, **MoveFirst,** and **MoveLast** methods, which correspond to the movement arrows on the data control.

3. Key the following statements:

```
    datAddresses_Database.RecordSet.MoveNext
End If
```

FIGURE 10.18
The last button to be added.

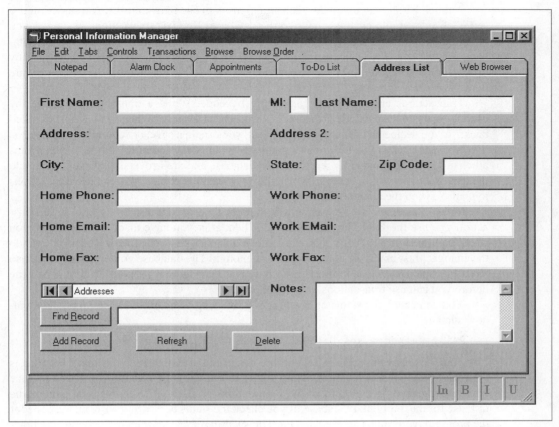

4. Run the program, change to the **Address List** tab, and change the **Address List Data Locked** menu item so that the file isn't read-only.

   The first record in the file is one we have added, so it should be okay to delete it.

5. Select the **Delete** button, and the dialog box appears. Click **Yes**, and the next record in the database appears. Because we are now on the next record, we need to verify that the record is actually gone.

6. Move to the first record in the file. The record should not have changed because you just deleted the previous record, which was the first record, and the current record is now the first record.

7. Add a new record to the file, refresh the file, and then delete that new record.

8. Do this a few more times until you are certain the program is working properly. Then exit the program.

10.7   Using Transactions

One of the problems with databases is recovering the data when someone makes an error keying data or deleting records. Suppose, for example, you are using this program to access your Addresses database and you delete the wrong record. The only way to get the data back is to rekey it or restore it from a backup, if you are lucky enough to have a backup current enough to get back the deleted record without erasing other changes you may have made to the file before deleting the record.

A much better way to handle such situations is to use **transactions.** A transaction is a series of recoverable changes made to the database. You use transactions whenever you want the opportunity to verify a series of changes before committing the data to the database. For example, if you are using some type of financial database and are making a lengthy series of changes, you might want to be able to cancel all the changes if the final totals are out of balance.

Transactions are controlled completely by code. While a transaction is open, any changes made to the database are stored in the transaction and can then be undone, or "rolled back." If you decide all the changes are correct, you can then save, or "commit," the changes.

Normally, when you first open a database, it is in "auto-commit" mode, which means all changes are automatically written to the database and are irreversible (unless you undo the changes by hand). In cases in which this is not a good choice, you can use transactions to control when the changes are to occur.

Visual Basic has three commands to support the use of transactions. To start a transaction you use the **BeginTrans** command. Then, after you have made your changes, you use either the **CommitTrans** command to save the changes to the file or **Rollback** to undo the changes. Just using the commands is not enough. The database you are using must also have the capability to use transactions. There is a **Transaction** property that must be True before you can use transactions on the database.

You can check the status of this property by using a statement in the immediate window such as

```
Print datAddresses_Database.Database.Transactions
```

You could also have used an If Test before you used the BeginTrans command, but that is unnecessary. Once a database is set up, either it will allow transactions or it won't. Once you have checked on the status of the Transactions property, it will always be either True or False for that particular database. If you check the status before you write all the code for the program, you can be assured that the Transaction status will remain the same, and however you use transactions in your program will be correct.

It is important to note that transactions are not tied to one database. That is, if you have a program that uses data from several databases at the same time, and a transaction has recorded changes to these databases, when the data are either committed or rolled back, the pending changes in all the affected databases are either committed or rolled back.

Let's begin by checking to be sure our database will allow transactions.

1. Run the program and pause it.

2. Key **Print datAddresses_Database.Database.Transactions** in the immediate window. The result should be –1, which indicates True. Therefore, this database will allow us to use transactions.

Although you can use multiple transactions—that is, you can have several active transactions going at the same time—we will create our program so that there is only one transaction in use. We will use a menu to put our three transaction commands in, and initially, only the **Begin Transaction** option will be available. Then, after the transaction has begun, we will turn the **Begin Transaction** option off and turn the other two options on.

3. Exit the program, open the Menu Editor, and add the following after the **Controls** menu:
   a. **T&ransactions** as the menu name.
   b. **&Begin Transaction** with the control name **mnuBegin_Trans** as the first menu item.
   c. A separator bar.
   d. **&Roll back all changes** with the control name **mnuRoll_Back**, making sure it is disabled (Enabled check box turned off).

e. &Commit all changes with the control name **mnuCommit,** making sure it is disabled.

Another consideration is that a transaction must have somewhere to store the changes you are making to the database. This requires you to set up a database **workspace** for the program.

4. Exit the Menu Editor, change to the module, and key the following statement:

```
Global gwrkAddresses As Workspace
```

Workspace is a defined type that Visual Basic uses for things such as database and transaction storage. What the workspace is used for is determined by the way the program uses it.

5. Open the code window for the **Begin Transaction** option.

First we need to set up the workspace for use with the statement

```
Set gwrkAddresses = DBEngine.Workspaces(0)
```

This statement defines the workspace as a workspace for the **DBEngine**, or the DataBase Engine, which is the tool Visual Basic uses to talk to databases.

Then we need to begin the transaction within the defined workspace, using the statement

```
wrkAddresses.BeginTrans
```

To finish the routine, we need to turn off the menu item for beginning the transaction and turn on the menu items for the rollback and commit.

HINT: When working with transactions, remember that the database must not be read-only when you turn on the transaction. Otherwise, the BeginTrans statement will be ignored.

6. Key the two statements given above and add the three commands for the menu items as:

```
mnuBegin_Trans.Enabled = False
mnuRoll_Back.Enabled = True
mnuCommit.Enabled = True
```

7. Switch to the code window for the **mnuRoll_Back_Click** procedure, and key the following statements:

```
    intResult = MsgBox ("You have indicated that you want to roll
  ⮡ back all the changes you have made to this database. This
  ⮡ means that they will all be undone and none will be stored in
  ⮡ the file. Is this what you want to do?", vbYesNo +
  ⮡ vbExclamation, "Roll Back Warning")
If intResult = vbYes Then
    gwrkAddresses.RollBack
    datAddresses_Database.Refresh
    mnuBegin_Trans.Enabled = True
    mnuRoll_Back.Enabled = False
    mnuCommit.Enabled = False
End If
```

Two things are important in this routine. First, we roll back the transactions in the workspace. Then we also refresh the database. Without this refresh, the displayed database would consist of just the rolled-back transactions. By refreshing the database, we get back to the original database that existed before the transaction.

8. Switch to the code window for the **mnuCommit_Click** procedure, and key the following statements:

```
    intResult = MsgBox ("You have indicated that you want to commit
    ⤷ all the changes you have made to this database. This means
    ⤷ that they will all be irreversibly stored in the file. Is
    ⤷ this what you want to do?", vbYesNo + vbExclamation, "Commit
    ⤷ Warning")
If intResult = vbYes Then
    gwrkAddresses.CommitTrans
    mnuBegin_Trans.Enabled = True
    mnuRoll_Back.Enabled = False
    mnuCommit.Enabled = False
End If
```

Though we need to refresh the database after a rollback, it is important that we not refresh the file while in the midst of a transaction, or the changes will be lost just as though we had used the RollBack command. Thus, we should put an If Test in the code for the **Refresh** button.

9. Switch to the code window for the **Refresh** button, and build an If Test around the existing statement as follows:

```
If Begin_Trans.Enabled Then
    datAddresses_Database.Refresh
Else
    MsgBox "You cannot refresh the file while a transaction is
    ⤷ active. Conclude your transaction first.", vbExclamation,
    ⤷ "Refresh Warning"
End If
```

We still aren't quite finished. When we are using workspaces with transactions, Visual Basic needs some additional reference tools added. This is done using the **References...** option on the **Project** menu.

10. Select the **References...** option on the **Project** menu.

Now you see a dialog box much like the dialog box for adding components. The one you need to add is the **Microsoft DAO 3.51 Object Library**.

11. Find this item in the list, and click the check box to turn it on. Exit the dialog box.

With all these changes, there are several things we must test.

12. Run the program, switch to the **Address List** tab, and turn off the **Data Locked** menu item.

13. Make a change to the first record in the file, and move to another record and then back to be sure the program can still make changes.

14. Select the **Begin Transaction** option, and then pull down the menu to be sure the other two items are now enabled.

15. Select the **Refresh** button to be sure the message appears as it is supposed to, and then exit the message box.

16. Make a change to the first record in the file, move to another record, and then move back to the first record.

Note that the record is changed. The difference is that this change has not been sent to the database yet. It is only temporary.

17. Select the **Commit all changes** item, and the warning box appears. Click the **Yes** button, and then move to another record and back to the first record. The record is still changed. Now the change is permanent.

18. Select the **Begin Transaction** option, change the first record, and move to another record and back. The change is still there.

19. Select the **Roll back all changes** option, click the **Yes** button, and the change is undone.

20. Make other changes that are committed and rolled back. Do this several times until you are convinced the program is working properly. Then exit the program and save it.

Remember that you can actually use several transactions at the same time. We chose to use only one to avoid complicating matters. You can experiment with using multiple transactions on your own if you wish.

10.8   Using SQL

Thus far, when accessing a database table, we have been using the entire table. There will be times, however, when you want to see not all the data but only a selected part of the data. For example, you may want to see just the records for those people who live in a particular state. To designate a part of the table, you can specify a **query** using **SQL**, or **Structured Query Language.** A query is simply a series of "English-like" commands and parameters that have special meaning to the underlying databases. When the query returns the specified part of the database, it is called a **Dynaset** (for dynamic set) because it is dynamic, or changeable.

A query is created with a **Select** statement. Because the format of the Select is complicated, with many pieces, it is easier to look at an example and break it down. For instance, we want to see a list of the addresses that have Texas as the entry in the State field. We would use a query similar to

```
Select * From Addresses Where [State] = 'TX'
```

The query begins with the **Select** command. All queries begin with this command. Following that is an asterisk. In a query you can specify which of the fields of the table you want to capture in the Dynaset. This position of the query is where the fields are specified. The asterisk (called a **wildcard character**) simply means to put all the fields from the table into the Dynaset. If we wanted just the first and last name and the home phone number, for example, we would specify the first part of the Select statement as

```
Select FirstName, LastName, HomePhone
```

rather than

```
Select *
```

Next comes the table we want to access, **Addresses**. If we didn't want to limit the query, we could stop the query here. But if we used the query

```
Select * From Addresses
```

we would simply get all the fields from the Addresses table.

Note that we used the name of the database table, not the name of the data control. Because we are going to use this query to create the Dynaset for the data control, we don't use the name of the data control in the query.

Where is the keyword that indicates we want a further classification of our query. Following Where, we have to specify what limiting specifications we want to use, such as **[State] = 'TX'** in our sample. When the field name is two words, we surround the name with brackets to signify the entire field name, such as **[Zip Code]**. Some database programs do not allow spaces in the field names; others do. Using brackets allows us to take care of such situations, and there is no harm in using the brackets even when the field is one word.

Finally, we enclosed the literal for the state in single quotes. This is necessary because it is a text-type entry. If we were looking up a numeric field, the quotes would not be used.

To see how a query works, we will add a menu item to the program and run the query from there.

1. Add a new menu called **&Browse** and add an item called **&SQL**.

2. Open the code window for the new **SQL** menu item and add the following code:

```
datAddresses_Database.RecordSource = "Select * From Addresses
↳ Where [State] = 'TX'"
datAddresses_Database.Refresh
```

We Refresh the database so the query will be used to display the database records.

3. Run the program, switch to the **Address** tab, and select the **SQL** menu item.

Note that the record displayed automatically changes to the one for Edward from TX.

4. Switch to the next record. It is a TX record also.

5. Switch to the next record. It is the last one and is TX also.

You can select from part of a field if you wish.

6. Exit the program and change the SQL statement in the **SQL** menu procedure to

```
datAddresses_Database.RecordSource = "Select * From Addresses
↳ Where left([HomePhone],3) = '256'"
```

The left function compares the area code (the first three digits) of the HomPhone field to '256' so we will find only those records.

7. Run the program, switch to the **Address** tab, and select the **SQL** menu item.

8. Look through the records and note that the HomePhone of each of them begins with 256.

An important thing to remember about such queries is that the dynaset is dynamic. It can be changed while the database is still locked.

9. Try to change some of the data, and you see that the program tells you the data are locked. Turn off the lock and try to change the data again. This time it works.

10. Try a few more uses of the SQL statement until you are thoroughly familiar with the way it works. You might try selecting all the first names that begin with a certain letter, or try to select a certain city. Then exit the program.

Browsing the Database

In order to better understand how queries work, we will add a new display to our program. One of the problems with the display we are currently using is that it shows only one record at a time. All database programs have a feature called **browse** that allows you to display many records at the same time and specify which fields you want displayed by using a query. We will add a browse display to our program.

To display the data in a table format of rows and columns as a relational database is designed, we will use a new tool called a **Grid** (or **FlexGrid** in this case).

1. Open the Components dialog box and turn on the **Microsoft FlexGrid Control 6.0**.

2. Change to the **Address List** tab, and add a grid to your Tabbed Control using the new tool shown in Figure 10.19. Use the control name **grdAddresses_Browse** and size it as shown in Figure 10.20.

3. Set the Visible property to False; we don't want the grid to hide the rest of the display when the user is not browsing the database.

FIGURE 10.19
The FlexGrid tool.

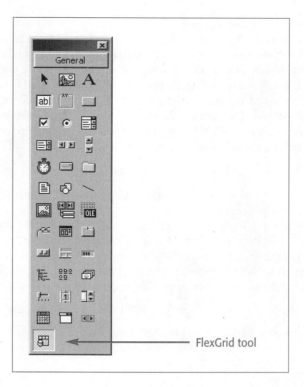

FlexGrid tool

FIGURE 10.20
The FlexGrid tool added.

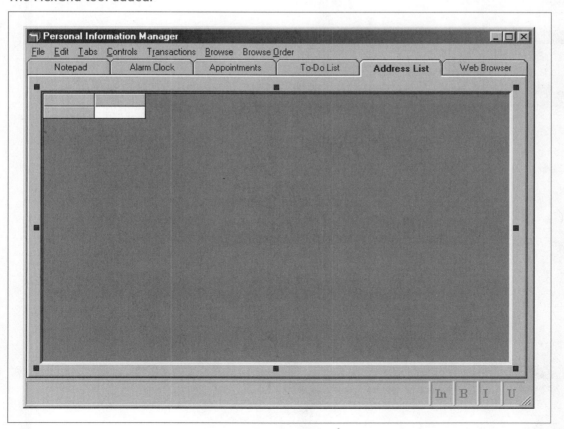

As you can see, a grid displays a series of rows and columns, the intersection of which is called a **cell.** The contents of the cells can be read from and written to during runtime. A grid is designed so the top row can contain column labels and the leftmost column can contain row labels. In our grid we need column labels, but we don't need row labels. The row and column for the labels are set up by two properties called **FixedRows** and **FixedCols.** The fixed rows and columns are displayed in a different color and do not scroll as the user scrolls the grid. They are fixed on the screen and are always displayed. The initial value for each property is 1 so that there is one fixed row and one fixed column. Because we don't want a fixed column, you need to set FixedCols to 0.

4. Change to the FixedCols property and change it to **0** (zero).

The cell in the second row and first column just became white. This is because it is no longer fixed.

We want our grid to have 14 columns (one for each of our fields) and 1000 rows so that we will have plenty of room to display our data. After we learn just how many rows there actually are by reading the records in the selected Dynaset, we will reduce the number of rows in the grid so that the data fit precisely. The number of rows and the number of columns are set by the **Rows** and **Cols** properties, respectively.

5. Change the Rows property to **1000** and the Cols property to **14**.

Now you will see a display like the one shown in Figure 10.21.

FIGURE 10.21
The updated grid.

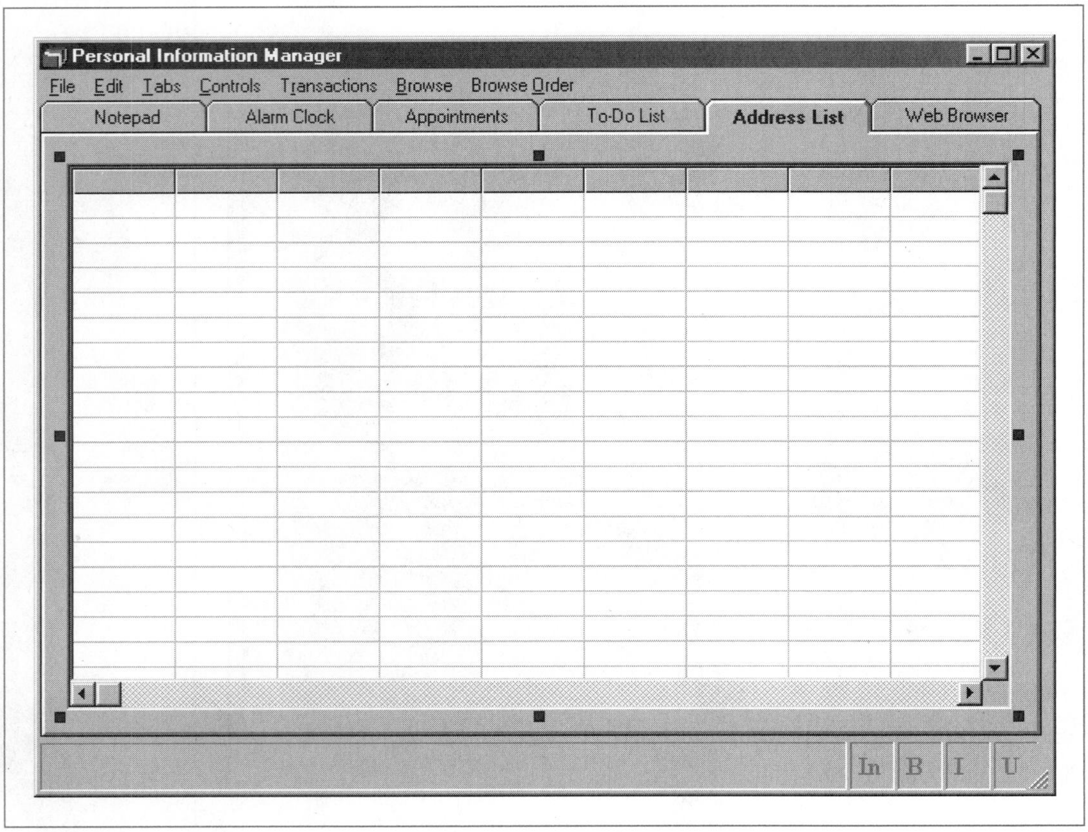

In a grid, a single cell or a group of cells can be selected. This is enabled with the **High-light** property. We don't intend to select elements in this grid, so the highlight can be turned off by changing the value of the Highlight property to False.

6. Change the Highlight property to flexHighlightNever.

To change to this display from the display of the single records, we will need to add some more menu items. We added the Browse menu when we added the SQL routine. So we simply need to add a few more items in the **Browse** menu.

7. Open the Menu Editor, add a separator line under the **SQL** menu item, and then add the following items:

    a. **&Browse Address Database** with the control name **mnuBrowse**

    b. **&Return to Single Record Display** with the control name **mnuReturn**

    c. A separator line

    d. **&Select** with the control name **mnuSelect**

The Browse Address Database will need to make the grid visible and then call a procedure to display the data. We will use a procedure so that we can display the data in more ways than the way they are displayed in the database. The statements to do these two functions are

```
grdAddresses_Browse.Visible = True
Display_Browse ("Select * From Addresses")
```

Display_Browse is the procedure we are going to set up, and we are going to pass **"Select * From Addresses"** to it as a parameter.

8. Open the code window for the **Browse Address Database** menu item, and key the two foregoing statements.

Now we need to add the procedure.

9. Move the cursor to an empty line, and key the statement

```
Sub Display_Browse(strSQL As String)
```

In Windows, when a process is going to take a bit of time, you generally see an hourglass on the screen instead of the normal cursor. This is an indication to you to wait for whatever is happening to finish. Because it may take a few seconds for Visual Basic to display the data in the grid, we will use this same technique.

There is a special property for that called **MousePointer**. It allows you to change the mouse pointer to something besides the default pointer. There are 17 pointer styles available, as shown in Table 10.1.

The one we want is the hourglass, which uses the predefined constant ccHourglass and requires the statement

```
MousePointer = ccHourglass
```

10. Key the MousePointer statement into the procedure.

Next we need to specify the widths of the columns of the grid. This requires the **ColWidth** property, which has the format

```
Gridname.ColWidth(Column number) [= Widthvalue]
```

The number of the column is used as an index for the command. For example, if you want to specify the width of the first column in the grid (which is actually column number 0), you would use the following statement:

```
grdAddresses_Browse.ColWidth(0) = 1860
```

Constant	Value	Description
ccDefault	0	(Default) Shape determined by the object.
ccArrow	1	Arrow.
ccCross	2	Cross (crosshair pointer).
ccIbeam	3	I Beam.
ccIcon	4	Icon (small square within a square).
ccSize	5	Size (four-pointed arrow pointing north, south, east, and west).
ccSizeNESW	6	Size NE SW (double arrow pointing northeast and southwest).
ccSizeNS	7	Size N S (double arrow pointing north and south).
ccSizeNWSE	8	Size NW, SE. (double arrow pointing northwest and southeast).
ccSizeEW	9	Size E W (double arrow pointing east and west).
ccUpArrow	10	Up arrow.
ccHourglass	11	Hourglass (wait).
ccNoDrop	12	No drop.
ccArrowHourglass	13	Arrow and hourglass.
ccArrowQuestion	14	Arrow and question mark.
ccSizeAll	15	Size all.
ccCustom	99	Custom icon specified by the MouseIcon property.

Normally you have to define your grid columns as a standard width and then run the application, adjust the columns to the proper width for the data, figure out which column you are looking at, and display that width. You can do this by moving the cursor over the proper statement in the code, and Visual Basic will display the width for you. Either way you do it, however, you need to determine the appropriate width of the column and then change all your ColWidth statements. To save you the trouble, we will give you the appropriate widths. They are shown in Table 10.2.

11. Key the appropriate ColWidth statements for the grid columns, following the example given earlier.

Now we need to put the column headings into the grid so the user will know what data are being displayed in each column. To do this, we need to position the cursor on the first row and move from the first column to the others as we define the titles. These positions are specified with the **Row** and **Col** properties. Thus, to position the cursor on the first row and column, we would use the statements

```
grdAddresses_Browse.Row = 0
grdAddresses_Browse.Col = 0
```

12. Key these statements.

To put the title into the cell pointed to by the Row and Col statements, you use the **Text** property:

```
grdAddresses_Browse.Text = "First Name"
```

TABLE 10.2
The widths of the columns in the grid.

Column Number	Width
0	1860
1	345
2	1860
3	1860
4	1860
5	1860
6	480
7	735
8	1125
9	1125
10	1950
11	1950
12	1125
13	1125

To put in the second title, you need to move to the next column:

```
grdAddresses_Browse.Col = 1
grdAddresses_Browse.Text = "MI"
```

You don't need another Row statement, because all the titles will be put in the first or the zeroth row.

13. Key these three statements into the procedure, and add the code for the rest of the column titles.

Next we need to do the query. You have already seen what the query looks like. This one will be similar to the one used in the SQL routine, but it will be a bit more generic because we will be using the SQL statement passed into the subroutine as the parameter. The statement we will need is

```
datAddresses_Database.RecordSource = strSQL
```

Then we need to refresh the database to cause the Dynaset to be opened for our use.

```
datAddresses_Database.Refresh
```

14. Key these two statements into the procedure.

Now we have our Dynaset and can loop through it to display the records. The Dynaset is, essentially, just like a regular table, and it is processed the same way. When the Dynaset is opened with the Refresh statement, the current record is the first one in the Dynaset. Remember, however, that the first record in the Dynaset will not necessarily be the first record in the table because not all the records in the table are in the Dynaset. They are in this case, because the SQL we specified for the Browse is to get all the data, but we have already seen how we can make the Dynaset smaller. After the first record is displayed, we can get the next record in the Dynaset by using the **MoveNext** statement.

We are going to process the Dynaset and display the data in the rows of the grid, so we will need a counter to keep track of the row where the current record should be put. The counter we will use is

```
intRow_Number = 1
```

15. Key this statement.

To process the Dynaset, we will use a Do Until loop and access the records until we reach the end of the Dynaset. In a fashion similar to file processing, we can use an **EOF** method to check for the end of the Dynaset. The Do Until command we need is

```
Do Until datAddresses_Database.RecordSet.EOF
```

16. Key this statement.

Next we need to tell Visual Basic in what column and row in the grid we are going to display the data.

```
grdAddresses_Browse.Row = intRow_Number
grdAddresses_Browse.Col = 0
```

17. Key these statements.

To put the data in the grid, we need to be able to access the specific field in the Dynaset. When we displayed the data on the other form, we used bound controls, and Visual Basic automatically placed the data for us. However, the FlexGrid control is not a bound control. We will have to specify each of the fields individually.

A Dynaset can be thought of as a sort of two-dimensional array. The current record pointer specifies the row of the Dynaset, and we specify the column or field by referencing the name of the field. Thus, to specify the First Name field would require the following statement:

```
grdAddresses_Browse.Text = datAddresses_Database.Recordset
 ⮑("FirstName")
```

Then we move to the next column with the Col statement and specify the Middle Initial field:

```
grdAddresses_Browse.Col = 1
grdAddresses_Browse.Text = datAddresses_Database.Recordset
 ⮑("MiddleInitial")
```

This same scheme is used for each of the fields.

18. Key the foregoing statements and the statements to display the rest of the fields, which have the database field names shown in Table 10.3.

Now we have a problem. If the field in the database is blank, we will get an error when we try to display it in the grid. The name fields are specified in the database not to allow blank fields, but any of the rest of the fields can be left null when the record is created or changed. We need to check whether the field in the database is null before we write it in the grid. This requires an If Test similar to the following:

```
If datAddresses_Database.Recordset("Address1") > "" Then
    grdAddresses_Browse.Text = datAddresses_Database.Recordset
     ⮑("Address1")
End If
```

19. Put If Tests around all the assignment statements.

Now we are ready to move to the next record in the Dynaset:

```
datAddresses_Database.Recordset.MoveNext
```

TABLE 10.3
The names of the fields in the Database table

Display Name	Database Name
First Name	FirstName
MI	MiddleInitial
Last Name	LastName
Address	Address1
Address2	Address2
City	City
State	State
Zip Code	ZipCode
Home Phone	HomePhone
Work Phone	WorkPhone
Home Email	HomeEmail
Work Email	WorkEmail
Home Fax	HomeFax
Work Fax	WorkFax

and to increase the row number:

```
        intRow_Number = intRow_Number + 1
Loop
```

20. Key these statements.

Now that we know how many records actually need to be displayed in the grid as given in intRow_Number, we can change the specified number of rows that the grid contains so there will be only as many rows as we have data items.

```
    grdAddresses_Browse.Rows = intRow_Number
```

21. Key this statement.

Finally, because we have finished processing the database, we can change the mouse pointer back to the default form:

```
    MousePointer = ccDefault
```

22. Key the MousePointer statement.

All that is left is to switch back to the original display from the Browse display. We have a menu item set up for this.

23. Switch to the code for the **Return to Single Record Display** menu item, and key the appropriate Visible statement to hide the Browse grid.

Now we can test the program to be sure the new code works properly.

24. Run the program, switch to the **Appointment List** tab, and select the **Browse Address Database** menu item. The grid should be displayed with the data in the appropriate columns.

25. After you have examined the display, switch back to the single-record display using the menu.

    Note that there is nothing in the display.

26. Move to the first record and then move around in the records.

    As you can see, the data are still there. The problem is that the query moved the record pointer beyond the end of the data. Not only that, but when a smaller Dynaset is selected, that Dynaset will still be selected when we switch back to the single-record display unless we reset the database by doing a query on all the data.

27. Exit the program and open the procedure for the **Return to Single Record Display** menu item.

28. Key the following two statements before the Visible statement:

    ```
    datAddresses_Database.RecordSource = "Select * From Addresses"
    datAddresses_Database.Refresh
    ```

29. Now try the program again. Switch to the Browse grid and then back to the single-record display. Note that the data appear just as they should.

30. Exit the program and save it.

Ordering the Database

Now that we have a form to browse the database, let's explore another SQL feature. One of the things you can do with a query is put the Dynaset into sequence. As you may have noticed, the Dynaset is currently displayed in first-name order. The first name is the first portion of the index of the file, so the file is automatically in that order. We can actually specify that the Dynaset be ordered on any of the fields. All that is required is adding the **Order By** keywords as part of the query, followed by the name of the field by which we want the Dynaset ordered. For example, if we wanted our Dynaset to be in last-name order, the SQL statement would be

```
Select * From Addresses Order By LastName
```

HINT: The Order By specification must be the last specification in the Select statement. For example, if you are using a Where clause, the Order By clause must follow it.

Let's add a menu system to our browse form so that we can have the file ordered by any of the four fields and in either ascending or descending order.

1. Add a new **Browse &Order** menu with submenus for **&Ascending** and **&Descending** plus a menu item for each of the 14 fields under each of the submenus. Make the set of ascending menu items a control array named **mnuAscending_Fields**, and the control array of descending menu items should be called **mnuDescending_Fields**. This will allow you to determine the menu item chosen by number.

2. Open the code window for any of the options of the **Ascending** submenu (they all use the same procedure).

   We know which field is being chosen from the menu because of the index, so we can set up a Case structure to specify the particular field needed in the Select clause by using a structure similar to the following:

```
Select Case Index
    Case 1
        Display_Browse ("Select * From Addresses Order By FirstName")
```

3. Key these statements and finish the Case structure using the database field names given in the previous section. Then use the statement to make the grid visible just in case it is not.

To display the data in descending order, all you need to do is use the **DESC** keyword following the field by which you are ordering, so the previous statement would become

```
Display_Browse ("Select * From Addresses Order By FirstName Desc")
```

4. Copy the code for the Ascending routine, switch to the code window for any of the options of the **Descending** submenu, paste the code there, and key the DESC keyword at the end of the Select statements.

5. Run the program, and test each of the new menu items to be sure they are all sorting the Browse display properly. After you have verified each of them, exit and save the program.

Selecting a Smaller Dynaset

As we mentioned earlier, you can specify a smaller Dynaset by selecting the fields you want displayed to see fewer fields or by using the Where clause to specify the type of records you want, such as those with TX as the state. We don't want to limit the number of fields displayed, because our code specifies the use of all the fields. We can, however, easily limit the number of records in the Dynaset with the Where clause. To do this, we will set up a new form for the user to select and enter the pieces of the Select clause that the Display_Browse subroutine needs.

1. Set up a new form named **frmAddresses_Selection** that looks like the one in Figure 10.22 with the following considerations:

a. Turn off the Control Box property and erase the Caption property to turn off the title bar.

b. The text box at the top is called **txtSelect_Clause** and has the Text property filled with what is shown in the figure.

c. The Display Selection button is called **cmdDisplay_Selection**.

d. The Cancel button has the control name **cmdCancel_Button**.

e. The first list is called **lstDatabase_Fields** and will contain the field names from the database.

FIGURE 10.22
The selection form.

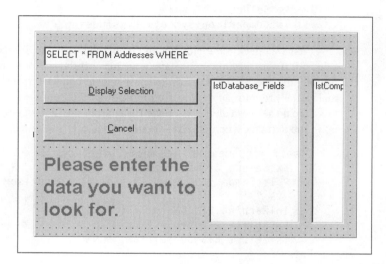

f. The second list (the narrow one) is called **lstComparison_Symbols** and will contain the various selection symbols (=, <, etc.)

g. The label with the warning in it is called **lblWarning** and has a font size of 18 with a foreground color of Red. Set the Visible property to False so that the label will not be visible initially.

What we want to do with this form is put the appropriate code in the text box, which we will then pass to the Display_Browse routine. To do this, we will give the user most of the Select clause in the text box and then let the user select the field name from the first list and the selection symbol from the second list. When the item in the list is selected, we want to append it to what is already in the text box. To do this, we need to verify that all the elements are added to the text box in the proper sequence. The label will be used to warn the user of the need to key in the appropriate data. It will be turned on after the comparison symbol is selected.

The first thing we need to do is have the **Select** menu item in the **Browse** menu call up the new form.

2. Open the code on the PIM form for the **Select** menu items, and key the statement necessary to load the Select form. Make sure it is modal.

3. Switch to the code for the lstDatabase_Fields list on the Select form.

All you need do here is add the appropriate field from the list to the end of what is already in the text box. The following statement will accomplish this:

```
txtSelect_Clause = txtSelect_Clause & " [" &
⮡ lstDatabase_Fields.List(lstDatabase_Fields.ListIndex) & "]"
```

Note that we automatically put the brackets around the field name. Again, the brackets are necessary only when the field name is made up of more than one word, but there is no harm in using the brackets, and it's a good habit to teach users in case they need to create queries of their own.

4. Key the foregoing statement.

Now we need to do the same type of thing for the symbol list. This is a bit more complicated, though, because we want to be sure the user has selected the Field Name list before selecting the symbol. We need an If Test that begins as follows:

```
If lstDatabase_Fields.ListIndex = -1 And lstComparison_
⮡ Symbols.ListIndex <> -1 Then
   MsgBox "You must select a database field for the Select
   ⮡ statement before selecting the symbol.", vbExclamation,
   ⮡ "Selection Error"
   lstComparison_Symbols.ListIndex = -1
```

First we check the Fields list and then make sure the Symbols list hasn't already been selected. If this msgbox is displayed, we turn off the symbols list, because if we are in this routine, the user or the program has just selected an item from the list. Turning the list off makes the program automatically run through this routine again. We need to be sure that there are no selected elements on the Else part of the If Test, or the selected symbol will end up in the text box when the list is being turned off. So the rest of the If Test is

```
ElseIf lstComparison_Symbols.ListIndex <> -1 Then
   txtSelect_Clause = txtSelect_Clause & " " &
   ⮡ lstComparison_Symbols.List(lstComparison_Symbols.ListIndex)
   ⮡ & " '"
   lblWarning.Visible = True
   txtSelect_Clause.SetFocus
   txtSelect_Clause.SelStart = 99
End If
```

Note here that we turned on the warning label to inform the user of the need to key the rest of the data for the Select clause. Then we moved the insertion point to the end of whatever is currently in the txtSelect_Clause text box.

5. Change to the code for the symbol list and key the foregoing If Test.

Now, as soon as the user begins to key the data, we should turn off the warning label.

6. Open the code for the text box.

You will be in the Change routine. As soon as the user begins to key into the text box, the Change routine is triggered. This is where we need to be to turn off the label.

7. Key the appropriate statement to turn off the label.

Next we need to exit the form without doing anything if the user selects the **Cancel** button.

8. Switch to the code for the **Cancel** button, and key the appropriate statement.

All we have left is the code for the **Display** button. We need to begin here with tests to be sure that both of the lists have been selected and to display an error message if they haven't. This will require code similar to

```
If lstDatabase_Fields.ListIndex = -1 Then
    MsgBox "You must select a database field for the Select
    ⮑ statement.", vbExclamation, "Selection Error"
ElseIf lstComparison_Symbols.ListIndex = -1 Then
    MsgBox "You must select a symbol for the Select statement.",
    ⮑ vbExclamation, "Selection Error"
```

9. Key these statements.

Then we need to make sure, insofar as possible, that the user has keyed the appropriate data to finish the Select clause. We can make sure there is a single quote at the end, but that is not enough. We have already placed a single quote in the text box following the selected symbol. We also need to be certain that the warning label has been turned off, because this is done only after the user has keyed something into the text box. So we need to add the following to the If Test:

```
ElseIf Right(txtSelect_Clause, 1) <> "'" Or lblWarning.Visible =
⮑ True Then
    MsgBox "You must enter the data you want to select surrounded
    ⮑ by single quotes on the end of the Select statement.",
    ⮑ vbExclamation, "Selection Error"
    txtSelect_Clause.SetFocus
    txtSelect_Clause.SelStart = 99
```

10. Key these statements.

Then we are ready to display the data on the Browse grid by finishing the If Test with

```
Else
    frmPIM.Display_Browse (txtSelect_Clause)
    frmPIM.grdAddresses_Browse.Visible = True
    Unload frmAddresses_Selection
End If
```

11. Key this code.

Now it is time to test the program.

12. Run the program, switch to the **Address List** tab, select the **Select** menu item, pick **State** in the Field list and = in the Symbol list, and key **TX'** for the data. Click the **Display Selection** button, and make sure that only records with TX in the state field are in the list.

13. Try other combinations and make sure the error tests are working. When you have checked everything, exit the program.

> **HINT:** You can, of course, combine your selection query with the ordering queries we created earlier. One method of doing so is to check the menu item for the order you selected and then test for the checked item in a fashion similar to the way we tested for the disabled button. Once found, the Order By code is added to the query. Remember that the Order By clause must be at the end.

10.9 Accessing External Databases

To access an **external** database like those created with programs such as **FoxPro, Paradox,** and **dBASE,** your data control will need to specify the **Connect** property. This property simply tells Visual Basic what database program the database came from and what the password is, if one is necessary. To see how this works, we will access a database that was created in **FoxPro 2.5**®.

1. Open a new project and add a data control.
2. Key **A:\CH-10** into the DatabaseName property for the data control. Note that the name of the database is not part of this entry. With external databases, the name of the database is put in the RecordSource property.
3. Key **School** in the RecordSource property.
4. Key **FoxPro 2.5** in the Connect property.
5. Add two text boxes to the form.
6. Use the name of the data control as the DataSource for both text boxes.
7. Use the Last_Name field for the DataField property of the first text box and the First_Name field for the DataField property of the second text box.
8. Save the program as **External**.
9. Run the program, and you should have George as the last name and Monica L. as the first name. Change to a few more records to verify that the data control is functioning properly and then exit the program.

10.10 A Few More Comments

We have only scratched the surface of the processing power of Visual Basic when it comes to databases. We could write an entire book just on using databases in Visual Basic. Indeed, such books have been written. You can find them at your local bookstore if you want more information on Visual Basic and databases.

Though we do not intend to spend any more time working through database access code, we feel it is important to mention a few more important things regarding Visual Basic and databases.

Visual Basic has an entire series of **aggregate functions** for finding things such as

- The first or last record in a series
- The minimum or maximum value in a series

- How many records meet the specified criteria
- The sum or average of a specified field in the Dynaset

You can limit the number of records in a Dynaset by using keywords such as **Distinct** and **DistinctRow**. For example, you could use a query to select records so that there would be no duplicates in the name field.

You can also combine tables from the same database or different databases by joining them on a field that is common to both tables. For example, we could have a separate table in the Addresses database that has the state names rather than the abbreviations. Then we could join the Addresses and State Name tables on the state field, and then the Dynaset would contain not only the state field (the code) but also the name of the state from the State Name table. This would allow us to display the state name instead of the abbreviation.

The Data Control gives you easy access to the database fields. Sometimes, however, you may want to access the database without using the Data Control. This is done through the **OpenDatabase** method. After the database is opened, the program can move through the elements of the database recordset just as we specified for accessing the records of the Dynaset when we set up the browse function. Then the data are displayed field by field with statements similar to the ones we used:

```
grdAddresses_Browse.Text = datAddresses_Database.Recordset
  ("FirstName")
```

This is the form we used in this chapter. Another form that this statement can take is

```
grdAddresses_Browse.Text = datAddresses_Database.Recordset!
  FirstName
```

This gives you a database field reference of Recordset!FirstName instead of Recordset ("FirstName"). You can use whichever form you find more convenient.

Even this list of additional functions doesn't begin to do justice to the power of Visual Basic and databases. This book doesn't cover all the database possibilities, and neither does the Visual Basic user's guide. The Help system has more information than the Visual Basic user's guide, but without knowing what you are looking for, you will find it of little value. You will need to use an outside source for further study.

10.11 The Visual Data Manager

To use Visual Basic as an interface to a database, you have to have a database. It's best to have the appropriate database program (such as Microsoft Access) to use to create your databases, but when you don't, Visual Basic has a special **Add-Ins** program called the **Visual Data Manager** that can be used to create and manipulate databases. The Visual Data Manager can be used to add records to and delete records from the database as well as to search for information in the database.

Creating the Patients Table

We will use the VisData program to create a database to store data about dental patients.

1. Pull down the **Add-Ins** menu and select the **Visual Data Manager...** option to see the form of the VisData program as shown in Figure 10.23.

The first thing we need to do is create a new database. This is done with the **New** option of the **File** menu.

FIGURE 10.23
The Visual Data
Manager.

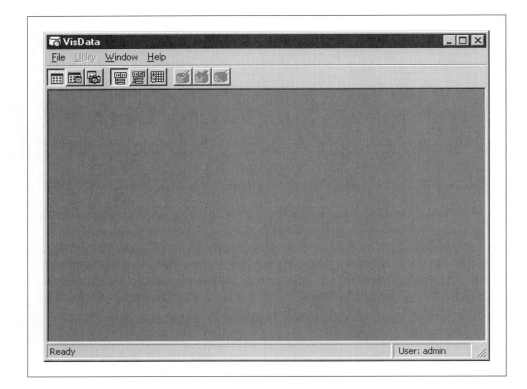

2. Pull down the **File** menu and select the **New** option. This presents you with a list of database formats you can use to create the database. Highlight **Microsoft Access** and select **Version 7.0 MDB** from the next submenu.

3. Select the Ch-10 folder on your work disk using the dialog box presented. Key **Patients** in the Filename text box, and click the *Save* button. This will present you with two new workspaces within the VisData workspace as shown in Figure 10.24 (the workspace arrangement may be different).

You have just created a new database. The two workspaces allow you to work with that database. The SQL workspace allows you to create queries for the database, whereas the Database Window workspace shows the various components of the database. Currently, the only components of the database are the properties of the database itself.

The first thing to do with a new database is to specify what tables are to be in the database and, with these, what fields. This means we need to define a new table.

4. Right-click the Properties entry in the Database Window workspace and select **New Table** from the small menu that appears. This will present you with the dialog box shown in Figure 10.25.

The first table we want to create is called **Patient Data**.

5. Key **Patient Data** in the Table Name entry box, and then click the **Add Field** button to see the dialog box shown in Figure 10.26.

For each of the fields in the database table, we must specify a unique name, the type of field, and the size. The field types available are given in Table 10.4. These data types are defined essentially the same way they are in Visual Basic itself.

All of these field types except Text have a predefined field size that cannot be changed. You can specify the length of a text field.

The first field that needs to be set up is the Last Name field.

FIGURE 10.24
The workspaces for the
new Patients database.

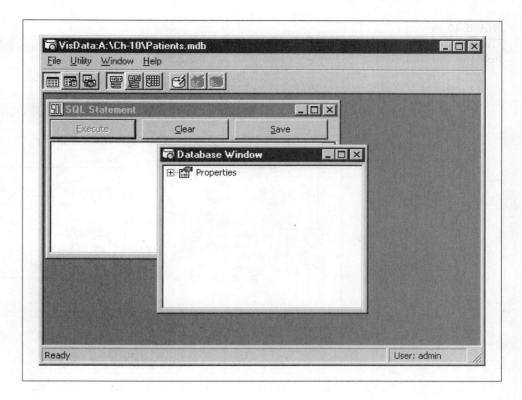

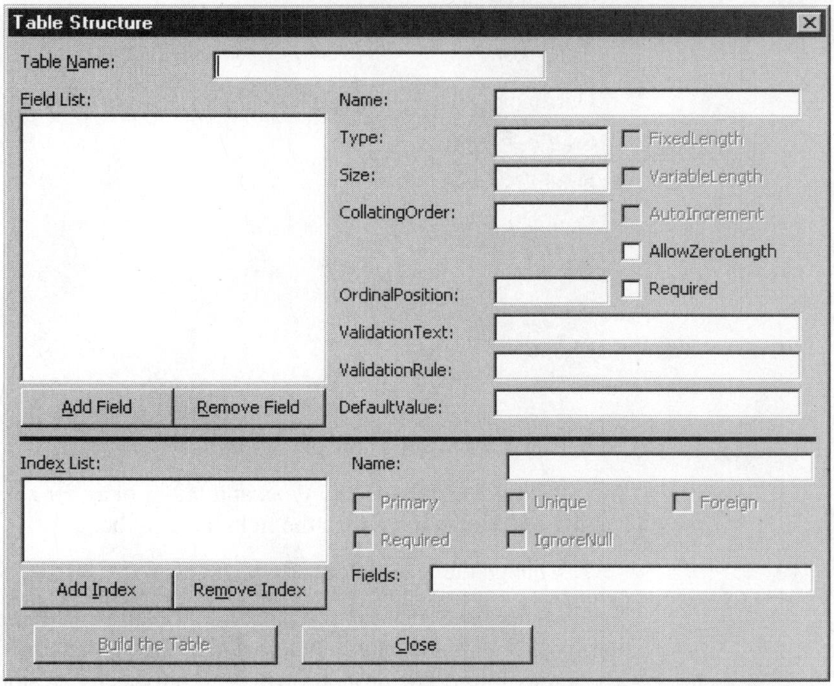

FIGURE 10.25
The Table Structure
dialog box.

FIGURE 10.26
The form to add new fields to the database.

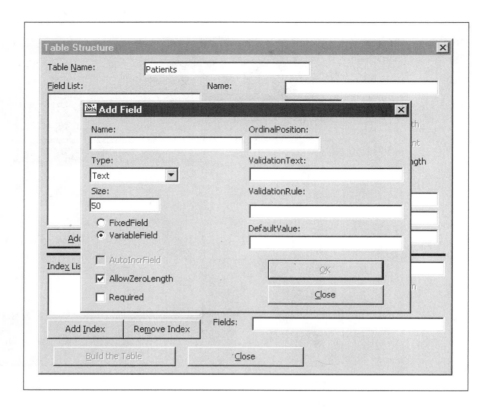

TABLE 10.4
The data types available for table field definition.

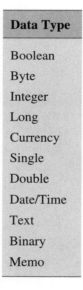

Data Type
Boolean
Byte
Integer
Long
Currency
Single
Double
Date/Time
Text
Binary
Memo

6. Key **LastName** in the Name field.

Text is the default data type, and this is okay for a name field, but the length defaults to 50, and that is more than the field needs to be.

7. Change the Size field to **20**.

Under the Size entry box, the program allows the specification of whether the field is of fixed or variable length. It defaults to variable length. This means that 20 characters will be a maximum. The program will need only as much storage space as the data in the field require to be stored. If you use a FixedField, every field will require 20 characters of storage, whether there are any data in the field or not. We will leave all our fields as Variable Field.

Under the Fixed/Variable option are three check boxes. The first one is unavailable, but the other two are important. The first lets you specify whether the field is allowed to be zero length, which means empty. The second lets you specify whether the field is required. Because we are going to use the LastName as part of the index of the table, we don't want it to be null (AllowZeroLength) and we do want to require it.

8. Turn off the AllowZeroLength check box, and turn on the Required check box. The dialog box should now look like the one shown in Figure 10.27.

9. Click the **OK** button to store this field and move to add another field.

If you move the Add Field dialog box aside, you will see the field specification for the field you just added in the Table Structure dialog box.

10. Move the Add Field dialog box as shown in Figure 10.28.

11. Add the remaining fields to the table structure as shown in Table 10.5.

12. Click the **Close** button after entering all the field data. Now the Table Structure dialog box appears as shown in Figure 10.29.

We want this table to be indexed by the LastName and FirstName fields.

13. Click the **Add Index** button to see the dialog box shown in Figure 10.30.

As mentioned, we want to create a key of LastName and then FirstName. We want to call the index **Primary**.

14. Key **Primary** in the Name field.

15. Click LastName in the Available Fields list and then click FirstName. This makes the Add Index dialog box appear as shown in Figure 10.31.

Note that this dialog box allows you to specify whether this index is the Primary index. In our case it is the Primary index, so we will leave this check box checked. A Primary index is the index by which the records are ordered by default. Thus, our table will be ordered by LastName. The other check box of interest is **Unique**. If you deselect this, you will allow the user to create two records in the table with the same index. If this is a Secondary index, it doesn't necessarily have to be unique. But if it is the Primary index, as ours is, it is best that it be unique. Processing the table is more difficult if there are duplicate indices. So you will leave this check box checked as well.

FIGURE 10.27
The Add Field dialog box with the first field set up.

FIGURE 10.28
The added field specifications shown in the Table Structure dialog box.

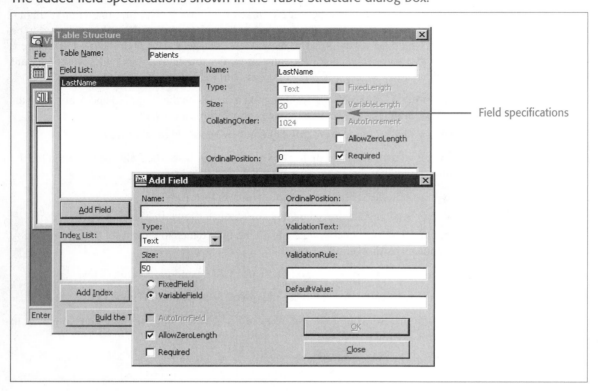

TABLE 10.5
The rest of the field specifications.

Field name	Data Type	Size	AllowZeroLength	Required
FirstName	Text	20	No	Yes
LastVisitDate	Date/Time	N/A	N/A	No
NextAppointment	Date/Time	N/A	N/A	No
Balance	Currency	N/A	N/A	No

16. Click the **OK** button and then click the **Close** button to exit the dialog box. Now the Table Structure dialog box shows the index we just created (Figure 10.32).

The index display shows the name of the index, the options chosen, and the fields that make up the index.

The last step in creating the table is to use the **Build the Table** button.

17. Click the **Build the Table** button. After a minute or so, the Table Structure dialog box vanishes, returning you to the main VisData window.

The Database Window now shows the table in its workspace (Figure 10.33).

FIGURE 10.29
The Table Structure dialog box after all the fields are added.

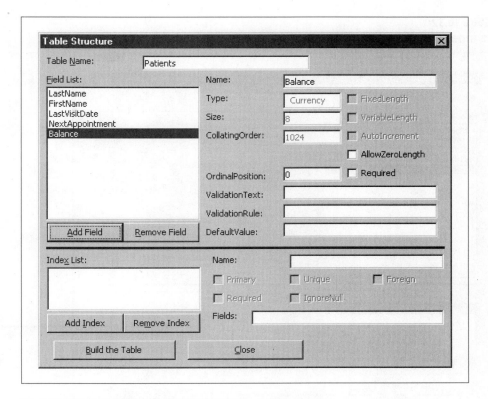

FIGURE 10.30
The Add Index dialog box.

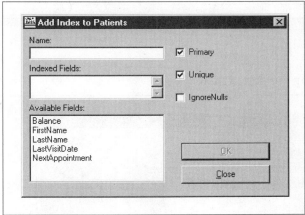

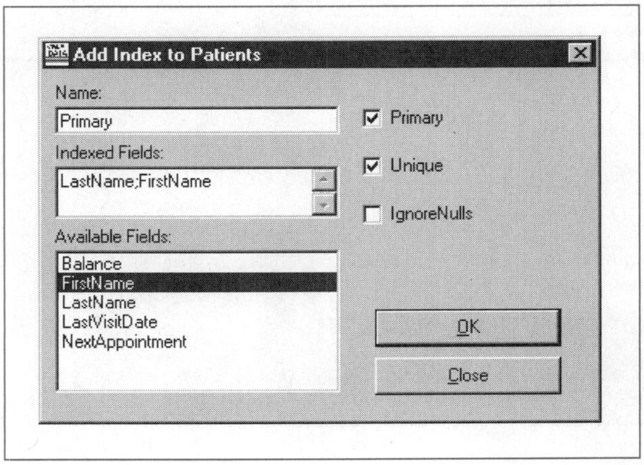

FIGURE 10.31
The Add Index dialog box after the Primary index is set up.

FIGURE 10.32
The index specifications shown in the Table Structure dialog box.

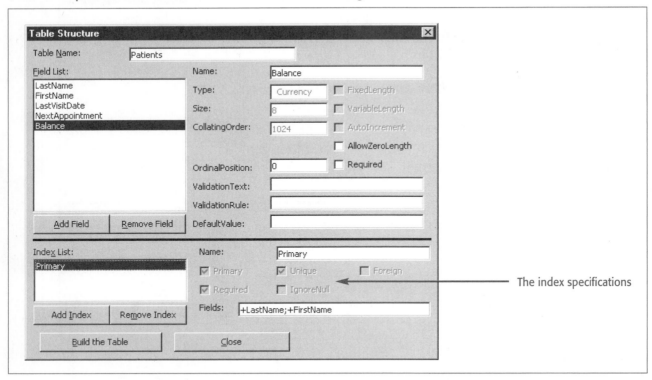

The index specifications

FIGURE 10.33
The Database Window, showing the added table.

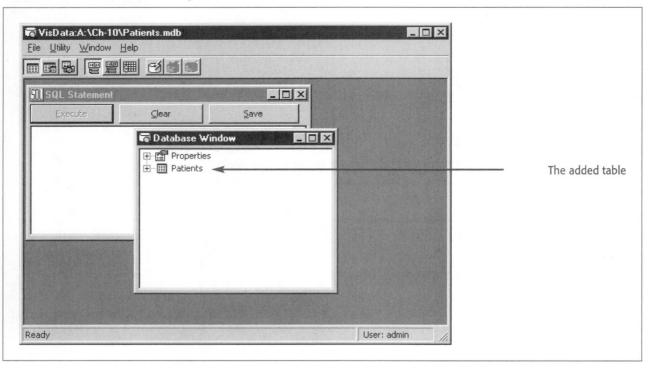

The added table

Adding Data to a Table

Now that the table has been created, we need to add some data. This can be done with Vis-Data also.

1. Right-click the Patients item in the Database Window workspace, and a small menu pops up. Select the **Open** option from the menu, and the dialog box for field entry appears as shown in Figure 10.34.

   This dialog box lets you enter data for the records you want to create in the database. Each of the fields is listed, and there is a data control like the one you learned to use in this chapter. It functions the same way.

2. Key the following data into the fields:
   - LastName: Fredericks
   - FirstName: Harold
   - LastVisitDate: 4/15/00
   - NextAppointment: 10/15/00
   - Balance: 12.50

3. Click the **Update** button to add the record to the table. The program prompts you for verification. Click the **Yes** button.

4. Click the **Add** button to clear the first record so that another can be entered. Enter the following data, and then click the **Update** button and the **Yes** button when prompted.
   - LastName: Club
   - FirstName: Sam
   - LastVisitDate: 12/15/99

FIGURE 10.34
The dialog box for data entry.

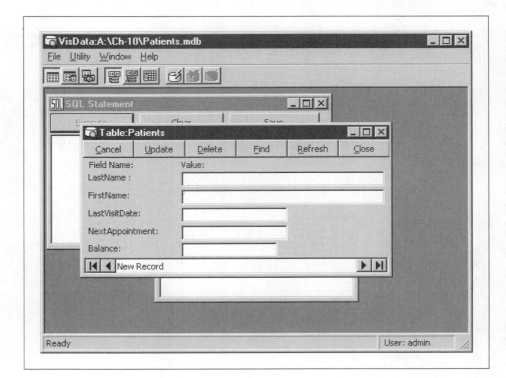

HINT: Visual Basic and Access are Y2K-compliant, so using year-2000 dates works properly.

■   NextAppointment: 12/16/00

■   Balance: 0

5. Click the **Close** button to exit the data entry form and click the **Yes** button on the commit dialog box.

Just as we created a browse mode in our program, VisData has one too. The three buttons in the middle of the button bar (⊞⊞⊞) indicate the type of form you are going to see. Currently the **Data Control** button (⊞) is selected, so you saw the form with the data control on it. To see the browse form, you need to select the Grid Control (⊞).

6. Click the Grid Control (⊞) and then double-click the Patients item icon in the Database Window workspace to see the form displayed in Figure 10.35.

You can enter data into the table using the browse form.

7. Key the data into the table as shown in Figure 10.36.

8. Click the line beneath the one you just keyed. The program will ask whether you want to commit the changes. Click the **Yes** button.

There are additional features in this program, but this gives you a general understanding of the program. It is easy to use if you want to do basic database creation, table building, and data entry. If you want the format of the entry to differ in any way from what this program presents, however, you have to build your own database interface programs.

FIGURE 10.35
The Grid Control form of the Patients database table.

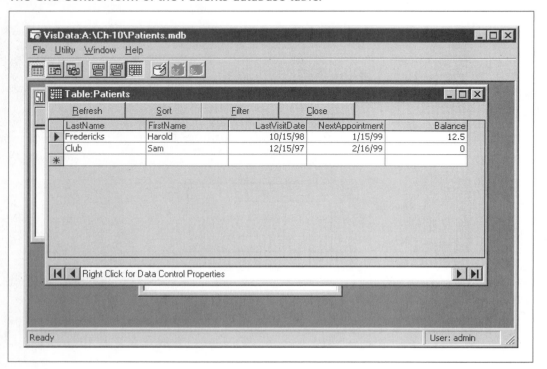

FIGURE 10.36
The data entered directly into the browse form.

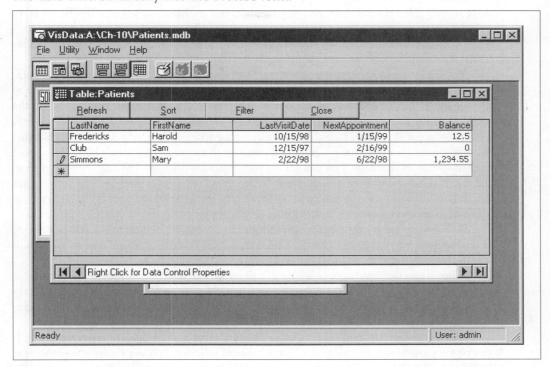

9. Practice with the program until you are thoroughly familiar with the way it works, and then exit the program.

10. Exit Visual Basic and shut the system down properly.

10.12 Debugging Your Programs

When working with databases, don't forget that if you are going to use transactions, the DAO object library must be turned on. Otherwise, the Workspaces statements will give you errors. Should you ever get errors on such statements, your first response should be to check your references list to be sure the DAO object library is enabled.

Though you can use nested transactions and it can be useful to do so, you need to be sure that the transactions are handled properly. You must always finish inside transactions before working with outside transactions.

If a program is exited when a transaction is in progress, the transactions are automatically rolled back. If a transaction has been started, you should not allow users to exit your program without warning them that the transaction will be rolled back. You might give them the option at that point either to commit or to roll back the changes.

Also remember, when working with transactions, that the database must not be read-only when you turn on a transaction. Otherwise, the BeginTrans statement will be ignored. It might be best to check the status of the database when the transaction is selected, warn the user that the database is locked, and not allow the transaction setup. We didn't do this in our program, but you might want to add the code yourself.

If you use the CommitTrans or Rollback method without first using the BeginTrans method, an error occurs. When using transactions, you should always make sure your program has used the BeginTrans method before allowing the user to commit or rollback the transaction. That's why we enabled the menu items only after the transaction had been started. This is related to changing the database so that it isn't read-only. As we have noted, if it is read-only, the BeginTrans statement will be ignored, and then when the program tries to commit or roll back the changes, an error will occur, stating that the Begin-Trans statement has not been used to set up the transaction.

You need to remember that you set up a Data Control so that it points to a specific database in a specific location. If you move the database to another location, you will have to change the Database property of the Data Control so that it once again corresponds to the location of the database. If you run the program without changing the Database property, your program will tell you it can't find the database when it tries to establish the links that the bound controls need. The program will continue to execute, but it won't be able to access or display any of the data. You can set up your program using an INI file with the path to the database as one of the fields in the INI file. Then, when your program reads this path, the DatabaseName property can be set so the database can be found on this path. This technique or similar ones lend more flexibility to your programs.

Remember that if you want multiple users to access a database using your program, you cannot set up your Data Control to be exclusive. If you do, only one user at a time will be able to access data from the database.

When using the ReadOnly property in a program that also allows the user to update the data, you must use a routine to warn the user that changes are not stored if the ReadOnly property is left on. Otherwise, the user may think that the specified changes have been made when they have not.

Whenever your program is adding or deleting records, you need to refresh the file. It can be very confusing for the user if, after a record is added, it is not found where the user believes it should be. New records are added at the end, and the user will not know this. By refreshing the file, you can put the record where the user expects to find it.

A common error message that is encountered when you are working with databases is "Object variable or With block variable not set." This can be caused by a variety of small mistakes. Probably the most common is trying to access data from the Data Control before the Data Control is active, such as when you use a MoveFirst statement in the Form_Load procedure. Because the form is not yet on the desktop, the Data Control is not active and the control is not yet pointing at any data. Thus, if you use the MoveFirst statement, you are telling the program to move through data it doesn't yet have access to. When you see this type of error, the first thing you want to look at is the order of the elements within the program.

10.13   Command and Menu Summary

In this chapter you learned about the following properties:

- **Col** is used to point to a particular column in a FlexGrid control.
- **Cols** is used to specify the number of columns in a FlexGrid control.
- **ColWidth** is used to specify the width of a column in a FlexGrid control.
- **Connect** is used to give Visual Basic any additional information needed to connect to an external database.
- **DatabaseName** allows you to specify the database that the data control is to access.
- **DataField** allows you to specify which field of the table you want displayed in the bound control.
- **DataSource** allows you to specify what data control the bound control is to use.
- **Exclusive** allows you to tell Visual Basic whether you want to be the only user allowed to access the database.

- **FixedCols** specifies the number of fixed columns in a FlexGrid control.
- **FixedRows** specifies the number of fixed rows in a FlexGrid control.
- **HighLight** lets you specify whether or not selected cells in a FlexGrid control will be highlighted.
- **MousePointer** lets you change the shape of the mouse pointer.
- **Options** lets you specify various access settings, such as read-only, for your database during runtime.
- **ReadOnly** lets you specify that the database being accessed will not allow any changes to be made.
- **RecordSet** lets you point to the object to which the database control is referring.
- **RecordSource** gives the Data Control access to the tables within the database.
- **Row** lets you specify the FlexGrid row that you are referencing.
- **Rows** is used to specify the number of rows in a FlexGrid control.
- **Transaction** lets you test a database to see whether it allows transactions.

In this chapter you learned about the following methods:

- **AddNew** updates the current database record and blanks out the bound controls so that you can key a new record.
- **BeginTrans** lets you start a transaction.
- **CommitTrans** lets you save the pending transactions to the database(s).
- **DataChanged** allows you to check whether a change has been made to the data in a bound control.
- **Delete** lets you delete the current database record.
- **EOF** allows you to test for the end of the Dynaset as you are accessing the records.
- **FindFirst** lets you access the first record that matches the specified criteria.
- **FindLast** lets you access the last record that matches the specified criteria.
- **FindNext** lets you access the next record after the current one that matches the specified criteria.
- **FindPrevious** lets you access the first record prior to the current one that matches the specified criteria.
- **MoveFirst** lets you access the first record in the table.
- **MoveLast** lets you access the last record in the table.
- **MoveNext** lets you access the next record after the current one in the table.
- **MovePrevious** lets you access the record just before the current one in the table.
- **OpenDatabase** lets you open a database for access.
- **Refresh** closes and reopens the database.
- **RollBack** lets you undo any pending transactions without saving them to the database(s).

In this chapter you learned about the following objects:

- **DBEngine** is the object Visual Basic uses to talk to databases.
- **Workspace** allows you to set up a work area for processing Dynasets.

In this chapter you learned about the following keywords:

- **DESC** is the portion of a query that indicates that the order is to be descending.
- **From** is the part of an SQL query that specifies the table that is to be used to create the Dynaset.

- **Order By** is the part of an SQL query that specifies the field that is to be used when sorting the Dynaset.
- **Select** begins an SQL query specification.
- **Where** is the part of an SQL query that specifies the selection criteria that are to be used to create the Dynaset.

In this chapter you learned about the following event:

- **Validate** occurs before a new record becomes the current record when the Data Control or the related commands are used to change records.

In this chapter you learned about the following prefixes:

- **dat** is for the Data Control.
- **grd** is for the FlexGrid Control.

In this chapter you learned about the following tools:

- The Data Control allows you to access database records.
- The FlexGrid allows you to show data as a table of rows and columns.

10.14   Performance Check

1. When using a Data Control to access a database, the two properties that you must always use are

   _____

   and _____ .

2. If the database is external, you must also use this property:

   _____

3. If you are in a multiuser environment and you don't want other users to have access to your database while you are using it, you should use this property:

   _____

4. When you use a text box into which the Data Control can automatically put data, that text box is called

   _____ .

5. The two controls specifying the connection between a text box and a Data Control are

   _____

   and _____ .

6. When a database is used to display records, the one being displayed is referred to as the

   _____ .

7. If you want to set up the file in your database program so that the user cannot change it, you should use the property

   _____ .

8. Every bound control has a special property that can be checked to see whether the data displayed in the control have been changed. This property is

   _____ .

9. The special method to close and reopen a database is called

   _____ .

10. What is the purpose of the FindFirst method?

    _____

11. The three methods related to the FindFirst method are

    _____ ,

    _____ ,

    and _____ .

12. Explain what the AddNew method does.

    _____

13. When a new record is added to a database table, where is that record put in relation to the other records in the table?

_____

14. The data control has arrows that can be used to change from one database record to another. There are also methods that can be used for the same purpose. These methods are

_____ ,

_____ ,

_____ ,

and _____ .

15. What property can be used to check whether or not your current database allows transactions?

_____

16. You have started a transaction and discover an error in the data you have entered. What method can be used to erase the changes that have been made?

_____

17. What does SQL mean?

_____

18. When a query is used to extract a part of a database, that database portion is called a

_____ .

19. Suppose your database has a field called Quantity Ordered. Show how you could enter that field name in a query.

_____

20. When you display your database so that there is more than one record on the screen at a time, you are using a feature called

_____ .

10.15 Programming Exercises

Note: Depending on how many of these exercises you do and which ones require the creation of new databases, you may run out of room on your work disk. If that is the case, format a new disk with a Ch-10 folder and create the new database on that disk. No files are needed other than the PIM applications and the ones mentioned in the particular exercise.

1. You have been assigned the task of setting up a program to access the Publishers table of the Bibliography database. This exercise will give you practice working with a single database table. At the computer, do each of the following:

   a. Get into Visual Basic and put your work disk in drive A.

   b. Add a Data Control to the form with the name and control name **datPublishers**.

   c. Change the DatabaseName property so that it will access the **Bibliography** database found in your Ch-10 folder. Change the RecordSource property to use the **Publishers** table. Change the Exclusive property to **True**.

   d. Add nine labels and nine text boxes, and arrange them and the Data Control until your form looks like the one in Figure 10.37.

   e. Change the Datasource property of each of the text boxes to the **datPublishers** data control.

   f. Change the DataField property of each text box to the appropriate field.

   g. Save the program as **Publishers Data.** Test the program to be sure it works properly. Then exit it, exit Visual Basic, and shut the system down properly.

2. You have been assigned the task of setting up a program to access the Titles table of the Bibliography database. This exercise will give you practice working with a single database table. At the computer, do each of the following:

FIGURE 10.37
The form for
Programming Exercise 1.

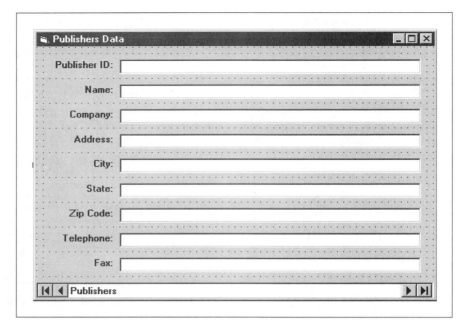

a. Get into Visual Basic and put your work disk in drive A.

b. Add a Data Control to the form with the name and control name **datTitles**.

c. Change the DatabaseName property so that it will access the **Bibliography** database found in your Ch-10 folder. Change the RecordSource property to use the **Titles** table. Change the Exclusive property to **True**.

d. Add labels and text boxes, and arrange them and the Data Control until your form looks like the one in Figure 10.38.

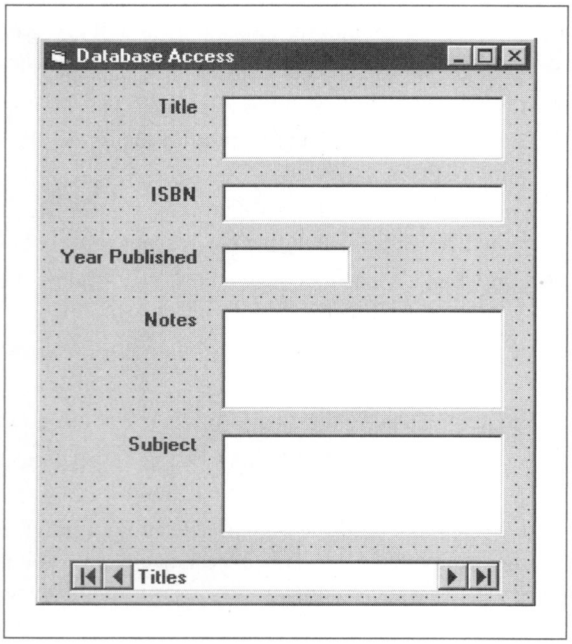

FIGURE 10.38
The form for
Programming Exercise 2.

e. Change the Datasource property of each of the text boxes to the **datTitles** Data Control.

f. Change the DataField property of each text box to the appropriate field.

g. Save the program as **Titles Data.** Test the program to be sure it works properly. Then exit it, exit Visual Basic, and shut the system down properly.

3. You need to have the data from three tables in the Bibliography database displayed at the same time. This exercise will give you practice working with multiple database tables. At the computer, do each of the following:

a. Get into Visual Basic and put your work disk in drive A.

b. Create a form like the one shown in Figure 10.39 with the following considerations:

1) The three Data Controls are set up to match the table names shown in the control in the figure.

2) Title, ISBN, Year Published, Publisher ID, and Author ID all come from the Titles table.

3) Publisher is looked up in the Publishers table using the Publisher ID in the Titles table with the FindFirst command.

4) Author is looked up in the Authors table using the Author ID in the Titles and the FindFirst command.

c. Save the program as **Three Tables**. Run the program to be sure it works properly. Then exit the program, exit Visual Basic, and shut the system down properly.

4. You work at an automotive repair facility that does everything from tune-ups to sound systems to body repair. They have a database set up that keeps track of the various repair stations where all the employees work. Your job is to create a program that will display the employees' names and the stations where they are authorized to work. Each employee can be authorized to work at up to five stations. This exercise will give

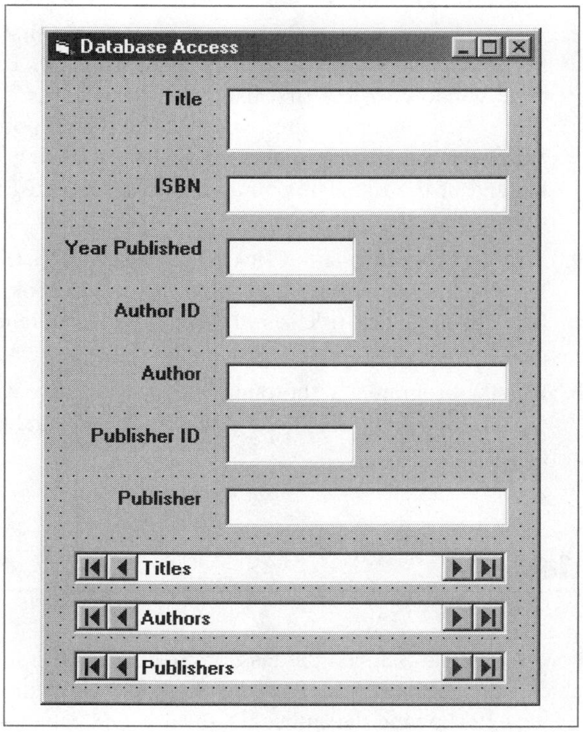

FIGURE 10.39
The form for
Programming Exercise 3.

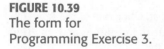

you practice working with two tables in one program. At the computer, do each of the following:

a. Get into Visual Basic and put your work disk in drive A.

b. Create a new program and add two Data Controls connected to the **Work Place** database. The first one should be attached to the **Workstations** table, the second to the **StationNames** table.

c. Add a text box and label for the employee name. Add labels and text boxes for the five workstation numbers (called **Station1** through **Station5**) in the Workstations table. These should be attached to the Workstations table.

d. Add five more text boxes (or labels) where you can write the station name that you use to match against the workstation number in the StationNames table.

e. Save the program as **Workstations**. Run the program to be sure it is working properly, then exit the program, Visual Basic, and the system.

5. A friend has been experimenting with a program to read a database and add the data to two lists. The program is supposed to read the Book database and display all the years in the first list. Then, when one of the years is selected, the book titles are displayed in the second list. The problem is that the program is not working. Your friend has asked you for help. At the computer, do each of the following:

a. Get into Visual Basic and put your work disk in drive A.

b. Load the **Book Lists** program.

c. Save the form and project with **Fixed** appended to the end.

d. Run the program. Immediately you get an error. If you recall, we mentioned this error in the "Debugging Your Programs" section. The problem is that the Data Control is not yet active. This code needs to be moved to the Form_Activate procedure.

e. Move the code and run the program again. You get another error. Click the **OK** button and look carefully at the offending statement. It is the Do Until statement. The problem is the EOF. You cannot use the EOF directly subordinate to the Data Control. You must use the Recordset method. Add the method.

f. Run the program. Now the years show up in the first list. Click one of the years. No titles show up in the other list. What's wrong? Exit the program and open the code window for the first list. After the records in the database are read (in the Form_Activate procedure), where is the record pointer? It's at the end of the file. When the records are read again, there are none because the pointer is already at the end of the file. The pointer needs to be repositioned. Add a MoveFirst statement before the loop.

g. Run the program again. Click 1977 in the first list. The title shows up in the Title list. Click 1981 in the Year Pub. list. Another book shows up in the list. The problem is that the first title is still there. Another statement is missing. Add the appropriate statement.

h. Run the program and thoroughly test it to be sure it is now working properly. Exit the program and print all the elements. Exit Visual Basic, and then shut the system down properly.

10.16 Performance Mastery

1. You have been assigned the task of creating a program that will display the Authors table of the **Bibliography** database. It should allow the user to move from one record to the next, showing the author ID, the author's name, and the list of the books written by the author. The titles of the books will have to be back-referenced in the Titles table by the Author ID (AU_ID). Use a list box to display the list of books. Design and create the program, save it as **Authors**, and thoroughly test it before printing it out.

2. You volunteer for the flower society. You have been asked to create a database that the chairperson can use to classify the members' entries in the local flower show. The database needs to be able to store the person's name, the category, the color, and the name of the flower entered. Use the VisData program to create the database, and make up some data to be entered. Then write a program that can be used to display the data. Use the Data Control and bound controls. Be sure the user of the program can add new records and delete the records of those members who have decided to withdraw from the contest. Design and create the program, save it as **Flower Show**, and thoroughly test it before printing it out.

3. A friend has been working on a database program that accesses the **Books** database (found in your Ch-10 folder). She has the program set up to access the database, but she needs help adding code for the buttons and the **Data Locked** menu item on the **File** menu. Load the **Database** program and add the appropriate code for the buttons and menu item. You will note that she has not followed the coding standards that you have been following. Save the program as **Database Updated** and thoroughly test it before printing it out.

4. You showed the Patients database you created in this chapter to a dentist friend, and he has asked you to expand the concept by writing a program to display the data. Use the Data Control and bound controls. Make sure the user of the program can add new records and delete ones for those patients who have never kept an appointment. Design and create the program, save it as **Patient Record**, and thoroughly test it before printing it out.

5. Your mother is a teacher's aide at a local school. The teacher she helps out needs a database that can be used to store her students' grades and a program that can be used to display those grades. Create a database called **Math Grades** in which each student can have up to ten grades. Then write a program that can be used to display the grades, average them, and display an A if the average is 91–100, a B if the average is 81–90, a C if the average is 71–80, a D if the average is 61–70, and an F if the average is below 61. The program should allow the creation of new records and the entry of new grades for the students. Design and create the program, save it as **Math Grades**, and thoroughly test it before printing it out.

6. Read through Programming Exercise 4 in the previous section. This is a good exercise, but it is incomplete. You need to be able to add new records to the Workstations table so that new employees can be authorized for the stations, and you need to be able to add new stations into the Station Names table. Create a program that will do all that the one in Programming Exercise 4 does and will allow new records to be added to both tables. Design and create the program, and save it as **Table Updates**. Thoroughly test the program and then print it out.

7. You have been asked by a personnel officer to create a database that can be used to store information about the personnel. She wants to be able to store the name, the date of hire, whether the person is salaried or hourly, and how many days of vacation that person has accumulated. Create a database called **Personnel Database** to store these data. Make up enough data to add at least five records to the database. Then write a program to display the data. The program should allow new entries to be added, as well as allowing entries to be removed for those employees who are no longer with the company. Design and create the program, and save it as **Personnel Data**. Thoroughly test the program and then print it out.

8. You work for Widgets International and have been given the assignment of creating a database called **Widget Database** that can be used to store various information about

Product	Quantity on Hand	Cost	Selling Price
Red widget	150	15.25	30.25
Blue widget	125	16.27	30.25
Yellow widget	235	18.24	30.25
Widget holder	147	5.24	9.95
Extra blades	321	2.16	3.45
Strap	12	1.25	4.15
Cleaning kit	76	7.65	12.50

the products that your company sells. The database should store the product name, the cost of the product, the quantity on hand, and the selling price. Then you need to write a program that can be used to display the data stored in the database as well as the total profit when all the products are sold (the difference between the cost and the selling price). Use the data shown in Table 10.6 in the program. Design and create the program, and save it as **Widget Database Display**. Thoroughly test the program before printing it out.

9. You work for Widgets International. Your boss has asked you to create a database that can be used to store the data shown in Table 10.7 (called **Widget Sales**). Then you are to write a program that will display a list of the various products that the company sells. When an item is selected from the list, the program should look up the related record and display the quarterly sales for the three sales areas in labels and on a bar graph. To use a list, your program will have to read through all the records in the database upon loading. Design and create the program, and save it as **Widget Sales Graph**. Test the program and then print it out.

Product	Southern Area	Western Area	Eastern Area
Red widget	15,225	17,897	16,435
Blue widget	12,345	32,456	16,543
Yellow widget	14,567	19,423	12,456
Widget holder	9,357	12,983	6,231
Extra blades	1,346	2,984	6,534
Strap	5,245	6,298	3,490
Cleaning kit	6,298	4,298	4,991

Additional Tools

11.1 Chapter Objectives

After finishing this chapter, you will be able to:

- Draw lines, boxes, dots, and circles in a Picture Box.
- Print text in a Picture Box in various colors.
- Demonstrate the use of drag-and-drop techniques.
- Print reports on a printer using the Print command.

11.2 Introduction

The next element of the PIM program that we want to work with is the To-Do list. What we want to create is a way for the user to input a list of projects and then classify them as to priority and whether they are active, completed, or overdue. To do this, we would like to be able to have a list where we can use different colors to show the status. That is, we want to be able to show active projects in black, overdue projects in red, and completed projects in magenta. We will use a Tabbed Control to display the projects, and the completed projects will be moved to a special tab. Then, if a project is moved from completed status back to active status, we want it to be displayed in magenta.

In the past we have worked with text boxes, labels, and lists. They all have nice features, and Visual Basic takes care of a lot of the work for us automatically, but they all have drawbacks that prevent us from using them for the To-Do list. More than anything else, none of them allows us to display different lines of text in different colors. Therefore, we will put the list in a **Picture Box**. A Picture Box is designed to allow images to be added to or created by the program, and everything placed in a Picture Box becomes part of the **bitmap** within the Picture Box. A bitmap is simply a mapping of all the bits that make up the drawing, and a Picture Box is a place to store and create bitmaps.

Because everything in a Picture Box becomes part of the bitmap, this includes any text that is written in the box. This has the disadvantage of making us do all the textual work ourselves. That is, if we put text in a Picture Box, the text becomes part of the bitmap and is no longer text and cannot be manipulated as text. We cannot select it as we can select it in a text box or list. We cannot use cut and paste as they can be used in a text box. But using a Picture Box does allow us to do some of the other things we want to be able to do, including displaying the separate lines of text in different colors.

11.3 A Look at the PIM

As always, we will begin the chapter with a look at how the PIM will perform when we are finished with the chapter.

1. Copy the PIM project and all the associated files from the Ch-10 folder on the disk you used in Chapter 10 to the Ch-11 folder on your work disk.

2. With your new work disk in drive A, launch the PIM application from the Ch-11 folder on your work disk.

The PIM looks almost the same as it did in the last chapter, but we have added elements to the **To-Do List** tab.

3. Click the **To-Do List** tab to see the display shown in Figure 11.1.

FIGURE 11.1
The To-Do List tab display.

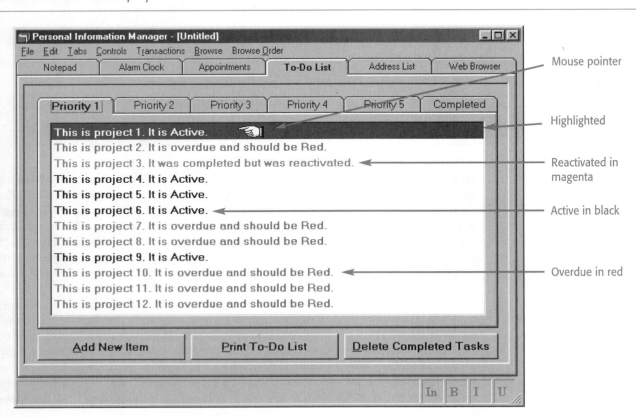

As you can see, active projects are shown in black and overdue projects in red. There is one project in the list that was completed and then reactivated; it is shown in magenta. For you more easily to follow the figures in the text, the dates used for the projects are hardcoded in the program. Normally this would not be done.

As you move the mouse pointer over the projects, the one the pointer is over will become highlighted just as though this were a list and the mouse pointer will change shape as shown in Figure 11.1.

4. Move the pointer over the projects to see the highlight.

The six tabs include five for the five priorities and one for completed projects. To change priorities on a project, you simply drag the project from one priority tab and drop it on another tab.

5. Click the first item in the workspace and hold the button down to see the drag-and-drop icon shown in Figure 11.2.

6. Drag the icon to the **Priority 3** tab and then drop it there.

The project disappears from the **Priority 1** tab.

7. Click the **Priority 3** tab and you see that the project is there.

If a project is completed, you can drop it on the **Completed** tab.

8. Switch back to the **Priority 1** tab. Drag project 5 and drop it on the **Completed** tab.

FIGURE 11.2
The highlighted project and the drag-and-drop icon.

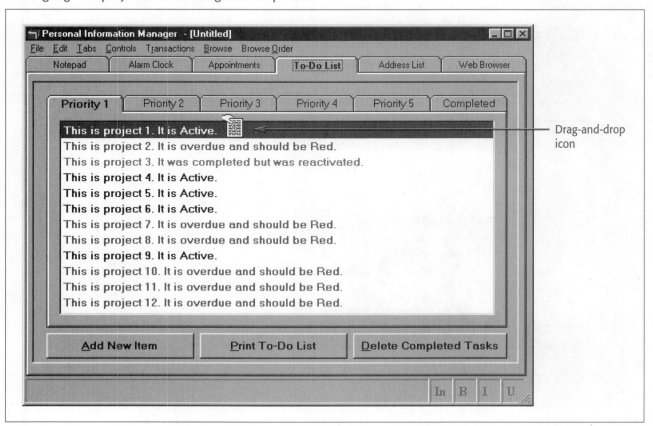

Drag-and-drop icon

9. Change to the **Completed** tab and see the project there.

   It is now magenta.

10. Drag the completed project and drop it on the **Priority 4** tab. Switch to that tab. The project is magenta here also.

    You can add new projects by using the **Add New Item** button.

11. Click the **Add New Item** button to see the form shown in Figure 11.3.

    Using this form, you can key a description, select a priority, and enter the due date.

12. Key **This is a sample project.** in the Description text box. Select a priority of 4, and enter a date that seems appropriate using the MM/DD/YY format, such as 12/15/00. Click the **OK** button.

> **HINT:** The format of the date shows only two digits for the year but it actually stores four digits and is Y2K-compliant.

The project will be in the **Priority 4** tab workspace. Not only have you recorded the date the project is due, but you have also automatically recorded when the project was added

FIGURE 11.3
The form to add a new project.

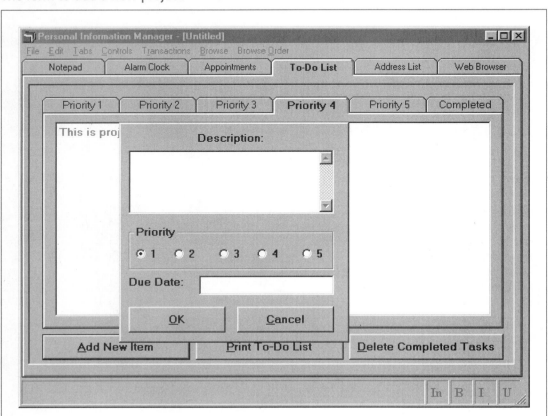

to the list. Because the user may wish to view these dates, we have added a small display much like the ToolTips displays.

13. Highlight the new item you just added to the **Priority 4** tab, and click and hold down the right mouse button. You will see a display similar to the one in Figure 11.4.

    If you have moved projects that you no longer need to the **Completed** tab, they can be deleted with the **Delete Completed Tasks** button.

14. Drag project 5 and drop it on the **Completed** tab. Switch to the **Completed** tab to see the project there.

15. Click the **Delete Completed Tasks** button. You see a warning dialog box. Click the **Yes** button, and the project disappears.

    It is handy to be able to print out a list of the tasks you have to do. The **Print To-Do-List** button lets you do this.

16. Click the **Print To-Do List** button, and the list prints on the printer.

17. Play with the program a bit more until you are familiar with the new functionality, and then minimize it in case you want to play with it some more as you add to your program.

    Now that you have seen how the program will work at the end of the chapter, it is time to make those additions to our PIM program from Chapter 10.

FIGURE 11.4
The display of the project dates.

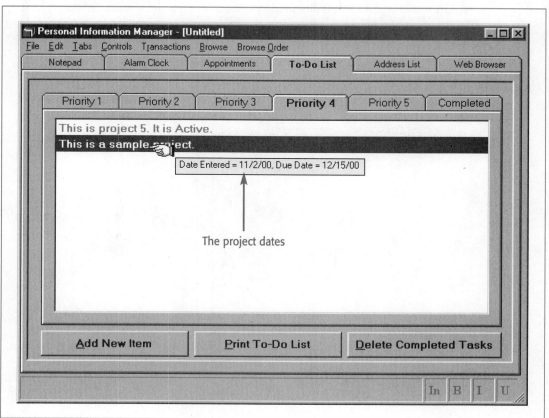

11.4 Adding the Picture Box

Because we want to be able to specify priorities for our projects, we need some way to separate the projects into groups. We are already familiar with the Tabbed Control, so we will use it for this separation.

1. Launch Visual Basic.

2. Load the PIM program you copied into the Ch-11 folder.

The inset you saw in the sample PIM program is created using the **Picture Box.** Normally a Picture Box is used to show graphic images, but in this case, we want to use it as an aid to visually separate the new Tabbed Control for the To-Do list from the original Tabbed Control.

3. Switch to the **To-Do List** tab. Add a Picture Box using the tool shown in Figure 11.5. Size and position the Picture Box as shown in Figure 11.6. Add a Tabbed Control called **tabTo_Do**, set up six tabs on one line, name them as shown in Figure 11.6, and add the three buttons shown.

As mentioned earlier, we are also going to use a Picture Box to display the projects. So we need to add a Picture Box to each of the **Priority** tabs.

4. Add a Picture Box to the **Priority 1** tab. Size and position the Picture Box as shown in Figure 11.7, and give it the control name **picTo_Do**. Make the font **Arial, bold,** and **10** point.

In addition to the settings mentioned in step 4, we need to set the **AutoRedraw** property to True. The AutoRedraw property tells Visual Basic to redraw what has been drawn in the Picture Box if the box is obscured by some other program element. Without this property turned on, if you launch another program that covers the box and then move that program out of the way, what was drawn in the box will not be redisplayed.

FIGURE 11.5
The Picture Box control.

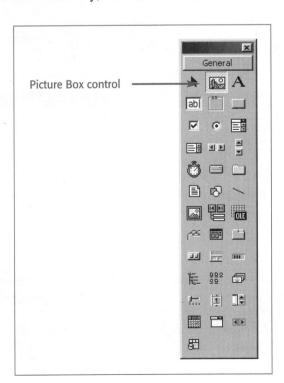

Picture Box control

FIGURE 11.6
The To-Do List display.

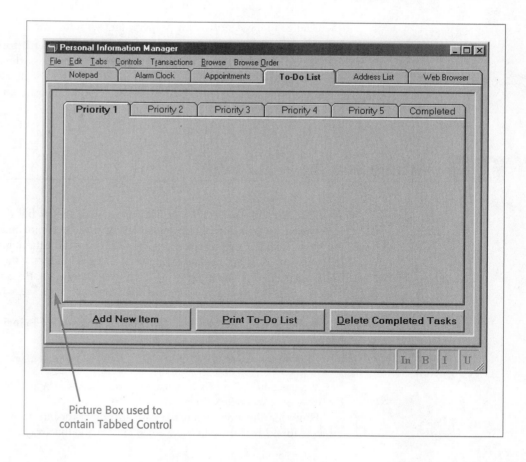

Picture Box used to
contain Tabbed Control

FIGURE 11.7
The Priority 1 tab with
the Picture Box added.

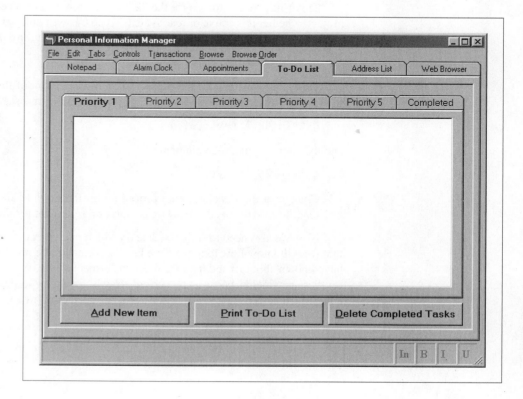

5. Change to the AutoRedraw property and set it to True.

6. Copy the Picture Box and paste it into each of the other **Priority** tabs as a control array. This will make it easy to refer to the Picture Boxes in the code. Be sure the control array index matches the label on the tab [**Priority 1** should be picTo_Do(1) and so on], though the tab itself will be one less because the tabs are numbered from zero.

11.5 Writing into the Picture Box

We will store our To-Do list in a database called **To-Do**, but to make manipulating those data easier, we will store the data in an array in the program and manipulate the data from the array. Because we are going to have to process the data frequently, displaying the data in the lists by reading the data from the database would slow the program down too much. Thus, we need to set up an array in which to store the data. Because we have a series of priority Picture Boxes that we want to write the data into, we will store the data in multi-dimensional array.

To begin with, we have one **Completed** tab and five **Priority** tabs, so we will have to begin with an array structure similar to

```
gstrTo_Do_Array(6)
```

We used the "g" prefix because this array needs to be global; we will need to reference the array on a secondary form.

However, this one dimension isn't sufficient for our needs. We will want to store 12 projects for each of the tabs, so we need to expand the array to

```
gstrTo_Do_Array(6,12)
```

This will give us storage for the 72 projects, but we also need to store the status of the project: whether it is active or reactivated. To do this we could set up another array, but why not just make further use of the current array? Let's add a third dimension, as in

```
gstrTo_Do_Array(6,12,2)
```

This allows us to store the project in the first element of the third dimension and the status in the second. That is, for priority 1, project 3, the message would be in element

```
gstrTo_Do_Array(1,3,1)
```

and the status would be in element

```
gstrTo_Do_Array(1,3,2)
```

1. Change to the (Declarations) procedure on the module and add the Global variable length (no size specified) string declaration statement for the array.

Now we also need to store the date on which the project was added to the To-Do list so that we will know how long we have been working on the project (or at least how long we have known about it) and the date when the project is due. We cannot use our current array for these new fields, because the current array is a string-type array and we want to store the dates in a date-type array. For this we will set up another three-dimensional array:

```
gdtmTo_Do_Dates(6,12,2)
```

The first element of the third dimension will be used to store the start date, and the second will be used for the due date.

2. Add the Global statement for this new array. It should be declared as a Date type. This makes it Y2K-compliant automatically.

To practice with this array and the Picture Boxes, we will put some dummy data into the arrays. You need to note a few things about these assignments. First, they are only for the first-priority Picture Box, because there are no elements where the first index is two or more. This is so that the other boxes will remain empty. Later you will learn how to set up the code to drag an entry from one priority box to another. To make this manipulation easy to see, it is better if the other priority boxes are empty. Second, the dates shown are only examples. You should use dates appropriate for your time frame. The due dates for the active projects should be after the current date so that they will still be active. The due dates for the overdue projects should be before the current date so that they will all be overdue. Also note that the colors in which the data are to be shown are designated in the message. That is, active projects will be displayed in black, and overdue projects will be displayed in red. The reactivated project will be shown in magenta.

3. Switch to the Form_Load procedure of the PIM form and key the following statements at the end of the current statements:

```
gstrTo_Do_Array(1, 1, 1) = "This is project 1. It is Active."
gstrTo_Do_Array(1, 1, 2) = "Active"
gdtmTo_Do_Dates(1, 1, 1) = #9/15/00#
gdtmTo_Do_Dates(1, 1, 2) = #9/29/00#
gstrTo_Do_Array(1, 2, 1) = "This is project 2. It is overdue and
↳ should be Red."
gstrTo_Do_Array(1, 2, 2) = "Active"
gdtmTo_Do_Dates(1, 2, 1) = #9/15/00#
gdtmTo_Do_Dates(1, 2, 2) = #9/22/00#
gstrTo_Do_Array(1, 3, 1) = "This is project 3. It was completed
↳ but was reactivated."
gstrTo_Do_Array(1, 3, 2) = "Reactive"
gdtmTo_Do_Dates(1, 3, 1) = #9/15/00#
gdtmTo_Do_Dates(1, 3, 2) = #9/29/00#
gstrTo_Do_Array(1, 4, 1) = "This is project 4. It is Active."
gstrTo_Do_Array(1, 4, 2) = "Active"
gdtmTo_Do_Dates(1, 4, 1) = #9/15/00#
gdtmTo_Do_Dates(1, 4, 2) = #9/29/00#
gstrTo_Do_Array(1, 5, 1) = "This is project 5. It is Active."
gstrTo_Do_Array(1, 5, 2) = "Active"
gdtmTo_Do_Dates(1, 5, 1) = #9/15/00#
gdtmTo_Do_Dates(1, 5, 2) = #9/29/00#
gstrTo_Do_Array(1, 6, 1) = "This is project 6. It is Active."
gstrTo_Do_Array(1, 6, 2) = "Active"
gdtmTo_Do_Dates(1, 6, 1) = #9/15/00#
gdtmTo_Do_Dates(1, 6, 2) = #9/29/00#
gstrTo_Do_Array(1, 7, 1) = "This is project 7. It is overdue and
↳ should be Red."
gstrTo_Do_Array(1, 7, 2) = "Active"
gdtmTo_Do_Dates(1, 7, 1) = #9/15/00#
gdtmTo_Do_Dates(1, 7, 2) = #9/22/00#
gstrTo_Do_Array(1, 8, 1) = "This is project 8. It is overdue and
↳ should be Red."
gstrTo_Do_Array(1, 8, 2) = "Active"
gdtmTo_Do_Dates(1, 8, 1) = #9/15/00#
gdtmTo_Do_Dates(1, 8, 2) = #9/22/00#
gstrTo_Do_Array(1, 9, 1) = "This is project 9. It is Active."
gstrTo_Do_Array(1, 9, 2) = "Active"
```

```
gdtmTo_Do_Dates(1, 9, 1) = #9/15/00#
gdtmTo_Do_Dates(1, 9, 2) = #9/29/00#
gstrTo_Do_Array(1, 10, 1) = "This is project 10. It is overdue and
  ↳ should be Red."
gstrTo_Do_Array(1, 10, 2) = "Active"
gdtmTo_Do_Dates(1, 10, 1) = #9/15/00#
gdtmTo_Do_Dates(1, 10, 2) = #9/22/00#
gstrTo_Do_Array(1, 11, 1) = "This is project 11. It is overdue and
  ↳ should be Red."
gstrTo_Do_Array(1, 11, 2) = "Active"
gdtmTo_Do_Dates(1, 11, 1) = #9/15/00#
gdtmTo_Do_Dates(1, 11, 2) = #9/22/00#
gstrTo_Do_Array(1, 12, 1) = "This is project 12. It is overdue and
  ↳ should be Red."
gstrTo_Do_Array(1, 12, 2) = "Active"
gdtmTo_Do_Dates(1, 12, 1) = #9/15/00#
gdtmTo_Do_Dates(1, 12, 2) = #9/22/00#
```

Now that we have the data assigned, we can write them into the Picture Boxes. We will set up a subroutine for writing the data into the Picture Boxes. The first time we want to write the data is when the user selects the **To-Do List** tab.

4. Open the code window for the Tabbed Control.

There is still some code there from our previous use of the tabs (see Figure 11.8). If you recall, it unchecks the menu items and then checks the one for the tab selected. We will write the new code after the current code.

Because we are going to use a subroutine to write the data, we simply need to call the subroutine. But we need to call it only when the **To-Do List** tab is selected. Thus, we need an If Test like the following:

```
If tabPIM.Tab = 3 Then
    Display_The_Projects
End If
```

Remember that the Tab method indicates which of the tabs is currently selected. The fourth tab (numbered from zero) is the **To-Do** tab, so we need to reference the tab numbered 3.

5. Key the foregoing statements after the code already in the procedure.

FIGURE 11.8
The code currently in the tabPIM_Click event procedure.

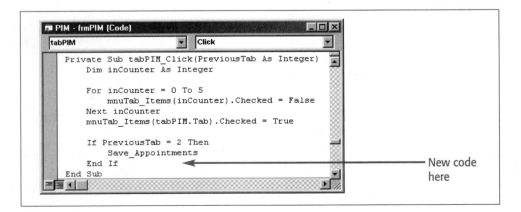

Now we must actually write the data into the Picture Boxes. That means we first need to create the **Display_The_Projects** procedure.

6. Create a public subroutine called **Display_The_Projects** by adding **Publc** before the substatement. The subroutine needs to be public because we will have to call it from the form later in the chapter.

To display the data, we will need to loop through the first two indices of our three-dimensional array. Remember that the first index points to the priority, the second to the number of the project, and the third contains the text for the active status. To write all 72 of the messages in the appropriate Picture Boxes, we will need an outside loop going through the six tabs and then an inside loop going through the 12 projects. We will hard-code the third dimension since it contains the data. So we must begin with

```
For intCounter_Outside = 1 To 6
    picTo_Do(intCounter_Outside).Cls
    For intCounter = 1 To 12
```

Note that between the For statements we inserted a **Cls** statement. This "clear screen" statement erases whatever is currently in the Picture Box. This is necessary because soon you will be removing projects from the Picture Box, and because the text we are going to write in the Picture Box becomes part of the bitmap as soon as it is written there, the only way to erase any excess text is to erase the entire Picture Box. We are using the outside counter as the index of the Picture Boxes because there are six Picture Boxes.

The first thing we need to do inside the outside loop is check whether the array element contains a project. There are two elements of each of the projects (the third dimension of the array): the project message and the status. If either of them is in the array, there is a project assigned to that array element. We simply need to check the element to see if there is a message or status. We will check for the message with the statement

```
If gstrTo_Do_Array(intCounter_Outside, intCounter, 1) > "" Then
```

If the element is greater than an empty string, there has to be something in it. Next we need to check the date. There are two possible states for it: current and overdue. We need to check the due date, which is stored in the second element of the third index of the gdtmTo_Do_Dates array, which gives us an If Test such as

```
If gdtmTo_Do_Dates(intCounter_Outside, intCounter, 2) < Date Then
```

This checks whether the date stored in the array is less than the current date in Date. If it is, we want to display the project in red because it is overdue. We need to change the foreground color of the Picture Box (the color of the elements put in the Picture Box) to red with a statement such as

```
picTo_Do(intCounter_Outside).ForeColor = vbRed
```

Note that the outside counter (the one that ranges from 1 to 6) is used because it is the one that points to the Picture Boxes.

If the project is "Active" but not overdue, then we want to display it in black, which means the foreground color should be black:

```
ElseIf gstrTo_Do_Array(intCounter_Outside, intCounter, 2) =
⮑ "Active" Then
    picTo_Do(intCounter_Outside).ForeColor = vbBlack
```

If the project is not "Active," it is "Reactive" and should be displayed in magenta:

```
Else
    picTo_Do(intCounter_Outside).ForeColor = vbMagenta
End If
```

Now that we know what the color of the project is, we are ready to actually display it. This requires the use of the **Print** method, but we need to do something else first. In a Picture Box, everything is displayed at the current cursor position. If we want something to be displayed in a particular position, we need to move the cursor to that position. When printing text, Visual Basic automatically adjusts the cursor to the next appropriate text position from Print statement to Print statement. But for our purposes, the next appropriate text position is not quite far enough down from the previous line. Therefore, we need to position the cursor ourselves. This is done with two properties, **CurrentX** for the horizontal position and **CurrentY** for the vertical position. The edge of any object is always zero, but we don't want to print the text right on the edge of the Picture Box. We will offset the CurrentX position by 50 with the statement

```
picTo_Do(intCounter_Outside).CurrentX = 50
```

Then we need to figure out the vertical position where the text needs to be printed. To determine how tall each line of text would be, you can use the **TextHeight** method with a statement in the immediate window such as

```
Print picTo_Do(1).TextHeight("Sample")
```

This gives a result of 240. However, experimenting with the text in the window reveals that a height of 300 seems more appropriate; it puts a bit more spacing between the printed lines. Using 300, however, puts the text right on the upper edge of the display area, so we will offset it downward by 40 twips. This means we need the CurrentY statement to be similar to the following:

```
picTo_Do(intCounter_Outside).CurrentY (intCounter - 1) * 300 + 40
```

This statement uses intCounter because it is the one that is counting the 12 projects we want displayed. Then we multiply it by 300 to move the pointer down 300 twips at a time. But intCounter begins with 1, so if we used intCounter straight and offset by 300, we would print the first line at position 300. We want the first one printed not at 300 but at 0. Thus we reduce intCounter by 1 before we multiply by 300. Then we add 40 to it so that it moves down a bit more, as we discussed earlier.

Now that we have the color set properly and know where the project is to be printed, we are finally ready to print it with a statement like

```
picTo_Do(intCounter_Outside).Print gstrTo_Do_Array(intCounter_
⮑ Outside, intCounter, 1)
```

Then we can end the If Test and the loops with the following statements:

```
        End If
    Next intCounter
Next intCounter_Outside
```

This gives us an entire routine as shown in Figure 11.9.

7. Save the program and then run it and click on the **To-Do List** tab.

You should have 12 lines printed in the Picture Box as shown in Figure 11.10. If you set up the dates properly, the active ones should be black, the overdue ones should be red, and the reactivated one should be magenta.

8. Switch to another tab. The Picture Box there should be empty.

9. Exit from the program.

FIGURE 11.9
The code in the Display_The_Projects procedure.

```
PIM - frmPIM (Code)                                                      _ □ ×
(General)                              ▼   Display_The_Projects            ▼
  Public Sub Display_The_Projects()
      Dim intCounter As Integer
      Dim intCounter_Outside As Integer
      Dim Date_In As Date

      Date_In = #9/23/2000#
      For intCounter_Outside = 1 To 6
          picTo_Do(intCounter_Outside).Cls        ' Clear the picture box
          For intCounter = 1 To 12               ' Set the color and print the project
              If gstrTo_Do_Array(intCounter_Outside, intCounter, 1) > "" Then
                  If gdtmTo_Do_Dates(intCounter_Outside, intCounter, 2) < Date_In Then
                      picTo_Do(intCounter_Outside).ForeColor = vbRed
                  ElseIf gstrTo_Do_Array(intCounter_Outside, intCounter, 2) = "Active" Then
                      picTo_Do(intCounter_Outside).ForeColor = vbBlack
                  Else
                      picTo_Do(intCounter_Outside).ForeColor = vbMagenta
                  End If

                  ' Position the insertion point then Print the project

                  picTo_Do(intCounter_Outside).CurrentX = 50
                  picTo_Do(intCounter_Outside).CurrentY = (intCounter - 1) * 300 + 40
                  picTo_Do(intCounter_Outside).Print gstrTo_Do_Array(intCounter_Outside, intCounter, 1)
              End If
          Next intCounter
      Next intCounter_Outside
  End Sub
```

FIGURE 11.10
How your form should look with the 12 lines printed.

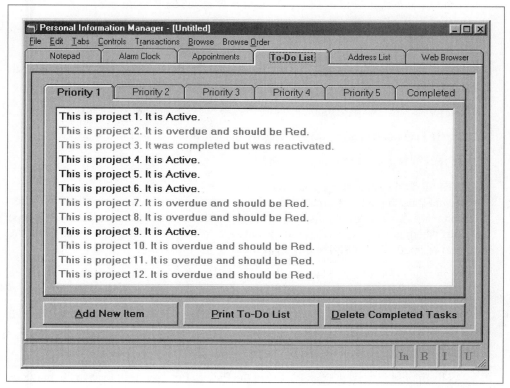

11.6   Highlighting the Lines

Because we want to be able to do several things with the lines printed in the Picture Box, we want to be able to highlight them. One way to do this would be to reprint the line with a reversed font, such as white on black. Unfortunately, Windows does not have a standard reversed font. We will have to reverse the font ourselves. We are displaying the text in a Picture Box, so we can easily reverse the font by displaying a box and then reprinting the line of text on top of the box. Remember that everything that is displayed in a Picture Box becomes part of the bitmap. Therefore, if we display a box in the Picture Box, it will cover the currently displayed text. Then, to redisplay the text, we can print right on top of the box because we are just printing into the Picture Box again.

When using a Picture Box, we can print lines, rectangles, squares, circles, ellipses, and dots. To draw a box (rectangle or square), we use the **Line** method and just add a parameter. The format of the Line method is

```
Object.Line (Starting_X, Starting_Y) - (Ending_X, Ending_Y),
↳[Color], [B][F]
```

The format specifies that a line is to be drawn from Starting_X to Ending_X horizontally and from Starting_Y to Ending_Y vertically. A line can be drawn horizontally, vertically, or diagonally just by changing the starting and ending positions. A completely horizontal line is drawn when the same Starting_Y and Ending_Y positions are used. To draw a completely vertical line, we use the same Starting_X and Ending_X positions.

The **[Color]** parameter is used to specify the color of the line as it is drawn. Thus, to draw the line in blue, we use

```
Object.Line (Starting_X, Starting_Y) - (Ending_X, Ending_Y), vbBlue
```

To draw a box rather than a line, we need only append a B to the end.

```
Object.Line (Starting_X, Starting_Y) - (Ending_X, Ending_Y),
↳vbBlue, B
```

This command would print a box with a blue border. We want our box to be filled with color, so the border won't matter. We can leave it out by using the method that follows:

```
Object.Line (Starting_X, Starting_Y) - (Ending_X, Ending_Y), , B
```

The **[F]** parameter can be used to specify that the box is to be filled:

```
Object.Line (Starting_X, Starting_Y) - (Ending_X, Ending_Y), , BF
```

We will do the same thing a different way.

Visual Basic has a lot of capabilities when it comes to drawing boxes and other objects. You can make them hollow by displaying the border in a color, or you can specify a fill type as solid (which is what we will use) or as any of a variety of patterns. To specify that the box is to be solid, the **FillStyle** property is used:

```
Object.FillStyle = Stylenumber
```

Stylenumber can be any of the values shown in Table 11.1.

We want the projects to be highlighted as we move the mouse over them, so we need to use the MouseMove event for highlighting.

1. Open the code window for the MouseMove event of the Picture Box.

As the mouse is moved up and down in the Picture Box, we need to save the previous cursor position, so if the cursor moves out of the range of the highlighted line, the previ-

TABLE 11.1
The values and descriptions of the FillStyle settings.

Predefined Constant	Setting	Description
vbFSSolid	0	Solid
vbFSTransparent	1	(Default) Transparent
vbHorizontalLine	2	Horizontal line
vbVerticalLine	3	Vertical line
vbUpwardDiagonal	4	Upward diagonal
vbDownwardDiagonal	5	Downward diagonal
vbCross	6	Cross
vbDiagonalCross	7	Diagonal cross

ously highlighted line can be unhighlighted while the new current line is highlighted. That means we need to have a variable to save that last position. Thus, the first line in this routine must be

```
Static intSave_Y As Integer
```

2. Key this statement into the procedure.

It has to be Static so that the value will always be retained as Visual Basic enters and exits this procedure.

The next statement we need is to set the FillStyle. That statement is

```
picTo_Do(Index).FillStyle = vbFSSolid
```

3. Key this statement.

Because we printed only 12 lines in the Picture Box, we need to be sure we are not trying to highlight a line below the 12 we know can be in the box. We must check this with an If Test such as

```
If Int(Y / 300) < 12 Then
```

4. Key this statement into the procedure.

This statement takes the current Y position (vertical), divides it by 300, and converts that result to an integer with the **Int** function. The Int function simply takes the specified number and removes whatever decimal portion there is. This leaves just the integer portion. It truncates the decimal portion; it does no rounding. If the number were 15.7, the Int function would yield 15, not 16. Because we are allowing each of our lines to be 300, if we divide Y by 300 and take the integer, we will get a number between zero and the height of the Picture Box. If that number is more than 11, we don't want to run the routine. That gives us 12 lines, 0 through 11.

If we are within our boundaries, we need to begin by erasing the display of whatever was previously highlighted. We do this by displaying the highlight box in white. To do this, we need to specify the fill color for the box with the **FillColor** method, as follows:

```
picTo_Do(Index).FillColor = vbWhite
```

5. Key this statement as the first statement inside the If Test.

Then we need to draw the box on top of whatever box was already displayed with the statement

```
picTo_Do(Index).Line (1, Int(intSave_Y / 300) * 300)-(8570,
↳ Int(intSave_Y / 300) * 300 + 300), vbWhite, B
```

This statement draws a box (the B at the end) from X position 1 to X position 8570, which is the width of the inside of the Picture Box, and from Y position Int(intSave_Y / 300) * 300 to Y position Int(intSave_Y / 300) * 300 + 300. Remember that intSave_Y is the Y position from the last time the MouseMove procedure was executed. By dividing it by 300 and taking the integer, we get an integer from 0 to 11. Then we multiply it by 300 to get the proper position. Finally, we add 300 to the end position so that we will have the start at one point and the end at the same point plus 300. This gives us a box that covers the area where the line was printed.

6. Key this statement into the procedure.

We have now deleted the text for the line by drawing a box on top of it, so we need to print it again. Rather than calculating where the line should be printed, it is easier simply to print all the lines because we already have a routine to do that.

```
Display_The_Projects
```

7. Key this statement.

Now we are ready to print the highlight box. Our printed lines are black, green, and red, so we will highlight in blue. Because we want to highlight only those lines where we actually print a project, we begin this portion of the routine by testing whether there is a project on this line. We do this by testing the element of the array with the following If Test:

```
If gstrTo_Do_Array(tabTo_Do.Tab + 1, Int(Y / 300) + 1, 1) > ""
↳ Then
```

8. Key this statement.

This statement points to the appropriate Picture Box by determining which tab the program is on and then adding 1 to it, because the tabs are numbered from 0 but the Picture Boxes are numbered from 1. The second index is calculated by dividing the current Y position by 300 and taking the integer. Again, this gives us a number from 0 to 11, but we need a number for the index from 1 to 12, so we simply add 1 to the integer. Then the third index is checked to see whether anything is stored for the project. If there is a project, we need to change the FillColor to blue (so that the highlight box will be displayed in blue) and then draw the box.

```
picTo_Do(Index).FillColor = vbBlue
picTo_Do(Index).Line (1, Int(Y / 300) * 300)-(8570, Int(Y / 300) *
↳ 300 + 300), vbBlue, B
```

9. Key these statements.

We drew the box over the text that we printed in the same spot, so we print the text again. But we don't want to print it in the regular color. If we did, we could just print all the lines again with our display routine. With the box in blue, we print the text in white so that it will stand out better. So we print just the one line.

To begin with, we change the ForeColor to white so that the text will be printed in white.

```
picTo_Do(Index).ForeColor = vbWhite
```

FIGURE 11.11
The code for the MouseMove event procedure.

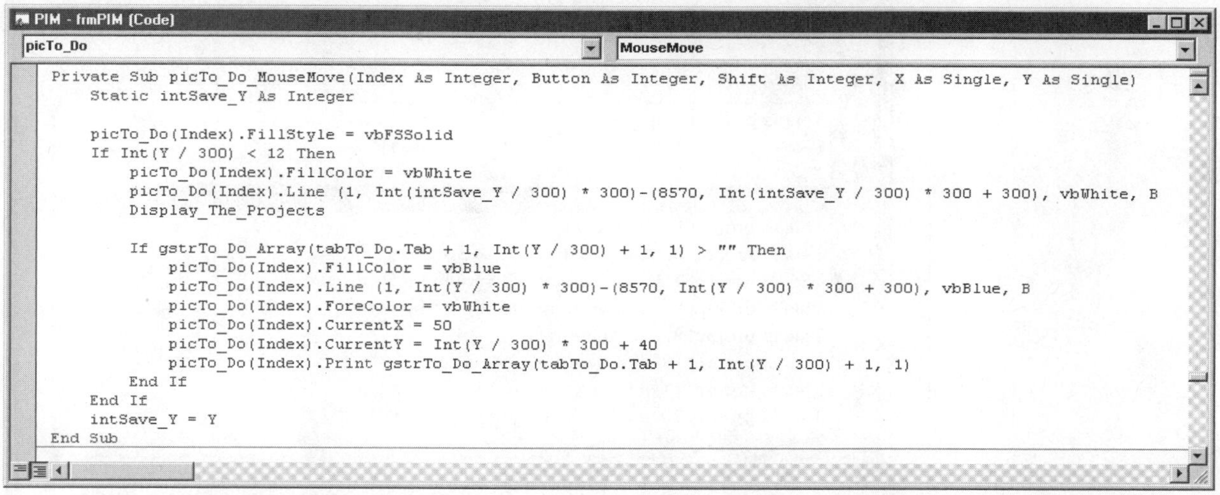

```
PIM - frmPIM (Code)
picTo_Do                                              MouseMove

    Private Sub picTo_Do_MouseMove(Index As Integer, Button As Integer, Shift As Integer, X As Single, Y As Single)
        Static intSave_Y As Integer

        picTo_Do(Index).FillStyle = vbFSSolid
    If Int(Y / 300) < 12 Then
        picTo_Do(Index).FillColor = vbWhite
        picTo_Do(Index).Line (1, Int(intSave_Y / 300) * 300)-(8570, Int(intSave_Y / 300) * 300 + 300), vbWhite, B
        Display_The_Projects

        If gstrTo_Do_Array(tabTo_Do.Tab + 1, Int(Y / 300) + 1, 1) > "" Then
            picTo_Do(Index).FillColor = vbBlue
            picTo_Do(Index).Line (1, Int(Y / 300) * 300)-(8570, Int(Y / 300) * 300 + 300), vbBlue, B
            picTo_Do(Index).ForeColor = vbWhite
            picTo_Do(Index).CurrentX = 50
            picTo_Do(Index).CurrentY = Int(Y / 300) * 300 + 40
            picTo_Do(Index).Print gstrTo_Do_Array(tabTo_Do.Tab + 1, Int(Y / 300) + 1, 1)
        End If
    End If
        intSave_Y = Y
    End Sub
```

10. Key this statement.

   Then we position the cursor as we did earlier in the display routine.

   ```
   picTo_Do(Index).CurrentX = 50
   picTo_Do(Index).CurrentY = Int(Y / 300) * 300 + 40
   ```

11. Key these statements into the procedure.

   Next we print the line of text and close the nested If Test.

   ```
           picTo_Do(Index).Print gstrTo_Do_Array(tabTo_Do.Tab + 1, Int
           ⮡(Y / 300) + 1, 1)
       End If
   End If
   ```

12. Key these statements into the procedure.

   Finally, we store the Y position so that the highlight box can be erased:

   ```
   intSave_Y = Y
   ```

13. Key this statement into the procedure.

   This gives us an entire routine as shown in Figure 11.11.

14. Run the program and select the **To-Do List** tab.

   The text should be in the Picture Box, and as you move the mouse from the top to the bottom of the Text Box, each of the lines, in turn, should become highlighted in blue with white text and then change back as the mouse is moved to the next line (see Figure 11.12).

15. After you have tested the program and are sure it is working properly, exit it.

FIGURE 11.12
The To-Do list, showing the highlighted text.

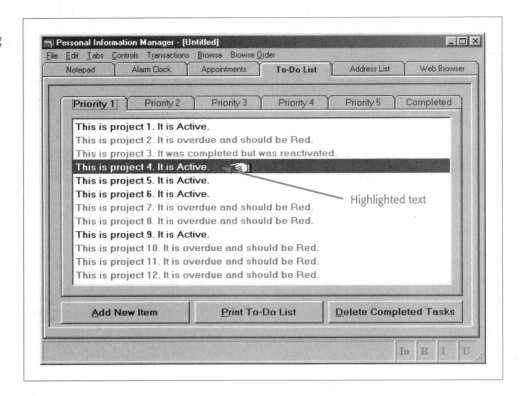

11.7   Using Drag-and-Drop

One of the nice features of many Windows programs is being able to drag an element from one portion of the program and drop it somewhere else. We would like to be able to do that with our projects. We would like to be able to drag a project from one priority and drop it on another priority so that it will show up in the other priority Picture Box. Though this may sound difficult, it really isn't too hard because, once again, Visual Basic handles most of the details for us.

Most Visual Basic objects are already set up for drag-and-drop. All we need to do is set a couple of properties to enable the feature. In the case of a Picture Box, there are two properties that we will use. The first is the **DragMode** property.

1. Select the Picture Box on the **Priority 1** tab, switch to the DragMode property, and pull down the list.

As you can see, there are only two possible states for this property, **Automatic** and **Manual** (the default). If the property is set to Manual, you have to turn on drag-and-drop yourself. Dragging can be turned on by using the **Drag** method, like this:

```
Object.Drag Action
```

where the **Action** parameter is one of the values shown in Table 11.2.

This command is generally used in the Click event for the object, so dragging is enabled when the object is selected. This technique is sometimes necessary for objects such as lists, for which dragging needs to be disabled so that clicking the object will still allow the object to be selected.

Using the Drag method isn't hard, but for our program, we will make drag-and-drop automatic.

TABLE 11.2
The values of the Action parameter of the Drag method.

Predefined Constant	Value	Description
vbCancel	0	Cancels drag operation
vbBeginDrag	1	Begins dragging object
vbEndDrag	2	Ends dragging and drops object

2. Change the property to **Automatic**.

3. Do the same for the other five Picture Boxes.

This gives us the Drag portion of drag-and-drop, and we can test just this part to see if it works.

4. Run the program and select the **To-Do List** tab.

5. Drag the Picture Box to the top of the screen.

You will see a box the size of the Picture Box moving as you move the mouse (see Figure 11.13). This is the default shape used for drag-and-drop. It is the shape of the item being

FIGURE 11.13
The drag-and-drop shape used.

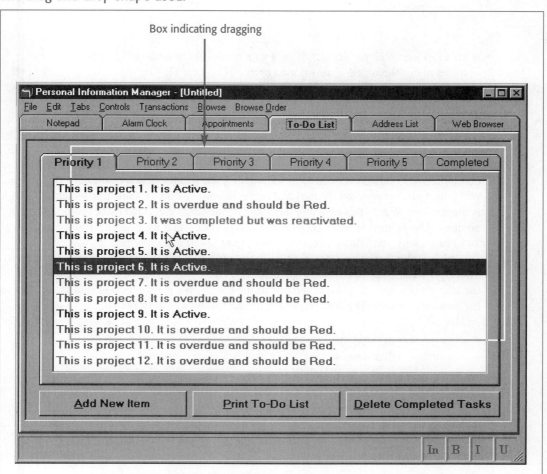

dragged. In some cases this is okay. If we were dragging the text in a text box, for example, the shape of the drag indicator would be the shape of the text box. This would look appropriate. In this case, however, the shape of the Picture Box is too large, so we will change it into an icon.

A number of drag-and-drop icons are available. We will use one that seems to be appropriate. The property for this is **DragIcon**.

6. Exit the program, change to the DragIcon property, select the pull-down list, change to the Misc folder within the Icons folder of the location where the student files are stored on your system, and select the **DragDrop.ico** icon. Do the same for the other five Picture Boxes.

This icon is for dragging one page. Though we are not actually dragging a page of text, it is an icon that looks appropriate for our use.

7. Run the program and try dragging the project from the Picture Box again. This time your icon looks like a hand holding a piece of paper (▤).

8. Exit the program.

Now that we have the drag, we are ready to put the drop portion together. This is done where we want to drop what we are dragging. Most objects have several events related to drag-and-drop. The one we need to use is called **DragDrop**, and the object is the To-Do Tabbed Control.

9. Change to the code window for the To-Do List Tabbed Control. Open the DragDrop event procedure.

> **HINT:** One of the parameters of the DragDrop event procedure is **Source**. It contains the name of the object that dropped onto this object. That is, if you dragged from a text box called txtInput_Data, in the DragDrop procedure, Source would contain txtInput_Data. If the program is dropping from several sources, knowing this enables you to determine which of the sources the data come from.

The first thing we need to do is determine which of the tabs the dragged element is being dropped onto. This is done by calculating the width of each of the tabs (the project will have to be dropped on the tab) and using that dimension to determine which of them it is dropped on. We do this by using the width of the control divided by 6, because there are six tabs. The control is 8655 twips wide, and dividing that by 6 yields 1443. Each tab is 1443 twips wide, and this is what we need to use in our calculations.

Along with that, we need to find the first empty spot in the array of projects for that tab. That is, if we already have four projects in the Picture Box and need to drop another one on the tab, we will have to put it at the end of the others. We need a loop to find the project in the array that is null. This can be done with the following Do Loop:

```
intCounter = 1
Do While gstrTo_Do_Array(Int(X / 1443) + 1, intCounter, 1) <> ""
⮑And intCounter < 12
    intCounter = intCounter + 1
Loop
```

Note that the conditional also checked to make sure that intCounter is less than 12. Because there is room for only 12 projects in the workspace and we have only 12 elements in the gstrTo_Do_Array array, we need to be sure that there are not already 12 projects in the workspace.

10. Add the foregoing code to the DragDrop event procedure.

Now we have a problem. We know the Picture Box and the line for placing the text. We also know from which Picture Box we are dropping a line. What we don't know is which line in that Picture Box we want to drop. In this DragDrop event procedure, there is no indication of what is taking place in the workspace; we have to make that determination somewhere else. As we move the cursor to highlight the project to be dropped, the Mouse-Move procedure knows which line has been selected. Thus, we need to capture the line number as we print the highlight in the Picture Box.

11. Switch back to the MouseMove procedure for the Picture Box, move to the statement that prints the highlighted line in the Picture Box (the end of the If Test), and insert the following statement after it (see Figure 11.14).

```
mintCurrent_Line = Int(Y / 300) + 1
```

This statement performs the same type of calculation on Y that we have performed before to determine which line is being highlighted.

12. Switch back to the DragDrop event procedure.

Because we don't want to drop the project (since there are already 12 projects in the workspace), we begin this next section with a large If Test:

```
If gstrTo_Do_Array(Int(X / 1443) + 1, intCounter, 1) <> "" And
↳ intCounter = 12 Then
    MsgBox "You are only allowed 12 projects of each priority. This
    ↳ project will not be dropped on this tab.", vbExclamation,
    ↳ "Project Error"
Else
```

FIGURE 11.14
Where to insert the new line of code in the MouseMove event procedure.

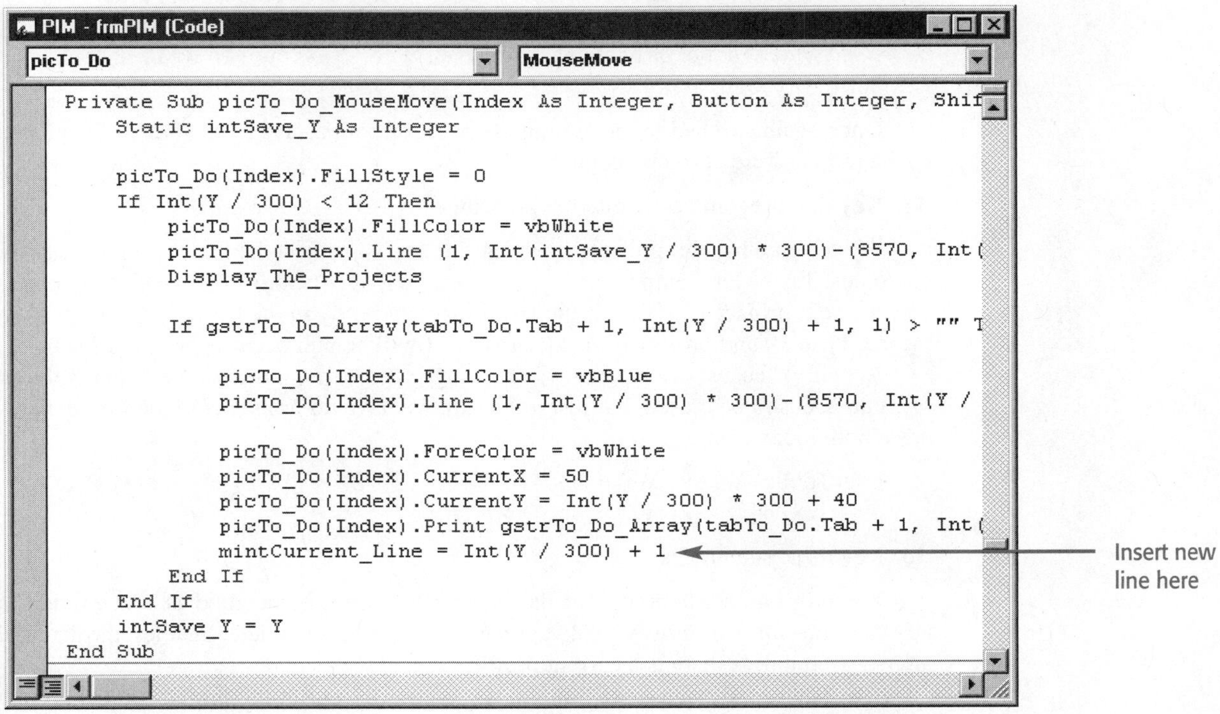

```
PIM - frmPIM (Code)

picTo_Do                              MouseMove

    Private Sub picTo_Do_MouseMove(Index As Integer, Button As Integer, Shif
        Static intSave_Y As Integer

        picTo_Do(Index).FillStyle = 0
        If Int(Y / 300) < 12 Then
            picTo_Do(Index).FillColor = vbWhite
            picTo_Do(Index).Line (1, Int(intSave_Y / 300) * 300)-(8570, Int(
            Display_The_Projects

            If gstrTo_Do_Array(tabTo_Do.Tab + 1, Int(Y / 300) + 1, 1) > "" T

                picTo_Do(Index).FillColor = vbBlue
                picTo_Do(Index).Line (1, Int(Y / 300) * 300)-(8570, Int(Y /

                picTo_Do(Index).ForeColor = vbWhite
                picTo_Do(Index).CurrentX = 50
                picTo_Do(Index).CurrentY = Int(Y / 300) * 300 + 40
                picTo_Do(Index).Print gstrTo_Do_Array(tabTo_Do.Tab + 1, Int(
                mintCurrent_Line = Int(Y / 300) + 1      ←——— Insert new
            End If                                                    line here
        End If
        intSave_Y = Y
    End Sub
```

If there are already 12 projects in the workspace that this project is to be dropped into, we display an error message to the user.

13. Add the foregoing code to the procedure.

Now that we have the line number we need, we can add the project to the array for the tab that is being dropped onto with the following code:

```
gstrTo_Do_Array(Int(X / 1443) + 1, intCounter, 1) =
 gstrTo_Do_Array(tabTo_Do.Tab + 1, mintCurrent_Line, 1)
gstrTo_Do_Array(Int(X / 1443) + 1, intCounter, 2) =
 gstrTo_Do_Array(tabTo_Do.Tab + 1, mintCurrent_Line, 2)
gdtmTo_Do_Dates(Int(X / 1443) + 1, intCounter, 1) =
 gdtmTo_Do_Dates(tabTo_Do.Tab + 1, mintCurrent_Line, 1)
gdtmTo_Do_Dates(Int(X / 1443) + 1, intCounter, 2) =
 gdtmTo_Do_Dates(tabTo_Do.Tab + 1, mintCurrent_Line, 2)
```

Note that we have to copy both the regular array and the dates array. Otherwise, there would be no start and due dates associated with the copied project. We also copied both elements of the third index so that we could get the project message, the status, and both dates.

14. Add the foregoing code.

We now have to remove the dropped project from the array of the tab that dropped the project; it is now related to the new tab, not to the one it came from. We do this by moving each element down from the next to the previous. If we need to remove project 5, we move project 6 to project 5, project 7 to project 6, and so on. This is done with the following code:

```
For intCounter = mintCurrent_Line To 11
    gstrTo_Do_Array(tabTo_Do.Tab + 1, intCounter, 1) =
     gstrTo_Do_Array(tabTo_Do.Tab + 1, intCounter + 1, 1)
    gstrTo_Do_Array(tabTo_Do.Tab + 1, intCounter, 2) =
     gstrTo_Do_Array(tabTo_Do.Tab + 1, intCounter + 1, 2)
    gdtmTo_Do_Dates(tabTo_Do.Tab + 1, intCounter, 1) =
     gdtmTo_Do_Dates(tabTo_Do.Tab + 1, intCounter + 1, 1)
    gdtmTo_Do_Dates(tabTo_Do.Tab + 1, intCounter, 2) =
     gdtmTo_Do_Dates(tabTo_Do.Tab + 1, intCounter + 1, 2)
Next intCounter
```

Once again, we had to move both elements of both arrays to be sure all the elements of the project were correctly copied.

15. Key the foregoing code into the procedure.

We are moving the projects down in the list, so project 12 is the only element that could possibly be left behind with a project that no longer belongs. We need to erase the elements from project 12. Then, if the last project currently in the list is 11, and if we move project 11 to 10 and project 12 to 11, project 11 will be null because project 12 is null.

Actually, because we are always checking just the first index element, that's the only one that needs to be erased, but just to be sure we have no problems in the future, we will erase both index elements.

```
gstrTo_Do_Array(tabTo_Do.Tab + 1, 12, 2) = ""
gstrTo_Do_Array(tabTo_Do.Tab + 1, 12, 1) = ""
```

16. Key these statements.

We didn't bother to empty the date array. Because it is specified as a date field, it really can't be emptied anyway. It always has to have the proper date. Besides, the date fields are not used unless there is a current project for them.

This leaves only one more thing to do. We need to print the projects in the windows with the display routine and close the If Test.

```
        Display_The_Projects
    End If
```

17. Key these two statements.

The entire routine looks like the one shown in Figure 11.15.

18. Run the program.

19. Switch to the **To-Do List** tab. Drag one of the projects from the **Priority 1** tab and drop it on one of the tabs. Change to that tab and make sure the project is now in that workspace.

20. Change back to the first priority tab, and drag-and-drop another project onto the same tab onto which you dropped the first one. Change to that tab and make sure there are now two projects there.

21. Continue to experiment with the program until you have assured yourself that it is working properly. Be sure to try dropping a project back onto the first tab.

FIGURE 11.15
The code for the DragDrop event procedure.

```
PIM - frmPIM (Code)                                                    _ □ ×

tabTo_Do                              ▼   DragDrop                           ▼

Private Sub tabTo_Do_DragDrop(Source As Control, X As Single, Y As Single)
    Dim intCounter As Integer

    ' Move project to the other tab picture box

    intCounter = 1
    Do While gstrTo_Do_Array(Int(X / 1443) + 1, intCounter, 1) <> "" And intCounter < 12
        intCounter = intCounter + 1
    Loop

    If gstrTo_Do_Array(Int(X / 1443) + 1, intCounter, 1) <> "" And intCounter = 12 Then
        MsgBox "You are only allowed 12 projects of each priority. This project will not b
    Else

        ' Move the project from tab to tab (in the arrays)

        gstrTo_Do_Array(Int(X / 1443) + 1, intCounter, 1) = gstrTo_Do_Array(tabTo_Do.Tab +
        gstrTo_Do_Array(Int(X / 1443) + 1, intCounter, 2) = gstrTo_Do_Array(tabTo_Do.Tab +
        gdtmTo_Do_Dates(Int(X / 1443) + 1, intCounter, 1) = gdtmTo_Do_Dates(tabTo_Do.Tab +
        gdtmTo_Do_Dates(Int(X / 1443) + 1, intCounter, 2) = gdtmTo_Do_Dates(tabTo_Do.Tab +

        ' Move the projects down in the array to replace the one moved

        For intCounter = mintCurrent_Line To 11
            gstrTo_Do_Array(tabTo_Do.Tab + 1, intCounter, 1) = gstrTo_Do_Array(tabTo_Do.Ta
            gstrTo_Do_Array(tabTo_Do.Tab + 1, intCounter, 2) = gstrTo_Do_Array(tabTo_Do.Ta
            gdtmTo_Do_Dates(tabTo_Do.Tab + 1, intCounter, 1) = gdtmTo_Do_Dates(tabTo_Do.Ta
            gdtmTo_Do_Dates(tabTo_Do.Tab + 1, intCounter, 2) = gdtmTo_Do_Dates(tabTo_Do.Ta
        Next intCounter

        ' Erase the last elements

        gstrTo_Do_Array(tabTo_Do.Tab + 1, 12, 2) = ""
        gstrTo_Do_Array(tabTo_Do.Tab + 1, 12, 1) = ""

        Display_The_Projects
    End If
End Sub
```

11.8   Changing the Status

We set up the **Completed** tab so that by dropping the projects on the tab, we could indicate that they are completed. The problem is that when we drop them on the **Completed** tab, we don't change the status of the projects, so they still display as active and overdue. We need to change the status to Complete when the projects are dropped on the **Completed** tab and then reactivate them if they are dropped back onto one of the **Priority** tabs.

This entails adding an If Test in the DragDrop procedure to determine what tab the project is being dropped onto. This If Test should be placed after the project has been moved to the new tab and before the project in the current tab is erased.

The routine that is needed is

```
If Int(X / 1443) + 1 = 6 Then
    gstrTo_Do_Array(Int(X / 1443) + 1, intCounter, 2) = "Complete"
ElseIf tabTo_Do.Tab + 1 = 6 Then
    gstrTo_Do_Array(Int(X / 1443) + 1, intCounter, 2) = "Active"
End If
```

As you can see, this If Test determines whether the tab being dropped on is 6 and, if it is, changes the status to Complete. If not, it checks to see if the tab the project is being removed from is 6. If it is, the project is reactivated.

1. Exit the program and insert the foregoing code between the lines to insert the project in the new tab and the lines to remove the project from the current tab (as shown in Figure 11.16).

FIGURE 11.16
The insertion point for the new code in the DragDrop event procedure.

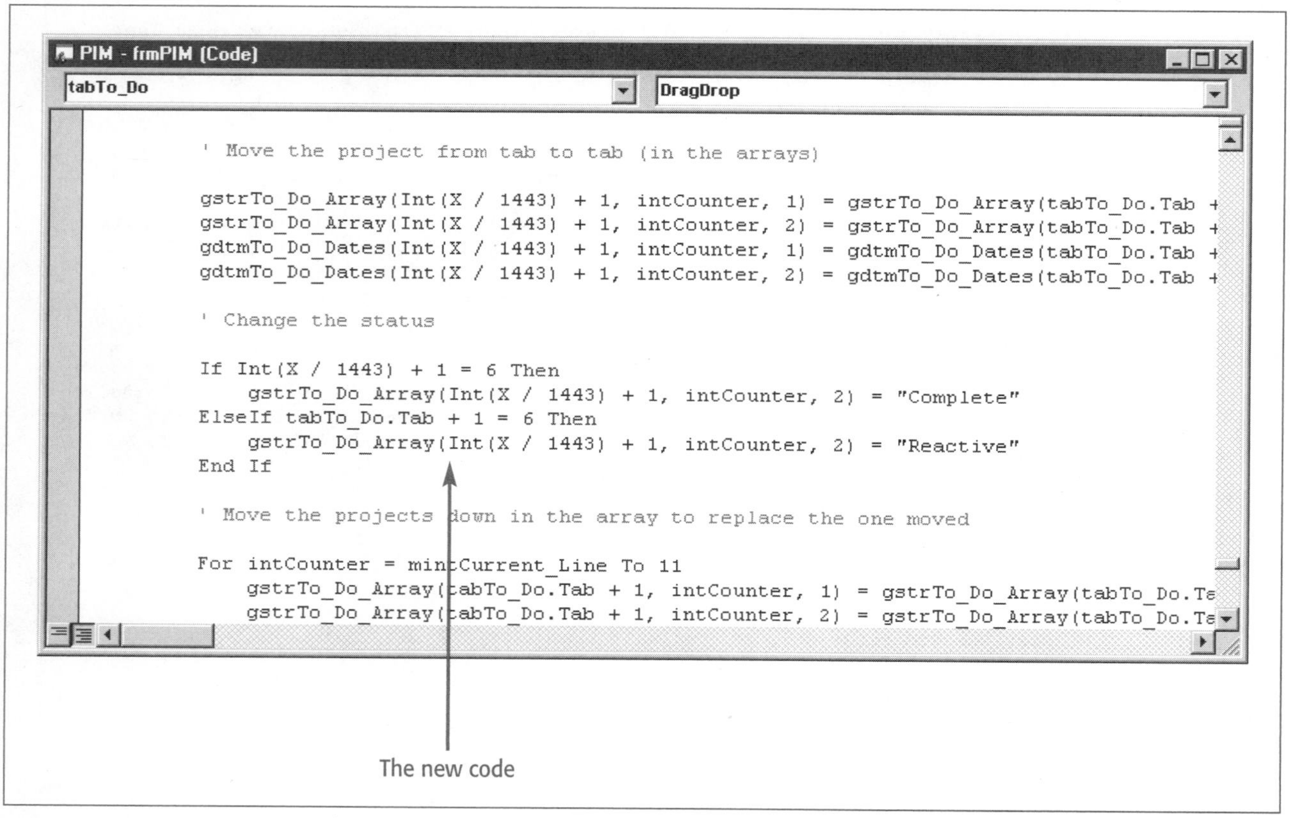

```
' Move the project from tab to tab (in the arrays)

gstrTo_Do_Array(Int(X / 1443) + 1, intCounter, 1) = gstrTo_Do_Array(tabTo_Do.Tab +
gstrTo_Do_Array(Int(X / 1443) + 1, intCounter, 2) = gstrTo_Do_Array(tabTo_Do.Tab +
gdtmTo_Do_Dates(Int(X / 1443) + 1, intCounter, 1) = gdtmTo_Do_Dates(tabTo_Do.Tab +
gdtmTo_Do_Dates(Int(X / 1443) + 1, intCounter, 2) = gdtmTo_Do_Dates(tabTo_Do.Tab +

' Change the status

If Int(X / 1443) + 1 = 6 Then
    gstrTo_Do_Array(Int(X / 1443) + 1, intCounter, 2) = "Complete"
ElseIf tabTo_Do.Tab + 1 = 6 Then
    gstrTo_Do_Array(Int(X / 1443) + 1, intCounter, 2) = "Reactive"
End If

' Move the projects down in the array to replace the one moved

For intCounter = min Current_Line To 11
    gstrTo_Do_Array(tabTo_Do.Tab + 1, intCounter, 1) = gstrTo_Do_Array(tabTo_Do.Ta
    gstrTo_Do_Array(tabTo_Do.Tab + 1, intCounter, 2) = gstrTo_Do_Array(tabTo_Do.Ta
```

The new code

2. Run the program. Drag a few elements from the **Priority 1** tab and drop them on the **Completed** tab. They should now be in the **Completed** tab's workspace and should be gone from the **Priority 1** workspace.

3. Drop an element from the **Completed** tab to some other tab. It should show up there in magenta or red, depending on whether it is overdue. (Magenta is the color we decided to use to designate the projects that have been reactivated.)

4. Continue to test the program until you are certain it is working properly; then exit the program.

11.9 Displaying the Dates

The one element of the projects that we have yet to deal with, other than using the due date to display the projects in the appropriate color, is the dates. This is good information that should be available to the user, so we need to determine how to display these dates. We could use the ToolTips display, but displaying the tips is not under our program's control. We would rather be in control of when and where the dates appear. We could also use the status bar for this (that is essentially what it was set up for), but we will do something a bit different instead. We will set up a small text box in which to display the dates. We will add the text box to the form itself rather than to the Picture Box. That way, we need only one text box rather than one for each Picture Box.

1. Add a text box to the form (see Figure 11.17) with the following considerations:
   a. The Height property is **330**.
   b. The BackColor is yellow.
   c. The BorderStyle is **1 - Fixed Single**.
   d. The Appearance is **0 - Flat**.
   e. The Visible property is False.

FIGURE 11.17
The new text box.

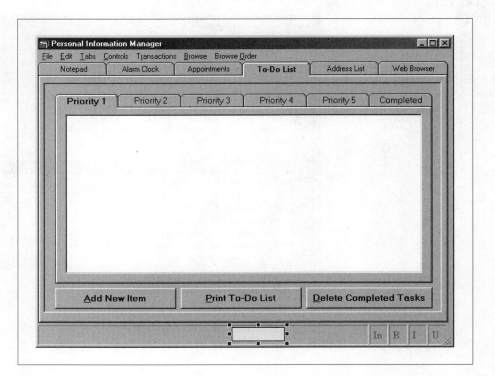

f. Position the text box over the status bar so that you can see where it is.

We want this text box to display when the user right-clicks the projects. Therefore, we need to use the MouseDown event.

2. Change to the MouseDown procedure for the Picture Box.

We need an If Test to be sure the right mouse button is pressed. Then the code in that If Test should position the text box just under the highlight box, display the dates, and turn on the text box. The necessary code is

```
If Button = vbRightButton Then
    txtDisplay.Text = " Date Entered = " & gdtmTo_Do_Dates(Index,
    ↳ Int(Y / 300) + 1, 1) & ", " & "Due Date = " &
    ↳ gdtmTo_Do_Dates(Index, Int(Y / 300) + 1, 2) & " "
    txtDisplay.Top = 1380 + Int(Y / 300) * 300 + 300
    txtDisplay.Left = 720 + X + 200
    txtDisplay.Width = TextWidth(txtDisplay.Text) + 100
    txtDisplay.Visible = True
End If
```

3. Key this code in the procedure.

In the txtDisplay.Text assignment statement, we display both the Date Entered (element 1) and the Due Date (element 2), separated by a comma. The label is offset from the X position by 720 so that it will be in the workspace and by another 200 so that the label will not be displayed right under the mouse cursor, but will be displayed near the cursor.

We used a new function in the procedure. The **TextWidth** function returns the width of the specified text. We use this to determine how wide the text box should be so it can display all the text we put in it. The extra 100 twips are an allowance for the space at the beginning and end of the text. The TextWidth function uses the width of the underlying form to determine this width. We need to be sure the font characteristics of the form and the text box are the same. The only change needed to either is to change the Font Style to **Bold**.

4. Call up the Font dialog box for the text box and change the Font Style to **Bold**.

FIGURE 11.18
The date display.

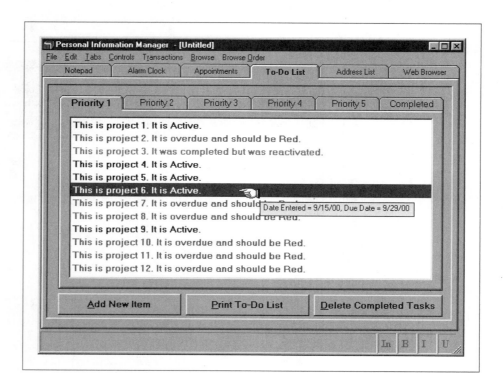

5. Do the same for the form.

This procedure turns on the display; somehow, it will have to be turned off. Well, because it is turned on in the MouseDown event procedure, the logical place to turn it off is in the MouseUp procedure. This way, the dates will be displayed while the right button is held down and will vanish when the button is released.

6. Change to the MouseUp procedure, and key the appropriate statement to turn the label off.

7. Run the program, change to the **To-Do List** tab, and right-click on one of the projects. The dates should appear in the label just under the highlighted project, as shown in Figure 11.18. Release the mouse button, and the label should disappear.

8. Exit the program.

11.10   Adding a New Project

There are only four things left to do to finish the To-Do list.

■ Use the **Add New Item** button to add a new project.

■ Print a report of the projects using the **Print To-Do List** button.

■ Use the **Delete Completed Tasks** button to remove all the projects from the Completed Picture Box and that portion of the array.

■ Attach the array to the database so that the projects will be read from and stored there.

Here we will use the **Add New Item** button to create a new project. In the next section we will explore how to send a report to the printer. The last two items will be left as exercises at the end of the chapter.

To add a new project, we need to get three things from the user:

■ The project message

■ The due date

■ The priority

To get these things, we will create a new form.

1. Create a new form called **frmAdd_To_Do** as shown in Figure 11.19, with the following considerations:

    a. The project description is a multiline text box called **txtTo_Do_Description**. Add a vertical scroll bar.

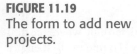

FIGURE 11.19
The form to add new projects.

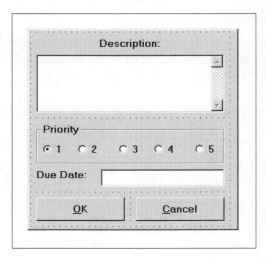

   b. The option buttons are a control array called **optTo_Do_Priorities**.

   c. The text box is called **txtDue_Date**.

   d. The buttons have the standard names.

   e. Turn off the control menu and erase the default caption so that there will be no title bar.

The first thing we need to do is call up the form when the user clicks the **Add New Item** button. The problem is that we don't want to display the dialog box if the priority Picture Box already has 12 projects in it. Because we can't add more than 12 elements, we must test for this and warn the user. The code we need is

```
intCounter = 1
Do While gstrTo_Do_Array(tabTo_Do.Tab + 1, intCounter, 1) <> ""
↳ And intCounter < 12
    intCounter = intCounter + 1
Loop
If gstrTo_Do_Array(tabTo_Do.Tab + 1, intCounter, 1) <> ""
↳ And intCounter = 12 Then
    MsgBox "You are only allowed 12 projects of each priority. You
        ↳ cannot add another project to this priority.", vbExclamation,
        ↳ "Project Error"
Else
    frmAdd_To_Do.Show 1
    Display_The_Projects
End If
```

   2. Change to the code for the **Add New Item** button, and key the foregoing statements.

On the form itself, the program needs to unload the form and save the data into the array when the user clicks the **OK** button.

   3. Change to the code for the **OK** button on the new form.

The first thing we need to do here is figure out which of the priority option buttons was clicked. This tells us in which priority tab workspace and which array element the new project is to be placed. It is done as follows:

```
For intCounter = 1 To 5
    If optTo_Do_Priorities(intCounter).Value = True Then
        intPriority = intCounter
    End If
Next intCounter
```

   4. Key this code into the procedure.

intPriority will contain the priority number that can be used to determine where the null place is in the array and then used again to put the data into the array. To find the first empty spot in the array, we will use code like that we used before:

```
intCounter = 1
Do While gstrTo_Do_Array(intPriority, intCounter, 1) <> "" and
↳ intCounter < 12
    intCounter = intCounter + 1
Loop
```

   5. Key this code into the procedure.

Now we know where to put the data in the array, and we will use the following statements to do it.

```
gstrTo_Do_Array(intPriority, intCounter, 1) = txtTo_Do_Description
gstrTo_Do_Array(intPriority, intCounter, 2) = "Active"
```

```
gdtmTo_Do_Dates(intPriority, intCounter, 1) = Date
gdtmTo_Do_Dates(intPriority, intCounter, 2) = txtDue_Date
```

6. Key this code into the procedure.

   The last thing is to unload the form.

7. Key the final statement into the procedure.

   The code for the **Cancel** button is easy. We just need to unload the form.

8. Change to the code for the **Cancel** button and key the appropriate statement to unload the form.

9. Run the program. Select the **Add New Item** button, and the message box appears. Because there are already 12 projects in the first priority, another cannot be added and the program caught it.

10. Add a few projects to other priorities to be sure the program is working properly, and then exit the program.

11.11 Printing Reports

> **WARNING:** You must have a printer networked or attached and online to use the code in the next section.

Thus far, when printing from our programs, we have used the PrintForm method. This is useful for printing many things, but often we want to print from our programs in a report format. In this section we will explore many printing techniques and will print the To-Do List and add a print function to the notepad.

Printing the To-Do List

When printing a report, we use the **Printer** object and many of the same methods and properties that we have already explored. To print text on the printer, the **Print** method is used just as it is used to print text into a Picture Box. That is, to print a message on the printer, you use a statement like the following:

```
Printer.Print "This is a sample message"
```

Not only is the Print method used, but we can also use drawing methods such as Line. Printing to a printer is much like drawing in a Picture Box. We can print and draw on the Printer object using any appropriate method, and the page is actually printed when either the **NewPage** or the **EndDoc** method is used. The **NewPage** method tells Visual Basic that you are through with this page and ready to print on the next page. It prints the page and positions the print position at the upper left corner of the next page. The **EndDoc** method is used to tell the printer you are finished printing the current document.

When a report is printed, normally a **heading** is printed at the top of each page. At a minimum, a heading usually contains the page number and a report title. Other elements of a heading might include the name of the person printing the report, the date and/or time the report was printed, and the name of the program from which the report was printed. When there are too many elements to print in a heading, a **footing**, which is printed at the bottom of each page, can also be used.

A heading may be printed several times when a report is printed, so we will use a called procedure to print ours.

1. Open the code window for the **Print To-Do List** button, and key **Print_Headings**.
2. Create a new public subroutine called **Print_Headings**.

A heading is generally printed with a larger font than the rest of the report so that it will stand out just as headings do in a newspaper or book. To set font characteristics, we use the same properties we have used before. That is, to set the font name and font size, we use

```
Printer.FontName = "Arial"
Printer.FontSize = 16
```

3. Key these statements into the Print_Headings procedure.

To print the page number, we will use a special property called **Page**. Visual Basic automatically keeps track of the current page number in this property. It begins as 1 and is automatically incremented when the NewPage method is used or when you print beyond the bottom of the page and a new page is automatically generated. The following statement is used to print the page number in the heading.

```
Printer.Print "Page " & Printer.Page;
```

The semicolon at the end is used to tell the printer that the next thing printed after this statement is to be printed on the same line.

The print position can be moved in several different ways. A literal filled with spaces can be printed:

```
Printer.Print "              ";
```

A number of spaces can also be printed using the String function:

```
Printer.Print String(25, " ");
```

or using the **Spc** function designed for the same purpose when printing:

```
Printer.Print Spc(25);
```

The **Tab** function positions the print position at the specified position:

```
Printer.Print Tab(50);
```

The CurrentX property, however, lets us position the cursor more precisely using a statement such as

```
Printer.CurrentX = 4000
```

4. Key this statement into the procedure.

As we discussed earlier, the CurrentX property moves the print position horizontally, and the CurrentY property moves the print position vertically. Thus, using these properties, we can move the print position up, down, left, or right to position the cursor wherever necessary for printing the next item.

Each of the elements of a heading can be printed using the same or different font characteristics. For this report, we have chosen to print the page number with a font size of 16, but we are going to print the report title in bold with a font size of 20. This is done with the following statements:

```
Printer.FontSize = 20
Printer.FontBold = True
Printer.Print "TO-DO LIST"
```

5. Key these three statements into the procedure.

Now it would be nice to draw a line under the heading. We could use the Underline method, but because we used two fonts of different sizes in the heading, the underlines would have different thicknesses. Besides, we want the line to be farther under the heading than an underline, and we want the line to be thicker. So we will use the Line method to draw the line. The statement we need is

```
Printer.Line (1, 400)-(12000, 440), vbBlack, BF
```

This prints the line from print position 1, 400 and draws a black box to print position 12000, 440. It gives us a thick line just under the heading.

This completes printing of the heading. Before exiting this procedure, however, we need to set the font characteristics for printing the regular portions of the report. Otherwise, after completion of the heading procedure, the rest of the report would be printed with the font characteristics used for the heading. Thus, we need the following statements:

```
Printer.FontName = "Times New Roman"
Printer.FontSize = 12
Printer.FontBold = False
Printer.Print
```

The last line here is used to create a blank line between the heading and the first line printed after the heading.

6. Key these statements into the procedure.

7. Run the program, switch to the To-Do list, and print the report. All you will get is the heading, but it is a good test to determine whether the printing is working.

With the heading printed, it is time to turn our attention back to the printing of the list itself.

8. Exit the program and switch back to the code for the **Print To-Do List** button.

We want to print a limited number of lines of text on the page before we print the page and begin a new page, so we keep track of the number of lines on the page and give that counter a starting value with the following statement:

```
intLine_Counter = 4
```

9. Key this statement after the Print_Headings statement.

Because there are six tabs that can contain projects, we need a loop such as

```
For intOutside_Counter = 1 To 6
```

10. Key the For statement.

Next we want to print, above each of the groups of projects, a heading designating the priority. To do so we reset the font characteristics:

```
Printer.FontName = "Arial"
Printer.FontSize = 14
Printer.FontBold = True
```

11. Key these statements.

We print a different heading if the project group is one of the priority groups or the completed group. This means we need an If Test like the following:

```
If intOutside_Counter < 6 Then
    Printer.Print "Priority " & Trim(Str(intOutside_Counter)) &
    ⤷ "Projects"
Else
    Printer.Print "Completed Projects"
End If
```

12. Key this If Test.

Now we are ready to print the projects, and we change the font:

```
Printer.FontName = "Times New Roman"
Printer.FontSize = 12
Printer.FontBold = False
```

13. Key these statements.

If there are no projects of any particular priority, we would like to print an appropriate message. To know when to print the message, we need a flag such as

```
blnWas_Line_Printed = False
```

14. Key this statement.

Next we need a loop to print the 12 projects within the priority group.

```
For intCounter = 1 To 12
    If gstrTo_Do_Array(intOutside_Counter, intCounter, 1) <> "" Then
        Printer.Print gstrTo_Do_Array(intOutside_Counter,
        ↳ intCounter, 1); " —>Date Entered = " & gdtmTo_Do_Dates
        ↳ (intOutside_Counter, intCounter, 1) & ", " & "Due Date = "
        ↳ & gdtmTo_Do_Dates(intOutside_Counter, intCounter, 2)
        blnWas_Line_Printed = True
        intLine_Counter = intLine_Counter + 1
```

Note that we set the flag indicating that a project was printed and that we increment the line counter.

15. Key these statements into the procedure.

Because we are printing various elements of the list with different font sizes, there is no precise way to determine exactly how many printed lines will constitute a full page. Sometimes you will have to print several samples before you arrive at the correct number of lines to use. In this program, we will use 55 lines per page, as in

```
If intLine_Counter >= 55 Then
```

16. Key this statement.

Now we need to use the NewPage method to print the current page and then print the headings.

```
            Printer.NewPage
            Print_Headings
            intLine_Counter = 4
        End If
    End If
Next intCounter
```

17. Key these statements.

Now, if no projects were printed under the heading, we print a message using the If Test as follows (with a test for the end of the page like the one we just used):

```
        If blnWas_Line_Printed = False Then
        Printer.Print "No Projects of this priority"
        intLine_Counter = intLine_Counter + 1
        If intLine_Counter >= 55 Then
            Printer.NewPage
            Print_Headings
            intLine_Counter = 4
        End If
    End If
End If
```

18. Key these statements.

Next we print a couple of blank lines to put some space between the project groups.

```
Printer.Print
Printer.Print
intLine_Counter = intLine_Counter + 2
If intLine_Counter >= 55 Then
    Printer.NewPage
    Print_Headings
    intLine_Counter = 4
End If
Next intOutside_Counter
```

19. Key these statements.

That leaves just one thing to do. We need to tell the program we are finished with the report with the EndDoc method.

```
Printer.EndDoc
```

20. Key this statement.

21. Run the program, switch to the To-Do list, and print the report. You should get a report with 12 projects showing in the first priority group and a "No Projects" message under the heading for all the other groups.

22. Drag and drop several of the projects on other priority tabs. Print the report again to be sure the projects are showing up where they are supposed to.

23. Exit the program.

Printing the Notepad Document

Printing the Notepad document is done by using the same basic print methods and properties. Because the text in the Notepad workspace may have long lines that the text box wraps automatically, we will have to concern ourselves with these long lines and create a print routine that will word-wrap. We will also use a dialog box that shows the progress of the printing by displaying the file name and the page currently being printed. This really wasn't necessary when we were printing the To-Do list, because the printing didn't take long. Printing a document, on the other hand, might take a while, and displaying a progress dialog box is helpful to the user.

We could add a menu item (usually on the **File** menu) to allow the user to print the document, but the Notepad has a set of buttons, so we will simply add a new button.

1. Add a button next to the other buttons on the Notepad tab as shown in Figure 11.20.

2. Change the caption to **P** and the control name to **cmdPrint_Notepad**.

3. Change the Left property to **1460** and the Top property to **520** to align the new button with the others.

To be consistent with the other buttons, we will want the ToolTips display to show up when the mouse is moved over the new button.

4. Key **Print** in the ToolTipText property.

We should also have a message appear in the status bar when the mouse is moved over the button, as we have for the other buttons. The MouseMove event procedure should have the following code:

```
staPIM_Status.Panels(1).Text = "This button will print the Notepad
⮡ document."
```

FIGURE 11.20
The Notepad with the **Print** button added to the button bar.

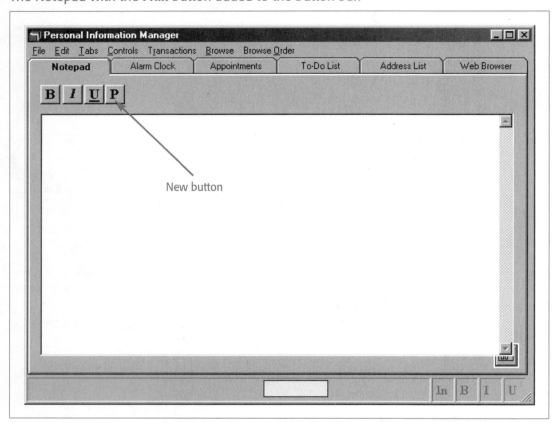

5. Switch to the code for the MouseMove event of the **Print** button, and key this statement.

Let's begin the print procedure by changing the MousePointer to the hourglass so that the user knows something is in process.

```
Screen.MousePointer = vbHourglass
```

The next thing we want to do is print the heading. This will require a call to the **Print_Notepad_Heading** procedure.

6. Switch to the cmdPrint_Notepad_Click procedure, and add the MousePointer statement and the appropriate call statement.

7. Create a new private subroutine called **Print_Notepad_Heading**. Add the following code to the procedure:

```
Printer.FontName = "Arial"
Printer.FontSize = 12
Printer.Print "Page " & Printer.Page;
Printer.CurrentX = 5000

' Search for the dash on the Caption

    intSearch = InStr(frmPIM.Caption, " -")
    Printer.Print Mid(frmPIM.Caption, intSearch + 3);
```

This gives us the page number on the left side of the heading and the file name from the caption of the title bar where it is placed when the file is saved or loaded. If the printing is done before the file is saved, the file name will be printed as "[Untitled]" because this is the default name shown on the title bar.

On this heading, we want to print the date on the right side. This is done with the statements

```
Printer.CurrentX = 10500
Printer.Print Date
```

8. Key these two statements.

Next we will draw a line under the heading with the statement

```
Printer.Line (1, 300)-(12000, 320), vbBlack, BF
```

9. Key this statement.

Then we change the font to what we want to use for the normal printing and print a blank line for spacing.

```
Printer.FontName = "Times New Roman"
Printer.FontSize = 12
Printer.FontBold = False
Printer.Print
```

10. Key these statements.

Finally, we want to show a progress form so that the user will know the progress of the printing process. This can be done with the following statements:

```
frmPrint_Display.Show
frmPrint_Display.lblFilename = "Printing: " & pnlButton_Bar.Caption
frmPrint_Display.lblPage = "Now Printing Page " & Printer.Page
DoEvents
```

11. Key these statements.

We have a statement to show a progress form, so we had better add the form to the program.

12. Create a new form (see Figure 11.21) with two labels, **lblFilename** (the top one) and **lblPage**. Erase the caption and turn off the ControlBox so that there will be no title bar.

The statements we added to the heading procedure change these labels so that they display the proper data.
Now we are ready to work through the rest of the print procedure.

13. Switch back to the cmdPrint_Notepad_Click procedure.

The last statement in this procedure thus far is the call to the heading procedure. Following that, we need to set the line counter.

```
intLine_Counter = 4
```

FIGURE 11.21
The printing progress form.

14. Key this statement.

Then we need a special counter to count the characters as they are printed across the page. Because this is a document and there are carriage returns only at the ends of the paragraphs, we need to determine when we have reached the edge of the page. The easiest way to do this is to count the characters as we print them across the page. This is done with the following counter:

```
intCharacter_Counter = 1
```

15. Key this statement.

Now we loop through all the characters that are displayed in the Notepad workspace text box.

```
For intCounter = 1 To Len(txtNotepad)
```

16. Key this statement into the procedure.

Normally we would have to print a line or two of text to determine how many characters can be printed on a line before we need to print a carriage return, but we have already determined the proper number through testing. When intCharacter_Counter reaches 110, we are ready for a new line. Unfortunately, we can't just print a carriage return when we reach 110 (if we did, we would split words). We need a test to determine when we have printed 110 or more characters and the next character is a space. If it is, then we know we are between words. We need an If Test like the following:

```
If intCharacter_Counter > 110 And Mid(txtNotepad, intCounter, 1) =
↳" " Then
```

17. Key this statement.

This is actually a rather unsophisticated test. We might have a word that extends beyond 110 and is so long that it extends beyond the edge of the printed page. If that happens, the rest of the letters of the word are simply printed beyond the edge of the page and are not visible when printed. Also, most word processors allow words with a dash to be divided at the dash. Ours won't do that, though it isn't difficult to accomplish. All you would need to do is check for a blank for the regular end of a word or a dash if the word is divided and print the dash (if there is one) on the first line and the rest on the next line. We won't bother with that.

Within the If Test, we know we are ready for another line, so the next statement should print a carriage return.

```
Printer.Print vbCrLf;
DoEvents
```

18. Key these statements.

Now that we have begun a new line, we need to reset the character counter and increment the line counter.

```
intCharacter_Counter = 1
intLine_Counter = intLine_Counter + 1
```

19. Key these two statements.

We have just printed a new line, so we need to see whether a new page needs to be started.

```
    If intLine_Counter >= 55 Then
        Printer.NewPage
        Print_Notepad_Heading
        intLine_Counter = 4
    End If
Else
```

20. Key these statements.

After the Else, we know we can just print the character because we are not ready to move to another line. But there is the possibility that the next character is a carriage return at the end of a paragraph. If it is, there are actually two characters: a carriage return and a line feed. We want to print the vbCrLf character to handle both of these characters and strip off the line feed that the text box has. Then we adjust the counters and test for a new page as before. All this is done with

```
If Mid(txtNotepad, intCounter, 1) = vbCr Then
    Printer.Print vbCrLf;
    intCounter = intCounter + 1
    intCharacter_Counter = 1
    intLine_Counter = intLine_Counter + 1
    If intLine_Counter >= 55 Then
        Printer.NewPage
        Print_Notepad_Heading
        intLine_Counter = 4
    End If
Else
```

21. Key these statements into the procedure.

If the character is not a carriage return, we simply print the character and count it.

```
        Printer.Print Mid(txtNotepad, intCounter, 1);
        intCharacter_Counter = intCharacter_Counter + 1
      End If
    End If
Next intCounter
```

22. Key these statements.

Then we need to tell the printer we are finished, reset the button and mouse pointer, and unload the printing progress form.

```
Printer.EndDoc
Screen.MousePointer = vbDefault
Unload frmPrint_Display
```

23. Key these statements.

That's it. We are ready to test the program.

24. Run the program. Load **Sample Document.txt** from the Ch-8 folder on your work disk.

25. Print the document. Check to be sure the text in the paragraphs is being wrapped properly. To see whether the heading procedure is called and is working properly, you can copy and paste the text in the workspace several times until there is enough to run over onto another page. Exit the program when you are satisfied that it is working properly.

11.12   Other Graphics Methods

You saw how useful it is to be able to draw graphics when you are manipulating a Picture Box. Well, as we noted earlier, the Line method is only one of several graphics methods available. To experiment with a few more methods, you will create a new program.

1. Create a new program with a Picture Box on the form.

The PSet Method

If you just want to draw a dot in the Picture Box, the **PSet** method is the one to use. The form of the method is PSet(X,Y), where X is the horizontal position and Y is the vertical position. To cause a dot to appear in the Picture Box precisely one inch from the top and left, you would use the command

```
Picture1.PSet (1440, 1440)
```

1. Open the code window for the MouseDown procedure, and key this PSet statement.

2. Run the program (you can save it as **Graphics Practice** if you wish) and click the Picture Box.

The dot appears in the Picture Box, but it is only one twip wide and is virtually impossible to see. Let's make it a bit bigger. This can be done with the **DrawWidth** method, as in

```
Picture1.DrawWidth = 10
```

3. Exit the program and insert this statement before the other. Run the program and click the Picture Box.

Now the dot appears much larger. The dot is drawn in the current foreground color, of course.

4. Exit the program, change the foreground color to green, and run the program again.

Now the dot is green.

You can position the dot anywhere in the Picture Box, including the place where you click the box. This is done by using the X and Y coordinates that are already given to you in the MouseDown event.

5. Exit the program and change the PSet statement to use the X and Y coordinate variables. Run the program again, and notice that as you click the Picture Box, the dots appear where you click.

The Circle Method

The other graphics method we are going to look at here is the **Circle** method. It is used as the Line method is, although it has several more parameters that you can change to draw ellipses and arcs as well as circles. The only parameter we are going to deal with, however, is **Radius**—the distance from the center to the edge of the circle. If you need to know more about the Circle method and the other parameters it can use, you can look it up in the user's manual or the Help system.

The form of the Circle method is

```
Object.Circle (X, Y), Radius
```

The X and Y parameters give the coordinates of the center of the circle, and the Radius gives the distance to the edge of the circle from the center. We will use the command in the MouseDown event again so that we will get a circle drawn around the point where we click the Picture Box.

1. Exit the program and change the PSet statement to

```
Picture1.Circle (X, Y), 100
```

2. Run the program and click the Picture Box.

You get what seems to be a very large dot with a small hole in the middle. Remember that you set the DrawWidth to 10. This means the circle is being drawn with a line width of 10. You need to change this.

3. Exit the program and change the DrawWidth to **2**.

4. Run the program again and click the Picture Box. This time you get a circle.

   Just as in the box command, you can specify the type of fill you want to use. If you use the Fillstyle of VbFSSolid, you get a solid circle.

5. Exit the program and add the Fillstyle statement above the Circle statement. Run the program and click the Picture Box.

   Now you have a solid circle, but the center of the circle is black. You have a black circle with a green border. The foreground color is used for the border of a circle or box, but the fill color must be specified separately.

6. Exit the program and add a Fillcolor statement above the circle command. Make the fill color green. Run the program and click the Picture Box.

   Now you have a solid green circle.

7. Exit the program and change the Fillstyle to VbDiagonalCross. Run the program and click the Picture Box.

   Now you have crosshatching in the circle.

8. Continue to experiment with the commands, changing the Fillcolor, Fillstyle, and DrawWidth until you are satisfied that you understand what each command is doing. Then exit the program.

11.13 Debugging Your Programs

There are a few problems you might encounter when using the Printer object. When printing documents, you need to be sure your line wrapping function is working properly. It is easy to tell by simply reading through the printed text and comparing it against the original document displayed in the program. If the two agree, your function is probably working correctly. Remember that you might encounter a word or two that appears at the right edge of the wrap and is longer than the program is set up to handle. If so, you may need to adjust your routine or rewrite the sentence in question so that it uses a shorter word.

The printer will not print the pages of your document unless you use the NewPage method, the text prints off the page, or you use the EndDoc method. If you forget to use EndDoc, the last page of the document will not print until the user exits the program. Upon that event, the contents of printer buffers will be sent to the printer.

When using the Line method, you need to be sure to specify the parameters properly. The X parameters refer to the horizontal positioning, the Y parameters to the vertical positioning. If you specify them incorrectly, the line or box you are drawing will be oriented incorrectly.

When using the DragDrop features, you must be sure to set up both ends of the transaction. The element that is to be dragged must be set up as manual or automatic and the icon chosen if necessary. Then whatever objects you are dropping onto must have the appropriate code to receive the data being dropped. Dropping an object onto another one that is not set up to receive the appropriate type of data will not cause the program to generate any type of error; the data just will not be received.

11.14 Command and Menu Summary

In this chapter you learned about the following properties:

■ **AutoRedraw** tells Visual Basic to redraw the graphic automatically when the window has been obscured by another window.

- **CurrentX** and **CurrentY** are special properties that contain the current coordinates of the mouse pointer within that object.
- **DragIcon** specifies the icon to be used to indicate dragging.
- **DragMode** specifies whether setup for the dragging of an object is to be automatic or manual.
- **DrawWidth** is used to specify the width of the line used to draw graphics elements.
- **FillColor** specifies the color that is to be used when a box or circle is filled.
- **FillStyle** specifies the style of fill that will be used as a box or circle is created.
- **Page** keeps track of the current page number for the Printer object.

In this chapter you learned about the following methods:

- **Circle** draws a circle in the workspace. There are several parameters that allow you to create arcs and ellipses as well as circles.
- **Cls** clears any runtime graphics and text from a form or Picture Box.
- **Drag** turns on the drag-and-drop capability for an object where the DragMode is set to Manual.
- **EndDoc** signals the printer that you have finished printing the document.
- **Line** draws a line in the workspace. It also draws a box if a B is appended to the end of the command.
- **NewPage** signals the printer to print the current page and begin a new one.
- **Print** is used to display text in a Picture Box or on a sheet of paper when the object is Printer.
- **PSet** draws a dot in the workspace.

In this chapter you learned about the following commands and functions:

- **Int** translates a numeric phrase into an integer value.
- **Spc** specifies the number of spaces to be printed.
- **Tab** specifies the print position to move to on the current print line.
- **TextHeight** is used to determine the height, in twips, of a text phrase.
- **TextWidth** tells you the width of a text phrase.

In this chapter you learned about the following event:

- **DragDrop** is executed when an object is dropped on another object.

In this chapter you learned about the following prefix:

- **pic** is for Picture Boxes.

In this chapter you learned about the following Object:

- **Printer** refers to the printer attached to the computer.

In this chapter you learned about the following Tool:

- lets you add a Picture Box to the form.

11.15   Performance Check

1. Why must you set the AutoDraw property to True when drawing in a Picture Box?

   _____

2. What does the PSet method draw?

   _____

3. What method is used to draw a line?

   _____

4. What method is used to draw a box?

   _____

5. What method is used to draw an ellipse?

   _____

6. Besides the position of the center, what else needs to be specified to draw a circle?

   _____

7. When you use the Line method and add a B at the end, what can be specified between the positions and the B?

   _____

8. What property is used to create a fill pattern?

   _____

9. What property is used to specify the color for a fill pattern?

   _____

10. What command is used to erase a Picture Box image?

    _____

11. What method is used to change the thickness of a line being drawn?

    _____

12. What property is used to change the DragDrop icon?

13. What method is used to display text in a Picture Box?

    _____

14. What method is used to determine the height of a portion of text?

    _____

15. What property tells you the current horizontal position of the cursor?

    _____

16. What does the property DragMode specify?

    _____

17. When you drop one object onto another, what event is triggered?

    _____

18. What method is used to enable drag-and-drop when the DragMode is specified as Manual?

    _____

19. What parameter is available in the DragDrop event procedure to determine the object that dropped onto the current object?

    _____

20. What is the Spc function used for?

    _____

21. What property contains the current page number when you are printing on the printer?

    _____

22. What method is used to signal the printer that the document is finished?

    _____

11.16 Programming Exercises

1. You like the drag-and-drop technique you learned in this chapter. You decide to practice dragging other objects. This exercise will give you practice using the drag-and-drop techniques. At the computer, do each of the following:

   a. Get into Visual Basic with your work disk in drive A.

   b. Create a new program, and add a Picture Box, text box, label, and list.

   c. Change the DragMode of the text box and label to Automatic.

   d. In the DragDrop event procedure for the Picture Box, put an If Test. If Source is the name of the text box, print the text box text in the Picture Box. If Source is the name of the label, print the caption of the label in the Picture Box. Otherwise, print the selected item from the list.

   e. The list cannot be set to automatic; otherwise, clicking the list will start the dragging, and the list element will not be selected. When the user clicks the list, use the Drag method to turn on the drag-and-drop capabilities. As soon as you click the list, you will be dragging the item. This is not a true drag-and-drop.

   f. Run the program and test it until you are satisfied that it is working properly. Then exit the program and save it as **Drag-and-Drop**.

   g. Exit Visual Basic and shut the system down properly.

2. You decide you need more practice with the drag-and-drop capabilities of Visual Basic. This exercise will give you practice using the drag-and-drop techniques. At the computer, do each of the following:

   a. Get into Visual Basic with your work disk in drive A.

   b. Create a program that has a large Picture Box to drop into, three other smaller Picture Boxes, three labels, and three text boxes.

   c. Set the DragMode property on all objects except the large Picture Box to Automatic.

   d. Using the Picture property of the three small Picture Boxes, load a different icon into each of them.

   e. Set up an If Test in the DragDrop routine of the large Picture Box to test the Source and drop the appropriate element into the Picture Box on the basis of the value of Source. If the source is a label or text box, you need to print the appropriate element in the Picture Box. If the source is one of the smaller Picture Boxes, you can use the Picture property to assign the icon stored in the small Picture Box to the large Picture Box.

   f. Run and test the program until you are satisfied that it is working properly. Then exit the program and save it as **Triple Drag-and-Drop**.

   g. Exit Visual Basic and shut the system down properly.

3. You like being able to see which projects have been completed by simply selecting the Completed tab. The problem is that you would also like to know when the project was completed. You decide to change the program so that it will store a third date, the date when the project was completed. This exercise will give you practice working with the array and with the drag-and-drop routines in the program. At the computer, do each of the following:

   a. Get into Visual Basic with your work disk in drive A.

   b. Load your PIM program from the work disk.

   c. Change the date array so that it has three elements in the third array element. The third element will be used to store the date completed.

   d. Change the DragDrop routine so that it will store the date completed in the new array element when the project is dropped on the Completed tab.

   e. Change the display of the label so that it will display the date due and the date completed instead of the date started. This will require you to use an If Test.

   f. Execute and thoroughly test the program, and then resave it.

   g. Exit Visual Basic and shut the system down properly.

 4. A friend of yours has been working on a program that uses drag-and-drop but cannot seem to get the program to work. He has asked for your help. At the computer, do each of the following:

   a. Get into Visual Basic with your work disk in drive A.

b. Load **Name Drag** from the Ch-11 folder on your work disk.

c. Run the program, and you see names appear in the list. Click the list. Nothing is selected. Drag the mouse to the text box. You see the large box being moved, but dropping on the text box accomplishes nothing.

d. Exit the program.

Because you cannot select when the DragMode is set to Automatic, you need to change it to Manual. But this alone is not enough. You need to use the Drag method.

e. Set the DragMode of the list to Automatic.

f. Open the code window for the Click event of the list, and key the statement

```
lstNames.Drag 1
```

g. Run the program, click one of the names in the list, and then drag it and drop it on the Text Box. Nothing happens. Exit the program.

h. Open the code window for the DragDrop event of the text box. Examine the statement there carefully. Fix the statement.

i. Run the program, click one of the names in the list, and then drag it and drop it on the text box. Now the name appears in the text box. Drag another name and drop it in the box. The name changes to the new one.

j. Continue to experiment with the program until you are certain it is working correctly. Then exit the program.

k. Exit Visual Basic and shut the system down properly.

11.17 Performance Mastery

1. You decide to practice a bit more with drawing objects. Create a program with three buttons: one for a line, one for a circle, and one for a rectangle. When you click one of the buttons, the other two buttons should become disabled until the processing of the current button is complete. The next two clicks should be in the Picture Box workspace.

   a. For the line, the first of these two clicks will be the beginning of the line and the second the end of the line.

   b. For the circle, the first click will be the center of the circle and the second the radius point.

   c. For the rectangle, the first click will be the upper left corner and the second the lower right corner.

   Design and create the program, and then save it as **Drawing Practice**. Thoroughly test the program and then print all the elements.

2. You want to have a program that will allow you to use five different notepads. Create a program using a tab of the Tabbed Control for each of the five notepads. Set the program up so that you can highlight text in one notepad and drop that text at the end of the text in any of the other notepads. Design and create the program, and then save it as **Drop Notepads**. Thoroughly test the program and then print all the elements.

3. You decide to write a program to get more practice dragging and dropping elements. Create a program with eight labels: one of each of the normal eight colors and an additional, larger label. Set up the program so that the smaller labels can be dropped on the larger one and the color of the larger label will change to the color of the smaller label that was dropped. Design and create the program, and then save it as **Color Drop**. Thoroughly test the program and then print all the elements.

4. You work at a large office where people are coming and going all the time. The secretary has asked you to create a program she can use to keep track of who's present and

who's not. Create a program that has two lists: one for those who are in and another for those who are out. Write the program so that you can drop the names from one list to the other. To do this, you will have to set the drag mode of the lists to Manual and then turn on the Drag method when the name in the list is selected. When dropped, the name will simply be added to the new list. Design and create the program, and then save it as **Drop In-Out**. Thoroughly test the program and then print all the elements.

5. You want to practice with the Line method and you decide to create a program that will allow the user to use the Line method to create line drawings. The program should begin a new line at the point where the user clicks the Picture Box and end the line where the user clicks a second time. There should be three buttons or menu items: one to erase the image, one to stop the line from being drawn after the first click (the program should ignore the second click and not draw the line), and one to erase the previous line (you can redraw the line in white to erase the line). You should also have seven color labels so that the user can select the colors in which the lines are to be drawn. The color missing (there are eight colors) is white; you will use that for the background color of the Picture Box. Design and create the program, and then save it as **Line Drawings**. Thoroughly test the program and then print all the elements.

6. One of the things we didn't do in this chapter is set up the routine to delete the completed projects. Update the program now so that it will do so. When users select the button, they should get a warning message before they actually delete the elements from the Completed tab and the six elements of the array. Resave the program and then thoroughly test it.

7. One of the things we didn't do in this chapter is enable reading and storing of the projects in the database. Update the program now so that it will do so. You should save the data from the array into the database whenever the data in the array are changed. Resave the program and then thoroughly test it.

8. You work for a company that creates bitmap images for advertising campaigns. You have been assigned the task of creating a program that can be used to preview the available graphics. Create a program with an Image box and the appropriate tools to find the bitmap images (BMP extension) on the disk. Set up the program so that you can drop the image from the File List Box onto the Image box. To do this, you will have to set the drag mode of the File List Box to Manual and then turn on the Drag method when the filename in the File List Box is selected. Then, when the file is dropped on the Image box, you will have to use the **LoadPicture** function to load the bitmap into the Image box. You can use the Visual Basic help file to discover how to use the LoadPicture function if necessary. Design and create the program, and then save it as **Drop Bitmaps**. Thoroughly test the program and then print all the elements.

9. You work for a company that creates short music files for television and radio advertising. You have been assigned the task of creating a program that can be used to preview the available music files. Create a program with a MultiMedia control and the appropriate tools to find the music files (RMI or MID extension) on the disk. Set up the program so that you can drop the filename from the File List Box onto the MultiMedia control. To do this you will have to set the drag mode of the File List Box to Manual and then turn on the Drag method when the file name in the File List Box is selected. Then, when the file is dropped on the MultiMedia control, you will have to use the appropriate commands to play the file. Design and create the program, and then save it as **Drop Music**. Thoroughly test the program and then print all the elements.

10. You work for a company that creates sound-effects files for television and radio advertising. You have been assigned the task of creating a program that can be used to preview the available sound-effect files. Create a program with a MultiMedia control and the appropriate tools to find the sound-effects files (WAV extension) on the disk. Set up

the program so that you can drop the file name from the File List Box onto the Multi-Media control. To do this, you will have to set the drag mode of the File List Box to Manual and then turn on the Drag method when the file name in the File List Box is selected. Then, when the file is dropped on the MultiMedia control, you will have to use the appropriate commands to play the file. Design and create the program, and then save it as **Drop Wave Files**. Thoroughly test the program and then print all the elements.

Linking Applications

12.1 Chapter Objectives

After finishing this chapter you will be able to:

- Explain how manual, automatic, and notify links between applications differ.

- Discuss the difference between destination and source applications.

- Explain how to create design-time links.

- Demonstrate how to create automatic and manual runtime links.

- Demonstrate how to create destination and source applications.

- Demonstrate how to execute macro commands in a linked application.

- Demonstrate how to use the OLE Container Control.

12.2 Introduction

You already know that you can run several Windows applications at the same time. You have also learned that you can pass data back and forth between applications using the clipboard by cutting and pasting. What you don't know yet is that the passing of data between applications can be set up so that it will happen automatically. That is, you can link data in one of your applications to a point in another application, and then when you change the data in your first application, the data in the other application will change automatically. This capability is called **Dynamic Data Exchange,** or **DDE.**

DDE will allow you to create an object in one Windows application, such as text in a text box or an image in a picture box; use that object in a different application by linking the two applications; and then, if the object is changed in the original application, automatically update it in the linked application. Not only that, but in many applications you can use an extension of DDE called **object linking and embedding,** or **OLE,** and then when you want to change the object in the linked application, you merely click on the object, and the original application will automatically be loaded so that the object can be changed.

For example, suppose you have created a logo in your favorite graphics program. You can save the file to disk, copy it to the clipboard, and then paste that copied logo into your word processor using a special paste option designed specifically for the purpose. Once the pasted logo is in the word processor, if you decide you want to change the logo, you can click it, and the graphics program will automatically open with the logo file already loaded. Or, if the application is set up properly, a subset of the graphics program can open in the current application, and the graphic can be edited right there.

Many Windows DDE and OLE applications already exist, but the real power lies in the hands of the programmer who can create DDE and OLE applications that can be used to tie into existing applications. In this chapter, we will explore DDE and OLE and discover some of the possibilities. We'll use two programs created in Visual Basic specifically for the purpose of seeing just how one application can be linked to another. This will show you not only how DDE works but also how Visual Basic applications that use DDE can be created. Then we will see how OLE objects can be used in your programs so that the data from other applications can be edited in your own Visual Basic applications.

12.3 How DDE Works

Applications that support DDE fall into two categories. **Source** applications are those that can send data to other applications. Paint, for example, is a source application. Other applications can accept data that has been sent from other applications and are called **destination** applications. Some applications can be used as both source and destination, though many are only one or the other. Figure 12.1 shows the interaction between source and destination applications.

When a source application is set up, the link between the two applications can be done three different ways: by an **automatic link,** a **manual link,** or a **notify link.** Suppose, for example, that we want Excel (a spreadsheet) to be the source application, and we are going to create a destination application in Visual Basic. If we use a manual link and change the data in Excel, the data are not automatically updated in the Visual Basic application. The Visual Basic application must tell Excel to update them. The problem is that Excel does not send any information to the Visual Basic application indicating that the data have been changed. The Visual Basic application (or the person using the application) has to determine that the data have been changed and then request the data.

Because of this, a notify link can be used instead. Here, when the data are changed in Excel, it sends a notification to the Visual Basic application, which can then ignore the notice or request an update of the data.

If it is important for the data always to be correct in the Visual Basic application, you will want to use an automatic link. Then, when the Excel data are changed, the data in the Visual Basic application are updated automatically.

FIGURE 12.1
Illustration of how a source application and a destination application interact.

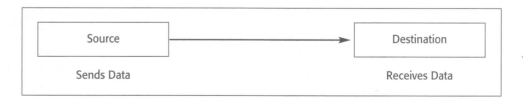

In Visual Basic, four types of controls can act as destinations: text boxes, Picture Boxes, labels, and grid cells. We can, for example, create a text box on a form and link that to another application. Then data changed in the other application will be automatically updated in our application. Only forms can act as sources in Visual Basic, although the data actually come from the controls on the form. For example, if we have a form called frmSource that has a text box on it, frmSource is the source, but the data entered into the text box are the data read by the destination application.

It is important to note that DDE works through the clipboard. As data are copied from one application to another, those data pass through the clipboard. As you are creating your DDE applications, you can watch what's happening by observing the data in the clipboard.

Now that we know something about how DDE works, let's see how to set up links and pass data from one application to another.

12.4 Destination Links at Design Time

Setting up destination links at design time is easy in Visual Basic. The easiest way to understand how it works is to experience it.

1. Launch Windows Explorer. Copy the Ch-12 folder from wherever it is stored on your system onto a blank diskette to be used as your new work disk.

2. Load Visual Basic and create a text box called **txtReceive** and a Picture Box called **picReceive** on the form (see Figure 12.2). Delete the text in the text box.

3. Launch the **Source** application from the Ch-12 folder on your practice disk, and you see a form like the one in Figure 12.3. This gives you the source application and your new Visual Basic program on the screen at the same time. We want this because we are going to link the applications.

Note that this application has several objects that we can use to send data to other applications. The grid has both text and graphics, and there is an additional text box. What we want to do is establish a link between this application and the text box on the form. When we create the link at design time, the link will be automatic. Neither manual nor notify links are available during design time.

FIGURE 12.2
The Receive form.

FIGURE 12.3
The form of the Source application.

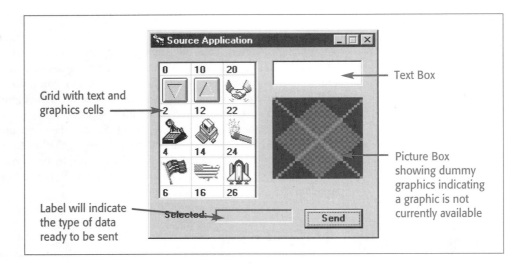

4. Size your Visual Basic form so that it and the application are side by side on the desktop as shown in Figure 12.4. To make the application easier to see, close all the windows except the form window, as shown in the figure.

5. Switch to the text box in the source application, key **Go to Text Box**, and click the **Send** button.

Note that the Selected: label specifies that there is currently text selected. If we selected the text in the grid, the label would specify Grid.Text, and if we selected one of the images in the grid, the label would show Grid.Picture.

Selecting the **Send** button copies the text to the clipboard. Copying the data to the clipboard is the first step in the linking process. In order to tell the destination application to create a link, there have to be data on the clipboard to link to.

6. Switch to the Visual Basic form, pull down the **Edit** menu, and select the **Paste Link** option.

The text we keyed and copied appears in the text box (Figure 12.5). We have just linked the text in the source application to the text in the text box on the form. The **Paste Link** option is similar to the **Paste** option, but by using this option, you established the link to the data back in the source. The best part is that now, when we change the text in the source, the text in the Text Box will automatically change too.

7. Switch to the source application and insert "**insert**" in between "to" and "text" as shown in Figure 12.6. Note that the text is also automatically changed in the text box.

We set up the Picture Box on the Visual Basic form to demonstrate that you can link pictures just as easily as you link text.

8. Select the shuttle image in the source application, and note that the large dummy pattern changes to reflect the selection and that the Selected: label shows Grid.Picture.

9. Select the **Send** button, switch to the form, select the Picture Box, and select the **Paste Link** option from the **Edit** menu. The shuttle image now appears on the form as shown in Figure 12.7.

The image can be updated by simply selecting another image in the grid.

10. Click the match in the grid, and the match automatically appears in the Picture Box on the form.

FIGURE 12.4
The source application and the Visual Basic form.

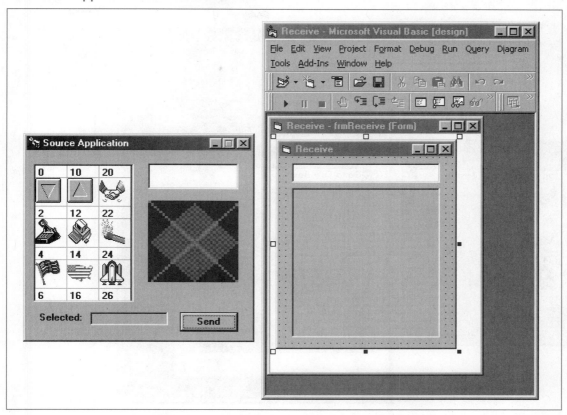

The best part about linking these applications is that both of the links are active at the same time. You have just seen how the image link is active. Now you will see how the text link is still active too.

11. Change the text in the source application text box and watch how that change is reflected in the text box on the form. Then change the picture to another and see that the one on the form also changes. Continue to change the data and the image until you are satisfied that both links are active. Then minimize the source application, and exit the application and save it as **Receive**.

Because most of the things we do in Visual Basic are guided by properties or methods, you might expect that the information about this link—whether it is automatic, manual, or notify, what application the text is linked to, and so on—would be available in Visual Basic properties. You would be correct. All the information about this link is available in four properties: **LinkMode**, **LinkTopic**, **LinkItem**, and **LinkTimeout**. Visual Basic has already set up these properties for us, so let's check and see what's in them.

The LinkMode Property

The first of these properties is the **LinkMode** property.

1. Switch to the Picture Box on your program form and select the LinkMode property.

You will note that this property has a value of Automatic. As previously mentioned, there are three possible settings for this property: automatic, manual, and notify. There is actually

FIGURE 12.5
The source is now linked to the form.

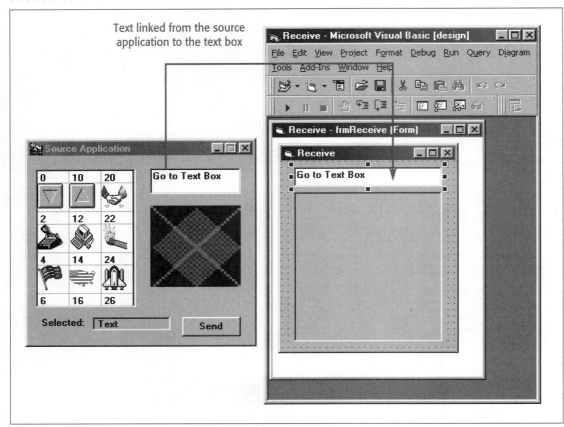

a fourth setting available, **None**, which simply means there is no link established. When you first set up a Picture Box and before you establish and update the link, the LinkMode property is None. Once you update a link, however, the LinkMode property becomes Automatic.

All design-time links are automatic. In order to set up a manual or notify link, the application needs to have some way to update the link after it has been established, and that requires code. Because no code can be applied to the application before it is executing, all the design-time links must be automatic.

The LinkTopic Property

Having an automatic link means that this application is connected to some external data source. To discover where that source is, we need to check the **LinkTopic** property.

1. Change to the LinkTopic property.

    Note that this property is

    ```
    Source|frmSource
    ```

This property value consists of two parts, the application name and the document name. Every Windows application that uses DDE is assigned a special DDE application name. Because the compiled name of the source application is Source, that is the first part of this property value. Other applications have DDE names such as WinWord for Microsoft Word for Windows and Excel for Microsoft Excel.

FIGURE 12.6
The change in the source application is reflected in the form.

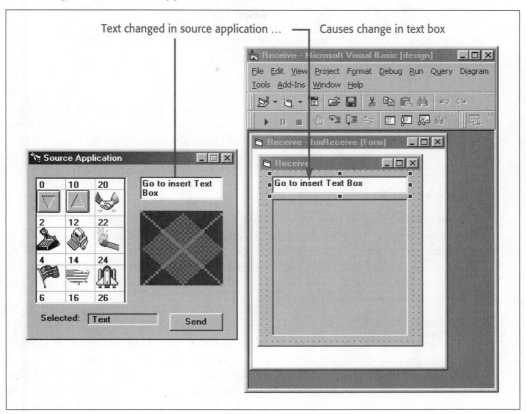

FIGURE 12.7
Now the shuttle picture in the grid is linked to the Picture Box on the form.

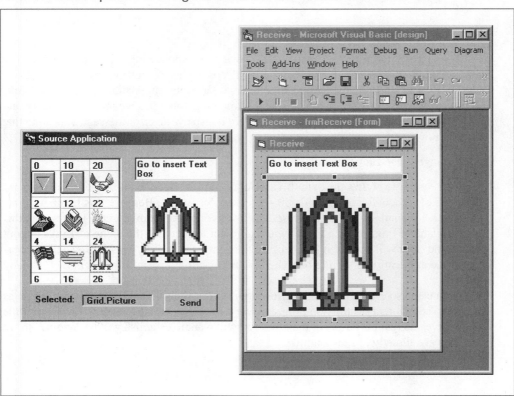

The second part of this property is the document from which the data came. All Visual Basic source applications use the form as the source "document," so the source name is frmSource. In other applications, such as WinWord, the name of the actual document in use would show in the property value. For example, if you linked to the document file Link.doc (doc is WinWord's standard extension), the value of the property would be

```
WinWord|Link.doc
```

Notice that between the application name and the document name there is a vertical separation bar (|). This symbol is usually found on the keyboard as the shifted part of the backslash key (\). You must use the appropriate symbol when you are creating these links (which you will do shortly), or the application will be confused and will not work properly.

The LinkItem Property

Just knowing which application and document the data come from is not enough. We also need to know from where in the document the data come. If we are linked to an application where there are precise addresses for the data elements, such as the cells in a spreadsheet, **LinkItem** contains that address. A word processor document has no such addresses, so the only link that can be there is a generic one, whereas a Visual Basic link is linked to the object on the form from which the data came.

1. Change to the LinkItem property.

This property contains either txtSource (if you have the text box selected) or picGrid (if you have the picture box selected). Both txtSource and picGrid indicate the object on the source form the data came from. If you had been linked to a word processor, your value would be something like **DDE_LINK**. This certainly doesn't tell us much, but it is enough for the application to locate the data to which it is linked. If there are multiple links to the same document, the second LinkItem value is DDE_LINK2, the third is DDE_LINK3, and so on.

The LinkTimeout Property

For one application to be linked to another, that other application must be available. The link we put in our application is a design-time link. But when we run the application, the system will try to find the application to which we have our application linked. The **Link-Timeout** property is where you can specify how long you will give the system to try and locate the application to which it is linked before it displays an error message indicating that it could not find the application for which it was looking.

1. Change to the LinkTimeout property.

This property shows the default value of 50. The LinkTimeout property is measured in tenths of a second, so the value 50 represents 5 seconds. Because this number corresponds to 5 seconds of real time, on some slower computers it might take longer than this to establish the link. In such cases, you may want to increase the value of LinkTimeout so that the error will not occur just because the computer is slow. This is especially important if the application is timing out when the application it is linked to is, in fact, already loaded.

You can also establish a link to allow your design-time Visual Basic program to act as source to some other destination program. We will not try this, because using design-time links serves no real purpose. All the links you will want to establish will be runtime, so we will proceed directly to runtime links.

12.5   A Runtime Destination Link Application

To establish a link from our source application to our Visual Basic application during runtime, we must have a way to tell Visual Basic what the various link values are. We need some option such as a menu **Paste Link** option, where we can put the necessary code. This is a sample application and we don't need a menu structure; instead, we will just add a button to our form.

1. Stretch the form, add a button underneath the Picture Box, and label it **Link**.

2. Switch to the code for the **Link** button.

For this link to work, we need to assign values to the three link properties of interest (we don't need to worry about LinkTimeout, because it has a default value of 5 seconds). We need to give values to LinkTopic, LinkItem, and LinkMode.

3. LinkTopic will have to be assigned to our source application and frmSource. Key the following statement:

```
txtReceive.LinkTopic = "Source|frmSource"
```

4. LinkItem needs to be given the location of the object on the form we want to link to. Key the following statement:

```
txtReceive.LinkItem = "txtSource"
```

Note that we are linking to txtSource. We can actually link to txtSource or picGrid (the picture that is being sent), but that will require that we determine what type of data is being sent by the source application, and we are not ready for that yet.

5. We want this to be an automatic link, so the value of LinkMode must be vbLinkAutomatic. Key this statement:

```
txtReceive.LinkMode = vbLinkAutomatic
```

> **HINT:** Remember that we could actually use the value of 1 instead of the constant vbLinkAutomatic. The code is simply easier to understand (which means it is better programming style) when we use constants with variable names meaningful to their function.

That's it. We're ready to see if it works.

6. Change to the source application, change the value in the text box (otherwise, you will be sending the wrong information to the clipboard, and no link will be established), and select the **Send** button.

7. Run the application and select the **Link** button.

The text in the source application text box appears in the text box in the new application. This is an automatic link between the applications, so if we change the value in the source, the value in the text box will also change.

8. Switch to the source application and change the value in the text box. As you do, the value in the text box in the new application changes too.

Changing the LinkItem

Our text box can be linked to either the text box or the grid (text or image) in the source application. And, as we saw earlier, we can actually have the graphics and text linked at the same time. We can see how this works with a few changes in our code.

1. Exit the application and switch to the code window for the **Link** button.

We are going to set up an If Test so that when the user selects the **Link** button, the application will determine what data are on the clipboard and then link to either the text box or the Picture Box. To do this, we will have to have some way to determine what is on the clipboard. This requires using the **Clipboard** object and the **GetFormat** method. **Clipboard** refers to the Windows clipboard where the data are transferred between applications. As we will discover later, several other methods are available for interfacing with it besides GetFormat.

The GetFormat method is used to determine the format that is available on the clipboard. You can test for link information, for text, for a bitmap, and for several other formats with which we won't concern ourselves. Initially, we should probably make sure that it is appropriate to link to the data on the clipboard. This is done by testing for the link information. If no link information is available, a link cannot be established.

2. Key the following code before the existing code.

```
If Not Clipboard.GetFormat(vbCFLink) Then
    MsgBox "There is no appropriate data on the clipboard.",
    ⌐ vbExclamation, "Linking error"
```

The GetFormat method simply tests what's on the clipboard. **vbCFLink** is a special constant that specifies linking information (the CF stands for Clipboard Format). The If Test is determining whether there is any linking information on the clipboard. If there is not, we want to inform the user and then not proceed with any linking.

Now, assuming that there is linking information on the clipboard, we can test to determine whether the data on the clipboard with the linking information consist of text, which is tested using the predefined variable **vbCFText,** or a picture, which is tested using **vbCFBitmap.** We do this with the If Test

```
ElseIf Clipboard.GetFormat(vbCFText) Then
```

3. Insert this statement.

If this test is True, we are ready to link text, so the next three statements in the code are appropriate, but we will need to add an Else on the end of them so that we can link the image. Then the statements to link to the image are

```
        picReceive.LinkTopic = "Source|frmSource"
        picReceive.LinkItem = "picGrid"
        picReceive.LinkMode = vbLinkAutomatic
End If
```

4. Add this code to the end of the procedure (don't forget the Else).

Now, to make sure the If Tests are working properly, we will copy some code to the clipboard. That way, any linking information that was on the clipboard will be erased.

5. Select some code and copy it to the clipboard.

6. Run the program and select the **Link** button. The error message should appear. Select the **OK** button.

Now we need to be sure the text linking will still work.

7. Change the data in the Source text box and select the **Send** button. The text should appear in the Receive text box. Change the data in the Source text box. The changes should be reflected in the Receive text box.

Okay, that works. Now we need to see whether we can link to the Picture Box.

8. Select one of the images in the grid on the Source form, and the picture on the Receive form changes. We are still linked from the design-time link we set up. To be sure the program is working, we have to break that link.

9. Exit the program, change to the properties for the Picture Box, and delete the value in LinkItem.

Immediately, Visual Basic displays a warning. That's because we have severed the link. Now we can run the program and test the new linking code.

10. Exit the warning, change the graphic in the grid (so that it will not be the same as the one showing in Receive), select Send, and then select the **Link** button. The Receive image now matches the Source image. Change the Source image, and watch the one in the Receive program change too.

11. Try changing the text again and note that it is still linked. Make several more changes to each until you are satisfied that the links are indeed working. Then exit and save the application.

A Manual Link

Most of the time, we will want the data in the destination application to be updated as soon as the data in the source application are changed. There are times, however, when instant updating is not feasible. Suppose, for example, that the data being sent are being used in extensive calculations. If the data are sent before the calculations using the previous number are finished, the calculations may end up in error. In such cases, we will want to be able to signal the source when to send the data. If we were using the data in a calculation, the code itself could signal the source, but because we are just experimenting, we will add a button to our form so that we can signal the source when to send the data.

1. Add a second button to the form and call it **Retrieve**.

If our link is to be a manual one, we will need to change the code in the **Link** button.

2. Switch to the code for the **Link** button and change the LinkMode statements to **vbLinkManual** (be sure to change both of them).

Now we need to add the code for the **Retrieve** button. All that's needed is an If Test similar to the one in the **Link** button code, with the property statements changed so that they use the **LinkRequest** method instead.

```
If Not Clipboard.GetFormat(vbCFLink) Then
    MsgBox "There are no appropriate data on the clipboard.",
    ↳ vbExclamation, "Retrieving error"
ElseIf Clipboard.GetFormat(vbCFText) Then
    txtReceive.LinkRequest
Else
    picReceive.LinkRequest
End If
```

3. Key this code.

4. Change the text in the Source text box and select the **Send** button. Then run the Receive application and select the **Link** button. This time, nothing happens.

5. Select the **Retrieve** button, and now the data in the text box are updated.

6. Change the text again. Note that the text in the Receive application doesn't change. Select the **Retrieve** button, and the text is updated.

7. Practice changing and updating the text some more, and then try changing and updating the Picture Box until you are satisfied that it is working properly.

8. Exit the application.

A Notify Link

Manual links are fine, but it might be nice to be notified by the source application when the data have been changed. If you use a notify link rather than a manual one, this will occur. Each object has a **LinkNotify** event that is executed when the data the object is linked to are changed. To try this out, we will need to make a few changes and a few additions to our application.

When using a manual link, we could actually use code in the LinkNotify event that updated the linked field. This would not be much different from having an automatic link. We want to notify the rest of the program only when an update to a linked field has been made. The easiest way to do this is with a flag field.

1. Change to the (General) procedure of the form and add the following two declarations:

```
Dim mblnPicture_Ready As Boolean
Dim mblnText_Ready As Boolean
```

The first time the program is executed, both of these fields need to be turned on so that the program is ready to receive its initial link. You will need to add the following code to the form Load procedure.

```
mblnText_Ready = True
mblnPicture_Ready = True
```

2. Switch to the Form_Load procedure and add these statements.

Next, the LinkMode properties need to be changed in the **Link** button code so that the mode is notify rather than manual.

3. Switch to the code for the **Link** button and change the two LinkMode statements to

```
vbLinkNotify
```

Now we are ready to set up the code in the LinkNotify events of the two objects on our form.

4. Change to the LinkNotify event of the text box and key the following statement:

```
mblnText_Ready = True
```

5. Switch to the LinkNotify event of the Picture Box and key the following statement:

```
mblnPicture_Ready = True
```

The last step is to change the code for the **Retrieve** button. Currently, the If Test checks for the format and then updates the link. Now, however, it will need to verify that the link has been updated by checking the mblnText_Ready and mblnPicture_Ready fields.

6. Switch to the **Retrieve** button procedure and change the If Test to

```
If Not Clipboard.GetFormat(vbCFLink) Then
   MsgBox "There are no appropriate data on the clipboard.",
    ⮑ vbExclamation, "Retrieving error"
ElseIf Clipboard.GetFormat(vbCFText) Then
```

```
        If mblnText_Ready = False Then
            MsgBox "The text has not been updated.", vbExclamation,
            ⤷ "Retrieve Error"
        Else
            txtReceive.LinkRequest
            mblnText_Ready = False
        End If
    Else
        If mblnPicture_Ready = False Then
            MsgBox "The picture has not been updated.", vbExclamation,
            ⤷ "Retrieve Error"
        Else
            picReceive.LinkRequest
            mblnPicture_Ready = False
        End If
    End If
```

7. Run the program and establish the links for both the text box and the Picture Box. Then select the **Retrieve** button without changing any of the Source data. An error message should appear.

8. Exit the message box, update the data, and then select the **Retrieve** button again. This time, the data in your application should have been updated.

9. Practice with the application until you are satisfied that it is working properly, and then exit the program.

Switching Text Links

Thus far we have been linked only to the text box of the source application, but there is text in the grid also (the numbers). It would be nice to be able to switch to whichever of these fields we want. For this we will need to be able to determine which of the fields is sending the data to be linked to. We saw earlier how to check the format of the data in the clipboard. We can use a similar technique to retrieve the link itself, and that will tell us which field is sending the data.

Currently, the **Link** button has the following code to create the link to the text box.

```
ElseIf Clipboard.GetFormat(vbCFText) Then
    txtReceive.LinkTopic = "Source|frmSource"
    txtReceive.LinkItem = "txtSource"        ◄──────── Replace this statement
    txtReceive.LinkMode = vbLinkNotify
Else
```

All we need to do to fix it so that it will link to either the text box (txtSource) or the grid numbers (txtGrid) is to set up a couple of extra statements.

1. Delete the current LinkItem statement and replace it with

```
strLink = Clipboard.GetText(vbCFLink)
intApost = stInStr(strLink, "!")
txtReceive.LinkItem = Right(strLink, Len(strLink) - intApost)
mblnText_Ready = True
```

The first statement brings in the link information and stores it in the variable strLink. As you will recall, the link information consists of the three parts, the first two separated by the line symbol (|) and the other two by an exclamation point (!). The second statement searches for that exclamation point, and the third assigns the item found after that exclamation point to the LinkItem property. The last statement turns on the update field. If we link to another field, the LinkNotify event does not get executed, and our mblnText_Ready field will still be false. Thus, we set it to on.

2. Run the program, change the text in the Source text box, and link that into the Receive text box. Update the text a couple of times to be sure it is working properly. Then select one of the numbers in the grid, send it, and link it.

Note that the text did not change. You still need to retrieve it.

3. Select the **Retrieve** button. Now the text changes to whatever number you selected. Select a few other numbers and update them in the Receive program. Also link the Picture Box again to be sure it still works.

4. Practice with the program a bit more until you are sure it is working properly, and then exit the program.

5. Exit the Source application also. We won't be needing it any more.

12.6   Runtime Source Links

Thus far we have explored only runtime destination links. Often, we will want to have a runtime source, so let's see what code is necessary for them.

1. Start a new project, add a Picture Box, turn on the AutoRedraw property, and load the **Source.bmp** file from the Ch-12 folder on your work disk into the Picture property as shown in Figure 12.8. Then add a text box called **txtSender**, a button with the caption **Send**, a label with a border called **lblData_Type_Out** (Figure 12.8) that will be used for output, and another label for the label on the first.

2. Save the form as **frmSender** and the project as **Sender**.

Because we have two different types of data to send to the destination application, our application will need to be able to determine which type of data we want to send when the **Send** button is selected. The easiest way to do this is to set a code so that we will know which of the objects on the form was previously selected to send the data. This means we need a field to keep track of this code.

3. Open the code window for the (General) procedure and declare **mstrData_Type** as a string.

FIGURE 12.8
The form for the Sender program.

4. Switch to the procedure for the Change event for the text box and key the following:

```
mstrData_Type = "Text"
lblData_Type_Out = "Text"
```

This sets the code so that we know which object was selected and displays the word Text in the label so that we can see what type of data is ready to be sent. We used the Change event because it doesn't do any good to send the text if it hasn't been changed, and the program will determine when the text was changed in the Change event.

5. Add similar code to the Click procedure for the Picture Box.

6. Open the code window for the **Send** button.

Now we are ready to add the code to establish the link from this application to another application. In doing this, we need to remember that all the DDE operations are done through the clipboard. Accordingly, we should begin our code with a statement to erase whatever may be remaining in the clipboard from previous uses; otherwise, our link may become confused with previous links.

7. Key the following statement:

```
Clipboard.Clear
```

There are actually only two pieces of information the other application will need to know: where the data are located in the original application and what that information is. But this information is different for the Picture Box and the text box, so we will need to determine which type of data is being sent by using the mstrData_Type field in an If Test:

```
If mstrData_Type = "Picture" Then
```

8. Key this beginning statement of the If Test.

To send the location data, we will first assign them to a temporary variable. This isn't actually necessary, but it's easier to see the link information when it is in its own assignment statement.

```
strLink = "Sender|frmSender!picSender"
```

Our linking information includes the Windows name for the application, Sender; the name of the form the data is coming from, frmSender (remember that all Visual Basic sources are forms, not objects); and the object name, picSender. Note that we use the vertical bar (|) between the application name and the form name and use an exclamation point (!) between the form name and the object name, as we discussed earlier. These separators must be used exactly as shown, or the application will not link properly. Visual Basic will not tell you what is wrong; the application simply will not work.

9. Key the foregoing statement.

Now we need to send this information to the clipboard. Because the link information is text, we will need to send text to the clipboard. The clipboard can pass a variety of data between applications, so there are several different methods we can use on the statement to transfer the data. The one we need for text is **SetText**:

```
Clipboard.SetText strLink, vbCFLink
```

We are sending strLink to the clipboard. At the end of the statement is the special variable vbCFLink that we used earlier. It contains a special code telling the application that this is linking information, not just regular data, being sent to the clipboard. It also indicates that because these are not the actual data, additional data will be coming soon. Our next statement should be the one to send those data. What we want to send is the picture. This requires a different clipboard method, **SetData**:

```
Clipboard.SetData picSender.Picture
```

10. Key these two statements and, using similar statements for the text box, finish the If Test. Note that the txtSender.Text should be sent to the clipboard with the SetText method, not the SetData method.

11. Run the application and click the picture box. Note that Picture shows up in the Data: label. Select the **Send** button.

This sends the link information and the picture to the clipboard. If you looked in the clipboard, you would see the picture but not the link information. Though we cannot see the link information, the destination application knows where to look for it.

Now we need an application that can receive our picture. For this, we will use a special Visual Basic program created just for the purpose.

12. Launch the **Destination** program from the Ch-12 folder on your disk, and you see a display similar to the one in Figure 12.9.

Note that this form has two text boxes and a picture box to receive the data we are sending, along with a series of display boxes to tell us what type of data is available and where those data came from. Right now, for example, upon our selecting the **Check Data** button, it should tell us that picture data are available, and the data in the other three boxes should exactly match the three parts of what we send to the clipboard as our link data. Let's see.

13. Select the **Check Data** button, and you see precisely what we just discussed: Picture as the type of data and Sender, frmSender, and picSender as the application, topic, and link item, as shown in Figure 12.10.

Now all we need to do is paste the link into our document.

14. Select the **Paste Link** option from the **Edit** menu, and you see the dialog box shown in Figure 12.11.

This dialog box once again gives us the same information as the source of the data. Note, however, that the data type is Bitmap. Because a picture box can hold several types of data, the Paste Link dialog box is more specific than the label on the main form.

HINT: Though this is a Visual Basic program constructed specifically for this chapter's experiences, the dialog box you see here is similar to the ones you will find in other applications, such as Word and Excel.

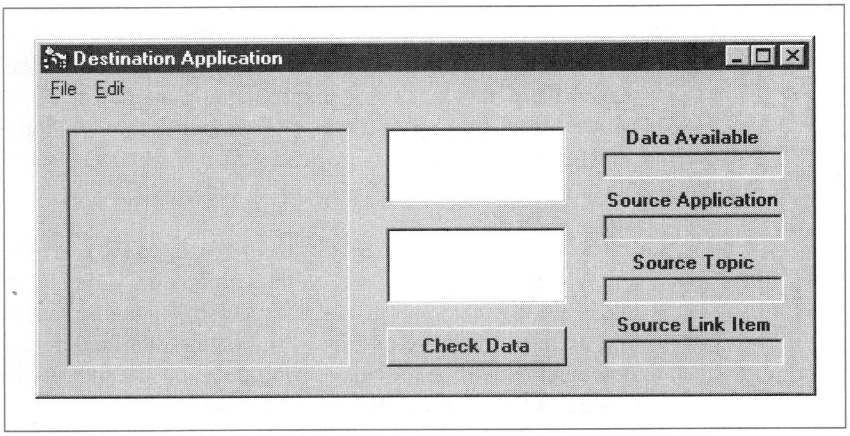

FIGURE 12.9
The Destination application form.

FIGURE 12.10
The link data from the Sender program.

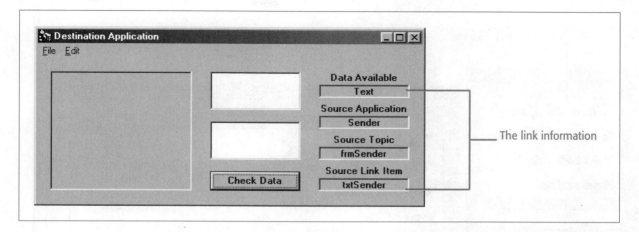

FIGURE 12.11
The Paste Link dialog
box.

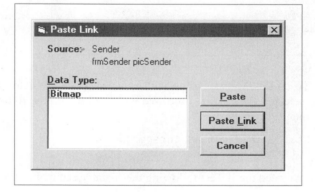

15. Select the **Paste Link** button, and the image appears in the picture box as shown in Figure 12.12.

16. Key some text in the text box and select the **Send** button. Switch to the Destination application, select the top text box, and use the Paste Link to link the two text boxes. Then switch back to the Sender text box and modify the data there. Note that the data in the text box in the Destination application are also updated.

17. Paste the link into the second text box and watch the text in both boxes change as you change the text in the Sender text box. This, of course, means that both text links are active at the same time.

Updating the Link

We have made it possible to update the text boxes, but because the picture is merely copied from disk, there is no way to change it to be sure our automatic link to the Destination application is working correctly.

1. Exit the application and switch to the code window for the **Send** button.

In this routine, we will add code to draw some boxes in the image, so it will be changed. We will set up the routine so that the first time the button is selected, the link is established and the picture sent, and then every other time it is selected, a box will be drawn and the link updated. We don't really care where the boxes appear in the drawing, so we will draw them in random locations in the image.

FIGURE 12.12
The image linked into the Destination application.

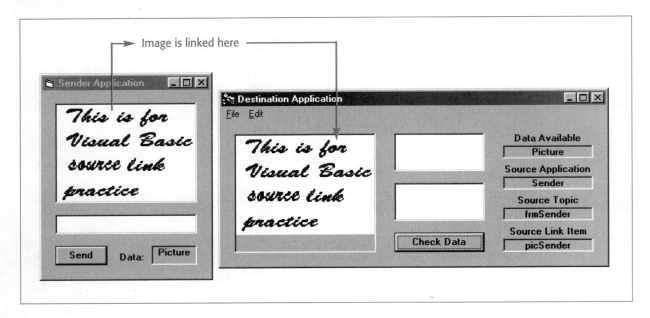

To do this, we will begin with a static variable to determine whether the button has been selected for the first time. We will need to add the following code before the Clear statement.

```
Static intFirst as Integer
intFirst = intFirst + 1
```

Then we need the If Test following the If statement that is already there.

```
If intFirst = 1 Then
```

Then the Else statement should follow the other three statements that are already there.

2. Key these statements and indent the code between the If and Else statements.

To draw boxes in random locations, we need to determine the coordinate positions of the corners randomly. Visual Basic has a function, **Rnd**, that we can use to generate a random number between 0 and 1. We can then use that number to calculate the X and Y coordinate positions by using the following statements:

```
intFirst_X = picSender.ScaleWidth * Rnd
intFirst_Y = picSender.ScaleHeight * Rnd
intSecond_X = picSender.ScaleWidth * Rnd
intSecond_Y = picSender.ScaleHeight * Rnd
```

And then we use these variables to draw the box:

```
    picSender.Line (intFirst_X, intFirst_Y)-(intSecond_X,
    ↳ intSecond_Y), , B
End If
```

3. Key these statements following the Else. Remember that the missing paramater is for the color and the B specifies a box.

Now we're ready to test the application again.

4. Run the application and select the **Send** button.

You get the same result as before, because the first selection of the **Send** button does the same thing as before. The difference comes after subsequent selections of the button.

5. Select the **Send** button again.

Note that a box appears in the Sender application, but the updated image is not automatically copied into the Destination application's Picture Box. The reason is subtle. It seems that when an image is copied into a Picture Box, it is an element. Simply drawing boxes in the Picture Box does not change the underlying image. There is a way around the problem. All we need to do is tell Visual Basic to update the image when the user selects the **Send** button.

6. Exit the application and add the following statement just above the End If statement that was just added.

```
picSender.LinkSend
```

The **LinkSend** statement merely tells Visual Basic to update the link.

7. Run the application and link the picture. Then, on subsequent selections of the **Send** button, you will see boxes appear in both Picture Boxes indicating that the link is being updated as shown in Figure 12.13.

> **HINT:** The random-number function will always generate the same sequence of random numbers every time you run the application. The numbers are generated by using the previously generated number in the calculation (called the **seed number**) to determine the next number. The seed number used to generate the first random number is always the same unless you use a special function, **Randomize**, to make that first seed number random as well. If you use Randomize before your random-number calculations, then every time the application is run, a different set of boxes will be drawn because a different set of random numbers will be generated.

8. Practice the links a few more times until you are satisfied that everything is working as it should, and then exit the application.

FIGURE 12.13
The boxes as they are duplicated in the Destination application because of the link.

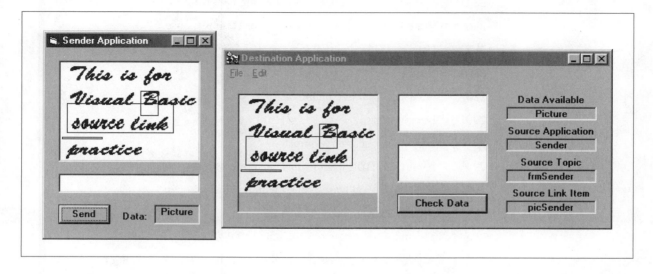

12.7	**Handling DDE Errors**

A number of things can go wrong when we are using DDE applications. Table 12.1 shows a list of the more common ones.

These errors are trappable, like the file errors that we discussed a few chapters ago. You will probably never see most of them, but there is at least one that may come up. If you are using an application that is supposed to send data to a particular application, such as Source, and Source is not active, you will get error 282, "No foreign application responded to a DDE initiate." What this means is that your application tried to talk to Source, but the system couldn't find Source. To handle such problems, we simply trap the errors as we trapped file errors, with the On Error GoTo statement, and then load the appropriate application.

1. Start a new project, and add a text box called **txtConnect** and a button. Label the button as **Link** and open the code window for the button.

We are going to create this application so that it is similar to the destination application we set up earlier. That is, it is going to ask for a link to Source, but this time we won't load Source, so it won't be available to link to.

The first statement in your code, then, should be the On Error GoTo statement:

```
On Error GoTo Link_Error
```

Next we need to add the code to establish the link:

```
txtConnect.LinkTopic = "Source|frmSource"
txtConnect.LinkItem = "txtSource"
```

TABLE 12.1
DDE errors

Error	Meaning
280	The DDE channel has not been fully closed, waiting for a response
281	No more DDE channels
282	No foreign application responded to a DDE initiate
283	Multiple applications responded to a DDE initiate
284	DDE channel locked
285	Received negative DDE acknowledgment from foreign application
286	Timeout occurred while waiting for DDE response
287	User hit DDE attention key
288	Destination is busy
289	No data for DDE data message
290	Data in wrong format
291	Foreign application terminated
292	An invalid DDE channel has been referenced
293	A DDE method was invoked with no channel open
294	Invalid DDE link format
295	The message queue was filled and a DDE message was lost
296	A paste link has been executed on a channel with an existing paste link

```
txtConnect.LinkMode = vbLinkAutomatic
Exit Sub
```

Next we need to create the error routine. We begin with the label

```
Link_Error:
```

Then we need the If Test determining what error was found:

```
If Err = 282 Then
```

If the application did encounter this error, it means that Source wasn't loaded. We need to display for the user an error dialog box related to that:

```
intReturned = MsgBox("Source has not been loaded. Do you want
 to load it now?", vbYesNo + vbQuestion, "Linking Error")
```

This message box will display the **Yes** and **No** buttons. If the user selects the **Yes** button, we want to launch Source so that the link can be established. Thus, if intReturned is vbYes, we want to launch Source and then resume execution at the Create_Link label. We want simply to exit the procedure if No is selected; remember that we must use an Exit Sub statement when No is selected, or we will get an error related to the fact that we exited an error routine without a Resume statement.

```
    If intReturned = vbYes Then
        lngTemp = Shell("A:\Ch-12\Source.exe")
        Resume
    End If
    Exit Sub
End If
```

The purpose of the **Shell** function is to communicate to Windows. In this case it will launch Source from the Ch-12 directory on drive A. The lngTemp variable is used to store the result of the Shell function, which is the Windows identification for the program you ran. If the function has an error and the program is not launched, lngTemp will be zero.

2. Key all the foregoing code, exit Destination if it is still loaded, save this application as **Error**, and then run the application.

3. Select the **Link** button, and the dialog box should appear. Select **Yes**.

After a minute or so, the minimized version of Source should appear on the desktop, and the text should disappear from the text box. There is nothing currently in the Source text box, so no data will be sent to the text box. But it is easy to tell whether the link was established.

4. Call Source to the desktop and enter something in the text box. That will now appear in the text box in the new application, indicating that the link is functioning properly.

5. Exit the applications.

12.8   Final Notes on DDE

We have covered a lot of DDE ground, but there are still a few important topics we have not discussed. For example, you can execute macro commands in a number of Windows applications from your Visual Basic applications. You can also refuse to let an application set up a link to your current application if that link is deemed inappropriate for some reason. Let's explore each of these ideas separately.

Executing Macro Commands in Other Applications

> **HINT:** This will be a very short introduction to using a macro in Excel. If you do not know anything about Excel macros, you may find the LinkExecute difficult to understand even with the given explanation. Don't let that bother you. This section is included merely to show you the possibilities of Visual Basic. You can add to your knowledge later as you become experienced with the macro commands of whatever program you plan to interface to your Visual Basic applications.

We just saw how we can launch an application that is not currently available by using the Shell function. With some Windows applications, we can go another step beyond simply launching the application to executing macro commands in the other application. Excel and Word, for example, will let another application send commands to them.

The method to execute commands in the linked application is **LinkExecute**. Each of the commands to be executed must be enclosed in square brackets ([]), and the entire string of commands must be enclosed in quotation marks. Here is a sample of the LinkExecute statement for executing a macro in Excel:

```
txtExcel_Link.LinkExecute "[Formula.GOTO(""R4C1"")]
 ↳ [Formula(""=SUM(R[-3]C:R[-1]C)"")]"
```

This tells Excel (which would be the application we would be linked to for this particular command) to branch to cell A4 (row 4, column 1) and then add up the column.

The first of the two commands (enclosed in square brackets) is Formula.GOTO (""R4C1""). The word Formula is the lead-in to a macro command, and ""R4C1"" is the cell address. The pair of quotation marks before and after the cell reference are there because the entire command string must be enclosed in quotation marks, and if we just used regular quotation marks around the cell, the first mark would end the quotation mark at the beginning of the command string. Using two double quotation marks together tells Visual Basic that the literal itself is to contain a double quotation mark and that it is to be ignored as part of the double quotation marks surrounding the entire command string.

The second command, Formula(""=SUM(R[-3]C:R[-1]C)""), gives Excel the summation command =SUM(R[-3]C:R[-1]C). This says to add up the cells in the range from the current row less 3 (row 4 − 3 = row 1) in the current column to the current row less 1 (row 4 − 1 = row 3) in the current column. It refers to the current column because no column number is specified. You might wonder why we don't just use the regular Excel summation command =SUM(A1:A3). The reason is simple. That is the summation command, not the **macro** summation command. A macro can be used in any cell, so it is important that the macro use references to the current cells, not absolute references like A1 and A3.

Following the execution statement, we need to link to cell A4 so that we can retrieve the result of the calculation. That requires the following three link statements:

```
txtExcel_Link.LinkTopic = "Excel|Sheet1"
txtExcel_Link.LinkItem = "R4C1"
txtExcel_Link.LinkMode = vbLinkAutomatic
```

As you can see, executing commands in another application requires only two things: You have to know whether the application will allow remote command execution (most Windows applications that use macros will), and you have to know how to write the macro commands for that other application. The easiest way to accomplish the second part is to create a macro that does what you want to accomplish in that application itself and then examine the stored code of that macro and copy it to your Visual Basic application. This won't always work, but it is a starting point.

> **HINT:** You need to be extremely careful when entering your macro commands in the LinkExecute method, because the application receiving the commands will not necessarily tell you if your macro command is incorrect. Instead, it may simply hang, forcing you to exit the application and, possibly, restart Windows.

The LinkOpen and LinkClose Events

Two events that we haven't discussed are the **LinkOpen** and **LinkClose** events. As you can imagine, the LinkOpen event occurs when a link is established between a Visual Basic application and another application, and the LinkClose event occurs when a link is terminated. Both events occur in source and destination applications.

The LinkOpen event can prove handy in certain situations. Suppose you have written an application that can be linked to any number of applications on a network, but if you let the applications continue to be linked to your application ad infinitum, the system starts to slow down. As a matter of fact, you have discovered that significant drag on the system begins to occur after ten applications have established links. With the LinkOpen event, you can determine when another link is being requested, and by keeping track of the current number of links, you can refuse to allow the link if accepting it would create too many links.

The LinkOpen event has Cancel as a parameter. You can add additional code to this procedure as with any other procedure, but the key to accepting or refusing the link is the parameter. If you leave Cancel with its initial False value, the link will be established. If, on the other hand, you change the value of Cancel to True, the link will be refused.

Using a count of the number of active applications also yields a use for the LinkClose event. When one of the limited number of applications closes, that should free up one of the ten available linking slots. You might want to use the LinkClose event to reduce the number of active links that you have counted so that another will then be available.

12.9 A Few Examples of OLE

OLE is essentially an extension of what DDE can do for you. There are, however, several things that OLE allows you to do that DDE doesn't. We will explore a few of these in this section.

As we noted earlier, OLE stands for Object Linking and Embedding, and a data item used in an OLE operation is generally referred to as an **Object**. An object can be, for example, a word processor document created in a program such as Microsoft Word or a spreadsheet originally created in a spreadsheet program such as Excel. But not everything OLE can do for you requires a new type of object. OLE can, for example, help you with the drag-and-drop techniques you learned in the previous chapter.

OLE Drag-and-Drop

One of the things you can do with some of the many OLE tools Visual Basic offers is drag-and-drop from one application to another. In Chapter 11 you learned how to drag-and-drop within an application, but there are many Windows applications that can drag-and-drop from one application to another. As you will see, Visual Basic makes this capability easy to incorporate.

1. Start a new application and add a text box.

2. Change to the **OLEDragMode** property and change it to Automatic. This will allow you to drag automatically from the text box. Change to the Text property and change it to **This is the Dragged text**.

3. Load another copy of Visual Basic and start a new application. Add a text box to this form and call it **txtReceiving**.

4. Change to the **OLEDropMode** property and change it to Automatic. This will allow this new application to receive data automatically. Run your new application.

5. Switch back to the first application and run it.

6. Highlight just some of the text, and drag-and-drop it on the other text box.

Note that the text has been erased in the first application and that Text1 is still in the receiving text box. You simply added to the text already in the text box. As you might expect, there is a way to avoid adding to what is already there and to avoid deleting the text from the first text box. This requires that the OLEDropMode be set to Manual and then some code be written.

7. Exit both applications and switch to the OLEDropMode property of the receiving application. Change the property to Manual.

8. Open the code window for the **OLEDragDrop** event of the receiving application.

There are a series of parameters here, most of which you should already be familiar with, but we are interested in only two of them at the moment. The **Data** parameter holds the name of the object that is dropping the text. We say text because that is what is being dropped in this case, but images and other types of data can also be dropped, just as in the last chapter. To get the text from the originating application, we use the **GetData** method and then tell the application, by using a parameter, what type of data we are getting. The type of data is text this time, so we will want to use vbCFText as the parameter, which gives us the statement

```
txtReceiving.Text = Data.GetData(vbCFText)
```

This sets the application up to copy and not move, so it will not delete the text from the sending application.

9. Key this statement and then run the application. Key some new text in the sending application, highlight some of it, and drag-and-drop it on the receiving application.

Now the text will remain in the sending application, and just the dropped text appears in the receiving text box. We assigned the data to the text box, so whatever was in there first was erased. Because we are controlling how the dropped text is handled, we could have added it at the end of what was in the text box or put it before what was already there.

If we want to control the text but also want to delete the text from the sending application, we will need to set the **Effect** parameter. It can be set to three possible values: 0 (constant is **vbDropEffectNone**), which means that the receiving application cannot accept the data so nothing will be done, 1 (constant is **vbDropEffectCopy**) for copying, which means the receiving application will receive the data and the sending application will not be changed, and 2 (constant is **vbDropEffectMove**) for moving, which will cause the data in the sending application to be deleted.

10. Exit the receiving application.

11. Add the following statement in front of the one already there.

```
Effect = vbDropEffectMove
```

12. Highlight some of the text in the sending application, and drag-and-drop it on the receiving application.

This time the text is deleted from the sending application.

13. Exit both applications and save them if you wish.

Dragging from Explorer

One of the major features of using OLE in Windows is the capability of most programs to automatically open files that have the proper format for the program by dragging the file name from Windows Explorer. This is not as difficult as it might seem. In this section we will explore how to do it.

1. Start a new project and add a picture box to the form. Save the form as **frmExplorer** and the program as **Drag from Explorer**.

2. Set the Dropmode of the picture box to **Manual**. Set the Autosize property to **True** so that the picture box will automatically adjust to the size of the image.

3. Open the code window for the OLEDragDrop event.

If we are going to read the file name of the file to be dropped onto our application directly from Explorer, it is important that the object being dropped onto our application is actually coming from Explorer. We can determine that by checking the format of what is being dropped. This is done with the GetFormat method:

```
If Data.GetFormat(vbCFFiles) = False Then
```

4. Key this statement.

As we said earlier, the Data parameter of the OLEDragDrop event contains the name of the dropping application. If we check the format of Data, we are checking the format of what is being dropped from the application. If the dropping application is Explorer, we should be getting a list of files. Checking the format for vbCFFiles will tell us if the proper data are being dropped.

If the format is not proper, the dropping is being done from some other application, and we don't want to work with it. Thus we need an error message:

```
Msgbox "The format of what is being dropped is incorrect.",
  ⤷ vbExclamation, "Dropping Error"
```

5. Key this statement into the procedure.

After this we need to get the file name from Explorer. Because Explorer can select multiple files, we don't get a single file name; we get an array. We will assume that the user is dropping only one file, so we will extract just the first element of the array with the following code:

```
Else
    strFilename = Data.Files(1)
```

Files is the property that contains the array of filenames.

6. Key these statements into the procedure.

After getting the file name, we need to determine whether the file is of the proper type to display in a picture box. The easiest way to do this is to let Visual Basic determine whether the file has the proper format by using an error routine such as

```
        On Error GoTo File_Format_Error
        picExplorer.Picture = LoadPicture(strFilename)
        Exit Sub
    End If
File_Format_Error:
        MsgBox "The format of this file is incorrect.",
          ⤷ vbExclamation, "Dropping Error"
    Exit Sub
```

The LoadPicture method simply loads the specified file into the picture box. The path and file name of the picture are given as the parameter.

7. Key the rest of the code. Run the program. Launch Explorer.

8. Change to the Windows folder on your hard disk. It contains some bitmaps that are suitable to load into the picture box.

9. Drag the file name of any file (not a BMP file) and drop it onto the picture box. You will get the invalid format error.

10. Find a BMP file and drop that file name onto the picture box. The file should appear in the Picture Box.

11. Drop a few more files onto the picture box until you are satisfied that everything is working properly. Then exit the program.

The OLE Container Control

Linking text or graphics from one application to another by dragging and dropping is a nice technique, but Visual Basic will actually let you embed an application object so that the data can be worked on in a pseudo-application of the original application or link to the application. When the object in the Visual Basic program is accessed, the original application is automatically launched so that the data can be worked on in the original application. We will look at both techniques in this section.

To do what we have just discussed, you must use the **OLE Container Control**.

1. Start a new program and draw an OLE Container Control on the form using the tool shown in Figure 12.14. Your form should look like the one shown in Figure 12.15.

After you have released the **Mouse** button when drawing the control on the form, you will see the dialog box shown in Figure 12.16.

This dialog box lets you determine how the control is used. On the left is the specification that lets you choose whether this is a new, empty control or one that is to be created from an existing file. If it is new, you pick the type of container it is to be from the list of Object Types. If you select Create from File, the dialog box will change to the one shown in Figure 12.17, which allows you to select the file you want loaded into the control. You no longer need to choose the type of container; that will be determined by the file that you choose to load. That is, if you pick a Word document, the container becomes a Word document container. If you choose an Excel spreadsheet, the container becomes a spreadsheet.

In this instance we want to load a file from the Ch-12 folder.

2. Click the **Create from File** option button to get the Insert Object dialog box.

FIGURE 12.14
The OLE Container Control tool.

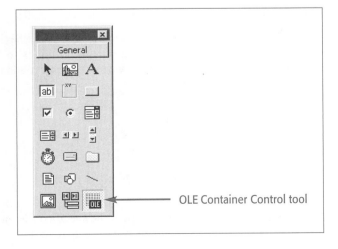

FIGURE 12.15
The form with the OLE Container Control.

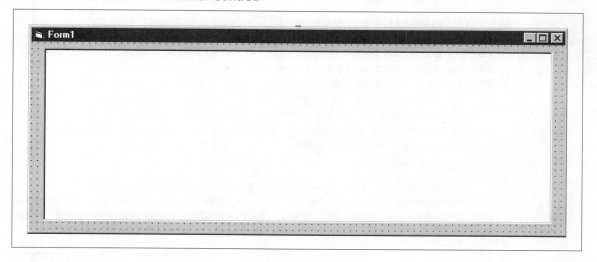

FIGURE 12.16
The Insert Object dialog box for the OLE Container Control.

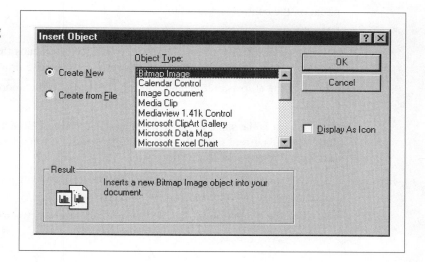

FIGURE 12.17
The form of the dialog box when the container is to be loaded with an existing file.

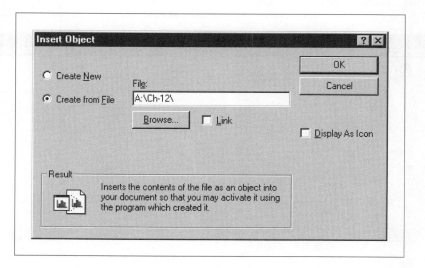

3. Click the **Browse** button and select the **Spread Sheet.xls** file from the Ch-12 folder on your work disk, but don't click the **OK** button on the above dialog box yet.

On this dialog box we can also specify whether the document is to be embedded, which is the default, or linked. If we want the document to be linked, we merely select the Link check box. If the document is linked, when we select the control while the program is running, the application in which the document was originally created will launch and you will be switched to that application. If the application isn't on your computer, you will get an error and will not be able to edit the document. You may or may not have Excel on your computer, so we will not link the document. We will only embed it. When it is embedded, you can make changes to the document, but those changes will not be reflected in the original document (in other words, Spread Sheet.xls will not be updated).

4. Click the **OK** button.

This will load into your control the spreadsheet shown in Figure 12.18.

Note that the spreadsheet has one line displayed in a larger font and that the lines around the data indicate the spreadsheet. This is actually an Excel spreadsheet with all that implies, but before we explore that, we need to look at a few important properties.

The Class Property   When you loaded the Excel spreadsheet into the control, you automatically set the **Class** property. This is the property that tells Visual Basic what type of application the control is related to.

1. Change to the Class property.

The value of this property is Excel.Sheet.5. This means that this control contains an Excel worksheet that was created with a version of Excel 5 or above.

2. Click the ellipsis button, and you see a list of the applications that this control can contain.

This list is the same as the list you saw in the Insert Object dialog box. If you change the class, the current contents of the control will have to be removed; they will no longer correspond to the new application type.

3. Select one of the classes (except Excel.Sheet.5), and you see a warning dialog box that tells you the current contents will be deleted.

4. Click the **No** button so that the spreadsheet will stay in the control.

FIGURE 12.18
The spreadsheet loaded into your control.

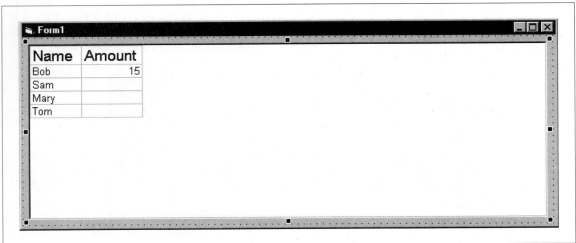

The SourceDoc Property   Another property that is important is the **SourceDoc** property. This specifies the document that is currently linked or embedded in the control.

1. Change to the SourceDoc property.

This shows the Spread Sheet file name and the path that file came from (A:\Ch-12\Spread Sheet.xls). If you want to change to a different file in the control, you can select it from this.

2. Click the ellipsis button.

The Insert Object dialog box you saw earlier appears. This is used the same way as the first dialog box you saw. You can link or embed a file or start a new, empty instance of the control.

3. Select the **Cancel** button to exit this dialog box.

The SizeMode Property   The **SizeMode** property specifies how the OLE Container Control is sized and how the image contained is displayed. There are four possible values for the SizeMode property, the first of which is **0 - Clip**. This causes the image loaded into the control to be clipped so that it fits within the control's borders. If the image is smaller than the borders, the image is simply placed within. This is the default mode in which the image is currently displayed.

The second possible value is **1 - Stretch**, which causes the image to be stretched to fit within the borders of the control. This may cause the image to be distorted if the image is shaped differently from the control.

1. Switch to the SizeMode property and change the value to **1 - Stretch**. You see the distorted image shown in Figure 12.19.

As you can see, this is probably not the best setting for a spreadsheet. You may want to set your control as Stretch when you are using bitmap images and other such images that you want to fill the form or control.

The third setting is **2 - AutoSize**, which causes the control to be sized to fit the data loaded.

2. Change the property setting to **2 - AutoSize**.

The control shrinks down to the size of the original spreadsheet data (Figure 12-20). If you add more lines or columns to the spreadsheet, the original size is maintained.

FIGURE 12.19
The spreadsheet control when the SizeMode property is set to **1 - Stretch**.

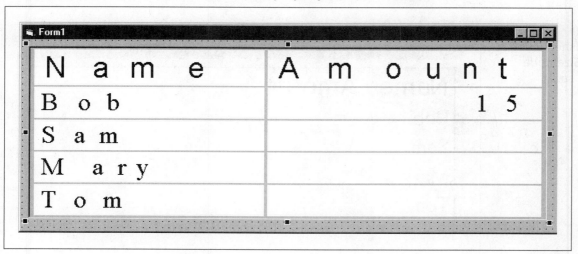

FIGURE 12.20
The spreadsheet control when the SizeMode property is set to **2 - AutoSize**.

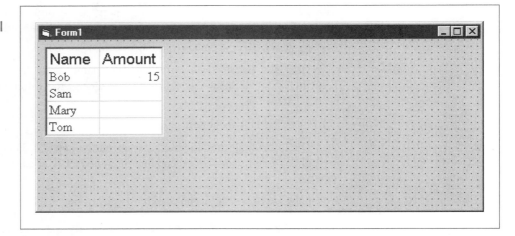

The last setting is **3 - Zoom**. With this setting, Visual Basic resizes the object to fit within the borders of the control without changing the original proportions of the object.

3. Change the setting to **3 - Zoom** and then resize the control to fill the form as it was earlier.

Now the spreadsheet expands to fill as much of the control as possible without becoming distorted, as shown in Figure 12.21.

4. Change the setting back to **0 - Clip**.

How the Container Works   As we have said, because this file is embedded, not linked, the data in the application are not linked to the file, and any changes to the data are local to the application and do not affect the file from which the data came.

1. Run the program.

You can open the spreadsheet for use in two ways. You can double-click the control or right-click and then choose the **Edit** option from the menu that appears. The other option on the menu is **Open**, and this will open the original file in the original application—in this case, an Excel spreadsheet in Excel.

2. Double-click the control, and the spreadsheet is ready to use as a normal spreadsheet except that all you see is the area currently loaded, as shown in Figure 12.22.

FIGURE 12.21
The spreadsheet control when the SizeMode property is set to **3 - Zoom**.

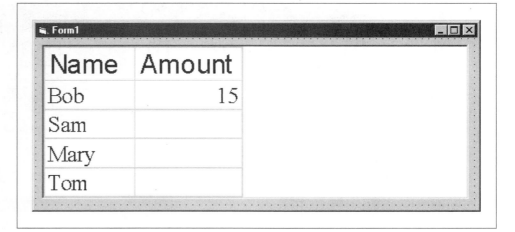

FIGURE 12.22
The spreadsheet ready for editing.

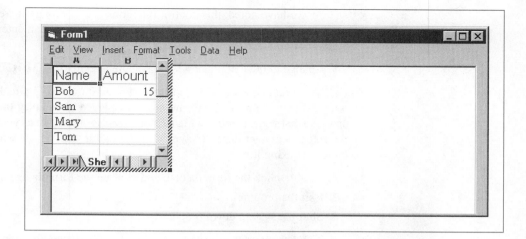

You can expand the area of the spreadsheet by dragging the borders.

3. Expand the spreadsheet two rows and one column by dragging the lower right corner (Figure 12.23).

4. Key the following numbers under the 15 in the amount column: **25**, **12**, and **44** (see Figure 12.24).

FIGURE 12.23
The spreadsheet with the added rows and column.

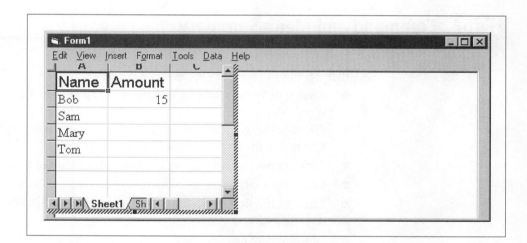

FIGURE 12.24
The spreadsheet container after the total has been calculated.

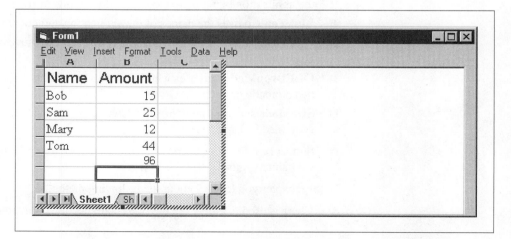

As we have noted, this control functions just as though it were an Excel spreadsheet, including the use of formulas and functions. That is, we can enter a formula to add up the column of numbers.

5. Change to the cell under 44 and key the formula **=SUM(B2:B5)** and press **Enter**.

The total of the column appears as 96, as shown in Figure 12.24. If you are familiar with Excel, you know that formulas are displayed in an entry line at the top of the work-space so that you can tell at a glance what your formulas are as you highlight the cells. Well, the Excel container doesn't have that feature, but you can see what's stored in any cell by double-clicking it.

6. Double-click the formula cell, and you see the formula again.

7. Exit the program.

8. Shut the system down properly.

The data revert to what they were. As we mentioned, this container was embedded, not linked, so the data were not connected to the file. When you exit, it simply goes back to its original value, just as a text box goes back to whatever was originally entered into it before the program was run. You have created an initial value for the container, and it will always maintain that initial value unless you change it.

12.10   Command and Menu Summary

In this chapter you learned about the following properties:

- **Class** tells Visual Basic the type of application to which an OLE Container Control is related.

- **Files** is an array of file names that is the result of a drop from an application that has a format of file names such as Windows Explorer.

- **LinkExecute** is used to execute commands in a linked application.

- **LinkItem** contains the address in the linked application where the data are.

- **LinkMode** tells the linked application what type of link is being used: automatic, manual, notify, or none.

- **LinkTimeout** contains the length of time during which the system can try to locate the application being linked to before displaying an error.

- **LinkTopic** passes the names of the application and document that are being linked.

- **OLEDragMode** specifies whether a drag in an OLE drag-and-drop procedure is to be automatic or manual.

- **OLEDropMode** specifies whether a drop in an OLE drag-and-drop procedure is to be automatic or manual.

- **SizeMode** specifies how the OLE Container Control is sized and how the image contained is displayed.

- **SourceDoc** specifies the document that is currently linked or embedded in an OLE Container Control.

In this chapter you learned about the following methods:

- **Clear** is used to empty the previous contents of the clipboard.

- **GetData** is used to get data from a sending application.
- **GetFormat** is used to check what type of data is currently on the clipboard.
- **GetText** is used to retrieve text from the clipboard.
- **LinkNotify** tells the linked application when the data the object is linked to are changed.
- **LinkRequest** is used to update a manual link or a notify link.
- **LinkSend** transfers the contents of an updated image to the destination application.
- **LoadPicture** loads the specified file into a picture box.
- **SetData** is used to send image data to the clipboard.
- **SetText** is used to send text to the clipboard.

In this chapter you learned about the following functions:

- **Randomize** is used to begin the process of calculating random numbers by generating a random seed number from which to generate the other numbers.
- **Rnd** is used to generate random numbers between 1 and 0.
- **Shell** allows the application to launch other applications.

In this chapter you learned about the following events:

- **OLEDragDrop** occurs when an object is dropped from another application.
- **LinkOpen** occurs when a link is established between a Visual Basic application and another application.
- **LinkClose** occurs when a link between two applications is terminated.

In this chapter you learned about the following Toolbox tool:

- ▣ adds an OLE Container Control to the form.

12.11   Performance Check

1. Is a form a source or a destination?

2. What are the four types of destinations in Visual Basic?

3. What advantage does an automatic link have over a manual link?

4. What advantage does a notify link have over an automatic link?

5. What is the LinkMode property for?

6. What does the LinkTopic contain?

7. If your application is linked to Word, what does the LinkItem property contain?

8. What is the default value of the LinkTimeout property in seconds?

9. What is the Windows DDE name for Microsoft Word?

_____

10. What does LinkRequest do?

_____

11. What object does the Clear command work with?

_____

12. What is the vbCFLink variable used for?

_____

13. What does LinkSend do?

_____

14. What is the Rnd function for?

_____

15. What is a seed number?

_____

16. What is the Randomize statement for?

_____

17. What does GetText do?

_____

18. What did we do after trapping the DDE error in this chapter?

_____

19. What is the LinkExecute method for?

_____

20. When might the LinkOpen event come in handy?

_____

21. When an object is dropped from another application, what event is triggered in the Visual Basic application?

_____

22. What property specifies how the OLE Container Control is sized?

_____

23. What property specifies the document that is currently linked or embedded in an OLE Container Control?

_____

24. What property tells Visual Basic the type of application to which the OLE Container Control is related?

_____

25. What technique is the Event method related to?

_____

12.12   Programming Exercises

1. You have been assigned the task of printing mailing labels. You need to print an entire page of labels addressed to the same address. Because this program will have to print labels from a variety of other programs, you decide to get the program ready by writing two Visual Basic applications: one to input the data for the labels and the other to extract the data from the first and then print the labels. This exercise gives you practice linking two Visual Basic applications and linking data into multiple labels. At the computer, do each of the following:

   a. Get into Visual Basic and put your work disk in drive A.

   b. Create a new project with appropriate labels and text boxes for entry of name, address, city, state, and zip code.

   c. Create an extra label where the data can be combined into the form of a label so they can be sent to the other application.

   d. Add a Link button to the form and there put the code for combining the data in the form of a label (use a return after the name, the address, and the rest), sending the link and label to the other application.

   e. Save the form as **frmLabeler** and the project as **Labeler**.

f. Create a new application (compile the first application or load a second copy of Visual Basic) with ten labels (five rows, two labels per row) large enough to receive the label being sent. Add the labels as a control array so that the label can be assigned using a loop.

g. Add an **Edit** menu with the items **Paste Link** and **Print the Labels**.

h. Add code to the **Paste Link** button that will get the link and data from the clipboard assigning the data to the labels.

i. Add code to the **Print the Labels** button to print the labels by printing the form.

j. Save the files and project as **Print Labels** and run Labeler. Select the **Link** button and then the **Paste Link** option in the label printer. The ten labels should appear on the form.

k. Be sure you have a printer attached and turned on, and select the **Print the Labels** option.

l. Exit the applications, Visual Basic, and the system.

2. You are going to be assigned the job of writing an application that will pass data to Excel and then use Excel's capabilities to calculate the result. You are not yet sure exactly what the Excel formulas are to be, so in your spare time you decide you will get some practice by writing an application that will send data to Excel, perform some simple calculations on the numbers, and then transfer the result back to the application to be displayed. This exercise will give you practice linking a Visual Basic application to Excel and sending Excel macro commands. You will need to have Excel on your computer in order to do this exercise. At the computer, do each of the following:

a. Get into Visual Basic and put your work disk in drive A.

b. Create a new application and add to the form the following (see Figure 12.25):

1) The three Text Boxes on the left are named **txtNumber_In_1**, **txtNumber_In_2**, and **txtNumber_In_3**.

2) The three labels with a border on the right side are called **lblAddition**, **lblSubtraction**, and **lblMultiplication**.

3) Add an **&Edit** menu with the options **&Copy** and **&Execute Excel Commands**.

c. Launch Excel (you can set the program up to do it automatically if you wish).

d. The **Copy** option should send link information to the clipboard on the basis of which control is active (there are three text boxes). You will need to use code similar to the following for this:

```
Clipboard.Clear
strLink = "Excel Calculations|frmExcel_Calculations!" &
  ⮑ Screen.ActiveControl.Tag
Clipboard.SetText strLink, vbCFLink
Clipboard.SetText Screen.ActiveControl.Text
```

FIGURE 12.25
The form for
Programming Exercise 2.

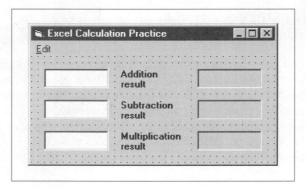

  e. The **Calculate** option must make an automatic link to cells A4 for the addition, A5 for the subtraction, and A6 for the multiplication. The addition formula should simply add up the column. The subtraction should subtract A2 from A1 and subtract A3 from that result, and the multiplication should just multiply the three fields together.

  f. Save the application as **Excel Calculations**.

  g. Run the application.

  h. Select the first text box, key **100**, and select the **Copy** option. Switch to Excel, select cell A1, and use the Paste Link option on the Paste Special dialog box to paste the linked number

  i. Switch back to your program, select the second text box, key **50**, and select the **Copy** option. Switch to Excel and paste the link into cell A2.

  j. Switch back to your program, select the third text box, key **20**, and select the **Copy** option. Switch to Excel and paste the link into cell A3.

  k. Select the **Execute Excel Commands** menu item. This should make the calculation results appear in the labels.

  l. Change one or more of the numbers, and the results change. Test the application by changing the numbers several times until you are certain the program is working properly. Then exit the program and print all the elements.

  m. Exit the applications, exit Visual Basic, and shut the system down properly.

3. You like being able to load files by dragging the file names from Explorer, but you want to go one step further. You want the program to be able to load bitmaps, text, and any other types of files that might be on your disk. At the computer, do each of the following:

  a. Get into Visual Basic and put your work disk in drive A.

  b. Create a new application and add an OLE Container Control to the form. You can specify it as containing any type of file.

  c. Change the OLEDropAllowed property to True. This allows the Container Control to accept files dropped from other applications.

  d. Save the form as **frmContainer** and the program as **Container Practice**.

  e. Run the program. Drag the **Sample.doc** file from the Ch-12 folder on your work disk and drop it on the Container Control. The file will be displayed as a Word file.

  f. Drag the **Spread Sheet.xls** file from the Ch-12 folder on your work disk and drop it on the Container Control. The file will be displayed as an Excel spreadsheet. This is the file you used in the chapter.

  g. Find a BMP file in the Windows folder on your hard drive, and drag-and-drop it on the Container Control. Note that it will also open.

  h. Experiment a bit more until you are familiar with the way the program is working, and then exit the program, Visual Basic, and the system.

12.13   Performance Mastery

1. You are soon going to need to create a program with a grid to link to other programs. In anticipation of this assignment, you have decided to practice by creating a program that has a grid with three rows of images and four rows of text that can be linked to other programs (such as the one you used in this chapter). This exercise will give you practice linking programs and using a grid. Design and create the program, test it using the destination program you created in this chapter (which you may have to modify slightly for this program), and then save it as **Grid Link**.

2. You have been given the task of creating a pair of linked programs. The first one is to allow the input of ten names. After they are input (call this program **Link Input**), they are to be linked to a second program (called **Link Sort**) that will sort them and display the sorted list. The easiest way to do this is to place the names in a dummy text field separated by commas. Then the sort program can link to that field, separate the names, and put them in the sorted list (Sorted property set to True). Make the link automatic so that every time a name is changed in the Link Input program, the list will be resorted and updated in the Link Sort program. The Link Sort program should have a sorted list box, and when the data are updated, all the names should be input from Link Input, added to the list, and then taken from the list and displayed in ten text boxes. This exercise will give you practice linking multiple programs. Design, create, and thoroughly test the programs before printing out all the elements.

3. You work for a company that creates sound-effect files for television and radio advertising. You have been assigned the task of creating a program that can be used to preview the available sound-effect files. Create a program with a MultiMedia control and set up the control so file names from Explorer can be dropped onto the control and then played automatically. Be sure the program will print out appropriate error messages if the dropping is done from some program other than Explorer or if the file dropped doesn't have the proper format. Design and create the program, and then save it as **Explorer Sound**. Thoroughly test the program and then print all the elements.

4. To be sure you understand how to work with Windows Explorer, you decide to write a program that can be used to accept a drop from Explorer and display all the file names in a list. The program should then allow the user to select one of the file names from the list and drop it on a Picture Box or a text box, and if the file is of the appropriate type, the bitmap or text data should appear in the box. The program should display all the appropriate error messages if the formats are incorrect at any point. Design and create the program, and then save it as **Explorer Filenames**. Thoroughly test the program and then print all the elements.

5. You are soon going to be working on a program that will make extensive use of the OLE capabilities of lists. You decide to write a set of sample programs to practice the necessary techniques. The first program (called **List Sender**) should have a list of names that will allow multiple items to be selected. This program should then have a **Send** button to send the selected items to a second program. The second program (called **List Receiver**) should receive the list and divide the selections up into five labels, one name per label. If more than five names are selected, the second program should display an appropriate error message. Design, create, and then thoroughly test the programs. Print all the elements of both programs when you are finished.

6. You are soon going to begin working on an extensive project using a lot of OLE. You decide to write a program to practice some of the techniques you may have to use. Write a program, called **Color Send**, that has eight color labels, one for each of the major colors. Under those labels put one text box with the visible property set to False. When one of the color labels is clicked, display the name of the color in the text box and send a link to another program from that text box. In the second program, called **Color Receive**, create a text box to receive the text sent and then a label that the program can change to represent the color sent from the first program. Use a button to create the link. Design, create, and then thoroughly test the programs. Print all the elements of both programs when you are finished.

7. You are soon going to begin working on an extensive project using a lot of OLE. You decide to write a program to practice some of the techniques you may have to use. Write a program, called **Sound Send**, that will have the tools necessary to allow the user to locate and select a sound file. When the name of the file is selected in the File List box, send that file name to another program where the sound file is played. Call that second

program **Sound Play**. Design, create, and then thoroughly test the programs. Print all the elements of both programs when you are finished.

8. You are soon going to begin working on an extensive project using a lot of OLE. You decide to write a program to practice some of the techniques you may have to use. Write a program, called **First Text**, that will have two text boxes. Initially put some text in the first text box. Add **Send** and **Link** buttons to the form. Create a second program, called **Second Text**, that has a text box to receive the text from the first program. You will need **Link** and **Send** buttons in the second program as well. When the first program sends the text and the link information, the **Link** button in the second program should be used to link the text into the text box. Then the **Send** button will be used to send the link and the text back to the first program. That program's **Link** button should link the text into the second text box. Thus, every time the text is changed in the first text box in the first program, the text in the second text box should change as well. Design, create, and then thoroughly test the programs. Print all the elements of both programs when you are finished.

9. You are soon going to begin working on an extensive project using a lot of OLE. You decide to write a program to practice some of the techniques you may have to use. Write a program, called **Text Drag**, that will have two text boxes. Initially put some text in the first text box. Add a **Link** button to the form. Create a second program, called **Text Drop**, that has a text box to receive the text from the first program. You will drag the text from the first text box and drop it in the text box in the second program. When the second program receives the text, it will need to establish an automatic link to the text box in the first program. Then send link information back to the first program. That program's **Link** button should link the text into the second text box. After the text is dropped and linked, every time the text is changed in the first text box in the first program, the text in the second text box should change as well. Design, create, and then thoroughly test the programs. Print all the elements of both programs when you are finished.

10. You are soon going to begin working on an extensive project using a lot of OLE. You decide to write a program to practice some of the techniques you may have to use. Write a program, called **Picture Send**, that has a control array of eight picture boxes. Load the Picture Boxes with the Moon01.ico through Moon08.ico icons from the Ch-5 folder. Use a timer to send a different image each second, starting with the first and looping back to the first after sending the last. Create a second program, called **Picture Receive**, that will receive the sent image and display it in a picture box. The image should change in the receiving program every time it changes in the sending program and should pass through the phases of the moon. Design, create, and then thoroughly test the programs. Print all the elements of both programs when you are finished.

11. Because the PIM program has a notepad, you decide to fix the program so that you can drag a file name from Explorer and automatically open the text file in the notepad. Change the program so that it will do this. You will need to copy the program from the work disk you used in Chapter 11.

Browsing the Web

13.1   Chapter Objectives

After finishing this chapter you will be able to:

- Describe the Internet, the World Wide Web, and the difference.
- Explain what a URL is and what the elements of a URL are.
- Demonstrate how to use a WebBrowser control in a program and how that control can be used to access a Web page.
- Demonstrate the use of the various WebBrowser methods.
- Demonstrate the use of the PictureClip control.

13.2   Introduction

We have only one element of the PIM left to add, the **Web browser**. This portion of the program will allow you to access the World Wide Web, which is often simply called the Web. We will begin by discussing the Web and how it is related to the Internet. Then we will plunge right in and add a Web browser to our PIM program. Along the way we will learn how to use a couple of other tools and, as always, we will learn a few new programming techniques.

13.3   The Internet and the World Wide Web

You have probably already signed onto the Internet many times using one of the available browser programs, such as **Internet Explorer** from Microsoft. When you sign onto the Internet, you are actually connecting to a huge series of computers that themselves are connected to one another by a series of phone lines, coaxial cable (like TV cable), and satellite links. This system of linked computers had its humble beginnings many years ago when a small group of research scientists developed the system so they could share their research with one another. As word spread about the system, more scientists and other persons such as college professors began using it and the number of users and connected computers continued to grow. Now it is estimated that there are upwards of 100 million users and that number continues to grow each day.

The documents that these early Internet users sent back and forth were strictly text-based. Quickly, however, it became obvious that just text was not sufficient for their needs. They began sending text and images, which evolved into **hypertext documents,** documents that contain links to other portions of the same document or to other documents. These links take the form of underlined text, buttons, or even defined areas of images.

So what's the difference between the Internet and the World Wide Web? Or is there a difference? Are they the same thing? Common usage might suggest that the two are indeed the same thing, but technically they are not. The Internet is the network of computers, storage devices, connections, and the software that controls these systems and the access to them. The Web, on the other hand, is the set of hypertext-linked documents, which are called **Web sites**, to which the Internet allows access by saving these sites on the available storage devices. The Internet also allows users to use **E-mail (electronic mail)**, gain access to archived files such as old news reports, and participate in discussion groups (called **chat rooms**) on a virtually endless selection of topics.

Web sites always begin with a starting or **home page**. This page generally contains an introductory message explaining what the Web site is about, with links to other Web pages or even other Web sites. Web pages are constructed using a special scripting language called **HTML**, which stands for **HyperText Markup Language**. Although HTML is very precise, like most computer languages, it is not difficult to use once you learn the syntax. But rather than go to that much effort, most people who need to create Web pages use a Web authoring program that allows you to create Web pages without understanding HTML at all.

To access a Web site with a browser program, you need to know the **URL**, or **universal resource locator,** of the site. This is the address of the Web site so the browser will know where, on the vast Internet network, the site is located. A typical home page URL is **http://www.yahoo.com**. Its URL elements follow.

1. **http://** is the scheme, the manner in which the browser is to interpret the data. The colon and separator slashes are part of the scheme and are required. The three most common schemes are:

   - **http, HyperText Transfer Protocol,** tells the computer that the file being transferred contains hypertext links.

   - **ftp, File Transfer Protocol,** tells the computer that the file being transferred is simply to be downloaded or uploaded and stored in the previously designated location.

2. **www** is the host or computer name. The name is generally www, though it can have other formats such as **search, movies, music,** or any of thousands of others. A home page will almost always be www, while subsequent pages will often have a different format indicator.

3. **yahoo** is the domain on which the home page of the site is actually located. The domain name is generally the name of the company or organization sponsoring the site, but it might be a person's name or just some word that the person who created the Web site decided to use.

4. **com** is the **domain suffix,** which identifies the type of organization that set up the site. There are many of these, but the four most commonly used are:

   - **com,** for commercial institutions or companies such as Microsoft, Yahoo, or Disney

- **edu,** for educational institutions, such as Yale and Rutgers
- **gov,** for government institutions, such as the IRS and the White House
- **org,** for nonprofit organizations or societies, such as the American Red Cross and the American Bar Association

There is a special organization that is actually responsible for setting up the URLs. When a company, organization, or person wants to put a Web site together, they submit a request to the **Internet Network Information Center** and if there is not already a Web site with the same **domain name** (in this case, yahoo.com), the request will be granted in just a few days. If the submitted domain name duplicates an existing one, the one submitted will have to be changed in some manner.

Most people don't want to host a Web site but merely to have access to the Internet. To do this, you must have a computer, a **modem**, which is a hardware device that connects your computer to the outside world via a phone line, or some other method of accessing the Internet such as the service provided by your school, and an **Internet Service Provider (ISP)**. An ISP is a company that leases phone lines to gain access to the Internet and then provides its subscribers with a local phone number and the appropriate software to allow them the necessary access. The ISP charges its subscribers a small monthly fee, usually about $20, for its services.

In this book we will assume you are already using a computer system that is or can be connected to the Internet. We will not discuss how such connections are made. If you work on your home computer and are not currently set up, you should contact a local or national company such as America Online or Microsoft (Microsoft Network or MSN) and they will instruct you on how to set up your system.

13.4 Looking at the Pim

As usual, before we begin looking at how to add to the PIM, we will take a brief look at the new features we are going to add to the program.

1. Copy the Ch-13 folder from wherever it is located on your system onto your work disk. If there isn't room, start a new disk, but be sure you set up folders for Ch-8, Ch-10, and Ch-11 and copy all the necessary files onto this new disk. Remember, the PIM is expecting certain files to be on the work disk and if they are not there the program will not work.

2. Launch the PIM application from the Ch-13 folder on your work disk. Switch to the **Web Browser** tab to see a display similar to the one shown in Figure 13.1.

> **HINT:** You will need to sign onto the Internet before you can actually run the PIM. If you need assistance with that part of the process, you will need to discuss it with your lab assistant or instructor.

Notice that the Browser automatically linked to the Yahoo! Web site home page. This is the same page that will be brought up when you click the **Home** button on the toolbar. This Web page, like most Web pages, is changed frequently, so you will not see precisely what is shown in Figure 13.1. Notice, however, that the page appears just as it would if you had brought it up in any other browser. It has headings, buttons, and underlined text links.

On the tabbed display, you see the Web browser workspace as well as the Address bar and the toolbar. The Address bar is a pull-down list where the last 25 Web pages visited are listed. All the pages visited while you are using the browser are automatically saved to a file

FIGURE 13.1
The Web Browser tab
display.

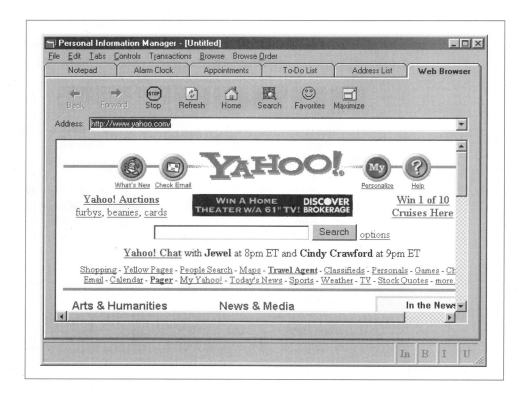

when the program is exited. Then, when the program is loaded, these files are automatically loaded into the Address list.

3. Highlight the address in the Address entry box, key **http://www.Microsoft.com**, and press **Enter**. This will cause the program to link to the Microsoft home page, which will appear similar to the page shown in Figure 13.2.

Now there will be two links stored in the Address list.

4. Pull down the Address list to see the two addresses as shown in Figure 13.3.

Above the Address bar is the toolbar with many of the standard browser tools. Notice that the **Back** button is now available. When you first ran the program it was not available. If you look back at Figure 13.1, you see the **Back** button is dimmed and unavailable. The program is set up to automatically use the intelligence of the Visual Basic Web browser control to know when there are sites to drop back to and when you can move forward to another.

5. Click the **Back** button and the browser again contains the Yahoo! site and the **Forward** button becomes available. Now the **Back** button is unavailable. You have moved back through the pages as far as you can.

6. Click the **Forward** button and the browser returns to the Microsoft Web site and the **Back** button again is available, while the **Forward** button is disabled.

The toolbar buttons are set up like buttons you see in many Windows applications. The button looks flat on the toolbar until you move the mouse over it and then it appears as a button.

7. Move the mouse over the buttons and you see them change, as illustrated with the **Stop** button in Figure 13.4.

FIGURE 13.2
The Microsoft home page.

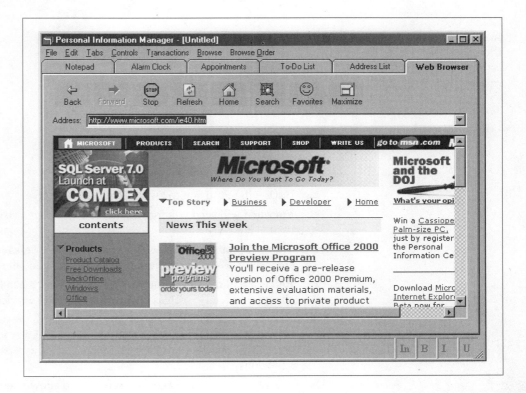

FIGURE 13.3
The Address list.

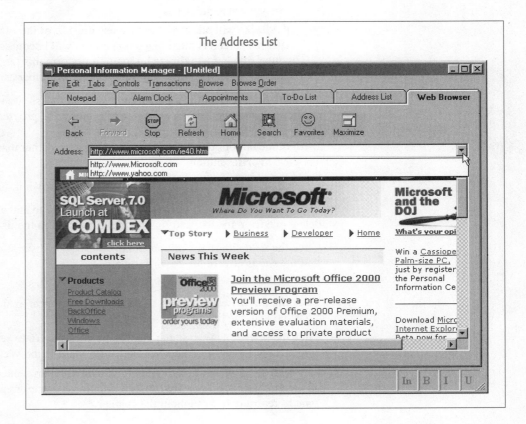

FIGURE 13.4
An illustration of how
the button appears
when the cursor is
moved over the tool.

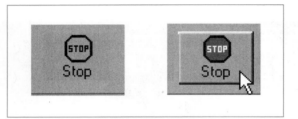

The definitions of the buttons are as follows:

- **Back** will return you to a Web page just visited.
- **Forward** will send you forward in the list of pages visited after **Back** has been used.
- **Stop** will stop the downloading of a Web page. This is generally used when you are visiting a Web page that seems to be taking too much time to download.
- **Refresh** will reload the current Web page. This is handy for Web pages that change frequently, such as ones that monitor stock prices.
- **Home** will reload the first page you visited when the program loaded. In the current program, that is the Yahoo! home page. Later you may want to change your Home button site to some other page, such as a page of stock market quotations.
- **Search** will load the Yahoo! search page to allow you to search for Web sites.
- **Favorites** will allow you to set up a selection of Web pages you like to visit often. These pages will generally show up in the Address list as well, but since the Address list will only hold 25 addresses, it is nice to have somewhere else to store your favorite pages.
- **Maximize** will allow you to increase the size of the PIM window to maximum. After the screen is maximized, the button will become a **Restore** button. The regular title bar **Maximize** button will perform this function, but browsers generally have this function available on the toolbar as well.

To the right of the toolbar there is a progress bar that shows up when you are accessing a Web site. Just like the **Back** and **Forward** buttons, the progress bar uses methods made available by the Web browser control.

Most of the buttons don't cause any visual changes other than loading a Web page, except for the **Favorites** button.

8. Click the **Favorites** button to see the dialog box shown in Figure 13.5.

Notice that this dialog box has buttons to allow you to add a Web site to the Favorites list, delete one from the list, and link to one of the sites in the list.

9. Click the **Add site to list** button and the dialog box disappears. What you didn't see is that the site is now in the Favorites list.
10. Pull down the Address list and click the Yahoo! Web site.
11. Click the **Favorites** button to see the dialog box appear again. This time the Microsoft Web site is in the list.
12. Click the Microsoft Web site in the list and click the **Go to selected site** button. The dialog box disappears and the Microsoft Web site is in the Web browser again.
13. Play with the program a bit more until you have experimented with each of the buttons on the toolbar. When you are finished, minimize the program, since you will probably want to return to it throughout the chapter.

FIGURE 13.5
The Favorites dialog
box.

13.5   Adding the Web Browser

The first thing we need to do is add the **WebBrowser control** to the Web Browser tab.

1. Launch Visual Basic, load the PIM program from your Ch-11 folder, and save the forms, module, and project to the Ch-13 folder.

For you to add the WebBrowser control to your project, the control will first need to be added to Visual Basic as it is an external component.

2. Press **Ctrl-T** to load the **Components** dialog box, scroll the list, and click the **Microsoft Internet Controls** item.

Since you already have the **Components** dialog box on the screen, you will add another control that we will use later in the chapter.

3. Scroll the list, click **Microsoft PictureClip Control 6.0**, and click the **OK** button to exit the dialog box.

Now you will see three new controls in the toolbox. The one you want at this moment is the WebBrowser control as indicated in Figure 13.6.

4. Switch to the Web Browser tab in the PIM program, click the WebBrowser control in the toolbar, and draw the WebBrowser on the tab as shown in Figure 13.7. Be sure not to place the top of the control any higher than illustrated (Top property is 1680), since you need to leave room for the other controls to be added above the browser.

5. Change the control name of the WebBrowser control to **webPIM**.

Now that you have the WebBrowser control set up, you should verify that it works.

FIGURE 13.6
The WebBrowser
control.

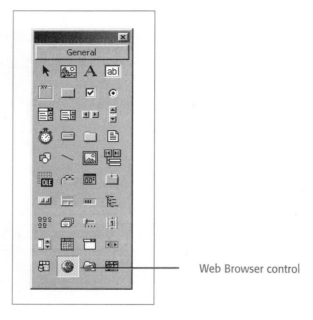

Web Browser control

6. Open the code window for the Form_Load procedure and add the following line of code to the end of the procedure:

```
webPIM.Navigate "http://www.yahoo.com"
```

This statement tells the WebBrowser control to retrieve a Web page using the **Navigate** method. We won't actually leave this code here. We just added it to be sure the control is going to work as it is supposed to.

FIGURE 13.7
The WebBrowser
control added to the
Web Browser tab.

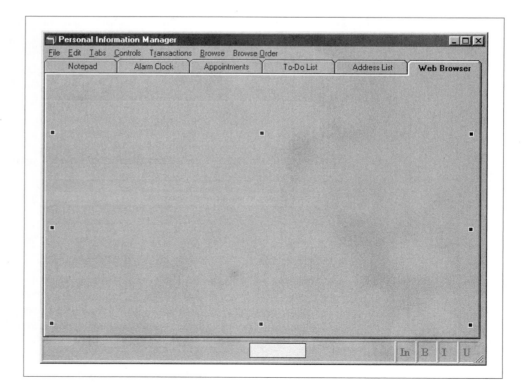

FIGURE 13.8
The Yahoo! home page.

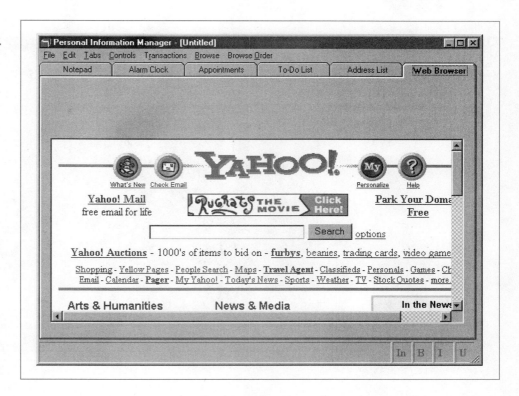

7. Remember to connect to the Internet and then run the program and click the Web Browser tab to be sure the Yahoo! Web site is loaded. If everything works as it should, you will see the Yahoo! home page as shown in Figure 13.8.

8. Exit the program.

13.6   The Address Bar

Next, we want to add the Address bar, which is simply a combo list box.

1. Switch to the Web Browser tab and add a Dropdown combo list box and size and position it as shown in Figure 13.9. Change the control name to **cboAddress**.

We want to direct most of the Web site access through this list. Thus, we want to set up a home page and immediately put it in the Address list.

2. Set up a module-level variable called **mstrWeb_Home** and then switch to the Form_Load procedure.

3. Move to the bottom of the procedure, delete the statement we added a minute ago, and key the following statements:

```
mstrWeb_Home = "http://www.yahoo.com"
cboAddress = mstrWeb_Home
cboAddress_KeyPress (Asc(vbCr))
```

The first statement sets the home page Web site address to the Yahoo! home page. The second statement puts the home page address in the Address list and the third statement uses the Address list KeyPress procedure to look up the Web site by passing the procedure

FIGURE 13.9
The Web Browser tab
with the Dropdown
combo list box added.

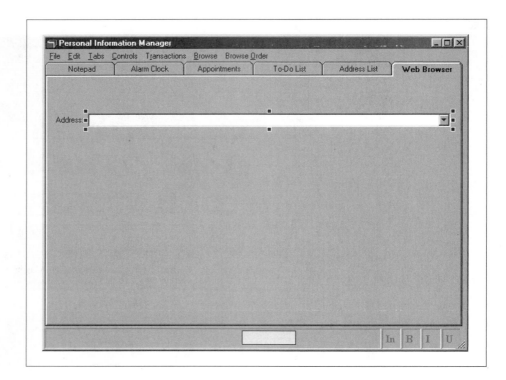

the ASCII code for the **Enter** key, 13. This being the case, we need to write the KeyPress procedure.

We don't want to look up the Web site as the user is keying into the Address list entry box. We want to do it only when the user is finished and signals it by pressing the **Enter** key. The first thing we want to do in the KeyPress procedure is make sure we are processing only when the **Return** key is pressed. This requires the following statement:

```
If KeyAscii = Asc(vbCr) Then
```

4. Change to the cboAddress_KeyPress procedure and key the previous statement.

Now we need to use whatever is in the list to get the Web site. This is done with the **Navigate** statement as follows:

```
webPIM.Navigate cboAddress.Text
```

5. Key the previous statement into the procedure.

Since we want to save the URLs of the visited Web sites in the Address list, we need to add this address to the list. Remember that just keying (or assigning) to the combo list entry box does not automatically add the item to the list. That must be done in the code separately. Since we will need to use this same routine again later in the program, we will create a subroutine called **Add_To_Address_List** to do it. The last two statements in this procedure are:

```
    Add_To_Address_List
End If
```

6. Key these two statements into the procedure.

Now we want to create the new subroutine.

7. Create a new procedure called **Add_To_Address_List**.

This procedure will add the address in the Address entry box into the list. We don't want to continually put the same address in the list, so we will begin by searching the list to see if the URL in the entry box is already listed. That will require the following routine:

```
blnWas_Found = False
For intCounter = 0 To cboAddress.ListCount - 1
    If cboAddress.Text = cboAddress.List(intCounter) Then
        blnWas_Found = True
    End If
Next intCounter
```

First we set a flag variable to False (blnWas_Found) so if we find the item in the list we can set the flag to True. This way, at the end of the loop we will know if the address was found in the list.

8. Key the previous code into the procedure.

Now we need to determine whether the address was found and, if not, put it in the list:

```
If blnWas_Found = False Then
  ' cboAddress.AddItem cboAddress.Text, 0
End If
End If
```

Notice we are adding the new address as item 0 (zero). This will put it at the top of the list, so the latest Web sites visited are always shown at the top of the list.

9. Key the rest of the routine into the procedure.

10. Run the program and switch to the Web Browser tab. You should see the Yahoo! home page.

11. Key **http://www.Microsoft.com** into the Address list entry box and press **Enter**. You should now see the Microsoft home page.

12. Pull down the Address list. You should have both of the visited pages in your list.

13. Click the Yahoo! URL.

Nothing happens, because selecting an item in the list sets off the Click event, not the KeyPress event. We can fix this problem easily.

14. Exit the program and switch to the code window for the cboAddress_Click procedure. Key the following statement in this procedure:

```
cboAddress_KeyPress (Asc(vbCr))
```

15. Restart the program and change to the Web Browser tab. The Yahoo! Web site should be displayed again.

16. Key **http://www.Microsoft.com** into the Address list entry box and press **Enter**. Pull down the Address list and click the Yahoo! URL. This time, the Yahoo! Web site should be reloaded.

17. Experiment with the program a bit more, linking to additional Web sites. You might try some or all of the following:

- **http://www.NASA.gov**, the NASA Web site
- **http://www.MTV.com**, the MTV Web site
- **http://www.Yale.edu**, the Yale University Web site
- **http://www.CBS.com**, the CBS television network Web site
- **http://www.NBC.com**, the NBC television network Web site

- ■   **http://www.ABC.com**, the ABC television network Web site
- ■   **http://ESPN.Sportszone.com**, the ESPN cable television network Web site
- ■   **http://www.Disney.com**, the Disney Web site
- ■   **http://www.RedCross.org**, the American Red Cross Web site

18. When you are finished, exit the program.

13.7   Adding the Browser Buttons

As you saw when you experimented with the finished PIM program, the Web Browser buttons are special in that they look flat until the mouse is moved over them and then they become regular buttons with graphics on them instead of just captions. You will learn how those buttons are created in this section.

1. Switch to the Web Browser tab and add a command button as shown in Figure 13.10. The button has a width of **855**, a height of **615**, the Left property is **240**, and the Top property is **480**. Change the control name to **cmdWeb** and the Visible property to **False**. We don't want the button to be visible initially.

FIGURE 13.10
The new Web browser button.

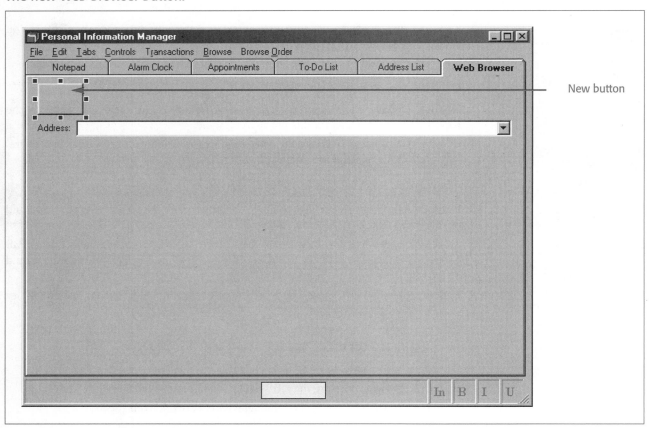

2. Change the **Style** property to **1 - Graphical**. This allows us to put a graphic on the button rather than just the normal text caption.

We will add the rest of the buttons as a control array, but will put a PictureBox control on top of the button first. Then we will duplicate the pair of controls. This is easier because the PictureBox control must be positioned very precisely or you will not achieve the desired effect.

3. Add a PictureBox control as shown in Figure 13.11 with the following considerations:
   - Height is 615
   - Width is 810
   - Left is 285
   - Top is 510
   - The control name is **picWeb**

4. Now copy this pair of controls (the button and picture box) and paste and position seven sets of them as shown in Figure 13.12.

The PictureClip Control

Now that we have the buttons and overlaid picture boxes, we need some graphics to display in the controls. This is where the second control you added earlier comes in. The **Picture-Clip control** allows you to store a group of images and then, by telling the program the

FIGURE 13.11
The PictureBox control.

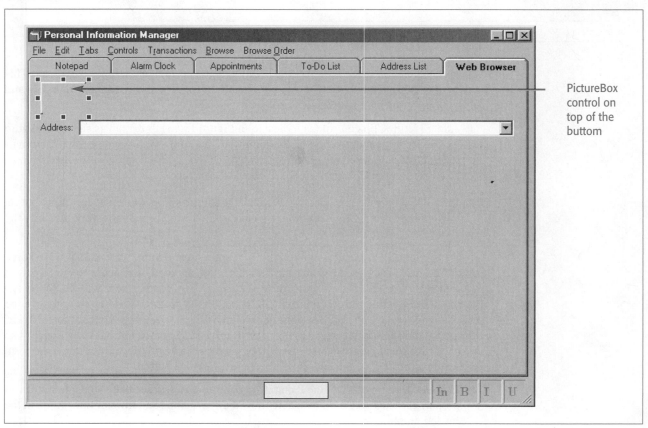

PictureBox control on top of the buttom

FIGURE 13.12
The rest of the button/picture box pairs.

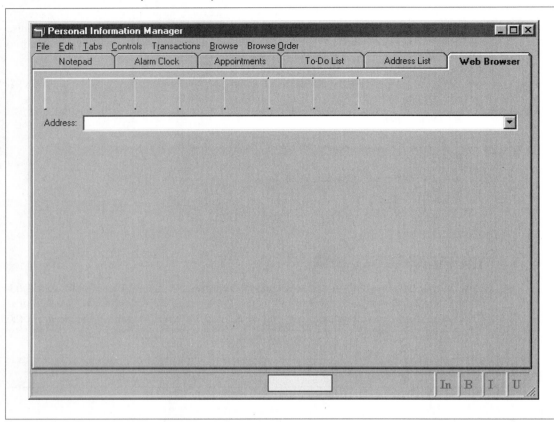

appropriate position in the group, you pull out only the portion of the image you want. This is done by setting up the group of images as a table. It will be easier for you to understand this by simply working with the control.

1. Add a PictureClip control (as indicated in Figure 13.13) to the tab as shown in Figure 13.14. The size and position of the control are not important, because it will automatically be resized when the graphic is loaded and the control is not visible when the program is running. Change the control name to **clpWeb**.

2. Switch to the Properties window and click the **Picture** property. Click the ellipse button and load the **Icon_Clip.bmp** image from the Ch-13 folder on your work disk into the control as shown in Figure 13.15.

Look carefully at the graphic you just loaded into the control. Notice that it has three rows of images. The first two rows are replacements of each other, while the third row is extra images. We will use the first row in the PictureBox controls that will lie flat on the Tabbed control, while the second row will be put on the buttons. The button will have the colored image and the PictureBox control will have the grayed image. The leftmost two images on the third line will be used to make the **Back** and **Forward** buttons unavailable. The rightmost two images on the third line will be used on the **Maximize** button when the form has been maximized, so the button will become a **Restore** button.

3. Examine the properties of the PictureClip control. You will see there are **Cols** and **Rows** properties. These are used to specify how many columns and rows of images are in the loaded graphic.

FIGURE 13.13
The PictureClip control.

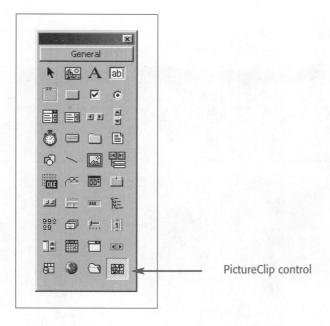

PictureClip control

FIGURE 13.14
The PictureClip control added to the tab.

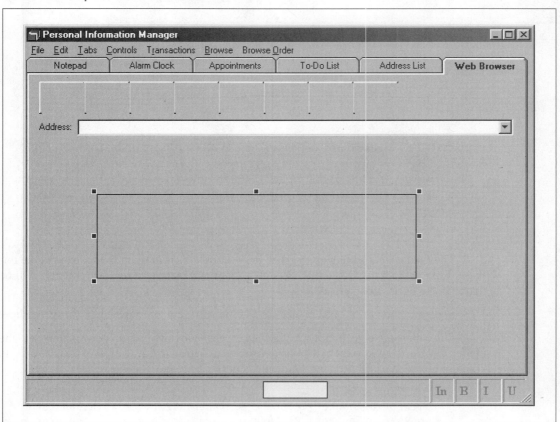

FIGURE 13.15
The PictureClip control with the graphic added.

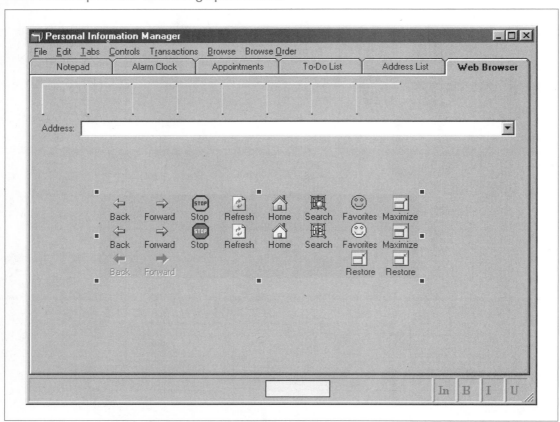

4. Change the **Cols** property to **8** and the **Rows** property to **3**.

> **HINT:** The images saved in a PictureClip control must be positioned very carefully. Visual Basic will use the Cols and Rows specifications to determine what portion of the graphic is used. If one of the images in the graphic is slightly larger or smaller than the rest or the spacing is off slightly, the portions of the graphic will not be separated properly.

The final step of setting up the Web browser buttons is to write the code to put the images from the PictureClip control into the buttons and picture boxes. Initially, this will be done in the Form_Load procedure.

5. Switch to the Form_Load procedure and move the cursor to the end of the procedure.

Since there are eight buttons in the control array and the first button, by default, has the index of zero, we will want to loop from 0 to 7 to assign an image to each of the buttons and picture boxes. We will need the following code:

```
For intCounter = 0 To 7
    picWeb(intCounter).Picture = clpWeb.GraphicCell(intCounter)
    cmdWeb(intCounter).Picture = clpWeb.GraphicCell(intCounter + 8)
Next intCounter
```

Both the picture boxes and the command buttons use the **Picture** property to assign the image to the control. That image is retrieved from the PictureClip control using the **GraphicCell** property, pointing at the particular image by position in the table of images. Since there are eight images in each row, the related item in the second row will need to be offset by 8. That's why we are using the counter and adding 8 to it (**intCounter + 8**). The two **Back** button images are 0 and 8, the two **Forward** button images are 1 and 9, and so on.

6. Insert this code in the procedure.

The problem with this is that the **Back** and **Forward** buttons should not show as being available, so we will want to use the extra images we have stored in the PictureClip graphic, on the third row, so they will look disabled. This means we need two more statements:

```
picWeb(0).Picture = clpWeb.GraphicCell(16)
picWeb(1).Picture = clpWeb.GraphicCell(17)
```

This will assign the two leftmost images on the third row to the **Back** and **Forward** buttons.

7. Add these two statements to the procedure.

Using the MouseMove Procedure

Now you need to do one more thing to make this all work properly. We are going to use the MouseMove event to change the display from the picture box to the button, so we need to be sure the **Back** and **Forward** buttons do not allow that to happen until Web sites have been visited appropriately.

1. Set the Enabled property of the **Back** and **Forward** buttons to False.

As we mentioned, we are going to use the MouseMove event of the picture boxes to switch the display from the picture boxes to the buttons, but if we are going to turn on one button, we need to be sure all the other buttons are turned off. Instead of trying to determine which button was on before we try to turn on another, we will simply turn them all off. To do this, we will set up a procedure called **Redo_Web_Buttons** as follows:

```
Sub Redo_Web_Buttons()
    Dim intcounter As Integer
    For intcounter = 0 To 7
        picWeb(intcounter).Visible = True
        cmdWeb(intcounter).Visible = False
    Next intcounter
End Sub
```

Notice that this procedure counts from 0 to 7 to set the Visible property of the picture boxes to True so they will be on and the Visible property of the buttons to False so they will be off. This way, all of the buttons are off and all of the picture boxes are on.

2. Move to the end of the current procedure and key the previous procedure.

Now we need to set up the MouseMove procedures to turn on the appropriate button while turning off the rest. Since the PictureBox control is the control that is visible when you are moving the mouse over the toolbar, we will need to use the MouseMove procedure of the picWeb control array. We begin by turning off all the buttons with the procedure we just created:

```
Redo_Web_Buttons
```

3. Switch to the picWeb_MouseMove procedure and key the previous statement.

Next, we need to turn on the appropriate command button and turn off the picture box. This can be done by pointing at them using the Index value provided by the MouseMove procedure. The statements we need are:

```
cmdWeb(Index).Visible = True
picWeb(Index).Visible = False
```

4. Key the previous two statements into the procedure.

This will allow the buttons to be turned on and off as the mouse is moved over the picture boxes, but what happens if the user moves the mouse off one of the buttons and onto the Tabbed control? We need to reset the Web buttons there also.

5. Change to the tabPIM_MouseMove procedure and key the call to the Redo_Web_Buttons procedure following the other statement already in the procedure.

This is all we need to turn the buttons on and off.

6. Run the program, switch to the Web Browser tab, and move the mouse over the toolbar. The icons should change to buttons one by one as you move the mouse from picture box to picture box. Move the mouse off the buttons and onto the Tabbed control. All of the buttons should now be only picture box icons.

Clicking the Buttons

Now that we have the procedures properly set up to allow the user to see the buttons, we need the functioning code behind these buttons. This will, of course, need to be added in the cmdWeb_Click procedure.

The Back and Forward Buttons

1. Change to the cmdWeb_Click procedure.

Since the command buttons are a control array, this procedure has an Index variable to tell us which of the buttons is clicked. We will use a Case construct to determine which one is clicked. We begin with

```
Select Case Index
    Case 0 ' Back
```

The code for the **Back** button is simple. We mentioned earlier that the WebBrowser control has many properties and methods to help us use the control. One of these will automatically keep track of the Web pages as they are visited. Thus, to go back to a previously visited Web page, all we need to do is use the **GoBack** method as follows:

```
webPIM.GoBack
```

2. Key the above statement into the procedure.

This isn't the end of the story for the **Back** button, however. Remember that currently the Back picture box is disabled, so moving the mouse over it will not trigger a change to the button and therefore the button cannot be clicked. We need some way to determine when to turn the picture box on so the button will also be enabled. The WebBrowser control has a special event called **CommandStateChange** that we can use to determine if any Web page has been visited. This event is executed whenever the value of the WebBrowser navigation forward or backward counter has changed. As we mentioned, the WebBrowser control automatically keeps track of which Web pages have been visited, but it also keeps track of how many pages you should be able to return to (GoBack) or go forward to (**GoForward**, which we will look at in a moment).

3. Change to the webPIM_CommandStateChange procedure.

This event procedure uses two parameters, **Command** and **Enable**. Command tells us which Web pages visited counter value has changed (the one for GoBack or the one for GoForward), while the Enable parameter tells us whether the command is to be enabled (True) or disabled (False). In other words, after we load the first Web page into the program and then change to a second one, the CommandStateChange event will be executed. The Command parameter will contain the value indicating that the Back counter value has changed, and the Enable parameter will be True, indicating that we are able to use the GoBack method. Now, after we use the GoBack method, we will have returned to the previous page and there will be no more Web pages to go back to. This will actually cause the CommandStateChange event to be triggered twice. The first time will be for the Back counter value. It will have been changed and the Enable parameter will now be False, since this was the last page there was to return to. The second time the CommandStateChange event is triggered, the Command parameter will indicate the Forward counter value and the Enable parameter will be True, indicating that we can now move forward through the list of Web pages.

The Command value of 1 indicates the Forward counter, while 2 indicates the Back counter. Thus, we will need to begin our procedure code with

```
If Command = 1 Then ' Navigate forward
```

4. Key the previous statement into the procedure.

Then we need to test the Enable parameter. If it is True, we need to change the picture in the Forward picture box to the second image in the PictureClip control, since it is the one that doesn't look disabled. Then we need to enable the picture box so the MouseMove event can be triggered. This means we need the following code:

```
If Enable = True Then
    picWeb(1).Picture = clpWeb.GraphicCell(1)
    picWeb(1).Enabled = True
Else
```

5. Key this code into the procedure.

If the Enable parameter is False, we need to do just the opposite. We need to reassign the image from the PictureClip control that indicates the picture box is disabled, and then actually disable the picture box so the MouseMove will no longer change it to the button:

```
    picWeb(1).Picture = clpWeb.GraphicCell(17)
    picWeb(1).Enabled = False
End If
```

6. Add this code to the procedure.

The Command parameter can contain values other than 1 and 2, so to be safe, the rest of the If Test should actually make sure the Command parameter value is 2:

```
ElseIf Command = 2 Then
```

7. Key this statement.

The final portion of this If Test checks the Enable parameter and, based on the value, changes the picture box for the **Back** button in the same manner as we changed the picture box for the **Forward** button.

8. Compose and key the appropriate statements.

That's it for the CommandStateChange event procedure. Now you need to add the code for the **Forward** button.

9. Change back to the cmdWeb_Click procedure and key the following two statements:

```
Case 1 ' Forward
    webPIM.GoForward
```

As you can see, the **GoForward** method is used the same way the GoBack method is used.

10. Close the Case construct so you can test the program.

11. Run the program and switch to the Web Browser tab.

     Both the **Back** and **Forward** buttons should appear disabled.

12. Key **http://www.Microsoft.com** into the Address list entry box and press **Enter**.

     Now the **Back** button should be enabled.

13. Move the mouse over the **Back** button and the button should actually appear. Click the **Back** button and the program should switch back to the Yahoo! Web site.

     The **Back** button should be disabled again and the **Forward** button should be enabled.

14. Click the **Forward** button and the Microsoft Web site should appear again, the **Back** button should be enabled again, and the **Forward** button should again be disabled.

15. Play with the functionality a bit more and then exit the program.

The Stop Button   The **Stop** button can be used when you are downloading a Web page that seems to be taking too much time. By stopping the downloading you can move onto another task in the program, such as accessing a different Web page.

The method used to stop download is very simple, it is **Stop.** The method is shown in the following statements, which need to be added to the Case construct already begun:

```
Case 2 ' Stop
    webPIM.Stop
```

1. Switch back to the code window and key the previous two statements.

2. Run the program, switch to the Web Browser tab, key **http://www.Microsoft.com** into the Address list entry box, and press **Enter**. Immediately click the **Stop** button. The downloading of the Web page will stop and the Yahoo! Web page will still be in the browser unless you are not quite fast enough. It is possible that a portion of the Microsoft Web page will now be in the browser, but it will not finish downloading.

3. Try the button a few more times and then exit the program.

The Refresh Button   The next button on the toolbar is the **Refresh** button. This is used when you are viewing a Web page that changes frequently, such as one showing stock market values. When you refresh the Web page, the WebBrowser control simply downloads it again so you have the most current copy of the page available.

Here again, the method used is simple. You merely use the **Refresh** method as given here:

```
Case 3 ' Refresh
    webPIM.Refresh
```

1. Switch back to the code window for the webPIM_Click procedure and key the previous two statements.

2. Run the program, switch to the Web Browser tab, and click the **Refresh** button. Though it may be hard to tell, the Yahoo! Web page should have been downloaded into the browser again.

3. Practice with this button and different Web pages until you are satisfied that the **Refresh** button is working. If you are running the program during a weekday, you might try linking to the Yahoo! Stock Quotes area and then refreshing that Web page. Since the stock market values change constantly, you should see some different values when you refresh the page.

4. Exit the program when you are finished.

The Home Button When we began this chapter, one of the first things we did was set up a special variable called **mstrWeb_Home** in which to store our initial home page. Now we are going to utilize that variable. When the user clicks the **Home** button, we want to put our home page into the Address list and link to that Web page. We need the following statements added to the webPIM_Click procedure:

```
Case 4 ' Home
    cboAddress.Text = strWeb_Home
    cboAddress_KeyPress (Asc(vbCr))
```

1. Switch back to the code window for the webPIM_Click procedure and key the previous three statements.
2. Run the program, switch to the Web Browser tab, key **http://www.Microsoft.com** into the Address list entry box, and press **Enter**.
3. Click the **Home** button and the Yahoo! Web page should reappear.

We set up our program to have the Yahoo! Web page as our internal home page. After this chapter is finished, you can change your home page to something else more appropriate to your tastes. Perhaps you would prefer to begin at the MTV home page or, if your program is going to be used mainly by children, you may want the home page to link to the Disney home page. If you watch stocks, you may want to make your home page one of the many stock market sites available.

The Search Button The next button we are going to discuss is the **Search** button. Just as the **Home** button brings up a Web page we decided to use, so does the **Search** button. Since we have been using Yahoo! for our internal home page, we will use Yahoo!s search page for our search page as well. This means that we need to assign the URL for the search page to the Address list entry box and then press the **Enter** key, in a similar fashion to the way we used the home page. We need the following statements:

```
Case 5 ' Search
    cboAddress.Text = "http://search.yahoo.com"
    cboAddress_KeyPress (Asc(vbCr))
```

1. Switch back to the code window for the webPIM_Click procedure and key the previous three statements.
2. Run the program, switch to the Web Browser tab, and click the **Search** button. The Yahoo! search page should appear in the browser as shown in Figure 13.16.
3. Click the **Home** button and the Yahoo! Web site home page should reappear.
4. Click the **Search** button again and the search page should reappear.

You may wish to try using the Yahoo! search engine before going to the next section in the chapter. We will not discuss how to do Internet searches, as it is outside the scope of this book. If you need assistance doing Internet searches, you should check with your lab assistant or instructor.

5. Exit the program when you are finished experimenting.

The Favorites Button As you saw when you practiced with the PIM program at the beginning of this chapter, the **Favorites** button will actually call up a dialog box for the storage of the selected pages. To call up the dialog box, you will need to add the following code to the cmdWeb_Click procedure:

```
Case 6 ' Favorites
    frmAdd_Favorite.Show 1
```

1. Switch back to the code window for the webPIM_Click procedure and key the previous two statements.

FIGURE 13.16

The Yahoo! search page.

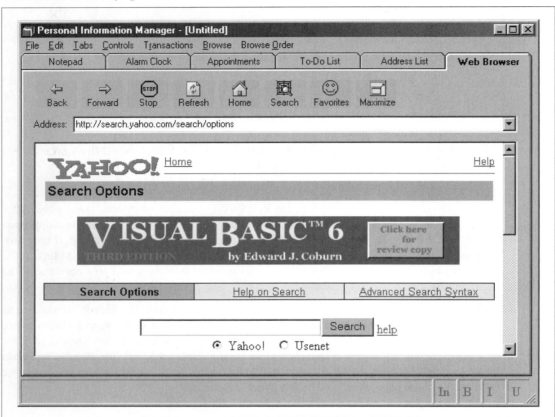

Now you need to create the new dialog box.

2. Add a new form, called **frmAdd_Favorites**, to the project as shown in Figure 13.17. The workspace is a list box called **lstFavorites**. Give the buttons the names **cmdAdd**, **cmdDelete**, **cmdGoTo**, and **cmdCancel**.

Since this is to be a list of favorite Web pages, we will save the captured pages so we can redisplay them when this dialog box is opened. That means we will read the file and add them to the list on this form using the Form_Load procedure.

3. Change to the Form_Load procedure for the new form.

Since this is to be an input file, and the first time the user runs the program there will be no file, we will set up the program so that won't matter. To do this, we need to use the On Error statement:

```
On Error GoTo File_Not_Found
```

When we open the file for input, if the file is not there, an error will occur, transferring program control to the **File_Not_Found** label. Since we will be saving the file after capturing a Web page in the list, we don't really need to create the file here. So at the error label, the program doesn't have to do anything. The label will simply enable the program to skip around the statements for reading the data from the file.

4. Key the On Error statement and the label, leaving a couple of blank lines between for the entry of the rest of the statements of the procedure.

FIGURE 13.17
The Favorites dialog box.

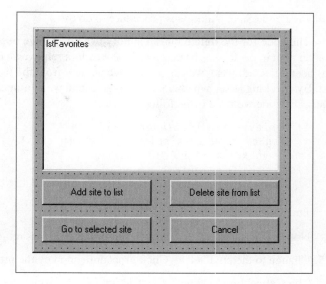

5. Key an appropriate Open statement to open the file **Favorites.txt** for input. Then write a Do-loop to input the Web pages and add them to the lstFavorites list box. Remember, you cannot input directly into the list box. You have to input into a temporary variable and then add that item to the list.

When the **add** button is clicked, we first need to determine whether the current Web page is already in the list. We don't want to allow the user to add the same page to the list multiple times. That would do the user no good. Thus, we need to loop through the current list to see if the Web page currently in the Address list box is already in the lstFavorites list. If it is, we want to display an error. If it is not, we want to put it in the list. This will require the following code:

```
intcounter = 0
Do Until intcounter > webFavorites.ListCount - 1 Or
↳ webFavorites.List(intcounter) = frmPIM.cboAddress.Text
    intcounter = intcounter + 1
Loop
If webFavorites.List(intcounter) = frmPIM.cboAddress.Text Then
    MsgBox "This page is already in the list.", vbExclamation, "Add
        ↳ Error"
Else
    webFavorites.AddItem frmPIM.cboAddress.Text
End If
```

6. Change to the cmdAdd_Click procedure and key the above statements.

After the Web page is added to the list, we want to save all the items in the list to the Favorites.txt file and then unload the form. Since we also want to save the Web pages in the list when we delete one, we will create a separate procedure (called **Save_Addresses**) for saving the pages. Thus, the final two statements in this procedure are:

```
Save_Addresses
Unload frmAdd_Favorite
```

7. Key these two statements.

In the Save_Addresses procedure, we simply open the file, print the Web pages into the file from the list, and then close the file.

8. Create the Save_Addresses procedure to do this.

The code for the **delete** button is not difficult. All we need to do is first check to see that an item in the list has been selected. We cannot remove an item from the list unless one has been selected. Also, we cannot remove an item from the list if there are no items in the list. By checking to see whether an item is selected, we eliminate both of these possibilities. Thus, the code we need is the following:

```
If webFavorites.ListIndex = -1 Then
    MsgBox "You must select a site in the list first",
    ↳ vbExclamation, "List Error"
Else
    webFavorites.RemoveItem (webFavorites.ListIndex)
    Save_Addresses
End If
```

Notice that we saved the addresses after the item was removed from the list.

9. Change to the cmdDelete_Click procedure and key the previous code.

The **Cancel** button simply needs to unload the form.

10. Change to the cmdCancel_Click procedure and key the appropriate statement.

The last button is the button to allow the user to link to the Web page selected in the list. Just as we cannot remove an item from the list if one is not selected, we don't want to try to link to a page if one is not selected. The code for the cmdGoTo_Click should be:

```
If webFavorites.ListIndex = -1 Then
    MsgBox "You must select a site in the list first",
    ↳ vbExclamation, "List Error"
Else
    frmPIM.cboAddress.Text =
    ↳ lstFavorites.List(webFavorites.ListIndex)
    frmPIM.cboAddress_KeyPress (Asc(vbCr))
    Unload frmAdd_Favorite
End If
```

We check to see if an item is selected and if it is, we copy it to the Address list on the frmPIM form and then press the **Enter** key to cause the program to link to the page.

11. Change to the cmdGoTo_Click procedure and key the previous statements.

This is all the code for the new form. Let's try the program.

12. Run the program, switch to the Web Browser tab, and click the **Favorites** button. Your dialog box should appear.

13. Click the **Add page to list** button. The form should disappear.

14. Switch to the Microsoft Web page using the URL given prevously.

15. Click the **Favorites** button again and the Yahoo! URL should be in your list. Click the URL in the list and click the **Go to selected page** button.

16. The dialog box should disappear and the Yahoo! Web page should again be in your browser.

17. Click the **Favorites** button again. Click the URL in the list and click the **Delete page from list** button. The URL should vanish from the list.

18. Play with the program a bit more to be sure it is functioning properly before exiting.

The Maximize Button   The last button on the toolbar is the **Maximize** button. This is actually a dual-function button. It will first maximize the window and then change to a

Restore button so the window can be automatically restored to its original size. This means we need to work two different cases, the window not maximized (so we will maximize it), and the window maximized (so we will restore it).

1. Switch to the cmdWeb_Click procedure again and key the start of this portion of the Case construct:

```
Case 7 ' Maximize
```

Since there is no way to tell which image has been placed in the picture box or the **command** button (it will be either Maximize or Restore), we will need to use a new property so we can sense the size of the window. That property is **WindowState**. We can test this property to determine whether the window is maximized with the following If Test:

```
If frmPIM.WindowState = vbMaximized Then
```

2. Key the previous statement into the procedure. vbMaximized is a predefined constant for the value of 2.

Now, if the window is maximized, we want to set it back to its original or normal size. We do this by assigning a new value to the WindowState property:

```
frmPIM.WindowState = vbNormal
```

3. Key the previous statement into the procedure. vbNormal is a predefined constant for the value of 0.

Since the window was maximized, we know the picture box and the **command** button must currently represent the restore function. We need to change the image in both the picture box and the **command** button with the following two statements:

```
picWeb(7).Picture = clpWeb.GraphicCell(7)
cmdWeb(7).Picture = clpWeb.GraphicCell(15)
```

4. Key the previous two statements into the procedure. You may want to look back at the PictureClip image to satisfy yourself that the correct images are being used.

If the window is not currently maximized (False on the If Test), we want to maximize it. We need another assignment statement for the WindowState property:

```
Else
    frmPIM.WindowState = vbMaximized
```

5. Key these two statements into the procedure.

Then we need to change the images to represent the restore function. Remember, the two rightmost images on the third row of the PictureClip image are for the restore. This gives us the final statements of the Case construct:

```
        picWeb(7).Picture = clpWeb.GraphicCell(22)
        cmdWeb(7).Picture = clpWeb.GraphicCell(23)
    End If
End Select
```

6. Key the previous statements into the procedure.

Since we have now used the **Maximize/Restore** button, we will need to reset all the buttons with the procedure we set up for the purpose:

```
Redo_Web_Buttons
```

7. Key the previous statement into the procedure.
8. Run the program, switch to the Web Browser tab, and click the **Maximize** button.

Notice that though the form becomes maximized, the Tabbed control and the status bar remain the sizes they were (see Figure 13.18). This is not what we wanted. When we maximize the form, we want the elements on the form to be adjusted as well. We will do that next.

Adjusting the Window Elements   As you just discovered, maximizing the window does not adjust any of the elements of the window. Each element of the form that is related to the size of the form will have to be adjusted individually. This is done in the **Form_Resize** procedure.

1. Exit the program and switch to the Form_Resize procedure.

We actually only want to allow the form to be maximized if we are on the Web Browser tab. Therefore, this procedure will begin with the following If Test:

```
If tabPIM.Tab <> 5 Then
    frmPIM.WindowState = vbNormal
    picWeb(7).Picture = clpWeb.GraphicCell(7)
    dWeb(7).Picture = clpWeb.GraphicCell(15)
End If
```

FIGURE 13.18
The maximized window.

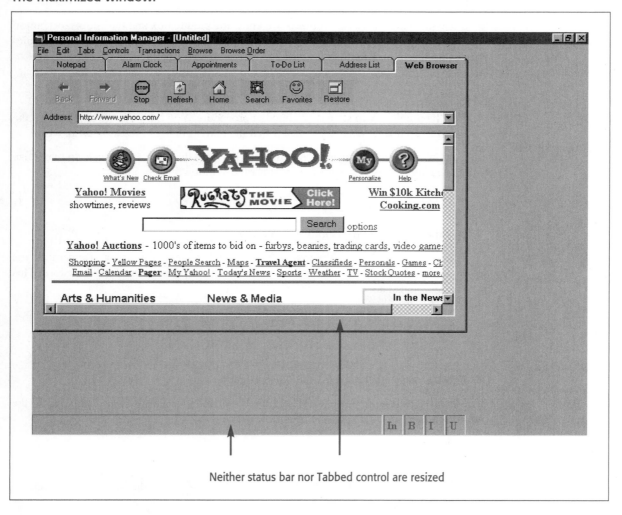

Neither status bar nor Tabbed control are resized

Notice that we tested to see if the tab is 5, the Tab number of the Web Browser tab. If it isn't 5, we restore the window to normal size and change the button images so they represent the maximize function.

2. Key the previous If Test into the procedure.

Now we need to determine the size of the various elements of the window in relationship to the window itself so they can be adjusted as the size of the window changes. Adjusting the size of the elements presents us with one small problem: An error will occur if we attempt to change the size of one of the elements when the window is minimized. Thus, we need to first determine that the window is not minimized:

```
If frmPIM.WindowState <> vbMinimized Then
```

3. Key this statement into the procedure.

There are five properties that need to be adjusted when the window is resized: the height and width of the Tabbed control, the height and width of the WebBrowser control, and the width of the first element of the StatusBar control. As you may recall from Chapter 7, we don't adjust the width of the status bar itself, but of the first element, which, in effect, changes the width of the entire status bar.

If you were to check the needed sizes, you would discover that the first element of the status bar needs to be 2040 twips less than the width of the form. The first statement we need is:

```
frmPIM.staPIM_Status.Panels(1).Width = frmPIM.Width - 2040
```

Then the difference between the height of the form and the height of the Tabbed control is 1215, while the difference in width is 195. This gives us the next two statements:

```
frmPIM.tabPIM.Height = frmPIM.Height - 1215
frmPIM.tabPIM.Width = frmPIM.Width - 195
```

Finally, the height difference of the WebBrowser control is 3255 and the difference in width is 705, to give us these statements:

```
    webPIM.Height = frmPIM.Height - 3255
    webPIM.Width = frmPIM.Width - 705
End If
```

4. Key the previous statements into the procedure.

One more thing needs to be done to make sure the elements of the window are changed to the proper size. If you have adjusted the size of the window while on the Web Browser and then switched to another tab, it would be nice if the window automatically resized itself for the other tab. To do this, we need to add more code to the tabPIM_Click procedure.

5. Switch to the tabPIM_Click procedure and move the cursor to the end of the procedure.

The code we need is the following If Test:

```
If tabPIM.Tab <> 5 Then
    frmPIM.WindowState = vbNormal
    frmPIM.Height = 7350
    frmPIM.Width = 9600
End If
```

As you can see, first we make sure that the tab is not the Web Browser, then we change the WindowState to normal and adjust the size of the window. Since we are adjusting the window size, the Web Browser elements will be adjusted as well: resizing the window causes execution of the Form_Resize event.

6. Key the previous If Test.

7. Run the program, switch to the Web Browser tab, and click the **Maximize** button. This time, the various elements adjust themselves as well.

8. Click the **Restore** button and the window returns to its previous size and the elements automatically adjust.

9. Click the **Maximize** button and then click one of the other tabs. The window resizes itself. Click the Web Browser tab and notice that the **Restore** button has once again become a **Maximize** button.

10. Play with the program a little more until you are satisfied that everything is working as it should. Be sure to resize the window by dragging the border and then change to another tab to be sure the window will resize itself properly. Exit the program.

13.8   The Progress Bar

There is only one more element of the Web browser to add. When you are accessing a Web site, it is always nice to know the progress, of the download. If there is virtually no progress, you can always stop the download and try another site. To add a progress bar, we need to introduce a new control and make use of another WebBrowser control event.

1. Switch to the Web Browser tab and add a label to the tab, positioning it as shown in Figure 13.19. Change the name of the label to **lblWeb**. Change the caption to **100%** as

FIGURE 13.19
The progress label.

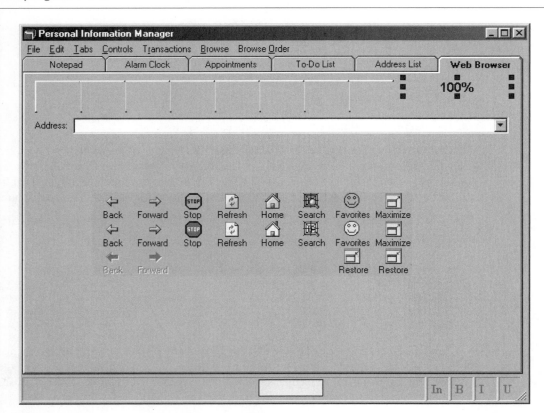

shown in Figure 13.19. Change the Visible property to **False**, since we don't want the label to appear except when we are actually downloading a Web page.

Next, you need to add a new control, called a **ProgressBar** control.

2. Add a ProgressBar control to the tab as shown in Figure 13.20 and size and position it as shown in Figure 13.21. Change the control name to **pbrWeb** and change the Visible property to **False**.

This control has Min and Max properties that we will set to 0 (which is the default) and 100 respectively. We want the progress bar to show the percentage of completion.

3. Change the Max value to 100.

To know this percentage value as the Web page is loaded, we will use the **ProgressChange** event.

4. Change to the webPIM_ProgressChange procedure.

Notice that this event has two parameters, **Progress** and **ProgressMax**. The ProgressMax value represents the total time that the download should take, while the Progress value represents the portion of the ProgressMax completed so far. When the download is complete, the Progress variable will have a value of –1. To use these values, we will need an If Test to be sure the download is not complete (when the value of Progress will be –1):

```
If Progress >= 1 Then
```

Next, we need to set the maximum value of the progress bar using the ProgressMax parameter:

```
prbWeb.Max = ProgressMax
```

Since the Progress parameter contains the completed portion of the ProgressMax parameter and we want to represent that value as a portion of 100 percent, we will need to convert it with the following statement:

```
prbWeb.Value = Progress * 100 / ProgressMax
```

FIGURE 13.20
The ProgressBar control.

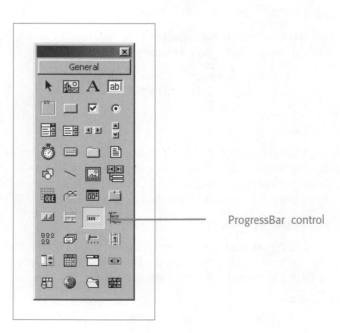

ProgressBar control

FIGURE 13.21
The ProgressBar control added to the tab.

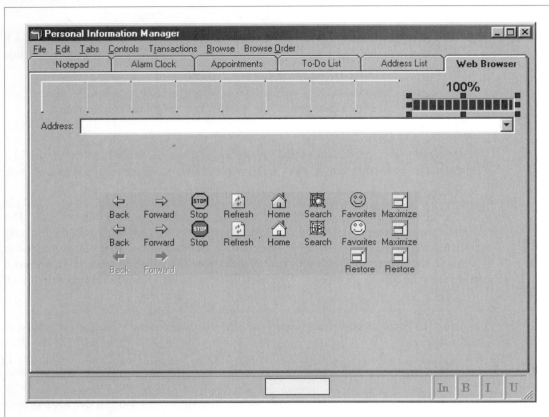

Then we need to use a similar calculation for the percentage label:

```
lblWeb.Caption = Str(Progress * 100 / ProgressMax) & " %"
```

Next, we need to make the label and progress bar visible, since we set the Visible property to False when we added them to the tab.

```
    lblWeb.Visible = True
    prbWeb.Visible = True
Else
```

5. Key the previous statements.

The Else portion of the If Test is executed if the value of the Progress variable is less than 1. If the download is complete, the Progress variable will actually have a value of –1. In this portion of the If Test, we need to turn the Visible properties back off. If the downloading is complete, we don't want the label and progress bar to still be visible.

6. Key the appropriate two statements.

Lastly, we need to write the URL of the downloaded Web page into the Address entry box. To do this, we need to use the **LocationURL** property. It will always contain the latest URL displayed in the WebBrowser control. The statement needed will be

```
cboAddress.Text = webPIM.LocationURL
```

7. Key this statement into the procedure.

Remember that just putting the URL in the Address list entry box does not add it to the list, so we will need to call the procedure we set up earlier to add that URL to the list (the procedure was called Add_To_Address_List). The final three statements of the procedure are then

```
      Add_To_Address_List
    End If
End Sub
```

8. Run the program and switch to the Web Browser tab. Key the URL for another Web site into the address bar and press **Enter**. You should see the progress label and bar appear, indicating the downloading progress.

9. Click one of the links in the new Web page and after the Web page has loaded, pull down the Address list to be sure the page was added to the list.

10. Practice with the program until you are satisfied that everything is working properly, then exit the program.

13.9   Saving the Addresses

The only thing we have left is to save the addresses from the Address list. We could do it as we have done with other file-saving procedures and save the file after each address is added to the list. This, however, takes time, and time is important when you are using a Web browser. Instead, we will save the list when the user exits the program. If you think back to Chapter 6, we created an **Exit** item on the **File** menu and set up a message box to verify that the user actually wished to exit the program. Now, however, we are going to move that code into the Form_QueryUnload procedure. This procedure was also discussed in Chapter 6. It is an event procedure that occurs when the user clicks the **Close** button on the title bar or uses the **Close** option on the **Control** menu.

What we want to do is move the code from the mnuExit_Click procedure to the Form_QueryUnload procedure and then add a little more code.

1. Change to the mnuExit_Click procedure and key the following statement:

```
Form_QueryUnload 0, 0
```

This will make the program execute the Form_QueryUnload procedure when the user picks the **Exit** option from the **File** menu. The two zeros on the end are the parameters that the Form_QueryUnload procedure requires.

2. Highlight and cut the rest of the code from mnuExit_Click.

3. Switch to the Form_QueryUnload procedure and paste the code there. You should have the following code in the procedure:

```
intResult = MsgBox("You have indicated you want to exit from the
program. Is this
↳ what you want?", vbQuestion + vbYesNo, "Exit Program?")
If intResult = vbYes Then
    End
End If
```

We want to add the code for saving the addresses before the End statement. Remember that we only want to save the latest 25 addresses, which will actually be at the top of the list.

4. Add the appropriate code to save the first 25 addresses into a file called **WebSites.txt** in the Ch-13 folder on drive A.

This If Test needs an Else clause. If the user clicks the **No** button on the message box to signal that the user really does not want to exit the program, we need to cancel the QueryUnload operation. The QueryUnload procedure is not ordinary in that if you exit the procedure in a normal fashion, the program is exited. Thus, if the user indicates that he or she does not want to exit, we need to tell the procedure not to by setting the **Cancel** parameter to a value other than zero. The Else clause of the If Test is:

```
Else
    Cancel = 1
```

5. Key the rest of the If Test.

6. Run the program and switch to the Web Browser tab. Change the browser to another Web site. Now you should have two addresses in the list.

7. Click the **Close** button on the title bar and click the **Yes** button on the dialog box. This should save the two Web sites in the file.

8. Run the program again and switch to the Web Browser tab. Pull down the Address list. There should be two addresses in the list. Select the other Web page URL (you are already on the Yahoo! Web page). The browser should have switched to the other page.

9. Practice with the program using all the Web Browser features you have added in this chapter until you are satisfied that everything is working properly. Then exit the program and shut the system down properly.

13.10   Debugging Your Programs

There are few problems you can have when working with the WebBrowser control as long as you use the methods and events properly. Most of the methods are easy to use since they consist mainly of one-word methods, such as GoBack, GoForward, and Stop, and require no parameters.

If you wish to save the URLs of the Web pages visited, you need to store whatever is found in the LocationURL property.

Using the PictureClip control is more complicated. The images you store in the control must be precisely positioned. Since the control separates the images by simply dividing the available image size into the specified number of rows and columns, the spacing around all the images must be done carefully. If there is just a small amount of extra space around one of the images, it can upset the alignment of all the images.

13.11   A Final Observation

Well, that concludes this chapter on the Web Browser and this chapter concludes our book. We have covered a lot of Visual Basic ground, but we have truly only scratched the surface. There are still many functions, options of functions, properties, and methods that we haven't had the time to explore, many additional tools that we haven't even mentioned, and many statements we have used only one or two ways when they can be used in numerous ways. The joy of programming is to constantly uncover new and exciting ways to create applications and then design those new applications.

We have discovered powerful functions, statements, forms, and objects, but we have only given you the Visual Basic tools to create new applications. The imagination, drive, and determination to create those applications must belong to the individual programmer. Enjoy the experience!

13.12 Command and Menu Summary

In this chapter you learned about the following properties:

- **Cols** lets you specify the number of columns of images stored in a PictureClip control
- **GraphicCell** lets you specify the portion of the image stored in a PictureClip control that is to be used.
- **LocationURL** contains the latest URL downloaded into a WebBrowser control.
- **Rows** lets you specify the number of rows of images stored in a PictureClip control.
- **Picture** lets you store an image in a control such as a command button or a picture box.
- **WindowState** lets you test the state (normal, minimized, or maximized) of a window.
- In this chapter you learned about the following methods:
- **GoBack** allows you to return the WebBrowser control to a Web page previously visited.
- **GoForward** allows you to go forward in the list of Web pages visited by the WebBrowser after having used the GoBack method.
- **Navigate** allows the WebBrowser control to retrieve a Web page.
- **Refresh** makes the current Web page in the WebBrowser control to be reloaded.
- **Stop** stops the downloading of a Web page.
- In this chapter you learned about the following events:
- **CommandStateChange** occurs whenever the back and forward counters of the list of visited Web pages changes.
- **ProgressChange** occurs when the downloading progress of the Web page being loaded into a WebBrowser control changes.
- **Resize** occurs when the form size is changed.
- In this chapter you learned about the following Toolbox tools:
- adds a PictureClip control to the form.
- adds a ProgressBar control to the form.
- adds a WebBrowser control to the form.

13.13 Performance Check

1. What is a hypertext document?

2. What is HTML?

3. What is a URL?

4. What is an ISP?

5. What is the difference between the Internet and the World Wide Web?

6. What method is used to retrieve a Web page in the WebBrowser control?

7. What do the letters HTTP stand for?

8. What property did we change so a button will display an image?

9. What two properties are used to indicate how many images are stored in a PictureClip control?

10. What property is used to load the image into a PictureClip control?

11. What property is used to assign an image to a PictureBox control?

12. What property is used to assign a particular portion of a PictureClip control to another object?

13. What is the difficult part of using the PictureClip control?

14. What event is used to determine whether we can use the GoBack method while using a WebBrowser control?

15. What method is used to stop downloading a Web page in the WebBrowser control?

16. What property allows you to maximize a window?

17. What event is executed when a window is resized?

18. What event is executed when the status of a downloading Web site changes?

19. What property contains the URL of the Web page currently displayed in a WebBrowser control?

20. When using the QueryUnload event, what parameter must you change the value of to cancel exiting the program?

13.14   Programming Exercises

1. You have a favorite stock that you like to watch and you decide to write a program so the stock price will constantly be displayed and updated automatically. At the computer, do each of the following:

   a. Get into Visual Basic with your work disk in drive A so you can store the program when it is complete.

   b. Create a new program and add a WebBrowser control and a Timer control to the form. Remember that you have to add the WebBrowser control to the Toolbox using the Components dialog box.

   c. Change the height of the WebBrowser control to 1800 and the width to 5500. This will allow the display of the stock to fit as shown in Figure 13.22.

FIGURE 13.22
The display of the IBM stock price.

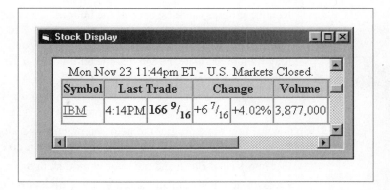

d. Key the appropriate command in the Form_Load procedure so the Web page will automatically be loaded when the program is run. The Web site URL you need is **http://quote.yahoo.com/q?s=ibm&d=v1**. This will load the IBM stock. If you want to load a different stock, just replace "ibm" in the URL with the ticker symbol for the stock you want to watch. If that doesn't work for you, run the PIM program, click the **Stock Quotes** link, enter the stock symbol for the stock you are interested in, and when the page comes up, copy the URL out of the Address list entry box.

e. Set the Interval property of the Timer control to **65000**, which is about one minute. Then, in the Timer control Timer event, key the appropriate statement to refresh the WebBrowser. This way, the stock price will be redisplayed about once a minute.

f. Run the program and adjust the display so it shows the stock in the WebBrowser workspace as illustrated in Figure 13.22. When the WebBrowser refreshes, it will readjust the display as you have it set so the stock will continually be positioned properly in the window.

g. When you have run the program long enough to satisfy yourself that it is running properly, exit the program and shut the system down properly.

2. You are a fan of TV and the movies and would like to have easy access to the various TV and movie schedules. At the computer, do each of the following:

a. Get into Visual Basic with your work disk in drive A so you can store the program when it is complete.

b. Create a new program and add a WebBrowser control and six buttons in a control array above the WebBrowser, to the form. Remember that you have to add the WebBrowser control to the Toolbox using the Components dialog box.

c. Label the buttons ABC, NBC, CBS, FOX, Movies, and Sched.

d. In the Click procedure for the buttons use a Case construct to navigate to each of the sites, which are:

- ABC: http://www.ABC.com
- NBC: http://www.NBC.com
- CBS: http://www.CBS.com
- FOX: http://www.FOX.com
- Movies: http://movies.yahoo.com
- Sched.: http://tv.yahoo.com

e. Set up the Form_Load procedure so that it will load the Movies Web page.

f. Run the program and test each of the buttons. You may want to add a progress bar so you can see the progress of the downloading. You may also want to adjust the URLs given so your program gets to the precise page you want. For example, you may want to navigate the Movies site until you find the page with the movie schedules for your locale and then copy that URL and use it instead of the one given.

g. When you have satisfied yourself that the program is running properly, exit the program and shut the system down properly.

3. You decide to write a program to help you practice working with the PictureClip control by animating a series of images. At the computer, do each of the following:

a. Get into Visual Basic and put your work disk in drive A.

b. Create a new program and add a PictureClip control to the form. Remember, the control must be added to the Toolbox first, using the Components dialog box. Load the Moon_Images.bmp file from the Ch-13 folder on your work disk into the control. Change the Cols property appropriately.

c. Add a Timer control to the form. Set the Interval property to 200. You may want to adjust this as you experiment with the finished program.

d. Using a Static variable, create a routine in the Timer procedure of the Timer control so that each time the timer is executed, the next image in the PictureClip control is substituted for the one currently there. When the counter exceeds the available number of images, it should be set back to zero.

e. Add an Image control to the form in which to display the images and change the Stretch property to True. This will cause the image put in the control to expand to fill the side of the control.

f. Run the program to be sure the moon images are properly animated and then save the program as **Moon Animation**.

g. Print the program elements and then exit Visual Basic and shut the system down properly.

13.15   Performance Mastery

1. You decide to write a program to get more practice working with the PictureClip control by animating a series of images. Create a program with a PictureClip control and load into it the **Butterfly_Images.bmp** file from the Ch-13 folder on your work disk. Add a Timer control to control the change of the images, and use an Image control to display the images. Design, create, and then save the program as **Butterfly**. Thoroughly test the program before printing all the program elements.

2. You monitor information on four different Web pages. You decide to write an application that will let you do just that, constantly monitor all the pages. Create a program with four WebBrowser controls, each one of them loading a different Web page when the program is run. Then add a text box and four option buttons, one for each of the windows. If the user enters a URL in the text box, that Web page should be downloaded into the WebBrowser control represented by the selected option button. Design, create, and then save the program as **MultiWeb**. Thoroughly test the program before printing all the program elements.

3. You are going to be assigned a task using the PictureClip control later, so you decide to write a program to get more practice working with the control by animating a series of images. Create a program with a PictureClip control and load into it the **Running_Man.bmp** file from the Ch-13 folder on your work disk. Add a Timer control

to control the change of the images, and use an Image control to display the images. As you change the image, change the Left property of the image so it will seem as if the image is running across the form. You will need to make the man run off the right edge of the form and then reposition the Image control to the left side of the form. If you use a negative value for the Left property when moving the image back to the left, you can make it appear as if the man is running onto the form. Design, create, and then save the program as **Running Man**. Thoroughly test the program before printing all the program elements.

4. You work for a company that creates Web pages for its customers. You need to create a program that will make it easy for customers to view sample pages. Create an application that has a menu of Web page URLs and a WebBrowser control. When a menu item is chosen, read the menu name and link to that Web page. Design, create, and then save the program as **Web Menus**. Thoroughly test the program before printing all the program elements.

5. You work for a company that creates Web pages for its customers. You need to create a program that will make it easy for customers to view sample pages. Create an application that has a Tabbed control with a WebBrowser control on each of the six tabs. Choose six different Web pages to appear on the tabs and load the pages when the program is initially executed. Design, create, and then save the program as **Web Tabs**. Thoroughly test the program before printing all the program elements.

Using ActiveX Controls

A Bit of History

One of the nice things about Visual Basic is that you don't have to continually rewrite the same pieces of code—reinventing the wheel. For example, you wouldn't want to have to write the code to draw a button on your form in every program in which you need to use a button. Microsoft recognized this need for **reusable components** in the very first version of Visual Basic. But it also recognized that not every program would need every available tool. Therefore, it created these reusable components, called them tools, and distributed them with Visual Basic as **VBX** files. VBX stands for Visual Basic eXtensions, a term that makes sense because VBX files *extend* the versatility of Visual Basic.

In Visual Basic 4, Microsoft extended the capabilities of many of the VBX components so that they incorporated OLE, and changed the names of these components to OCX. Another reason why Microsoft changed the name of the components is that Visual Basic 4 moved from the 16-bit realm to the 32-bit realm. VBX components are 16-bit, whereas OCX components are 32-bit. **16-bit** means that internally, items and commands used 16 bits for storage. Windows 3.1 was a 16-bit operating system. With the improvements in Windows after Windows 3.1, the interfaces were designed around a 32-bit architecture, allowing larger data structures and faster processing.

In Visual Basic 5, Microsoft moved the component technology farther yet and called the reusable components **ActiveX controls.** ActiveX components began as Web tools for use on the World Wide Web. They have been expanded, however, to incorporate OLE and other important elements of the older OCX components.

Visual Basic 5 includes many of both types of components, OCX and ActiveX. The Check Box control, for example is an OCX control, whereas the Common Dialog Control is an ActiveX control.

Creating an ActiveX control is much like creating a program in Visual Basic. You start with a form and put controls on the form. When you compile an ActiveX control, an OCX file is created and Visual Basic takes care of the rest of the details. Then when you have the OCX file, you can add it to your programs just like any other control.

The difference is that an ActiveX control is not a form but a control. It cannot run independently, as a program can. It must be compiled as an OCX and then used within an object, which is called the **container,** in another program. Also, the properties that it is normal for a form to have are not necessarily the same for an ActiveX control, and most of them are not available. Besides, most of the properties you would want to be able to change would be properties not for the control but for the objects on the control, and those are not available. Thus, if we want to create an ActiveX control with a label and we want to use the ForeColor property for that label, we have to create that property ourselves. You will soon see how that is done.

A.2   Creating an ActiveX Control

To create an ActiveX control and work with it before compiling it, you need to start with a regular application and then add to it.

1. Get into Windows and launch Visual Basic with a Standard EXE project.

Now we need to add a second project for the ActiveX control. This actually forms a project group with two separate projects as shown in the Project Explorer, as indicated in Figure A.2.

2. Select the **Add Project** option of the **File** menu and you will see the standard Add Project choice screen. Select the **ActiveX Control** project, as shown in Figure A.1, and click the **Open** button. This will give you the control and a program form as shown in Figure A.2.

Notice that the ActiveX Control window doesn't have a title bar. That's because it is not a form. It is simply a workspace for creating an ActiveX Control that can then be added to other projects. Also, the form layout window will not show the position of the control. Its position is determined by the object you use as a container for the control.

3. Select the Project1 entry in the Project Explorer window and change the name of the project to **Shape_Program** and then select the Project2 entry and change the name of the project to **Shape_Control.**

Next, we need to change the control name of the ActiveX Control itself.

FIGURE A.1
The ActiveX Control icon for adding an ActiveX Control.

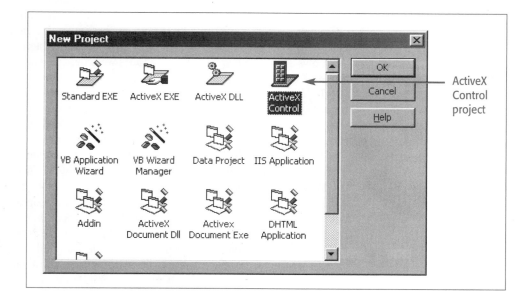

FIGURE A.2
The project group with the Standard and the ActiveX Control project added.

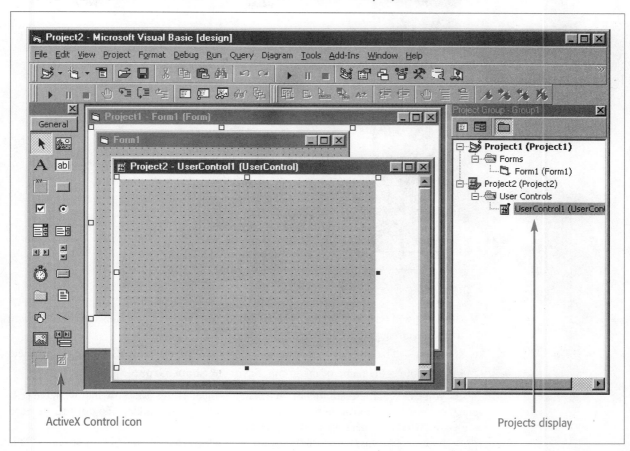

4. Select the ActiveX Control workspace and change the control name to **acxShapeLabel** (acx for ActiveX).

We want to create an oval with a label in it that can be used to label other projects. This will be just a simple control, but it will show you the basics of creating an ActiveX control. With this new knowledge, you can create controls that you want to create and that will be more useful for your purposes.

5. Add a shape to the form using the **Shape** control as shown in Figure A.3. Change the control name of the shape to **shpOval**.

6. Change the Shape property to **2 - Oval.** Size and position the oval as shown in Figure A.4. By leaving a bit of room around the shape you leave room for the border to be resized.

Whatever size you make your ActiveX control is the size that it will have in the program in which it is used. To see this, we will use the control in the other project that is part of this project group. Remember that the control cannot be executed by itself. It must be contained within an object in another program. But first, let's save the project group.

7. Save the project and the first thing Visual Basic will ask for is the name of the form. Save it as **frmShape**.

8. Next comes the name of the first project. Save it with the name already given.

FIGURE A.3
The Shape control.

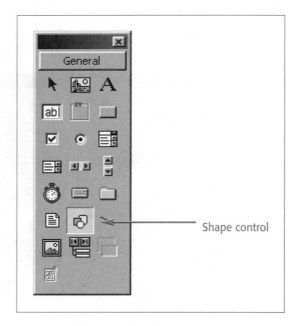

Shape control

9. Next you will be asked for the name of the control (with the ctl extension). Save it with the name already shown.

10. Next you will be asked for the name of the ActiveX control project. Save it as specified.

11. Finally comes the name of the group. Save it as **Shape Group**.

As you can see, there are lots of pieces in a project group. But now that we have one, we can put our new control on the form of the new project we added. To do that, we need to close the window where we are creating the control.

Look at the bottom right corner tool in the Toolbox (as indicated in Figure A.2). This is the tool for the ActiveX control we are creating. Right now it is disabled. It will stay that way until we close the control workspace window.

FIGURE A.4
The position and size of the oval.

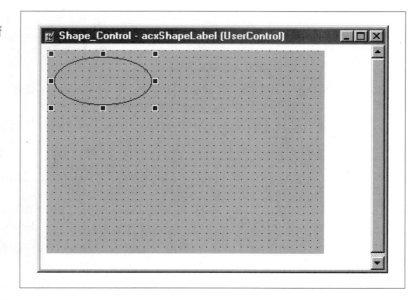

FIGURE A.5
The form with the shape control added.

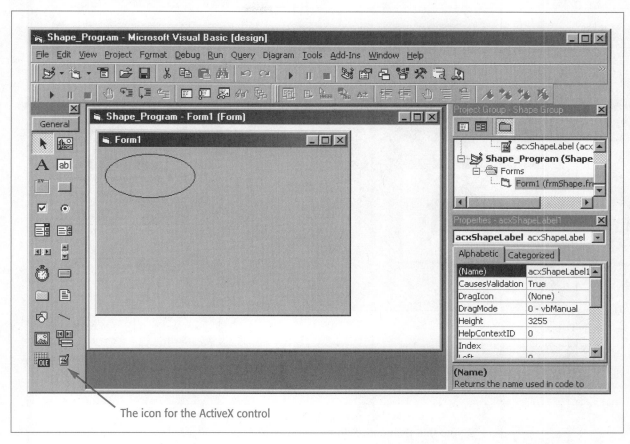

The icon for the ActiveX control

12. Switch to the control workspace window and close it.

Now the icon we were discussing is enabled.

13. Double-click the ActiveX Control icon to add a shape control to the form as shown in Figure A.5.

A.3   Changing the ActiveX Control

Note that all the grid dots have disappeared (at least the ones in the figure have; your new form may be larger). That's because the control is much larger than it needs to be for the shape and it is covering the entire form, obscuring the alignment dots. That can be changed.

1. Switch to the Project window and reload the ActiveX control workspace by double-clicking the listing in the Project window.

2. Click the program form. Note that the control has diagonal lines on it. This indicates that the control cannot be worked with when the control workspace window is open.

3. Switch back to the control workspace window and reduce the size of the control workspace to the size illustrated in Figure A.6.

FIGURE A.6
The resized control workspace.

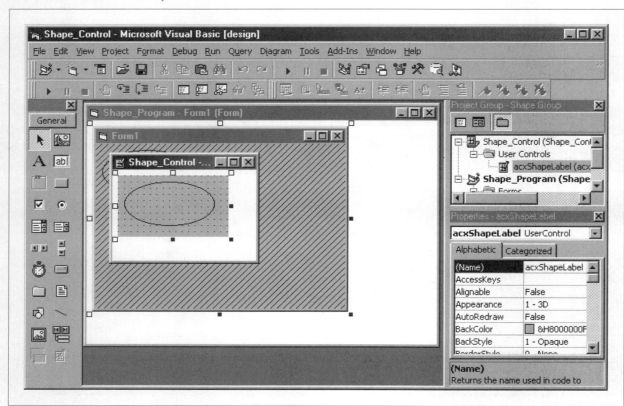

Note that the control on the form is still the same size it was before. To get it to the proper size, you need to delete the current one and add a new one. But let's work on the control itself a bit first.

4. Add a label inside the control called **lblShape**. Change the font name to **Arial** and the size to **12**, and make it **Bold**. Change the Alignment to **2 - Center**, change the ForeColor to yellow, and change the BackStyle to **0 - Transparent**. Your label should look like the one shown in Figure A.7.

   Note that the control on the form still has not changed. As we have said, the control on the form will need to be deleted and readded.

5. Select the control on the form and delete it. Close the control workspace. Double-click the control icon to add a new control to the form (see Figure A.8).

FIGURE A.7
The added label.

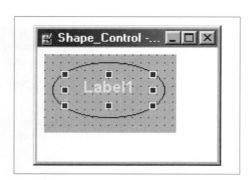

FIGURE A.8
The new control.

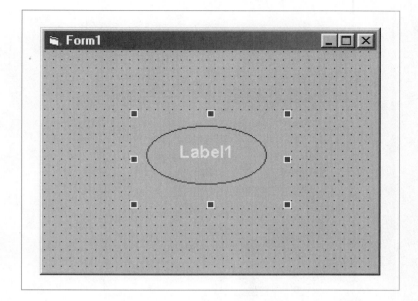

A.4   Setting Up the Properties

As we mentioned earlier, none of the properties associated with the objects added to the control are available to the control.

1. Select the control and look at the list of properties. The entire list is shown in Figure A.9.

   As you can see, there are none of the normal properties you might associate with a label and a shape. To have properties for the control that the programmer can change, we must add them. To begin with, we will add a Caption property so that the user can change the caption of the label.

2. Open the control window and then the code window for the control. The code window must be open for the next step.

3. Select the **Add Procedure...** option on the **Tools** menu to see the dialog box shown in Figure A.10.

   We want to create a property called Caption.

4. Key **Caption** as the property name, and select **Property** as the **Type**. Click the **OK** button to exit the dialog box.

   This causes two new procedures to appear in the code window as shown in Figure A.11. The **Get** procedure makes the property available to Visual Basic for reading. The **Let** procedure is used to set the property value. To define a read-only property, you use a Get procedure without the corresponding Let procedure.

   These procedures are used essentially the same way every time they are used. Note that the Get procedure is designated as Variant and that the parameter in the Let procedure is also Variant. These two declarations must be the same, but as in other instances, using a variant is not the best idea. Thus, we need to change the declarations to String.

5. Change both of the declarations to **String** as in this code line:

```
Public Property Get Caption () As String
```

FIGURE A.9
The list of available
properties.

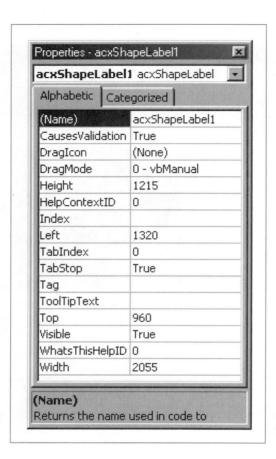

In the Get procedure you assign a value to the procedure name that represents the property in the project that is being changed. The caption we want our Caption property to change is lblShape.Caption, so this is what we assign to the procedure and property name, using a statement like the following:

```
Caption = lblShape.Caption
```

6. Key this statement in the Get procedure.

FIGURE A.10
The Add Procedure
dialog box.

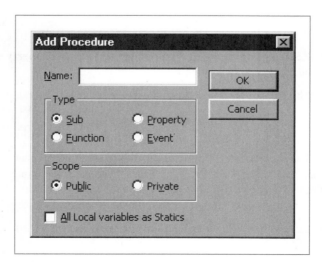

FIGURE A.11

The two new procedures for adding a property.

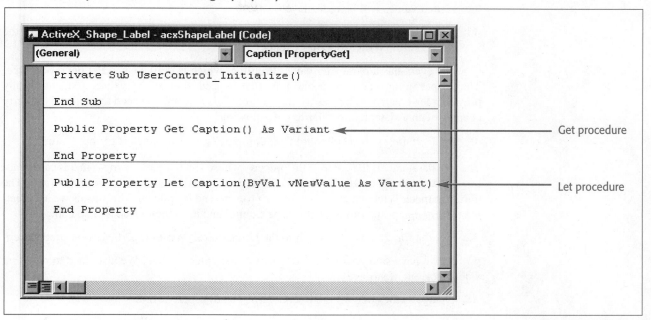

The Let procedure has a parameter called **vNewValue**. This parameter (which can be renamed to something more suitable if you wish) will contain whatever the Caption property of the control is changed to by the user. This needs to be assigned to the property of the object that the property is designed to change. Once again, that property is the lblShape Caption. This requires the statement

```
lblShape.Caption = vNewValue
```

7. Key this statement in the Let procedure.

Let's see how the property works.

8. Close the code workspace window, and switch to the form to which you added the control.

Note that the properties of the control now include a Caption property.

9. Change the value of the Caption property to **Sample** and press **Enter**.

The caption of the label is now Sample. We aren't finished with the Caption property, however.

10. Run the program. Note that the caption of the label reverts to **Label1**. Exit the program.

We need to tell Visual Basic to save the changes that the user might make to the new property. To do that, we need to use the UserControl events that all ActiveX controls have. The two we are interested in are **UserControl_ReadProperties** and **UserControl_WriteProperties.**

The **WriteProperties** event is executed when the user has changed one of the properties of the ActiveX (UserControl) control and the program in which the control is used is either executed or saved. If the property changes were not saved, then the next time the user used the program, the properties would revert to their original values.

The ReadProperties event is executed when the control is displayed. If the property values are not first written with the WriteProperties event, they cannot be read properly, and the original values will be redisplayed.

11. Open the code workspace for the control and display the code for the UserControl_WriteProperties event.

The event has a parameter called PropBag, which is defined as a **PropertyBag** type. The PropertyBag type is a special type that is used to store the values assigned to any programmer-created properties for the control. This is where we need to write the property changes with a statement similar to the following:

```
Call PropBag.WriteProperty("Caption", lblShape.Caption, "Label")
```

The first parameter is the name of the property whose value we are saving—in this case, Caption. The second parameter is the value we want stored—lblShape.Caption this time. The third parameter is the default value for the property and is optional. This means we are creating the Caption property for the lblShape Control and its default value will be Label.

12. Key the foregoing statement into the UserControl_WriteProperties event procedure.

As we have said, this is only one part of the value storage. We also need to read that value back out of storage.

13. Change to the code for the UserControl_ReadProperty event.

This event also uses the PropBag parameter defined as a PropertyBag type. Because the PropertyBag is where the property values are stored, this is where they will need to be read. This is done with the statement

```
lblShape.Caption = PropBag.ReadProperty("Caption", "Label")
```

As before, the first parameter here is the name of the property (Caption), and the second parameter is the default value.

14. Key the foregoing statement into the UserControl_ReadProperty event procedure. This gives you the code shown in Figure A.12.

Now we are ready to test the program again.

15. Close the control window (if you have it open). Change the Caption property to **Sample** and run the program. Now the caption of the label retains the new value.

16. Exit the program. Switch to the form. The caption of the label is still Sample. This means that the change to the value is retained, as it should be.

Just to be sure we understand the process of creating a property, we will create a few more properties. This time, we want a property that allows us to change the inside color of the oval. Unlike the case with most objects, the inside color of a shape is not the BackColor. To change the inside color, you use the **FillColor** property. Let's set up a property for this.

17. Switch to the code window for the control and select the **Add Procedure...** option of the **Tools** menu.

18. Key **FillColor** as the property name and select the **Property** option button. Click the **OK** button to exit the dialog box.

We now have the Get and Let procedures as before. They require the same type of code we used before. The Get procedure requires the statement

```
FillColor = shpOval.FillColor
```

19. Key this statement into the Get procedure.

FIGURE A.12
The code for the control thus far.

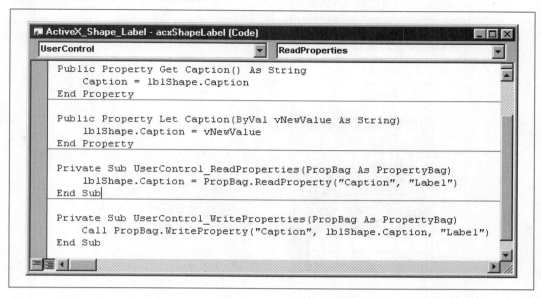

```
ActiveX_Shape_Label - acxShapeLabel (Code)
UserControl                          ReadProperties

Public Property Get Caption() As String
    Caption = lblShape.Caption
End Property

Public Property Let Caption(ByVal vNewValue As String)
    lblShape.Caption = vNewValue
End Property

Private Sub UserControl_ReadProperties(PropBag As PropertyBag)
    lblShape.Caption = PropBag.ReadProperty("Caption", "Label")
End Sub

Private Sub UserControl_WriteProperties(PropBag As PropertyBag)
    Call PropBag.WriteProperty("Caption", lblShape.Caption, "Label")
End Sub
```

The Let procedure requires the statement

```
shpOval.FillColor = vNewValue
```

20. Key this statement.

These procedures are declared as Variants just as the first set of procedures were. That time, we changed the declarations to String. This time, however, we will change to a special data type called **OLE_Color**. This will allow the program to use the color dialog boxes that are normally used in property lists for color-type properties.

21. Change the declarations for both procedures to **OLE_Color** as in the following:

```
Public Property Get FillColor() As OLE_Color
```

Next, we need to change two of the Shape object properties on the control form.

22. Switch to the control workspace window, select the shape, and switch to the FillStyle property.

Note that the current value is 1 - Transparent. It needs to be a value that will cause something to be displayed when the FillColor is changed. We will use **0 - Solid**, but you can experiment later with other patterns.

23. Change the FillColor property to **0 - Solid**.

The FillColor of the shape becomes black. This is the default color for the FillColor of the shape. We could change it to something else here, but let's leave it and let the user decide what color is best. The forecolor of the label is yellow, so the caption will show up just fine against the black background.

24. Close the control workspace window. Switch to the form, select the control, and switch to the FillColor property. Note that it now has a pull-down list.

25. Click the arrow, and the color selection dialog box appears as shown in Figure A.13.

FIGURE A.13
The color selection
dialog box.

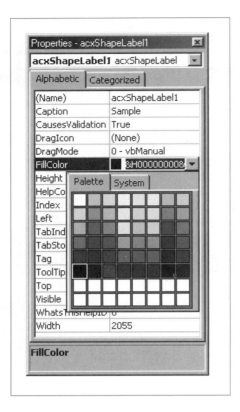

26. Click the red color box, and the FillColor of the shape becomes red.

This won't cause the color to be saved, however. Remember that the WriteProperties and ReadProperties procedures need to contain the code to write and read back the property value changes. In Figure A.14, you will see the code needed for saving the FillColor value.

The default values for these statements represent the numeric value (in hexadecimal as +HFF0000) of the color blue. The value you use for the default value is not important. It is simply better if there is a default value in the command.

27. Key the two new statements and then run the program. The FillColor of the shape will stay red.

28. Exit the program. The FillColor is still red, which means it is being saved properly.

The other three properties we want to set up for the control are BorderColor, BorderWidth, and ForeColor. We want them to allow the user to change the color and width of the border of the shape and the color of the font of the label. The additional code needed for these properties is shown in Figure A.15.

To add the code shown, you need to add the procedures as we did before with the Add Procedure dialog box. Then you need to add the code to the WriteProperties and ReadProperties procedures as given in Figure A.15.

29. Make the appropriate changes to the code.

Now there are two additional properties for the control.

30. Change the Border Width value to **4** and the BorderColor value to blue. This will give you a control like the one shown in Figure A.16.

FIGURE A.14
The new code for saving the value changes to the FillColor property.

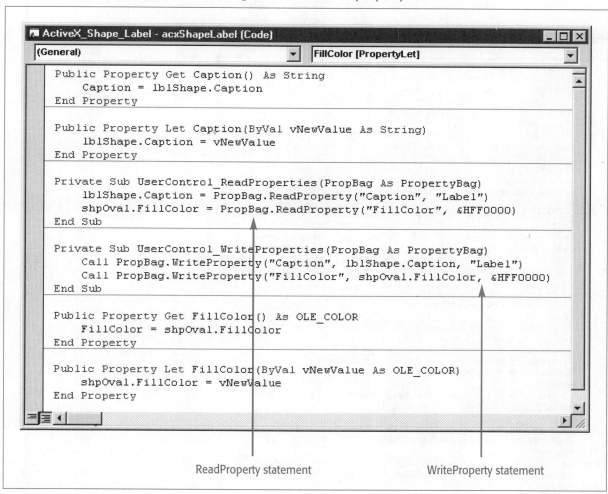

```
ActiveX_Shape_Label - acxShapeLabel [Code]                        _ □ ×
(General)                          ▼    FillColor [PropertyLet]              ▼

    Public Property Get Caption() As String
        Caption = lblShape.Caption
    End Property

    Public Property Let Caption(ByVal vNewValue As String)
        lblShape.Caption = vNewValue
    End Property

    Private Sub UserControl_ReadProperties(PropBag As PropertyBag)
        lblShape.Caption = PropBag.ReadProperty("Caption", "Label")
        shpOval.FillColor = PropBag.ReadProperty("FillColor", &HFF0000)
    End Sub

    Private Sub UserControl_WriteProperties(PropBag As PropertyBag)
        Call PropBag.WriteProperty("Caption", lblShape.Caption, "Label")
        Call PropBag.WriteProperty("FillColor", shpOval.FillColor, &HFF0000)
    End Sub

    Public Property Get FillColor() As OLE_COLOR
        FillColor = shpOval.FillColor
    End Property

    Public Property Let FillColor(ByVal vNewValue As OLE_COLOR)
        shpOval.FillColor = vNewValue
    End Property
```

ReadProperty statement   WriteProperty statement

FIGURE A.15

The additional code for the two new properties.

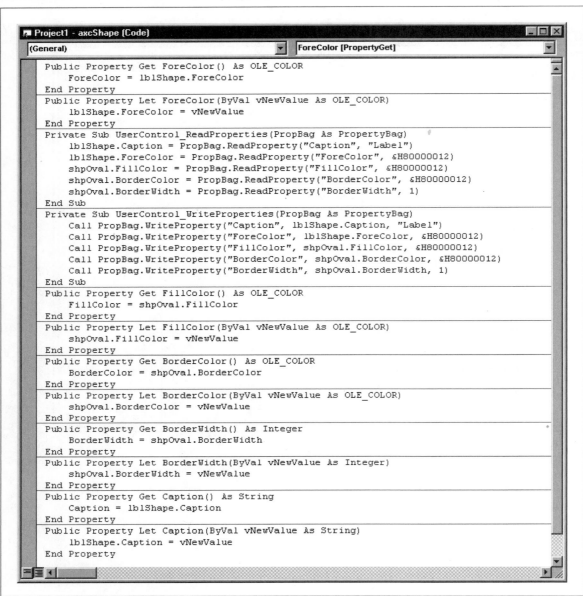

```
Public Property Get ForeColor() As OLE_COLOR
    ForeColor = lblShape.ForeColor
End Property
Public Property Let ForeColor(ByVal vNewValue As OLE_COLOR)
    lblShape.ForeColor = vNewValue
End Property
Private Sub UserControl_ReadProperties(PropBag As PropertyBag)
    lblShape.Caption = PropBag.ReadProperty("Caption", "Label")
    lblShape.ForeColor = PropBag.ReadProperty("ForeColor", &H80000012)
    shpOval.FillColor = PropBag.ReadProperty("FillColor", &H80000012)
    shpOval.BorderColor = PropBag.ReadProperty("BorderColor", &H80000012)
    shpOval.BorderWidth = PropBag.ReadProperty("BorderWidth", 1)
End Sub
Private Sub UserControl_WriteProperties(PropBag As PropertyBag)
    Call PropBag.WriteProperty("Caption", lblShape.Caption, "Label")
    Call PropBag.WriteProperty("ForeColor", lblShape.ForeColor, &H80000012)
    Call PropBag.WriteProperty("FillColor", shpOval.FillColor, &H80000012)
    Call PropBag.WriteProperty("BorderColor", shpOval.BorderColor, &H80000012)
    Call PropBag.WriteProperty("BorderWidth", shpOval.BorderWidth, 1)
End Sub
Public Property Get FillColor() As OLE_COLOR
    FillColor = shpOval.FillColor
End Property
Public Property Let FillColor(ByVal vNewValue As OLE_COLOR)
    shpOval.FillColor = vNewValue
End Property
Public Property Get BorderColor() As OLE_COLOR
    BorderColor = shpOval.BorderColor
End Property
Public Property Let BorderColor(ByVal vNewValue As OLE_COLOR)
    shpOval.BorderColor = vNewValue
End Property
Public Property Get BorderWidth() As Integer
    BorderWidth = shpOval.BorderWidth
End Property
Public Property Let BorderWidth(ByVal vNewValue As Integer)
    shpOval.BorderWidth = vNewValue
End Property
Public Property Get Caption() As String
    Caption = lblShape.Caption
End Property
Public Property Let Caption(ByVal vNewValue As String)
    lblShape.Caption = vNewValue
End Property
```

FIGURE A.16
The control after the
two new properties are
changed.

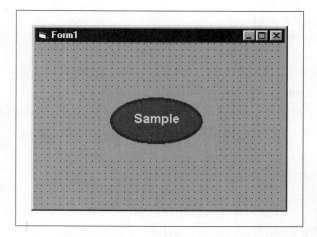

A.5   Setting Up the Toolbox Icon

The icon in the Toolbox for the new control is the standard, default icon for ActiveX controls. It would be better if we had an icon designed specifically for our control. The toolbox doesn't actually use icons; it uses bitmaps. Therefore, we have created a bitmap designed specifically for our new control.

1. Switch to the control workspace window. Switch to the ToolBoxBitmap property.

2. Click the ellipsis button to get the Load Bitmap dialog box. Change to the App-A folder on your work disk, and load the ActiveX Bitmap.BMP file.

3. Close the control workspace window. Now the icon in the Toolbox for the control looks like the current state of the shape (see Figure A.17).

FIGURE A.17
The new Toolbox icon
for the ActiveX control.

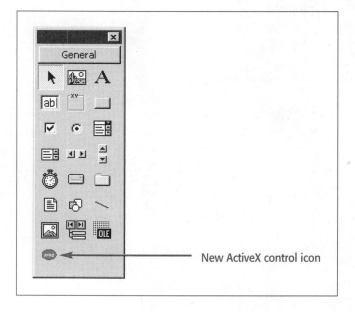

New ActiveX control icon

A.6   Compiling Your Control

Compiling an ActiveX control is similar to compiling a regular program.

1. Switch to the control workspace window.
2. Pull down the **File** menu and select the **Make acxShapeLabel.ocx** option.

   You see the normal Make Project compile dialog box.

3. Change the Save in: folder reference to the App-A folder on your work disk, and click the **OK** button to compile the OCX.

A.7   Using the New Control in Another Program

Now that the control is compiled, it can be used in any subsequent program.

1. Launch a new version of Visual Basic and start a new Standard EXE program.
2. Press **Ctrl-T** to open the Components dialog box. You will see the **ShapeControl** component somewhere in the list. If it is not there, click the **Browse** button and use the dialog box to locate the OCX file.
3. Turn this component on and then exit the dialog box.

   You have the new tool in the Toolbox.

4. Add a shape control to your form.

   It is added with its defaults of Label1 for the caption and a black FillColor.

5. Adjust the properties to be sure they work properly.

   Your newly compiled ActiveX control can be distributed to others by simply giving them the compiled OCX. Then they can add it to their Components dialog box with the **Browse** button.

6. Exit the program, all other programs, and Visual Basic, and shut the system down properly.

Standard Prefixes

B.1   Introduction

Objects and variables should be named with a consistent prefix. This makes it easy to identify the type of object or variable. We have used such prefixes throughout the book. In this appendix, you will find a list of the standard prefixes used here and additional ones suggested for elements that were not discussed in the book.

B.2   Suggested Prefixes for Controls

Control Type	Prefix	Example
3D Panel	pnl	pnlCaps_Lock_Button
Animated button	ani	aniFlashing
Calendar control	cal	calAppointments
Check box	chk	chk
Combo box	cmo	cmoPatients
Command button	cmd	cmdExit
Common Dialog Control	cdg	cdgOpen
Communications	com	comInput
Data control	dat	datBiography
Data-bound combo box	dbcbo	dbcboDoctors
Data-bound grid	dbgrd	dbgrdNurses
Data-bound list box	dblst	dblstTasks

Control Type	Prefix	Example
Directory list box	dir	dirSingle_Display
Drive list box	drv	drvMultiple_Display
FileListBox	fil	filSearching
Form	frm	frmPIM
Frame	fra	fraOptions
Gauge	gau	gauNotice
Graph control	gra	graMonthly_Income
Horizontal scroll bar	hsb	hsbDrawing
Image	img	imgDisplay
ImageList	ils	ilsPhotos
Key status	key	keyCaps
Label	lbl	lblShape
Line	lin	linTop_Edge
ListBox	lst	lstEmployee
ListView	lvw	lvwFootings
MAPI message	mpm	mpmInput
MAPI session	mps	mpsStudent
MCI	mci	mciVideo
Menu	mnu	mnuClear_All
MIDI child form	mdi	mdiNotepad
MonthView	mnv	mnvAppointments
MSFlexGrid	grd	grdAssociates
MS Tab	mst	mstAppointments
OLE	ole	oleDrivers
OptionButton	opt	optLead_Time
Outline	out	outChart
Pen Bedit	bed	bedFirstName
Pen Hedit	hed	hedLastName
Pen ink	ink	inkImport
Picture	pic	picShow_Off
PictureClip	clp	clpUpper_Left
ProgressBar	pbr	pbrHours_Worked
Report	rpt	rptTimecards
RichTextBox	rtf	rtfAmount_Input

Control Type	Prefix	Example
Shape	shp	shpOval
Slider	sld	sldMileage
Spin	spn	spnColor
StatusBar	sta	staDisplay
Tabbed control	tab	tabObjectives
TabStrip	tsp	tspProperties
TextBox	txt	txtName_Input
Timer	tmr	tmrWatch
Toolbar	tlb	tlbActions
TreeView	tre	treOrganization
UpDown	upd	updPointer
VerticalScrollBar	vsb	vsbTime_Display
WebBrowser	web	webPim

B.3   Suggested Prefixes for Variables

Variable Type	Prefix	Example
Boolean	bln	blnFlag
Byte	byt	bytUptown
Currency	cur	curMoney_Input
Date (Time)	dtm	dtmWeekly
Double	dbl	dblControl_Value
Integer	int	intCounter
Long	lng	lngDistance
Single	sng	sngResult_Amount
String	str	strKey_In
User-defined records	udr	udrGroup_Data
User-defined type	udt	udtEmployer
Variant	vnt	vntResult_Array

B.4   Suggested Prefixes for Scopes

Because variables can have different scopes, it is useful to use a scope-indicating prefix character. The following characters are suggested:

Scope	Prefix	Example
Global	g	gintCounter
Module or form	m	mstrComment

Visual Basic Menu System

The images that follow show you the various Visual Basic menus. The menus are given in the order in which they appear on the menu bar. After each image is a list giving a brief explanation of these options. The options are listed in the order in which they appear in the menu.

FIGURE C.1

The **File** menu.

New Project (shortcut key **Ctrl-N**) erases the current project and begins a new one. If you have made changes to the current project since the last time it was saved, Visual Basic asks whether you want to save the changes to the current project before it is erased.

Open Project... (shortcut key **Ctrl-O**) lets you load a previously saved project.

Add Project... lets you add an additional project to a project group.

Remove Project removes the currently selected project from a project group.

Save Project Group lets you save a project group to disk.

Save Project Group As... lets you create a duplicate project by saving an existing project with a different name.

Save (form or control name) (shortcut key **Ctrl-S**) allows you to save the currently selected form or control to disk.

Save (form or control name) As... lets you create a duplicate form or control by saving the selected form or control with a different name.

Save Selection allows you to save the currently selected tables and the relationships between them when using the Database designer.

Save Change Script allows you to display the **Save Change Script** dialog box, which can be used to save the Transact-SQL statements generated during your editing session using the Table and Database designers.

Print... (shortcut key **Ctrl-P**) lets you print all of your program or just selected parts of it.

Print Setup... displays the standard Print Setup dialog box with options to specify the printer, page orientation, paper size, and paper source, as well as other printing options.

Make (Project Name).exe... lets you make an EXE file that can subsequently be run through Windows without the need for loading Visual Basic first.

Make Project Group creates a separate executable file for each project in the group you select.

List of Latest Projects shows the latest four projects that have been worked on.

Exit allows you to exit the Visual Basic system.

FIGURE C.2
The **Edit** menu.

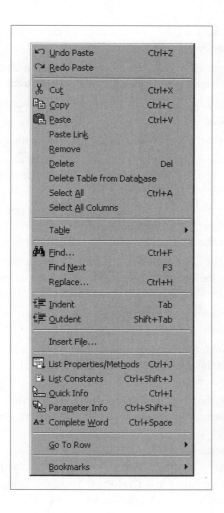

Undo (activity) (shortcut key **Ctrl-Z**) lets you undo whatever activity you just performed (such as a paste).

Redo (activity) lets you carry out again the activity that you just used the Undo option to undo (such as redoing the Paste function).

Cut (shortcut key **Ctrl-X**) copies the selected code to the clipboard while removing it from the current location.

Copy (shortcut key **Ctrl-C**) copies the selected code to the clipboard without removing it from its current location.

Paste (shortcut key **Ctrl-V**) copies the code found on the clipboard into the current location in the code window.

Paste Link allows you to paste a link to a valid DDE source. It is available only when the Clipboard contains a valid DDE source and the selected control is a valid DDE link.

Remove allows you to remove a table from your Database designer diagram.

Delete (shortcut key **Del**) erases the selected code.

Delete Table from Database allows you to delete a table from a Database designer database. Initially, the table is marked for deletion and it is then permanently deleted from the database when the diagram is saved.

Select All (shortcut key **Ctrl-A**) lets you select all the code in the active code window.

Select All Columns allows you to select all the columns in the Diagram pane of an input source window of the Query designer.

Table is a submenu for options used in the Table and Database designers. The options are Set Primary Key, Insert Column, and Delete Column.

Find... (shortcut key **Ctrl-F**) lets you search for a specified entry through all or just a section of the code.

Find Next (shortcut key **F3**) lets you search for another instance of the search entry.

Replace... (shortcut key **Ctrl-H**) lets you search for a specified entry and change that entry to something else. You can choose to have each change verified or change all instances without prompting.

Indent (shortcut key **Tab**) shifts all lines in the selection to the next tab stop. All lines in the selection are moved the same number of spaces to retain the same relative indentation within the selected block.

Outdent (shortcut key **Shift-Tab**) shifts all lines in the selection to the previous tab stop. All lines in the selection are moved the same number of spaces to retain the same relative indentation within the selected block.

Insert File... allows you to insert code from another source into the current position in the code window.

List Properties/Methods (shortcut key **Ctrl-J**) opens in the code window a pull-down list box that contains the properties and methods available for the object currently displayed in the code window.

List Constants (shortcut key **Ctrl-Shift-J**) opens in the code window a pull-down list box that contains the valid constants for a property that you typed and that preceded the equals sign (=).

Quick Info (shortcut key **Ctrl-I**) allows you to display the syntax for the variable, function, statement, method, or procedure that is selected in the code window.

Parameter Info (shortcut key **Ctrl-Shift-I**) shows, in the code window, a pop-up that contains information about the parameters of the initial function or statement.

Complete Word (shortcut key **Ctrl-Space**) allows Visual Basic automatically to fill in the rest of the word you are typing once you have entered enough characters for the word to be identified.

Go To Row is a submenu of rows to go to in the Results pane of the Query and View designers.

Bookmarks is a submenu that gives you options to create or remove bookmarks in the code window, move to the next or the preceding bookmark, or clear all the bookmarks.

FIGURE C.3
The **View** menu.

Code (shortcut key **F7**) calls up the code window for the selected object.

Object (shortcut key **Shift-F7**) calls up the form to which the code in the code window refers.

Definition (shortcut key **Shift-F2**) displays the location in the code window where the variable or procedure under the pointer is defined.

Last Position (shortcut key **Ctrl-Shift-F2**) allows you to move the cursor quickly to a previous location in your code.

Object Browser (shortcut key **F2**) displays the Object Browser dialog box, which lists the object libraries, type libraries, classes, methods, properties, events, and constants you can use in code, as well as the modules and procedures you have defined in your project.

Immediate Window (shortcut key **Ctrl-G**) displays the Immediate window, which you can use to display information from your program by using debugging statements in your code or by typing commands directly into the window.

Locals Window displays the Locals window with the list of the values of all the variables in the current stack.

Watch Window displays the current watch expressions in the Watch window.

Call Stack (shortcut key **Ctrl-L**) displays the list of the procedure calls in the application that have started but have not been completed.

Project Explorer (shortcut key **Ctrl-R**) displays the Project Explorer window, which displays a hierarchical list of the currently open projects and their contents.

Properties Window (shortcut key **F4**) displays the Properties window, which lists the design-time properties for a selected form, control, class, user control, property page, user document, or menu.

Form Layout Window displays the Form Layout window, in which you can preview and position your forms where you want them to appear in your application.

Property Pages (shortcut key **Shift-F4**) displays the property pages for a user control so that you can change a control's properties at design time.

Table is a submenu that enables you to collapse and expand the selected window in the Diagram pane of the Database, Query, and View designers.

Zoom is a submenu that enables you to zoom a Database designer diagram by a fixed percentage.

Show Panes is a submenu that enables you to hide and show panes in the Query and View designers.

Toolbox displays the standard Visual Basic controls as well as any other controls you have added to your project using the Components dialog box.

Data View Window allows you to display the Data View Window, which allows you to manipulate the structure of your database.

Color Palette displays the Color Palette dialog box, which allows you to change a form's or control's colors.

Toolbars is a submenu that allows you to turn on or off the various Toolbars available in Visual Basic. The names of the available toolbars follow (see Appendix D for more information on the toolbars).

- **Debug**, which contains buttons for common debugging tasks
- **Edit**, which contains buttons for common editing tasks
- **Form Editor**, which contains buttons specific to editing a form
- **Standard**, which is the default toolbar
- **Customize**, which you can use to customize or create toolbars and customize your menu bar

Visual Component Manager allows you to display the Visual Component Manager, which allows you to organize, find, and insert components into a Visual Studio project.

FIGURE C.4
The **Project** menu.

Add Form allows you to insert a new or existing form into your active project by using the Add Form dialog box.

Add MDI Form allows you to insert a new or existing MDI form into your active project by using the Add MDI Form dialog box.

Add Module allows you to insert a new or existing module or class module into your active project by using the Add Module or Add Class Module dialog box.

Add Class Module allows you to insert a new or existing module or class module into your active project by using the Add Module or Add Class Module dialog box.

Add User Control allows you to insert a new or existing user control into your active project by using the Add User Control dialog box.

Add Property Page allows you to insert new or existing property pages into your active project by using the Add Property Page dialog box.

Add User Document allows you to insert a new or existing User Document into your active project by using the Add User Document dialog box.

Add DHTML Page allows you to add a new DHTML page to your DHTML project.

Add Data Report allows you to add a new Data Report so you can display fields and records from the underlying table or query.

Add WebClass allows you to add a new WebClass to an existing Web applicaiton.

Add Data Environment allows you to add a new Data Environment to a project being managed by the Data Environment Designer.

Add File (shortcut key **Ctrl-D**) allows you to add an existing file to the current project.

Remove (item name) allows you to remove the currently selected item from your project.

References... allows you to add an object library, type library, or project reference to your project. This makes another application's objects available in your code.

Components... (shortcut key **Ctrl-T**) allows you to add controls, designers, or insertable objects (such as a Microsoft Word document) to the Toolbox by using the Components dialog box.

(Project name) Properties... allows you to view the project properties for the selected project by using the Project Properties dialog box.

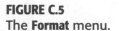

FIGURE C.5
The **Format** menu.

Align is a submenu that allows Visual Basic to align two selected objects so that they align on the left, on the right, on the center position horizontally, on the top, on the bottom, on the center position vertically, or in the left top corner to the nearest Grid dot.

Make Same Size is a submenu that allows Visual Basic to resize the last of two or more objects so that they are the same in Width, Height, or Both.

Size to Grid adjusts the positions of the selected object(s) to fit the nearest gridlines on the form.

Horizontal Spacing is a submenu that allows you to change the horizontal space between selected objects. The options are

- **Make Equal**, which moves the selected objects so that there is equal space between them, using the outermost objects as ending points

- **Increase**, which increases horizontal spacing by one grid unit

- **Decrease**, which decreases horizontal spacing by one grid unit

- **Remove**, which removes the horizontal space so that the objects are aligned with their edges touching

Vertical Spacing is a submenu that allows you to change the vertical space between selected objects. The options are

- **Make Equal**, which moves the selected objects so that there is equal space between them, using the top and bottom objects as the ending points.

- **Increase**, which increases vertical spacing by one grid unit

- **Decrease** which decreases vertical spacing by one grid unit

- **Remove**, which removes the vertical space so that the objects are aligned with their borders touching

Center in Form is a submenu that allows you to center selected objects on the central axes of the form either horizontally or vertically.

Order is a submenu that allows you to change the order of the selected objects on a form. You can bring the selected item to the front (shortcut key **Ctrl-J**) or send it to the back (shortcut key **Ctrl-K**).

Lock Controls allows you to lock all controls on the selected form in their current positions so that you don't inadvertently move them once they are in the desired location.

FIGURE C.6
The **Debug** menu.

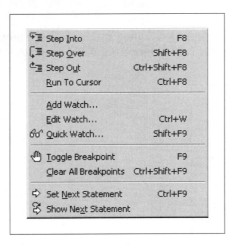

Step Into (shortcut key **F8**) lets you execute your program one statement at a time (single step).

Step Over (shortcut key **Shift-F8**) lets Visual Basic treat a procedure call as a single step.

Step Out (shortcut key **Ctrl-Shift-F8**) allows you to execute the remaining lines of a function in which the current execution point lies. The next statement displayed is the statement following the procedure call.

Run to Cursor (shortcut key **Ctrl-F8**) allows you to run the application to a statement further down in your code where you want execution to stop.

Add Watch... is used to give Visual Basic an expression to keep track of and show you the result of in the Immediate window.

Edit Watch (shortcut key **Ctrl-W**) allows you to modify a watch already created. This can be called up by double-clicking the watch in the Immediate window.

Quick Watch... (shortcut key **Shift-F9**) lets you automatically add a variable watch by selecting the variable in code and then selecting this option.

Toggle Breakpoint (shortcut key **F9**) lets you turn a breakpoint on or off.

Clear All Breakpoints (shortcut key **Ctrl-Shift-F9**) removes all breakpoints previously set.

Set Next Statement (shortcut key **Ctrl-F9**) can be used to change the current line in your application execution.

Show Next Statement lets you highlight the next statement to be executed.

FIGURE C.7
The **Run** menu.

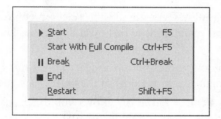

Start (shortcut key **F5**) is used to start execution of the program. When the program is paused, this option changes to **Continue** to allow you to continue execution where it left off (still shortcut key **F5**).

Start With Full Compile (shortcut key **Ctrl-F5**) is used to start execution of the program after it is compiled.

Break (shortcut key **Ctrl-Break**) allows you to pause the execution of the program.

End is used to terminate the execution of the program.

Restart (shortcut key **Shift-F5**) is used to restart the execution of a program from the current line.

FIGURE C.8
The **Query** menu.

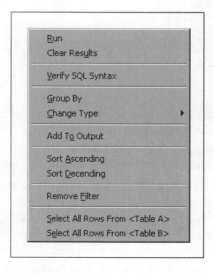

Run allows you to execute the current query, stored procedure, or other SQL statement in the Query Designer.

Clear Results allows you to clear the results of a query in the Query Designer.

Verify SQL Syntax allows you to check the SQL statement in the Query Designer against the database to determine whether the statement uses correct syntax.

Group By allows you to change the current query in the Query Designer to an aggregate query that summarizes and groups data. If the current query is already an aggregate query, the selected query reverts to a nonaggregate query.

Change Type is a submenu that allows you to change the current query in the Query Designer to another type such as Select, Insert, Insert Values, Update, Delete, or Make Table.

Add To Output allows you to add the selected column or columns in the Query Designer to the list of columns so they will appear in the result set of a Select query.

Sort Ascending allows you to add the selected column or columns in the Query Designer to the list of columns to sort by and specifies Ascending in the Sort By column.

Sort Descending allows you to add the selected column or columns in the Query Designer to the list of columns to sort by and specifies Descending in the Sort By column.

Remove Filter allows you to remove search conditions for the selected column or columns in the input source window of the Query Designer.

Select All Rows From <Table A> allows you to specify an outer join in the Query Designer that includes rows from this, the first table, even if there are not related rows in the second selected table.

Select All Rows From <Table B> allows you to specify an outer join in the Query Designer that includes rows from the first table even if there are not related rows in this, the second selected table.

FIGURE C.9
The **Tools** menu.

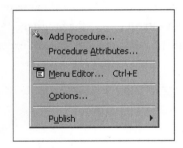

Add Procedure... allows you to insert a new Sub, Function, Property, or Event procedure into the active module.

Procedure Attributes... allows you to set the attributes for each property and method specified for an item by using the Procedure Attributes dialog box.

Menu Editor (shortcut key **Ctrl-E**) opens the dialog box that allows you to create a menu for the application.

Options... allows you to set attributes of the Visual Basic programming environment by using the Options dialog box. The tabs on the dialog box are Editor, Editor Format, General, Docking, Environment, and Advanced.

Publish is a submenu with options that allow you to translate your project into a Web document format.

FIGURE C.10
The **Add-Ins** menu.

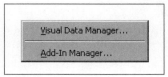

Visual Data Manager... opens the Visual Data Manager application so that you can access and manage data.

Add-In Manager... allows you, by using the Add-In Manager dialog box, to load and unload add-ins that extend the Visual Basic development environment.

FIGURE C.11
The **Window** menu.

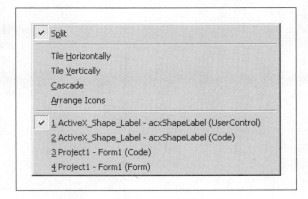

Split allows you to divide the code window into two displays of equal size.

Tile Horizontally arranges the forms and the code windows horizontally.

Tile Vertically arranges the forms and code windows vertically.

Cascade arranges the forms and code windows so that they overlap in a cascade.

Arrange Icons arranges the minimized forms and code windows so that they are aligned at the bottom of the Visual Basic workspace.

Window List shows the list of all open form and code windows.

FIGURE C.12
The **Help** menu.

Contents... brings up the MSDN Library window with the first, Contents, tab selected.

Index... brings up the MSDN Library window with the second, Index, tab selected.

Search... brings up the MSDN Library window with the third, Search, tab selected.

Technical Support... gives you information about the various ways you can get help from Microsoft if you are having difficulty with Visual Basic.

Microsoft on the Web gives you a list of Microsoft Web sites where you can get additional information about Visual Basic and other topics.

About Microsoft Visual Basic provides important information about Visual Basic.

Tool Bar Buttons and Toolbox Tools

The following sections illustrate the icons on the five toolbars. Then there is a short description of each of these tools. After that there is a labeled illustration of the toolbox, followed by a brief description of each of these tools. The toolbox shows only those tools we used in the text along with those tools that either already were in the toolbox or were added when we added a component.

The Standard tool bar icons are briefly defined in the following list.

📴 lets you add an additional project to the project group.

📝 lets you add an additional form or module to the application.

📋 (shortcut key **Ctrl-E**) calls up the Menu Editor window.

📂 (shortcut key **Ctrl-O**) lets you load a previously saved project.

💾 is used to save the project to disk.

✂ (shortcut key **Ctrl-X**) copies the selected code to the clipboard while removing it from the current location.

📋 (shortcut key **Ctrl-C**) copies the selected code to the clipboard without removing it from its current location.

📋 (shortcut key **Ctrl-V**) copies the code found on the clipboard into the current location in the code window.

🔍 (shortcut key **Ctrl-F**) lets you search for a specified entry through all the code or just a section of it.

↩ (shortcut key **Ctrl-Z**) lets you undo whatever activity you just performed (such as a paste).

↪ lets you carry out again the activity that you just used the Undo option to undo (such as redoing the Paste function).

▶ allows you to execute your program.

FIGURE D.1
The Standard tool bar.

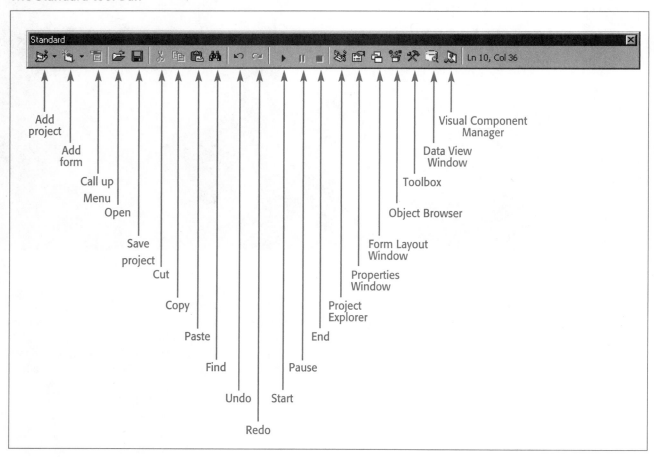

![II] allows you to pause the execution of your program.

![■] allows you to terminate the execution of your program.

![icon] (shortcut key **Ctrl-R**) displays the Project Explorer window, which displays a hierarchical list of the currently open projects and their contents.

![icon] (shortcut key **F4**) displays the Properties window, which lists the design-time properties for a selected form, control, class, user control, property page, user document, or menu.

![icon] displays the Form Layout window, where you can preview your forms and position them where you want them to appear in your application.

![icon] (shortcut key **F2**) displays the Object Browser dialog box, which lists the object libraries, type libraries, classes, methods, properties, events, and constants you can use in code, as well as the modules and procedures you have defined in your project.

![icon] displays the standard Visual Basic controls and any other controls you have added to your project using the Components dialog box.

![icon] allows you to display the Data View Window, which allows you to manipulate the structure of your database.

FIGURE D.2
The Debug tool bar.

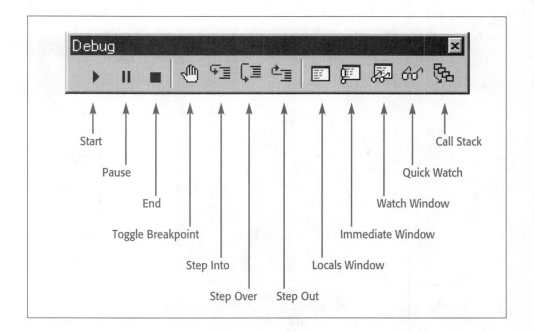

allows you to display the Visual Component Manager, which allows you to organize, find, and insert components into a Visual Studio project.

calls up a dialog box that allows you to add and remove the icons from the Add-In Toolbar.

calls up several dialog boxes that guide you through the creation of an ActiveX Control.

calls up a series of dialog boxes to help you convert forms in your current project into ActiveX documents.

calls up several dialog boxes that guide you through the creation of an application.

calls up a dialog box to help you build your class and collection hierarchy for your Visual Basic Project.

calls up a series of dialog boxes to help you create a form with objects bound to a local or remote data source.

calls up a series of dialog boxes that help you set up a property page for your ActiveX Control.

(shortcut key **F5**) is used to start execution of the program.

(shortcut key **Ctrl-Break**) allows you to pause the execution of your program.

allows you to terminate the execution of your program.

(shortcut key **F9**) lets you turn a breakpoint on or off.

(shortcut key **F8**) lets you execute your program one statement at a time (single step).

(shortcut key **Shift-F8**) lets Visual Basic treat a procedure call as a single step.

displays the Locals window with the list of the values of all the variables in the current stack.

FIGURE D.3
The Form Editor tool
bar.

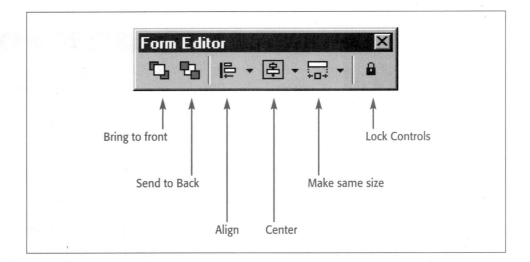

(shortcut key **Ctrl-G**) displays the Immediate window, which can be used to display information from your program by using debugging statements in your code or by typing commands directly into the window.

displays the current watch expressions in the Watch window.

(shortcut key **Shift-F9**) lets you automatically add a variable watch by selecting the variable in code and then selecting this option.

(shortcut key **Ctrl-L**) is used to display the Calls dialog box.

(shortcut key **Ctrl-J**) lets you send the specified object to the front of the ZOrder.

(shortcut key **Ctrl-K**) lets you send the object to the back of the ZOrder.

is a pull-down list of alignment options that allows Visual Basic to align two selected objects so that they align on the left, on the right, on the center position horizontally, on the top, on the bottom, on the center position vertically, or in the left top corner to the nearest Grid dot.

is a pull-down list that allows you to center selected objects on the central axes of the form either horizontally or vertically.

is a pull-down list that allows Visual Basic to resize the last of two or more objects so that they are the same in width, height, or both.

allows you to lock all controls on the selected form in their current positions so that you don't inadvertently move them once they are in the desired location.

displays in the code window a list box that contains the properties and methods available for the selected object.

displays in the code window a list box that contains the constants that are valid choices for the property you typed and that precede the equals sign (=).

displays the syntax for a selected function, method, or procedure.

displays in the code window a pop-up that contains information about the parameters of the function in which the pointer is located.

FIGURE D.4
The Edit tool bar.

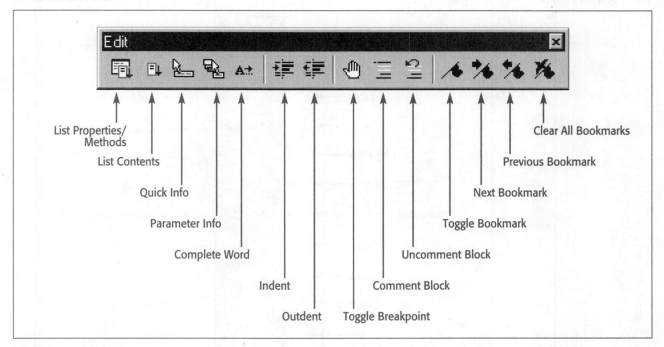

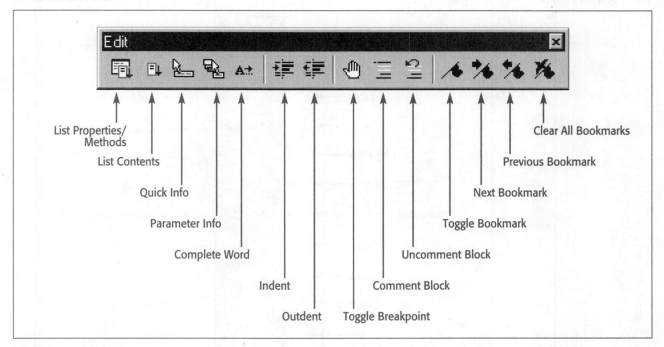 allows Visual Basic automatically to finish the word you are typing.

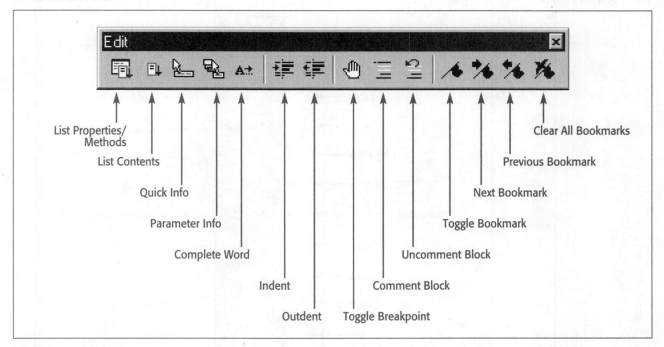 (shortcut key **Tab**) shifts all lines in the selection to the next tab stop. All lines in the selection are moved the same number of spaces to retain the same relative indentation within the selected block.

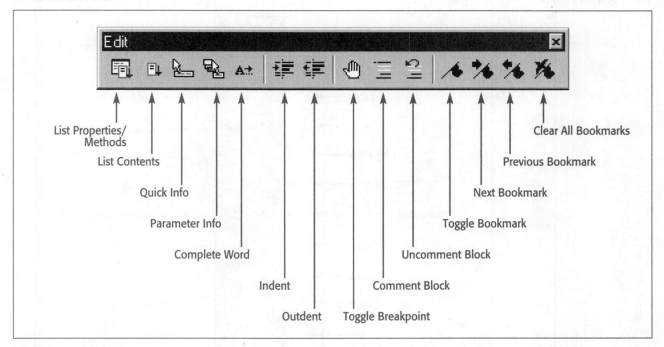 (shortcut key **Shift-Tab**) shifts all lines in the selection to the previous tab stop. All lines in the selection are moved the same number of spaces to retain the same relative indentation within the selected block.

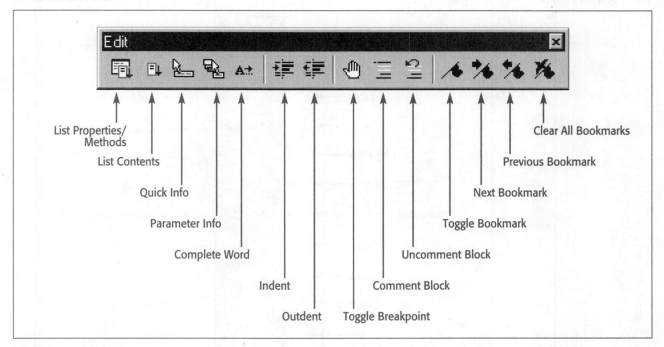 (shortcut key **F9**) lets you turn a breakpoint on or off.

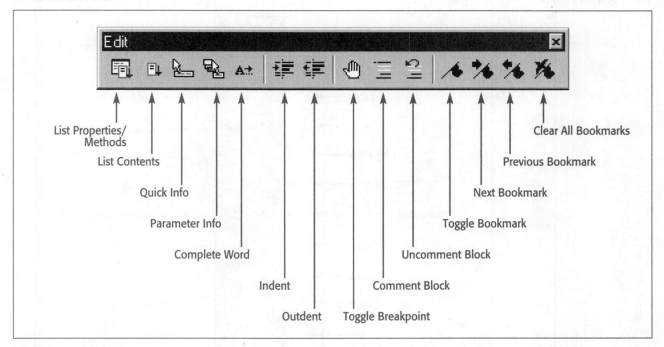 allows you to make comments out of all statements in the selected block of code.

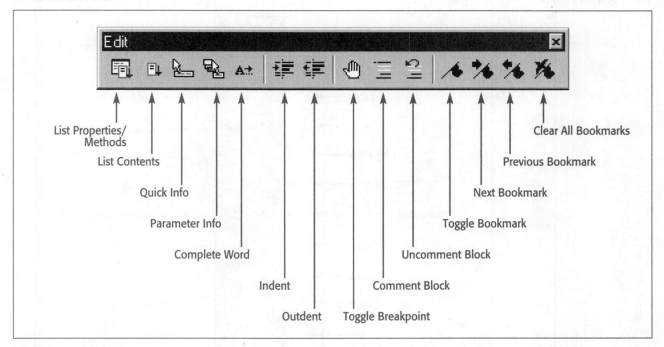 allows you to remove the comment character from all the statements in a selected block of code.

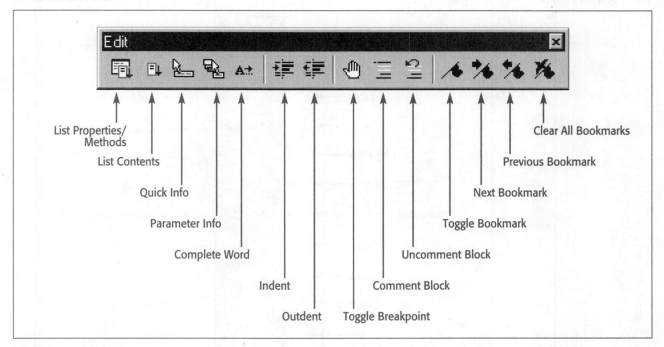 allows you to turn a bookmark on or off for the active line in the code window.

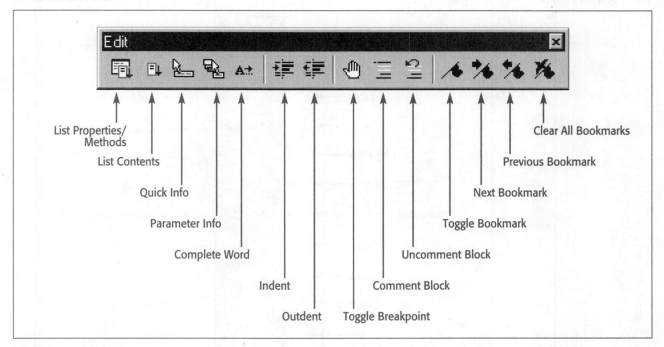 moves the focus to the next bookmark.

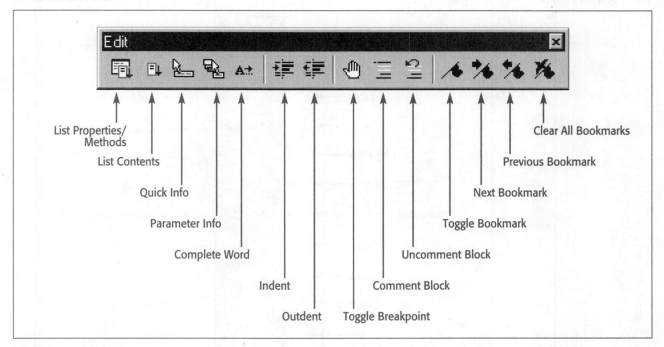 moves the focus to the previous bookmark.

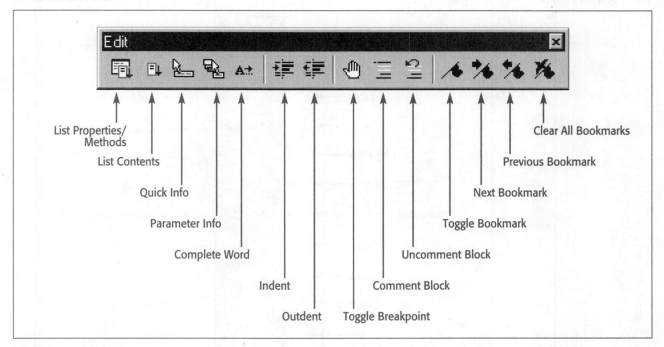 removes all bookmarks set in a project.

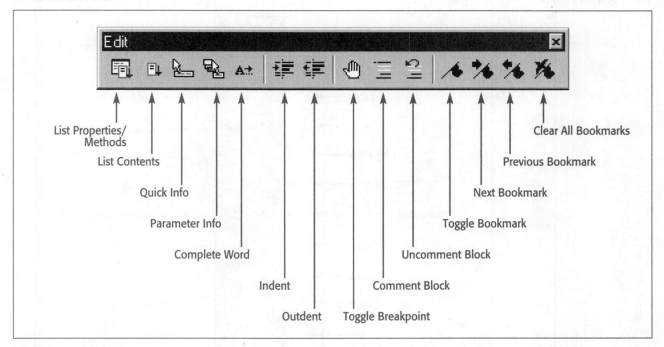 The Pointer allows you to do normal mouse manipulations on your forms.

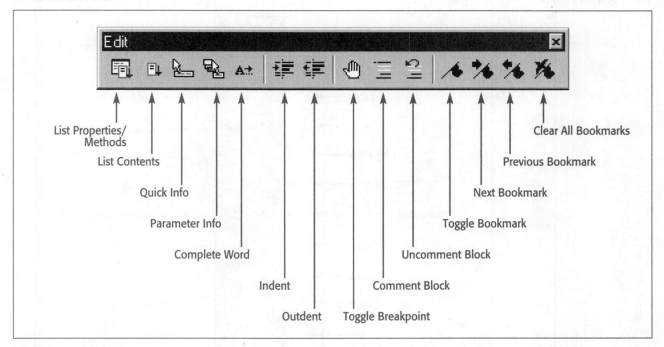 The PictureBox acts as a storage place for graphic images.

 The Label is used for labeling elements in your program.

FIGURE D.5
The Toolbox tools.

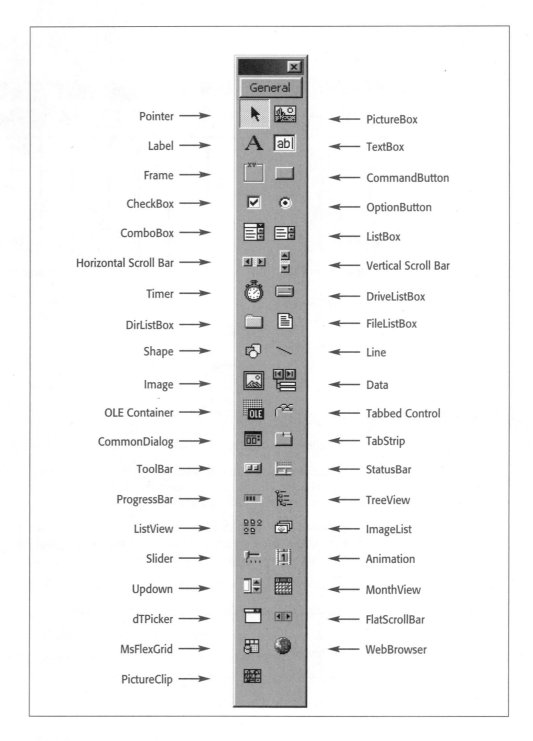

[abl] The TextBox is used to get input from the user.

[xv] The Frame allows you to group objects on the form.

■ The CommandButton allows you to add to the form a button that can be sensed when the user clicks it.

[✓] The CheckBox can be checked or unchecked by the user.

The OptionButtons work as a group so that when one is turned on, all the rest are automatically turned off by Visual Basic.

The ComboBox allows you to set up a variety of different list formats.

The ListBox presents a list of items from which the user can select one or more.

The Horizontal Scroll Bar lets the user scroll the attached object horizontally (under program control).

The Vertical Scroll Bar lets the user scroll the attached object vertically (under program control).

The Timer can be used in your program to determine how often the timer code should be executed.

The DriveListBox provides a pull-down list of available drives that allow the user to change drives.

The DirListBox adds a list that allows the user to change the directory.

The FileListBox allows the user to pick the needed file from the list.

The Shape Control allows you to draw shapes on your forms.

The Line Control allows you to draw lines on your forms.

The Image Control allows the user to store images on the form.

The Data Control allows you to access database records.

The OLE Container allows you to make OLE connections.

The Tabbed Control is a tool that has a defined number of tabs where different objects can be placed.

The CommonDialog Control allows you to add to your form one of a series of standard dialog box access controls (such as a Save As dialog box).

The TabStrip is a tool that has a defined number of tabs where different objects can be placed.

The Toolbar lets you set up a toolbar and add buttons that are automatically the same size.

The StatusBar provides a window, usually at the bottom of a parent form, through which an application can display various kinds of status data.

The ProgressBar can be used to show the progress of a program's functioning by adjusting the size of the displayed colored bar.

The TreeView displays a hierarchical list of Node objects, each of which consists of a label and an optional bitmap.

The ListView allows you to display items arranged into columns with or without column headings and display accompanying icons and text.

The ImageList allows the programmer to store images in an array format so that the images can be referenced by index.

The Slider allows the programmer to set up a slider with or without tick marks. The slider can be moved by dragging it, clicking the mouse to either side of the slider, or using the keyboard.

The Animation control is used to create buttons that display animations when clicked.

The UpDown control has a pair of arrow buttons that the user can click to increment or decrement a value that is displayed in an associated control.

The MonthView allows the user to pick a date from the calendar.

The DTPicker (DateTimePicker) allows you to provide a formatted date field that allows easy date selection through a drop-down calendar interface similar to the MonthView control.

The FlatScrollBar is a two-dimensional scroll bar until the mouse passes over it and it gains the three-dimensional look.

The MSFlexGrid allows you to show data as a table of rows and columns.

The WebBrowser allows you to display Web pages in a Web workspace.

The PictureClip allows you to load an array of images and extract a particular portion of the image by its placement position.

Glossary

access key A key that lets you select a button or menu by holding down the **Alt** key and pressing the underlined key.

aggregate functions Database functions for determining specific calculation on a series of records.

And One of the connectives used to join two parts of an If Test.

append The process of adding records to the end of a sequential file.

application Another name for a program.

application windows The windows that an application uses to operate.

array A series of variables that can be referred to by a common variable name.

ascending The sorting order in which the elements are arranged from smallest to largest.

ASCII The coding standard used for the code translation of the keystrokes sent to the computer.

aspect The value that lets you change a circle into an ellipse.

assignment statement A statement that allows you to store a value in a variable.

automatic link A DDE link in which the linked data are automatically updated wherever they are changed.

AVI The file extension of multimedia animation files.

beta copy A copy of a program that is sent to potential users so they can test it.

binary digits (or **bits**) The elemental storage switches a computer uses when it stored data. It takes eight or more bits to represent a stored character or a pixel on the display.

binary tree An indexing structure without cycles that begins by assigning the initial element as the root and subsequent elements as branches from that root. The branches are continually made to the left of the root or other nodes if the new item is less that the current node and are made to the right if the new item is greater than the current node.

bitmap A type of image file.

bits See **binary digits**.

boolean operator See **relational operator**.

bound controls Controls that are used to display database data through their connection to a Data Control.

breakpoint A point in the program where the execution of the program will temporarily stop.

browse A database feature that allows you to display many records at the same time and specify which fields you want displayed by using a query.

buffer A temporary storage area in the computer.

bug See **logic error**.

button bar An element of many Windows applications, in which often-used menu functions are shown as buttons.

buttons Program elements that represent program functions. Buttons can be selected by clicking on them, by using **Alt** and the underlined letter, or by using the **Tab** key to highlight the button, and then pressing **Enter**.

byte A variable type that can be used to store a one-character value.

Call Stack dialog box A dialog box that shows a list of the nesting order of the procedures that are currently in use.

call The optional command used to execute a procedure.

cell The intersection of a row and a column in a grid.

character class Part of the metacharacter pattern-matching used when searching Visual Basic code.

chat room An Internet discussion group.

check digit A number created by adding the values of each of the numeric storage codes when a disk is copied. After the disk is copied, this number is compared with the check digit created from the original disk. If the numbers match, it is a good copy.

Clipboard The Windows program used to store elements that are cut or copied from one program for transfer to another program.

code window A Visual Basic window in which you key the code to be executed when the associated program element is selected.

code workspace The part of the code window where the code is entered.

compile-time error A syntax-type error that is found when a program is executed.

compiling The process of translating Visual Basic code into a special set of instructions that the computer can interpret better and faster than the English code and graphical forms that make up the program.

concatenation The process of combining two or more strings into one.

condition A test that defines a relationship between two elements.

connective An If Test element that allows two or more conditionals to be used as a single test.

constant A stored value, in a program, whose value cannot be changed.

context-sensitive help Help windows that contain information about what you are currently working on.

control array An array of program objects.

control menu box The small box in the upper-left corner of most windows that contains menu functions relating to manipulating the window and interacting with the Windows environment.

controls Visual Basic elements added to a form.

counter variable The variable used on a For-Next loop to determine how many times the loop has executed.

currency A data type that stores numbers with a fixed decimal point of four positions.

current line The line that the execution has currently been stopped on when single-stepping through your program.

current record The record from the database that is currently being displayed in the bound controls.

data aware Another name for a bound control.

database A type of formatted data storage that allows programs to access the data easily.

date variable A special variable used to store dates and time.

dBASE A commercial database program.

DBEngine The database engine Visual Basic uses to talk to databases.

DDE See **dynamic data exchange**.

debugging The process of finding and repairing errors in your programs.

declaration The process of specifying the variable name and type so the variable can be accessed.

delimited file A file in which there are commas between the fields and quotation marks around the string fields.

descending The sorting order in which the elements are arranged from largest to smallest.

design-time errors Errors that are made as you key the code.

desktop The screen display representing the top of your desk, where each of the tasks being worked on is shown in a window.

destination application The application in a DDE conversation that receives the data.

dialog box A type of window in which the application asks for additional information.

Distinct and **DistinctRow** Query keywords that can limit the number of records selected for a Dynaset.

Do. . . Loop See **loop**.

docking Visual Basic's way of keeping the elements of the programming environment arranged so the windows that contain them don't overlap.

documentation The information created to help the user operate the program or the programmer maintain it.

DoEvents The command that releases control from the program to Windows so events such as a mouse click on a button can be detected.

domain suffix The portion of the URL that identifies the type of organization that set up the Web site.

Double Variable used to store numbers that have a decimal point with an unspecified number of decimal positions. Can store numbers much larger than a Single variable can.

drag-and-drop The programming technique that allows certain types of data to be copied or moved from one program element to another by dragging it from the first element and dropping it on the second element.

dragging Moving an element by clicking and holding the button down on it while moving the mouse.

dynamic A type of array in which the number of elements can be changed.

dynamic data exchange The process of linking data in one application to a point in another application so when you change the data in the first application, the data in the other application will change automatically.

Dynaset The records selected from the database by a query.

electronic mail (e-mail) A system that allows computer users to send messages back and forth.

ellipsis A group of three dots that, when used on a menu item, indicates that additional information will be needed when you are using that particular item.

end-of-file marker The marker that is automatically put on the end of the data in the file so that a program can sense when there is no more data in the file.

event-driven programming A programming method in which the program flow is controlled by the user interacting with objects drawn on the screen.

events Predefined user actions that Visual Basic recognizes and respond to.

explicit declaration A variable declaration using Dim, Static, or Global.

exponential notation A numeric representation of a number and how many decimal positions it requires.

external database A database created with a program other than Microsoft Access.

field A portion of a record that contains a specific part of the data of the record.

file A collection of data stored on disk.

File Transfer Protocol (FTP) The portion of the URL that tells the computer that the file being transferred is simply to be downloaded or uploaded and stored in a previously designated location.

filter A method of telling a file access common dialog box which files should be accessed (such as those with TXT as an extension).

floating-point numbers Numbers that have a decimal point with an unspecified number of decimal positions.

flowchart A type of program design in which the program elements are represented by boxes of various shapes and sizes that are connected to illustrate the program flow.

focus The currently active object has the application focus.

font A particular style and design of the characters in a character set.

footing Information printed at the bottom of each page of a report.

form The window where the objects of an application are placed.

format The manner in which information is displayed.

form-level The scope of a variable whose value is available to procedures on that form only.

Forms Layout window The window that shows an image of the desktop with the positioning of the various forms that make up your project.

For-Next A type of looping structure that has an automatic counter, an end-point test, and an automatic branch.

FoxPro A commercial database program.

function A procedure that returns a value as a result of the code within it.

global A program element that has scope through the entire element.

glossary items Items in a help system window that offer definitions of terms.

graphical user interface (GUI) An interface in which you communicate with the system by selecting the icon that represents the task to be accomplished and the associated files.

heading Information printed at the top of each page of a report.

Help system The system of instructions that explain how Visual Basic (or an other Windows program) works.

home page The initial Web page arrived at on a Web site.

home position The upper left corner of a Visual Basic object.

Hypertext Markup Language (HTML) The language used to create Web pages.

Hypertext Transfer Protocol (HTTP) The portion of the URL that tells the computer that the file being transferred contains hypertext links.

hypertext documents Documents that contain links to other portions of the same document or to other documents.

icon A small image, displayed on the desktop, that represents a program function.

immediate window The Visual Basic window in which you can monitor various program elements as the program executes.

implicit declaration Variables that are defined when used are implicitly declared.

index The number representing the current position in an array. Also, the file containing the key and record pointer into the main file of an indexed file.

indexed file A file method that consists of two files, the main file with all the data and a sorted index file containing only the key and a pointer to the related record in the main file.

INI The extension for a file that provides initial information to a program.

Internet Explorer The Web browser furnished by Microsoft for users of Windows 95 and 98.

Internet Network Information Center The center responsible for assigning the URLs for Web sites.

Internet Service Provider (ISP) A company that leases phone lines to gain access to the Internet and then provides its subscribers with a local phone number and the appropriate software to allow them access.

key A unique field within a record that allows that record to be accessed within the random access file.

launch The process of starting a program.

literal Text in quotes used in assignment or similar statements.

local When the scope of an element is less than global, it can be local to a form, a module, or an object.

logic error An error that Visual Basic will not locate for you and that will not interfere with the operation of the program although the results of the program will be incorrect.

long An integer variable type that requires twice as much storage as an integer but can store much larger numbers.

loop A series of statements that are reused by branching from the bottom of the series to the top so they can be executed again.

macro A series of commands executed automatically in sequence.

manual link A DDE link in which the linked data are not automatically updated when they are changed, but are updated only on instruction from the program into which the data are linked.

Maximize button The window button that allows you to make the window as large as possible on the desktop.

menu bar The part of the window in which the pull-down menus are indicated by name.

Menu Editor The dialog box that allows you to create menus for your programs.

metacharacters Special characters used for pattern matching when searching for instances in the code window.

method An object property that is available only during runtime.

MID The file extension of multimedia MIDI music files (see also RMI).

military time A time format in which hours after 12:00 noon are specified as hours added to 12; 1:00 PM is 13:00, 2:00 PM is 14:00, and so on.

Minimize button The window button that allows you to reduce the window to an icon.

mod See **modulo arithmetic**

modal A desktop form that the user must complete before being allowed to switch to any other window or application.

modem A hardware device that connects a computer to the outside world via a phone line.

module A special code window where you can place only declarations and code, no objects.

modulo arithmetic A test to determine when a number is evenly divisible by another number.

multimedia The use of sound, graphics, and video on a computer.

Multimedia Control The control in Visual Basic that allows you to use multimedia files.

multiple-character wildcard The asterisk (*) metacharacter used to match zero or more characters when searching your code.

nesting Placing one loop or other type of structure inside a like structure.

notify link A DDE link in which the linked data are not automatically updated when they are changed, but a notification is sent to the linked program that can be used to cause the receiving application to update the data.

numeric variable A storage location for data for calculation.

numeric wildcard The number symbol (#) metacharacter used to match any one numeric character (0 through 9) when searching your code.

object linking and embedding (OLE) An extension of DDE in which linked data can be changed by having the original application automatically loaded.

on-line help A help system that is always available for the user through the menu system.

Or One of the connectives used to join two parts of an If Test.

order of operations The order in which calculations are performed.

Output The file mode that allows data to be stored in the file.

Paradox A commercial database program.

parameter Data used in a statement or passed to a function or subroutine by the calling statement.

paste The process of copying data from the clipboard into an object.

Personal Information Manager (PIM) An application with personal management tools such as an address list, a notepad, and an appointment scheduler.

pixels The dots that make up a video display.

pop-up menu A menu that appears on the desktop when you click or right-click the mouse.

post-test A test performed at the end of the loop.

predefined constant A constant already defined within Visual Basic.

pretest loop A test performed at the beginning of the loop.

Printer The object that allows you to print outprint on a printer.

procedure The code for an event or standalone section of code that can be called from multiple positions in the program.

procedure call A method of executing a procedure without triggering an event.

procedure stepping See **Step Over**.

program A series of instructions that directs the computer to perform one or more tasks.

program documentation Documentation that is put directly in the program coding in the form of comments.

project The collection of all parts that make up a Visual Basic program.

Project window   The Visual Basic window that lets you see the names of all the parts of your program.

properties   The set of characteristics of an object.

Properties window   The window of the Visual Basic interface that shows you the properties available for the selected object.

pseudocode   A type of program design in which program instructions are written in English rather than program code.

query   A request to the database to set up a Dynaset with only the records requested in the request.

radius   The distance from the center to the edge of a circle.

random   A file access method that lets records be accessed directly by record number.

record   A portion of a file that is made up of a series of fields. Each record will consist of the same fields.

relational interface   The method of creating a database file in which the data are stored in tables made up of rows and columns of data. The tables can be connected through a relationship between a field in one table and a field in another.

relational operator   The part of an If Test that tells Visual Basic what type of comparison to perform.

RMI   File extension used for multimedia MIDI music files (see also **MID**).

rollback   A feature that allows you to cancel any database changes made when the database is handled by a transaction.

runtime errors   Errors that occur as the program is executing.

runtime   The time when a program is executing.

scientific notation   See **exponential notation**.

scope   The range or level of statements or procedures that recognize a variable, constant, or procedure.

scroll bars   Small bars on the right edge or bottom of a window that allow the window to be scrolled.

seed number   The initial number used for random-number generation.

separator lines   The lines in a menu that separate groups of similar options.

sequential   A file processing method that allows access to the records only in the order in which they are stored in the file.

Setup Wizard   The special program that helps you set up programs for distribution to users who may not have Visual Basic on their computers.

shortcut key   A key that allows a menu option to be executed without pulling down the menu.

single-character wildcard   The question mark (?) metacharacter used to match any one character when searching code.

single   Variable used to store numbers that have a decimal point with an unspecified number of decimal positions.

single-step (Step Into)   The process of executing a program one statement at a time.

sizing handles   Small boxes on an object that let you change the size of the object by dragging them.

sorting   A process of putting a list into some type of sequence.

split line   The division of the debug window that allows you to see watches in the upper portion and use the lower portion for debugging.

SQL   See **Structured Query Language**.

status bar   A display, usually at the bottom of a form, that gives the user information about the status of the program.

Step Over   Executing a procedure as a single step when single-stepping through a program.

string variable   A variable that is used to store text in any form.

Structured Query Language (SQL)   A series of "English-like" commands and parameters that have special meaning to the underlying database and are used to extract the specified part of the database.

submenu   A menu that is pulled down from a higher-level menu.

subroutine   See **procedure**.

subscript   See **index**.

substring   A portion of a larger string.

syntax   The methods and rules of writing programs in a language.

syntax errors   See **design-time errors**.

test and debug   See **debugging**.

text string   See **literal**.

title bar   The portion of the window that gives the title of the application or the function of the window.

Tool bar   The portion of the program that has tool icons or buttons that represent menu options.

Toolbox   The portion of the Visual Basic program in which you select the program controls to be placed on your form.

transaction   A series of recoverable changes made to a database.

trappable errors   Runtime errors that can be trapped, allowing an error message to be given to the user so the problem can be corrected and the application allowed to continue.

twip   A window measurement equal to 1/1440 of an inch.

universal resource locator (URL)   The address of a Web page.

user-generated errors   Errors that are caused by the user in the normal course of operating a program.

user's guide   Written program documentation that explains to a user how the program operates.

variable   Temporary storage location for a value.

variant   A special type of variable that Visual Basic automatically changes to hold whatever type of data is being assigned to it.

vbp   The file extension Visual Basic uses on project files.

Visual Data Manager   The Visual Basic tool that lets you create and manipulate databases.

watch   A Visual Basic debugging tool that allows you to specify values that you want displayed in the watch portion of the debug window.

WAV   The file extension of multimedia sound effects files.

Web browser   A program that allows the user to view Web pages.

Web sites   A set of hyperlinked documents that can be viewed with a Web browser.

What's This?   A small display window that gives the user information about a program element.

wildcard character   The part of a query that specifies that all fields within the database are to be included.

window frame   The edge of the window that allows you to adjust the size of the window.

window workspace   The portion of the window in which the work of the application is done.

Index